T0192114

Lecture Notes in Computer Science 13491

Marco Dorigo · Heiko Hamann ·
Manuel López-Ibáñez · José García-Nieto ·
Andries Engelbrecht · Carlo Pinciroli ·
Volker Strobel · Christian Camacho-Villalón (Eds.)

Swarm Intelligence

13th International Conference, ANTS 2022
Málaga, Spain, November 2–4, 2022
Proceedings

Springer

Editors
Marco Dorigo (iD)
Université Libre de Bruxelles
Brussels, Belgium

Manuel López-Ibáñez (iD)
University of Manchester
Manchester, UK

Andries Engelbrecht (iD)
Stellenbosch University
Stellenbosch, South Africa

Volker Strobel (iD)
Université Libre de Bruxelles
Brussels, Belgium

Heiko Hamann (iD)
University of Lübeck
Lübeck, Germany

University of Konstanz
Konstanz, Germany

José García-Nieto (iD)
University of Málaga
Málaga, Spain

Carlo Pinciroli (iD)
Worcester Polytechnic Institute
Worcester, MA, USA

Christian Camacho-Villalón (iD)
Université Libre de Bruxelles
Brussels, Belgium

ISSN 0302-9743   ISSN 1611-3349 (electronic)
Lecture Notes in Computer Science
ISBN 978-3-031-20175-2   ISBN 978-3-031-20176-9 (eBook)
https://doi.org/10.1007/978-3-031-20176-9

This Springer imprint is published by the registered company Springer Nature Switzerland AG
The registered company address is: Gewerbestrasse 11, 6330 Cham, Switzerland

Preface

These proceedings contain the papers presented at ANTS 2022, the Thirteenth International Conference on Swarm Intelligence, which took place during November 2–4, 2022. The conference was hosted by the University of Málaga, Spain. The ANTS series started in 1998 with the First International Workshop on Ant Colony Optimization (ANTS'98). Since then ANTS, which is held bi-annually, has gradually become an international forum for researchers in the wider field of swarm intelligence. In 2004, this development was acknowledged by the inclusion of the term "Swarm Intelligence" (next to "Ant Colony Optimization") in the conference title. Starting in 2010, the ANTS conference has been officially devoted to the field of swarm intelligence as a whole, without any bias towards specific research directions; this is reflected in the current title of the conference.

This volume contains 33 papers selected from 45 initial submissions. Of these, 19 were accepted as full-length papers and 14 were accepted as short papers. This corresponds to an overall acceptance rate of 73%. Also included in this volume are four extended abstracts.

Each paper was subject to peer review and decisions on acceptance were based on the reviews of at least three experts in the field. Papers of members of the organizing committee were handled by a conflict-of-interest chair.

All the contributions were presented as posters. The full-length papers were also presented orally in a plenary session. Selected extended versions of the best papers presented at the conference will be published in a special issue of the journal *Swarm Intelligence*.

We take this opportunity to thank the large number of people that were involved in making this conference a success. We express our gratitude to the authors who contributed their work, to the members of the international Program Committee, and to the additional referees for their qualified and detailed reviews.

We hope the reader will find this volume useful both as a reference to current research in swarm intelligence and as a starting point for future work.

August 2022

Marco Dorigo
Heiko Hamann
Manuel López-Ibáñez
José García-Nieto
Andries Engelbrecht
Carlo Pinciroli
Volker Strobel
Christian Camacho-Villalón

Organization

Organizing Committee

General Chairs

Marco Dorigo	Université Libre de Bruxelles, Belgium
Heiko Hamann	University of Konstanz, Germany

Local Organization and Publicity Chairs

Manuel López-Ibáñez	University of Málaga, Spain
José García-Nieto	University of Málaga, Spain

Technical Program Chairs

Andries Engelbrecht	Stellenbosch University, South Africa
Carlo Pinciroli	Worcester Polytechnic Institute, USA

Publication Chair

Volker Strobel	Université Libre de Bruxelles, Belgium

Paper Submission Chair

Christian Camacho-Villalón	Université Libre de Bruxelles, Belgium

Program Committee

Ashraf Abdelbar	Brandon University, Canada
Martyn Amos	Northumbria University, UK
Jacob Beal	BBN Technologies, USA
Giovanni Beltrame	Polytechnique Montréal, Canada
Tim Blackwell	Goldsmiths, University of London, UK
Darko Bozhinoski	Delft University of Technology, The Netherlands
Alexandre Campo	Université Libre de Bruxelles, Belgium
Marco Castellani	University of Birmingham, UK
Stephen Chen	York University, Canada
Christopher Cleghorn	University of the Witwatersrand, South Africa
Maurice Clerc	Independent Consultant on Optimisation, France
Leandro Coelho	Pontifícia Universidade Católica do Parana, Brazil
Carlos Coello Coello	CINVESTAV-IPN, Mexico

Sanjoy Das	Kansas State University, USA
Guido de Croon	Delft University of Technology, The Netherlands
Gianni Di Caro	Carnegie Mellon University, USA
Karl Doerner	University of Vienna, Austria
Mohammed El-Abd	American University of Kuwait, Kuwait
Eliseo Ferrante	Vrije Universitat Amsterdam, The Netherlands
Simon Garnier	New Jersey Institute of Technology, USA
Roderich Gross	University of Sheffield, UK
Kyle Harrison	University of New South Wales Canberra, Australia
Kiyohiko Hattori	University of Electro-Communications, Japan
Mary Katherine Heinrich	Université Libre de Bruxelles, Belgium
Tim Hendtlass	Swinburne University, Australia
Yara Khaluf	Ghent University, Belgium
Simone Ludwig	North Dakota State University, USA
Vittorio Maniezzo	University of Bologna, Italy
Alcherio Martinoli	École Polytechnique Fédérale de Lausanne, Switzerland
Massimo Mastrangeli	Delft University of Technology, The Netherlands
Michalis Mavrovouniotis	University of Cyprus, Cyprus
Yi Mei	Victoria University of Wellington, New Zealand
Bernd Meyer	Monash University, Australia
Nicolas Monmarché	Université de Tours, France
Roberto Montemanni	Istituto Dalle Molle di Studi sull'Intelligenza Artificiale, Switzerland
Frank Neumann	University of Adelaide, Australia
Ben Niu	Shenzhen University, China
Ann Nowe	Vrije Universiteit Brussel, Belgium
Kazuhiro Ohkura	Hiroshima University, Japan
Michael Otte	University of Maryland, USA
Jacopo Panerati	University of Toronto, Canada
Konstantinos Parsopoulos	University of Ioannina, Greece
Orit Peleg	University of Colorado Boulder, USA
Paola Pellegrini	IFSTTAR, France
Gilbert Peterson	US Air Force Institute of Technology, USA
Michal Pluhacek	Tomas Bata University in Zlin, Czech Republic
Günther Raidl	Vienna University of Technology, Austria
Pawel Romanczuk	Humboldt University of Berlin, Germany
Andreagiovanni Reina	Université Libre de Bruxelles, Belgium
Andrea Roli	University of Bologna, Italy
Erol Şahin	Middle East Technical University, Turkey
Roman Senkerik	Tomas Bata University in Zlin, Czech Republic
Kevin Seppi	Brigham Young University, USA
Thomas Stützle	Université Libre de Bruxelles, Belgium
Dirk Sudholt	University of Passau, Germany
Munehiro Takimoto	Tokyo University of Science, Japan
Mohamed S. Talamali	Sheffield Hallam University, UK

Danesh Tarapore   University of Southampton, UK
Guy Theraulaz   Paul Sabatier University, France
Dhananjay Thiruvady   Deakin University, Australia
Vito Trianni   Italian National Research Council, Italy
Elio Tuci   Université de Namur, Belgium
Ali Emre Turgut   Université Libre de Bruxelles, Belgium
Vivek Shankar   Polytechnique Montréal, Canada
  Varadharajan
Mostafa Wahby   University of Lübeck, Germany
Rolf Wanka   Friedrich-Alexander-Universität Erlangen-Nürnberg,
                              Germany
Justin Werfel   Harvard University, USA
Carsten Witt   Technical University of Denmark, Denmark
Masahito Yamamoto   Hokkaido University, Japan
Zhi-Hui Zhan   South China University of Technology, China

Additional Reviewers

Nicolas Bredeche   Sorbonne University, France
Nicolas Coucke   Université Libre de Bruxelles, Belgium
Edmund Hunt   University of Bristol, UK
Raina Zakir   Université Libre de Bruxelles, Belgium

Contents

Full Papers

Extended Abstracts

A Geometry-Sensitive Quorum Sensing Algorithm for the Best-of-N Site Selection Problem

Grace Cai(✉) and Nancy Lynch

Computer Science and Artificial Intelligence Laboratory, MIT, Cambridge, MA, USA
gracecai@mit.edu, lynch@csail.mit.edu

Abstract. The house hunting behavior of the Temnothorax albipennis ant allows the colony to explore several nest choices and agree on the best one. Their behavior serves as the basis for many bio-inspired swarm models to solve the same problem. However, many of the existing site selection models in both insect colony and swarm literature test the model's accuracy and decision time only on setups where all potential site choices are equidistant from the swarm's starting location. These models do not account for the geographic challenges that result from site choices with different geometry. For example, although actual ant colonies are capable of consistently choosing a higher quality, further site instead of a lower quality, closer site, existing models are much less accurate in this scenario. Existing models are also more prone to committing to a low quality site if it is on the path between the agents' starting site and a higher quality site. We present a new model for the site selection problem and verify via simulation that is able to better handle these geographic challenges. Our results provide insight into the types of challenges site selection models face when distance is taken into account. Our work will allow swarms to be robust to more realistic situations where sites could be distributed in the environment in many different ways.

1 Introduction

Swarms of birds, bees, and ants are able to coordinate themselves to make decisions using only local interactions [3,14,18]. Modelling these natural swarms has inspired many successful swarm algorithms [7]. One such bio-inspired algorithm comes from the house hunting behavior of ants. Models of the ants' behavior when selecting a new nest serve as the basis for swarm algorithms which seek to select the best site out of a discrete number of candidate sites in space [17].

Many variations of the best-of-N site selection problem have been studied for swarms [22]. For example, when sites are of equal quality, choosing one is a symmetry-breaking problem [9,23]. Situations with asymmetric site qualities and costs (where higher quality sites have a higher cost of being chosen) have also been studied – for example, when one of two candidate sites is significantly larger than the other (making it harder for agents to detect other agents favoring the larger site, even when it is of higher quality) [4].

© Springer Nature Switzerland AG 2022
M. Dorigo et al. (Eds.): ANTS 2022, LNCS 13491, pp. 1–13, 2022.
https://doi.org/10.1007/978-3-031-20176-9_1

However, most site selection models are mainly tested on small numbers of candidate nest sites that are equidistant from the agents' starting location (also known as the home nest) [6,15]. In many applications of the site selection problem such as shelter seeking, sites will not be distributed so uniformly.

This equidistant setup fails to capture two important geographical details that existing algorithms struggle with in making accurate decisions. Firstly, nests that are closer to the home nest are advantaged because they are more likely to be found. Even so, house hunting ants can still choose higher quality sites that are much further than lower quality, closer sites. We have found that existing site selection models often commit to the closer site even when there is a better, further option. Secondly, using sites equidistant from the home nest eliminates the possibility of some nests being in the way of others. Site selection models often trigger consensus on a new site after a certain quorum population of agents have been detected in it. If a low quality nest is on the path from the home nest to a high quality nest, agents travelling between the home nest and the high quality nest could saturate the path and detect a quorum for the lower quality nest that is in the way instead of the highest quality nest.

This paper aims to create a new algorithm that can successfully account for a more varied range of nest distributions, allowing agents to successfully choose higher quality nests even when they have the disadvantage of being further from the agents' starting location or there are other lower quality nests in the way. The model should also perform with similar accuracy compared to existing models on the default setup with equidistant candidate nest sites. We show via simulation that incorporating a quorum threshold that decreases with site quality allows for increased accuracy compared to previous models. We also show that setups where candidate sites are in the way of each other or are of similar quality can make it harder for site selection models to produce accurate results.

Section 2 describes the house hunting process of ants and overviews existing swarm models. Section 3 describes our model. We provide details on the implementation of our model, test accuracy and decision time in different geographic situations, and report the results in Sect. 4. We discuss these results in Sect. 5. Lastly, we suggest future work in Sect. 6. The full simulation code can be found at [1].

2   Background

2.1   Ant House Hunting

When the *T. albipennis* ants' home nest is destroyed, the colony can find and collectively move to a new, high quality nest. To do so, *T. albipennis* scouts first scan the area, searching for candidate nests. When a nest is found, the scouts wait a period of time inversely proportional to the nest quality before returning to the home nest. There, they recruit others to examine the new site in a process known as forward tandem running. Tandem runs allow more ants to learn the path to a new site in case the ants decide to move there. When an ant in a candidate nest encounters others in the site at a rate surpassing a threshold rate (known as the quorum threshold), ants switch their behavior to carrying other members of the colony to the new nest. Carrying is three times faster than tandem runs and accelerates the move to the new nest [13,14].

This decision-making process allows ants to not only agree on a new nest, but also to choose the highest quality nest out of multiple nests in the environment. This is true even if the high quality nest is much further from the home nest than the low quality nest [8,19]. Franks [8] found that with a low quality nest 30 cm from home and a high quality nest 255 cm from home, 88% of ant colonies successfully chose the high quality nest even though it was 9 times further.

2.2 House Hunting and Site Selection Models

To better study the ants' behavior, models have been designed to simulate how ants change behavior throughout the house hunting process [15,24]. These models, initiated by Pratt [15], allow simulated ants to probabilistically transition through four phases – the Exploration, Assessment, Canvassing, and Transport phases. The Exploration represents when the ants are still exploring their environment for new sites. When an ant discovers a site, it enters the Assessment phase, in which it examines the quality of the site and determine whether to accept or reject it. If the ant accepts the site, it enters the Canvassing phase, which represents the process of recruiting other ants via forward tandem runs. Finally, if a quorum is sensed, the ant enters the Transport phase, which represents the carrying behavior used to move the colony to the new site.

These models, however, assume that when an ant transitions from the Exploration phase to the Assessment phase, it is equally likely to choose any of the candidate nest sites to assess. This assumes that any nest is equally likely to be found, which is unlikely in the real world because sites closer to the home nest are more likely to be discovered. To our knowledge, house hunting models have not tried to model situations where nests have different likelihoods of being found, as is the case when nests have different distances from the home nest [24].

The corresponding problem to house hunting in robot swarms is known as the *N-site selection problem* [22]. Agents, starting at a central home site, must find and choose among N candidate nest sites in the environment and move to the site with highest quality. Unlike house hunting models, which do not physically simulate ants in space, swarm models set up ants in a simulated arena and let them physically explore sites and travel between them.

Inspired by ant modelling, [6] and [17] have modeled swarm agents using four main states – Uncommitted Latent, Uncommitted Interactive, Favoring Latent, and Favoring Interactive (with [6] adding a fifth Committed state to emulate having detected a quorum). Uncommitted Latent agents remain in the home nest while Uncommitted Interactive agents explore the arena for candidate sites. Favoring Interactive agents have discovered and are favoring a certain site and recruit other agents to the site, while Favoring Latent agents remain in the new site to try and build up quorum. Agents probabilistically transition between these states based on environmental events (e.g. the discovery of a new site) and eventually end up significantly favoring a new candidate nest or committed to it. Other swarm models for N-site selection typically use a similar progression through uncommitted, favoring, and committed type phases [12].

One setup where a high quality site was twice as far as a low quality one was successfully solved in [17], but for the most part these models and their variations have mainly been tested in arenas with two candidate sites equidistant from the home nest [2,6,11,16]. Our model aims to analyze the behavior of these models in more varied site setups and improve upon them.

3   Model

We first describe our new discrete geographical model for modeling swarms. Then we discuss the individual restrictions, parameters, and agent algorithms needed for the house hunting problem specifically.

3.1   General Model

We assume a finite set R of agents, with a state set SR of potential states. Agents move on a discrete rectangular grid of size $n \times m$, formally modelled as directed graph $G = (V, E)$ with $|V| = mn$. Edges are bidirectional, and we also include a self-loop at each vertex. Vertices are indexed as (x, y), where $0 \leq x \leq n - 1$, $0 \leq y \leq m - 1$. Each vertex also has a state set SV of potential states.

We use a discrete model so the model can be simulated in a distributed fashion on each vertex to reduce computation time.

Local Configurations: A *local configuration* $C'(v)$ captures the contents vertex v. It is a triple $(sv, myagents, srmap)$, where $sv \in SV$ is the vertex state of v, $myagents \subseteq R$ is the set of agents at v, and $srmap : myagents \to SR$ assigns an agent state to each agent at v.

Local Transitions: The transition of a vertex v may be influenced by the local configurations of nearby vertices. We define an **influence radius** I, which is the same for all vertices, to mean that vertex indexed at (x, y) is influenced by all valid vertices $\{(a, b) | a \in [x - I, x + I], b \in [y - I, y + I]\}$, where a and b are integers. We can use this influence radius to create a local mapping M_v from local coordinates to the neighboring local configurations. For a vertex v at location (x, y), we produce M_v such that $M_v(a, b) \to C'(w)$ where w is the vertex located at $(x + a, y + b)$ and $-I < a, b < I$. This influence radius is representative of a sensing and communication radius. Agents can use all information from vertices within the influence radius to make decisions.

We have a local transition function δ, which maps all the information associated with one vertex and its influence radius at one time to new information that can be associated with the vertex at the following time. It also produces directions of motion for all the agents at the vertex.

Formally, for a vertex v, δ probabilistically maps M_v to a quadruple of the form $(sv_1, myagents, srmap_1, dirmap_1)$, where $sv_1 \in SV$ is the new state of the vertex, $srmap_1 : myagents \rightarrow SR$ is the new agent state mapping for agents at the vertex, and $dirmap_1 : myagents \rightarrow \{R, L, U, D, S\}$ gives directions of motion for agents currently at the vertex. Note that R, L, U, and D mean right, left, up, and down respectively, and S means to stay at the vertex. The local transition function δ is further broken down into two phases as follows.

Phase One: Each agent in vertex v uses the same probabilistic transition function α, which probabilistically maps the agent's state $sr \in SR$, location (x, y), and the mapping M_v to a new suggested vertex state sv', agent state sr', and direction of motion $d \in \{R, L, U, D, S\}$. We can think of α as an agent state machine model.

Phase Two: Since agents may suggest conflicting new vertex states, a rule L is used to select one final vertex state. The rule also determines for each agent whether they may transition to state sr' and direction of motion d or whether they must stay at the same location with original state sr.

Probabilistic Execution: The system operates by probablistically transitioning all vertices v for an infinite number of rounds. During each round, for each vertex v, we obtain the mapping M_v which contains the local configurations of all vertices in its influence radius. We then apply δ to M_v to transition vertex v and all agents at vertex v. For each vertex v we now have $(sv_v, myagents_v, srmap_v, dirmap_v)$ returned from δ.

For each v, we take $dirmap_v$, which specifies the direction of motion for each agent and use it to map all agents to their new vertices. For each vertex v, it's new local configuration is just the new vertex state sv_v, the new set of agents at the vertex, and the $srmap$ mapping from agents to their new agent states.

3.2   House Hunting Environment Model

The goal of the house hunting problem is for agents to explore the grid and select the best site out of N sites to migrate to collectively. We model sites as follows.

A set S, $|S| = N$ of rectangular sites are located within this grid, where site s_i has lower left vertex (x_i^1, y_i^1) and upper right vertex (x_i^2, y_i^2). Each site s_i also has a quality $s_i.q \in [0, 1]$. To represent these sites, we let the vertex state set be $SV = S \cup \{\emptyset\}$ for each vertex, indicating which site, if any, the vertex belongs to. Furthermore, we denote the site s_0 to be the *home nest*. In the initial configuration, all agents start out at a random vertex in the home nest, chosen uniformly from among the vertices in that nest.

3.3   Agent States and Transition Function

The agent state set SR is best described in conjunction with the agent transition function α. Agents can take on one of 6 core states, each a combination of one of three preference states (Uncommitted, Favoring, Committed), and two activity states (Nest, Active). The state model can be seen in Fig. 1.

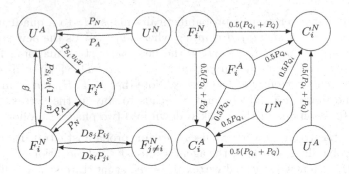

Fig. 1. State model. $\{U, F, C\}$ denote preference states. The superscript $\{N, A\}$ denotes the activity state, and a subscript i denotes that an agent is favoring or committed to site i. The transitions for Uncommitted and Favoring states are shown on the left, and transitions from Uncommitted and Favoring to Committed states are on the right.

Uncommitted Nest (U^N) agents stay in the home nest to prevent too many agents from flooding the environment. They have a chance of transitioning to Uncommitted Active (U^A) agents, which try to explore the arena and discover new sites. U^A agents move according to the Levy flight random walk, which has been shown to be used by foraging ants [21]. U^N agents transition to U^A with probability P_A, and U^A agents transition to U^N agents with probability P_N. This results in an expected $x = \frac{P_A}{P_A+P_N}$ percent of uncommitted agents are active, whereas $1 - x$ agents remain in the nest. Prior work [17] lets $P_N = 9P_A = L$, where L is the inverse of the average site round trip time, chosen to promote sufficient mixing. This leads to 10% of the agent population being active.

Uncommitted Active agents have a chance P_{S_i} of discovering a new nest, which is 1 if a new nest is within influence radius and 0 otherwise. If they discover a nest s_i, they explore and accept it with probability $s_i.q$ (the quality of s_i). They then have an $x\%$ chance of transitioning to Favoring Active, and a $(1 - x)\%$ chance of transitioning to Favoring Nest.

Favoring agents (F_i^A, F_i^N) prefer the site s_i that they discovered. Favoring Active (F_i^A) agents remain in site s_i to build quorum. Favoring Nest (F_i^N) agents return to the home nest to recruit others to site s_i. Favoring Nest agents transition to Active with the same probability P_A and Favoring Active agents transition back to Nest agents with probability P_N, creating the same effect where an expected 90% of the favoring agent population is F_i^A while the rest are F_i^N.

F_i^N agents have a probability β of abandoning their nest, which is 1 if the time spent without seeing other agents surpasses t_β. F_i^A agents can be inhibited by other F_i^A agents as follows. The chance an agent favoring nest i is converted to favoring nest j is $Dr_j P_{ij}$, where the factor of D is the probability of agents messaging each other (to prevent excessive messaging). r_j is the number of agents favoring s_j that have the agent within their influence radius. After an agent hears of the new site s_j, it visits the site to evaluate $s_j.q$ and changes its preference to s_j if $s_j.q > s_i.q$. Thus, the condition P_{ij} is 1 when $s_j.q > s_i.q$ and 0 otherwise.

U^A agents and F_i^N agents can detect a quorum and commit to a site when q agents in the site are within their influence radius. The quorum size scales with site value as $q = \lfloor (q_{MIN} - q_{MAX}) * s_i.q + q_{MAX} \rfloor$, where q_{MAX} and q_{MIN} are the maximum and minimum possible quorum threshold respectively. The condition P_Q is 1 when quorum is satisfied and 0 otherwise. Agents in any Favoring or Uncommitted state will transition to the committed state, if they encounter an agent already in quorum. The condition P_{Q_i} is 1 when another quorum agent for s_i is encountered and 0 otherwise. Furthermore, agents have an $\frac{1}{2}$ chance of transitioning to Committed Active (C_i^A) and a $\frac{1}{2}\%$ chance of Committed Nest C_i^N after having detected or been notified of a quorum.

C_i^N agents head to the home nest to inform others of the move, while C_i^A agents randomly wander the grid to find stragglers. Agents in quorum states continue to wander until they have sensed quorum for t_Q time steps, whereupon they return to the new selected site s_i.

The resulting agent state set SR is a product of the 6 core states needed in the state model as well as a number of auxiliary variables such as an agent's destination, the names of the sites it favors or has sensed quorum for, and parameters for an agent's random walk when exploring the grid.

Since in the house hunting problem (unlike other problems like task allocation), an agent never modifies the environment, an agent's proposed new vertex state is always the same as the old vertex state. Therefore, phase two of δ is not needed to reconcile conflicting vertex state suggestions from agents.

The transition function α, which for each agent returns a proposed new vertex state sv', agent state sr' and direction of motion works as follows. The agent never modifies the grid, so $sv' = sv$. The agent state sr' and direction d are calculated according to the core transitions and the auxiliary variables needed to keep track of those transitions. For example, when an agent is headed towards a site, the direction d is calculated to be the next step towards the site. When an agent is staying within a site, the direction d is calculated to be a random walk within the site boundaries.

The total set of variables parameters is $\{P_A, P_N, D, t_Q, t_\beta, q_{MIN}, q_{MAX}\}$, as well as the site locations $(x_i^1, y_i^1), (x_i^2, y_i^2)$ and quality $s_i.q$. In Sect. 4, we explore how changes in q_{MIN}, q_{MAX}, and the site locations and quality impact the accuracy, decision time, and split decisions made by the model.

4   Results

The model was tested in simulation using Pygame, with each grid square representing $1\,cm^2$. Agents moved at $1\,cm/s$, with one round representing one second. We chose this speed because even the lowest cost robots are still able to move at $1\,cm/s$ [20]. Agents had an influence radius of 2. All simulations were run using 100 agents, and a messaging rate of $1/15$. We let the abandonment timeout $t_\beta = \frac{5}{L}$ and the quorum timeout $t_Q = \frac{1}{L}$.

For each set of trials, we evaluated accuracy (the fraction of agents who chose the highest quality nest), decision time (the time it took for all agents to arrive at the nest they committed to), and split decisions (the number of trials where not all agents committed to the same nest).

4.1   Further Nest of Higher Quality

House hunting ants are capable of choosing further, higher quality sites over closer, lower quality ones [8]. When the far site and the near site are of equal value, ants consistently choose the closer one. To test our model's ability to produce the same behavior, we replicated the experimental setups in [8].

Three different distance comparisons were tested, with a further, higher quality nest of quality 0.9 being 2x, 3x, and 9x as far as a lower quality nest of quality 0.3 on the path from the high quality nest to the home nest. We included a control setup for each of these distance comparisons where both the far and close nest were quality 0.3. The arena size was $N = 16, M = 80$ for the 2x case, $N = 18, M = 180$ for the 3x case, and $N = 18$, $M = 300$ for the 9x case.

We tested our model using two different quorum parameters. In one test, we had $q_{MIN} = q_{MAX} = 4$, intended to represent the behavior of previous models with a fixed quorum threshold. In the other setup, $q_{MIN} = 4$ and $q_{MAX} = 7$, allowing our model to use the new feature of scaling the quorum threshold with site quality. We ran 100 trials for each set of parameters.

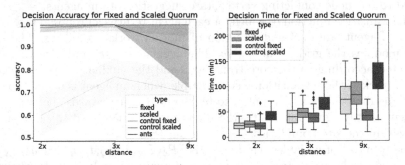

Fig. 2. Decision Time and Accuracy for far nests 2, 3, and 9 times as far from the home nest. Fixed quorum indicates the fixed threshold value of 4, and scaled quorum indicates $q_{MIN} = 4, q_{MAX} = 7$. The accuracy for the actual ants is taken from [8].

As seen in Fig. 2, using a scaled threshold significantly improved accuracy from using a fixed one. In the control case, both the fixed and scaled quorum threshold achieved high accuracy, with all accuracies being greater than 99%. In cases where the far site was of higher quality, the decision time for fixed and scaled quorum was comparable. However, the scaled quorum threshold took significantly (Welch's T-test, $p = 0.05$) more time in the control case to decide.

Furthermore, as seen in Fig. 2, our model successfully chose the further site with comparable (or significantly higher in the 9x case) accuracy than ants themselves, indicating that our model is on par with the ants.

4.2   Effects of Lower Quality Nest Being in the Way

To isolate the effects of the low quality nest being in the way of the high quality nest, we tested our model where the high quality nest (quality 0.9) was one of $\{2, 3, 4, 5, 6, 7, 8, 9\}$ times further than the low quality nest (quality 0.3), but in opposite directions of the home nest. We compared model performance when the low quality nest was in the way of the home nest. We ran tests with $N = 18$, $M = 300$, with the low quality nest always 30 cm from home. We again tested a fixed ($q_{MIN} = q_{MAX} = 4$) and scaled ($q_{MIN} = 4, q_{MAX} = 7$) quorum threshold on these setups. 100 trials were conducted for each set of parameters.

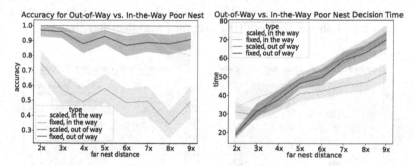

Fig. 3. Decision Time and Accuracy for far nests 2–9 times further than the close nest for both fixed and scaled quorums. In the in-the-way setup, the home nest, low quality nest, and high quality nest were lined up in that order. In the out of way setup, the low quality nest, home nest, and high quality nest were lined up in that order.

Figure 3 shows that for the out-of-way setup, the scaled quorum performs significantly (Welch's T-test, p = 0.05) more accurately than the fixed quorum on all far nest distances. For the in-the-way setup, the scaled quorum performs significantly better (Welch's T-test, p = 0.05) when the far nest is 3x further or more. Note it is harder for the fixed quorum to solve the in-the-way problem accurately compared to the out-of-way problem (Welch's T-test, p = 0.05). It is likewise harder for the scaled quorum to solve the in-the-way problem when the far nest is $\{3, 4, 6, 7, 8, 9\}$ times further (Welch's T-test, p = 0.05), showing that the in-the-way problem is harder to solve for site selection algorithms.

For distances 3x or further, there is no significant difference between the decision times for the fixed out-of-way, scaled out-of-way, and scaled in-the-way setups. For distances 5x and further, the fixed quorum takes significantly less time than the other setups but suffers in decision accuracy (Welch's T-test, p = 0.05) compared to the other three setups.

4.3   Effects of Magnitude of Difference in Site Quality

Because site quality affects the quorum threshold, we expect it to be harder for agents to correctly choose a high quality far site when it is only slightly better than nearby lower quality sites. This is because the difference in quorum threshold is less pronounced for sites of similar quality. For two equidistant nests, the algorithm should consistently choose the best site as it has in past work, so the absolute difference in site quality should not matter.

To test these effects, we used the setup in Sect. 4.1 where the further nest was 2x (60 cm) as far as the in-the-way close nest (30 cm), and compared it to an equidistant setup where both candidate nests were 30 cm away from the home nest in opposite directions. We tested both a fixed quorum $q_{MAX} = q_{MIN} = 4$ and a scaled quorum on these setups $q_{MAX} = 7, q_{MIN} = 4$. We varied the quality of the near nest in the set of potential values $\{0.3, 0.6, 0.9\}$, corresponding to quorum thresholds of $\{6, 5, 4\}$ respectively, with the far nest having quality 1.0. (In the equidistant case, we varied the quality of one nest while the other had quality 1.0.) Fig. 4 shows the resulting accuracy and decision time.

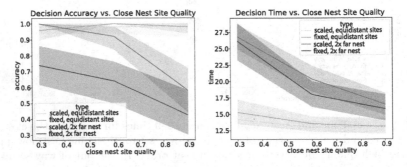

Fig. 4. Decision Accuracy and Time given varying differences in site quality between the near and the far nest.

As predicted, a smaller difference in site quality/quorum threshold led to significantly (Welch's T-test, $p = 0.05$) lower decision accuracy for the non-equidistant setup. In the equidistant setup, agents were able to achieve a near-100% outcome regardless of magnitude of differences in site quality. However, in the unbalanced setup, we confirmed that for larger differences in site quality, the algorithm comes to a more accurate decision, showing that non-equidistant candidate nest setups cause sensitivity to absolute site value differences that can't be seen in the equidistant setup.

5 Discussion

The results demonstrate our model's ability to improve accuracy when choosing from a higher quality, further site and a lower quality, closer site. This improvement comes at the cost of a higher decision time when converging on a lower quality site, because the quorum threshold for low quality sites is higher in our model. This higher decision time is reasonable and represents hesitance when committing to a poor quality option in the hopes of finding a better one.

Our model also demonstrated the extra difficulty that comes with a lower quality site being in the path from the home nest to a high quality site. Qualitative observation showed that agents travelling back and forth between the far site and the home nest often unintentionally contributed to a quorum in the poor quality, in-the-way site as they travelled through it. We showed that using a scaled quorum threshold as opposed to a fixed one is an effective way of significantly increasing decision accuracy. However, even if the closer, poor quality site is completely out of the way of the far, high quality site, Fig. 3 shows that using a scaled quorum can still help to improve accuracy.

Figure 4 shows that our model is still successful when candidate sites are equidistant from home, as is most commonly tested. We also show that an equidistant setup is not influenced by the absolute difference between candidate site qualities. Contrarily, in the setup with a further, high quality nest, it is harder to make an accurate decision the smaller the quality difference between the high and low quality nests. Note that it is also less grievous of an error to choose the low quality nest when the quality difference is small.

We observed a shorter decision time in conjunction with lower accuracy, similar to the time-accuracy trade-off in natural swarms [5,10]. In each set of 100 trials run, there were at most 2 split decisions, indicating our model succeeds in keeping the swarm together even when migrating to the further nest.

6   Future Work

While our model has made strides in being more accurate when choosing between sites with different geographical distributions, many site setups have yet to be tested. Future work could introduce obstacles to the environment, or try to adapt the house hunting model to an arena with continuous site values.

Our model suggests that a quorum threshold that scales with site quality leads to more accurate site selection. Future work could explore if actual ants do the same and use this information to create more accurate models.

Lastly, while our model is hard to analyze without making simplifications (because it involves agents physically moving in space), future work could try to develop analytical bounds. One method we envision is simplifying the chance of each site being discovered to a fixed probability and trying to model agent population flow between the different model states, similar to [16], which does this for candidate sites all with an equal chance of discovery.

Acknowledgements. This work was supported by NSF awards CCF-1461559, CCF-1810758, and CCF-2139936.

References

1. Cai, G.: Geometric Swarm Modelling (2022). https://doi.org/10.5281/zenodo.6508646

2. Cai, G., Sofge, D.: An urgency-dependent quorum sensing algorithm for N-site selection in autonomous swarms. In: Proceedings of the 18th International Conference on Autonomous Agents and MultiAgent Systems, pp. 1853–1855 (2019)
3. Camazine, S., Visscher, P.K., Finley, J., Vetter, R.S.: House-hunting by honey bee swarms: collective decisions and individual behaviors. Insectes Soc. **46**(4), 348–360 (1999)
4. Campo, A., Garnier, S., Dédriche, O., Zekkri, M., Dorigo, M.: Self-organized discrimination of resources. PLoS ONE **6**(5), e19888 (2011)
5. Chittka, L., Dyer, A.G., Bock, F., Dornhaus, A.: Bees trade off foraging speed for accuracy. Nature **424**(6947), 388 (2003)
6. Cody, J.R., Adams, J.A.: An evaluation of quorum sensing mechanisms in collective value-sensitive site selection. In: 2017 International Symposium on Multi-Robot and Multi-Agent Systems (MRS), pp. 40–47 (2017). https://doi.org/10.1109/MRS.2017.8250929
7. Fan, X., Sayers, W., Zhang, S., Han, Z., Ren, L., Chizari, H.: Review and classification of bio-inspired algorithms and their applications. J. Bionic Eng. **17**(3), 611–631 (2020)
8. Franks, N.R., et al.: Can ant colonies choose a far-and-away better nest over an in-the-way poor one? Anim. Behav. **76**(2), 323–334 (2008)
9. Hamann, H., Schmickl, T., Wörn, H., Crailsheim, K.: Analysis of emergent symmetry breaking in collective decision making. Neural Comput. Appl. **21**(2), 207–218 (2012)
10. Heitz, R.P.: The speed-accuracy tradeoff: history, physiology, methodology, and behavior. Front. Neurosci. **8**, 150 (2014)
11. Khurana, S., Sofge, D.: Quorum sensing re-evaluation algorithm for N-site selection in autonomous swarms. In: ICAART (1), pp. 193–198 (2020)
12. Parker, C.A.C., Zhang, H.: Cooperative decision-making in decentralized multiple-robot systems: the best-of-N problem. IEEE/ASME Trans. Mechatron. **14**, 240–251 (2009)
13. Pratt, S.C.: Behavioral mechanisms of collective nest-site choice by the ant temnothorax curvispinosus. Insectes Soc. **52**(4), 383–392 (2005)
14. Pratt, S.C.: Quorum sensing by encounter rates in the ant *Temnothorax albipennis*. Behav. Ecol. **16**(2), 488–496 (2005)
15. Pratt, S.C., Sumpter, D.J., Mallon, E.B., Franks, N.R.: An agent-based model of collective nest choice by the ant *Temnothorax albipennis*. Anim. Behav. **70**(5), 1023–1036 (2005)
16. Reina, A., Marshall, J.A., Trianni, V., Bose, T.: Model of the best-of-N nest-site selection process in honeybees. Phys. Rev. E **95**(5), 052411 (2017)
17. Reina, A., Valentini, G., Fernández-Oto, C., Dorigo, M., Trianni, V.: A design pattern for decentralised decision making. PLoS ONE **10**(10), e0140950 (2015)
18. Reynolds, C.W.: Flocks, herds and schools: a distributed behavioral model. In: Proceedings of the 14th Annual Conference on Computer Graphics and Interactive Techniques, pp. 25–34 (1987)
19. Robinson, E.J., Smith, F.D., Sullivan, K.M., Franks, N.R.: Do ants make direct comparisons? Proc. R. Soc. B: Biol. Sci. **276**(1667), 2635–2641 (2009)
20. Rubenstein, M., Ahler, C., Nagpal, R.: Kilobot: a low cost scalable robot system for collective behaviors. In: 2012 IEEE International Conference on Robotics and Automation, pp. 3293–3298. IEEE (2012)
21. Sims, D.W., Humphries, N.E., Bradford, R.W., Bruce, B.D.: Lévy flight and Brownian search patterns of a free-ranging predator reflect different prey field characteristics. J. Anim. Ecol. **81**(2), 432–442 (2012)

22. Valentini, G., Ferrante, E., Dorigo, M.: The best-of-N problem in robot swarms: formalization, state of the art, and novel perspectives. Front. Robot. AI **4**, 9 (2017)
23. Wessnitzer, J., Melhuish, C.: Collective decision-making and behaviour transitions in distributed ad hoc wireless networks of mobile robots: target-hunting. In: Banzhaf, W., Ziegler, J., Christaller, T., Dittrich, P., Kim, J.T. (eds.) ECAL 2003. LNCS (LNAI), vol. 2801, pp. 893–902. Springer, Heidelberg (2003). https:// doi.org/10.1007/978-3-540-39432-7_96
24. Zhao, J., Lynch, N., Pratt, S.C.: The power of social information in ant-colony house-hunting: a computational modeling approach. bioRxiv, pp. 2020-10 (2021)

An Approach Based on Particle Swarm Optimization for Inspection of Spacecraft Hulls by a Swarm of Miniaturized Robots

Bahar Haghighat[1,2(✉)], Johannes Boghaert[1,3], Zev Minsky-Primus[1],
Julia Ebert[1], Fanghzheng Liu[4], Martin Nisser[4], Ariel Ekblaw[5],
and Radhika Nagpal[1,2]

[1] Harvard University, Boston, MA, USA
bahar.haghighat@princeton.edu
[2] Princeton University, Princeton, NJ, USA
[3] Swiss Federal Institute of Technology in Zürich (ETHZ), Zürich, Switzerland
[4] Massachusetts Institute of Technology (MIT), Cambridge, MA, USA
[5] MIT Media Lab Space Exploration Initiative, Cambridge, MA, USA

Abstract. The remoteness and hazards that are inherent to the operating environments of space infrastructures promote their need for automated robotic inspection. In particular, micrometeoroid and orbital debris impact and structural fatigue are common sources of damage to spacecraft hulls. Vibration sensing has been used to detect structural damage in spacecraft hulls as well as in structural health monitoring practices in industry by deploying static sensors. In this paper, we propose using a swarm of miniaturized vibration-sensing mobile robots realizing a network of mobile sensors. We present a distributed inspection algorithm based on the bio-inspired particle swarm optimization and evolutionary algorithm niching techniques to deliver the task of enumeration and localization of an *a priori* unknown number of vibration sources on a simplified 2.5D spacecraft surface. Our algorithm is deployed on a swarm of simulated cm-scale wheeled robots. These are guided in their inspection task by sensing vibrations arising from failure points on the surface which are detected by on-board accelerometers. We study three performance metrics: (1) proximity of the localized sources to the ground truth locations, (2) time to localize each source, and (3) time to finish the inspection task given a 75% inspection coverage threshold. We find that our swarm is able to successfully localize the present sources accurately and complete the predefined inspection coverage threshold.

1 Introduction

Many industries, such as agriculture, bridge and wind turbine maintenance, and space exploration are actively investing in robotic inspection [8–10, 24]. The overarching goal is to reduce the risk, cost, and service downtime by supporting human inspection. Deploying robots becomes particularly useful when inspection must be carried out in dangerous conditions or over extended periods of time. In

© Springer Nature Switzerland AG 2022
M. Dorigo et al. (Eds.): ANTS 2022, LNCS 13491, pp. 14–27, 2022.
https://doi.org/10.1007/978-3-031-20176-9_2

particular, long-term space infrastructure deployments will benefit from robotic inspection [3]. Across a long deployment time, damages caused by structural fatigue and micrometeoroid and orbital debris (MMOD) become non-negligible [16]. Identifying and mending such damages before they become a source of major structural failure is critical. As an example, the International Space Station (ISS) has now been in operation for over two decades. As the structure ages, failures arise [1,16]. In the near future, this could also apply to the Lunar Gateway space station and the lunar surface Base Camp of NASA's Artemis program. Regular inspection is instrumental to extending lifetime of such deployments.

Vibration sensing and analysis methods are widely used in structural health monitoring [30,33]. In aerospace applications, in particular, the accelerometer-based Wing Leading Edge Impact Detection System (WLEIDS) was set up and flown on all shuttle flights after the 2003 fatal accident of the Columbia space shuttle. Currently, more than 80 accelerometers are in operation on the ISS for structural dynamics monitoring [33]. The underlying theoretical methods for vibration analysis are based on the vibration response or modal analysis of an a priori known structure [6,13]. The signal processing and failure identification methods depend on the specific target systems [38]. Standard practices typically involve deployment of a large set of static sensors with fixed sampling rates [15].

An automated inspection task may be performed by using a network of static sensors (deployed pre- or post-construction) or a single mobile robot (deployed post-construction). There are, however, multiple benefits in using a swarm of mobile robots. Swarms are known for their resilience to failure of individual units. Compared to fixed sensor networks, used in many environmental monitoring applications, robot swarms provide dynamic and flexible coverage performances [7]. Minimizing the complexity and cost of the individual robotic units is required for achieving low-cost swarm operations. This drive for simplicity has been the motivation behind employing bio-inspired algorithms and miniaturized robots.

An automated inspection task can be formulated based on the well-studied source localization task [11,21,23], that involves three components: (i) finding a cue, (ii) tracing the cue to a source location, and (iii) confirming a localized source. We formulate our inspection task as a repetition of a source localization task until a termination condition is reached. This requires two high-level search behaviors: a *local search* behavior to localize a new source in the search space and a *global search* behavior to maximize exploration and coverage of the search space. In what follows, we briefly review the literature for both search behaviors. **Global search** methods aim to maximize coverage through (i) a random or (ii) a systematic exploration of the search space. Lévy flights and Brownian motion random walks explore a search space randomly [27,28,36]. The basic lawnmower problem in an unobstructed environment and the traveling salesman problem are examples of systematic exploration methods. Being NP-hard [4,5], there is no guaranteed way to determine the optimal solution to these problems in order to cover the search space, however, near optimal solutions are possible [20]. **Local search** methods aim to localize a source [19]. Three main categories of these search methods can be identified: (i) reactive, (ii) heuristic cognitive, and (iii) probabilistic cognitive methods. **Reactive** search methods, such as gradient-based and bug algorithms, guide the search by relying solely on the latest observations made by the robots. These methods are typically simple and require little memory and computational resources [31,34,37], but have been shown to perform poorly in complex search scenarios [11,21]. Cognitive methods combine incoming observations with previously gathered information to guide the search [19]. **Heuristic cognitive** search methods see the source localization problem as an optimization problem. The objective function to be optimized can, in the case of an odor source localization problem for instance, be the gas concentration sensed by the robots [19]. Heuristic methods typically lend themselves well to multi-robot search scenarios [19]; by design, their mathematical optimization counterparts deploy multiple agents as candidate solutions that explore the search space. The most known bio-inspired example of heuristic optimization methods are the Particle Swarm Optimization (PSO) [14] and the Cuckoo Search (CS) [39]. PSO-based multi-robot search has been studied in [18,32]. **Probabilistic cognitive** search methods use probabilistic inference to derive the distribution of the cue in the search space [19,37]. This derivation requires a known dispersion model for any given cue and environment [19] and is often based on the Bayesian inference framework, such as Hidden Markov Models (HMMs) [29] and Particle Filters (PFs) [22]. Another example in this category is infotaxis, which uses an entropy-reduction principle [35]. Probabilistic cognitive search methods are applicable only as long as their underlying model assumptions hold and accurate cue dispersion models are available; for this reason, these methods remain less applicable to localizing failure sources using vibration cues.

We believe that small-scale vibration-sensing robot swarms have a great potential for a variety of structural health monitoring tasks. In this work, we contribute towards realizing such potential by presenting a simulation and algorithmic framework that enables a simulated swarm of miniaturized robots to inspect simplified spacecraft hull surface models. To the best of our knowledge, our work is the first to propose and demonstrate the utility of vibration-sensing surface-inspecting robot swarms. We plan to conduct and present real robot experiments in future works. In this work, we contribute and combine two main elements:

- **Localizing an *a priori* unknown number of failure sources:** Unlike source localization, in inspection tasks the number of failure sources is *a priori* unknown. We address this by employing a PSO-based heuristic local search as well as a coverage maximizing Lévy random walk global search.
- **Using vibration sensing for localizing the failure sources:** Compared to odor sensing paradigms, vibration sensing remains under-addressed in autonomous inspecting robot swarms. We employ a realistically modeled vibration signal (ANSYS software) on simplified spacecraft surface sections.

2   Problem Statement

We formally define the inspection task that we set out to undertake as the repeated localization of any multitude of *failure sources* on a 2.5D (a 2D curved)

(a) Simulated robot   (b) Real robot   (c) Simulated robot   (d) Real robot

Fig. 1. We use a realistic model of the Rovable robot in our simulation experiments. The real Rovable robot (b, d) and its simulation model created in Webots (a, c) have similar physical properties. For scale, each wheel is 12mm in diameter.

surface in orbit, using a swarm of robots that sense the vibration signal as a *cue*, until a termination condition based on the overall surface coverage level is met.

A *failure source* is then defined as a feature that disturbs the normal functioning of a system. Detecting a failure source requires knowledge of the functional state of the system. We hypothesize that failure sources such as cracks and fissures on the surface result in creation of specific vibration signal profiles that are detectable in the presence of endemic or induced vibration energy [2]. In our modeling of the failure sources, we further simplify the points of mechanical failure as sources of induced vibration applying force to the surface following a sinusoidal pattern at a frequency 1 Hz, which falls within the mid-frequency range of the vibratory regime of the ISS [25]. The amplitude of the sinusoidal load, set to 1N, is chosen such that the resulting acceleration values are within the ISS acceleration spectrum ranging from below a micro-g to 10 milli-g [25]. The *cue* is then the acceleration signal that is sensed during the inspection task.

3   Simulation Framework

Our simulation framework serves as the virtual environment in which we deploy and study our inspecting robot swarm. Two main software components are used: the ANSYS software, which we use for creating realistic vibration signals propagating on a surface that models a shell structure in orbit, and the Webots robotic simulator [26], which we use for simulating the operation of our robots.

Within Webots, we have three main components: (i) a realistic robot model of a 3-cm sized 4-wheeled robot with magnetic wheels, (ii) ferromagnetic target surfaces that the robots traverse to inspect, and (iii) a (supervisor controller) script that passes on the vibration data to the robots, emulating the function of a black box that contains an acceleration sensor and a processing unit that returns the maximum observed acceleration amplitude. The robot model shown in Fig. 1 is based on the Rovable robot. Originally designed as a mobile wearable robot, Rovables can sense acceleration using their on-board IMUs [12]. Rovables are capable of wireless communication and low-power localization using their wheel encoders and on-board IMUs for inertial-based navigation. The robots are able to carry loads of 1.5N and can adhere to ferromagnetic surfaces using

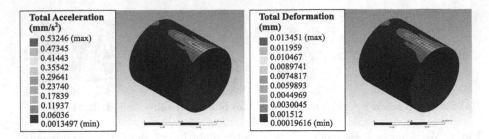

Fig. 2. We use a cylindrical surface of 4m length in ANSYS to model a simplified spacecraft hull and empirically tune the elastic support parameter to 10^{-4} N/mm^3 and the load case amplitude to 1N to mimic the vibration regime of the ISS [25]. Vibration propagation is strongly biased along the axial length.

their magnetic pincher-wheels. A newer version of the robot is equipped with a vertically-mounted linear actuator for inducing vibrations, which could potentially be utilized as an alternative to using endemic vibrations energy. All basic operations of Rovables have been tested in zero gravity conditions in multiple real-life parabolic flights. In this paper, we study the zero gravity conditions in simulation. Within Webots, the Rovable proto file captures the physical properties of the real robot, such as mass, center of mass, and surface contact properties.

The simulated Rovables are additionally assumed to have knowledge of the map of the environment as well as their own locations on the map using a global positioning sensor. Knowledge of the map is a realistic assumption because spacecraft hulls are routinely modeled in extensive detail. A loss-free infinite-range communication channel is also assumed between the robots. The robots share their locations on the map and use this information for collision avoidance.

Within ANSYS, we use the Transient Analysis to subject the surface model to a sinusoidal load case of 1 N at 1 Hz representing a vibration source. To represent the placement of the surface model in orbit, we use an elastic support boundary condition that involves the notion of foundation stiffness expressed in N/mm^3. This is typically used to model soil supported or submersed structures. We empirically set the foundation stiffness parameter to 10^{-4} N/mm^3 by running a series of simulations and evaluating the results in discussion with a human expert. The resulting deformation amplitude for the applied load case is 13 μm. Figure 2 shows the surface model used for the empirical calibrations. In order to reduce the computational cost of the data processing and export pipeline, we create data files that approximate the time-dependent acceleration data obtained from ANSYS with 2D Gaussian distributions that represent the amplitude of the acceleration data on the surface. This data is then retrieved by the (supervisor controller) script in our Webots simulation and is passed to the simulated robots according to their location at each simulation step.

Algorithm 1. Inspection Algorithm Overview

1: **run** Lévy Random Walk (RW)   ▷ Initialize
2: **while** *coverage* < 75% **do**
3:     **if** *robot* in collision **then**   ▷ Collision avoidance
4:         **run** Collision Avoidance (CA)
5:     **else if** *cue* picked up or recruited into niche **then**   ▷ Local search
6:         **run** Particle Swarm Optimization (PSO)
7:         **if** *cue* is a *source* **then**   ▷ Source confirmation
8:             **declare** *source*
9:             **run** Directed Walk (DW)   ▷ Re-initialization
10:             **return to** Lévy Random Walk (RW)
11:         **end if**
12:     **else**
13:         **run** Lévy Random Walk (RW)   ▷ Global search
14:     **end if**
15:     **update** *coverage*   ▷ Update coverage
16: **end while**

---

4 Proposed Algorithm

The overall structure of our inspection algorithm is shown in Algorithm 1. We use a multi-modal variation of the PSO algorithm that takes advantage of a niche formation behavior to allow parallel search for multiple sources as our local search strategy combined with a random walk approach as our global search strategy. Formation of niches happens simultaneously as the robots switch from global to local search upon sensing a cue. We do not consider merging of the niches, if robots from two niches come close they repel each other. There are four main control states in the algorithm, which we explain briefly in this paragraph and in more detail in the following ones. In the absence of any prior sensing of a cue, the robots start in the Random Walk (RW) state, performing an unbiased Lévy random walk around the environment until they sense a cue. Upon sensing a cue, the robot will start performing a biased random walk in the Particle Swarm Optimization (PSO) state while simultaneously forming a niche by recruiting a second robot for a second opinion on the source location. Once a robot is finished localizing a source, it starts in the Directed Walk (DW) state and moves to an unexplored area in the environment and the niche is dismantled. The robot will execute the Collision Avoidance (CA) state at any point in time if it is closer than a threshold distance to a static obstacle or moving robot in the environment.

For each particle i, dimension j, and time step t, the PSO velocity update is:

$$v_{ij}^t = \omega * v_{ij}^{t-1} + c_1 * \text{rnd}()^t \times \left(p_{\text{best}_{ij}} - x_{ij}^{t-1}\right) + c_2 * \text{rnd}()^t \times \left(g_{\text{best}_{ij}} - x_{ij}^{t-1}\right) \tag{1}$$

where p_{best} and g_{best} are respectively the positions of the best values observed by the individual i and the corresponding niche. The inertia term $\omega = 0.15$, $c_1 = 0.35$, and $c_2 = 0.5$ are weights that balance exploration and exploitation in the search space. The niche formation behavior is part of the local search behavior and allows for confirming an identified source location. Here, we consider niches of size 2. In particular, once a robot is in the vicinity of a source and starts the PSO state, it engages in niche formation by recruiting its nearest neighbor within a maximum range of 1m. The recruited robot then starts in PSO state.

After localizing a source, a robot engages in a directed walk behavior, moving towards unexplored parts of the environment. This is achieved by using a sliding window approach to identify the least covered areas and then performing a roulette wheel sampling where the likelihood of selecting a less covered goal position increases quadratically and inversely with surface coverage level there. Upon localization, a source is marked on the coverage map as a circular obstacle region with a radius determined by the range a cue was first perceived from by an approaching robot, deterring the robots from the cue of a discovered source.

Collision avoidance is performed using the artificial potential field (APF) method based on (i) a map of the environment in which the boundaries of the arena and the obstacles are known and (ii) by communicating with other robots to obtain their location on the map. Each obstacle contributes a repulsive term to update a robot's velocity. The repulsive term i in dimension j for robot r is:

$$v_{i,j}^r = w_i \times \left(\frac{1}{d_i^r} - \frac{1}{\theta_i} \right) \times \left(\frac{x_j - p_{i,j}}{(d_i^r)^3} \right) \tag{2}$$

where d_i is the distance from the robot to obstacle i, x_j is the robot's position in dimension j and $p_{i,j}$ is the closest point on obstacle i in dimension j. The threshold θ_i is the distance to the obstacle i below which the robot will engage in collision avoidance. The threshold and weight values depend on the obstacle. There are three obstacle types: (i) static, which includes the arena boundaries and the obstacles ($w = 0.075\,\mathrm{m}$, $\theta = 5 \times 10^{-4}$), (ii) dynamic, which includes a moving robot ($w = 0.12\,\mathrm{m}$, $\theta = 3 \times 10^{-4}$), and (iii) niche, which includes a robot that is part of a niche ($w = 0.75\,\mathrm{m}$, $\theta = 5 \times 10^{-4}$).

Given enough time, we would like that all the sources present in the search environment be successfully localized. We employ a Lévy random walk for the global search behavior. The Lévy random walk assigns a random orientation (angle) and a random step length (magnitude) to the robot, following a Lévy distribution. This exploratory random walk guarantees full coverage of the search environment asymptotically. We terminate the inspection based on a predefined coverage threshold and using a coverage map that is shared between the robots.

The shared coverage map is represented as a grid-based map of $10 \times 10\,\mathrm{cm}$ cells. As the robots move across the surface, sense the acceleration cue, and localize sources, they update the shared coverage map using their internal sensor model. We use a simplified sensor model that is a two dimensional Gaussian distribution of $\mathcal{N}(\mu = 0\,\mathrm{m}, \sigma_x = \sigma_z = 0.1\,\mathrm{m})$. To update the coverage map based on a single robot's observation, the sensor model Gaussian distribution centered around the location of the reporting robot is superimposed on the coverage map by comparing the coverage value in the map and the coverage value from the sensor model at each point. The coverage value in the map is then replaced by the maximum of the two values. The same update rule is applied for merging coverage information from multiple robots to update the shared coverage map (Fig. 3).

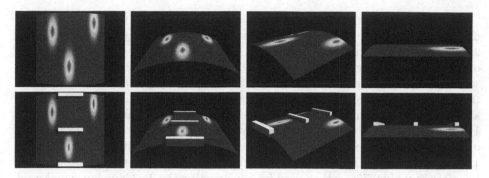

Fig. 3. The columns show different angles of the two surfaces shown in the rows. We study two surface models in our simulation experiments in Webots, one with no obstacles in Scenario I (top row) and one with three cuboid obstacles in Scenario II (bottom row). The three vibration sources and the cue spread are visualized. The acceleration cue spread is affected by the presence of obstacles.

5 Simulation Experiments

We used the Amazon Web Services (AWS) cloud platform for batch simulations. Each simulation instance was launched on a 4-core CPU with 8 GB of RAM.

5.1 Experimental Objectives

Our desired objective for a given inspection experiment is threefold. We would like that the swarm succeeds (i) in localizing all the sources (localization success), (ii) in reaching the coverage threshold for terminating the inspection (termination success), and (iii) that all of the robots in the swarm manage to maneuver around in the search space, without getting lost or stuck, sensing the cue to the source locations while avoiding obstacles (maneuverability success).

To quantify the swarm performance on these aspects, we take inspiration from metrics used in the fields of source localization and target search and consider three performance metrics [17,40]. In each scenario, we quantify (i) the source localization accuracy, that is the proximity of a confirmed source location to its ground truth location, (ii) the time to find each source present in the search space, and (iii) the time to reach the coverage threshold termination criterion. To gain insight into the control dynamics of the inspecting swarm, we look at the time the robots spend in each of the control states described in Sect. 4.

5.2 Experimental Scenarios

The real-world inspection problem that underlies our research is a complicated undertaking. Within the scope of this work, we study two simplified problems. We consider two experimental scenarios. In each scenario, we deploy a swarm of size $N = 8$ robots to inspect the surfaces for sources of vibration.

Scenario I comprises a 2.5D curved cylindrical surface with projected flat dimensions of 4×4 m. The ANSYS simulations involve a full cylindrical surface of 2mm thickness, 4m radius, and 6m axial length. The surface section is a quarter of the full cylinder with the arena edges 1m away from the cylinder edges. The sources of vibration are at locations $(x = 2\,\text{m}, z = 3\,\text{m})$, $(x = 1\,\text{m}, z = 1\,\text{m})$, and $(x = 3.5\,\text{m}, z = 0.5\,\text{m})$ on the projected surface reference frame, with the origin at the top-left corner. The entire surface is subject to a foundation stiffness of $10^{-4}\frac{\text{N}}{\text{mm}^3}$, and the mesh is sized uniformly with cells of 10×10 cm. At the location of each vibration source, we apply a sinusoidal load case with an amplitude of 1N and frequency 1 Hz. The peak amplitude at steady state at each mesh node, i.e. after roughly 9.75s, is then used for constructing the 2D Gaussian signal used in Webots (see Sect. 3). For Scenario I, we use $\mathcal{N}(\mu = 0\,\text{m}, \sigma_x = 0.15\,\text{m}, \sigma_z = 0.45\,\text{m})$ scaled by 0.7708 for all three sources. For Scenario II, we use $\mathcal{N}(\mu = 0\,\text{m}, \sigma_x = 0.1\,\text{m}, \sigma_z = 0.25\,\text{m})$ scaled by 0.6511 at location $(x = 2\,\text{m}, z = 3\,\text{m})$ and $\mathcal{N}(\mu = 0\,\text{m}, \sigma_x = 0.15\,\text{m}, \sigma_z = 0.45\,\text{m})$ scaled by 0.7334 and 0.7359 at locations $(x = 1\,\text{m}, z = 1\,\text{m})$ and $(x = 3.5\,\text{m}, z = 0.5\,\text{m})$, respectively.

Scenario II is an extension of Scenario I; we further increase the geometrical complexity of the search environment by introducing three cuboid obstacles representing features such as ridges or add-on sections on the surface.

6   Results

We obtained the results of 100 trials of the two simulation experimental scenarios described in Sect. 5. The random seed was fixed per robot. The robots' starting positions were randomized per trial. By simulating swarms of various sizes and observing the effect of robot density on inspection performance, we chose the swarm size $N = 8$. For the sake of brevity, those studies are not discussed here.

Figure 4 visualizes how presence of obstacles impacts the robots trajectories and their coverage performance by comparing two trials of the two scenarios.

The swarm performance results are shown in Fig. 5. We considered the three performance metrics described in Sect. 5: (i) source localization accuracy, (ii) time to localize each source and to reach the %75 coverage threshold, and (iii) time spent in each of the four main control states. In both experimental scenarios, we observed that the experimental objectives we laid out in Sect. 5.1 were successfully achieved. In particular, the robots managed to successfully localize all three vibration sources in the environment while traversing the 2.5D surfaces, performing obstacle avoidance, and sensing the vibration cue. The complexity of the search environment increases from Scenario I to Scenario II. This increase in complexity clearly affects the inspection completion time, i.e., the time the %75 coverage threshold is reached, as well as the time each of the three sources are discovered (indicated by S_i for $i = \{1, 2, 3\}$ in Fig. 5b, f). This is also visible in the time progress of discovering sources as shown in Fig. 5d, h, where the solid line and shaded area represent the average and one standard deviation interval over 100 trials, respectively. The same effect can be noted by comparing the time spent in the RW control state between the two scenarios (Fig. 5c, g). We can

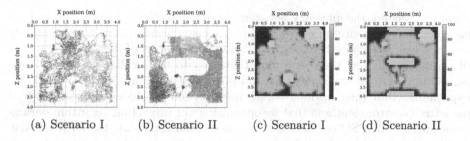

(a) Scenario I   (b) Scenario II   (c) Scenario I   (d) Scenario II

Fig. 4. Obstacles affect robot trajectories and overall coverage maps. Trajectory and coverage plots for two trials of Scenario I (a, c) and Scenario II (b, d) are compared. Trajectory of each robot is depicted in a different color (a, b). Higher coverage level is shown in warmer color (c, d). Upon localization, a source is marked on the coverage map as a circular region with a radius determined by the range a cue was first perceived from by an approaching robot. Because the spread of the cue is larger along the z axis, the size of the marked regions differ depending on the direction of approach. (Color figure online)

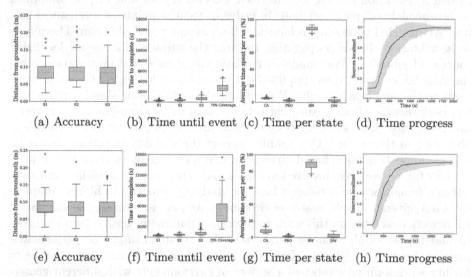

(a) Accuracy   (b) Time until event   (c) Time per state   (d) Time progress

(e) Accuracy   (f) Time until event   (g) Time per state   (h) Time progress

Fig. 5. The robots manage to successfully achieve all the experimental objectives laid out in Sect. 5.1. The presence of obstacles negatively impacts the swarm's temporal performance but appears to have minimal impact on the source localization accuracy. We study three main performance metrics in Scenario I (top row) and Scenario II (bottom row): the localization accuracy (a, e), the time elapsed before the discovery of a source and before reaching the %75 coverage threshold (b, f), and the time spent by the robots in each of the four main control states (c, g). The plots show results for 100 simulation experiments per scenario.

explain the variation in source localization accuracy (Fig. 5a, e) by considering three main factors. First, the more time the robots spend in the PSO versus the CA control state, the higher their chances will be to achieve a better localization accuracy. Second, the interplay between the shape and spread of the cue and the placement of the sources in the arena plays a significant role in how accurately a source can be localized. Lastly, the various parameters of the inspection algorithm determine how the robots find their way to the localized sources. These parameters were all empirically set and none was systematically optimized. We hypothesize that their optimal values may depend on the overall geometry of the search environment and that by optimizing our inspection algorithm parameters, such as the PSO coefficients, the random walk step size, the APF collision avoidance parameters, the niche size, and the maximum niche recruitment range we can enhance the various swarm performance metrics, including the source localization accuracy.

7   Conclusion

We developed a simulation and algorithmic framework that enables studying a swarm of vibration sensing miniaturized wheeled robots that inspect simplified surface models of spacecraft hulls in order to localize points of mechanical failure. We modeled points of mechanical failure as sources of vibration. The robots sense vibration signals propagating through the surface as a cue for localizing sources of vibration. We simulated realistic vibration signal propagation using the ANSYS software, then simplified data transfer by fitting 2D Gaussian functions to the simulation results. We used the Webots robotic simulator to study the performance of our inspecting robot swarm in two experimental scenarios involving three sources on 2.5D cylindrical surfaces in presence and absence of obstacles on the surface. Our results support the viability of robot swarms for surface inspection tasks based on sensing vibration signals through the surface.

Our future work will involve leveraging and extending the modeling and algorithmic framework we developed here for studying scenarios of higher complexity. First, given a specific search environment, we plan to leverage the simulation framework developed in this work to perform a parameter optimization in order to find the set of algorithmic parameters that result in improved performance metrics. Second, we plan to develop a fully automated simulation pipeline to facilitate randomized studies of a variety of environments with different geometries. In particular, we plan to automate the process of simulating the vibration signal from ANSYS such that the data is directly accessible by the simulated robots within Webots. Third, we plan to implement realistic constraints in the communication range and bandwidth of the simulated robots within Webots.

Our hope is that this work supports and inspires studies of vibration-sensing robot swarms as a flexible solution for structural surface inspection applications.

Acknowledgements. We thank Dr. Harald Wild from ETH Zürich for his help with the ANSYS simulations. This work was supported by a Swiss National Science Foundation (SNSF) postdoctoral fellowship award P400P2_191116, an Office of Naval Research (ONR) grant N00014-22-1-2222, and a National Aeronautics and Space Administration (NASA) grant 80NSSC21K0353.

References

1. Russian cosmonauts find new cracks in ISS module. Reuters (2021). https://www.reuters.com/lifestyle/science/russian-cosmonauts-find-new-cracks-iss-module-2021-08-30/
2. Abu-Mahfouz, I., Banerjee, A.: Crack detection and identification using vibration signals and fuzzy clustering. Procedia Comput. Sci. **114**, 266–274 (2017)
3. Aloor, J.J., Sajeev, S., Shakya, A.: Space Robotics versus Humans in Space (2020)
4. Arkin, E.M., Fekete, S.P., Mitchell, J.S.: Approximation algorithms for lawn mowing and milling. Comput. Geom. **17**(1–2), 25–50 (2000). A preliminary version of this paper was entitled The lawnmower problem and appears in the Proceedings of the 5th Canadian Conference on Computational Geometry, Waterloo, Canada, pp. 461–466 (1993)
5. Arkin, E.M., Hassin, R.: Approximation algorithms for the geometric covering salesman problem. Discret. Appl. Math. **55**(3), 197–218 (1994)
6. Avci, O., Abdeljaber, O., Kiranyaz, S., Hussein, M., Gabbouj, M., Inman, D.J.: A review of vibration-based damage detection in civil structures: from traditional methods to Machine Learning and Deep Learning applications. Mech. Syst. Signal Process. **147**, 107077 (2021)
7. Bayat, B., Crasta, N., Crespi, A., Pascoal, A.M., Ijspeert, A.: Environmental monitoring using autonomous vehicles: a survey of recent searching techniques. Curr. Opin. Biotechnol. **45**, 76–84 (2017). https://doi.org/10.1016/j.copbio.2017.01.009
8. Bualat, M., et al.: Autonomous robotic inspection for lunar surface operations. In: Laugier, C., Siegwart, R. (eds.) Field and Service Robotics, vol. 42, pp. 169–178. Springer, Cham (2008)
9. Carbone, C., Garibaldi, O., Kurt, Z.: Swarm robotics as a solution to crops inspection for precision agriculture. KnE Eng. **3**(1), 552 (2018)
10. Carrillo-Zapata, D., et al.: Mutual shaping in swarm robotics: user studies in fire and rescue, storage organization, and bridge inspection. Front. Robot. AI **7**, 53 (2020)
11. Chen, X., Huang, J.: Odor source localization algorithms on mobile robots: a review and future outlook. Robot. Auton. Syst. **112**, 123–136 (2019)
12. Dementyev, A., et al.: Rovables: miniature on-body robots as mobile wearables. In: Proceedings of the 29th Annual Symposium on User Interface Software and Technology, Tokyo Japan, pp. 111–120. ACM (2016). https://dl.acm.org/doi/10.1145/2984511.2984531
13. Doebling, S., Farrar, C., Prime, M., Shevitz, D.: Damage identification and health monitoring of structural and mechanical systems from changes in their vibration characteristics: a literature review. Technical report LA-13070-MS, 249299 (1996). https://doi.org/10.2172/249299
14. Eberhart, R., Kennedy, J.: Particle swarm optimization. In: Proceedings of the IEEE International Conference on Neural Networks, vol. 4, pp. 1942–1948 (1995)
15. Ganesan, V., Das, T., Rahnavard, N., Kauffman, J.L.: Vibration-based monitoring and diagnostics using compressive sensing. J. Sound Vib. **394**, 612–630 (2017)
16. Hyde, J.L., Christiansen, E.L., Lear, D.M.: Observations of MMOD impact damage to the ISS. In: International Orbital Debris Conference. No. JSC-E-DAA-TN75127 (2019)
17. Jain, U., Tiwari, R., Godfrey, W.W.: Multiple odor source localization using diverse-PSO and group-based strategies in an unknown environment. J. Comput. Sci. **34**, 33–47 (2019)

18. Jatmiko, W., Sekiyama, K., Fukuda, T.: A PSO-based mobile sensor network for odor source localization in dynamic environment: theory, simulation and measurement. In: 2006 IEEE International Conference on Evolutionary Computation, Vancouver, BC, Canada, pp. 1036–1043. IEEE (2006). https://doi.org/10.1109/CEC.2006.1688423
19. Jing, T., Meng, Q.H., Ishida, H.: Recent progress and trend of robot odor source localization. IEEE Trans. Electr. Electron. Eng. tee.23364 (2021)
20. Karapetyan, N., Benson, K., McKinney, C., Taslakian, P., Rekleitis, I.: Efficient multi-robot coverage of a known environment. In: 2017 IEEE/RSJ International Conference on Intelligent Robots and Systems (IROS), pp. 1846–1852 (2017). http://arxiv.org/abs/1808.02541
21. Kowadlo, G., Russell, R.A.: Robot odor localization: a taxonomy and survey. Int. J. Robot. Res. 27(8), 869–894 (2008)
22. Li, J.G., Meng, Q.H., Li, F., Zeng, M., Popescu, D.: Mobile robot based odor source localization via particle filter. In: Proceedings of the 48h IEEE Conference on Decision and Control (CDC) held jointly with 2009 28th Chinese Control Conference, Shanghai, China, pp. 2984–2989. IEEE (2009)
23. Lilienthal, A., Loutfi, A., Duckett, T.: Airborne chemical sensing with mobile robots. Sensors 6(11), 1616–1678 (2006)
24. Liu, Y., Hajj, M., Bao, Y.: Review of robot-based damage assessment for offshore wind turbines. Renew. Sustain. Energy Rev. 158, 112187 (2022)
25. McPherson, K., Hrovat, K., Kelly, E., Keller, J.: ISS researcher's guide: acceleration environment. Technical report, National Aeronautics and Space Administration
26. Michel, O.: WebotsTM: professional mobile robot simulation. arXiv:cs/0412052 (2004)
27. Palyulin, V.V., Chechkin, A.V., Metzler, R.: Levy flights do not always optimize random blind search for sparse targets. Proc. Natl. Acad. Sci. 111(8), 2931–2936 (2014)
28. Pang, B., Song, Y., Zhang, C., Wang, H., Yang, R.: A swarm robotic exploration strategy based on an improved random walk method. J. Robot. 2019, 1–9 (2019)
29. Pang, S., Farrell, J.: Chemical plume source localization. IEEE Trans. Syst. Man Cybern. Part B (Cybern.) 36(5), 1068–1080 (2006)
30. Park, J.: Special feature vibration-based structural health monitoring. Appl. Sci. 10(15), 5139 (2020)
31. Persson, E., Anisi, D.A.: A Comparative study of robotic gas source localization algorithms in industrial environments. IFAC Proc. Vol. 44(1), 899–904 (2011)
32. Pugh, J., Martinoli, A.: Inspiring and modeling multi-robot search with particle swarm optimization. In: 2007 IEEE Swarm Intelligence Symposium, Honolulu, HI, USA, pp. 332–339. IEEE (2007)
33. Richards, W.L., Madaras, E.I., Prosser, W.H., Studor, G.: NASA applications of structural health monitoring technology. In: International Workshop on Structural Health Monitoring, No. DFRC-E-DAA-TN11102 (2013)
34. Russell, R., Bab-Hadiashar, A., Shepherd, R.L., Wallace, G.G.: A comparison of reactive robot chemotaxis algorithms. Robot. Auton. Syst. 45(2), 83–97 (2003)
35. Vergassola, M., Villermaux, E., Shraiman, B.I.: Infotaxis as a strategy for searching without gradients. Nature 445(7126), 406–409 (2007)
36. Viswanathan, G.M., Buldyrev, S.V., Havlin, S., da Luz, M.G.E., Raposo, E.P., Stanley, H.E.: Optimizing the success of random searches. Nature 401(6756), 911–914 (1999)
37. Voges, N., Chaffiol, A., Lucas, P., Martinez, D.: Reactive searching and infotaxis in odor source localization. PLoS Comput. Biol. 10(10), e1003861 (2014)

38. Fan, W., Qiao, P.: Vibration-based damage identification methods: a review and comparative study. Struct. Health Monit. **10**(1), 83–111 (2011)
39. Yang, X.S., Deb, S.: Cuckoo search via Levy flights. In: 2009 World Congress on Nature & Biologically Inspired Computing (NaBIC), Coimbatore, India, pp. 210–214. IEEE (2009)
40. Zhang, J., Gong, D., Zhang, Y.: A niching PSO-based multi-robot cooperation method for localizing odor sources. Neurocomputing **123**, 308–317 (2014)

Automatic Design of Multi-objective Particle Swarm Optimizers

Daniel Doblas[1], Antonio J. Nebro[1,2](✉) [ID], Manuel López-Ibáñez[3] [ID],
José García-Nieto[1,2] [ID], and Carlos A. Coello Coello[4] [ID]

[1] ITIS Software, Universidad de Málaga, Málaga, Spain
{dandobjim,ajnebro,jnieto}@uma.es
[2] Departamento de Lenguajes y Ciencias de la Computación, Universidad de Málaga,
Málaga, Spain
[3] Alliance Manchester Business School, University of Manchester, Manchester, UK
manuel.lopez-ibanez@manchester.ac.uk
[4] Departamento de Computación, CINVESTAV-IPN, Mexico City, Mexico
ccoello@cs.cinvestav.mx

Abstract. Multi-objective particle swarm optimizers (MOPSOs) have
been widely used to deal with optimization problems having two or more
conflicting objectives. As happens with other metaheuristics, finding the
most adequate parameters settings for MOPSOs is not a trivial task,
and it is even harder to choose structural components that determine the
algorithm's design. Thus, it is an open question whether automatically-
designed MOPSOs can outperform the best human-designed MOP-
SOs from the literature. In this paper, we first design and develop
a component-based architecture and an algorithmic template, called
AMOPSO, for the auto-design and auto-configuration of MOPSOs using
jMetal and we integrate it with irace, an automatic-configuration tool.
Second, by taking as our starting point two algorithms (OMOPSO and
SMPSO), we conduct a study focused on automatically generating three
AMOPSO variants by using different well-known multi-objective benchmarking problem families (ZDT, DTLZ, and WFG) as *training* problems
for automatic design, and then we analyze whether they improve upon
the initial versions of the algorithms and how their components differ.
Experiments show that the two AMOPSO variants obtained from using,
respectively, the ZDT and DTLZ problems for training are able to statistically outperform the SMPSO and OMOPSO algorithms in all three
benchmark families previously indicated.

1 Introduction

Multi-objective particle swarm optimizers (MOPSOs) are popular techniques to
solve optimization problems composed of two or more conflicting objectives [17],
and new proposals appear regularly in international conferences and journals.
In this context, given the large number of possible algorithm's combinations
and configurations, it is often unclear what are the best design choices and

© Springer Nature Switzerland AG 2022
M. Dorigo et al. (Eds.): ANTS 2022, LNCS 13491, pp. 28–40, 2022.
https://doi.org/10.1007/978-3-031-20176-9_3

parameters settings to use in practice or which ones have the strongest impact on performance.

The automatic design and parameter configuration of metaheuristics [20] is an open research line that has as its main goal to provide users of these algorithms with tools able to obtain accurate configurations automatically. This way, given a set of problems to be solved, instead of using quick-search exhaustive (time-consuming) methods to configure a metaheuristic manually by performing pilot tests where the values of the parameters are adjusted in an *ad-hoc* manner, the idea is to use statistically-driven automatic configuration tools.

Our motivation emerges in the typical scenario where, given a set of problems to be solved, an expert user of a given algorithm can afford to set its parameters manually by performing pilot tests in which the parameter values are adjusted in some way, using experience or intuition. This is usually a trial-and-error process in which a limited number of configurations is explored, possibly suffering from human biases and incorrect assumptions. If we consider another scenario in which a non-expert user of the algorithm intends to solve a problem in a certain domain, such user will not have the experience to even attempt such a trial-and-error process and will simply use the default algorithmic parameters taken from the literature.

In this paper, we propose an auto-design framework that allows instantiating many different variants of multi-objective Particle Swarm Optimizers (MOP-SOs), some of them already available from the literature. In this framework, choosing a design and tuning the parameters of a MOPSO are conducted by means of irace [11], an automatic configuration tool, with the goal of identifying good configurations for well-known multi-objective continuous optimization benchmarks. For testing purposes, we study which design options, in combination with parameters settings, actually contribute the most to the performance of the automatically generated algorithms by comparing them with other configurations that instantiate well-known MOPSOs from the literature.

In this regard, the current paper is contextualized by the involvement of authors in the proposal of SMPSO [13] (an algorithm that remains as a very competitive Pareto-based MOPSO), the design and implementation of the jMetal framework for multi-objective optimization with metaheuristics [14], and the development of the irace package for automatic algorithm configuration [11]. Our objectives are then twofold: first, we aim to provide a software platform for MOPSO auto-configuration combining jMetal and irace and; second, we aim to conduct a study on the performance of algorithms generated from the developed auto-configurable MOPSO (AMOPSO) on three classic benchmarks of continuous optimization problems.

Our work follows the line started in [15], in which the combination of jMetal and irace to provide an auto-designed and auto-configurable version of NSGA-II [5] was described. In this regard, few similar studies have been presented in past references [4,10]. In the former, a context-free grammar approach was used to implement the algorithms and two tools were used for the auto-tuning: grammatical evolution and irace; the DTLZ benchmark problems [6] were used and SMPSO was chosen as a reference algorithm. Although we share similar goals, we rely on the use of jMetal, so that the resulting software becomes available to the community in a release of a framework which is widely known in the field; additionally, we consider a wider set of configurable features, as well as structural algorithmic component decisions in the generation of new variants. PSO-X [4] is comparable to the scale of our proposed framework by including a comprehensive number of characteristics of PSO, but it is focused on single-objective algorithms, so structural decisions concerning external archive management (including the role of archived particles in the velocity update) are not taken into account.

The remainder of this article is organized as follows. The next section is devoted to introduce the software tools used to develop the proposed framework. Section 3 describes the design and development decisions taken to generate the auto-MOPSO approach. Our experimental settings, as well as our comparisons and discussions are given in Sect. 4. Finally, our conclusions and some possible future steps in this research line are described in Sect. 5.

2   Software Tools

In this section, we briefly describe jMetal and irace, which are the two software tools we have used in this work.

jMetal [7,14] is an open source, Java-based framework for multi-objective optimization with metaheuristics that has become a widely used tool for many researchers in the area. The jMetal project started in 2006 and it is continuously evolving, and the main topic that is guiding currently its evolution is to adapt it to enable the auto-configuration and auto-design of multi-objective metaheuristics.

Elitist iterated racing, in particular the implementation available in the irace package [11] from version 2.0 and higher, is a method for the automatic configuration of optimization algorithms, i.e., to find accurate settings of a given algorithm for a given set of training instances of a problem. In this context, an algorithm configuration is a complete assignment of values to all required parameters of an algorithm. In irace, algorithm configurations are sampled from a sampling distribution, uniformly at random at the beginning, but biased towards the best configurations found in later iterations. At each iteration, the generated configurations and the "elite" ones from previous iterations are raced [3] by evaluating them on training problem instances. A statistical test is used to decide which configurations should be eliminated from the race, taking into account that an elite configuration cannot be outperformed by a configuration evaluated in fewer problem instances. When the race terminates, the surviving configurations become elites for the next iteration and are used to bias the sampling of new configurations. A complete description of elitist iterated racing is provided in its original paper [11].

3   Approach for Developing an Auto-configurable MOPSO

A number of MOPSOs are included in jMetal, from which two remarkable versions are OMOPSO [18] and SMPSO [13]. These algorithms are still considered as very competitive, and are both characterized by using an external archive to store the non-dominated solutions after the search process. Although they share a common PSO template, they are not ready to be used for automatic configuration because the template is not designed to configure its internal components in a flexible way, nor it allows to build a particular MOPSO instance in a declarative manner, which is a requirement for using automatic configuration methods.

The adopted approach to deal with these limitations is the same as applied in [15]. We have designed a new template for MOPSOs where their internals are represented as components that can be easily combined. The template is based on t1the pseudo-code included in Algorithm 1.

Algorithm 1. Pseudo-code of the MOPSO template.

createInitialSwarm()
evaluateSwarm()
initializeVelocity()
initializeLocalBest()
initializeGlobalBest()
while terminationConditionIsNotMet() **do**
    updateVelocity()
    updatePosition()
    perturbation() // mutation
    evaluateSwarm()
    updateGlobalBest()
    updateLocalBest()
end while
returnGlobalBest()

We can observe that the *run()* method follows the steps of a generic MOPSO algorithm, including a perturbation phase. All the components of a MOPSO are instances of classes representing them, so creating a particular MOPSO will consist of creating an instance of the *ParticleSwarmOptimizationAlgorithm* class with its concrete components.

There is a catalog of components of each type. The current components are taken from the implementations of OMOPSO and SMPSO but, with the purpose of only generating valid algorithmic designs while at the same time allowing a high degree of flexibility in the number of available designs, we have made some assumptions and some features of the algorithms have been relaxed. This way, we consider that all the auto-designed MOPSOs (AMOPSOs from now on) have an external bounded archive to store the non-dominated solutions found in the search, and that an archive will be used to store the global best particles. The type of archive is an available design choice. In addition, the perturbation is based on applying a mutation operator with a given frequency.

Both OMOPSO and SMPSO can be created using the template by selecting their proper components, but for OMOPSO we have made two simplifications regarding its original implementation. First, OMOPSO uses an archive based on epsilon dominance, but we have removed this feature because the epsilon value must be adjusted per problem and the size of the epsilon archive cannot be fixed beforehand. Second, the perturbation in the original OMOPSO combines uniform and non-uniform mutation; we simplify this scheme by adopting the perturbation of SMPSO, based on applying polynomial-based mutation.

The full set of configurable parameters in our AMOPSO framework and their domains is shown in Table 1. In this paper, we fixed the value of several components and parameters of the framework, as described in the caption (e.g., *defaultVelocityInitialization* and *defaultGlobalBestUpdate* in the case of *velocityInitialization* and *globalBestUpdate*, respectively) because currently our framework does not contain useful alternatives to those components, but we mention them as our plan is to add additional choices in the near future. We describe briefly the parameters in the following.

We assume in this study that the archive size is fixed to 100 particles and the swarm size can range between 10 and 200. There are three choices for the bounded external archive, which adopt different schemes to remove solutions of the archive when it becomes full. The *crowdingDistanceArchive* is based on applying the crowding distance density estimator of NSGA-II [5], the *hypervolumeArchive* applies the hypervolume contribution [1], and the *spatialSpreadDeviationArchive* was proposed in the FAME algorithm [19].

There are three strategies to initialize the swarm: random, based on a latin hypercube sampling, and the scheme used in scatter search algorithms (see for example [16]). The speeds of the particles are initialized by default to 0.0. The perturbation is based on applying a mutation operator to the particles of the swarm with a frequency F between 1 and 10 (i.e., particles in the positions F, $2F$, $3F$, ..., in the swarm), and there are three mutation operators to choose from, with their corresponding control parameters. As the mutation probability is problem dependent and it is usually set to $1/n$ (where n is the number of problem variables), we have defined a *mutationProbabilityFactor*, which is a value between 0.0 and 2.0, in such a way that the effective mutation probability will be the multiplication of that factor and $1/n$.

There are four strategies for computing the inertia weight: constant (a value between 0.1 and 1.0), random, linear increasing and linear decreasing, the three last with minimum and maximum weight values in the ranges $[0.1, 0.5]$ and $[0.5, 1.0]$, respectively.

The two alternatives for velocity updating are the default one, corresponding to the classical scheme that is used in OMOPSO, and the constraint speed mechanism applied in SMPSO (see [13,18] for further details). The $C1$ and $C2$ coefficients take values from the ranges $[1.0, 2.0]$ and $[2.0, 3.0]$, respectively.

Table 1. Parameter space of AMOPSO. In addition, archiveSize = 100, velocityInitialization = defaultVelocityInitialization,   perturbation = frequencySelection-MutationBasedPerturbation,   localBestInitialization = defaultLocalBestInitialization, globalBestInitialization = defaultGlobalBestInitialization, globalBestUpdate = default-GlobalBestUpdate,   localBestUpdate = defaultLocalBestUpdate,   positionUpdate = defaultPositionUpdate.

Parameter	Domain	
swarmSize	$[10, 200] \subset \mathbb{N}$	
externalArchive	{ crowdingDistanceArchive, hypervolumeArchive, spatialSpreadDeviationArchive }	
swarmInitialization	{ random, latinHypercubeSampling, scatterSearch }	
mutation	{ uniform, polynomial, nonUniform }	
mutationProbabilityFactor	$[0.0, 2.0] \subset \mathbb{R}$	
mutationRepairStrategy	{ random, round, bounds }	
uniformMutationPerturbation	$[0.0, 1.0] \subset \mathbb{R}$	**if** mutation=uniform
polynomialMutationDistributionIndex	$[5.0, 400.0] \subset \mathbb{R}$	**if** mutation=polynomial
nonUniformMutationPerturbation	$[0.0, 1.0] \subset \mathbb{R}$	**if** mutation=nonUniform
mutationFrequency	$[1, 10] \subset \mathbb{N}$	
inertiaWeightComputingStrategy	{ constant, random, linearIncreasing, linearDecreasing }	
weight	$[0.1, 1.0] \subset \mathbb{R}$	
weightMin	$[0.1, 0.5] \subset \mathbb{R}$	
weightMax	$[0.5, 1.0] \subset \mathbb{R}$	
velocityUpdate	{ defaultVelocityUpdate, constrainedVelocityUpdate }	
c1Min	$[1.0, 2.0] \subset \mathbb{R}$	
c1Max	$[2.0, 3.0] \subset \mathbb{R}$	
c2Min	$[1.0, 2.0] \subset \mathbb{R}$	
c2Max	$[2.0, 3.0] \subset \mathbb{R}$	
globalBestSelection	{ binaryTournament, random }	
velocityChangeWhenLowerLimitIsReached	$[-1.0, 1.0] \subset \mathbb{R}$	
velocityChangeWhenUpperLimitIsReached	$[-1.0, 1.0] \subset \mathbb{R}$	

The default policies for initializing and updating the local best are that each particle is its local best at the beginning and the local best is updated if the particle dominates it. The selection of the global best consists in taking solutions from the external archive by applying a random or a binary tournament scheme.

The default position update also applies the classical strategy, but if the resulting position of a particle is lower than the lower bound of the allowed position values, the position of the particle is set to the lower bound value and the velocity is changed by multiplying if by value in the range $[-1, 1]$. The same applies in the case of the upper bound.

4   Experimentation

In this section, we intend to validate our proposal of combining jMetal and irace and the AMOPSO template. Our goals are: (1) to quantify the improvements that can be obtained with automatically designed MOPSOs with AMOPSO over SMPSO and OMOPSO when solving the three classical problem benchmark families ZDT [21], DTLZ [6] and WFG [8] (in all cases, we focus on problems with two objectives); and (2) to analyze the configurations found to determine common patterns in components and parameters or to identify whether some of them appear to be particularly relevant.

The first step is to use irace with the AMOPSO template by considering the design space detailed in Table 1. The two configurations of AMOPSO that reproduce SMPSO and OMOPSO have been included in irace as initial configurations. Each run of an AMOPSO configuration on a single problem instance stops after 25 000 solution evaluations and returns 100 solutions. When a run finishes, irace receives as fitness value the product of the normalized hypervolume (that is, $1 - HV_{of}/HV_{rf}$, where HV_{of} and HV_{rf} stand for the hypervolumes of the obtained front and reference front, respectively) times the IGD+ [9] quality indicators corresponding to those 100 solutions. Such a fitness metric was proposed previously in the context of the automatic design of multi-objective evolutionary algorithms [2]. Since functions within a benchmark family are quite different from each other and we wish to generate a configuration that performs well for all functions and, hopefully, generalizes over them, we define a block of instances as evaluating a configuration on each individual function within the benchmark. The racing approach within irace dynamically decides how many runs per block are necessary to discard a configuration (the minimum is 5 runs per block). Each execution of irace was stopped after 100 000 AMOPSO runs, which required roughly 7 h of computation time on a 128-core Linux virtual machine. Using this setup, we executed irace three times, one per benchmark problem family, leading to three different configurations of AMOPSO. We refer to them as $AMOPSO_z$, $AMOPSO_d$, and $AMOPSO_w$, where the subscripts z, d, and w refer to the ZDT, DTLZ and WFG benchmark families.

The second step is to perform a comparative study on all three problem families between SMPSO, OMOPSO and the AMOPSO designs obtained from each benchmark. We include NSGA-II in this study to use its results as a baseline. It is configured with a population size of 100 and the variation operators are SBX (probability: 0.9, distribution index: 20.0) and polynomial-based mutation (probability: $1/n$, distribution index: 20.0). Our methodology consisted in performing 25 independent runs per configuration and reporting the median and interquartile range of the hypervolume quality indicator values. The Friedman's ranking and Holm's post-hoc multiple-comparisons tests (at a 5% level of significance) have been applied to check if there are significant differences between the distribution of results.

4.1   Analysis of the AMOPSO Configurations Found

Table 2 details the parameters settings of SMPSO, OMOPSO and the AMOPSO designs for each of the benchmarks. At a first glance, we observe that there are two common components in the AMOPSO variants: the hypervolume contribution-based external archive and the uniform mutation. While the benefits of

Table 2. Settings of the MOPSO algorithms. (CD: crowding distance, HV: hypervolume contribution, LHS: latin hypercube sampling, SS: scatter search). The subscripts z, d, and w in AMOPSO stand, respectively, for the designs generated from the ZDT, DTLZ and WFG problems.

Parameter	SMPSO	OMOPSO	AMOPSO$_z$	AMOPSO$_d$	AMOPSO$_w$
swarmSize	100	100	22	11	43
externalArchive	CD	CD	HV	HV	HV
swarmInitialization	Random	Random	Random	SS	LHS
mutation	Polynomial	Polynomial	Uniform	Uniform	Uniform
mutationProbabilityFactor	1.0	1.0	0.06	0.12	0.18
mutationRepairStrategy	Bounds	Round	Random	Random	Round
polynomialMutDistIndex	20.0	20.0	N/A	N/A	N/A
uniformMutPerturbation	N/A	N/A	0.60	0.72	0.18
nonUniformMutationPert	N/A	N/A	N/A	N/A	N/A
mutationFrequency	6	6	8	8	7
inertiaWeightStrategy	Constant	Random	Lin.Inc	Constant	Lin.Inc.
weight	0.1	N/A	N/A	0.11	N/A
weightMin	N/A	0.1	0.19	N/A	0.23
weightMax	N/A	0.5	0.82	N/A	0.64
velocityUpdate	Constr	Default	Constr	Constr	Default
c1Min	1.5	1.5	1.73	1.80	1.19
c1Max	2.5	2.0	2.49	2.46	2.22
c2Min	1.5	1.5	1.32	1.05	1.29
c2Max	2.5	2.0	2.15	2.54	2.20
velocityChangeLowerLimit	−1.0	−1.0	0.18	0.14	−0.98
velocityChangeUpperLimit	−1.0	−1.0	−0.32	−0.75	−0.78

adopting an archive using the hypervolume to store the global best particles were analyzed in [12], the adoption of uniform mutation is not so common as, in general, polynomial-based mutation seems to be the most widely used mutation operator in the context of continuous multi-objective optimization.

A remarkable observation is that the swarm sizes are considerably smaller than the usual setting (i.e., if S solutions are to be found, both the swarm and the external archive have a size of S). This means that the algorithms foster the intensification of the search, performing a higher number of internal iterations.

We also observe that the AMOPSO$_z$ and AMOPSO$_d$ configurations share most of the components and many of their parameter values have roughly similar ranges, suggesting that either of these AMOPSO variants could have similar performance with the ZDT and DTLZ problems. The values of the parameters that adjust the velocity when the particle positions go out of range are striking; while in SMPSO and OMOPSO these values are −1.0, resulting in velocity reversal, the velocity adjustments in AMOPSOz and AMOPSOd in the case of the lower limits are very small, so that the resulting velocity is very significantly reduced.

Table 3. Median and interquartile range of the hypervolume quality indicator values of the compared algorithms. Cells with dark gray background and light gray background represent, respectively, the best and second best indicator values.

	NSGAII	SMPSO	OMOPSO	AMOPSO$_z$	AMOPSO	AMOPSO$_d$	AMOPSO$_w$
ZDT1	$6.60e-01_{4.9e-04}$	$6.62e-01_{1.0e-04}$	$6.61e-01_{3.2e-04}$	$6.62e-01_{7.7e-06}$	$6.62e-01_{4.8e-06}$	$6.62e-01_{4.8e-06}$	$6.62e-01_{1.3e-04}$
ZDT2	$3.26e-01_{3.3e-04}$	$3.29e-01_{1.6e-04}$	$3.28e-01_{3.3e-04}$	$3.29e-01_{1.6e-05}$	$3.29e-01_{1.3e-05}$	$3.29e-01_{1.3e-05}$	$3.29e-01_{6.7e-05}$
ZDT3	$5.15e-01_{3.0e-04}$	$5.15e-01_{4.7e-04}$	$5.14e-01_{1.5e-03}$	$5.16e-01_{1.4e-05}$	$5.16e-01_{1.2e-05}$	$5.16e-01_{1.2e-05}$	$5.16e-01_{4.7e-03}$
ZDT4	$6.57e-01_{4.5e-03}$	$6.61e-01_{1.9e-04}$	$0.00e+00_{0.0e-04}$	$6.62e-01_{1.0e-05}$	$6.62e-01_{1.5e-05}$	$6.62e-01_{1.5e-05}$	$0.00e+00_{0.0e+00}$
ZDT6	$3.90e-01_{2.0e-03}$	$4.01e-01_{7.7e-05}$	$4.01e-01_{5.6e-05}$	$4.01e-01_{1.3e-05}$	$4.01e-01_{1.9e-05}$	$4.01e-01_{1.9e-05}$	$4.01e-01_{1.5e-05}$
DTLZ1	$4.90e-01_{4.6e-03}$	$4.94e-01_{4.2e-04}$	$0.00e+00_{0.0e+00}$	$4.95e-01_{3.4e-05}$	$4.95e-01_{1.9e-05}$	$4.95e-01_{1.9e-05}$	$0.00e+00_{0.0e+00}$
DTLZ2	$2.09e-01_{3.4e-04}$	$2.10e-01_{8.9e-05}$	$2.10e-01_{1.8e-04}$	$2.11e-01_{9.0e-05}$	$2.11e-01_{1.2e-05}$	$2.11e-01_{1.2e-05}$	$2.11e-01_{1.4e-04}$
DTLZ3	$0.00e+00_{5.2e-02}$	$2.10e-01_{1.2e-01}$	$0.00e+00_{0.0e+00}$	$2.11e-01_{1.3e-01}$	$2.11e-01_{2.7e-03}$	$2.11e-01_{2.7e-03}$	$0.00e+00_{0.0e+00}$
DTLZ4	$2.09e-01_{2.1e-01}$	$2.10e-01_{1.1e-04}$	$2.10e-01_{4.5e-04}$	$2.11e-01_{3.2e-05}$	$2.11e-01_{1.7e-05}$	$2.11e-01_{1.7e-05}$	$2.11e-01_{2.7e-04}$
DTLZ5	$2.11e-01_{2.9e-04}$	$2.12e-01_{1.0e-04}$	$2.12e-01_{1.0e-04}$	$2.13e-01_{7.7e-05}$	$2.13e-01_{6.1e-06}$	$2.13e-01_{6.1e-06}$	$2.12e-01_{1.7e-04}$
DTLZ6	$1.83e-01_{4.6e-02}$	$2.12e-01_{5.8e-05}$	$2.12e-01_{5.6e-05}$	$2.13e-01_{5.9e-06}$	$2.13e-01_{6.9e-06}$	$2.13e-01_{6.9e-06}$	$2.13e-01_{1.1e-05}$
DTLZ7	$3.34e-01_{2.0e-04}$	$3.35e-01_{1.1e-04}$	$3.34e-01_{3.3e-04}$	$3.35e-01_{6.8e-06}$	$3.35e-01_{4.8e-06}$	$3.35e-01_{4.8e-06}$	$3.35e-01_{1.2e-04}$
WFG1	$4.82e-01_{1.1e-01}$	$1.16e-01_{6.0e-03}$	$1.95e-01_{7.9e-02}$	$1.32e-01_{3.1e-02}$	$1.27e-01_{7.0e-03}$	$1.27e-01_{7.0e-03}$	$3.63e-01_{1.4e-01}$
WFG2	$5.61e-01_{2.7e-03}$	$5.61e-01_{1.2e-03}$	$5.64e-01_{1.4e-04}$	$5.64e-01_{1.3e-04}$	$5.64e-01_{2.6e-04}$	$5.64e-01_{2.6e-04}$	$5.65e-01_{4.4e-05}$
WFG3	$4.92e-01_{6.0e-04}$	$4.93e-01_{3.8e-04}$	$4.94e-01_{1.5e-04}$	$4.95e-01_{1.8e-05}$	$4.95e-01_{1.9e-05}$	$4.95e-01_{1.9e-05}$	$4.95e-01_{4.0e-06}$
WFG4	$2.17e-01_{4.7e-04}$	$2.02e-01_{2.4e-03}$	$2.08e-01_{1.7e-03}$	$2.09e-01_{2.8e-03}$	$2.09e-01_{2.6e-03}$	$2.09e-01_{2.6e-03}$	$2.15e-01_{4.9e-03}$
WFG5	$1.95e-01_{4.5e-04}$	$1.96e-01_{5.5e-05}$	$1.96e-01_{9.1e-05}$	$1.97e-01_{4.2e-05}$	$1.97e-01_{4.4e-05}$	$1.97e-01_{4.4e-05}$	$1.97e-01_{6.4e-05}$
WFG6	$2.02e-01_{1.4e-02}$	$2.09e-01_{4.0e-04}$	$2.10e-01_{7.3e-05}$	$2.11e-01_{1.3e-05}$	$2.11e-01_{3.2e-05}$	$2.11e-01_{3.2e-05}$	$2.11e-01_{1.7e-05}$
WFG7	$2.09e-01_{3.5e-04}$	$2.09e-01_{4.5e-04}$	$2.10e-01_{1.0e-04}$	$2.11e-01_{1.1e-05}$	$2.11e-01_{1.2e-05}$	$2.11e-01_{1.2e-05}$	$2.11e-01_{4.2e-06}$
WFG8	$1.46e-01_{2.1e-03}$	$1.48e-01_{1.9e-03}$	$1.47e-01_{1.1e-03}$	$1.51e-01_{1.0e-03}$	$1.51e-01_{1.1e-03}$	$1.51e-01_{1.1e-03}$	$1.51e-01_{1.1e-03}$
WFG9	$2.37e-01_{1.6e-03}$	$2.35e-01_{6.3e-04}$	$2.37e-01_{9.8e-04}$	$2.39e-01_{1.4e-03}$	$2.40e-01_{1.3e-03}$	$2.40e-01_{1.3e-03}$	$2.41e-01_{1.3e-03}$

4.2   Comparative Analysis of the MOPSO Variants

We proceed to compare the three automatically-designed AMOPSO configurations (AMOPSO$_z$, AMOPSO$_d$, and AMOPSO$_w$) with NSGA-II, SMPSO, and OMOPSO. We evaluate all algorithms on all three benchmark families (ZDT, DTLZ and WFG). In the case of the AMOPSO variants, we expect that each variant will perform well on the benchmark used for automatically designing it. If, in addition, a variant performs well on the other two benchmark families, it will provide evidence that the performance of that variant generalizes to other problems, i.e., that AMOPSO variant would be a robust MOPSO.

Table 4. Average Friedman's rankings with Holm's Adjusted p-values (0.05) of compared algorithms for ZDT, DTLZ and WFG. Symbol * indicates the control algorithm and column at right contains the overall ranking of positions with regards to I_{HV}.

I_{HV} Hypervolume		
Algorithm	$Friedman's_{Rank}$	$Holm's_{Adj-p}$
*AMOPSO$_d$	**2.048**	-
AMOPSO$_z$	2.048	0.05e+00
AMOPSO$_w$	3.214	0.25e−02
SMOPSO	4.429	0.17e−02
OMOPSO	4.500	0.13e−02
NSGAII	4.762	0.01e−02

We report in Table 3 the values of the hypervolume quality indicator, where the best (highest) and second best values are highlighted in dark and light grey background, respectively. From this table, we can observe that the results of the AMOPSO$_z$ and AMOPSO$_d$ configurations are close in the ZDT and DTLZ problems, confirming the observation made in the previous section about the similarities of their configurations, and the AMOPSO$_w$ design only gets the best results in some of the WFG instances. According to the statistical Friedman's ranking and Holm's non-parametric tests (see Table 4), AMOPSO$_z$ and AMOPSO$_d$ perform similarly without significant differences in their distribution results, although showing the former higher ranking (hence acting as control algorithm denoted with *). The remaining variants AMOPSOw, SMPSO, OMOPSO, and NSGA-II show statistically lower performances, since the null hypothesis in Holm's test is rejected in their case.

Additionally, we have applied the Wilcoxon rank-sum test at a 5% level of significance (not included for space constraints) and it confirms that the difference between AMOPSO$_z$ and AMOPSO$_d$ is not significant in 14 out the 21 problems. The tests between AMOPSO$_z$ and SMPSO, whose hypervolume values in Table 3 are close in the ZDT and DTLZ problems, states that the differences are significant in all the cases but one; regarding AMOPSO$_d$ and SMPSO, all the differences are significant.

From this analysis, our selection would be either $AMOPSO_z$ or $AMOPSO_d$, as both yield the best overall approximations of the Pareto front in the three benchmarks according to Table 3. We were able to find a robust MOPSO variant by using their five and seven benchmark instances (respectively) for training, while reaching also competitive performance with regards to testing all the considered problems. In the case of $AMOPSO_w$, it just shows competitive performance for training WFG instances, but not for testing ZDT and DTLZ ones, which indicates some degree of over-fitting to this specific benchmark family.

5   Conclusions and Future Work

We have presented an approach to combine jMetal with the irace package to provide a tool for the automatic design and configuration of multi-objective particle swarm optimizers (MOPSO). Our proposal is based on developing a template for MOPSOs, called AMOPSO, by using the base components of the OMOPSO and SMPSO optimizers which are enriched with three possible external archives, three mutation operators, four strategies for computing the inertia weight, and two schemes for the update of the velocity. The resulting design space has been encoded as a parameter space to be tuned by irace to find the best design of AMOPSO given a set of input problems. The criterion used by irace to assess the performance of a given setting is the product of the normalized hypervolume and the IGD+ indicator.

To validate our approach, we have considered three well-known benchmark problems (ZDT, DTLZ, and WFG) and we have found three different variants of AMOPSO for each of them (named $AMPOSO_z$, $AMOPSO_d$, and $AMOPSO_w$). The analysis of the configurations of these auto-designed MOPSO algorithms reveals that common components include the use of an external archive based on the hypervolume contribution density estimator, the adoption of uniform mutation, and a reduced swarm size (between 11 and 43), while the external archive allows the algorithms to return a Pareto front approximation of 100 solutions.

These variants have been compared with respect to NSGA-II, SMPSO, and OMOPSO by computing the hypervolume quality indicator on three benchmark families. The results show that the AMOPSO variants found with the ZDT and DTLZ problems rank first according to the statistical Friedman ranking test, and both algorithms reach a competitive overall performance on all the problems adopted.

There are a number of lines for future work. We are particularly interested in an in-depth analysis of the AMOPSO configurations to determine which parameters have the highest influence in the search. Extending our study to cope with large-scale multi-objective problems and to apply the acquired experience to address the optimization of real-world problems are issues that we are interested in tackling.

Acknowledgements. This work has been partially funded by the Spanish Ministry of Science and Innovation via Grant PID2020-112540RB-C41 (AEI/FEDER, UE) and the Andalusian PAIDI program with grant P18-RT-2799. M. López-Ibáñez is a "Beatriz Galindo" Senior Distinguished Researcher (BEAGAL 18/00053) funded by the Spanish Ministry of Science and Innovation (MICINN). Carlos A. Coello Coello gratefully acknowledges support from CONACyT grant no. 2016-01-1920 (Investigación en Fronteras de la Ciencia 2016).

References

1. Beume, N., Naujoks, B., Emmerich, M.T.M.: SMS-EMOA: multiobjective selection based on dominated hypervolume. Eur. J. Oper. Res. **181**(3), 1653–1669 (2007). https://doi.org/10.1016/j.ejor.2006.08.008
2. Bezerra, L.C.T., López-Ibáñez, M., Stützle, T.: Automatically designing state-of-the-art multi- and many-objective evolutionary algorithms. Evol. Comput. **28**(2), 195–226 (2020). https://doi.org/10.1162/evco_a_00263
3. Birattari, M., Stützle, T., Paquete, L., Varrentrapp, K.: A racing algorithm for configuring metaheuristics. In: Langdon, W.B., et al. (eds.) Proceedings of the Genetic and Evolutionary Computation Conference, GECCO 2002, pp. 11–18. Morgan Kaufmann Publishers, San Francisco (2002)
4. Camacho-Villalón, C.L., Stützle, T., Dorigo, M.: PSO-X: a component-based framework for the automatic design of particle swarm optimization algorithms. IEEE Trans. Evol. Comput. (2021). https://doi.org/10.1109/TEVC.2021.3102863
5. Deb, K., Pratap, A., Agarwal, S., Meyarivan, T.: A fast and elitist multi-objective genetic algorithm: NSGA-II. IEEE Trans. Evol. Comput. **6**(2), 182–197 (2002). https://doi.org/10.1109/4235.996017
6. Deb, K., Thiele, L., Laumanns, M., Zitzler, E.: Scalable test problems for evolutionary multiobjective optimization. In: Abraham, A., Jain, L., Goldberg, R. (eds.) Evolutionary Multiobjective Optimization. AI&KP, pp. 105–145. Springer, London (2005). https://doi.org/10.1007/1-84628-137-7_6
7. Durillo, J.J., Nebro, A.J.: jMetal: a Java framework for multi-objective optimization. Adv. Eng. Softw. **42**(10), 760–771 (2011). https://doi.org/10.1016/j.advengsoft.2011.05.014
8. Huband, S., Hingston, P., Barone, L., While, L.: A review of multiobjective test problems and a scalable test problem toolkit. IEEE Trans. Evol. Comput. **10**(5), 477–506 (2006). https://doi.org/10.1109/TEVC.2005.861417
9. Ishibuchi, H., Masuda, H., Nojima, Y.: A study on performance evaluation ability of a modified inverted generational distance indicator. In: Silva, S., Esparcia-Alcázar, A.I. (eds.) Proceedings of the Genetic and Evolutionary Computation Conference, GECCO 2015, pp. 695–702. ACM Press, New York (2015)
10. de Lima, R.H.R., Pozo, A.T.R.: A study on auto-configuration of multi-objective particle swarm optimization algorithm. In: Proceedings of the 2017 Congress on Evolutionary Computation (CEC 2017), pp. 718–725. IEEE Press, Piscataway (2017). https://doi.org/10.1109/CEC.2017.7969381
11. López-Ibáñez, M., Dubois-Lacoste, J., Pérez Cáceres, L., Stützle, T., Birattari, M.: The irace package: iterated racing for automatic algorithm configuration. Oper. Res. Perspect. **3**, 43–58 (2016). https://doi.org/10.1016/j.orp.2016.09.002

12. Nebro, A.J., Durillo, J.J., Coello Coello, C.A.: Analysis of leader selection strategies in a multi-objective Particle Swarm Optimizer. In: Proceedings of the 2013 Congress on Evolutionary Computation (CEC 2013), pp. 3153–3160. IEEE Press, Piscataway (2013). https://doi.org/10.1109/CEC.2013.6557955

13. Nebro, A.J., Durillo, J.J., García-Nieto, J., Coello Coello, C.A., Luna, F., Alba, E.: SMPSO: a new PSO-based metaheuristic for multi-objective optimization. In: 2009 IEEE Symposium on Computational Intelligence in Multi-Criteria Decision-Making (MCDM), pp. 66–73 (2009). https://doi.org/10.1109/MCDM.2009.4938830

14. Nebro, A.J., Durillo, J.J., Vergne, M.: Redesigning the jMetal multi-objective optimization framework. In: Jiménez Laredo, J.L., Silva, S., Esparcia-Alcázar, A.I. (eds.) Proceedings of the Genetic and Evolutionary Computation Conference Companion, GECCO Companion 2015, pp. 1093–1100. ACM Press, New York (2015)

15. Nebro, A.J., López-Ibáñez, M., Barba-González, C., García-Nieto, J.: Automatic configuration of NSGA-II with jMetal and irace. In: López-Ibáñez, M., Auger, A., Stützle, T. (eds.) Proceedings of the Genetic and Evolutionary Computation Conference Companion, GECCO Companion 2019, pp. 1374–1381. ACM Press, New York (2019). https://doi.org/10.1145/3319619.3326832

16. Nebro, A.J., Luna, F., Alba, E., Dorronsoro, B., Durillo, J.J., Beham, A.: AbYSS: adapting scatter search to multiobjective optimization. IEEE Trans. Evol. Comput. 12(4) (2008)

17. Reyes-Sierra, M., Coello Coello, C.A.: Multi-objective particle swarm optimizers: a survey of the state-of-the-art. Int. J. Comput. Intell. Res. 2(3), 287–308 (2006)

18. Sierra, M.R., Coello Coello, C.A.: Improving PSO-based multi-objective optimization using crowding, mutation and ϵ-dominance. In: Coello Coello, C.A., Hernández Aguirre, A., Zitzler, E. (eds.) EMO 2005. LNCS, vol. 3410, pp. 505–519. Springer, Heidelberg (2005). https://doi.org/10.1007/978-3-540-31880-4_35

19. Santiago, A., Dorronsoro, B., Nebro, A.J., Durillo, J.J., Castillo, O., Fraire, H.J.: A novel multi-objective evolutionary algorithm with fuzzy logic based adaptive selection of operators: fame. Inf. Sci. 471, 233–251 (2019). https://doi.org/10.1016/j.ins.2018.09.005. https://www.sciencedirect.com/science/article/pii/S0020025518306959

20. Stützle, T., López-Ibáñez, M.: Automated design of metaheuristic algorithms. In: Gendreau, M., Potvin, J.-Y. (eds.) Handbook of Metaheuristics. ISORMS, vol. 272, pp. 541–579. Springer, Cham (2019). https://doi.org/10.1007/978-3-319-91086-4_17

21. Zitzler, E., Thiele, L., Deb, K.: Comparison of multiobjective evolutionary algorithms: empirical results. Evol. Comput. 8(2), 173–195 (2000). https://doi.org/10.1162/106365600568202

Automatic Extraction of Understandable Controllers from Video Observations of Swarm Behaviors

Khulud Alharthi[1,3]([✉]) [iD], Zahraa S. Abdallah[2] [iD], and Sabine Hauert[1,2] [iD]

[1] Bristol Robotics Laboratory, University of Bristol, Bristol, UK
khulud.alharthi@bristol.ac.uk
[2] Department of Engineering Mathematics, University of Bristol, Bristol, UK
[3] Department of Computer Science, College of Computers and Information
Technology, Taif University, Taif, Saudi Arabia

Abstract. Swarm behavior emerges from the local interaction of agents and their environment often encoded as simple rules. Extracting the rules by watching a video of the overall swarm behavior could help us study and control swarm behavior in nature, or artificial swarms that have been designed by external actors. It could also serve as a new source of inspiration for swarm robotics. Yet extracting such rules is challenging as there is often no visible link between the emergent properties of the swarm and their local interactions. To this end, we develop a method to automatically extract understandable swarm controllers from video demonstrations. The method uses evolutionary algorithms driven by a fitness function that compares eight high-level swarm metrics. The method is able to extract many controllers (behavior trees) in a simple collective movement task. We then provide a qualitative analysis of behaviors that resulted in different trees, but similar behaviors. This provides the first steps toward automatic extraction of swarm controllers based on observations.

1 Introduction

Swarm behavior emerges from simple rules which govern the interaction among the agents and between each agent with their surrounding environment. Birds flocking, fish schooling, and bee foraging are examples of swarm behaviors found in natural systems [25]. Inspiration has been taken from these natural systems to design robot swarms. Swarm robotics could be used in fire and rescue, storage organization, bridge inspection. Also, in a biomedical application where swarms of large numbers of miniature robots coordinate to detect, monitor, or treat medical conditions [4,22,24]. Swarm behavior is designed by defining the rules of local interaction between agents and their environment [3].

Extracting an understandable controller by watching a video of the overall swarm behavior can serve many purposes. It can be considered a design paradigm

---

Z. S. Abdallah and S. Hauert—Both authors have contributed equally to the work.

M. Dorigo et al. (Eds.): ANTS 2022, LNCS 13491, pp. 41–53, 2022.
https://doi.org/10.1007/978-3-031-20176-9_4

of swarm robotics by allowing for the automatic extraction of use-able rules for robot swarms just based on a demonstrated behavior of artificial or natural swarms. In addition, the readability of the controller can provide the swarm engineer with the ability to understand, control, or adapt the rules to new robots. Moreover, the method can be used to analyze the natural swarm system. For example, extracting these rules can help behavioral ecology studies interpret how these rules developed and whether the same rules evolved across different species [18]. Another application involves understanding the motion of a particular cell system, which can provide insight into the influence of new medical intervention on this system [9]. This method could also be also used to control natural swarm systems or learn the behavior directly from an online setting [2].

Using existing video observations of swarm behaviors as a source of learning has been investigated in several works. In the imitation learning context, a video of an ideal behavior is used to train a controller mostly in form of a neural network to produce a swarm imitating the demonstrated behavior [5,7,14,16,20, 23,27–29]. For the second context, video observations were used to learn about biological swarm behavior by analyzing their trajectories to investigate what components of the individual controller were crucial for the emergent behavior seen in different species [1,8,12,17,18,24,26].

Most of the proposed works do not provide high-level, understandable rules that can easily be adopted to external systems. In this work, we develop a method to automatically extract understandable controllers from a video observation of swarm behavior. The only input to the proposed method is the video observation of the swarm behavior with no information on the type of the swarm and no requirement of a training dataset. The extracted controller takes the form of a behavior tree to favour human readability [13,15]. An evolutionary algorithm is used to produce a similar emergent behavior to the original observed behavior. The fitness of the evolutionary algorithm is defined as the similarity between two behaviors assessed using eight swarm motion metrics.

The paper is organized as follows. Section 2 introduces an overview of the related works. Section 3 presents the components of the proposed extraction method of the swarm's local controller based on a video observation. Our results are analyzed and discussed in Sect. 4.

2   Related Works

The use of a video observation of swarm behavior as a source of learning can be beneficial in several ways. It can be considered an automatic design approach for swarm robotics. Also, it can provide insight into the underlying biological swarm mechanism. Thus, the human readability of the learned controller is highly regarded. In this section, we review works that used video observation to learn a swarm behavior.

Robot swarms are often seen as simple with (a) multiple robots that have (b) simple capabilities and (c) only local perception where (d) all of them collectively work to achieve specific behavior. Designing swarm behaviors that fit these characteristics comes with three important benefits: robustness, flexibility, and scalability [3,21]. Designing the rules that make up a swarm robot's local controller is done either manually or by a careful definition of optimization's objective function to find the rules automatically [3,10]. In either case, expertise about the desired swarm behavior is needed. Imitation learning eliminates this requirement and allows the extraction of the swarm controller from a demonstration of the desired emergent swarm performance.

Imitation Learning provides the robots with the ability to learn directly from an expert demonstration. This establishes a learning paradigm between the swarm robots as a learner and the original swarm behavior presented in a video as the teacher [23]. Different forms of these three components of imitation learning: the expert swarm demonstration, the learner swarm, and the learning mechanism have been proposed in several works. A teacher could take the form of offline behavioral data consisting of states and actions at different time steps. This behavioral data can be generated from a simulation of the target behavior. Depending on the sensing capabilities of the target behavior, the dataset could include images [14,27] or other inferred state descriptors [16,20,29]. The teaching data can also be generated by capturing the live behavior from a biological swarm [20,28]. A robot demonstrator in an online learning environment is another form of the teacher in the imitation learning process [5,7]. The imitation learning process either aims to train a machine learning model that can map the sensed information into action [16,27], to translate the observed trajectory into performable form and copy it to the learner robot directly [5,29], or to optimize a local controller using inverse reinforcement learning [28]. Most of the works conducted in offline imitation learning for swarms focus on extracting swarm controllers in different variations of neural network form, which are known to lack interpretability. These variations include: Graph Neural Network [29], Convolutional Neural Network (CNN) [27], Feed-Forward Neural Network [16], Recurrent Neural Network [20] or a mixture of them [14].

Some of the studies that propose methods to extract rules from video observations of swarms have a different goal than imitation learning. While imitation learning aims to gain the extracted rules as a learned task that produce the collective behavior robustly in the same or different environment, these works are only concerned with understanding the mechanism of the behavior observed in the video. Observation-based rule extraction uses parameter fitting techniques such as Bayesian inference, force matching and additive mixture [8,12,18]. These techniques receive an input of trajectories from the observed swarm behavior and rules with associated parameters. They then produce values for these parameters to indicate the impact of each of these rules on the emergent behavior. These rules include simple actions such as collision avoidance and aligning velocity. Strategies that the individual of the swarm follow all the time such as following a leader, following its neighbors or only following their own rules have been extracted and tested using fish and baboon observations [1,26].

Work by [17] proposed a turning-like classifier to differentiate between an imitated sample from the assessed controller and the original sample from the original controller. A co-evolutionary algorithm is used to optimize both the classifier to classify original behavior as original and behavior from the assessed controller as duplicate and also to optimize the assessed controller to deceive the classifier by making it classify their behavior as the original. Another method used a single monitoring robot to infer the parameter of the predefined rule of the swarm in a shared simulation setting [24].

Most of the proposed works do not provide high-level, understandable rules that can easily be adopted to external systems. This paper aims to not only imitate the behavior but also to provide human-readability of the local rules that lead to the observed behavior. In addition, no assumptions were made about the demonstrated behavior other than considering it is a swarm behavior. In this work, we aim to extract an understandable swarm controller in the form of a behavior tree with nine motion action nodes from a swarm video observation using an evolutionary algorithm and eight swarm metrics. The extracted behavior tree will explain the swarm observation using the list of leaf nodes built in the system. The no-context aspect of our extraction method with rich options of leaf nodes will make it applicable to a wide range of swarm observations. This work serves as a first step toward extracting more complex behavior trees with different leaf node types such as motion actions, transportation actions, communication, and sensing actions we aim to pursue in future works.

3   Methodology

Extracting robot controllers that result in an observed swarm behavior can be defined as an optimization problem with the following formula:

$$\min distance\left(OriginalSwarmMetrics, AssessedSwarmMetrics\right) \quad (1)$$

where:

Original Swarm Metrics is a vector of metrics describing the swarm motion presented in the video demonstration.

Assessed Swarm Metrics is a vector of metrics describing the swarm motion generated by simulating a behavior tree to be assessed.

The aim is to minimize the distance between the two vectors, with the assumption that if rules assessed generate swarm behaviors with similar metrics, then imitation has been successful. The controller extraction method starts by computing metrics describing the original swarm behavior. The next steps involve using the evolutionary method to optimize a behavior tree by: for each individual in the initial population, generating random behavior trees, simulating each individual copied over the homogeneous swarm, then measuring the metrics resulting from the swarm behavior, and assigning a fitness based on the distance between this assessed swarm metrics and the original swarm metrics. As generations evolve, high-performing behavior trees are selected, mutated, and crossed over to generate behavior trees that have similar metrics as the original swarm behavior. Figure 1 shows the general framework of the proposed method.

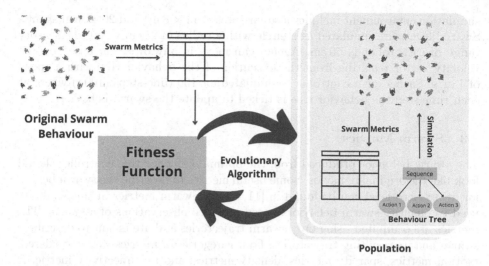

Fig. 1. Extraction method with artificial evolution to discover behavior trees that generate swarm behaviors with swarm metrics similar to those of the original swarm behavior.

3.1   Behavior Tree Controller

Swarm controllers in the form of behavior trees are implemented as a sequence node with three leaf nodes. The sequence node prompts each of its leaf nodes from left to right to execute and return success notifications unless any failure happens in any of the leaf nodes [15]. Leaf nodes can be any of the following nine types:

- Aggregation: move in the direction of neighboring robots.
- Dispersion: move away from neighbouring robots.
- Separation: avoid collision with neighbouring robots.
- Clustering: move towards the nearest robot to form multiple clusters.
- Random motion: move in the random direction.
- South-East force: move to the south-east direction.
- South-West force: move to the south-west direction.
- North-East force: move to the north-east direction.
- North-West force: move to the north-west direction.

A library of random controllers is generated to fill the initial population needed by the evolutionary algorithm. Each behavior tree is generated by randomly selecting three of the nine leaf node options.

3.2   Controller Execution

To produce the swarm trajectories for each swarm controller, a 2D simulation environment is built using C++ with OpenGL and python Matplotlib. The simulation environment includes a square area ($8\,\text{m} \times 8\,\text{m}$) and 20 swarm agents. Swarm agents are simulated as a circle with a radius of 25 cm where the sensory range of each robot is 50 cm. Agents can move in any direction based on the velocity vector resulting from the execution of the behavior tree with a speed of $1\,\text{m/s}$. Each swarm controller is simulated for 100 time-steps (100 s) where at each time step the behavior tree is ticked to update the swarm behavior.

3.3   Swarm Metrics

The swarm behavior produced from the optimal behavior tree controller should look like the original behavior. Some useful metrics to describe the swarm behavior at a macro level can be found in [11,13,19]. Swarm metrics in this work are used to quantify swarm behaviors based on video observations of a swarm. The metrics are computed using only swarm trajectories and are meant to describe a swarm and its resulting trajectories. Four categories of metrics were considered: motion metrics, sparsity metrics, density metrics, and a connectivity metric. A description of these metrics is provided in the following list. In this description, each agent is defined as a where, a is a composite of two vectors that store the location of the agent a in the x and the y direction. $distance$ is computed using Euclidean distance and n is the total number of agents in the swarm. Each of these metrics is a time-series vector as they are computed at each time-step.

Motion Metrics: This category of metrics is used to capture the direction, magnitude and frequency of the swarm motion. It includes three metrics: the center of mass, the maximum swarm shift and the swarm mode index.
1-Center of mass is computed as the average overall agent locations in the x and the y direction.
2-Maximum swarm shift is computed as the maximum distance moved among all agents measured at each time-step t.
3-Swarm mode index is used to measure the frequency of the swarm motion. It is computed as the distance between the center of mass and the swarm mode at each time-step t. The swarm mode is defined as a location in the x and the y direction with maximum frequency among all agents' locations. The frequency of location l in the x or the y direction is computed using the following formula

$$Frequency(l) = \sum_{\substack{i=1 \\ distance(l,l_i)<0.1}}^{n} 1 \tag{2}$$

Sparsity Metrics: These metrics describe how sparse the swarm is quantified using two metrics: the longest path and the maximum radius.
4-Longest path is the maximum distance traveled from the origin among all agents.
5-Maximum radius is defined as the maximum distance among the distances between center of mass of the swarm and each agent.

Density Metrics: Two metrics are used to capture the density, the average local density, and the average nearest neighbour distance.

6-Average local density is the sum of the number of agents in the local radius r of each agent averaged over the total number of agents.

7-Average nearest neighbour distance is the sum of the distance to the nearest neighbour of each agent averaged over the total number of agents.

Connectivity Metric: if the swarm state in each time-step t is considered a graph, with the nodes being the agents, then the connectivity of the swarm can be computed using the **8-Beta index**. The beta index is a metric that measures the connectivity of the graph by dividing the number of paths between nodes by the number of nodes in the graph. For the swarm beta index, the path is assumed to be connecting two agents if the distance between them is less than the average distance. Average distance is computed as the sum of the distances among all the agents over the total number of agents.

3.4 Fitness Function

The fitness function measures how similar the original swarm behavior is to the assessed swarm behavior based on the swarm metrics extracted from the recorded trajectories. It is defined as the euclidean distance between the original and assessed swarm metric vectors.

$$\sqrt{\sum_i (OriginalSwarmMetrics_i - AssessedSwarmMetrics_i)^2} \qquad (3)$$

Metrics are normalized to ensure each metric contributes equally to the fitness. For each metric, we store the maximum and a minimum values recorded over the whole population of the first generation and use it to normalize over the entire evolutionary run.

3.5 Evolutionary Algorithm

Genetic programming (GP) has been used to evolve behavior trees using operations that take into consideration their hierarchical structure [13,15]. In this work, behavior trees are evaluated by the fitness function where the goal of evolution is to minimize fitness. Elitism is used to copy the best three behavior trees to the next generation without any change. The remaining individuals are selected using tournament selection with a tournament size of three. The next steps include applying single-point crossover and single-point mutation with rates as shown in Table 1. In the single-point crossover, the cross point is chosen randomly and the two behavior trees swap their leaf nodes. The Mutation is done by choosing a random leaf node and changing its type to any of the other leaf node types. The behavior tree with the best fitness function in the final generation will then be chosen as the extracted swarm controller.

Table 1. Evolutionary parameters

Parameter	Value
Population size	50
Generations number	30
Elitism size	3
Tournament size	3
Crossover rate	0.5
Mutation rate	0.3

4   Results

In this section, we test the capability of the swarm metrics to capture the similarity of two swarm trajectories, we then evaluate the performance in correctly extracting original behavior trees. Finally, we provide a qualitative analysis of successful extractions, and extractions resulting in different trees.

4.1   Evaluation of Swarm Metrics

As a first step, we aimed to see which swarm metrics were useful in differentiating between similar or different behavior trees. To this end, we plot the discrimination power of each metric in Sect. 3.3 by comparing their values in two settings. First, the difference between metrics vectors of two swarm trajectories produced by the same controller is computed. In the second setting, the difference was computed based on two swarm trajectories produced by two different randomly generated controllers. 100 pairs of swarm trajectories were used in each setting. Figure 2 shows the ability of each metric to assess the similarity of two swarm observations. This result shows the distance between metrics for two different swarm behaviors resulting from two different trees is larger than the distance between metrics resulting from the same tree. Thus, demonstrating their discrimination potential. Although some metrics show a higher capability to discriminate than others, each of them can provide a different contribution to the fitness function.

4.2   Performance of the Controller Extraction Method

To quantify the performance of the extraction method, we randomly generate 100 behavior trees, each one used as the original swarm behavior from which a behavior tree needs to be extracted. To have a meaningful behavior, generations of the original behavior trees were constrained by preventing leaf nodes that have a canceling effect on each other from being presented in the same behavior tree such as aggregation node and dispersion node. The simulated swarm trajectories of these behavior trees are then used as an input to the controller extraction method. A Jaccard index is used to evaluate the produced controller

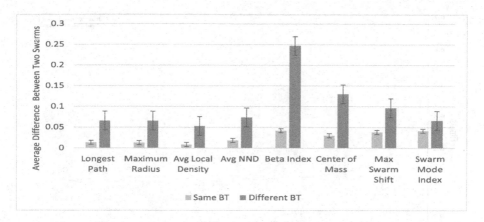

Fig. 2. The discrimination power of swarm metrics is apparent when the distance between metrics for swarm behaviors generated from the same behavior trees is smaller than the metrics coming from two different behavior trees.

by assessing the similarity of the extracted controller to the original behavior tree. This metric is used as ground truth to assess the exact similarity between behavior trees, and can not be used in the fitness which captures indirect metrics that can be extracted from the video observations. The Jaccard index is a measure of similarity between two texts and is computed by dividing the intersection of characters between the two strings over the union of all the characters [6]. When the Jaccard index is one, the two strings are the same, whereas zero indicates they are completely different. Here behavior trees are represented as strings. The method was able to achieve 0.868 average Jaccard similarity over the 100 behavior trees where 75 behavior trees out of 100 were the exact copy of the original behavior trees. The rest can be grouped into two groups. A high similarity group with a Jaccard index larger than or equal to 0.5 which includes 18 extracted controllers. The last 7 controllers have a Jaccard index less than 0.5 and are in the low similarity group. However, no controller was extracted with a zero similarity. That means the extracted controller in the worst-case will have at least one of the nodes the same as the original controller. Table 2 shows a summary of the method's performance. There is a significant improvement over the first generations as shown by the best fitness of all the 100 behavior trees in Fig. 3. The average fitness also demonstrates some learning but with larger

Table 2. Performance measures of the controller extraction method

Accuracy	75
Controllers with high similarity	18
Controllers with low similarity	7
Average Jaccard Index (all)	0.868

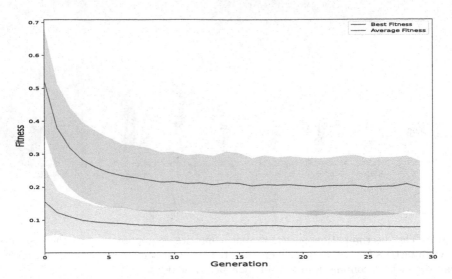

Fig. 3. The learning curve of the best fitness (in green) and the average fitness (in red) over the 30 generations shows a successful minimization of the distance between the original and the assessed swarm behavior metrics. (Color figure online)

distribution values than the best fitness. Increasing the number of leaf nodes of the behavior tree will increase the search space as well as the complexity of the problem. The performance of this method was tested against more complex behaviors coming from behavior trees with 4, 5 and 6 leaf nodes. The results obtained show the potential of this method as it was able to extract 70 exact behavior trees with four leaf nodes, 57 behavior trees with five and 43 with six leaf nodes. Although with 6 leaf nodes, the Jaccard similarity was 0.778, no controller was extracted with zero similarity. For each of these 43 extracted controllers, the method was able to search around 3,000 possibilities of behavior trees, which is not trivial space.

4.3   Qualitative Behavioral Analysis

An example of a produced controller along with the original controller is presented in Fig. 4. The original behavior tree includes: random motion node, aggregation node and North-East node. Aggregation node and North-East node were extracted successfully while random node was not. Overall, the random node faced a failed extraction 22 times out of 37. In 18 cases, the random node was confused with a separation node as shown in this example. This is not surprising since combining separation node and leaf nodes with opposite behavior such as aggregation and clustering could look similar to the motion of the random node. Separation nodes itself were wrongly extracted in just three cases out of 26.

Aggregation, dispersion, clustering and all the directional nodes except north-east node had zero failed extractions. In general, the directional nodes tend to be over-extracted even when they are not present in the original controller.

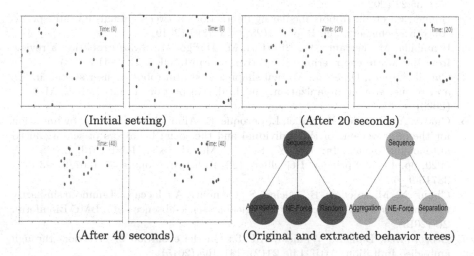

(Initial setting)   (After 20 seconds)

(After 40 seconds)   (Original and extracted behavior trees)

Fig. 4. An example of the output of the method with a high Jaccard similarity includes three screenshot of the controller and the behavior from the right to the left. The original behavior tree and their simulated behavior are shown in red whereas the extracted behavior tree and the imitated behavior are presented in green. (Color figure online)

5   Conclusion

Swarm behaviors in natural systems are inspiring in terms of their ability to provide these systems with robustness and flexibility. Extracting the rules from such systems is crucial for both the engineering of swarm robotics and the interpretability of the underlying dynamics of the swarm systems whether natural or artificial. Such extractions are also useful to understand and control artificial systems after observation. In this study, we developed an understandable swarm controller extraction method using an evolutionary algorithm and eight swarm metrics. To evaluate the method, we constructed a swarm dataset where each sample contains a behavior tree as swarm controller and corresponding simulated swarm trajectories. Our experimental results show the method can exactly extract 75 behavior trees out of 100 behavior trees while obtaining a 0.868 averaged Jaccard similarity. These results show the potential of the method in applications ranging from robotics to biology. In the future, more complex behavior trees and more action nodes will be considered such as transportation, communication and sensing nodes.

References

1. Amornbunchornvej, C., Berger-Wolf, T.: Framework for inferring following strategies from time series of movement data. ACM Trans. Knowl. Discov. Data **14**(3), 35:1–35:22 (2020)
2. Bonnet, F., et al.: Robots mediating interactions between animals for interspecies collective behaviors. Sci. Robot. **4**(28), eaau7897 (2019)
3. Brambilla, M., Ferrante, E., Birattari, M., Dorigo, M.: Swarm robotics: a review from the swarm engineering perspective. Swarm Intell. **7**(1), 1–41 (2013)
4. Carrillo-Zapata, D., et al.: Mutual shaping in swarm robotics: user studies in fire and rescue, storage organization, and bridge inspection. Front. Robot. AI **7**, 53 (2020)
5. Chatty, A., Gaussier, P., Kallel, I., Laroque, P., Alimi, A.M.: Learning by imitation for the improvement of the individual and the social behaviors of self-organized autonomous agents. In: Tan, Y., Shi, Y., Mo, H. (eds.) ICSI 2013. LNCS, vol. 7929, pp. 44–52. Springer, Heidelberg (2013). https://doi.org/10.1007/978-3-642-38715-9_6
6. Chung, N., Miasojedow, B., Michał, S., Gambin1, A.: Jaccard/Tanimoto similarity test and estimation methods for biological presence-absence data. BMC Bioinform. **20** (2019)
7. Erbas, M.D., Bull, L., Winfield, A.F.T.: On the evolution of behaviors through embodied imitation. Artif. Life **21**(2), 141–165 (2015)
8. Eriksson, A., Nilsson Jacobi, M., Nyström, J., Tunstrøm, K.: Determining interaction rules in animal swarms. Behav. Ecol. **21**(5), 1106–1111 (2010)
9. Ferguson, E.A., Matthiopoulos, J., Insall, R.H., Husmeier, D.: Inference of the drivers of collective movement in two cell types: dictyostelium and melanoma. J. R. Soc. Interface **13**(123), 20160695 (2016)
10. Francesca, G., Birattari, M.: Automatic design of robot swarms: achievements and challenges. Front. Robot. AI **3**, 29 (2016)
11. Harriott, C., Seiffert, A., Hayes, S., Adams, J.: Biologically-inspired human-swarm interaction metrics. Proc. Hum. Factors Ergon. Soc. Ann. Meeting **58**, 1471–1475 (2014)
12. Herbert-Read, J.E., Perna, A., Mann, R.P., Schaerf, T.M., Sumpter, D.J.T., Ward, A.J.W.: Inferring the rules of interaction of shoaling fish. Proc. Natl. Acad. Sci. **108**(46), 18726–18731 (2011)
13. Hogg, E., Hauert, S., Harvey, D., Richards, A.: Evolving behaviour trees for supervisory control of robot swarms. Artif. Life Robot. **25**(4), 569–577 (2020). https://doi.org/10.1007/s10015-020-00650-2
14. Hu, T.K., Gama, F., Chen, T., Wang, Z., Ribeiro, A., Sadler, B.: VGAI: end-to-end learning of vision-based decentralized controllers for robot swarms, pp. 4900–4904 (2021)
15. Jones, S., Studley, M., Hauert, S., Winfield, A.: Evolving behaviour trees for swarm robotics. In: Groß, R., et al. (eds.) Distributed Autonomous Robotic Systems. SPAR, vol. 6, pp. 487–501. Springer, Cham (2018). https://doi.org/10.1007/978-3-319-73008-0_34
16. Li, J., Tan, Y.: A two-stage imitation learning framework for the multi-target search problem in swarm robotics. Neurocomputing **334**, 249–264 (2019)
17. Li, W., Gauci, M., Groß, R.: Turing learning: a metric-free approach to inferring behavior and its application to swarms. Swarm Intell. **10**(3), 211–243 (2016). https://doi.org/10.1007/s11721-016-0126-1

18. Mann, R.P.: Bayesian inference for identifying interaction rules in moving animal groups. PLoS ONE **6**(8), e22827 (2011)
19. Manning, M.D., Harriott, C.E., Hayes, S.T., Adams, J.A., Seiffert, A.E.: Heuristic evaluation of swarm metrics' effectiveness. In: Proceedings of the Tenth Annual ACM/IEEE International Conference on Human-Robot Interaction Extended Abstracts, p. 17–18 (2015)
20. Maxeiner, H.: Imitation learning of fish and swarm behavior with Recurrent Neural Networks. Master's thesis, Dahlem Center for Machine Learning and Robotics (2019)
21. Nedjah, N., Junior, L.S.: Review of methodologies and tasks in swarm robotics towards standardization. Swarm Evol. Comput. **50**, 100565 (2019)
22. Peyer, K.E., Zhang, L., Nelson, B.J.: Bio-inspired magnetic swimming microrobots for biomedical applications (2012)
23. Prorok, A., Blumenkamp, J., Li, Q., Kortvelesy, R., Liu, Z., Stump, E.: The holy grail of multi-robot planning: learning to generate online-scalable solutions from offline-optimal experts. arXiv abs/2107.12254 (2021)
24. Ruangdech, S., Hauert, S., Homer, M.: Inferring swarm models using a single monitoring robot. In: Artificial Life Conference Proceedings, no. 31, pp. 278–279 (2019)
25. Şahin, E.: Swarm robotics: from sources of inspiration to domains of application. In: Şahin, E., Spears, W.M. (eds.) SR 2004. LNCS, vol. 3342, pp. 10–20. Springer, Heidelberg (2005). https://doi.org/10.1007/978-3-540-30552-1_2
26. Schaerf, T.M., Herbert-Read, J.E., Ward, A.J.W.: A statistical method for identifying different rules of interaction between individuals in moving animal groups. J. R. Soc. Interface **18**(176), rsif.2020.0925, 20200925 (2021)
27. Schilling, F., Lecoeur, J., Schiano, F., Floreano, D.: Learning vision-based flight in drone swarms by imitation. IEEE Robot. Autom. Lett. **4**(4), 4523–4530 (2019)
28. Yu, X., Wu, W., Feng, P., Tian, Y.: Swarm inverse reinforcement learning for biological systems. In: 2021 IEEE International Conference on Bioinformatics and Biomedicine (BIBM), pp. 274–279 (2021)
29. Zhou, S., Phielipp, M.J., Sefair, J.A., Walker, S.I., Amor, H.B.: Clone swarms: learning to predict and control multi-robot systems by imitation. In: 2019 IEEE/RSJ International Conference on Intelligent Robots and Systems (IROS), pp. 4092–4099 (2019)

Benchmarking Performances of Collective Decision-Making Strategies with Respect to Communication Bandwidths in Discrete Collective Estimation

Qihao Shan[✉][ID] and Sanaz Mostaghim[ID]

Chair of Computational Intelligence, Faculty of Informatics,
Otto von Guericke University, Magdeburg, Germany
{qihao.shan,sanaz.mostaghim}@ovgu.de

Abstract. Multi-option collective decision making is an emergent topic of study within the field of swarm intelligence. Many strategies have been proposed to enable decentralized and localized decision-making behaviors in intelligent swarms. However, many proposed strategies have very different requirements on the communication bandwidth and paradigm, which make a clear and fair comparison difficult. In this paper, we seek to investigate the performances of several promising decision-making algorithms in a discrete collective estimation scenario when the communication bandwidth and paradigm are controlled. The considered algorithms' performances are gauged via error, consensus time and failure rate. Among the considered algorithms, we have observed that distributed Bayesian belief sharing (DBBS) has superior performances in all three metrics, especially at higher communication bandwidths. On the other hand, ranked voting with Borda count (RV-BC) has comparable performances to the baseline algorithms at lower bandwidths, while slightly outperforms at higher bandwidths. We have concluded that the direct belief fusion mechanism that underpins DBBS is an efficient use of communication bandwidths in the experimental scenario investigated here. However, among the considered algorithms, its message size scales the quickest with the number of available options, which can potentially limit its viability.

1 Introduction and Related Works

In the study of swarm intelligence, collective decision making refers to the process where a swarm of agents reaches a particular global state using only local interactions among the agents as well as between the agents and the environment. Within the field of collective decision making, best-of-n problems encompass the class of decision-making scenarios with discrete options, from which the agents attempt to form a singular consensus on the most suitable one based on their interactions with the surrounding environment and each other [8]. In this paper, we focus on the discrete collective estimation scenario [5], which serves as a multi-option extension to the binary collective perception problem [7].

© Springer Nature Switzerland AG 2022
M. Dorigo et al. (Eds.): ANTS 2022, LNCS 13491, pp. 54–65, 2022.
https://doi.org/10.1007/978-3-031-20176-9_5

Many decision-making strategies inspired by naturally existing intelligent swarms have been proposed to perform decision making in best-of-n problems, such direct modulation of voter-based decisions (DMVD) [9] and direct modulation of majority-based decisions (DMMD) [10]. These opinion-based algorithms are characterized by an individual agent having an explicit representation of a favored option and trying to recruit its peers to its opinion during the decision-making process. There are also decision-making strategies proposed that take inspiration from sensor fusion as well as electoral process, such as distributed Bayesian belief sharing (DBBS) [5] and ranked voting algorithms [4]. These decision-making strategies were proposed to specifically address the multi-option decision-making scenario of discrete collective estimation. They seek to convey the relative preferences of the options by agents using direct communication, which can result in a higher communication bandwidth compared to the opinion-based methods such as DMVD and DMMD. On the other hand, DMVD and DMMD both require the agents to possess and broadcast uniquely identifying indices in their locality, which limits the scalability of the system. In contrast, DBBS in its current form, and ranked voting algorithms potentially, can function without uniquely identifying indices for the agents. These differences in communication bandwidth and paradigm make it difficult to accurately assess the viability of these decision-making strategies.

To provide a fair and accurate comparison among the various decision-making strategies, benchmark studies need to be conducted on them at similar communication bandwidths and communication paradigms. In this paper, we aim to gauge the performances of collective decision-making strategies from the perspective of communication bandwidths used, and observe the performances of considered algorithms in a discrete collective estimation scenario when the communication bandwidths are kept at equal levels and the communication paradigm kept to strictly peer-to-peer without identifiers.

2   Problem Statement

In this paper, we investigate a discrete collective estimation scenario. It has been used in previous studies on this topic [4,5]. It is a multi-option extension to the binary collective perception scenario investigated in [7] and a discrete variant of the continuous collective estimation problem investigated in [6]. The experimental environment is as shown in Fig. 1 (left), the arena is covered in black and white tiles, with the proportion of black tiles referred to as the fill ratio. N mobile robots roam the arena, whose task is to collectively determine the most likely fill ratio out of a series of H hypotheses. The robots can only communicate with their peers within a limited distance, and also only detect the color of the arena ground directly beneath themselves. The communication paradigm here is strictly peer-to-peer, and is only in the form of one robot broadcasting a message and another robot receiving it. An individual robot has no uniquely identifying indices. If multiple robots within a neighborhood are broadcasting at the same time, a random message would be picked up by a receiving robot.

Fig. 1. Illustration of experimental scenario (left) and arena patterns under concentrated distribution of environmental features (right)

In [4,5], Shan et al. has utilized decision-making strategies based on belief fusion and ranked voting respectively to perform the required task. They have also used a modified version of direct comparison (DC) and DMVD as baselines, due to their applications in binary collective perception problems shown in [1, 7]. We have modified the considered algorithms such that they have the same communication paradigm, and communication bandwidths that can be easily adjusted using parameters. Details will be presented in the next section.

Similar to previous literature on discrete collective estimation [5], we test the considered algorithms in two different environmental scenarios. The first is an environment where the distribution of tiles is random (Fig. 1 left), and the second is where black-color tiles are concentrated in distribution (Fig. 1 right).

3   Methodology

In this section, we present the details of the decision-making algorithms investigated in this paper. We will cover the decision-making mechanisms of each strategy considered and how we are controlling the communication bandwidth to achieve a fair comparison. For all decision-making strategies described here, the robots used a Bayesian statistics-based mechanism to compute the qualities of considered options. They are also programmed to perform random walk inside the arena by a low-level controller.

3.1   Control Mechanisms for Environmental Exploration

For all considered decision-making strategies, the robots use the same mechanism to explore the environment and obtain their own estimates of the likelihood of individual hypotheses on the fill ratio. The latter serves as the option qualities. These are the same as previous papers on the subject [4,5], and we will briefly cover them here.

The low-level mechanism that controls the movement of the robots is a finite-state machine with two possible motion states as shown in Table 1. At every control loop, a robot makes an observation of the color of the ground beneath

Table 1. Low-level control mechanism used to implement random walk

Motion	Transition condition
A. Moving Forward	Timer $exp(40)$s or Obstacle Detected
B. Turn in Random Direction	Timer $unif(0, 4.5)$s

itself, if it is moving forward in motion state A. Observation collection is limited to during forward motion in order to prevent an agent from collecting multiple observations at the same location. An observation is stored in vector $\underline{ob}$ that can be $\begin{bmatrix} 0 \\ 1 \end{bmatrix}$ or $\begin{bmatrix} 1 \\ 0 \end{bmatrix}$ depending on the color observed.

A robot's belief on the likelihoods of the fill ratio hypotheses are stored in vector $\underline{\rho}_n$, where each entry refers to the estimated likelihood of a corresponding hypothesis. After each observation, $\underline{\rho}_n$ is modified as follows.

$$\underline{\rho}_n = Normalize(\underline{\rho}_n \circ (K \cdot \underline{ob})) \tag{1}$$

$$K = \begin{bmatrix} 0.05 & 0.95 \\ 0.15 & 0.85 \\ \dots & \\ 0.95 & 0.05 \end{bmatrix} \tag{2}$$

Matrix K is of size $H \times 2$ and encodes all considered fill ratio hypotheses, where the first column represents white color and the second black color.

3.2 Opinion-Based Strategies: DC and DMVD

Algorithm 1 shows our implementation of DC and DMVD algorithms. Both algorithms are modified from implementations in binary collective perception scenarios [1,7], and they serve as baseline algorithms to gauge the performances of the other two recently proposed algorithms.

In line 4–6, robot n sample the color of the arena floor beneath itself and modifies its internal belief ρ_n on the likelihood of every fill ratio hypothesis. In line 7, the robot tries to collect the opinion of a random neighbor within its communication radius. If more than one robot nearby is broadcasting, the message from a random robot is received. In line 8–10, the robot updates its own opinion d_n using its corresponding decision rule. In line 11, the robot randomly mutates its current opinion to a neighboring hypothesis at a probability set by the mutation rate τ.

In previous implementations of the two algorithms, the robots use exploration and dissemination periods of configurable lengths to control the relative frequency of message transfer and decision making. In this paper, we use the parameter ϕ, denoting the broadcasting probability, to achieve similar effects. In line 12 of both algorithms, the robot broadcasts its opinion randomly for the rest of the control loop. We simulate the communication such that at any instant,

---

Algorithm 1: Opinion-based Strategies: DC and DMVD

    Input   : Initialized belief of robot n: $\underline{\rho}_n$
    Output: Converged decision: d_n

1 Initialize d_n with random valid values
2 Set broadcasting probability: ϕ and mutation probability: τ
3 **while** *Decisions in swarm have not converged* **do**
4   **if** *Robot n is moving forward in motion State A* **then**
5        $\underline{ob}$ = CollectObservation
6        $\underline{\rho}_n = Normalize(\underline{\rho}_n \circ (K \cdot \underline{ob}))$
7   (d_m, ρ_{m,d_m}) = CollectRandomNeighborOpinion
8   **if** *d_m is collected* **then**
9   DC : If $\rho_{m,d_m} > \rho_{n,d_n}$: $d_n = d_m$
10   DMVD: $d_n = d_m$
11    $d_n = RandomChoice([d_n + 1, d_n - 1], \tau)$
12   Broadcast d_n, ρ_{n,d_n} randomly at probability DC: ϕ; DMVD: $\phi \times \rho_{n,d_n}$

---

there is a certain probability for the robot to be broadcasting its opinion. For DMVD, this probability is the product of a configurable parameter ϕ and the computed quality of the robot's current opinion ρ_{n,d_n}. While for DC, it is just the parameter ϕ.

3.3 Ranked Voting-Based Strategy

Algorithm 2 shows our implementation of a ranked voting-based decision-making algorithm. We consider the best performing voting system investigated in previous work on the subject [4], Borda count, with similar modifications made to bring exploration and dissemination processes into one control loop.

    The robot performs the same exploration actions in Algorithm 2 line 5–7 to modify its own belief $\underline{\rho}_n$. It exchanges its opinion with its peers using the vector *ballot*. It contains the ranking of all available options starting from 0. The robot first attempt to collect a random neighbor's opinion $ballot'_m$ in Algorithm 2 line 8. Then in Algorithm 2 line 10 it tallies the result and updates its decision d_n using a Borda count voting system. RV-BC is subject to the same random mutation as in DMVD and DC shown in line 11 of Algorithm 2. *ballot* is then updated in line 14 of Algorithm 2, which produces a ranking of all available options using the internal belief of the robot $\underline{\rho}_n$. However, the current decision d_n would always be placed first in the ranking, regardless of its quality computed by the robot. The communication bandwidth of RV-BC is tuned via two parameters, broadcasting probability ϕ and ballot length η. The effect of ϕ is the same as in the previous subsection. On the other hand, when the ballot length η is smaller than the number of options, the robot shortens its ballot to length η by removing the least preferred options in line 13–14 of Algorithm 2. The shortened ballot is referred to as *ballot'* in the pseudocode.

Algorithm 2: Ranked Voting with Borda Count (RV-BC)

    Input   : Initialized belief of robot n: $\underline{\rho}_n$

    Output: Converged decision: d_n

1 Initialize d_n with random valid values

2 Set broadcasting probability: ϕ, ballot length: η and mutation probability: τ

3 Initialize $\underline{ballot}_n$ with ηs

4 **while** *Decisions in swarm have not converged* **do**

5   **if** *Robot n is moving forward in motion State A* **then**

6         $\underline{ob}$ = CollectObservation

7         $\underline{\rho}_n = Normalize(\underline{\rho}_n \circ (K \cdot \underline{ob}))$

8     $\underline{ballot}'_m$ = CollectRandomNeighborOpinion

9   **if** $\underline{ballot}'_m$ *is collected* **then**

10        $d_n = argmin(\underline{ballot}_n + \underline{ballot}'_m)$

11     $d_n = RandomChoice([d_n + 1, d_n - 1], \tau)$

12     $\underline{ballot}_n = MakeBallot(d_n, \underline{\rho}_n)$

13     $\underline{ballot}'_n = \underline{ballot}_n$

14     $\underline{ballot}'_n[\underline{ballot}'_n > \eta] = \eta$

15   Broadcast $\underline{ballot}'_n$ randomly at probability $\phi \times \rho_{n,d_n}$

3.4 Belief Fusion-Based Strategy: DBBS

Algorithm 3 shows our implementation of the DBBS algorithm, the implementation here is very similar to in [5], with the broadcasting probability ϕ similarly added.

The DBBS algorithm differs from other considered algorithms in that the robots share its belief $\underline{\rho}_n$ with each other and make the decision independently based on the combined beliefs of themselves and their peers in line 11 of Algorithm 3. The belief fusion process is controlled by two parameters λ and μ. λ is the decay rate of previously recorded beliefs of neighbors when adding new beliefs to the record (Algorithm 3 line 8), and μ is the decay rate of neighbors' beliefs when computing the outgoing message $\underline{\xi}_n$ (Algorithm 3 line 9). Both parameters tune the level of positive feedback in the decision-making process among the robots and should be set between 0 and 1.

4 Experiments and Results

In this section, we cover our experimental setup, including the assumptions and parameter settings used to control the communication bandwidths of the considered algorithms. Afterwards, we present our experimental results.

4.1 Experimental Setup

Our experiments are done in a simulated physics-based environment, as shown in Fig. 1 (left). It is 2-dimensional with a $2\,\text{m} \times 2\,\text{m}$ arena covered by 400 tiles. We simulate 20 mobile robots with the specification of e-pucks [3]. They have a

---

Algorithm 3: Distributed Bayesian Belief Sharing (DBBS)

Input: Initialized belief of robot n: $\underline{\rho}_n$, record of neighbors' beliefs : $\underline{\rho}'_n$
Output: Converged decisions: d_n

1 Set parameters: λ, μ and broadcasting probability: ϕ
2 **while** *Decisions in swarm have not converged* **do**
3   **if** *Robot n is moving forward in motion State A* **then**
4          $\underline{ob}$ = CollectObservation
5          $\underline{\rho}_n = Normalize(\underline{\rho}_n \circ (K \cdot \underline{ob}))$
6      $\underline{\xi}_m$ = CollectRandomNeighborOpinion
7   **if** $\underline{\xi}_m$ *collected* **then**
8          $\underline{\rho}'_n = Normalize(\underline{\rho}'^{\lambda}_n \circ \underline{\xi}_m)$
9      $\underline{\xi}_n = \underline{\rho}_n \circ \underline{\rho}'^{\mu}_n$
10   Broadcast $\underline{\xi}_n$ randomly at probability ϕ
11     $d_n = MaxIndex(\underline{\rho}_n \circ \underline{\rho}'_n)$

---

linear speed of $0.16\,\mathrm{m/s}$ and a rotational speed of $0.75\,\mathrm{rad/s}$. The communication range is set to $0.5\,\mathrm{m}$. The length of a control loop is set to $1\,\mathrm{s}$.

Table 2. Assumptions on the message format and sizes for all considered algorithms

Decision-making strategy	Message format
DMVD	short int (16 bits)
DC	short int + float (48 bits)
DBBS	$H\times$ float (320 bits)
RV-BC	$\eta\times$ short int (16η bits)

In this paper, when the robots are performing any considered algorithm, they use the message formats listed in Table 2 during their communication. We assume the robots are programmed using c++, and consider data types available for c++ for the message transfer and subsequent computation of the communication bandwidth used. In DMVD, the robots exchange only the index of their current decisions during dissemination, and we assume that the information is stored in a *short int* variable of 16 bits. Similarly, in DC, the robots exchange the index of their current decisions as well as the estimated qualities, which are stored using a *short int* and a *float* respectively, adding to a total of 48 bits. In DBBS, the robots exchange the estimated qualities of all considered options, which consists of H *float* variables, where H is the number of options. In this paper $H = 10$, thus the message size is 320 bits. And finally, in RV-BC, the robots exchange the rankings of the options, which is stored in η *short int* variables, with η being the ballot length parameter.

We investigate the performances of considered algorithms at 4 different bandwidth levels as shown in Table 3, together with the parameter settings for all

Table 3. Parameter settings for each investigated algorithm to reach the considered bandwidths levels

Decision-making strategy	Bandwidths			
	1.6 bits/s	3.2 bits/s	8 bits/s	16 bits/s
DMVD	$\phi = 0.1$	$\phi = 0.2$	$\phi = 0.5$	$\phi = 1$
DC	$\phi = 0.1/3$	$\phi = 0.2/3$	$\phi = 0.5/3$	$\phi = 1/3$
DBBS	$\phi = 0.005$	$\phi = 0.01$	$\phi = 0.025$	$\phi = 0.05$
RV-BC $\eta = 10$	$\phi = 0.01$	$\phi = 0.02$	$\phi = 0.05$	$\phi = 0.1$
RV-BC $\phi = 0.1$	$\eta = 1$	$\eta = 2$	$\eta = 5$	$\eta = 10$

considered algorithms to limit the communication bandwidths to those levels. In previous related works on collective perception [2] and discrete collective estimation [4,5], it has been observed that there is a trade-off between decision-making speed and accuracy. Thus, at each bandwidth level, we vary the other parameters that are independent of communication bandwidth for each considered algorithms and plot the Pareto frontiers of performances for different levels of communication. For DC, DMVD and RV-BC, the Pareto frontiers are obtained using the settings of $\tau = \{0, 0.01, 0.02, ...0.08\}$, while for DBBS, the Pareto frontiers are obtained using the settings of $\lambda = \{0.5, 0.6, 0.7, 0.8, 0.9\}$ and $\mu = \{0, 0.2, 0.4, 0.6, 0.8, 1\}$. We also assess the reliability of considered algorithms via the failure rates, which measures the proportion of experimental runs that fails to achieve a consensus within a time limit of 1200 s.

4.2   Experimental Results

The experimental results and the obtained Pareto frontiers between mean consensus time and mean absolute error are plotted in Fig. 2. The color coding of markers represents the failure rates.

As shown in Fig. 2(a), at the lowest considered bandwidth of 1.6 bits/s, all considered algorithms display clear trade-offs between decision speed and accuracy. They are also able to keep failure rates low at less than 0.1 for most parameter settings, except for DC with τ settings higher than 0.03 where the failure rates increase rapidly and approach 1 when $\tau \geq 0.05$. This is contrary to the more reliable performances of DC observed in [5]. Compared to DC, DMVD has comparable performances at high consensus time and can outperform DC at low consensus time. It also has lower failure rates across all parameter settings. Among the considered algorithms, DMVD can reach a consensus the fastest at low τ settings, although at a cost of higher error. DBBS is able to reach an error of zero in a shorter time than other considered algorithms, but has a hard time further reducing its consensus time. RV-BC has relatively poor performances in terms of decision time at error at this bandwidth level and its Pareto frontier is largely dominated by those of DBBS and DMVD. The upper left section of the Pareto frontier, produced by limiting the communication probability ϕ, results

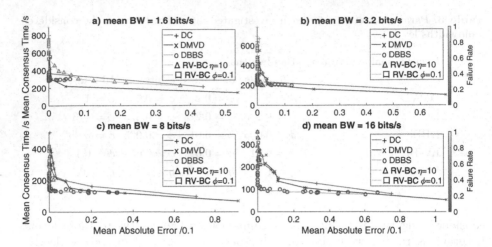

Fig. 2. Experimental results obtained by the considered algorithms in random environments

in very low error, but the consensus time is relatively high, while the lower right section, produced by limiting the ballot size η, results in relatively high error with not enough reduction in consensus time to outperform other considered algorithms significantly.

As shown in Fig. 2(b–d), as the communication bandwidth increases, all considered algorithms experience improvements in their performances, and are able to achieve progressively lower error at shorter decision time and lower failure rate. Among them, DBBS has the most significant improvements and progressively outperforms the other algorithms at the entire Pareto frontier at higher bandwidths. On the other hand, RV-BC has significant improvements in its error, but the algorithm has difficulties coming to a fast decision even at the highest communication bandwidth of 16 bits/s. At the same time, the performances of RV-BC become increasingly inelastic regarding the parameters and the results largely cluster together.

The performances of considered algorithms in environments with concentrated feature distribution are shown in Fig. 3. It can be observed that all considered algorithms experience a significant performance drop in all three metrics compared to in random environments. It is difficult for all algorithms to achieve an error of zero without experiencing high failure rates. This is especially apparent at low communication bandwidths shown in Fig. 3(a, b), where the data points at the top-left side of the Pareto frontiers have failure rates approaching 1. As the communication bandwidth increases, all considered algorithms experience a decrease in failure rate and decision time, but an increase in error.

Among the considered algorithms, DBBS still outperforms the others during most of the Pareto frontiers in terms of decision speed and accuracy, especially at higher communication bandwidths. It is also able to achieve lower failure rates at equivalent decision time, demonstrating its reliability in more difficult

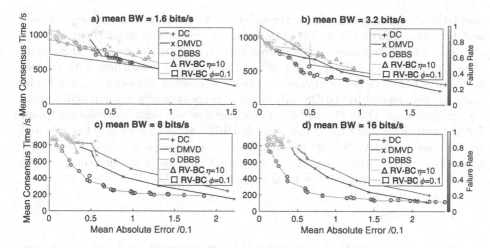

Fig. 3. Experimental results obtained by the considered algorithms in concentrated environments

environments. On the other hand, RV-BC displays slightly worse performances at lower bandwidths compared to DC and DMVD, while continue to display inelastic performances at higher bandwidths.

5   Discussion

Comparing the performances observed above with the results obtained in previous works on discrete collective estimation [4,5], we see that when controlling the communication bandwidth and paradigm, DC experiences a significant performance drop and is consistently comparable or worse compared to DMVD all along the Pareto frontier. This demonstrates that directly transmitting option qualities for comparison is not an efficient use of limited communication bandwidth. Also, DC suffers from the communication paradigm used here that restricts communication to peer-to-peer, which reduces the number of options seen by individual robots, and increasing the number of message transmissions needed for high-quality options to propagate among the robots. The same effects are also observed for RV-BC, which displays different performances compared to the results shown in [4]. However, despite its inelastic performances, it is still able to outperform the baselines at higher consensus time, especially at higher communication bandwidths. In contrast, DMVD is less impacted by the restriction in communication bandwidth and paradigm. This is because it only transmits the index of the chosen option to its peers, and the modulation of communication probability enables good options to propagate in a locality even when communication is only restricted to peer-to-peer.

DBBS still clearly outperforms the other considered algorithms when controlling the communication bandwidth, especially at higher bandwidths of 8 bits/s and 16 bits/s. On the other hand, the difference is not as prevalent at lower bandwidths. This confirms the results obtained in [5]. However, it should be noted that the results here are based on the assumptions regarding the message sizes made above, which scales differently for different considered algorithms with respect to the number of options. Therefore, when the number of options increase, the message size needed for DBBS will increase proportionally while it will largely be unaffected for DMVD and DC. Thus, there would exist a break-even point for the number of options, beyond which DBBS would not be viable compared to the baselines. RV-BC faces similar scaling message size when the number of options increase. However, the proportional increase is smaller compared to DBBS, since only the rankings need to be transmitted.

6   Conclusion

In this paper, we have investigated the performances of several collective decision-making strategies in a discrete collective estimation problem when controlling the communication bandwidth and paradigm. We aim to provide a fair and accurate assessment of the performances of previously proposed decision-making strategies that have different requirement to their communication bandwidths and paradigm. Thus, we have experimented on the considered algorithms at four bandwidth levels, where the communication paradigm is also restricted to only peer-to-peer. For every considered algorithm, we have varied the parameters that are independent of communication to plot the Pareto frontiers of their accuracy vs speed trade-off in the decision-making process. We have also taken into account of the reliability of considered algorithms using the failure rate.

Of the two newly proposed decision-making strategies, DBBS and RV-BC, we have observed that DBBS displays superior performances compared to other considered algorithms along the Pareto frontiers. On the other hand, RV-BC has comparable performances with the two baseline algorithms used at low bandwidths. It surpasses the baselines at high bandwidths, but is inelastic in its accuracy vs speed performance.

In future works, we aim to investigate how the performance relations produced here varies with the number of available options. Thus, we can provide the complete assessment of the discussed algorithms, and find out the limit of their relative viabilities.

References

1. Bartashevich, P., Mostaghim, S.: Benchmarking collective perception: new task difficulty metrics for collective decision-making. In: Moura Oliveira, P., Novais, P., Reis, L.P. (eds.) EPIA 2019. LNCS (LNAI), vol. 11804, pp. 699–711. Springer, Cham (2019). https://doi.org/10.1007/978-3-030-30241-2_58
2. Ebert, J.T., Gauci, M., Mallmann-Trenn, F., Nagpal, R.: Bayes bots: collective Bayesian decision-making in decentralized robot swarms. In: 2020 IEEE International Conference on Robotics and Automation (ICRA), pp. 7186–7192 (2020). https://doi.org/10.1109/ICRA40945.2020.9196584

3. Mondada, F., et al.: The e-puck, a robot designed for education in engineering. In: Proceedings of the 9th Conference on Autonomous Robot Systems and Competitions, vol. 1, no. 1, pp. 59–65 (2009). http://infoscience.epfl.ch/record/135236
4. Shan, Q., Heck, A., Mostaghim, S.: Discrete collective estimation in swarm robotics with ranked voting systems. In: 2021 IEEE Symposium Series on Computational Intelligence (SSCI), pp. 1–8 (2021). https://doi.org/10.1109/SSCI50451.2021.9659868
5. Shan, Q., Mostaghim, S.: Discrete collective estimation in swarm robotics with distributed Bayesian belief sharing. Swarm Intell. **15**(4), 377–402 (2021). https://doi.org/10.1007/s11721-021-00201-w
6. Strobel, V., Dorigo, M.: Blockchain technology for robot swarms: a shared knowledge and reputation management system for collective estimation. In: Swarm Intelligence: 11th International Conference, ANTS 2018, Rome, Italy, 29–31 October 2018, Proceedings, vol. 11172, p. 425. Springer, Heidelberg (2018)
7. Valentini, G., Brambilla, D., Hamann, H., Dorigo, M.: Collective perception of environmental features in a robot swarm. In: Dorigo, M., et al. (eds.) ANTS 2016. LNCS, vol. 9882, pp. 65–76. Springer, Cham (2016). https://doi.org/10.1007/978-3-319-44427-7_6
8. Valentini, G., Ferrante, E., Dorigo, M.: The best-of-N problem in robot swarms: formalization, state of the art, and novel perspectives. Front. Robot. AI **4**, 9 (2017). https://doi.org/10.3389/frobt.2017.00009
9. Valentini, G., Hamann, H., Dorigo, M.: Self-organized collective decision making: the weighted voter model. In: Proceedings of the 2014 International Conference on Autonomous Agents and Multi-Agent Systems, AAMAS 2014, Richland, SC, pp. 45–52. International Foundation for Autonomous Agents and Multiagent Systems (2014). https://doi.org/10.5555/2615731.2615742
10. Valentini, G., Hamann, H., Dorigo, M.: Efficient decision-making in a self-organizing robot swarm: on the speed versus accuracy trade-off. In: Proceedings of the 2015 International Conference on Autonomous Agents and Multiagent Systems, AAMAS 2015, Richland, SC, pp. 1305–1314. International Foundation for Autonomous Agents and Multiagent Systems (2015). https://doi.org/10.5555/2772879.2773319

Best-of-N Collective Decisions
on a Hierarchy

Fabio Oddi[1], Andrea Cristofaro[1], and Vito Trianni[2][✉]

[1] DIAG, Sapienza University of Rome, Rome, Italy
fabio.oddi@uniroma1.it, cristofaro@diag.uniroma1.it
[2] ISTC, National Research Council, Rome, Italy

Abstract. The best-of-N problem in collective decision making is complex especially when the number of available alternatives is larger than a few, and no alternative distinctly shines over the others. Additionally, if the quality of the available alternatives is not a priori known and noisy, errors in the quality estimation may lead to the premature selection of sub-optimal alternatives. A typical speed-accuracy trade-off must be faced, which is hardened by the presence of several alternatives to be analyzed in parallel. In this study, we transform a one-shot best-of-N decision problem in a sequence of simpler decisions between a small number of alternatives, by organizing the decision problem in a hierarchy of choices. To this end, we construct an m-ary tree where the leaves represent the available alternatives, and high-level nodes group the low-level ones to present a low-dimension decision problem. Results from multi-agent simulations in both a fully-connected topology and in a spatial decision problem demonstrate that the sequential collective decisions can be parameterized to maximize speed and accuracy against different decision problems. A further improvement relies on an adaptive approach that automatically tunes the system parameters.

1 Introduction

Collective decisions are key in many natural and artificial systems, from bacteria to social insects, from organizations to robot swarms [11,18,22,24]. A collective decision requires that a group of agents agrees on a common solution to a given problem. Generally speaking, a best-of-N collective decision problem presents multiple alternative solutions, each characterized by a quality value representing associated benefits and costs, and the best possible one must be chosen by a (qualified) majority or through full consensus. Intuitively, the larger is the number N of alternatives, the harder is the problem of selecting the best one. This is because a qualified majority is more difficult to form if individual choices can spread across many competing alternatives, and because correctly evaluating and comparing multiple alternatives becomes extremely cumbersome and can lead to spreading of individual biases. Indeed, previous studies on collective decision making revealed that increasing the number of alternatives negatively affects the

© Springer Nature Switzerland AG 2022
M. Dorigo et al. (Eds.): ANTS 2022, LNCS 13491, pp. 66–78, 2022.
https://doi.org/10.1007/978-3-031-20176-9_6

ability to make accurate decisions. First, the parameter space in which a decision deadlock is possible is larger when N increases, suggesting that the system may remain unable to collectively choose any alternative for a long time, and that sub-optimal alternatives could be selected [16]. Second, the time taken to select the best alternative increases exponentially with the number of available alternatives, in adherence with the Hick-Hyman's law of psychophysics [15].

In the face of the complexity of deciding among multiple alternatives, there is evidence that the path towards decision does not directly lead to a crisp choice of the best alternative [7]. Instead, it is likely that one or a group of alternatives is discarded quickly to reduce the problem dimensionality. This is the case for choices among spatially distributed alternatives in both individuals and collectives, where the feedback between body movements and decision making allows to select out alternatives when their reachability decreases [23]. Similarly, optimal decision heuristics in multi-alternative choice problems allow to focus attention on a limited number of alternatives, often as small as two, reducing the cognitive load for a comprehensive evaluation [6]. When evidence must be gathered about the available alternatives, a speed-accuracy trade-off arises, where higher accuracy can be achieved by collecting additional evidence, which slows down decision making [5]. Selective attention to different alternatives can be modulated according to value, which implies that low-quality alternatives are sampled less often [9]. On the other hand, adaptive sampling of alternatives postulates that increased sampling is dedicated to alternatives when quality uncertainty is higher [8]. Both these mechanisms suggest that sequential sampling and evidence accumulation in multi-alternative decision problems can lead to focusing on just the most interesting options, putting aside less valuable ones.

Correlations between alternatives (e.g., spatial location) may require optimal planning of the sampling effort. This problem has been addressed in robotics mapping, where a multi-resolution adaptive sampling can optimize evidence accumulation [10]. On the basis of the gathered evidence, (collective) decision making can lead to optimal deployment of robots in the area where working is most valuable [1,2]. In these studies, an m-ary tree is introduced to represent the spatial correlation between alternatives (i.e., areas where some work is required). This representation also drives the resolution of the evidence accumulation, enabling to observe multiple alternatives at the same time or to focus on subgroups.

Inspired by the above considerations, we study whether collective decision making can benefit from a hierarchical organization of the N available alternatives, which can direct the evidence accumulation and decision process. We choose a hierarchical organization as the most straightforward way of aggregating alternatives, by maintaining possible correlations (e.g., closeness in space) and recursively creating macro-alternatives that group together some of the available options. Our working hypothesis is that a complex decision process can be simplified by reducing it to a sequence of decisions between a smaller number of groups of alternatives. Evidence accumulation is performed at the group level, hence with a reduced resolution (i.e., aggregating randomly sampled values within a group). Decisions are collectively taken following a decentralized algorithm inspired by house-hunting honey bees [17], which can be controlled by a single parameter describing the ratio of interactions with respect to individual decision. We complete the algorithm with quorum sensing, which enables to efficiently serialize the decision making process over the defined hierarchy [14,21]. We show that the hierarchical approach allows to solve different decision problems with the same parameterization, while the non-hierarchical approach does not present a single parameterization that both maximizes accuracy and is capable of breaking deadlocks among equivalent alternatives. These results are robust to noisy evidence accumulation—owing to the possibility of agents to share their local knowledge and collectively minimize the estimation error—and to local quorum estimation. We also introduce an adaptive parameterization of the collective decision-making algorithm based on the residual uncertainty about the quality of alternatives. Thanks to this mechanism, it is possible to improve the speed-accuracy trade-off for all tested hierarchies. Finally, we demonstrate that the proposed approach can be adapted well to spatial best-of-N decisions.

2 Experimental Setup

2.1 Problem Description

In best-of-N decisions, N different alternatives are present, each characterized by a quality value v_i, $i \in [1, N]$. A group of M agents must collectively choose the alternative with the highest quality, or one of the equal-best alternatives. Without loss of generality, we assume that one alternative has maximum value (here, $v_M = 10$), while all other alternatives have the same, small value ($v_m = \kappa v_M$, $\kappa \in [0,1]$). We consider that a decision has been made by the group of agents when a quorum $Q \in (0.5, 1]$ is reached for one of the alternatives, that is, a minimum fraction Q of agents has selected the same alternative.

In our hierarchical problem formulation, the alternatives are organized in a m-ary tree, that is, a tree where each parent node has at most m children. Each alternative corresponds to a leaf node in the tree, while non-leaf nodes represent groups of alternatives. Given N alternatives, the minimum depth of an m-ary tree is $D = \lfloor \log_m N \rfloor$. Hence, a binary tree with depth $D = 5$ contains at most $N = 32$ alternatives. Conversely, when $m = N$, the depth of the tree is $D = 1$ meaning that there is no hierarchical organization of the alternatives, which are all children of the root node. A node at level $d \in \{0, \ldots, D\}$ of the tree entails a decision between at most m alternatives. We consider here only perfect m-ary trees, where each non-leaf node has exactly m child nodes and all leaf nodes are at the same depth. A tree node is labeled by n_j^d, where d is the depth and $j \in 1, \ldots, m^d$ is an univocal index. The sub-tree defined by n_j^d is referred to as S_j^d. The root node (n_1^0) is the starting point for collective decision making.

2.2 Collective Decision Process

The collective decision process extends a design pattern for decentralized decision making [17] with quorum sensing to move at different tree depth. We start by describing the ideal case in which agents have knowledge about the number and quality of the alternatives, as well as about the number of agents that are in their same sub-tree. Later, we relax these assumptions.

Agents with Perfect Knowledge. In the hierarchical collective decision model, at any time t an agent i is characterized by a tuple $a_i = \langle s_i, c_i \rangle$, where s_i is the node in which the agent resides, and c_i is a desired destination node. If $c_i = s_i$, the agent is said to be "uncommitted at s_i", that is, the agent has not selected a desired destination. Otherwise, c_i can be any children of s_i and the agent is said to be "committed to c_i". At start, all agents are initialized with the tuple $\langle n_1^0, n_1^0 \rangle$, that is, they are uncommitted at the root node. We denote with $\mathcal{P}_j^d$ the sub-population of agents residing at any node in the sub-tree starting from n_j^d. Note that $\mathcal{P}_1^0$ is the entire agent population, with $|\mathcal{P}_1^0| = M$.

Agents change their residence node only if a quorum of committed agents has been reached for the child node they are committed to. Specifically, an agent i residing in node $s_i = n_j^d$ and committed to the child node $c_i = n_l^{d+1}$ moves its residence to the latter if $|\mathcal{P}_l^{d+1}| \geq QM$. Once such a quorum is reached, all committed agents change their residence node, ensuring that a large fraction of the population moves down the hierarchical structure towards the leaf nodes. This also means that agents never need to move back to the parent node (but see below when imperfect quorum sensing is implemented). The process ends if a quorum is reached for one of the leaf nodes representing one of the available options. In other words, agents remain in their residing node unless a quorum is reached, and then move to the selected child node. Given that a sufficiently large quorum is the result of a collective decision, the agent population is expected to perform a sequence of D decisions leading to the selection of one leaf node.

The commitment state of an agent changes according to stochastic processes inspired by the decision process of house-hunting honeybees [17]. In particular, we exploit the parameterization extensively studied in [15,16]. To this end, the quality of a node must be considered, which must be a function of the group of alternatives that a node represents. Here, we consider that the quality of a node $v(n_j^d)$ is recursively computed as the maximum quality among the child nodes:

$$v(n_j^d) = \max_{n \in \mathcal{C}(n_j^d)} v(n), \tag{1}$$

where $\mathcal{C}(n_j^d)$ is the set of child nodes of n_j^d. This allows to propagate up in the hierarchy the best value of the underlying alternatives represented in the leaf nodes, without loosing in resolution. See Sect. 4 for a discussion.

At time t, an agent i uncommitted at n_j^d ($a_i = \langle n_j^d, n_j^d \rangle$) can spontaneously become committed to a randomly selected child node n_l^{d+1} with probability:

$$P_\gamma = k \frac{v(n_l^{d+1})}{v_M}, \tag{2}$$

where k is a tunable parameter chosen to scale the probability. At the same time, the agent i may get recruited by another agent $b \in \mathcal{P}_j^d$, with $a_b = \langle s_b, c_b \rangle$. This is implemented by choosing a random agent from $\mathcal{P}_j^d$ and computing the following recruitment probability:

$$P_\rho = \begin{cases} h\frac{v(c_b)}{v_M} & c_b \neq n_j^d \\ 0 & \text{otherwise} \end{cases}, \tag{3}$$

where h is a scaling factor. Note that commitment and recruitment are evaluated in parallel, requiring that $P_\gamma + P_\rho \leq 1$. Hence, we impose that $h + k = 1$.

When an agent i is committed to n_l^{d+1}, it can spontaneously become uncommitted at n_j^d with an abandonment probability inversely proportional to quality:

$$P_\alpha = k\frac{1}{1 + v(n_l^{d+1})}, \tag{4}$$

where k is the same scaling factor as in (2). Also, the agent i may get inhibited by another agent $b \in \mathcal{P}_j^d$, with $a_b = \langle s_b, c_b \rangle$. This is implemented by choosing a random agent from $\mathcal{P}_j^d$ and computing the inhibition probability:

$$P_\sigma = \begin{cases} h\frac{v(c_b)}{v_M} & c_b \neq n_j^d \wedge c_b \neq n_l^{d+1} \\ 0 & \text{otherwise} \end{cases}, \tag{5}$$

where h is the same scaling factor as in (3). Also in this case, we must enforce that $P_\alpha + P_\sigma \leq 1$, which is still the case if we ensure that $h + k = 1$.

Note that, with a flat hierarchy ($D = 1$), the collective decision process reduces to the standard best-of-N decisions previously studied [15,16]. In analogy with previous work, we introduce a single control parameter $r = \frac{h}{k}$ to tune the relative strength of stochastic processes based on interactions with other agents (i.e., recruitment and inhibition) with respect to spontaneous stochastic processes (i.e., commitment and abandonment).

Estimation of the Alternative Quality. Moving beyond the ideal case presented above, we introduce here the more realistic case in which agents are aware about the maximum number N of alternatives and their hierarchical organization, but are not aware of their quality, which is perceived with noise. At every decision step, an agent i makes an observation of a node n chosen according to its state: if the agent is uncommitted at n_j^d, it observes the child node selected for the computation of the commitment probability (2). Otherwise, the agent observes the desired destination c_i. If the observed node n is a non-leaf node, then a random leaf in the sub-tree of n is chosen for observation, and all parent nodes are updated according to (1). Upon observation of a leaf node n_j^D, agent i updates its quality estimate $\tilde{v}_i$ according to a moving average:

$$\tilde{v}_i(n_j^D) \leftarrow \begin{cases} v(n_j^D) + N(0, \sigma_j^D) & t_j^D = 0 \\ \lambda\tilde{v}_i(n_j^D) + (1 - \lambda)(v(n_j^D) + N(0, \sigma_j^D)) & \text{otherwise} \end{cases}, \tag{6}$$

where t_j^D counts the number of observations previously performed, λ represents the smoothing factor and σ_j^D represents the variance of a Gaussian noise. This simple exponential filter allows to rapidly converge on a stable estimation of the quality of the alternatives, and also allows to adapt to changing qualities—a possibility not explored in this study. Additionally, by limiting the observations to the sub-tree where an agent resides, the estimation is focused on the relevant alternatives, avoiding to waste time for those that have been discarded earlier.

To take advantage of the collective sensing abilities, agents exchange their current estimates upon interaction: when agent i interacts with agent b, it receives from b the quality estimates of all the N alternatives. These estimates are treated in the same way as independent observations to update the individual estimates with (6). Overall, this leads to a fast convergence towards the average.

Quorum Sensing. If agents cannot reliably count how many agents are committed to a given node, an estimate can be obtained by keeping memory of the last interactions. At every time step t, an agent i that interacts with another agent b records in a list $\mathcal{L}$ a tuple $\langle b, c_b, t_b = t \rangle$. In case an element is present in $\mathcal{L}$ with the same id b, the corresponding timestamp t_b is updated. Finally, old elements are purged from $\mathcal{L}$ when $t - t_b > T_M$, where T_M is a maximum period for retaining past interactions. As agents have only one interaction per time step, it follows that $|\mathcal{L}| \leq T_M$. Quorum sensing is implemented looking at the information in $\mathcal{L}$. An agent i committed to n_l^{d+1} counts the number L_l^{d+1} of elements in the list where $c_b \in S_l^{d+1}$. If L_l^{d+1} is larger than a threshold L_M, the agent has recently interacted with a sample of the population with the same commitment. Hence, the agent considers the quorum reached and changes its residing node to $s_i = n_l^{d+1}$. This estimation is however prone to errors, because of small samples or because old information does not represent any more the current population. Hence, a recovery mechanism allows robots to move to the parent node. Given that $\mathcal{L}$ shrinks if an agent resides in a node in which the population is small (e.g., when a real quorum was not actually reached), an agent uncommitted at n_j^d changes its residence to the parent node if $|\mathcal{L}| < L_m$, where $L_m < L_M \leq T_M$.

Adaptive Parameter Selection. The parameter $r = \frac{h}{k}$ can determine if and how fast the group converges to a shared choice [16]. High values correspond to fast but possibly inaccurate decisions, as social information is given more importance than individual quality estimation. To improve the decision making process, social feedback should increase when the uncertainty about the available options decreases. Agents measure uncertainty by learning two independent Gaussian models for each alternative—i.e., updating one model every second observation. Then, the Hellinger distance $H_d \in [0, 1]$ between the two is computed and associated to the corresponding leaf node. Non-leaf nodes receive the maximum distance of their children. High H_d corresponds to insufficient sampling, hence high uncertainty. An agent i committed to n_l^{d+1} uses the $H_d(n_l^{d+1})$ to compute a value $r_i = g(1 - H_d)$, where g is a gain to adjust the range. During the decision process, an agent i interacting with agent b receives from the latter the value r_b. This allows to tune the process strength after the uncertainty of the interacting agent, where low uncertainty corresponds to stronger interactions.

Decision Making on a Spatial Hierarchy. We also consider the spatial case in which agents have to identify the most valuable area within a given region. The region is divided in N areas, and a hierarchical organization is imposed recursively partitioning the region in smaller areas. The root node of the hierarchical structure represents the whole region, which is partitioned in m sub-regions, and each is recursively divided further until N areas are obtained. Similarly to the non-spatial setup, only one area has maximum quality v_M, while all other areas have the same quality $v_m = \kappa v_M$. We consider here the case of binary and quad-trees, usually employed to represent a 2D space. Agents move according to a random waypoint model [4]: an agent i selects a random position within the region corresponding to the node c_i within the hierarchy, and moves there at constant speed. To focus on the effects of spatiality, we ignore collisions, as if the agent body size were negligible with respect to the dimensions covered (e.g., in case of drones monitoring a large field [2]). In the future, this assumption can be relaxed via efficient velocity-obstacle collision avoidance [3].

The decision process is implemented through space as follows. An agent i randomly selects a position in c_i and moves there. Once the random position is reached, it broadcasts information about its ID i, its current state a_i, the current quality estimates for the N alternatives, and a timestamp t_i. Broadcast messages can be received within a limited communication radius R_c. Upon reception of a new message, an agent re-broadcasts it, and stores the information in a list $\mathcal{N}$ of detected neighbors, overwriting any older message from the same sender. Quality estimates are updated according to the information received from neighbors. Messages older than T_M are purged from $\mathcal{N}$. When the agent reaches the desired position, a noisy observation is made at the agent location, and the tree structure is updated accordingly. Then, the decision process takes place. If the agent is uncommitted at n_j^d, it computes the commitment probability for the child node n_l^{d+1} corresponding to the current agent position. A random neighbor is selected from $\mathcal{N}$ and the recruitment probability is computed. Similarly, if the agent is committed to n_l^{d+1}, the abandonment probability is computed with the latest quality estimate, and the inhibition probability from the randomly selected neighbor from $\mathcal{N}$. In any case, the information from the selected neighbor is used to update the list $\mathcal{L}$ for quorum sensing, similarly which is implemented as in the non-spatial case. Note that quorum is not computed on the list $\mathcal{N}$ because to avoid overestimating the opinion of the local population, and to keep the decision process aligned with the non-spatial case. Note also that in the spatial case, decisions are taken only when a new observation is made at the randomly selected position, contrary to the non-spatial case in which decisions occur at any time step. Hence, the spatial case evolves slowly, but an equivalence can be make looking at the average number of decisions made within the population.

3   Results

We measure accuracy as the percentage of runs (out of 100) in which the best alternative—or one of the equal-best when $\kappa = 1$—was correctly identified by at least QM agents. As a proxy for decision speed, we measure the convergence time taken by the agents to reach a collective decision. To this end, we employ the Kaplan-Meier estimator [12] to compute the empirical cumulative distribution of convergence times, censoring the runs that do not converge within the maximum allotted time. We fit a Weibull distribution and use the fitted function to compute average and standard deviation of the convergence times.

First of all, we consider the non-spatial case in which agents have perfect knowledge. We consider a relatively easy decision problem with $\kappa = 0.75$, a more difficult one with $\kappa = 0.85$, and a symmetry breaking problem with $\kappa = 1$. The parameter $r = \frac{h}{k}$ is used as control parameter to tune convergence speed. Figure 1 shows how the accuracy varies across problems for different configurations were flat, binary and quad-trees are employed (the latter only for $N = 16$). For any value of N we tested, the binary tree provides the highest accuracy when $r = 1$. A lower value ($r = 0.5$) is equally good unless $N \geq 16$ and $\kappa = 1$, where several runs do not terminate within the allotted time $\mathcal{T}$. Indeed, when r is small, the collective decision process cannot take full advantage of the positive and negative feedback loops, making symmetry breaking very difficult. Conversely, higher values of r may excessively rely on social information, which may lead to a loss in accuracy when the decision problem is difficult ($\kappa = 0.85$).

Non-hierarchical structures ($m = N$) struggle to consistently provide good results across all problem configurations, especially for large N. There exist parameterizations leading to good results (e.g., when $N = 16, r = 3$ for $\kappa \leq 0.85$, or $r = 5$ for $\kappa = 1$), but no single one performs systematically well across different

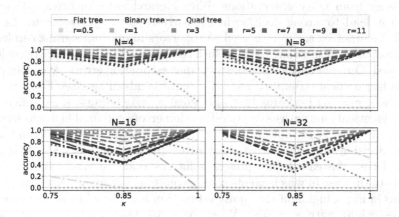

Fig. 1. Accuracy of different hierarchical structures ($m = 2, 4, N$, indicated by line type) for different values of $\kappa \in \{0.75, 0.85, 1\}$ with varying number of options N and parameter r (line color). Other parameters: $M = 100$, $Q = 0.8$, $\mathcal{T} = 1000$ time steps.

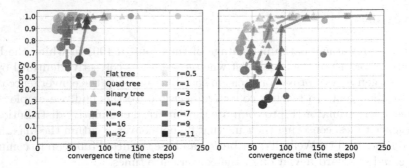

Fig. 2. Performance evaluation over 100 independent runs of different hierarchical structures ($m = 2, 4, N$) with varying number of options N (point color) and parameter r (color intensity). For each value of N, the Pareto frontier is displayed connecting points that are non-dominated. Dominated points are smaller than non-dominated ones. Left: $\kappa = 0.75$. Right: $\kappa = 0.85$. Other parameters as in Fig. 1.

values of k and N. Similarly, the quad trees deployed for $N = 16$ display a good overall performance for $r = 3$, but still not comparable with the binary trees.

Overall, we found that hierarchical decisions perform better as they allow to serialize the best-of-N problem in a sequence of smaller problems, which can be better parameterized to deal with different complexity levels. However, high accuracy may come at the cost of slowing down the decision process, and this could be especially the case if a long sequence of decisions must be performed. In Fig. 2, we study the speed-accuracy trade-off for $\kappa = 0.75$ (left) and $\kappa = 0.85$ (right).[1] In both cases, the hierarchical approach produces solutions that lay on the Pareto frontier, often dominating non-hierarchical solutions. Hence, fast convergence is ensured also in case of a sequence of D decisions.

When the quality of the alternatives is not known a priori, a (slow) estimation is necessary from noisy observations. With hierarchical structures, estimation errors may lead to wrong decision in the early stages (e.g., nearer to the tree root) that cannot be easily recovered. Also, errors in quorum sensing can lead a whole group down the wrong path. In such conditions, the flat hierarchy could be advantaged. Our simulations demonstrate that estimation errors have an impact, but still hierarchical structures provide a sensible advantage (see Fig. 3 and 4). In this case, $r = 0.5$ performs best also when $\kappa = 1$, because small differences between identical alternatives due to estimation errors get amplified, accelerating convergence towards any option. For $r \geq 1$, instead, estimation errors can lead to a wrong decision especially when alternatives are similar ($\kappa = 0.85$). Flat trees and quad trees instead do not present solutions that are systematically good, similarly to the case in which agents could exploit perfect knowledge. The Pareto diagrams in Fig. 4 highlight that noisy estimation leads to a loss in accuracy and speed, especially with $\kappa = 0.85$. When $N = 16$, binary trees are not always Pareto optimal, but lay close to the frontier and can be accepted.

---

[1] For $\kappa = 1$, decision speed is very similar across different configurations, and the trade-off is dominated by solutions with high r that quickly converge to any option.

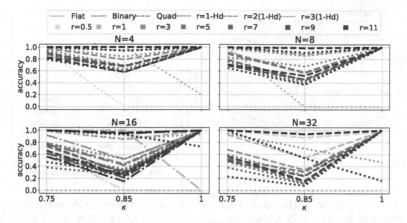

Fig. 3. Accuracy over 100 independent runs of different hierarchical structures with noisy observation and quorum sensing ($M = 100$, $Q = 0.8$, $\lambda = 0.8$, $\sigma_j^D = 1$, $T_M = 12$, $L_M = 10$, $L_m = 2$, $\mathcal{T} = 1000$ time steps). Black lines indicate the adaptive approach.

The slow evidence gathering process requires a small value of r to provide good accuracy, but this leads to a slow collective decision process. An adaptive approach can prove best if it gathers evidence to minimize uncertainties and increases speed when sufficient information is available. By linking the parameter r to the uncertainty, collective decisions can be both accurate and fast. Figure 3 and 4 show results of simulations with an adaptive approach, where the gain g has been tuned to maximize decision accuracy. An adaptive approach proves very advantageous especially with binary trees and complex decision problems, where both accuracy and speed are improved (see Fig. 4 right).

Finally, we analyse a proof of concept where mobile agents need to select the best area among N (see videos at [13]). Here, the adaptive approach is employed. Results shown in Fig. 5 demonstrate that binary trees provide the best solutions and also optimize the speed-accuracy trade-off. Hence, despite

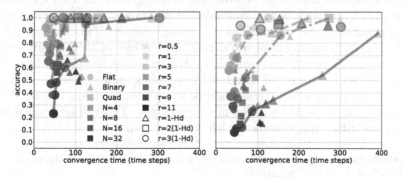

Fig. 4. Pareto diagram corresponding to simulations with noisy observation and quorum sensing. Left: $\kappa = 0.75$. Right: $\kappa = 0.85$. Other parameters as in Fig. 3.

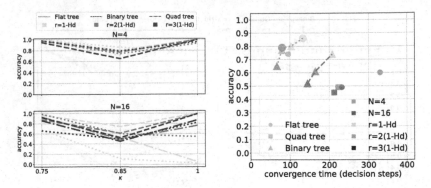

Fig. 5. Left: Accuracy of the spatial simulations for different configurations. Right: Pareto diagram for $\kappa = 0.85$. Other parameters: $M = 100$, $Q = 0.8$, $\lambda = 0.8$, $\sigma_j^D = 1$, $T_M = 100$, $L_M = 10$, $L_m = 2$, $\mathcal{T} = 10000$ time steps.

the spatial correlations that may slow down decision-making, the hierarchical approach outperforms non-hierarchical configurations. Somewhat surprisingly, quad trees do not lead to good performance, despite they are the best choice for representing 2D spaces. Further studies should be performed to verify if different parameterizations lead to better results.

4   Conclusions

This study demonstrates that collective decision making can benefit from a hierarchical representation of the alternatives. A number of assumptions have been made, such as the a priori knowledge of N and of the tree structure. Such assumption can be relaxed, providing agents with the ability to build the hierarchy on the fly—possibly in a collective, decentralized way—or discovering it through observations, should this be related to the decision problem. Another assumption is related to the propagation of the maximum value from the leafs up the tree, which requires knowledge of what leaf is being observed from any non-leaf node. If such knowledge is not available, all observations must be aggregated at the non-leaf node, for instance via a (moving) average. This however reduces the ability to distinguish between different alternatives at the beginning of the process, as preliminary experiments have demonstrated (data not shown). We hypothesize that, by means of an adaptive sampling approach (e.g., Thompson sampling [20]), better alternatives could be sampled more frequently, leading to approximate the propagation of the maximum value. This will be studied in the future, along with implementation with Kilobots [19].

Acknowledgments. Vito Trianni acknowledges partial support from the project TAILOR (H2020-ICT-48 GA: 952215).

References

1. Albani, D., Hönig, W., Nardi, D., Ayanian, N., Trianni, V.: Hierarchical task assignment and path finding with limited communication for robot swarms. Appl. Sci. **11**(7), 3115 (2021)
2. Albani, D., Manoni, T., Nardi, D., Trianni, V.: Dynamic UAV swarm deployment for non-uniform coverage. In: Proceedings of the 17th International Conference on Autonomous Agents and MultiAgent Systems, AAMAS 2018, pp. 523–531 (2018)
3. Bareiss, D., van den Berg, J.: Generalized reciprocal collision avoidance. Int. J. Robot. Res. **34**(12), 1501–1514 (2015)
4. Bettstetter, C., Hartenstein, H., Pérez-Costa, X.: Stochastic properties of the random waypoint mobility model. Wirel. Netw. **10**(5), 555–567 (2004)
5. Bogacz, R.: Optimal decision-making theories: linking neurobiology with behaviour. Trends Cogn. Sci. **11**(3), 118–125 (2007)
6. Brown, S., Steyvers, M., Wagenmakers, E.J.: Observing evidence accumulation during multi-alternative decisions. J. Math. Psychol. **53**(6), 453–462 (2009)
7. Busemeyer, J.R., Gluth, S., Rieskamp, J., Turner, B.M.: Cognitive and neural bases of multi-attribute, multi-alternative, value-based decisions. Trends Cogn. Sci. **23**(3), 251–263 (2019)
8. Cassey, T.C., Evens, D.R., Bogacz, R., Marshall, J.A.R., Ludwig, C.J.H.: Adaptive sampling of information in perceptual decision-making. PLoS ONE **8**(11), e78993 (2013)
9. Gluth, S., Spektor, M.S., Rieskamp, J.: Value-based attentional capture affects multi-alternative decision making. eLife **7**, e39659 (2018)
10. Jin, L., Rückin, J., Kiss, S.H., Vidal-Calleja, T., Popović, M.: Adaptive-resolution field mapping using Gaussian process fusion with integral kernels. IEEE Robot. Autom. Lett. **7**(3), 7471–7478 (2022)
11. Kameda, T., Toyokawa, W., Tindale, R.S.: Information aggregation and collective intelligence beyond the wisdom of crowds. Nat. Rev. Psychol. **1**, 345–357 (2022)
12. Kaplan, E.L., Meier, P.: Nonparametric estimation from incomplete observations. J. Am. Stat. Assoc. **53**(282), 457–481 (1958)
13. Oddi, F., Cristofaro, A., Trianni, V.: Videos associated to "Best-of-N collective decisions on a hierarchy" (2022). https://doi.org/10.5281/zenodo.6786939
14. Pavlic, T.P., Hanson, J., Valentini, G., Walker, S.I., Pratt, S.C.: Quorum sensing without deliberation: biological inspiration for externalizing computation to physical spaces in multi-robot systems. Swarm Intell. **15**(1–2), 171–203 (2021)
15. Reina, A., Bose, T., Trianni, V., Marshall, J.A.R.: Psychophysical laws and the superorganism. Sci. Rep. **8**(1), 4387–8 (2018)
16. Reina, A., Marshall, J.A.R., Trianni, V., Bose, T.: Model of the best-of-N nest-site selection process in honeybees. Phys. Rev. E **95**(5), 052411–15 (2017)
17. Reina, A., Valentini, G., Fernández-Oto, C., Dorigo, M., Trianni, V.: A design pattern for decentralised decision making. PLoS ONE **10**(10), e0140950–18 (2015)
18. Ross-Gillespie, A., Kümmerli, R.: Collective decision-making in microbes. Front. Microbiol. **5**(54) (2014)
19. Rubenstein, M., Ahler, C., Hoff, N., Cabrera, A., Nagpal, R.: Kilobot: a low cost robot with scalable operations designed for collective behaviors. Robot. Auton. Syst. **62**(7), 966–975 (2014)
20. Russo, D., Van Roy, B.: An information-theoretic analysis of Thompson Sampling. J. Mach. Learn. Res. **17**(1), 2442–2471 (2016)

21. Saha, A., Marshall, J.A.R., Reina, A.: Memory and communication efficient algorithm for decentralized counting of nodes in networks. PLoS ONE **16**(11), e0259736 (2021)
22. Sasaki, T., Pratt, S.C.: The psychology of superorganisms: collective decision making by insect societies. Annu. Rev. Entomol. **63**(1), 259–275 (2018)
23. Sridhar, V.H., et al.: The geometry of decision-making in individuals and collectives. Proc. Natl. Acad. Sci. U.S.A. **118**(50), e2102157118 (2021)
24. Valentini, G., Ferrante, E., Dorigo, M.: The best-of-N problem in robot swarms: formalization, state of the art, and novel perspectives. Front. Robot. AI **4**, 1–43 (2017)

Collective Decision-Making for Conflict Resolution in Multi-Agent Pathfinding

Sebastian Mai[✉][iD] and Sanaz Mostaghim[iD]

Faculty of Computer Science, Otto von Guericke University Magdeburg,
Magdeburg, Germany
{sebastian.mai,sanaz.mostaghim}@ovgu.de

Abstract. Multi-Agent Path Planning is important in many applications involving multiple mobile robots. In this paper, we present a novel algorithm to solve the Multi-Agent Pathfinding problem by using Collective Decision-making and indirect communication (stigmergy). We call this planning method Collective Conflict Resolution (CCR). The algorithm has two components: A mechanism to create a prioritization graph through collective decisions and a planning mechanism that is able to plan paths consistent with the priorities given by the graph. The CCR algorithm can be used both in global planning with full knowledge of all paths, and in decentralized settings with limited knowledge and communication. In our experiments, we compare our new planner with two state-of-the-art algorithms: Conflict-based Search (CBS) and Prioritized Planning. Furthermore, we analyze how a limited planning horizon can affect the planning cost. The results show that the proposed method offers a good trade-off between planning cost and solution quality, which results in a better success rate compared to Prioritized Planning, which sometimes does not find a solution. In addition, the algorithm is able to achieve a good solution quality with lower cost compared to the more complex CBS algorithm.

1 Introduction

Multi-Agent Pathfinding (MAPF) [20] is an important component of many Multi-Agent Systems, for example in drone swarms [10] or automated warehouses [9]. In this paper, we develop a novel approach to solve the MAPF problem by using Swarm Intelligence techniques: Collective Decision-making (CDM) [8] and (artificial) stigmergy. Our approach works similar to highway-based sub-optimal MAPF solvers like [3,4], but does not require predesigned highways. The algorithm consists of two components: (1) A prioritization (similar to those highways) between agents, which is created through a series of collective decisions. (2) A planning method that is able to plan paths consistent with the prioritization. Both components together are used to compute conflict free plans for all agents in a MAPF setting. The prioritization is attached to the map of the environment and is an emergent property of the system. In addition, the prioritization is a form of indirect communication between agents (stigmergy), similar to virtual

© Springer Nature Switzerland AG 2022
M. Dorigo et al. (Eds.): ANTS 2022, LNCS 13491, pp. 79–90, 2022.
https://doi.org/10.1007/978-3-031-20176-9_7

pheromones. In our experiments, we use the MAPF-benchkmark provided by [20]. We compare our planner to two other methods: Prioritized Planning [22] and Conflict-based Search [18] and analyze the impact of the planning horizon.

The remainder of this paper is structured as follows: In the next section, we will give a formal definition of the MAPF-problem and give an overview on methods to solving the MAPF-problem. In Sect. 3, we present our algorithm. Afterwards, we show the experiments used to analyze the algorithm and discuss the results of our analysis. Finally, we conclude the paper and outline questions for further research.

2   State of the Art

The problem of finding conflict-free paths for multiple agents with pre-defined start and goal positions in a graph is defined as the Multi-Agent Pathfinding Problem (MAPF) [20,21]. This problem is defined as follows: Given a roadmap-graph G with nodes v_n and edges $e_{m,n}$, we need to find conflict free paths $\Pi_i = \{\pi_i(t)|\forall t\}$ for all agents, that connect start and goal. We call the set of paths for all agent $S = \{\Pi_i|\forall i\}$ a solution to the problem. Additionally, the paths must be conflict free. A conflict can occur, when two agents use the same node, or edge of the graph at the same time-step. In this paper, a conflict is defined based on the condition of k-robust MAPF [1] with $k \leq 1$: Two agents i and j are in conflict if $\pi_i(t) = \pi_j(t \pm k)$. With $k = 0$ two agents occupy a node at the same time. The $k = 1$ robustness prevents multiple types of edge-conflicts (following conflict, swapping conflict, circular conflicts cf. [20,21]).

All the algorithms used within this paper use the same implementation of two low-level planners: A* and Spacetime-A* [19]. The well-known A* algorithm uses a heuristic function to perform a best-first search within the graph and is able to find the shortest path from start to goal position. However, the A* algorithm is not able to find paths in the presence of dynamic constraints, i.e. agent i is not allowed to use node n at time t. If those (temporary) constraints are present, we use the Spacetime-A* algorithm [19]. This algorithm expands the original roadmap graph G in time. The result is the graph G_t where for each node v_n in G we have τ nodes $v_n(t)$. The edges in G_t are directed, and connect two nodes $v_m(t), v_n(t + 1)$ if the two nodes are connected by an edge in G: $e_{m,n}(t, t + 1) \in G_t \iff e_{m,n} \in G$. In addition, we add an edge $e_{n,n}(t, t + 1)$ that connects $v_n(t)$ to $v_n(t + 1)$. This edge represents waiting at node n. The search in G_t makes it possible to include the dynamic constraints in planning, and it is sufficient to use G_t as an implicit graph which does not consume additional memory. Unfortunately, running Spacetime-A* is more costly than running the normal A* due to a larger search-space and the heuristic function we use in Spacetime-A*: The true cost of moving from node v_n to the goal location in G (which is found by running A*). To summarize: When planning paths for multiple agents, there may occur some *conflicts*. Conflicts happen between two agents i, j at a specific node v_c and a specific time $t_{i,c}$. From each conflict, a higher level planner can create *constraints*, which exclude a node v_c to be present within the path of agent i at time t_c: $p_i(t_c) \neq v_c$. If either agent i or j replan their path with the new constraint, the original conflict is resolved. However, new conflicts may occur which may require further replanning until eventually all conflicts are resolved or no plan consistent with the constraints can be found.

One of the simplest methods to solve the problem is called Prioritized search [22]. With this method, we create a priority order between agents. The highest priority robot plans its path without constraints. From this first plan, we generate dynamic constraints for planning the second robot's path. In this manner, we update the constraints and plan paths until we found a solution for all agents. This approach is simple and can be distributed well - robots only need to know their priority and communicate their plans to lower priority robots. However, the solutions obtained by prioritized planning tend to be suboptimal, and it is sometimes not possible to find a valid path for agents with lower priority.

The Conflict-based Search algorithm [18] revolves around finding and resolving conflicts. A conflict between two agents i and j at time t and node v_n can be resolved either by constraining the path of one of both agents i or j to omit visiting node v_n at time t. Each possible conflict resolution requires the algorithm to recompute the path of exactly one agent and may induce new conflicts. In the CBS algorithm, we use a best-first search on the constraints resolving the conflicts. The CBS algorithm is optimal and complete, i.e., the algorithm is able to find the optimal solutions for all solvable MAPF-problems. However, the algorithm is expensive because it queries the Spacetime-A* algorithm often.

The notion of "highway-layouts" is used by [3,4] which modify the cost of traveling along certain edges of the layout. This approach is able to reduce the planning cost with a small impact in the solution quality, and inspired our approach of generating a similar "highway-layout" through CDM. A similar concept (direction maps) is used by [11]. [12] uses imitation learning to solve the MAPF problem. A Graph-Neural Network can learn from an optimal MAPF solver and tries to predict the optimal path from local information. In [16] a mathematical model of fairness is used. The concept is based on building a solution with incomplete, local knowledge and the notion of privacy (agents do not disclose all their internal information). In our work, we only use the sum-of-cost metric, to evaluate the quality of a solution. Different applications call for multiple objectives (i.e. makespan, safety, ...) and some approaches exist, that use multi-objective optimization to find a better trade-off between different objectives [14,23].

Other methods in Multi-Agent planning resolve conflicts locally, most notably the velocity obstacle/reciprocal velocity obstacle [2]. This is similar to many methods used in swarm robotics, like steering behaviors [17] or artificial potential fields [7]. Those methods do not rely on deliberative planning, but rather use virtual forces to compute control outputs that attract the robots towards their goal. Some methods in SI use (virtual) pheromones for finding a short path to a site of interest, notably Ant-Colony Optimization [5] or pheromone-based foraging [6]. While those methods may be useful in the time expanded graph to find collision free paths, they can not be applied to our problem without modification because the methods rely on many agents traveling the same path while in our problem, this would constitute a conflict that must be avoided at high cost.

Algorithm 1: Collective Conflict Resolution

---

input : Graph G, start positions $\pi_i(t = 0)$, goal positions $\pi_i(t = \text{end})$
output: $S = \{\Pi_i | \forall i\}$
constraints $= \emptyset$;
$G_p = (\{v_n | \forall v_n \in G\}, \emptyset)$ **while** *conflicts* $\neq \emptyset$ **do**
    $S = \text{compute\_paths}(G, \text{constraints})$;
    $C = \text{find\_conflicts}(S)$;
    if $\exists c \in C$ *resolvable by* G_p **then**
        $c = \text{argmin } t_c$;
        $i, v_c, t_c = \text{low\_priority\_agent}(c)$;
        constraints $= \text{constraints} \cup (i, v_c, t_c)$
    else
        // Identify most urgent conflict
        $c = \underset{c_i \in C}{\text{argmax }} h(c_i)$;
        // Compute options and quality for CDM
        $\Omega = \{e_{m,c}, q(e_{m,c}) | \forall m, c = v_c\}$;
        // Apply decsion function
        $e_{m,c} = \text{CDM}(\Omega)$;
        // Remove edges from G_p and modify the cost in G and G_p
        $G_p = \text{implement\_decision}(e_{m,c}, G_p)$;
        $G, G_p = \text{update\_cost}(e_{m,c}, G, G_p)$;
    end
end

---

3   Collective Conflict Resolution

In this section, we present the Collective Conflict Resolution (CCR) algorithm. The algorithm finds a solution to the MAPF-problem by resolving conflicts through a series of collective decisions. An outline of the CCR-algorithm is given in Algorithm 1. The CCR algorithm is centered around detecting and resolving conflicts and then replan paths based on the proposed resolution. In contrast to CBS, the CCR algorithm does not search the full space of possible constraints that potentially resolve a conflict. The CCR algorithm uses collective decision-making to create a graph G_p, which we call priority-graph. G_p allows us to prioritize agents based on their travel directions. When an agent involved in a conflict travels in the direction indicated by G_p, other agents need to give way.

In the following, we describe how the agents use the priority-graph G_p to avoid conflicts and how G_p is modified, when G_p does not yet contain priorities for the next conflict.

3.1   Plan Paths Coherent with G_p

In this section, we assume that G_p is already populated and explain how the path-planning process for each agent works. Each edge in G_p indicates an edge that gives the right of way to enter a node v_n in the roadmap G. We guarantee that for each node $v_n \in G$, at most one edge $e_{m,n}$ exists in G_p. If the edge $e_{m,n}$ is present, it means that an agent i moving from node m to node n is allowed to move and while another agent j that enters node n from another direction has to wait until agent i has left or chose a different route).

At the beginning of path planning, each agent simply plans their path without any constraints. Now all agents exchange their (local) plans with a fixed time horizon τ and detect conflicts. In case a conflict is detected, we note the time t_c and location $\pi_i(t)$ of the conflict and try to resolve the conflict using G_p. This works as follows: All agents check, if there is an edge going into the node where the conflict occurs $\exists e_{x,\pi_i(t_c)}$. If the edge exists, we use the origin x of the edge $e_{x,\pi_i(t_c)}$ to create a constraint for one of the agents. If $\pi_i(t_c - 1) = x$, agent i has the right of way, and does not change its path, because it is using the edge $e_{x,\pi_i(t_c)}$. In case $\pi_i(t_c - 1) \neq x$, agent i will create a constraint to avoid node $\pi_i(t_c)$ at time t_c because it is using a different edge to enter node $\pi_i(t_c)$ and this edge has no priority. In this case, the agent will create a new plan using Spacetime A*, which adheres to the newly created constraint.

Figure 1 shows an example configuration with four agents. In this scenario, we have four agents and their planned path. The first conflict is between the two agents on C2 (green) and D3 (orange), which both plan to occupy the same node at $t = 1$. In this case, there is one priority edge C2$\longrightarrow$C3(gray arrow) which was already added to G_p. This priority edge gives the right of way to the green agent moving in the direction of the edge. This means the green agent will keep its planned path, while the orange agent has to replan its path while avoiding node C3 at $t = 1$. A solution to this problem could be that the agent waits at the current position, entering C3 at $t = 1$. Because of the k-robustness, the agent would then detect another conflict and replan its path again. If the agent waits for another time-step, the conflict is resolved and the plan would be valid. The orange agent would use the plan.

In the scenario, we also have another conflict. At $t = 2$, both the blue agent F7 and the yellow agent F8, plan to occupy node D8 at $t = 2$. When two agents are in conflict with each other, and $\nexists e_{x,\pi_i(t_c)}$, we need to extend the graph G_p (which is the case with the blue and yellow agent). This process is described in the following.

3.2   Modify G_p Through Collective Decision-Making

The graph G_p is extended, if one or more conflicts are detected by the agents within their time horizon τ. Because the decision space using all conflicts is too large, we use multiple sequential decisions to add an edge in G_p. In this process, first a conflict is chosen by computing the priority indicated as $h(c)$ for a conflict (Eq. 1). The priority is higher, when more agents use the location v_c of the conflict within their current path at any time. The priority is also higher, when the conflict occurs at an earlier time t_c. In the scenario from Fig. 1, three agents plan to use the node at different times. Hence, the priority of this conflict is $h(c) = 1/2 + 1/2 + 1/6 = 7/6$.

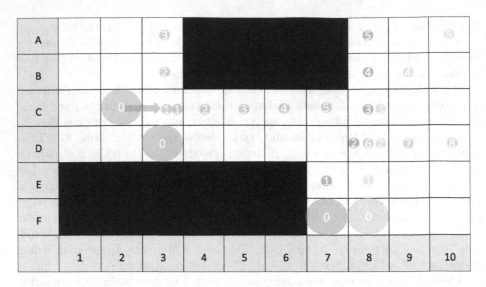

Fig. 1. Example scenario with four agents (large circle) and their planned path (small circle). The number within each circle show the time of each planned position. In the current setting, we have one priority edge (gray arrow). Obstacles are shown in black. (Color figure online)

Once a conflict is chosen, Collective Decision-making (CDM) is used to prioritize one edge leading to node v_c. In our application, we use CDM because we need to find a consensus between agents and the estimation of the quality of each solution uses local knowledge only known to each individual agent. In this CDM-process, the quality of each option is computed using spatial A* (instead of the more costly Spacetime-A*). This is denoted by $\mathcal{L}(\cdot)$: The length of the shortest path from start to goal-node in G, which only use those edges in G that are either equal to the priority edge existing in G_p or where no priority edge in G_p exists. If no path is found $\mathcal{L}(i, G, G_p) = \infty$. The quality for one edge $e_{m,n}$ is then determined by the negated cost increase l for agent i (Eq. 2). Each agent then references the loss of each option by the loss generated by the worst option (Eq. 3). This means, agents that are not affected by any of the options compute a quality of $q(i, e_{m,n}) = 0$ for all their options. In addition, options $e_{m,n}$ that completely block the path of an agent have are discarded if there is another option left because $l(i, e_{m,n}) = \infty$ for those options. If the agent has no options to find a path before adding the new priority edge, we use a quality of $q(i, e_{m,n}) = 0$. As a decision function, we use the direct-comparison method, which chooses the option with the overall highest quality among all agents. In the future, we want to know if decision-functions affect the quality of the solutions. Once an edge is chosen, we update the graph G_p by adding the new edge and replan the paths of all agents, to adhere to the newly created prioritization, before selecting the next conflict for decision-making.

$$h(c) = \sum_{\forall \pi_i(t) = v_c} \frac{1}{t} \tag{1}$$

$$l(i, e_{m,n}) = \mathcal{L}(i, G, G_p) - \mathcal{L}(i, G, G_p \cup \{e_{m,n}\}) \tag{2}$$

$$q(i, e_{m,n}) = l(i, e_{m,n}) - \min_{\forall e_{x,n} \in G} l(i, e_{x,n}) \tag{3}$$

The graph G_p is created during the collaborative (re-)planning of the agents and is an emergent property of the system. In case the agents rely on local communication with their neighbors and the graph is persistent throughout the whole experiment, we can also view the behavior as a form of stigmergy, where agents communicate indirectly through G_p to other agents that are not within the same neighborhood.

3.3 Limitations

Currently, when two agents use an edge to a node and both agents do not use the prioritized travel-direction, both agents will avoid the node in their next planned path. A better strategy could be used to resolve such second-order conflicts, but is currently not part of our approach. In addition, the algorithm is not complete, which means that for some scenarios it is impossible to find a solution, even when infinite resources are available for planning.

While most components of the algorithm can be distributed to multiple communicating agents, the current implementation relies on G_p, which is a centralized component. In the future, this limitation may be overcome by directly using the opinion of the agents. This has the drawback that the behavior of the system is more dynamic, and it is harder to analyze the emerging behavior.

4 Experiments

We implemented our algorithm in Python[1] and ran several experiments, using the benchmark maps from [20]. For each map, we run each planner configuration with 25 different scenarios, which are also provided by the benchmark [20].

Figure 2 shows the solution of our CCR planner for a scenario in the Maze environment. The solution contains no conflicts (paths cross, but agents do not occupy the same position at the same time). We can observe the prioritization created by the CDM process. On the right side of the map, there is a narrow passage in this passage, on agent was prioritized over the other and is able to pass the area before the agent coming from the top of the image is able to travel through the passage.

In addition, we see on the left of Fig. 2, that some of the agents pass each other, and a type of lane structure emerged, where agents traveling in the same direction use one lane and agents travelling in the other direction use another.

---

[1] The code is available at https://www.ci.ovgu.de/Research/Codes.html. The benchmark files are available at https://mapf.info.

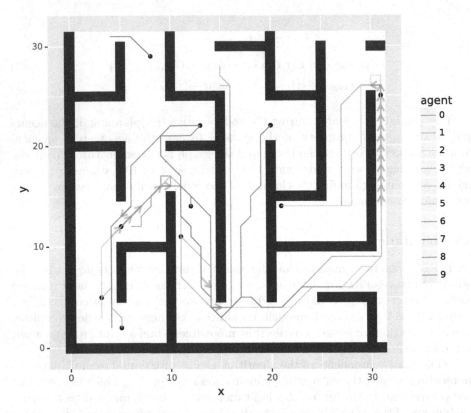

Fig. 2. CCR solution for the Maze environment. The black dots represent the starting positions of the agents, gray arrows show the priorities from G_p after planning.

In Fig. 3 we see another solution created by our planner, where we can gain more insight in the behavior of the planner. While the resulting plan is still conflict-free, this example shows a counter intuitive relation between the priority map and the plans of the agents. As an artifact of planning, sometimes priorities are created which are not used by any agent. An example for that is the priority at position $x = 9, y = 6$, which seemingly restricts the movement of the orange agent, without another agent using its priority. This happens if another agent replans its path despite having the priority (because another conflict requires to change the path of an agent). In this example, we can also see a "roundabout" emerging around the obstacle at position $x = 12, y = 15$.

In our experiments, we compare our CCR algorithm with two state-of-the art MAPF-algorithms: CBS [18] which is a more expensive, optimal solver and prioritized search [22] which uses less computational resources, but may not always find a good solution. In addition, we implemented a limited-horizon version of CBS [18], Prioritized Planning [22] and CCR, which ignores all conflicts beyond the horizon for planning paths to the goal location. To measure the cost of path planning, we count mean the number of times the (spatial) A* algorithm was

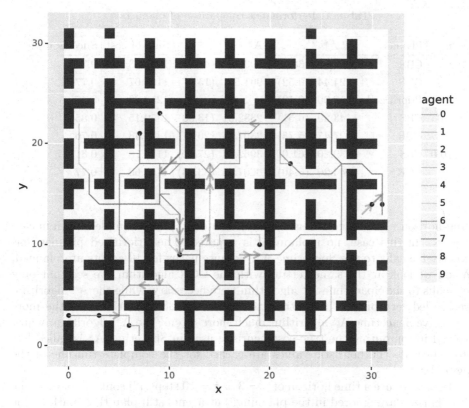

Fig. 3. CCR solution for the Room environment. The black dots represent the starting positions of the agents, gray arrows show the priorities from G_p after planning.

used in one scenario and the mean number of times the Spacetime-A* algorithm is called. In addition, we limit the run-time and memory-requirements for each planning run. If we use a limited time-horizon, a new plan is created and the behavior is simulated, if no horizon is used the plan does not change and is not recomputed. The quality of a plan is measured using the sum-of-cost metric, which is a common metric in many related approaches [20,21].

Table 1 shows the result of our experiments for the baseline CCR algorithm and the results for CBS [18] and Prioritize Planning [22] in the same setting. For each metric, we compute the mean value in each map and report the mean performance over all maps in the table. The mean number of A* and Spacetime-A* executions is only computed for the successful runs and in addition to the number of A* and Spacetime-A* executions, we report the number of executions normalized by the makespan (the length of the run on the particular map). We can observe that none of the used algorithms were successful in all cases, due to the limitations of the planner, and our constraints on computational resources. However, the CCR algorithm is able to achieve a good success rate, close to the success rate of CBS [18]. A key parameter when running the planner is the

Table 1. Performance comparison of planners

τ	Planner	ST A*		A*		Sum of cost	Success rate
∞	CBS	3369.53	(66.17)	593.09	(4.97)	1101.88	0.79
	CCR	24.44	(0.52)	961.50	(15.87)	1108.67	0.77
	Prioritized	10.00	(0.13)	–		1253.22	0.47
3.0	CBS	1143.29	(6.51)	2382.61	(13.00)	1459.15	0.85
	CCR	1227.47	(5.75)	2307.15	(20.41)	1439.48	0.76
10.0	CBS	4439.20	(61.09)	3962.44	(27.00)	1171.78	0.81
	CCR	1044.20	(6.40)	3607.36	(33.13)	1165.60	0.77

time-horizon τ. Our algorithms are implemented to plan a complete path in case $\tau = \infty$. In this case, no replanning is required. The Prioritized planner, has exactly ten calls to the Spacetime-A*, because paths for 10 agents are planned. When we look at the same setting with the CCR algorithm, we see that only few calls to the Spacetime-A* algorithm were necessary, while the A* algorithm was called very often[2]. In contrast to that, the CBS algorithm uses the more expensive Spacetime-A* algorithm much more often. The A* algorithm, which is used in computing the true-cost heuristic used in Spacetime-A* is called less often because the heuristic values are cached for the complete runtime of the algorithm.

In case we use a time horizon of $\tau = 3$ or $\tau = 10$ steps, all conflicts beyond the time horizon are ignored in the planning, but agents still plan their path to the goal. New information becomes available as the agents move and communicate. Hence, we recompute plans at every time-step. With $\tau = 3$ we see that CBS and CCR have similar cost and similar solution quality. While CBS is an optimal algorithm, here we restrict the information available to the algorithm and loose the properties of completeness and optimally. In addition, with a short planning horizon τ the CBS algorithm is aware of only few conflicts, which are resolved faster. The number in brackets show the number of A* and Spacetime-A* iterations normalized by the makespan of the solution. This gives an indication, how much computational effort is spent in each replanning step. We can observe that throughout the experiments, the CCR algorithm uses the A* algorithm more often (in creating G_p) and uses Spacetime-A* less often. When comparing the different versions in terms of their time-horizon, we see that with a short time-horizon CBS and CCR behave more similarly (in terms of their cost) and with a longer time-horizon CBS has a higher complexity (more conflicts are detected) but will also find better results.

---

[2] We do not report the number of calls to the A* algorithm for Prioritized planning because we use a caching mechanism for the true-cost heuristic. In our implementation, this value can not be compared fairly between Prioritized Planning and CBS/CCR.

5   Conclusion

In this paper, we present a novel algorithm to solve the Multi-Agent Pathfinding Problem (MAPF) [20]. The algorithm uses a prioritization Graph G_p to resolve conflicts through. This graph is created through a series of collective decisions and is an emergent result of the planning process. The planner of each individual robot is able to give way to other robots based on the priority graph. The algorithm is designed in a way that allows agents to rely on local information with the only exception of the priority graph G_p, which is shared between all agents.

Our experiments show, that the algorithm is able to achieve a good trade-off in planning effort and solution quality. In comparison to prioritized search [22] our algorithm (CCR) is more costly to run, but has a better success rate. CBS [18], is an algorithm which is guaranteed to find the optimal solution, but finding a plan with CBS uses more computational resources than our approach.

In the future, we intend to integrate our planner in the DrivingSwarm framework [15] with a discrete roadmap based on [13]. While planning is not a typical application scenario for swarm intelligence, our research shows that the emergent behavior present in Multi-Agent planning warrant questions for future research: How do different decision strategies impact the planning performance? In this work, we only use one decision function (direct comparison). In the future, we hope to analyze the impact of different decision-making methods on the planning performance. In addition, future research is needed to understand how local communication can replace the global information stored in the priority graph G_p and which emergent effects are present if we reduce the (local) information available to the agents.

References

1. Atzmon, D., Felner, A., Wagner, G., Stern, R., Bart, R.: k-robust multi-agent path finding. In: SoCS, vol. 1, pp. 157–158 (2017)
2. van den Berg, J., Lin, M., Manocha, D.: Reciprocal velocity obstacles for real-time multi-agent collision avoidance. In: Proceedings of IEEE International Conference on Robotics and Automation, pp. 1928–1935 (2007)
3. Cohen, L., Koenig, S.: Bounded suboptimal multi-agent path finding using highways. In: IJCAI International Joint Conference on Artificial Intelligence, January 2016, pp. 3978–3979 (2016)
4. Cohen, L., Uras, T., Koenig, S.: Feasibility study: using highways for bounded-suboptimal multi-agent path finding. In: Proceedings of the 8th Annual Symposium on Combinatorial Search, SoCS 2015, January 2015, pp. 2–8 (2015)
5. Dorigo, M., Stützle, T.: Ant colony optimization: overview and recent advances. Technical report, TR/IRIDIA/2009-013, IRIDIA, Université Libre de Bruxelles, Brussels, Belgium, May 2009
6. Font Llenas, A., Talamali, M.S., Xu, X., Marshall, J.A.R., Reina, A.: Quality-sensitive foraging by a robot swarm through virtual pheromone trails. In: Dorigo, M., Birattari, M., Blum, C., Christensen, A.L., Reina, A., Trianni, V. (eds.) ANTS 2018. LNCS, vol. 11172, pp. 135–149. Springer, Cham (2018). https://doi.org/10.1007/978-3-030-00533-7_11

7. Gazi, V., Passino, K.M.: Swarm Stability and Optimization. Springer, Heidelberg (2011). https://doi.org/10.1007/978-3-642-18041-5
8. Hamann, H.: Swarm robotics: a formal approach (2018). https://doi.org/10.1007/978-3-319-74528-2
9. Honig, W., Kiesel, S., Tinka, A., Durham, J.W., Ayanian, N.: Persistent and robust execution of MAPF schedules in warehouses. IEEE Robot. Autom. Lett. **4**(2), 1125–1131 (2019). https://doi.org/10.1109/LRA.2019.2894217
10. Honig, W., Preiss, J.A., Kumar, T.K., Sukhatme, G.S., Ayanian, N.: Trajectory planning for quadrotor swarms. IEEE Trans. Rob. **34**(4), 856–869 (2018). https://doi.org/10.1109/TRO.2018.2853613
11. Jansen, M.R., Sturtevant, N.R.: Direction maps for cooperative pathfinding. In: Proceedings of the 4th Artificial Intelligence and Interactive Digital Entertainment Conference, AIIDE 2008, pp. 185–190 (2008)
12. Li, Q., Gama, F., Ribeiro, A., Prorok, A.: Graph neural networks for decentralized multi-robot path planning (2019). http://arxiv.org/abs/1912.06095
13. Mai, S., Deubel, M., Mostaghim, S.: Multi-objective roadmap optimization for multiagent navigation (2022)
14. Mai, S., Mostaghim, S.: Modeling pathfinding for swarm robotics. In: Dorigo, M., et al. (eds.) ANTS 2020. LNCS, vol. 12421, pp. 190–202. Springer, Cham (2020). https://doi.org/10.1007/978-3-030-60376-2_15
15. Mai, S., Traichel, N., Mostaghim, S.: Driving swarm: a swarm robotics framework for intelligent navigation in a self-organized world. Accepted at ICRA 2022 (2022)
16. Raymond, A., Malencia, M., Paulino-Passos, G., Prorok, A.: Agree to disagree: subjective fairness in privacy-restricted decentralised conflict resolution. Front. Robot. AI **9**, February 2022. https://doi.org/10.3389/frobt.2022.733876
17. Reynolds, C.W.: Steering behaviors for autonomous characters. In: Game Developers Conference (1999). http://www.red3d.com/cwr/steer/gdc99/
18. Sharon, G., Stern, R., Felner, A., Sturtevant, N.: Meta-agent conflict-based search for optimal multi-agent path finding. In: Proceedings of the 5th Annual Symposium on Combinatorial Search, SoCS 2012, pp. 97–104 (2012)
19. Silver, D.: Cooperative pathfinding. In: Proceedings of the First Artificial Intelligence and Interactive Digital Entertainment Conference, pp. 117–122 (2005). http://www.aaai.org/Library/AIIDE/aiide05contents.php
20. Stern, R., et al.: Multi-agent pathfinding: definitions, variants, and benchmarks. In: AAAI Conference on Artificial Intelligence (AAAI) (2019)
21. Surynek, P., Felner, A., Stern, R., Boyarski, E.: An empirical comparison of the hardness of multi-agent path finding under the makespan and the sum of costs objectives. In: Proceedings of the 9th Annual Symposium on Combinatorial Search, SoCS 2016 (SoCS), January 2016, pp. 145–146 (2016)
22. Van Den Berg, J.P., Overmars, M.H.: Prioritized motion planning for multiple robots. In: 2005 IEEE/RSJ International Conference on Intelligent Robots and Systems, IROS, pp. 430–435 (2005). https://doi.org/10.1109/IROS.2005.1545306
23. Weise, J., Mai, S., Zille, H., Mostaghim, S.: On the scalable multi-objective multiagent pathfinding problem. In: Accepted at Congress on Evolutionary Computing CEC 2020 (2020)

Controlling Robot Swarm Aggregation Through a Minority of Informed Robots

Antoine Sion[1], Andreagiovanni Reina[2], Mauro Birattari[2],
and Elio Tuci[1(✉)]

[1] Faculty of Computer Science, University of Namur, Namur, Belgium
{antoine.sion,elio.tuci}@unamur.be
[2] IRIDIA, Université Libre de Bruxelles, Brussels, Belgium
{andreagiovanni.reina,mauro.birattari}@ulb.be

Abstract. Self-organized aggregation is a well studied behavior in swarm robotics as it is the pre-condition for the development of more advanced group-level responses. In this paper, we investigate the design of decentralized algorithms for a swarm of heterogeneous robots that self-aggregate over distinct target sites. A previous study has shown that including as part of the swarm a number of informed robots can steer the dynamic of the aggregation process to a desirable distribution of the swarm between the available aggregation sites. We have replicated the results of the previous study using a simplified approach: we removed constraints related to the communication protocol of the robots and simplified the control mechanisms regulating the transitions between states of the probabilistic controller. The results show that the performances obtained with the previous, more complex, controller can be replicated with our simplified approach which offers clear advantages in terms of portability to the physical robots and in terms of flexibility. That is, our simplified approach can generate self-organized aggregation responses in a larger set of operating conditions than what can be achieved with the complex controller.

1 Introduction

Swarm robotics can be defined as "the study of how a large number of relatively simple physically embodied agents can be designed such that a desired collective behavior emerges from the local interactions among the agents and between the agents and the environment" [25]. Robot swarms aim to be robust, flexible and scalable due to their decentralized nature and their large group size. Brambilla et al. [2] and Schranz et al. [26] give an overview of the basic collective behaviors that robot swarms can display in order to achieve complex tasks such as coordinated motion, task allocation, self-assembly or aggregation, which is studied in this paper. Aggregation is used to group the swarm in a location—for example, to initiate a collaborative task that requires physical proximity among the robots. Inspiration for self-organized aggregation can be found in animals such as bees [29] or cockroaches [18].

© Springer Nature Switzerland AG 2022
M. Dorigo et al. (Eds.): ANTS 2022, LNCS 13491, pp. 91–103, 2022.
https://doi.org/10.1007/978-3-031-20176-9_8

Several approaches have been studied in swarm robotics to achieve aggregation. A popular method is to control the robots through probabilistic finite-state machines. Soysal and Şahin [28] analyzed the performance of a three-state finite-state machine while varying different transitional probabilistic parameters. Variations of the controller yielded different aggregation behaviors highlighting the importance of the evaluation metrics used such as cluster sizes or total distances between robots. Cambier et al. [4] studied the influence of cultural propagation in an aggregation scenario. Using a simple finite-state machine with two states, robots communicated with each other to modify the probabilistic parameters of their controllers. This behavioral plasticity has ensured adaptability to dynamic environments and performed better than classical approaches. Simpler methods have also been proposed to achieve self-organized aggregation as in [16] where the only sensor available to the robots is a binary sensor informing them on the presence of another robot in their line of sight. The controller did not require computation and the parameters were chosen via a grid search. This approach is validated with successful experiments with 1000 simulated robots and 40 physical robots. Francesca et al. [14] showed that self-organized aggregation can be achieved by robots controlled by probabilistic finite-state machines that are generated automatically.

Artificial evolution has also been used to evolve controllers resulting in self-organized aggregation [8]. Francesca et al. [15] evolved a neural network controller to perform self-organized aggregation and showed that the dynamics of the resulting collective behavior closely matches the one of a biological model that describes how cockroaches select a resting shelter. Kengyel et al. [20] studied aggregation in heterogeneous robot swarms where each robot ran one among four distinct behaviors inspired from aggregation in honeybees. The number of robots running the alternative behaviors were varied using an evolutionary algorithm. The results of the simulations show that through the cooperation of different types of behaviors, the heterogeneous swarm performs better than its homogeneous equivalent.

In this study, we revisit the methods illustrated in [13] to steer self-organized aggregation responses with the use of informed robots. Generally speaking, the use of informed individuals to steer the dynamic process leading to the group response is a method to guide self-organisation in distributed systems inspired by behaviors observed in biology. In a seminal study, Couzin et al. [6] studied the influence of informed individuals in collective decision making in the context of collective animal motion. The informed individuals had a preferred direction of motion and biased the collective decision in that direction. The rest of the swarm did not have any preferred direction of motion, nor was able to recognise informed individuals as such. The study shows that the accuracy of the group motion towards the direction known by the informed agents increases asymptotically as the proportion of informed individuals increases, and that the larger the group, the smaller the proportion of informed individuals needed to guide the group with a given accuracy. A recent study on cockroaches [3] has shown that a minority of individuals preferring one shelter over the other can influence the population to reach a consensus for only one site. The technique of using informed individuals to steer the collective dynamics has already been used in artificial systems with various types of collective behaviors. For example, informed individuals have been used in flocking [5,9,10] to guide the robot swarm in the desired direction, in collective decision making [7,23] to achieve adaptability, and in self-organized aggregation to differentiate between multiple sites [11–13,17].

In this paper, we replicate the experimental setup originally illustrated in [13] by showing that equally effective aggregation dynamics can be obtained with a largely simplified approach. The aggregation response described in [13] took place in a circular arena with two aggregation sites, the black and the white site (see Fig. 1a). The goal of the swarm was to distribute the robots between the two sites in a desired proportion (e.g. 70% of the robots on the white site and the remaining 30% on the black one) while minimizing the total proportion of informed robots. Non-informed robots treated both sites in the same way while informed robots were designed to systematically avoid one of the sites and to rest on the other. The swarm comprised a certain proportion of informed robots, among which there were those that selectively rested on the black site and those that rested only on the white site. The study shows that the proportion of robots on black/white site at the end of an aggregation process matches the proportion of informed robots resting only on the black/white site relative to the number of informed robots in the swarm (see Sect. 2 for more details). These aggregation dynamics can be achieved using a relatively low percentage of informed robots in the swarm—roughly 30% for a swarm of 100 robots.

In [13], the robots were controlled by a probabilistic finite-state machine illustrated in details in Sect. 2 and depicted in Fig. 1c. In this study, we question the nature of the mechanisms regulating the transition from state Stay ($\mathcal{S}$) to state Leave ($\mathcal{L}$), and the type of communication protocol involved in these mechanisms, by suggesting an alternative solution that largely simplifies the rule regulating the transition between these two states for non-informed robots. Following the "Occam's razor" principle, the solution we illustrate in this paper can represent a preferable alternative to the more complex solution proposed in [13] and can help the porting of the control system to the physical robots. Moreover, we remove differences both in behavior and in communication capabilities between informed and non-informed robots that, in our view, undermine the robustness of the aggregation process. For example, in [13], non-informed robots rest on an aggregation site if this is already inhabited by at least one informed robot that signals its presence on the site. Thus, an aggregation process can only be initiated by informed robots. This can significantly delay the aggregation process, in particular in those operating conditions in which the probability that an informed robot finds and rests on an aggregation site is relatively low. Additionally, this makes the swarm less robust to the loss of informed robots. In the extreme case of a loss of all informed robots, there will be no aggregation at all. With our approach, aggregation dynamics can emerge independently of the presence of informed robots. This increases the range of group responses that the swarm can generate without interfering with the effectiveness of the aggregation dynamics.

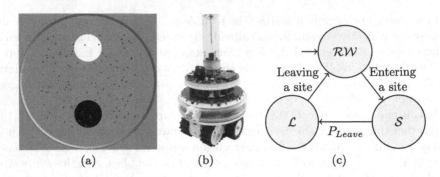

Fig. 1. (a) The simulated circular arena with the robots (blue dots) and the aggregation sites (black and white circles). (b) The Foot-bot robot [1]; image from www.swarmanoid.org. (c) The probabilistic finite-state machine controlling the robot behavior composed of three states; $\mathcal{RW}$ (Random Walk), $\mathcal{S}$ (Stay) and $\mathcal{L}$ (Leave). (Color figure online)

2   Materials and Methods

The experiments are ran using ARGoS [21], which is one of the best-performing simulators to run physics-based simulations for large-scale robot swarms [22]. The robots operate in a circular environment where the aggregation sites are circular areas located at equal distance between the center of the arena and its perimetric wall (Fig. 1a). One site is painted in black, the other in white; the arena floor is grey. We perform our experiments with a simplified model of the Foot-bot [1] (see Fig. 1b), a mobile robot that we equip with three types sensors: a ground sensor, an array of proximity sensors, and the range-and-bearing sensor. The ground sensor is located on the robot's underside, to detect the color of the ground; it returns 1, 0.5, and 0 when a robot is on a white, grey, and black floor, respectively. The proximity sensors use infrared (IR) signals to detect obstacles such as other robots or the arena walls. The range-and-bearing sensor is used by the robots to exchange simple communication signals when they are located at less than 0.8 m from each other.

A trial starts with the robots randomly placed in the arena following a uniform distribution, and it terminates after 30,000 s. As in [13], the swarm of size N is composed of informed robots (in proportion ρ_I) and non-informed ones (in proportion $1 - \rho_I$). During a trial, both informed and non-informed robots move randomly in the environment at 10 cm/s. Non-informed robots can rest on any aggregation site as soon as they enter into one of them. Informed robots selectively avoid to rest on one site and rest only on the other one. There are informed robots for black—which avoid to rest on the white site, and rest on the black aggregation site only—and informed robots for white—which avoid to rest on the black site, and rest on the white site only. Let N_{sb} be the number of informed robots for black, N_{sw} the number of informed robots for white, $\rho_{sb} = \frac{N_{sb}}{N_{sb}+N_{sw}}$ the proportion of informed robots for black relative to the total number of informed robots, and $\rho_{sw} = 1 - \rho_{sb}$ the proportion of informed robots for white relative to the total number of informed robots. Firat et al. [13] demonstrated that, with a relatively small proportion of informed robots in the swarm ($\rho_I \approx 0.3$) and for different values of ρ_{sb} and ρ_{sw}, the number of robots aggregated on the black site is approximately equal to $N \rho_{sb}$, while the number of those aggregated on the white site is approximately equal to $N \rho_{sw}$, for swarms of size $N = 50$ and for $N = 100$. Our objective is to replicate this aggregation dynamics with a largely simplified model illustrated below.

The primary difference between our model and the one introduced in [13] resides in the way in which the robots communicate while within an aggregation site. In [13], communication is needed by the robots to count how many informed robots are resting on the aggregation site within the communication range. In our model, communication is needed by the robots to count how many robots (including both informed and non-informed) are resting on the aggregation site within the communication range. This small difference between the two models derives from a rather substantial modification of the robots' communication system which we apply to the original model as illustrated in [13] to improve the robustness and flexibility of the swarm's behavior. In [13], informed robots emits signals (i.e., one bit signal), while non-informed robots can only receive these signals, they can not emit them. Contrary to [13], in our model, informed and non-informed robots are functionally identical with respect to communication; they can both send and receive signals. This implies that, contrary to [13], in our model communication signals indicate only the presence of spatially proximal robots within a site without saying anything about the identity of the signal's sender (i.e., whether it is an informed or a non-informed robot). Therefore, the results of our study can generalise to application scenarios where the communication is indirect, i.e., the robots count the neighbors in its view range without the need of an exchange of messages and without the need of distinguishing between informed and non-informed robots.

Both in [13] and in our model, the robots are controlled by a probabilistic finite state-machine (hereafter PFSM, see Fig. 1c), which is updated every 2 s and comprises three states: Random Walk ($\mathcal{RW}$), Stay ($\mathcal{S}$), and Leave ($\mathcal{L}$). However, in our model, the rules that regulate the transition between different states have been modified with respect to the original implementation as illustrated in [13]. In the following, we describe the PFSM and we illustrate the modifications we introduced with respect to [13].

At the beginning of a trial, the robots are in state $\mathcal{RW}$. They explore the environment while avoiding obstacles with an isotropic random walk based on straight motion and random rotation. The robots move straight for 5 s at a speed of 10 cm/s, and turn with turning angles taken from a wrapped Cauchy distribution [19]. The probability density function is the following:

$$f_\omega(\theta, \mu, \rho) = \frac{1}{2\pi} \frac{1 - \rho^2}{1 + \rho^2 - 2\rho \cos(\theta - \mu)}, \quad 0 < \rho < 1, \tag{1}$$

where μ is the average value of the distribution and ρ the skewness. With $\rho = 0$, the wrapped Cauchy distribution becomes uniform and there is no correlation between the movement directions before and after a turn. With $\rho = 1$, we have a Dirac distribution and the robot follows a straight line. Here we take $\rho = 0.5$. During this behavior, when the proximity sensors detect an obstacle (the wall or other robots), the robot stops and turns of an angle chosen uniformly in the interval $[-\pi, \pi]$. After turning, if there is no obstruction ahead, the robot resumes its normal random walk otherwise, it repeats the manoeuvre.

Both in our model and in [13], informed robots systematically transition from state $\mathcal{RW}$ to the state $\mathcal{S}$ when they enter their preferred site, otherwise they move randomly. While in $\mathcal{S}$, informed robots rest on the aggregation site. The condition that triggers the transition from state $\mathcal{RW}$ to the state $\mathcal{S}$ for non-informed robots is different in our model with respect to [13]. In particular, in [13], non-informed robots switch to state $\mathcal{S}$ if, while entering into an aggregation site, they perceive the presence of informed robots at the site. Contrary to [13], in our approach, non-informed robots systematically transition from state $\mathcal{RW}$ to state $\mathcal{S}$ whenever they enter into an aggregation site regardless of the presence of any other type of robot at the site. In both studies, when a robot enters an aggregation site, it continues moving forward for 10 s to avoid a congestion of robots on the perimeter of the site that could eventually hinder other robots from entering. Then, it rests on the site.

Both in our model and in [13], informed robots never leave the state $\mathcal{S}$. That is, once an informed robot finds its preferred site, it never leaves the site. Non-informed robots transition from state $\mathcal{S}$ to state $\mathcal{L}$ with a probability that is computed differently with respect to [13]. In [13], non-informed robots transition from state $\mathcal{S}$ to state $\mathcal{L}$ with a probability P_{Leave} computed as

$$P_{Leave} = \begin{cases} e^{-a(k-|n-x|)} & \text{if } n > 0, \\ 1 & \text{if } n = 0; \end{cases} \tag{2}$$

where n and x are the number of informed robots resting on the site within communication distance at this moment and at the moment of joining this site, respectively. Parameters a and k are fixed to $a = 2$ and $k = 18$. With Eq. (2), the transition from state $\mathcal{S}$ to state $\mathcal{L}$ is based on the temporal variation in the number of informed robots perceived at an aggregation site.

Contrary to [13], in our model the probability P'_{Leave} that regulates the transition from state $\mathcal{S}$ to state $\mathcal{L}$ for non-informed robots is computed as

$$P'_{Leave} = \alpha e^{-\beta n}, \tag{3}$$

with n the number of robots (including both informed and non-informed) within communication distance, $\alpha = 0.5$, and $\beta = 2.25$[1]. Contrary to [13], P'_{Leave} relies on the fact that any type of robot in the swarm can broadcast and perceive communication signals while resting on a site. This transforms P'_{Leave} into something that depends on the estimated local density of (any type of) robots, while

---

[1] The parameters α and β have been fine-tuned to achieve a symmetry-breaking behavior in a homogeneous swarm of $N = 100$ non-informed robots using the same arena setup illustrated in [13].

in [13] P_{Leave} depends on the variation in the number of informed robots in the neighborhood. Hence, P_{Leave} requires the robots to use memory and distinguish between types of robots, P'_{Leave} does not.

Both in [13] and in our approach a robot in state $\mathcal{L}$ exits an aggregation site by moving forward and avoiding obstacles. Once outside the site, it systematically transitions to state $\mathcal{RW}$.

To summarise, the main differences between the model illustrated in [13] and our model are the following: (i) in [13] informed robots only emit signals and non-informed robots only receive signals. In our models, both informed and non-informed robots send and receive communication signals. (ii) In [13], non-informed robots rest on a site only if they perceive the presence of informed robots, and leave a site with a probability that depends on the variation in the number of perceived informed robots. Hence, it requires memory of the past and a comparison between the present and the past state. In our model, non-informed robots systematically rest on an aggregation site, and they leave it with a probability that is determined by the current local density of robots (regardless of whether they are informed or non-informed) at the site. Therefore, our model is reactive and does not require any form of memory. In the next section, we show that the above mentioned modifications improve the robustness and the behavioral flexibility of the swarm.

3   Results

In this section, we compare the performance of swarms of robots controlled by the PFSM as originally illustrated in [13] and by our modified PFSM presented in Sect. 2. We evaluate the two approaches in several different conditions given by all the possible combinations of the parameters' values listed in Table 1. In particular, we vary the swarm size (N), the proportion of informed robots in the swarm (ρ_I), and the proportion of black (ρ_{sb}) and white (ρ_{sw}) informed robots. As in [13], while changing the swarm size, the swarm density has been kept constant by changing the diameter of the arena and of the aggregation sites (see Table 1 for details).

We recall that the task of the robots is to distribute themselves on each site in a way that the robots resting on the black and white sites should be equal to $N\rho_{sb}$ and $N\rho_{sw}$, respectively, with the proportion of informed robots ρ_I being

Table 1. Parameters values

Experiment parameters	Values
Swarm size (N)	$\{50, 100\}$
Proportion of informed robots (ρ_I)	$\{0.1, 0.2, 0.3, 0.4, 0.5\}$
Proportion of black informed robots (ρ_{sb})	$\{0.5, 0.6, 0.7, 0.8, 0.9, 1\}$
Arena diameter	12.9 m (for $N = 50$), 19.2 m (for $N = 100$)
Aggregation site diameter	2.8 m (for $N = 50$), 4.0 m (for $N = 100$)

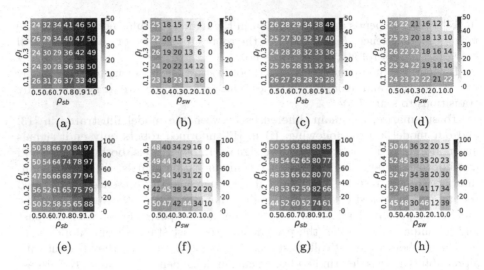

Fig. 2. Graphs showing the median over 20 trials of the number of robots on each site at time $t = 30,000$ s (end of trials) for $N = 50$ robots (top row) and $N = 100$ robots (bottom row). For our approach the results are shown in (a) and (e) with reference to the black site, and in (b) and (f) with reference to the white site. For the approach in [13], the results are shown in (c) and (g) with reference to the black site, and in (d) and (h) with reference to the white site. On all graphs, the y-axis refers to the proportion of informed robots in the swarm (ρ_I) and the shades of grey refer to the number of robots at each aggregation site with white indicating zero robots, and black indicating 50 robots in graphs on top row, and 100 robots in graphs on bottom row. The x-axis refers to (ρ_{sb}) in (a), (c), (e), and (g) and to (ρ_{sw}) in (b), (d), (f), and (h).

as small as possible. For each testing condition, and for each approach, we have run 20 trials. Figure 2 shows, for both approaches, the median over 20 trials of the number of robots resting on each site at the end of each trial (i.e., at time $t = 30,000$ s) for a swarm of $N = 50$ robots (see Fig. 2, graphs in top row) and for a swarm of $N = 100$ robots (see Fig. 2, graphs in bottom row). For our approach the results are shown in Figs. 2a and 2e with reference to the black site, and in Figs. 2b and 2f with reference to the white site. For the approach in [13], the results are shown in Figs. 2c and 2g with reference to the black site, and in Figs. 2d and 2h with reference to the white site.

With a swarm of $N = 50$ robots, both approaches perform relatively well, with the median of the number of robots resting on the black site increasing for progressively higher values of ρ_{sb} (see Figs. 2a, and 2c) and decreasing for progressively lower values of ρ_{sw} (see Figs. 2b and 2d). These trends can be clearly observed, for both approaches, for any values of ρ_I, even for the smallest tested value $\rho_I = 0.1$ (i.e., 10% of informed robots in the swarm). However, our approach performs better than the approach in [13] for values of $\rho_I > 0.3$ and $\rho_{sb} > 0.8$. In these conditions, our results are closer to the target robot distributions than the results obtained with the approach from [13] (see Figs. 2a, 2b, 2c,

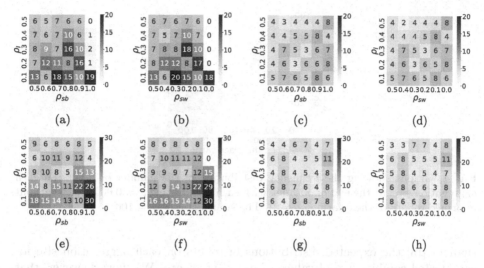

Fig. 3. Graphs showing the interquartile range over 20 trials of the number of robots on each site at $t = 30{,}000\,$s (end of trial). See the caption of Fig. 2 for more details.

and 2d, top right corners). With a larger swarm size $N = 100$, our results are closer to the target robot distributions for both $\rho_I < 0.3$ and $\rho_{sb} < 0.7$ (see Figs. 2e, 2f, 2g, and 2h, bottom left corners) and for $\rho_I > 0.3$ and $\rho_{sb} > 0.8$ (see Figs. 2e, 2f, 2g, and 2h, top right corners).

Figure 3 shows the interquartile ranges of the number of robots on each site at $t = 30{,}000\,$s for both approaches for a swarm size of $N = 50$ (graphs in top row) and $N = 100$ (graphs in bottom row). For low proportions of informed robots ($\rho_I < 0.3$), our approach shows a slightly higher variability in the final distribution of the swarms (Figs. 3a, 3b, 3e, and 3f) than the approach in [13] (see Figs. 3c, 3d, 3g, and 3h). However, at higher proportions of informed robots($\rho_I > 0.3$), the variability is roughly the same for the two approaches in the majority of the parameter configurations.

With our modified approach, we have run further tests with a swarm entirely made of non-informed robots (i.e., $\rho_I = 0$). The removal of informed robots from the swarm prevents the model illustrated in [13] from generating robots' aggregates, as the transition from state random walk $\mathcal{RW}$ to the state stay $\mathcal{S}$ (i.e., resting on the aggregation site) of non-informed robots is triggered by the perception of an aggregation site populated by informed robots. As shown in Fig. 4, in our model, a swarm without informed robots can break the environmental symmetry by repeatedly forming a single aggregate on either the black or the white aggregation site. The median of the number of robots not resting on any site at the end of the experiment is 4 with an interquartile range of 5. This shows that the modifications we made to the system as originally illustrated in [13] enlarges the swarm behavioral repertoire without loss of performance with respect to the results shown in [13]. The results of our tests show that our simplified model generates aggregates that match equally fine or even better

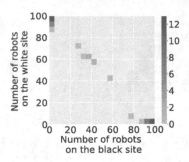

Fig. 4. Graphs showing the frequency distribution of the number of robots on each aggregation site, at the end of 50 runs, with each trial lasting $t = 30{,}000$ s, and without informed robots in the swarm ($\rho_I = 0$). The swarm size is $N = 100$.

than in [13] the expected distributions of robots on each aggregation site for each tested combination of values of ρ_I, ρ_{sb}, and ρ_{sw}. We show, however, that our approach generates a slightly higher between-trials variability than the one in [13]. This is due to the fact that when every robot can start the formation of clusters in the sites, as it is in our approach, clusters composed exclusively of non-informed robots can also appear. When the proportion of informed robots is low, the disruptive effect of these types of aggregates on the desired aggregation dynamics increases as well as with the between trials variability. We also show that, in the absence of informed robots in the swarm, the robots break the environmental symmetry by repeatedly generating a single aggregate on either the black or the white site. Since any aggregation behavior in the absence of informed robots is precluded to the swarm as modelled in [13], we conclude that the modifications introduced by us improve the robustness and the behavioral flexibility of the swarm.

4   Conclusions

We proposed a simplified version of an existing aggregation method using informed individuals in a swarm of robots. We have presented the results of a comparative study that quantitatively evaluates the effectiveness of two different algorithms in driving the aggregation dynamics in swarms of heterogeneous robots made of informed and non-informed robots. The original approach, illustrated in [13], is based on a finite-state machine controller by which individual robots only transit from state random walk $\mathcal{RW}$ (corresponding to random diffusion in the environment) to state Stay $\mathcal{S}$ (corresponding to resting on an aggregation site) when they end up on an aggregation site populated by informed robots. Moreover, the robots transit from state Stay $\mathcal{S}$ to state Leave $\mathcal{L}$ (corresponding to leaving the aggregation site) with a probability that depends on the variation in the perceived number of informed robots at the site during resting, thus requiring memory, however limited. The functional characteristics of this finite-state machine are supported by a communication protocol in which only informed robots can send signals and non-informed robots can receive signals. We have replicated the study illustrated in [13] with a simplified finite-state machine controller in which the robots rest on a site regardless of the presence of informed robots, and they leave the site with a memoryless probability that depends on the current perceived local density at the aggregation site of any type of robots. Moreover, we have re-established a functional equivalence in communication capabilities between informed and non-informed robots. That is, in our approach, there is no distinction in communication capabilities between the types of robots, both can send and receive messages that signal their presence at an aggregation site. This implementation choice allows the robots to estimate the robot density in their neighborhood without any need of distinguishing between robot types. Our comparative tests show that the swarms controlled by our approach generate aggregation dynamics that are never less performing than [13], and in some experimental conditions they are closer to the target robot distributions than the one observed with the approach illustrated in [13]. We showed that, our approach, contrary to the one introduced in [13], suffers from a slightly higher between-trials variability in the number of robots resting at each aggregation site at the end of a trial. We also show that our approach can generate a larger set of aggregation dynamics than in [13], since in the absence of informed robots the swarm controlled with our simplified approach systematically forms a single aggregate in one of the aggregation sites, while the swarm controlled by the approach in [13] never aggregates. Based on the "Occam's razor" principle of parsimony, we claim that due to its simplicity, effectiveness, and robustness to a larger set of operating conditions, our approach should be favored over the one introduced in [13] to control the aggregation dynamics using informed robots.

Future research directions will consider setups with three or more aggregation sites to verify if, with our approach, the expected distributions of robots at the aggregation sites are attained in more complex environments. We also plan to validate the approach illustrated in this paper with the physical robot Kilobots [24] using the Kilogrid platform [30]. This will allow the study of the convergence time of the system and the possible speedup of the dynamics [27].

Acknowledgements. This work was supported by Service Public de Wallonie Recherche under grant n° 2010235 - ARIAC by DIGITALWALLONIA4.AI; by the European Research Council (ERC) under the European Union's Horizon 2020 research and innovation programme (grant agreement No 681872); and by Belgium's Wallonia-Brussels Federation through the ARC Advanced Project GbO (Guaranteed by Optimization). A. Reina and M. Birattari acknowledge the financial support from the Belgian F.R.S.-FNRS, of which they are Chargé de Recherches and Directeur de Recherches, respectively.

References

1. Bonani, M., et al.: The MarXbot, a miniature mobile robot opening new perspectives for the collective-robotic research. In: 2010 IEEE/RSJ International Conference on Intelligent Robots and Systems, pp. 4187–4193. IEEE (2010)

2. Brambilla, M., Ferrante, E., Birattari, M., Dorigo, M.: Swarm robotics: a review from the swarm engineering perspective. Swarm Intell. **7**(1), 1–41 (2013). https://doi.org/10.1007/s11721-012-0075-2

3. Calvo Martín, M., Eeckhout, M., Deneubourg, J.L., Nicolis, S.C.: Consensus driven by a minority in heterogenous groups of the cockroach periplaneta americana. iScience **24**(7) (2021). https://doi.org/10.1016/j.isci.2021.102723

4. Cambier, N., Albani, D., Frémont, V., Trianni, V., Ferrante, E.: Cultural evolution of probabilistic aggregation in synthetic swarms. Appl. Soft Comput. **113**, 108010 (2021). https://doi.org/10.1016/j.asoc.2021.108010

5. Çelikkanat, H., Şahin, E.: Steering self-organized robot flocks through externally guided individuals. Neural Comput. Appl. **19**(6), 849–865 (2010). https://doi.org/10.1007/s00521-010-0355-y

6. Couzin, I.D., Krause, J., Franks, N.R., Levin, S.A.: Effective leadership and decision-making in animal groups on the move. Nature **433**, 513–516 (2005). https://doi.org/10.1038/nature03236

7. Masi, G.D., Prasetyo, J., Zakir, R., Mankovskii, N., Ferrante, E., Tuci, E.: Robot swarm democracy: the importance of informed individuals against zealots. Swarm Intell. **15**(4), 315–338 (2021). https://doi.org/10.1007/s11721-021-00197-3

8. Dorigo, M., et al.: Evolving self-organizing behaviors for a swarm-bot. Auton. Robot. **17**(2), 223–245 (2004). https://doi.org/10.1023/B:AURO.0000033973.24945.f3

9. Ferrante, E., Turgut, A.E., Huepe, C., Stranieri, A., Pinciroli, C., Dorigo, M.: Self-organized flocking with a mobile robot swarm: a novel motion control method. Adapt. Behav. **20**(6), 460–477 (2012). https://doi.org/10.1177/1059712312462248

10. Ferrante, E., Turgut, A.E., Stranieri, A., Pinciroli, C., Birattari, M., Dorigo, M.: A self-adaptive communication strategy for flocking in stationary and non-stationary environments. Nat. Comput. **13**(2), 225–245 (2013). https://doi.org/10.1007/s11047-013-9390-9

11. Firat, Z., Ferrante, E., Cambier, N., Tuci, E.: Self-organised aggregation in swarms of robots with informed robots. In: Fagan, D., Martín-Vide, C., O'Neill, M., Vega-Rodríguez, M.A. (eds.) TPNC 2018. LNCS, vol. 11324, pp. 49–60. Springer, Cham (2018). https://doi.org/10.1007/978-3-030-04070-3_4

12. Firat, Z., Ferrante, E., Gillet, Y., Tuci, E.: On self-organised aggregation dynamics in swarms of robots with informed robots. Neural Comput. Appl. **32**(17), 13825–13841 (2020). https://doi.org/10.1007/s00521-020-04791-0

13. Firat, Z., Ferrante, E., Zakir, R., Prasetyo, J., Tuci, E.: Group-size regulation in self-organized aggregation in robot swarms. In: Dorigo, M., et al. (eds.) ANTS 2020. LNCS, vol. 12421, pp. 315–323. Springer, Cham (2020). https://doi.org/10.1007/978-3-030-60376-2_26

14. Francesca, G., Brambilla, M., Brutschy, A., Trianni, V., Birattari, M.: AutoMoDe: a novel approach to the automatic design of control software for robot swarms. Swarm Intell. **8**(2), 89–112 (2014). https://doi.org/10.1007/s11721-014-0092-4

15. Francesca, G., Brambilla, M., Trianni, V., Dorigo, M., Birattari, M.: Analysing an evolved robotic behaviour using a biological model of collegial decision making. In: Ziemke, T., Balkenius, C., Hallam, J. (eds.) SAB 2012. LNCS (LNAI), vol. 7426, pp. 381–390. Springer, Heidelberg (2012). https://doi.org/10.1007/978-3-642-33093-3_38

16. Gauci, M., Chen, J., Li, W., Dodd, T.J., Groß, R.: Self-organized aggregation without computation. Int. J. Robot. Res. **33**(8), 1145–1161 (2014). https://doi.org/10.1177/0278364914525244

17. Gillet, Y., Ferrante, E., Firat, Z., Tuci, E.: Guiding aggregation dynamics in a swarm of agents via informed individuals: an analytical study. In: The 2019 Conference on Artificial Life: A Hybrid of the European Conference on Artificial Life (ECAL) and the International Conference on the Synthesis and Simulation of Living Systems (ALIFE), pp. 590–597. MIT Press (2019). https://doi.org/10.1162/isal_a_00225

18. Jeanson, R., et al.: Self-organized aggregation in cockroaches. Anim. Behav. **69**(1), 169–180 (2005). https://doi.org/10.1016/j.anbehav.2004.02.009

19. Kato, S., Jones, M.: An extended family of circular distributions related to wrapped Cauchy distributions via Brownian motion. Bernoulli **19**(1), 154–171 (2013). http://www.jstor.org/stable/23525635

20. Kengyel, D., Hamann, H., Zahadat, P., Radspieler, G., Wotawa, F., Schmickl, T.: Potential of heterogeneity in collective behaviors: a case study on heterogeneous swarms. In: Chen, Q., Torroni, P., Villata, S., Hsu, J., Omicini, A. (eds.) PRIMA 2015. LNCS (LNAI), vol. 9387, pp. 201–217. Springer, Cham (2015). https://doi.org/10.1007/978-3-319-25524-8_13

21. Pinciroli, C., et al.: ARGoS: a modular, parallel, multi-engine simulator for multi-robot systems. Swarm Intell. **6**(4), 271–295 (2012). https://doi.org/10.1007/s11721-012-0072-5

22. Pitonakova, L., Giuliani, M., Pipe, A., Winfield, A.: Feature and performance comparison of the V-REP, gazebo and ARGoS robot simulators. In: Giuliani, M., Assaf, T., Giannaccini, M.E. (eds.) TAROS 2018. LNCS (LNAI), vol. 10965, pp. 357–368. Springer, Cham (2018). https://doi.org/10.1007/978-3-319-96728-8_30

23. Prasetyo, J., De Masi, G., Ferrante, E.: Collective decision making in dynamic environments. Swarm Intell. **13**(3), 217–243 (2019). https://doi.org/10.1007/s11721-019-00169-8

24. Rubenstein, M., Ahler, C., Hoff, N., Cabrera, A., Nagpal, R.: Kilobot: a low cost robot with scalable operations designed for collective behaviors. Robot. Auton. Syst. **62**(7), 966–975 (2014). https://doi.org/10.1016/j.robot.2013.08.006

25. Şahin, E., Girgin, S., Bayindir, L., Turgut, A.E.: Swarm robotics. In: Blum, C., Merkle, D. (eds.) Swarm Intelligence. Natural Computing Series, pp. 87–100. Springer, Heidelberg (2008). https://doi.org/10.1007/978-3-540-74089-6_3

26. Schranz, M., Umlauft, M., Sende, M., Elmenreich, W.: Swarm robotic behaviors and current applications. Front. Robot. AI **7**, 36 (2020). https://doi.org/10.3389/frobt.2020.00036

27. Sion, A., Reina, A., Birattari, M., Tuci, E.: Impact of the update time on the aggregation of robotic swarms through informed robots (2022). Accepted to the SAB 2022 Conference

28. Soysal, O., Şahin, E.: Probabilistic aggregation strategies in swarm robotic systems. In: Proceedings 2005 IEEE Swarm Intelligence Symposium, SIS 2005, pp. 325–332 (2005). https://doi.org/10.1109/SIS.2005.1501639

29. Szopek, M., Schmickl, T., Thenius, R., Radspieler, G., Crailsheim, K.: Dynamics of collective decision making of honeybees in complex temperature fields. PLoS ONE **8**(10), 1–11 (2013). https://doi.org/10.1371/journal.pone.0076250

30. Valentini, G., et al.: Kilogrid: a novel experimental environment for the Kilobot robot. Swarm Intell. **12**(3), 245–266 (2018). https://doi.org/10.1007/s11721-018-0155-z

Decentralized Multi-Agent Path Finding in Warehouse Environments for Fleets of Mobile Robots with Limited Communication Range

Abderraouf Maoudj[(⊠)] and Anders Lyhne Christensen

SDU Biorobotics, MMMI, University of Southern Denmark (SDU), Odense, Denmark
{abma,andc}@mmmi.sdu.dk

Abstract. Mobile robots have already made their way into warehouses, and significant effort has consequently been devoted to designing effective algorithms for the related multi-agent path finding (MAPF) problem. However, most of the proposed MAPF algorithms still rely on centralized planning as well as simplistic assumptions, such as that robots have full observability of the environment and move at equal and constant speeds. The resultant plans thus cannot be executed directly on physical robots where these assumptions generally do not hold. To mitigate these issues, we consider the decentralized partially observable multi-robot setting where robots do not have access to the full state of the world. Instead, each robot coordinates with neighbors within a limited communication range. In the proposed approach, each robot independently plans its own path using A* without taking into account other robots, and the robots then solve potential conflicts locally as they occur. Experimental results obtained in various benchmark scenarios confirm that the proposed decentralized approach is effective and scales well to large numbers of robots.

1 Introduction

With the rapid development of low-cost sensors and computing devices, it is becoming increasingly feasible to deploy large-scale systems of mobile transportation robots in industrial environments. Nowadays, many industrial applications benefit from fleets of mobile robots transporting goods and materials between workstations and storage pipes [27]. The increased use of robot fleets has given rise to a number of challenging optimization problems, such as multirobot path planning [24] and multirobot scheduling [1].

Planning conflict-free paths for a team of mobile robots, known as the *multi-agent path finding* (MAPF) problem, remains a major challenge [15,20]. Given a set of agents, each with a pre-specified initial location and a pre-specified goal location in a known environment, MAPF is concerned with finding collision-free paths for the agents such that certain objectives are minimized. MAPF is inspired by real-world applications, such as automated warehouses [11], traffic management [3], and valet parking [12].

The original version of this chapter was revised: The quantitative results have been revised to accurately reflect the research findings. The correction to this chapter is available at https://doi.org/10.1007/978-3-031-20176-9_34

© Springer Nature Switzerland AG 2022, corrected publication 2023
M. Dorigo et al. (Eds.): ANTS 2022, LNCS 13491, pp. 104–116, 2022.
https://doi.org/10.1007/978-3-031-20176-9_9

MAPF is NP-hard to solve optimally [25]. As a result, a significant amount of research has been conducted and the resulting state-of-the-art algorithms can be divided into four categories [7]:

Systematic search algorithms are centralized planning approaches, which enable finding all possible solutions, including an optimal one. In this category, numerous algorithms have been proposed, such as the branch-and-cut-and-price (BCP) algorithm [5], pairwise symmetry reasoning [8], conflict-based search (CBS) algorithms and their variants [8,9]—which are currently among the most popular algorithms for solving the MAPF problem optimally. Although these planners achieve optimal or bounded sub-optimal solutions, they often suffer from a computational complexity that increases exponentially with the problem size.

Rule-based algorithms, in which the agents move step-by-step following ad-hoc rules [13]. For instance, the graph abstraction approach [16], the conflict classification-based algorithm [26], biconnected graphs [21], and parallel-push-and-swap (PPS) [17]. These algorithms are polynomial-time but can still fail to find solutions within a reasonable amount of time for large instances.

Learning-based algorithms use reinforcement learning techniques for finding cooperative and competitive behaviors for solving conflicts [15]. Different learning-based algorithms have been proposed in literature for solving MAPF, see for instance [2,18]. Even though learning-based approaches have proven to be more robust to uncertainties in practical applications than the algorithms discussed above, they do not provide guarantees on solution quality [13,18].

Priority-based algorithms, in which the MAPF problem is decomposed into a series of single-agent path planning problems, where the agents plan their paths sequentially according to a priority scheme. Popular algorithms include the prioritized planning algorithm [14], searching with consistent prioritization [10], the hierarchical cooperative A* approach (HCA), and priority inheritance with backtracking [13]. The prioritized planning algorithm provides a practical solution to applications with large numbers of robots. However, the quality of the resulting solutions depends on the choice of the prioritization scheme, especially in dense environments with limited path choices [23].

The algorithms described above rely on simplistic assumptions and have different objectives. Most of them assume that robots always move at their nominal speed, ignore kinematic constraints, and do not take into account imperfect plan-execution capabilities [4]: in practical scenarios, a robot may need to slow down or come to a complete halt when facing a challenging situation, such as entering a narrow corridor or turning on the spot. The execution will therefore deviate from the plan found offline, and variation in the robots' speeds can thus significantly affect the applicability of these approaches.

To overcome the aforementioned challenges, we propose a decentralized approach based on online conflict resolution, wherein each agent autonomously plans its path using A* while initially ignoring the other agents. Our approach does thus not require the robots to have complete information about the state of the environment. Instead, we consider that robots operate in a partially-observable

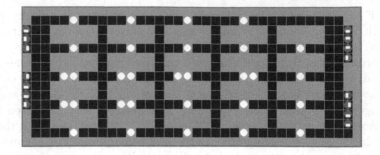

Fig. 1. Example of a warehouse layout. (Color figure online)

world, where each robot can only communicate with neighbors within its vicinity. Additionally, the proposed approach can be used in scenarios where agents have a sequence of goals, which makes it promising for practical scenarios, where agents are continually assigned new goal locations and are required to compute paths online [2].

2 Environment Model and Assumptions

In many practical applications, the layout of a warehouse is fixed, and robots can only move along a predefined roadmap [24]. Accordingly, in this study, we consider automated warehouses with predefined roadmaps, in which a set of m mobile robots $\{r_1, ..., r_m\}$ perform their assigned transportation tasks. The robots are assumed to know the roadmap and their own position and orientation in the map. Figure 1 illustrates an example of a warehouse layout modelled as a 36×15 grid map: the red circles and yellow circles represent the robots and their designated targets, respectively, the green squares represent obstacles, and the black squares represent free space where the robot can move.

In real-world scenarios, wireless communication can be noisy and the robots often have a limited field-of-view [2,19]. Therefore, to reduce the gap between simulation and real-world scenarios, we assume that each robot can only access the state of its neighbors within limited communication range (2 squares). At each time step, if robot j is in communication range of robot i, we say that robot j is in robot i's neighborhood $j \in N_i^t$.

A warehouse layout can be abstracted into an undirected graph $G = (V, E)$, where nodes V correspond to locations arranged in the grid and the edges E correspond to straight lines between locations that can be traversed by the robots. At every time step t, each robot i occupies one of the graph nodes n_i^t, referred to as the *location* of that robot at time t, and can choose to perform an *action* a_i. The action can be either `move` to an adjacent node or `wait` in its current node. The multi-agent path finding problem consists of computing collision-free paths for the team of agents from their current locations to their respective targets. The objective is to minimize the *sum-of-costs* (or *flow time*), that is, the sum over all agents of the time steps required to reach their target locations [22].

3 Proposed Approach

In this section, we present our decentralized cooperative multi-agent path finding approach (DCMAPF) enabling large-scale systems of autonomous mobile robots to operate effectively in shared warehouse environments.

The proposed DCMAPF is presented in Algorithm 1. DCMAPF has two phases: (i) *Path planning* and (ii) *Execution and motion coordination*. In the first phase, the robots individually plan the shortest paths from their initial location to their targets using A*. In the second phase, robots follow their planned paths while detecting and resolving local conflicts at each time step. To reduce the complexity of local coordination, we introduce a *leader-follower* concept for adjacent robots moving in the same direction. At time step t, robot k is a follower of robot i if $n_k^{t+1} = n_i^t$. Since followers relay messages, a leader can have an arbitrary number of followers, and the *followers* of robot i consist of robot k and its followers. If a conflict occurs, the leader negotiates on behalf of itself and its followers. Moreover, to achieve effective decentralized conflict resolution, manually designed local rules are adopted that determine which robot should be given priority. Giving priority to a robot means that it will move first, and a robot occupying the next node in higher priority robot's path must give way.

Hereinafter, the following concepts are used:

- *remainingNodes*: the local list of remaining nodes $n_i^0, ..., n_i^T$ in the planned path for robot i. The list is updated at each time step (a node is removed) and during conflict resolution (nodes are added if a robot needs to give way).
- *giveWayNode*: a free neighboring node that can be used by a robot to move out of the way and allow another, higher priority robot to pass.
- *numberRequestsMyNode*: the number of robots having their n_i^{t+1} or n_i^{t+2}, $\forall i \in \{1, ..., m\}$, equal to the robot's n_{id}^t.
- *numberFollowers*: the number of followers of the robot.

Upon starting the execution, all the robots are located in their initial nodes. In every time step, each robot i identifies all neighbors within communication range and sends them its local data, such as its next node n_i^{t+1}, *remainingNodes*, and *numberFollowers*. After receiving data from its neighbors, the robot checks for potential conflicts with its neighbors. Since conflict detection and handling is done online, only the robot's next node n_i^{t+1} is used for conflict detection. If a conflict is detected, the robots coordinate to solve the conflict as described in Algorithms 2 and 3 (details can be found in Sect. 3.1), then each robot calculates its action a_i and updates its *remainingNodes* accordingly. If no conflict is detected and if a robot has any followers, it checks if its immediate follower's path is longer than its own. If so, the robot gives way to its follower if it has a free neighboring node. This step is essential to avoid deadlocks in certain regions, such as narrow corridors.

In the subsequent step, the robot's action a_i and its updated *remainingNodes* list will be used in a post coordination process, see Algorithm 4. This process is executed by the robots involved in resolving conflicts in the previous steps to check for further potential conflicts resulting from their previous decisions. In

---

Algorithm 1: Proposed DCMAPF approach

---

input: map, n^0_{myID}, $Targets[]$

phase 1: Path planning
$remainingNodes \leftarrow A^*(\text{map}, n^0_{myID}, Targets[])$

phase 2: Execution and motion coordination

while $remainingNodes \neq \phi$ or $neighbors.remainingNodes \neq \phi$ **do**

    $n^t_{myID} \leftarrow remainingNodes[0]$
    $pathLength \leftarrow \text{Length}(remainingNodes)$
    $N^t_{myID} \leftarrow \textbf{GetNeighbors}()$
    send($n^{t+1}_{myID}, pathLength, numberFollowers, numberRequestsMyNode$)

    for i in N^t_{myID} **do**

        if $(n^{t+1}_{myID} = n^t_i$ $)$ and $(n^{t+1}_i = n^t_{myID})$ **then**
            $criticalNode \leftarrow \{n^{t+1}_{myID}, n^t_i\}$
            $a_{myID} \leftarrow \textbf{Algorithm3}(criticalNode, N^t_{myID})$

        else if $(n^{t+1}_{myID} = n^{t+1}_i$ $)$ **then**
            $criticalNode \leftarrow n^{t+1}_{myID}$
            $a_{myID} \leftarrow \textbf{Algorithm2}(criticalNode, N^t_{myID})$

        else
            //no conflict detected
            $nextAction \leftarrow \texttt{move}$
            follower$\leftarrow \textbf{GetMyFollower}()$
            if $(follower.pathLength > pathLength)$ **then**
                $giveWayNode \leftarrow \textbf{GetFreeNeighboringNode}()$
                if $(giveWayNode$ is not $None)$ **then**
                    Insert the $giveWayNode$ into $remainingNodes$

    $n^{t+1}_{myID} \leftarrow remainingNodes[0]$
    send(n^{t+1}_{myID}, $plannedAction$)
    $a_{myID} \leftarrow \textbf{PostCoordination}(n^{t+1}_{myID}, a_{myID})$
    if $(a_{myID} = \texttt{move}$ $)$ **then**
        move to n^{t+1}_{myID}
        Remove n^{t+1}_{myID} from $remainingNodes$

---

this process, detected conflicts are resolved using the same steps and algorithms as described above. Afterward, the robots involved in the negotiation process send their calculated action a_i and next node n^{t+1}_i ($\forall i \in N^t_i$) to their neighbors. Accordingly, leaders ensure that their followers adapt their actions to the outcome of the negotiation process. Once a robot i has calculated its a_i and updated its $remainingNodes$, the robot moves to n^{t+1}_i if $a_i = \texttt{move}$, or remains stationary in its current node n^t_i if $a_i = \texttt{wait}$. The steps presented in Algorithm 1 are reiterated until all robots have reached their target.

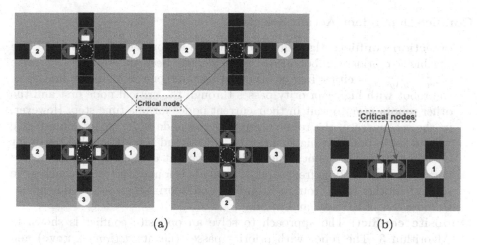

Fig. 2. Conflict illustrations and critical nodes. (a) Intersection conflicts, and (b) Opposite conflict.

3.1   Cooperative Conflict Resolution Strategy

In this work, we divide potential conflicts into the two types illustrated in Fig. 2: (i) *intersection conflict* and (ii) *opposite conflict (swapping conflict)*. The intersection conflict occurs when two or more robots have planned to pass through the same node in the same time step. In this type of conflict, there is only one critical node, which is the shared next node in the robots' paths. On the other hand, an opposite conflict occurs when two robots are located on two adjacent nodes and need to move in opposite directions. In this type of conflict, the robots' current nodes are the critical nodes.

The conflict resolution strategy has two steps. First, the robots negotiate to determine the highest priority robot (see below). In the second step, the robots calculate their actions to give way to the highest priority robot and to then pass through the critical node one by one.

Priorities: The procedure for defining the highest priority robot is based on six rules that prevent congestion and reduce the number of additional *giveWayNodes* necessary for the robots to pass through the critical node without collision. The following rules are applied in order and determine priority:

- `rule1`: a robot occupying a critical node is given priority.
- `rule2`: a robot moving out of another robot's way is given priority.
- `rule3`: the robot with the largest *numberFollowers* is given priority.
- `rule4`: a robot having a free neighboring node is given priority.
- `rule5`: the robot having the largest *numberRequestsMyNode* is given priority.
- `rule6`: the robot with the longest remaining path is given priority.

While the first three rules prevent deadlocks, the last three rules reduce the number of additional *giveWayNodes* introduced in the robots' path and thus enable the robots to avoid one another in fewer time steps.

Conflict-Dependent Action Selection:

Intersection conflict: Algorithm 2 details the action selection process. Once the highest priority robot (*PriorityAgent*) has been determined, the node $n^{t+2}_{PriorityAgent}$ is either free or occupied by another robot. In the first case, the robot with higher priority passes through the critical node first and the other robots have to wait in their current nodes for one time step. However, in the second case, the robot occupying the node $n^{t+2}_{PriorityAgent}$ must give way to the robot with higher priority to pass and the other robots wait for one time step. The robot requested to move out of the way chooses a free neighboring node. If no free neighboring node is found, the robot chooses the node of another robot from its neighbors and informs the concerned neighbor to move out of the way, and so on.

Opposite conflict: The approach to solve an opposite conflict is shown in Algorithm 3. The robot with priority passes (i.e. its *action* ← move) and the other robot moves out of the way to a free neighboring node. If no free neighboring node is found, the robot with lower priority chooses the node of its follower robot (move backward) and informs the follower to move out of the way.

Note that any neighboring node calculated during the conflict resolution process will be inserted as the first elements in the *remainingNodes* list of the robot. Accordingly, if the robot's action is move, then the robot selects the first node in its *remainingNodes*.

4   Experimental Results and Performances Analysis

In this section, we present the results of an extensive set of experiments conducted to assess the performance of *DCMAPF*. These tests were performed using benchmark maps with varying sizes, obstacles densities, and number of robots. We implemented *DCMAPF* in Python and the experiments were conducted on a workstation equipped with an AMD Ryzen 9 5950X 16-core CPU @3.40 GHz and 32 GB RAM.

4.1   Benchmarks and Setup

For our experiments, we chose three types of maps, *empty*, *random* and *warehouse* from the MAPF benchmark maps [20]. Specifically, we used the following maps: *empty-48-48*, *random-32-32-20*, *random-64-64-20*, and *warehouse-20-40-10-2-2*. For each combination of map and number of agents, we selected 25 scenarios from the MAPF benchmark.

We compared our *DCMAPF* approach to four state-of-the-art planners, namely: CBS with its improvement technique [8] as an optimal planner, EECBS [9] as a state-of-the-art bounded sub-optimal search-based planner, and PIBT and PIBT+ [13] as prioritized planners. Note that, for all planners, the implementations coded by their respective authors were used with default parameter settings [13]. The source code for these planners is available in [6].

Algorithm 2: Solve intersection conflict

---

input : criticalNode, N_i^t
output: a_{myID}

`step 1: Determine the highest priority agent`
$PriorityAgent \leftarrow$ **CheckPriorityRules()**
Action $\leftarrow$ Empty list
`step 2: Calculate the action`
Action[PriorityAgent] $\leftarrow$ **move**
if $(n_{PriorityAgent}^{t+2}$ *is Free)* **then**

> **for** i in N_i^t and $i \neq PriorityAgent$) **do**
> > Action[i]$\leftarrow$**wait**
>
> **if** *criticalNode is not Free* **then**
> > *giveWayNode* $\leftarrow$ **GetFreeNeighboringNode()**
> > Action[Agent occupying the criticalNode] $\leftarrow$ **move**
> > Insert the *giveWayNode* into the *remainingNodes* of the agent

else

> **for** i in N_i^t **do**
> > **if** $(n_i^t = n_{PriorityAgent}^{t+2})$ **then**
> > > Action[i]$\leftarrow$**move**
> > > *giveWayNode* $\leftarrow$ **GetFreeNeighboringNode()**
> > > Insert the *criticalNode* into the *remainingNodes* set of the agent
> >
> > **else**
> > > Action[i]$\leftarrow$**wait**

Return(*Actions[myID]*)

Algorithm 3: Solve opposite conflict

---

input : criticalNode, N_i^t
output: a_{myID}

`step 1: Determine the highest priority agent`
$PriorityAgent \leftarrow$ **CheckPriorityRules()**
Action $\leftarrow$ Empty list
`step 2: Calculate the action`
Action[PriorityAgent] $\leftarrow$ **move**
for i in N_i^t **do**

> **if** *(i $\neq$ PriorityAgent)* **then**
> > Action[i]$\leftarrow$**move**
> > *giveWayNode* $\leftarrow$ **GetFreeNeighboringNode()**
> > Insert the *giveWayNode* into the *remainingNodes* of the agent

Return(*Actions[myID]*)

Our comparison metrics are *sum-of-costs* and *success rate*, which is the percentage of the MAPF instances solved within a runtime limit. It is important to note that *CBS, EECBS, PIBT* and *PIBT+* are centralized planners and have

---

Algorithm 4: Post coordination

---

input : n_{myID}^{t+1}, a_{myID}
output: a_{myID}

$plannedAction \leftarrow a_{myID}$
step 1: Check for further potential conflicts
$N \leftarrow$ **GetNeighbors()**
for i *in* N **do**
    if $(n_{myID}^{t+1} = n_i^{t+1})$ *and (the action of robot i is* **move**$)$ **then**
        $criticalNode \leftarrow n_{myID}^{t+1}$
        $a_{myID} \leftarrow$ **Algorithm2**$(criticalNode, N_{myID}^t)$

step 2: Followers adapt their actions to those of their leader
Leader=**GetAgentOccupyingNextNode**(N_{myID}^t)
if $(a_{leader} = $ **wait** $)$ **then**
    $a_{myID} \leftarrow$ **wait**
else if $(a_{leader} = $ **move**$)$ *and* $(n_{leader}^{t+1} = n_{myID}^t)$ **then**
    $a_{myID} \leftarrow$ **move**
    $giveWayNode \leftarrow$ **GetFreeNeighboringNode()**
    Insert the $giveWayNode$ into the $remainingNodes$ of the agent
else
    $a_{myID} \leftarrow plannedAction$
Return(a_{myID})

---

access to the whole state of the system, whereas *DCMAPF* is a decentralized approach where the robots' decisions are based only on their local observation and messages shared between robots within a limited communication range. Since *DCMAPF* resolves conflicts online, we allowed a maximum of 300 time steps for 32 and 48-sized maps, and 600 time steps for the other maps. The other offline planners were given a time limit of 30 s to plan the paths for all robots as is commonly used [13,20]. An execution was considered unsuccessful if the robots failed to resolve a conflict or a planner failed to provide a solution within the time limit.

4.2 Results

The obtained results are presented in Fig. 3. The first clear trend is that the *DCMAPF* performs well in terms of success rate in all maps no matter the map size or the number of robots. Secondly, a prominent trend observed in all plots of the metric *sum-of-costs* is that *DCMAPF* outperforms the prioritized planners *PIBT* and *PIBT+* for small fleet sizes. Additionally, it is evident that the *sum-of-costs* of *DCMAPF* tends to increase relative to the other planners as the maps become more challenging with higher numbers of robots.

In maps with low obstacle densities, such as *empty-48-48*, all planners have very high success rates, except CBS that has lower success rate in most experiments involving more than 100 robots due to its computational complexity. In terms of solution cost, *DCMAPF* outperforms *PIBT* and *PIBT+* when the

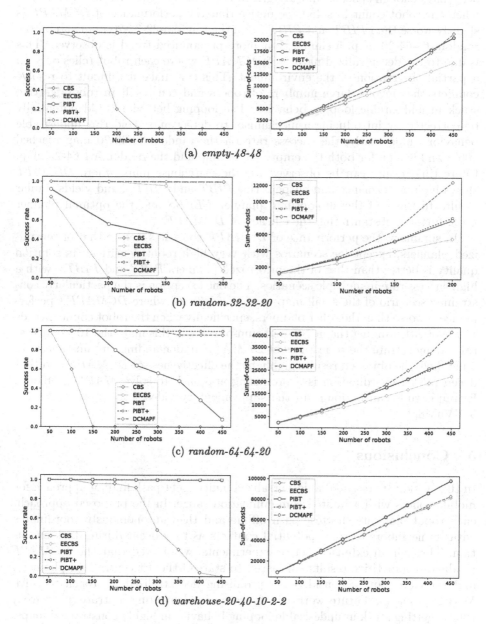

(a) *empty-48-48*

(b) *random-32-32-20*

(c) *random-64-64-20*

(d) *warehouse-20-40-10-2-2*

Fig. 3. Comparative results in terms of *success rate* and *sum-of-costs* of successful runs on four benchmark maps.

number of robots is less than 450 since in conflict resolution, robots with low priority have enough space to quickly give way to higher priority robots. However, when the robot count hits 450, we notice that the performance of *DCMAPF* is slightly worse than *PIBT* and *PIBT+*. On the random-32-32-20 map and on the random-64-64-20 map, a similar, but more pronounced trend is observed. This is due to the decentralized nature of *DCMAPF* where each robot relies only on a partial observation of the environment. This can make it difficult to resolve conflicts that involve large numbers of robots and can result in robots getting stuck in undesirable looping behavior. The looping behavior could potentially be corrected by introducing a mechanism to detect and avoid this undesirable behavior. Importantly, the success rate on the random-32-32-20 map reached 100% and is high for both the empty-48-48 map and the random-64-64-20 map. Interesting results can be observed for the warehouse map, where *DCMAPF* shows high performance and outperforms *PIBT* and *PIBT+*, and yields similar results to those of the sub-optimal planner *EECBS* and the optimal planner *CBS*, further substantiating the efficacy of *DCMAPF*.

In summary, the performance of *DCMAPF* compares well to that of centralized planners, except for scenarios with very high robot densities. Its solution quality is better than that of the prioritized planners *PIBT* and *PIBT+* with a high success rate in multiple scenarios. The one exception is the particularly constrained scenario of the small map *random-32-32-20*, where *DCMAPF's* performance is worse than the other planners, specifically when the robot count exceeds 150. Notwithstanding the increase in sum-of-costs in this map, the 100% success rates demonstrate the robustness of *DCMAPF* in demanding circumstances. In a nutshell, the obtained results highlight the effectiveness of *DCMAPF* and that decentralized coordination is a promising approach to solve *MAPF* problems. Example runs can be found in the supplementary video: https://youtu.be/5_5TdVuM8kI.

5   Conclusions

In this work, we presented a decentralized multi-agent path finding approach for mobile robots with a limited communication range. In the proposed approach, each robot plans its shortest path offline and then autonomously coordinates with its neighbors to solve potential conflicts as they occur during task execution. Through an extensive set of experiments, we showed that the *DCMAPF* produces competitive results compared to state-of-the-art centralized planners, and therefore can be considered a promising decentralized approach to solve MAPF problems. Future work will focus on implementing a strategy to avoid robots getting stuck in undesirable looping behavior in highly constrained maps.

Acknowledgements. This work was supported by the Independent Research Fund Denmark under grant 0136-00251B.

References

1. Bobanac, V., Bogdan, S.: Routing and scheduling in multi-AGV systems based on dynamic banker algorithm. In: Proceedings of the 16th Mediterranean Conference on Control and Automation, pp. 1168–1173. IEEE (2008)
2. Damani, M., Luo, Z., Wenzel, E., Sartoretti, G.: PRIMAL_2: pathfinding via reinforcement and imitation multi-agent learning-lifelong. IEEE Robot. Autom. Lett. **6**(2), 2666–2673 (2021)
3. Dresner, K., Stone, P.: A multiagent approach to autonomous intersection management. J. Artif. Intell. Res. **31**, 591–656 (2008)
4. Hönig, W., et al.: Multi-agent path finding with kinematic constraints. In: Proceedings of the Twenty-Sixth International Conference on Automated Planning and Scheduling (ICAPS), pp. 477–485. AAAI Press (2016)
5. Lam, E., Le Bodic, P.: New valid inequalities in branch-and-cut-and-price for multi-agent path finding. In: Proceedings of the International Conference on Automated Planning and Scheduling (ICAPS), pp. 184–192. AAAI Press (2020)
6. Li, J.: Source code for CBS, EECBS and PIBT. https://github.com/Jiaoyang-Li/CBSH2-RTC. https://github.com/Jiaoyang-Li/EECBS and https://github.com/Kei18/pibt2
7. Li, J., Chen, Z., Harabor, D., Stuckey, P., Koenig, S.: Anytime multi-agent path finding via large neighborhood search. In: International Joint Conference on Artificial Intelligence, pp. 4127–4135. IJCAI (2021)
8. Li, J., Harabor, D., Stuckey, P.J., Ma, H., Gange, G., Koenig, S.: Pairwise symmetry reasoning for multi-agent path finding search. Artif. Intell. **301**, 103574 (2021)
9. Li, J., Ruml, W., Koenig, S.: EECBS: a bounded-suboptimal search for multi-agent path finding. In: Proceedings of the AAAI Conference on Artificial Intelligence, pp. 12353–12362. AAAI Press (2021)
10. Ma, H., Harabor, D., Stuckey, P.J., Li, J., Koenig, S.: Searching with consistent prioritization for multi-agent path finding. In: Proceedings of the AAAI Conference on Artificial Intelligence, pp. 7643–7650. AAAI Press (2019)
11. Ma, H., Li, J., Kumar, T., Koenig, S.: Lifelong multi-agent path finding for online pickup and delivery tasks. In: Proceedings of the International Conference on Autonomous Agents and Multiagent Systems (AAMAS), pp. 837–845. IFAAMAS (2017)
12. Okoso, A., Otaki, K., Nishi, T.: Multi-agent path finding with priority for cooperative automated valet parking. In: 2019 IEEE Intelligent Transportation Systems Conference (ITSC), pp. 2135–2140. IEEE (2019)
13. Okumura, K., Machida, M., Défago, X., Tamura, Y.: Priority inheritance with backtracking for iterative multi-agent path finding. In: Proceedings of the Twenty-Eighth International Joint Conference on Artificial Intelligence (IJCAI-2019), pp. 535–542. IJCAI Organization (2019)
14. Rathi, A., Vadali, M., et al.: Dynamic prioritization for conflict-free path planning of multi-robot systems. arXiv preprint arXiv:2101.01978 (2021)
15. Reijnen, R., Zhang, Y., Nuijten, W., Senaras, C., Goldak-Altgassen, M.: Combining deep reinforcement learning with search heuristics for solving multi-agent path finding in segment-based layouts. In: 2020 IEEE Symposium Series on Computational Intelligence (SSCI), pp. 2647–2654. IEEE (2020)
16. Ryan, M.R.K.: Exploiting subgraph structure in multi-robot path planning. J. Artif. Intell. Res. **31**, 497–542 (2008)

17. Sajid, Q., Luna, R., Bekris, K.: Multi-agent pathfinding with simultaneous execution of single-agent primitives. In: International Symposium on Combinatorial Search, vol. 3, no. 1, pp. 88–96. AAAI Press (2012)
18. Sartoretti, G., et al.: Primal: pathfinding via reinforcement and imitation multi-agent learning. IEEE Robot. Autom. Lett. **4**(3), 2378–2385 (2019)
19. Stephan, J., Fink, J., Kumar, V., Ribeiro, A.: Concurrent control of mobility and communication in multirobot systems. IEEE Trans. Rob. **33**(5), 1248–1254 (2017)
20. Stern, R., et al.: Multi-agent pathfinding: definitions, variants, and benchmarks. In: Symposium on Combinatorial Search (SoCS), pp. 151–158. AAAI Press (2019)
21. Surynek, P.: A novel approach to path planning for multiple robots in bi-connected graphs. In: 2009 IEEE International Conference on Robotics and Automation, pp. 3613–3619. IEEE (2009)
22. Surynek, P., Felner, A., Stern, R., Boyarski, E.: Efficient SAT approach to multi-agent path finding under the sum of costs objective. In: Proceedings of the Twenty-second European Conference on Artificial Intelligence, ECAI, pp. 810–818. IOS Press (2016)
23. Van Den Berg, J.P., Overmars, M.H.: Prioritized motion planning for multiple robots. In: 2005 IEEE/RSJ International Conference on Intelligent Robots and Systems, pp. 430–435. IEEE (2005)
24. Yu, D., Hu, X., Liang, K., Ying, J.: A parallel algorithm for multi-AGV systems. J. Ambient. Intell. Humaniz. Comput. **13**(4), 2309–2323 (2022)
25. Yu, J., LaValle, S.M.: Structure and intractability of optimal multi-robot path planning on graphs. In: Proceedings of the Twenty-Seventh AAAI Conference on Artificial Intelligence, pp. 1443–1449. AAAI Press (2013)
26. Zhang, Z., Guo, Q., Yuan, P.: Conflict-free route planning of automated guided vehicles based on conflict classification. In: 2017 IEEE International Conference on Systems, Man, and Cybernetics (SMC), pp. 1459–1464. IEEE (2017)
27. Zhao, Y., Liu, X., Wang, G., Wu, S., Han, S.: Dynamic resource reservation based collision and deadlock prevention for multi-AGV. IEEE Access **8**, 82120–82130 (2020)

Decomposition and Merging Co-operative Particle Swarm Optimization with Random Grouping

Alanna McNulty[1], Beatrice Ombuki-Berman[1], and Andries Engelbrecht[2]($\boxtimes$) (iD)

[1] Department of Computer Science, Brock University, St. Catharines, Canada
{am17xy,bombuki}@brocku.ca
[2] Department of Industrial Engineering and Computer Science Division,
Stellenbosch University, Stellenbosch, South Africa
engel@sun.ac.za

Abstract. Particle swarm optimization (PSO) does not scale well to large-scale optimization problems (LSOPs). A divide-and-conquer approach towards solving LSOPs has been shown to be very effective in scaling PSO, resulting in a family of co-operative PSO (CPSO) algorithms. Recently, two adaptive co-operative PSO approaches have been developed to improve performance on non-separable problems, namely decomposition CPSO (DCPSO) and merging CPSO (MCPSO). Though DCPSO and MCPSO were shown to perform competitively, they are limited in their ability to explore variable groupings. This paper proposes incorporating random grouping of decision variables into DCPSO (RG-DCPSO) and MCPSO (RG-MCPSO) to better cope with complex variable dependencies. These algorithms were compared to results from five other decomposition-based approaches in order to determine if applying random grouping to DCPSO and MCPSO leads to an improvement in performance. The empirical results show that when applied to function optimization problems, RG-DCPSO was able to achieve the best overall final objective function values in environments with up to 1000 dimensions. The results also show that RG-MCPSO performs well for non-separable objective functions in large-dimensional spaces with 500 and 1000 dimensions.

1 Introduction

Large scale optimization problems (LSOPs) are optimization problems containing many decision variables. Many real-world LSOPs exist in the fields of manufacturing, engineering, data mining, and vehicle routing. Generally, optimization algorithms do not scale well to LSOPs. As a result, there have been many proposed modifications to optimization algorithms to allow for better performance for LSOPs. The main issue faced by optimization algorithms in LSOPs is referred to as the "curse of dimensionality": With a linear increase in the number of decision variables, the volume of the search space increases exponentially. In the case of particle swarm optimization (PSO), the size of the search space makes it difficult for PSO to effectively search for the global optimum. As the number of decision variables increases, the particles become more likely to leave the search space

© Springer Nature Switzerland AG 2022
M. Dorigo et al. (Eds.): ANTS 2022, LNCS 13491, pp. 117–129, 2022.
https://doi.org/10.1007/978-3-031-20176-9_10

completely, requiring the use of methods such as boundary constraint handling techniques to prevent swarm divergence [16]. A divide-and-conquer approach has previously been used to scale PSO to LSOPs. Co-operative PSO (CPSO) is one such approach, where the decision variables are divided into sub-swarms which are optimized independently [23]. Decomposition CPSO (DCPSO) is done by initializing an n_x-dimensional[1] swarm and decomposing it until each sub-swarm optimizes a single decision variable. Merging CPSO (MCPSO) initializes a CPSO and merges sub-swarms together at a fixed rate until all sub-swarms have been merged into one swarm. DCPSO and MCPSO have been shown to improve the scalability of PSO for LSOPs [4].

DCPSO and MCPSO are limited in their ability to consider variable dependencies. The variable groupings are deterministic and rigid, and can result in some inter-relations among dependent decision variables being missed. This paper proposes incorporating random grouping [11] of decision variables into DCPSO and MCPSO. Random grouping allows for a more dynamic and stochastic approach towards finding variable dependencies, while adding little computational overhead to the established algorithms.

The rest of the paper is outlined as follows: Sect. 2 gives the necessary background information, Sect. 3 discusses the proposed variants of PSO for LSOPs, Sect. 4 describes the experimental setup, Sect. 5 discusses the additional decomposition approaches used for comparison, Sect. 6 gives the experimental results, and Sect. 7 provides the final conclusion.

2   Background

The necessary background information on PSO and random grouping is provided in this section.

2.1   Particle Swarm Optimization

PSO is based on the flocking behaviour of birds, originally developed as a way to solve n_x-dimensional continuous-valued, boundary constrained optimization problems [8]. PSO has since been used in many applications, including neural network training [8], generating aesthetically pleasing images [1], swarm robotics [7], portfolio optimization [5], data clustering [24], RNA structure prediction [13], among many others [6,9,18].

A PSO swarm is made up of particles, which move through the n_x-dimensional search space until a stopping criterion is met. Each particle's position within the search space is a possible solution. Each particle also maintains its own velocity and personal best position. The velocity update function is as follows:

$$\mathbf{v}_i(t+1) = w\mathbf{v}_i(t) + c_1\mathbf{r}_{1i}(t)(\mathbf{y}_i(t) - \mathbf{x}_i(t)) + c_2\mathbf{r}_{2i}(\hat{\mathbf{y}}_i(t) - \mathbf{x}_i(t)) \quad (1)$$

---

[1] n_x is the number of decision variables.

where $\mathbf{v}_i(t)$ is the velocity of particle i at time t, $\mathbf{x}_i$ is the particle's current position, $\mathbf{y}_i$ is its personal best position, and $\hat{\mathbf{y}}_i$ is the neighbourhood best position. Shi and Eberhart introduced w as the inertia weight in [19]. c_1 is the cognitive coefficient, and determines the influence of the particle's current best position. Similarly, c_2 is the social coefficient, and determines the influence of the neighbourhood best. Both $\mathbf{r}_1$ and $\mathbf{r}_2$ are random vectors with components sampled uniformly over $[0, 1]$. The position update function is as follows:

$$\mathbf{x}_i(t + 1) = \mathbf{x}_i(t) + \mathbf{v}_i(t + 1) \tag{2}$$

After each particle's current position has been updated, the new position is evaluated using the objective function. If the new position is better than the old one, then the new position is taken to be that particle's new personal best position. Additionally, if a particle has a better position than the neighbourhood best, the neighbourhood best is replaced with this particle.

The PSO algorithm as it was originally introduced by Kennedy and Eberhart [8] runs into a problem referred to as the "curse of dimensionality" [23]. As the number of decision variables increases, the performance deteriorates, because with a linear increase in the number of decision variables, the size of search space increases exponentially. In LSOPs, particles may also start leaving the search space entirely, resulting in the swarm diverging [16].

Another problem experienced by PSO is referred to as "two steps forward and one step back" [23]. If the search space has many decision variables, a particle moving closer to the minimum in one dimension can decrease the objective function value of that particle even if the other dimensions worsen slightly. The personal best position of that particle is still completely overwritten, resulting in losing valuable information about the search space.

Oldewage et al. showed that stronger focus should be given on exploitation rather than exploration when applying PSO to solve LSOPs [14]. Previously introduced methods include applying velocity clamping to each particle [15], and adjusting the values of control parameters to better fit large-dimensional problems [17].

2.2   Co-operative Particle Swarm Optimization

The CPSO-S algorithm is a divide-and-conquer variation of PSO which splits an n-dimensional swarm into n one-dimensional sub-swarms [23]. Each of the resulting sub-swarms is optimized independently, using its own PSO. CPSO-S was designed to minimize the effects of the "curse of dimensionality".

CPSO is able to achieve stronger exploitation with respect to smaller sub-spaces of the search space. The pseudocode for CPSO is given in Algorithm 1. In this algorithm, n_x is the number of decision variables, K is the number of sub-swarms, $S_k.\hat{\mathbf{y}}_i$ is the neighbourhood best of the kth sub-swarm, $S_k.\mathbf{x}_i$ is the position of the ith particle in the current sub-swarm, $S_k.\mathbf{y}_i$ is the current best position of the ith particle in the current sub-swarm, $S_k.n_s$ is the number of particles in the kth sub-swarm, f is the objective function, and $\mathbf{b}$ is the context vector.

Algorithm 1. CPSO

$K_1 = n_x \bmod K$ and $K_2 = K - (n_x \bmod K)$;
Initialize $K_1 \lceil n_x / K \rceil$-dimensional and $K_2 \lfloor n_x / K \rfloor$-dimensional swarms;
while *stopping criterion is not met* **do**
    for *each sub-swarm* $S_k, k = 1, ..., K$ **do**
        for *each particle* $i = 1, ..., S_k.n_s$ **do**
            if $f(b(k, S_k.\boldsymbol{x}_i)) < f(b(k, S_k.\boldsymbol{y}_i))$ **then**
                $S_k.\boldsymbol{y}_i = S_k.\boldsymbol{x}_i$;
            end
            if $f(b(k, S_k.\boldsymbol{y}_i)) < f(b(k, S_k.\hat{\boldsymbol{y}}_i))$ **then**
                $S_k.\hat{\boldsymbol{y}}_i = S_k.\boldsymbol{y}_i$;
            end
        end
        for *each particle* $i = 1, ..., S_k.n_s$ **do**
            Update the velocity using Equation (1);
            Update the position using Equation (2);
        end
    end
end

CPSO-S_K allows the n_x-dimensional problem to be sub-divided into K sub-problems. The CPSO-S algorithm is a special case of CPSO-S_K where $K = n_x$. The CPSO-S and CPSO-S_K algorithms were introduced in [23].

The "context vector" is an important part of CPSO. Since the CPSO algorithm requires that the swarm is subdivided into sub-swarms and the objective function is only defined for an n_x-dimensional problem, there is no objective function defined for the lower-dimensional sub-swarms. The current best positions of each sub-swarm are stored in their corresponding indices of the context vector. The objective function value of the context vector is then used to determine the fitness of particles in sub-swarms. Once the CPSO-S is finished optimizing the swarm, the context vector represents the global best position. The context vector is illustrated in Fig. 1. One problem with the original CPSO approach is stagnation [23]. Stagnation occurs when every sub-swarm becomes stuck in a sub-optimal position. Since only one sub-swarm is being updated at a time, there is no way for the particles in the other sub-swarms to recognize when the other sub-swarms are stuck in a sub-optimal position. This problem does not occur with PSO [23], since PSO updates all dimensions at the same time. Another issue is variable dependencies, which are not properly addressed by CPSO since sub-swarms are optimized independently of each other.

2.3   Random Grouping

Random grouping randomly groups decision variables into sub-groups. The main benefit is that groupings of variables can be changed as the algorithm converges, allowing for more variable groupings to be explored. Random grouping has pre-

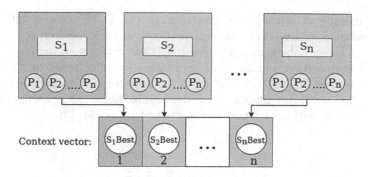

Fig. 1. An illustration of a context vector.

viously been incorporated into other biologically-inspired algorithms such as the artificial bee colony (ABC) algorithm [26], cooperative coevolving particle swarm optimization (CCPSO) [11], and has been shown to improve the performance of evolutionary algorithms for non-separable problems [25].

2.4   Decomposition and Merging Co-operative Particle Swarm Optimization

Decomposition CPSO (DCPSO) and merging CPSO (MCPSO) [4] were designed to avoid the problems experienced by CPSO as discussed in Sect. 2.2. The goal of these algorithms is to implement a balance between the exploration benefits gained from PSO and the exploitation benefits gained from a CPSO by having the decision variables grouped into different sub-swarms as the swarm converges.

DCPSO starts off with one n_x-dimensional swarm, and decomposes the swarm at regular intervals until there are n_x one-dimensional swarms. The decomposition approach leads to the exploitation benefits of using smaller sub-spaces of the entire search space by systematically neglecting variable dependencies. The fixed rate of decomposition is given by:

$$n_f = \frac{n_T}{1 + (\frac{log(n)}{log(n_k(t))})} \tag{3}$$

where n_T is the maximum number of objective function evaluations which will be done during the search process, n_f is the number of fitness evaluations which should be done between each decomposition step, n is the total number of dimensions, and $n_k(t)$ is the number of sub-swarms from each decomposition step, which is kept at a constant value of 2.

If a sub-swarm has an even number of dimensions, decomposing the swarm is easy. If the sub-swarm has an odd number of dimensions, then decomposition is done such that one sub-swarm contains $\lfloor \frac{n}{2} \rfloor$ decision variables and the second sub-swarm contains the rest [4].

MCPSO is essentially the opposite of DCPSO. MCPSO starts off optimizing the swarm as n_x one-dimensional sub-swarms using a CPSO-S. The sub-swarms are then merged at a fixed rate, given in Eq. (3). In the case of MCPSO, n_f is the number of fitness evaluations done between each merging step. MCPSO continues to merge sub-swarms together until there is one n_x-dimensional swarm.

The decomposition and merging approaches are illustrated in Fig. 2. Algorithm 2 describes DCPSO and MCPSO. The decomposition and merging condition is that a certain number of fitness evaluations has occurred since the previous decomposition or merging, determined using Eq. (3).

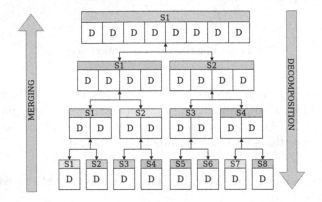

Fig. 2. Illustration of DCPSO and MCPSO.

3   Proposed Variants

This section introduces the proposed variants of DCPSO and MCPSO. The purpose of these two variants is to improve the performance of DCPSO and MCPSO by minimizing the effect of sub-optimal decompositions or merges that are done on the swarm. DCPSO and MCPSO are limited in their ability to explore variable dependencies. Once new sub-swarms have been created, the decision variables which are assigned to each sub-swarm remain fixed, thereby imposing different degrees of independence assumptions on decision variables. This can lead to DCPSO and MCPSO optimizing a sub-optimal swarm until the next decomposition or merging step takes place.

To address this problem, it is proposed that random grouping be applied at a fixed rate throughout the execution of DCPSO and MCPSO. Additional benefits of using random grouping are that it adds little computational overhead because all that is being changed is the groupings of decision variables, and no additional information about the current behaviour of the swarm is required.

Algorithm 3 represents the changes made to DCPSO and MCPSO to incorporate random grouping. A random grouping condition determines when decision variables are randomized over the sub-swarms. The random grouping condition used is that a certain number of fitness evaluations have been used up since the

---

Algorithm 2. DCPSO and MCPSO

---

    while *stopping criterion is not met* **do**
        if *decomposition or merging condition is true* **then**
            randomly decompose or merge the sub-swarms;
        end
        for *each sub-swarm $S_k, k = 1, ..., K$* **do**
            for *each particle $i = 1, ..., S_k.n_s$* **do**
                if $f(b(k, S_k.\boldsymbol{x}_i)) < f(b(k, S_k.\boldsymbol{y}_i))$ **then**
                    $S_k.\mathbf{y}_i = S_k.\mathbf{x}_i;$
                end
                if $f(b(k, S_k.\boldsymbol{y}_i)) < f(b(k, S_k.\hat{\boldsymbol{y}}_i))$ **then**
                    $S_k.\hat{\mathbf{y}}_i = S_k.\mathbf{y}_i;$
                end
            end
            for *each particle $i = 1, ..., S_k.n_s$* **do**
                Update the velocity using Equation (1);
                Update the position using Equation (2);
            end
        end
    end

---

last grouping. When random grouping is incorporated into DCPSO it is referred to as RG-DCPSO, and when random grouping is incorporated into MCPSO it is referred to as RG-MCPSO.

4 Experimental Setup

This section gives all of the information regarding the experimental setup, including parameters, benchmark functions, and statistical methods used.

4.1 Control Parameters

Values of $w = 0.729$ and $c_1 = c_2 = 1.494$ were used for each PSO algorithm. These values have been shown to perform well in [27], and satisfy stability conditions which guarantee that the swarm will reach an equilibrium state [3]. Every individual PSO sub-swarm which was created (at initialization as well as at every decomposition or merging step) contained 20 particles. The total number of objective function evaluations used for each run was taken from [2], and is $3000 \times n_x$. Additionally, $n_k(t)$ was kept as a constant of two for both DCPSO and MCPSO. Each algorithm was run 30 times on each function, and the average final global objective function value was taken for comparison.

4.2 Statistical Methods

The Kruskal-Wallis test [10] was used in order to check if there is at least one pair of algorithms on at least one problem whose performance differs with statistical

---

Algorithm 3. RG-DCPSO and RG-MCPSO

---

while *stopping criteria is not met* **do**
    if *random grouping condition is met* **then**
        randomize the dimensions across all sub-swarms;
    end
    if *decomposition or merging condition is true* **then**
        decompose or merge each S_k into $n_k(t)$ sub-swarms;
    end
    for *each sub-swarm* $S_k, k = 1, ..., K$ **do**
        for *each particle* $i = 1, ..., S_k.n_s$ **do**
            if $f(b(k, S_k.\boldsymbol{x}_i)) < f(b(k, S_k.\boldsymbol{y}_i))$ **then**
                $S_k.\mathbf{y}_i = S_k.\mathbf{x}_i$;
            end
            if $f(b(k, S_k.\boldsymbol{y}_i)) < f(b(k, S_k.\hat{\boldsymbol{y}}_i))$ **then**
                $S_k.\hat{\mathbf{y}}_i = S_k.\mathbf{y}_i$;
            end
        end
        for *each particle* $i = 1, ..., S_k.n_s$ **do**
            Update the velocity using Equation (1);
            Update the position using Equation (2);
        end
    end
end

---

significance. If it was determined that there is a significant difference between the results, the Mann-Whitney-Wilcoxon rank sum test [12] was used to compare each of them pairwise in order to determine which algorithm performed best. All statistical tests were run with a significance level of $\alpha = 0.05$.

If an algorithm performed better than another using the pairwise Mann-Whitney-Wilcoxon rank sum, then it "won", and was given a point, likewise the "losing" algorithm lost a point. If there was no statistically significant difference in performance, then the algorithms "tied" and neither algorithm gained or lost a point. The algorithms were then ranked according to the points each earned, starting with number of wins, followed by the number of losses, and then the number of ties. The ranking of algorithms was done separately for each benchmark problem type to demonstrate which algorithm performed best.

4.3   Benchmark Functions

All 20 benchmark functions from the CEC'2010 special session and competition on large-scale global optimization were used [22]. This benchmark set contains a variety of separable, partially-separable, and non-separable functions, and each function can be extended to use any number of dimensions.

4.4   The Random Grouping Condition of DCPSO and MCPSO

The random grouping condition, as mentioned in Sect. 3, is that a certain number of fitness evaluations has passed since the previous random grouping. Therefore, it was first necessary to find an appropriate number of fitness evaluations to use up in between the random groupings before comparing RG-DCPSO and RG-MCPSO to other algorithms. The performance measure used is the final average objective function value of the algorithm after 30 independent runs. The benchmark functions used were the functions from [22]. A brief comparison study was carried out which compared performance using 10, 30, 100, 200, 250, 300, 350, 400, 500, and 3000 objective function evaluations between random groupings. The asterisks in Table 1 indicate which value was found to have the best performance among those tested for each problem size, and were used for both RG-DCPSO and RG-MCPSO.

Table 1. Values used for random grouping condition

# of dimensions	30 FE	250 FE	350 FE	3000 FE
30				*
100	*	*		
500	*			
1000			*	

5   Compared Decomposition-Based Approaches

This section lists each of the additional decomposition-based approaches to CPSO which were compared to RG-DCPSO and RG-MCPSO: CPSO-S, MCPSO, DCPSO, recursive differential grouping (RDG) [21], and random adaptive grouping (RAG) [20]. These algorithms were selected because they are also decomposition-based, and have been used to compare to DCPSO and MCPSO in previous studies [2]. Values of $\alpha = 10^{-12}$ and $k = 10$ were used for RDG, because they were demonstrated to perform well in [21]. For RAG, a value of $T = 0.1 \times n_T$, and a sub-swarm size of 10 were used because Sopov et al. have demonstrated that these values lead to optimal results [20].

6   Experimental Results

This section summarizes the experimental results. Table 2 lists the points earned by each algorithm. "Sep." refers to the separable functions, "Single-Group" refers to single-group partially separable functions, $n_x/2m$ refers to $n_x/2m$-separable functions, n_x/m refers to n_x/m-separable functions, and "Non-Sep." refers to non-separable functions. "Total" sums up the points earned by each algorithm across all functions tested.

The points earned by each algorithm are listed in the order "W/L/T| Rank", where "W" indicates the number of wins, "L" indicates the number of losses, and "T" indicates the number of ties. "Rank" refers to the final ranking of each algorithm. The ranks should then be looked at column-wise to see which algorithm performed best for each benchmark type. The top-ranked algorithm has its rank indicated with a bold **1** for easier identification.

Table 2. Algorithm ranks (entries are given in the format W/L/T| Rank)

Algorithm name	Sep.	Single-Group	$n_x/2m$	n_x/m	Non-Sep.	Total
30 dimensions						
CPSO-S	6/5/6| 5	3/16/11| 7	8/11/10| 5	3/15/6| 6	10/0/8| 2	30/47/41| 4
DCPSO	11/4/3| 2	21/2/7| 1	21/3/6| 2	18/1/5| 1	5/5/8| 4	76/15/29| 2
RG-DCPSO	13/3/3| 1	20/2/9| 2	22/3/6| 1	18/1/5| 1	10/0/10| 1	83/9/33| 1
MCPSO	7/5/6| 3	4/15/11| 6	9/11/10| 4	4/15/5| 5	3/6/9| 5	27/52/41| 6
RG-MCPSO	7/5/6| 3	5/14/10| 5	9/11/10| 4	2/15/7| 7	5/3/8| 3	28/48/41| 5
RDG	5/11/2| 6	14/16/0| 3	13/15/2| 3	14/10/0| 3	4/14/0| 7	50/66/4| 3
RAG	1/17/0| 7	12/14/4| 4	1/29/0| 6	10/12/2| 4	2/11/5| 6	26/83/11| 7
100 dimensions						
CPSO-S	16/6/11| 3	10/16/4| 4	8/13/9| 4	6/13/5| 4	11/5/2| 2	51/53/31| 3
DCPSO	18/10/8| 4	23/2/5| 1	16/8/6| 2	16/7/1| 2	10/7/1| 3	83/34/21| 2
RG-DCPSO	24/7/10| 1	23/3/4| 2	30/0/1| 1	24/0/0| 1	18/0/0| 1	119/10/15| **1**
MCPSO	17/7/12| 2	8/17/5| 5	8/11/11| 3	6/13/5| 4	9/6/3| 4	48/54/36| 4
RG-MCPSO	10/16/8| 5	6/21/3| 7	7/19/3| 7	5/16/3| 6	6/12/0| 5	34/84/17| 6
RDG	11/25/0| 6	8/21/1| 6	7/17/6| 6	14/8/2| 3	4/14/0| 6	44/85/9| 5
RAG	3/28/5| 7	14/12/4| 3	10/18/2| 5	5/19/0| 7	2/16/0| 7	34/93/11| 7
500 dimensions						
CPSO-S	25/5/3| 1	6/16/8| 6	9/11/9| 5	5/11/8| 7	7/4/5| 4	52/47/33| 3
DCPSO	19/16/1| 5	24/3/3| 1	18/11/1| 2	12/9/3| 2	8/9/1| 5	81/48/9| 2
RG-DCPSO	27/12/0| 2	22/5/3| 2	23/7/1| 1	19/4/2| 1	12/6/2| 2	103/34 /8| **1**
MCPSO	21/9/6| 3	7/15/8| 5	10/10/10| 4	5/10/9| 6	9/4/5| 3	52/48/38| 4
RG-MCPSO	18/14/4| 4	8/14/8| 4	11/10/9| 3	6/10/7| 4	11/3/4| 1	54/51/32| 5
RDG	6/30/0| 6	5/25/0| 7	13/17/0| 6	12/10/2| 3	5/12/1| 6	41/94/3| 6
RAG	3/33/0| 7	18/22/0| 3	6/24/0| 7	9/14/1| 5	2/16/0| 7	38/109/1| 7
1000 dimensions						
CPSO-S	20/4/8| 2	6/16/16| 6	14/7/23| 4	10/10/26| 6	9/4/29| 4	68/41/102| 4
DCPSO	8/27/1| 6	19/6/6| 2	2/28/6| 7	0/23/7| 7	2/15/8| 7	31/99/28| 7
RG-DCPSO	23/12/5| 4	25/3/8| 1	20/9/11| 1	15/9/12| 1	13/7/12| 3	96/40/48| **1**
MCPSO	20/7/9| 3	7/13/19| 5	15/6/28| 2	13/7/32| 3	11/4/35| 2	66/37/123| 3
RG-MCPSO	23/5/8| 1	8/13/16| 4	15/6/25| 3	12/8/29| 4	12/2/33| 1	70/34/111| 2
RDG	10/25/1| 5	5/25/1| 7	16/14/1| 5	14/8/3| 2	6/11/4| 5	51/83/10| 5
RAG	6/30/0| 7	18/12/0/3	9/21/0 /6	11/10/3| 5	4/14/3| 6	48/87/6| 6

RG-DCPSO was consistently the top-performing algorithm across all dimension sizes that were tested. DCPSO was second in 30−, 100−, and 500−dimensional environments. RG-DCPSO was the top-performing algorithm for n_x/m, $n_x/2m$, and non-separable problems for 30− and 100−dimensional environments. DCPSO was ranked first for the single-group functions in 30−, 100−, and 500−dimensional environments, with RG-DCPSO being second. In 1000−dimensional spaces, RG-DCPSO was ranked first and DCPSO was ranked second for the single-group functions.

RG-MCPSO had poor relative performance for smaller-dimensional spaces, but improved as the size of the search space increased. RG-MCPSO took over for second position from DCPSO in 1000−dimensional problems. RG-MCPSO was the best-performing algorithm for the non-separable problems with 500 and 1000 dimensions. An important note is that while the PSO parameters selected for experimentation have been demonstrated to satisfy stability conditions, there is a range of possible values which could be used. Therefore, a possible next step would be to adjust the parameters of RG-MCPSO to see if this results in better performance.

7 Conclusion

The purpose of this paper was to incorporate random grouping into DCPSO and MCPSO. The final fitness values found by RG-DCPSO and RG-MCPSO were compared to those found by five other decomposition-based PSO methods. Search space sizes of $30, 100, 500$, and 1000 were used for comparison, and to demonstrate the ability of RG-DCPSO and RG-MCPSO to scale up to larger problems.

Results have shown that RG-DCPSO resulted in significantly improved performance for LSOPs. RG-MCPSO resulted for improved performance in large-scale non-separable objective functions. The better performance of RG-DCPSO is due to random grouping allowing for the greater exploration of variable dependencies.

In future work, RG-DCPSO and RG-MCPSO should be evaluated on objective functions in environments with more than 1000 dimensions, as well as on additional objective functions to ensure that they perform well in different environments. Additional testing should also be done to find the exact number of objective function evaluations which should be carried out between the random groupings in both DCPSO and MCPSO. The performance of RG-MCPSO improves as the number of dimensions increases, especially for the non-separable problems. Due to the stochastic nature of PSO algorithms, the choice of parameters used has a large impact on the final performance of the algorithm. Thus, experimenting with different PSO parameters which also satisfy stability conditions, especially in the case of RG-MCPSO, would be beneficial in demonstrating the full capabilities of the algorithms in optimizing functions in large-dimensional spaces.

References

1. Barry, W.: Generating aesthetically pleasing images in a virtual environment using particle swarm optimization. Ph.D. thesis, Brock University (2012)
2. Clark, M.: Comparative study on cooperative particle swarm optimization decomposition methods for large-scale optimization. Master's thesis, Brock University, March 2021. https://dr.library.brocku.ca/handle/10464/15031
3. Cleghorn, C.W., Engelbrecht, A.P.: Particle swarm convergence: an empirical investigation. In: Proceedings of the IEEE Congress on Evolutionary Computation, pp. 2524–2530. IEEE (2014)
4. Douglas, J., Engelbrecht, A.P., Ombuki-Berman, B.M.: Merging and decomposition variants of cooperative particle swarm optimization: new algorithms for large scale optimization problems. In: Proceedings of the 2nd International Conference on Intelligent Systems, Metaheuristics and Swarm Intelligence, pp. 70–77. ACM (2018)
5. Erwin, K., Engelbrecht, A.P.: Set-based particle swarm optimization for portfolio optimization. In: Dorigo, M., et al. (eds.) ANTS 2020. LNCS, vol. 12421, pp. 333–339. Springer, Cham (2020). https://doi.org/10.1007/978-3-030-60376-2_28
6. Hajihassani, M., Armaghani, D.J., Kalatehjari, R.: Applications of particle swarm optimization in geotechnical engineering: a comprehensive review. Geotech. Geol. Eng. **36**, 705–722 (2018)
7. Hereford, J.M.: A distributed particle swarm optimization algorithm for swarm robotic applications. In: IEEE International Congress on Evolutionary Computation, pp. 1678–1685. IEEE (2006)
8. Kennedy, J., Eberhart, R.: Particle swarm optimization. In: Proceedings of International Conference on Neural Networks, vol. 4, pp. 1942–1948 (1995)
9. Khare, A., Rangnekar, S.: A review of particle swarm optimization and its applications in solar photovoltaic system. Appl. Soft Comput. **13**(5), 2997–3006 (2013)
10. Kruskal, W.H., Wallis, W.A.: Use of ranks in one-criterion variance analysis. J. Am. Stat. Assoc. **47**(260), 583–621 (1952)
11. Li, X., Yao, X.: Cooperatively coevolving particle swarms for large scale optimization. IEEE Trans. Evol. Comput. **16**(2), 210–224 (2012)
12. Mann, H.B., Whitney, D.R.: On a test of whether one of two random variables is stochastically larger than the other. Ann. Math. Stat. **18**(1), 50–60 (1947)
13. Neethling, M., Engelbrecht, A.: Determining RNA secondary structure using set-based particle swarm optimization. In: Proceedings of the IEEE Congress on Evolutionary Computation (2006)
14. Oldewage, E.T.: The perils of particle swarm optimization in high dimensional problem spaces. Master's thesis, University of Pretoria (2017)
15. Oldewage, E.T., Engelbrecht, A.P., Cleghorn, C.W.: The merits of velocity clamping particle swarm optimisation in high dimensional spaces. In: Proceedings of the IEEE Symposium Series on Computational Intelligence, pp. 1–8 (2017)
16. Oldewage, E.T., Engelbrecht, A.P., Cleghorn, C.W.: Boundary constraint handling techniques for particle swarm optimization in high dimensional problem spaces. In: Dorigo, M., Birattari, M., Blum, C., Christensen, A.L., Reina, A., Trianni, V. (eds.) ANTS 2018. LNCS, vol. 11172, pp. 333–341. Springer, Cham (2018). https://doi.org/10.1007/978-3-030-00533-7_27
17. Oldewage, E.T., Engelbrecht, A.P., Cleghorn, C.W.: Movement patterns of a particle swarm in high dimensional spaces. Inf. Sci. **512**, 1043–1062 (2020)

18. Pluhacek, M., Senkerik, R., Viktorin, A., Kadavt, T., Zelinka, I.: A review of real-world applications of particle swarm optimization algorithm. In: Proceedings of the International Conference on Advanced Engineering Theory and Applications (2017)
19. Shi, Y., Eberhart, R.C.: Parameter selection in particle swarm optimization. In: Proceedings of Evolutionary Programming VII, pp. 591–600 (2005)
20. Sopov, E., Vakhnin, A., Semenkin, E.: On tuning group sizes in the random adaptive grouping algorithm for large-scale global optimization problems. In: Proceedings of the International Conference on Applied Mathematics Computational Science, pp. 134–13411 (2018)
21. Sun, Y., Kirley, M., Halgamuge, S.K.: A recursive decomposition method for large scale continuous optimization. IEEE Trans. Evol. Comput. **22**(5), 647–661 (2018)
22. Tang, K., Li, X., Suganthan, P.N., Yang, Z., Weise, T.: Benchmark functions for the CEC 2010 special session and competition on large-scale global optimization (2010)
23. Van den Bergh, F., Engelbrecht, A.P.: A cooperative approach to particle swarm optimization. IEEE Trans. Evol. Comput. **8**(3), 225–239 (2004)
24. Van der Merwe, D., Engelbrecht, A.: Data clustering using particle swarm optimization. In: Proceedings of IEEE Congress on Evolutionary Computation, vol. 1, pp. 215–220, December 2003
25. Yang, Z., Tang, K., Yao, X.: Large scale evolutionary optimization using cooperative coevolution. Inf. Sci. **178**(15), 2985–2999 (2008)
26. Zeng, T., et al.: Artificial bee colony based on adaptive search strategy and random grouping mechanism. Expert Syst. Appl. **192**, 116332 (2022)
27. Zhang, W., Ma, D., Wei, J., Liang, H.: A parameter selection strategy for particle swarm optimization based on particle positions. Expert Syst. Appl. **41**(7), 3576–3584 (2014)

Dynamic Spatial Guided Multi-Guide Particle Swarm Optimization Algorithm for Many-Objective Optimization

Weka Steyn[1] and Andries Engelbrecht[2][✉]

[1] Department of Industrial Engineering, Stellenbosch University,
Stellenbosch, South Africa
wekasteyn@gmail.com
[2] Department of Industrial Engineering and Computer Science Division,
Stellenbosch University, Stellenbosch, South Africa
engel@sun.ac.za

Abstract. The multi-guide particle swarm optimization (MGPSO) algorithm utilizes random tournament selection in determining the archive guide for the velocity update of a particle, choosing the least crowded solution of a static number of solutions in the external archive. This report aims to determine the feasibility of utilizing a linearly decreasing tournament size with the aim of improving initial exploration and final exploitation of the search space by the particle swarms. The archive guide for a given particle is determined from the nearest archive solutions with the aim of increasing swarm exploration efficiency. The proposed dynamic spatial MGPSO algorithm is compared with the original MGPSO algorithm and state-of-the-art algorithms specifically designed to solve many-objective optimization problems. The results show that the dynamic soatial guided MGPSO (DSG-MGPSO) scales well to many-objective problems, with performance very competitive to that of other many-objective optimization algorithms.

1   Introduction

The particle swarm optimization (PSO) algorithm is a metaheuristic swarm intelligence optimization algorithm, first proposed by Kennedy and Eberhart [10] to solve single-objective optimization problem by modelling the flocking behaviour of birds. The PSO algorithm was further developed in multi-objective variations used to solve multi-objective optimization problems (MOPs), including the multi-guide particle swarm optimization (MGPSO) algorithm proposed by Scheepers et al. [14]. The MGPSO algorithm was found to be very competitive with other multi-objective optimization algorithms (MOAs), including the non-dominated sorting genetic algorithm (NSGA-II) [4], multi-objective evolutionary algorithm (MOEA) [19], speed constraint multi-objective particle swarm optimization (SMPSO) algorithm [12], and velocity equated particle swarm optimization (VEPSO) [13] algorithm.

M. Dorigo et al. (Eds.): ANTS 2022, LNCS 13491, pp. 130–141, 2022.
https://doi.org/10.1007/978-3-031-20176-9_11

Steenkamp and Engelbrecht scaled the MGPSO algorithm to many-objective optimization problems (MaOPs) [17]. Erwin and Engelbrecht proposed the use of random control parameter sampling [6] from the MGPSO stability regions derived by Scheepers et al. [14]. This random sampling approach eliminated the need for computationally costly control parameter tuning. The MGPSO algorithm was found to perform competitively with other many-objective optimization algorithms (MaOAs) [17]. In an attempt to improve the scalability of the MGPSO algorithm to MaOPs, Steenkamp investigated the use of Knee-points [20]; however, this did not improve the performance of the MGPSO [16].

The MGPSO algorithm proposed by Scheepers et al. [14] utilizes a static archive selection size of two or three when determining the archive guide for a particle. This paper proposes the use of a linearly decreasing archive size, in conjunction with a spatial archive guide selection, as opposed to random selection, in an attempt to improve the performance of the MGPSO algorithm. The empirical results show that the proposed dynamic spatial guided MGPSO (DSG-MGPSO) perform very well compared with the original MGPSO and other many-objective algorithms.

Section 2 provides a brief overview of multi-objective optimization, the PSO algorithm and the MGPSO algorithm, providing figures, definitions and pseudo-code where needed. Section 3 provides greater insight to the proposed spatial archive, followed by Sect. 4, detailing the breakdown of the experimental procedure to be followed. Section 5 then showcases and discusses the obtained results. Lastly, the paper concludes with Sect. 6, providing a brief summary of the content discussed in the report and the obtained results.

2   Background

This section serves to provide all necessary information regarding multi-objective optimization problems and Pareto dominance (Sect. 2.1), many-objective optimization (Sect. 2.2), PSO (Sect. 2.3) and MGPSO (Sect. 2.4).

2.1   Multi-Objective Optimization

MOPs are optimization problems that have two or three conflicting and dependant objectives to be optimised. The solution for an MOP consists of multiple Pareto optimal solutions. A MOP is generally defined as [18]:

$$
\begin{aligned}
\text{minimize} \quad & \mathbf{f}(\mathbf{x}), \quad \mathbf{x} \in [x_{min}, x_{max}]^{n_x} \\
\text{subject to} \quad & \mathbf{g}_m(\mathbf{x}) = 0, \quad m = 1, \ldots, n_g \\
& \mathbf{h}_m(\mathbf{x}) \leq 0, \quad m = n_g + 1, \ldots, n_g + n_h
\end{aligned}
\tag{1}
$$

where $\mathbf{f}(\mathbf{x}) = (f_1(\mathbf{x}), \ldots, f_{n_k}(\mathbf{x}))$

The following definitions are important for dominance-based approaches towards solving multi- and many-objective optimization problems.

Definition 1: Pareto-Dominance. Assuming minimization, a decision vector $\mathbf{x}_1$ dominates a decision vector, $\mathbf{x}_2$ (i.e. $\mathbf{x}_1 \prec \mathbf{x}_2$), if and only if $\mathbf{x}_1$ is not worse than $\mathbf{x}_2$ in all objectives, i.e. $f_k(\mathbf{x}_1) \leq f_k(\mathbf{x}_2), \forall k = 1, \ldots, n_k$, and $\mathbf{x}_1$ is strictly better than $\mathbf{x}_2$ in at least one objective, i.e. $\exists k = 1, \ldots, n_k : f_k(\mathbf{x}_1) < f_k(\mathbf{x}_2)$.

Definition 2: Pareto-Optimal. A decision vector $\mathbf{x}^* \in F$ is Pareto-optimal if there does not exist a decision vector, $\mathbf{x} \neq \mathbf{x}^* \in F$ that dominates it. That is, $\nexists k : f_k(\mathbf{x}) < f_k(\mathbf{x}^*)$. An objective vector, $\mathbf{f}^*(\mathbf{x})$, is Pareto-optimal if $\mathbf{x}$ is Pareto-optimal.

Definition 3: Pareto-Optimal Set. The set of all Pareto-optimal decision vectors form the Pareto-optimal set P^*. That is, $P^* = \{\mathbf{x}^* \in F | \nexists \mathbf{x} \in F : \mathbf{x} \prec \mathbf{x}^*\}$.

Definition 4: Pareto-Optimal Front. Given the objective vector, $\mathbf{f}(\mathbf{x})$, and the Pareto-optimal solution set, P^*, then the Pareto-optimal front, $PF^* \subseteq O$, is defined as $PF^* = \{\mathbf{f} = (f_1(\mathbf{x}^*), f_2(\mathbf{x}^*), \ldots, f_{n_k}(\mathbf{x}^*)) | \mathbf{x}^* \in P^*\}$

2.2 Many-Objective Optimization

MaOPs consist of large numbers of objectives – at least four. According to Hughes, with an increasing number of objectives comes an increased number of non-dominated solutions, which decreases the ability of dominance-based algorithms to settle around the true Pareto-front [9]. Hughes hypothesized and proved that any Pareto-based optimization algorithm designed for multi-objective optimization, whilst effective, lose integrity as the number of objectives to be solved increases [9]. Due to the high computational cost of calculating accurate solutions to MaOPs, it is of great interest to scale relatively computationally inexpensive stochastic algorithms such as the MGPSO algorithm to accurately approximate the Pareto-fronts of MaOPs.

2.3 Particle Swarm Optimization

The particle swarm optimization (PSO) algorithm is a stochastic metaheuristic optimization algorithm inspired by natural flocks, developed by Kennedy and Eberhart [10], with the aim of solving single-objective optimization problems (SOPs). Movement of a particle in a swarm is influenced by its current, personal best, and neighbourhood best positions. Information about best positions found thus far is shared amongst particles in a swarm by use of neighbourhood topologies, the efficiencies of which were compared in [5,7]. The velocity and position update equations of the inertia PSO algorithm are [15]

$$v_i^d(t + 1) = wv_i^d(t) + c_1 r_{1i}^d(t)(y_i^d(t) - x_i^d(t)) + c_2 r_{2i}^d(t)(\hat{y}_i^d(t) - x_i^d(t)) \quad (2)$$

$$x_i^d(t + 1) = x_i^d(t) + v_i^d(t + 1) \quad (3)$$

where $v_i^d(t)$ and $x_i^d(t)$ represent the velocity and position of a particle i at iteration t in dimension d, respectively. The elements of the random vectors, $\mathbf{r}_1$ and $\mathbf{r}_2$, are sampled from a uniform distribution over $[0,1]$, and the control parameters c_1 and c_2 are user specified values which determine how much weight is given to a particle's personal best, $\mathbf{y}_i$, and neighbourhood best, $\hat{\mathbf{y}}_i$, position respectively.

2.4 Multi-Guide Particle Swarm Optimization

The multi-guide particle swarm optimization (MGPSO) algorithm is a multi-objective variation of the inertia PSO algorithm [15]. The MGPSO algorithm utilises n_k sub-swarms containing n_s particles each, and introduces an external archive of non-dominated solutions, which in turn serve as guides for the velocity update equation of the MGPSO algorithm, which is defined as follows [14]:

$$
\begin{aligned}
v_{i,k}^d(t+1) \quad = \quad & wv_{i,k}^d(t) + c_1 r_{1i,k}^d(t)(y_{i,k}^d(t) - x_{i,k}^d(t)) \\
+ \quad & \lambda_{i,k} c_2 r_{2i,k}^d(t)(\hat{y}_{i,k}^d(t) - x_{i,k}^d(t)) \\
+ \quad & (1 - \lambda_{i,k}) c_3 r_{3i,k}^d(t)(\hat{a}_{i,k}^d(t) - x_{i,k}^d(t))
\end{aligned}
\tag{4}
$$

where $\hat{a}_{i,k}^d(t)$ denotes the archive guide for dimension d of particle i in sub-swarm k at iteration t. The archive trade-off coefficient λ controls the amount of influence that the archive guide and neighbourhood best position has on the velocity of a particle. Elements of the vector, $\mathbf{r}_3$, are uniformly sampled from $[0,1]$ and c_3 is an additional control parameter.

The archive guide $\hat{a}_{i,k}^d(t)$ is randomly selected from the external archive of non-dominated solutions by means of tournament selection, where static tournament sizes of two or three are used [14]. The least crowded candidate solution is assigned as the archive guide to encourage exploration of the search space.

The MGPSO is summarized in Algorithm 1.

3 Proposed Dynamic Spatial Archive Guide

A spatial archive guide is proposed in the velocity update equation of the MGPSO algorithm. The MGPSO algorithm proposed by Scheepers et al. [14] randomly selects n_t number of solutions from the archive, of which the least crowded solution is selected as the archive guide for particle i. The archive solution partly determines the movement of the particle in the following iteration. The archive-guide of the velocity update equation subtracts $\mathbf{x}_i(t)$ from $\hat{\mathbf{a}}_i$. Theoretically, should $\hat{\mathbf{a}}_i$ be sufficiently far enough away from $\mathbf{x}_i(t)$, this can cause a strong positive acceleration of the particle in the direction of the assigned archive guide. While this ensures a thorough exploration of the search space, it is inefficient in the event that the particle at position $\mathbf{x}_i(t)$ is assigned an archive guide on the opposite end of the given search space, which can be more efficiently explored by a closer particle.

Algorithm 1. Multi-Guide Particle Swarm Optimization Algorithm

---

Input: Objective functions f_k for $k = 1, \ldots, n_k$
Output: Archive of non-dominated solutions

for $k \rightarrow 1$ to n_k do
  Initialize sub-swarm S_k to contain n_s number of particles
  for $i \rightarrow 1$ to n_s do
    Initialize personal best as $\mathbf{y}_{i,k} = \mathbf{x}_{i,k}$
    Evaluate $f_k(\mathbf{y}_{i,k})$
    Initialize velocity as $\mathbf{v}_{i,k} = 0$
    Initialize trade-off coefficients $\lambda_{i,k} \sim U(0,1)$
    Initialize neighbourhood best position $\hat{\mathbf{y}}_{i,k}$

for $t \rightarrow 1$ to n_t do
  for $k \rightarrow 1$ to n_k do
    for $i \rightarrow 1$ to n_s do
      if $f_k(\boldsymbol{x}_{i,k}(t)) < f_k(\boldsymbol{y}_{i,k}(t))$ then
        $\mathbf{y}_{i,k}(t) = \mathbf{x}_{i,k}(t)$
        if $f_k(\boldsymbol{y}_{i,k}(t)) < f_k(\hat{\boldsymbol{y}}_{i,k}(t))$ then
          $\hat{\mathbf{y}}_{i,k}(t) = \mathbf{x}_{i,k}(t)$

      if $\boldsymbol{x}_{i,k}(t)$ *is non-dominated* then
        if *archive is not at capacity* then
          insert $\mathbf{x}_{i,k}(t)$ into the archive
          remove dominated positions in the archive

        if *archive is at capacity* then
          remove most crowded position insert $\mathbf{x}_{i,k}(t)$ into the archive
          remove dominated positions in the archive

  for $k \rightarrow 1$ to n_k do
    for $i \rightarrow 1$ to n_s do
      Select $\hat{\mathbf{a}}_{i,k}(t)$ form archive using tournament selection
      for $d \rightarrow 1$ to n_d do
        Calculate $\mathbf{v}_{i,k}^d(t+1)$ using equation (4)
        $x_{i,k}^d(t+1) = x_{i,k}^d(t) + v_{i,k}^d(t+1)$

Return Archive

The proposed method addresses this potential inefficiency by making each particle aware of its proximity to every solution in the external archive, and only considering the n_t nearest solutions when determining the least crowded solution. When selecting the archive guide $\hat{\mathbf{a}}_{i,k}$ for each particle i in each sub-swarm S_k, the crowding distance of the external archive with respect to the selected archive guide is determined. For each particle, the Euclidean-distance, $e(\mathbf{x}_{i,k}(t), \mathbf{a}(t))$, to each solution, $\mathbf{a}(t)$, in the archive is calculated. The Euclidean distances are ranked in ascending order, and the external archive and the associated crowding distances are ranked accordingly. The n_t closest solutions are considered in the tournament selection, with a larger crowding distance being favoured.

4   Experimental Procedure

The performance of the dynamic spatial guided MGPSO (DSG-MGPSO) is compared against that of the controlling dominance area of solutions - speed constraint multi-objective particle swarm optimization (CDAS-SMPSO) [2], knee-point driven evolutionary algorithm (KnEA) [20], many-objective non-dominated sorting genetic algorithm III (NSGA-III) [3], and the many-objective evolutionary algorithm based on dominance and decomposition (MOEA/DD) [11]. For comparison, the DSG-MGPSO algorithm is also compared against a MGPSO with randomly sampled control parameter values, referred to as RMG-PSO. Both MGPSO algorithms sample control parameter values to satisfy the theoretically derived stability condition [6, 14],

$$0 < c_1 + \lambda c_2 + (1 - \lambda)c_3 < \cfrac{4(1 - w^2)}{1 - w + \cfrac{(c_1^2 + \lambda^2 c_2^2 + (1 - \lambda)^2 c_3^2)(1 + w)}{3(c_1 + \lambda c_2 + (1 - \lambda)c_3)^2}} \qquad (5)$$

with $|w| < 1$; w is uniformly sampled from $(-1, 1)$, λ is uniformly from $(0,1)$. The control parameters c_1, c_2 and c_3 are uniformly sampled from $(0,4)$.

Each algorithm is evaluated on 3, 5, 8, 10 and 15 objective WFG$_1$ to WFG$_9$ and DTLZ$_1$ to DTLZ$_7$ benchmark problems, and is executed for 30 independent runs of 2000 iterations. The 3, 5, 8, 10 and 15 objective problems are evaluated with 153, 126, 156, 110 and 135 candidate solutions respectively [17].

The solution sets achieved by each optimization algorithm are normalized in the range [0,1], and evaluated using the hyper-volume (HV) [21] with the Nadir point as reference, and the inverted generational distance (IGD) [1]. The mean values achieved for both HV and IGD are then compared using the wins/losses methodology proposed by Helbig and Engelbrecht [8]. This approach considers each environment period individually, and compares measures of performance for each algorithm across each individual change period. A Kruskal-Wallis test is used to confirm if a statistical significant difference exist between the different algorithms. If so, then pairwise Mann-Whitney-Wilcoxon rank sum tests with Hol correction is used to asses differences between each pair of algorithms. A win is rewarded to the superior algorithm and a loss to the inferior algorithm.

5   Empirical Analysis

This section discusses the results obtained from following the experimental procedure outlined in Sect. 4. Tables 1, 2, 3, 4 and 5 show the rankings of the algorithms for each of the evaluated benchmark problems. For each benchmark problem, the number of wins and losses achieved per algorithm are shown. Algorithms are ranked on the difference between wins and losses, with a rank of 1 being the best result. It is important to note that algorithms can tie for the same ranking, which indicates that there was no statistically significant difference between the mean HV or IGD values achieved by two or more algorithms. Each algorithm is given an overall (O) ranking for both HV and IGD per number of objectives.

Table 1. 3-objective and 5-objective DTLZ ranking tables

| | | 3-objective DTLZ | | | | | | | | | | | | | | | | 5-objective DTLZ | | | | | | | | | | | | | | | |
| | | HV | | | | | | | | IGD | | | | | | | | HV | | | | | | | | IGD | | | | | | | |
		1	2	3	4	5	6	7	O	1	2	3	4	5	6	7	O	1	2	3	4	5	6	7	O	1	2	3	4	5	6	7	O
CDAS-SMPSO	Wins	0	5	0	0	0	0	0	5	3	3	3	1	3	3	1	17	0	0	0	1	1	1	0	3	2	5	3	0	5	3	3	21
	Losses	5	0	5	4	3	4	5	26	2	2	2	4	2	2	2	16	5	5	5	4	4	4	5	32	1	0	2	5	0	2	2	12
	Rank	3	1	5	4	4	5	5	6	2	2	2	4	2	3	2	3	5	5	4	5	4	4	5	5	3	1	2	5	1	2	2	2
DSA-MGPSO	Wins	2	4	4	4	4	5	4	27	4	4	4	4	4	5	4	29	3	1	4	3	4	4	4	23	2	1	4	3	3	4	4	21
	Losses	0	1	0	0	0	0	0	1	0	0	0	0	0	0	0	0	1	3	0	0	0	0	0	4	1	3	0	1	1	0	0	6
	Rank	1	2	1	1	1	1	1	1	1	1	1	1	1	1	1	1	2	4	1	2	1	1	1	1	3	3	1	2	2	1	1	1
KnEA	Wins	2	2	3	3	0	3	2	15	2	2	2	3	2	2	1	14	5	3	1	0	0	0	3	12	5	3	1	1	0	2	0	12
	Losses	0	3	2	2	3	2	2	14	3	3	3	2	3	3	2	19	0	2	4	5	5	5	2	23	0	1	3	4	4	3	4	19
	Rank	1	4	2	2	4	3	3	3	3	3	3	2	3	4	2	4	1	3	3	6	5	5	2	4	1	2	3	4	4	3	4	4
MOEA/DD	Wins	1	1	1	2	2	2	2	11	1	1	1	2	1	1	1	8	2	4	2	3	3	3	1	18	1	3	1	5	2	1	2	15
	Losses	4	4	4	3	2	3	2	22	4	4	4	3	4	4	2	25	3	1	2	0	2	2	4	14	4	1	3	0	3	4	3	18
	Rank	2	5	4	3	2	4	3	4	4	4	4	3	4	5	2	5	3	2	2	2	2	2	4	2	5	2	3	1	3	4	3	3
NSGA-II	Wins	2	0	2	0	1	0	1	6	0	0	0	0	0	0	0	0	1	5	2	2	2	2	2	16	0	0	0	2	0	0	0	2
	Losses	0	5	3	4	3	4	4	23	5	5	5	5	5	5	5	35	4	0	2	3	3	3	3	18	5	5	5	3	4	5	4	31
	Rank	1	6	3	4	3	5	4	5	5	5	5	5	5	5	6	3	6	4	1	2	4	3	3	3	6	4	4	3	4	5	4	5
RMGPSO	Wins	2	3	4	4	4	4	4	25	4	4	4	4	4	4	4	28	3	1	4	3	4	4	4	23	2	1	4	3	3	4	4	21
	Losses	0	2	0	0	0	1	0	3	0	0	0	0	0	1	0	1	1	3	0	0	0	0	0	4	1	3	0	1	1	0	0	6
	Rank	1	3	1	1	1	2	1	2	1	1	1	1	1	2	1	2	2	4	1	2	1	1	1	1	3	3	1	2	2	1	1	1

5.1 HV Results

In terms of HV, the results are as follows: The CDAS-SMPSO algorithm performed worst overall for the 3-, 5- and 8-objective DTLZ benchmark problems. The DSG-MGPSO algorithm was the best overall performing algorithm, achieving seven best overall rankings for the 3-, 5- and 10-objective DTLZ and the 3-, 5-, 8- and 10-objective WFG benchmark problems. The DSG-MGPSO achieved a top three overall ranking for each of the evaluated benchmark problems in terms of HV, with no worst overall rankings. Similar results were achieved by the RMGPSO algorithm, with only three overall best rankings for the 3-,5- and 15-objective DTLZ benchmark problemss. The RMGPSO matched the performance of the DSG-MGPSO with the 5-objective DTLZ. The KnEA managed to achieve an overall top three rank for five of the 10 benchmark problems, with two overall worst rankings for the 8- and 15-objective WFG benchmark problems. The MOEA/DD was the worst performing algorithm, with five overall worst rankings for the 10- and 15-objective DTLZ, along with only two top three rankings. Lastly, the NSGA-III managed one overall best ranking for the 15-objective WFG benchmark.

Table 2. 8-objective and 10-objective DTLZ ranking tables

		8-objective DTLZ																10-objective DTLZ															
		HV								IGD								HV								IGD							
		1	2	3	4	5	6	7	O	1	2	3	4	5	6	7	O	1	2	3	4	5	6	7	O	1	2	3	4	5	6	7	O
CDAS-SMPSO	Wins	0	5	0	0	1	0	0	6	5	5	5	5	5	3	5	33	0	2	0	0	3	1	0	6	5	5	5	5	5	3	5	33
	Losses	5	0	5	5	2	5	5	27	0	0	0	0	0	0	0	0	5	0	5	3	2	4	5	24	0	0	0	0	0	2	0	2
	Rank	5	1	5	5	3	5	6	6	1	1	1	1	1	2	1	1	4	1	5	5	2	4	5	5	1	1	1	1	1	3	2	1
DSA-MGPSO	Wins	4	0	4	2	4	4	2	20	2	2	4	3	3	3	3	20	4	2	4	4	4	4	2	24	0	1	2	2	3	4	2	14
	Losses	0	3	0	2	0	0	3	8	1	2	1	1	1	0	1	7	0	0	0	0	0	0	2	2	3	2	2	2	1	0	2	12
	Rank	1	5	1	3	1	1	4	2	3	3	3	2	2	2	2	2	1	1	1	1	1	1	3	1	5	4	3	3	2	1	4	2
KnEA	Wins	2	0	1	1	0	1	5	10	1	0	1	2	0	1	1	6	2	2	1	3	1	2	4	15	3	4	1	4	0	2	1	15
	Losses	3	3	4	4	5	4	0	23	4	5	3	3	4	3	4	26	2	0	4	1	3	3	1	14	2	1	3	1	4	3	4	18
	Rank	3	5	4	4	5	4	1	5	5	5	4	4	4	4	4	5	2	1	4	3	3	3	2	3	3	2	5	2	4	3	5	3
MOEA/DD	Wins	3	4	3	5	2	3	1	21	2	4	1	1	2	1	2	13	2	0	2	0	1	0	1	6	4	0	4	1	2	0	3	14
	Losses	2	1	2	0	2	2	4	13	1	1	3	4	3	3	3	18	2	5	3	3	3	5	4	25	1	5	1	4	3	5	1	20
	Rank	2	2	2	1	2	2	5	3	3	2	4	5	3	4	3	4	2	3	3	5	3	5	4	6	2	6	2	4	3	5	2	4
NSGA-II	Wins	1	3	2	4	1	2	4	17	0	1	0	0	0	0	0	1	1	1	3	0	0	3	5	13	0	1	0	0	0	1	0	2
	Losses	4	2	3	1	3	3	1	17	5	4	5	5	4	5	5	33	4	4	2	3	5	2	0	20	3	2	5	5	4	4	5	28
	Rank	4	3	3	2	4	3	2	4	6	4	5	6	4	5	5	6	3	2	2	5	4	2	1	4	5	4	6	5	4	4	6	5
RMGPSO	Wins	4	0	4	2	4	4	3	21	2	2	3	3	3	3	3	19	4	2	4	3	4	4	2	23	0	1	1	2	3	4	2	13
	Losses	0	3	0	2	0	0	2	7	1	2	2	1	1	0	1	8	0	0	0	0	0	0	2	2	3	2	2	2	1	0	1	11
	Rank	1	5	1	3	1	1	3	1	3	3	3	2	2	2	2	3	1	1	1	2	1	1	3	2	5	4	4	3	2	1	3	2

Table 3. 15-objective DTLZ and 3-objective WFG ranking tables

		15-objective DTLZ																3-objective WFG																				
		HV								IGD								HV										IGD									
		1	2	3	4	5	6	7	O	1	2	3	4	5	6	7	O	1	2	3	4	5	6	7	8	9	O	1	2	3	4	5	6	7	8	9	O
CDAS-SMPSO	Wins	0	5	0	2	2	1	0	10	5	5	5	4	5	3	5	32	1	2	3	2	1	2	2	2	3	18	2	2	3	2	0	2	2	1	3	17
	Losses	5	0	5	3	2	4	5	24	0	0	0	0	0	2	0	2	3	2	2	3	3	3	3	3	2	24	2	2	2	3	4	3	3	3	2	23
	Rank	6	1	5	3	2	5	6	5	1	1	1	1	1	3	1	1	5	3	3	3	3	4	3	2	4	4	2	3	3	3	5	3	4	3	2	4
DSA-MGPSO	Wins	3	1	2	3	4	4	3	20	1	2	2	2	3	5	2	17	5	5	5	4	4	4	5	4	4	40	4	5	5	3	4	4	3	4	4	36
	Losses	0	1	1	1	0	0	2	5	2	1	1	2	1	0	2	9	0	0	0	0	0	0	0	0	0	0	0	0	0	1	0	0	0	0	0	1
	Rank	2	3	3	2	1	1	3	2	4	3	3	2	2	1	3	2	1	1	1	1	1	1	1	1	1	1	1	1	1	2	1	1	2	1	1	1
KnEA	Wins	2	2	2	5	2	3	4	20	1	2	1	4	0	2	1	11	0	2	1	3	3	3	3	3	2	20	0	2	1	5	3	3	3	3	2	22
	Losses	3	1	1	0	2	1	1	9	2	3	4	0	5	3	4	21	5	2	4	2	2	2	2	2	3	24	5	2	3	0	2	2	0	2	3	19
	Rank	4	2	3	1	2	3	2	3	4	4	4	5	1	5	4	6	3	5	2	2	2	3	3	3	3	3	3	5	3	4	1	2	2	2	3	3
MOEA DD	Wins	3	0	2	0	1	0	1	7	4	0	2	1	2	0	4	13	1	1	0	0	0	0	0	0	0	2	2	1	0	0	0	0	0	0	0	3
	Losses	1	5	0	4	4	5	4	23	1	5	1	4	3	5	1	20	2	4	5	5	5	4	5	5	4	39	1	4	5	5	3	4	5	3	4	34
	Rank	3	5	2	4	3	6	5	6	2	6	3	3	3	6	2	4	4	4	6	5	4	4	6	5	4	6	2	4	5	5	4	4	6	4	4	6
NSGA-III	Wins	1	1	1	0	0	2	5	10	0	1	0	0	1	1	0	3	4	0	2	1	1	0	1	1	0	10	1	0	1	1	1	0	1	0	0	5
	Losses	4	2	4	4	5	3	0	22	5	3	5	5	4	4	5	31	1	5	3	4	3	4	4	4	4	32	1	5	3	4	3	4	4	4	4	32
	Rank	5	4	4	4	4	1	4	6	4	6	5	6	4	4	5	5	6	2	5	4	4	3	4	5	4	5	5	4	4	3	4	5	5	4	4	5
RM-GPSO	Wins	4	1	4	3	4	3	2	21	1	3	2	2	3	4	2	17	2	4	4	4	4	4	4	4	4	34	2	4	4	3	4	3	4	4	4	32
	Losses	0	1	0	1	0	0	3	5	2	1	1	2	1	1	2	10	2	1	1	0	0	0	1	0	0	5	3	1	1	1	0	0	0	0	0	6
	Rank	1	3	1	2	1	2	4	1	4	2	3	2	2	2	3	3	3	2	2	1	1	1	2	1	1	2	4	2	2	2	1	1	2	1	1	2

Table 4. 5-objective and 8-objective WFG ranking tables

		5-objective WFG																				8-objective WFG																			
		HV										IGD										HV										IGD									
		1	2	3	4	5	6	7	8	9	O	1	2	3	4	5	6	7	8	9	O	1	2	3	4	5	6	7	8	9	O	1	2	3	4	5	6	7	8	9	O
CDAS-SMPSO	Wins	1	3	3	4	0	0	0	0	2	13	1	0	3	3	2	2	1	0	2	14	0	3	3	4	1	1	1	1	2	16	5	2	3	5	4	4	3	4	4	34
	Losses	2	2	2	1	5	5	5	5	1	28	2	2	2	2	3	3	3	5	1	23	5	2	2	1	2	4	3	4	1	24	0	2	2	0	1	1	1	0	0	7
	Rank	3	3	3	2	3	4	4	6	2	4	2	3	2	3	4	3	3	5	3	5	4	3	3	2	3	4	5	3	3	4	1	3	2	1	2	2	2	1	1	1
DSA-MGPSO	Wins	4	5	5	1	1	4	3	5	2	30	4	5	4	0	0	0	0	1	0	14	4	5	5	1	4	4	4	4	4	35	1	5	4	1	1	1	0	4	0	17
	Losses	0	0	0	2	1	0	1	0	1	5	0	0	0	3	4	4	3	3	4	21	0	0	0	2	0	0	0	0	0	2	3	0	0	3	2	3	3	0	4	18
	Rank	1	1	1	4	2	1	2	1	2	1	1	1	1	5	5	4	4	4	5	4	1	1	1	4	1	1	1	1	1	1	3	1	1	5	4	4	3	1	5	3
KnEA	Wins	0	2	1	5	5	3	5	3	5	29	0	0	0	5	5	5	5	5	5	30	3	1	1	0	0	0	0	0	0	5	0	0	0	1	0	0	0	0	3	4
	Losses	5	3	4	0	0	2	0	2	0	16	5	2	4	0	0	0	0	0	0	11	2	3	4	5	5	5	5	5	5	39	4	4	4	4	6	5	3	4	3	6
	Rank	5	4	5	1	1	2	1	3	1	3	3	3	3	4	1	1	1	1	1	1	2	4	5	6	5	6	5	6	4	6	4	4	4	4	6	5	3	4	3	6
MOEA DD	Wins	1	0	0	1	1	1	1	2	0	7	1	0	0	4	3	3	3	4	2	20	1	0	0	5	2	2	1	2	1	14	3	2	0	4	5	5	5	3	3	30
	Losses	3	5	5	2	1	3	3	3	4	29	2	2	4	1	2	1	1	1	1	15	3	5	5	0	2	3	1	2	4	25	1	2	4	1	0	0	0	2	0	10
	Rank	4	6	6	4	2	3	3	4	3	6	2	3	4	2	3	2	2	2	3	2	3	5	6	1	2	3	4	2	5	5	2	3	4	2	1	1	1	2	2	2
NSGA-III	Wins	2	1	2	0	1	1	1	1	0	9	1	0	2	0	4	3	3	3	2	18	1	1	2	1	1	3	2	2	2	15	3	0	2	2	1	3	3	1	2	17
	Losses	2	4	3	5	1	3	3	4	4	29	2	2	3	3	1	1	1	2	1	16	3	3	3	2	3	2	1	2	2	21	1	4	3	2	2	2	1	3	3	21
	Rank	2	5	4	6	2	3	3	5	3	5	2	3	3	5	2	2	2	3	3	3	3	4	4	4	4	2	3	2	4	3	2	4	3	3	4	3	2	3	4	4
RM-GPSO	Wins	4	4	4	1	1	4	3	4	2	27	4	4	4	0	0	0	0	1	0	13	4	4	4	1	4	4	2	4	3	30	1	4	4	0	1	0	0	1	0	11
	Losses	0	1	1	2	1	0	1	1	1	8	0	1	0	3	4	4	4	3	4	23	0	1	1	2	0	0	0	0	0	4	3	1	0	5	2	4	3	3	4	25
	Rank	1	2	2	4	2	1	2	2	2	2	1	2	1	5	5	4	5	4	5	6	1	2	2	4	1	1	2	1	2	2	3	2	1	6	4	6	3	3	5	5

Table 5. 10-objective and 15-objective WFG ranking tables

		10-objective WFG																				15-objective WFG																			
		HV										IGD										HV										IGD									
		1	2	3	4	5	6	7	8	9	O	1	2	3	4	5	6	7	8	9	O	1	2	3	4	5	6	7	8	9	O	1	2	3	4	5	6	7	8	9	O
CDAS-SMPSO	Wins	0	1	3	0	1	1	1	2	0	9	4	2	3	5	3	5	2	5	3	32	0	3	2	1	0	0	1	1	1	9	4	2	3	5	4	5	3	4	5	35
	Losses	3	3	2	1	3	3	2	2	2	21	0	3	2	0	1	0	1	0	1	8	3	0	3	4	5	4	4	4	4	31	0	1	2	0	0	0	0	0	0	3
	Rank	3	4	3	4	3	3	2	2	3	4	1	3	2	1	2	1	2	1	2	1	3	1	4	4	3	5	5	5	4	5	1	3	2	1	1	1	2	1	1	1
DSA-MGPSO	Wins	4	5	5	0	4	4	4	4	4	34	1	5	4	0	2	0	0	0	0	12	4	2	3	2	2	2	2	3	2	22	1	4	4	0	3	0	0	0	0	16
	Losses	0	0	0	1	0	0	0	0	0	1	3	0	0	4	2	4	4	1	4	22	0	0	0	2	0	1	1	0	3	7	3	0	0	3	1	4	4	0	4	19
	Rank	1	1	1	4	1	1	1	1	1	1	3	1	1	4	3	4	3	4	4	4	1	2	2	3	1	3	3	2	3	2	3	1	1	3	3	5	5	1	4	3
KnEA	Wins	3	0	1	0	3	3	0	1	0	11	0	0	1	4	4	3	5	0	5	22	3	0	1	0	1	0	0	0	0	5	0	0	1	0	0	2	2	0	3	8
	Losses	2	3	4	1	2	2	5	4	3	26	5	5	4	1	1	0	1	0	1	18	2	5	5	2	5	2	5	6	6	6	4	5	4	3	5	3	4	3	2	5
	Rank	2	5	5	4	2	3	3	4	5	5	4	5	4	2	1	2	1	4	1	2	2	5	5	2	5	2	6	6	5	6	4	5	4	3	5	3	4	3	2	5
MOEA DD	Wins	0	0	0	5	0	0	1	0	1	7	3	3	0	2	2	3	2	0	3	18	0	1	0	5	2	2	5	2	4	21	4	2	0	3	0	2	4	1	3	19
	Losses	3	4	5	0	5	5	2	5	2	31	2	1	5	2	0	1	1	1	1	14	3	1	5	0	0	1	0	1	0	11	0	1	5	1	4	1	0	2	1	15
	Rank	3	6	6	1	4	4	2	4	2	6	2	2	5	3	2	2	2	4	2	2	3	3	6	1	1	3	1	3	1	4	1	3	5	2	5	3	1	2	2	2
NSGA-III	Wins	0	3	2	0	1	1	1	2	0	10	4	1	2	2	0	2	2	0	2	15	0	2	3	4	2	5	2	2	4	24	3	1	2	3	2	2	3	0	2	18
	Losses	3	2	3	1	3	3	2	2	2	21	0	4	3	2	5	3	1	1	3	22	3	0	0	1	0	0	1	2	0	7	2	4	3	1	3	1	1	3	3	21
	Rank	3	3	4	4	3	3	2	2	3	3	1	4	3	3	5	3	2	4	3	3	3	2	2	2	1	1	3	4	1	1	2	4	3	2	4	3	4	3	4	3
RM-GPSO	Wins	4	4	4	0	4	4	4	4	4	32	1	3	4	0	1	0	0	0	0	9	4	1	3	2	2	2	2	4	3	23	1	2	4	0	3	0	0	0	0	10
	Losses	0	1	1	1	0	0	0	0	0	3	3	1	0	4	3	4	4	1	4	24	0	3	0	2	0	1	1	0	2	9	3	0	0	3	0	4	4	2	4	20
	Rank	1	2	2	4	1	1	1	1	1	2	3	2	1	4	4	4	3	4	4	5	1	4	2	3	1	3	3	1	2	3	3	2	1	3	2	5	5	3	4	4

5.2 IGD Results

In terms of IGD, the CDAS-SMPSO algorithm was the overall best performing algorithm, with a total of six overall best rankings for the 8-, 10- and 15-objective benchmark problems for both DTLZ and WFG. Furthermore, the CDAS-SMPSO algorithm managed to achieve a best three ranking for eight of the ten benchmark problems evaluated. The DSG-MGPSO was the second best performing algorithm, performing identical to the CDAS-SMPSO; however with a lower number of overall best rankings, which were for the 3- and 5-objective DTLZ and the 3-objective WFG benchmark problems. The IGD results highlight the advantage of using the spatial archive guide section, as the RMGPSO only managed one overall best ranking for the 5-objective DTLZ, and then as a tie with the DSG-MGPSO. Furthermore, the RMGPSO only managed six top three rankings as opposed to the eight from the DSG-MGPSO, as well as two overall worst rankings for the 5- and 10-objective WFG benchmark problems. The KnEA managed to achieve one overall best ranking for the 5-objective WFG benchmark problem and two worst overall rankings for the 8- and 15-objective WFG benchmark problems. The KnEA managed to achieve five top three overall rankings. The MOEA/DD achieved similar results to the KnEA, with no overall best rankings and only one overall worst ranking for the 3-objective WFG. The NSGA-III is the worst performing algorithm, with the least number of top three best rankings and five overall worst rankings for all of the DTLZ benchmark problems.

6 Conclusions

This article proposed the use of a spatial archive guide selection in an attempt to improve the scalability of the MGPSO algorithm to MaOPs. The proposed DSG-MGPSO algorithm was compared against other specifically designed MaOAs and a random archive guide selected RMGPSO as a baseline. Each algorithm was evaluated on the DTLZ and WFG benchmark problems for 3-, 5-, 8- 10- and 15-objectives. The obtained solution sets were evaluated for both HV and IGD, and compared using the wins/losses process by Helbig and Engelbrecht [8], and tabulated in ranking tables.

Both MGPSO variations were found to perform very well with regards to HV when compared against the other MaOAs, with the spatial archive guide selection providing slightly better performance over the regular RMGPSO algorithm. In terms of HV, the spatial archive guide selection used in the DSG-MGPSO far outperformed the RMGPSO algorithm, generally providing a more well distributed solution set. However, the DSG-MGPSO was only the second best performing algorithm in terms of IGD after the CDAS-SMPSO algorithm – though better than RMGPSO.

Overall, the spatial archive guide selection successfully scaled the MGPSO algorithm to better solve MaOPs, providing solution sets that are consistently close to the true Pareto front. However, whilst these solutions are generally well distributed, more work is needed in order to improve the distribution of solution sets found by the DSG-MGPSO.

Acknowledgements. The authors thank the National Research Foundation (NRF) for providing funding and the Centre for High Performance Computing (CHPC) for providing computational resources.

References

1. Coello Coello, C.A., Reyes Sierra, M.: A study of the parallelization of a coevolutionary multi-objective evolutionary algorithm. In: Monroy, R., Arroyo-Figueroa, G., Sucar, L.E., Sossa, H. (eds.) MICAI 2004. LNCS (LNAI), vol. 2972, pp. 688–697. Springer, Heidelberg (2004). https://doi.org/10.1007/978-3-540-24694-7_71
2. De Carvalho, A.B., Pozo, A.: Measuring the convergence and diversity of cdas multi-objective particle swarm optimization algorithms: a study of many-objective problems. Neurocomputing **75**(1), 43–51 (2012)
3. Deb, K., Jain, H.: An evolutionary many-objective optimization algorithm using reference-point-based nondominated sorting approach, part I: solving problems with box constraints. IEEE Trans. Evol. Comput. **18**(4), 577–601 (2013)
4. Deb, K., Pratap, A., Agarwal, S., Meyarivan, T.: A fast and elitist multiobjective genetic algorithm: NSGA-II. IEEE Trans. Evol. Comput. **6**(2), 182–197 (2002)
5. Engelbrecht, A.P.: Particle swarm optimization: global best or local best? In: Proceedings of the 11th Brazilian Congress on Computational Intelligence, pp. 124–135. IEEE (2013)
6. Erwin, K., Engelbrecht, A.P.: A tuning free approach to multi-guide particle swarm optimization. In: Proceedings of the IEEE Swarm Intelligence Symposium (2021)
7. Günther, M., Nissen, V.: A comparison of neighbourhood topologies for staff scheduling with particle swarm optimisation. In: Mertsching, B., Hund, M., Aziz, Z. (eds.) KI 2009. LNCS (LNAI), vol. 5803, pp. 185–192. Springer, Heidelberg (2009). https://doi.org/10.1007/978-3-642-04617-9_24
8. Helbig, M., Engelbrecht, A.P.: Analysing the performance of dynamic multi-objective optimization algorithms. In: Proceedings of the IEEE Congress on Evolutionary Computation, pp. 1531–1539 (2013)
9. Hughes, E.J.: Evolutionary many-objective optimisation: many once or one many? In: Proceedings of the IEEE Congress on Evolutionary Computation, vol. 1, pp. 222–227 (2005)
10. Kennedy, J., Eberhart, R.: Particle swarm optimization. In: Proceedings of the International Conference on Neural Networks, vol. 4, pp. 1942–1948 (1995)
11. Li, K., Deb, K., Zhang, Q., Kwong, S.: An evolutionary many-objective optimization algorithm based on dominance and decomposition. IEEE Trans. Evol. Comput. **19**(5), 694–716 (2014)
12. Nebro, A.J., Durillo, J.J., Garcia-Nieto, J., Coello, C.C., Luna, F., Alba, E.: Smpso: a new pso-based metaheuristic for multi-objective optimization. In: Proceedings of the IEEE Symposium on Computational Intelligence in Multi-Criteria Decision-Making, pp. 66–73 (2009)
13. Parsopoulos, K.E., Vrahatis, M.N.: Particle swarm optimization method in multi-objective problems. In: Proceedings of the ACM Symposium on Applied Computing, pp. 603–607 (2002)
14. Scheepers, C., Engelbrecht, A.P., Cleghorn, C.W.: Multi-guide particle swarm optimization for multi-objective optimization: empirical and stability analysis. Swarm Intell. **13**(3), 245–276 (2019)
15. Shi, Y., Eberhart, R.: A modified particle swarm optimizer. In: Proceedings of the IEEE International Conference on Evolutionary Computation, pp. 69–73 (1998)
16. Steenkamp, C.: Multi-guide particle swarm optimization for many-objective optimization problems. Master's thesis, Stellenbosch University (2021)
17. Steenkamp, C., Engelbrecht, A.P.: A scalability study of the multi-guide particle swarm optimization algorithm. Swarm Evol. Comput. **66**, 100943 (2021)

18. Van Veldhuizen, D.A., Lamont, G.B.: Evolutionary computation and convergence to a pareto front. In: Late Breaking Papers at the Genetic Programming Conference, pp. 221–228 (1998)
19. Zhang, Q., Li, H.: MOEA/D: a multiobjective evolutionary algorithm based on decomposition. IEEE Trans. Evol. Comput. **11**(6), 712–731 (2007)
20. Zhang, X., Tian, Y., Jin, Y.: A knee point-driven evolutionary algorithm for many-objective optimization. IEEE Trans. Evol. Comput. **19**(6), 761–776 (2014)
21. Zitzler, E., Thiele, L.: Multiobjective optimization using evolutionary algorithms - a comparative case study. In: Proceedings of the International Conference on Parallel Problem Solving from Nature, pp. 292–301 (1998)

Extracting Symbolic Models of Collective Behaviors with Graph Neural Networks and Macro-Micro Evolution

Stephen Powers[1]([✉])[ID], Joshua Smith[2][ID], and Carlo Pinciroli[1][ID]

[1] Department of Robotics Engineering, Worcester Polytechnic Institute,
Worcester, MA, USA
{spowers2,cpinciroli}@wpi.edu
[2] Worcester, MA, USA
smith.josh.95@proton.me

Abstract. Collective behaviors are typically hard to model. The scale of the swarm, the large number of interactions, and the richness and complexity of the behaviors are factors that make it difficult to distill a collective behavior into simple symbolic expressions. In this paper, we propose a novel approach to symbolic regression designed to facilitate such modeling. Using raw and post-processed data as an input, our approach produces viable symbolic expressions that closely model the target behavior. Our approach is composed of two phases. In the first, a graph neural network (GNN) is trained to extract an approximation of the target behavior. In the second phase, the GNN is used to produce data for a *nested* evolutionary algorithm called *macro-micro evolution (MME)*. The macro layer of this algorithm selects candidate symbolic expressions, while the micro layer tunes its parameters. Preliminary experimental evaluation shows that our approach outperforms competing solutions for symbolic regression, making it possible to extract compact expressions for complex swarm behaviors.

1 Introduction

Biological collective systems, such as fish schools and bird flocks, typically involve large numbers of individuals engaging in massively numerous interactions, with non-linear effects that produce complex and coordinated swarm-level behaviors. Identifying simple, yet effective, models to capture such interactions is typically difficult and it involves non-trivial data analysis and hypothesis testing [3].

In this paper, we propose an automatic approach to symbolic regression designed to facilitate modeling of collective behaviors. Given the raw data of the collective behavior, e.g., the trajectories of the agents or information about their pairwise interactions, our approach derives a human-readable symbolic expression that best approximates the input data. Our work is applicable to both natural sciences (e.g., to discover new models of collective behaviors), and in

---

J. Smith—Independent Researcher.

© Springer Nature Switzerland AG 2022
M. Dorigo et al. (Eds.): ANTS 2022, LNCS 13491, pp. 142–154, 2022.
https://doi.org/10.1007/978-3-031-20176-9_12

engineering (e.g., to extract approximate models of collective behaviors optimized in a centralized manner).

Several works aim to produce interpretable behavioral models obtained through optimization and evolutionary methods. Notable examples include the variants of AutoMoDe [1,8], novelty search to discover collective behaviors in minimalistic robots [2], grammatical evolution [7], and behavioral trees [11,15]. All these works produce a desired (and unknown) behavior for artificial agents (robots), rather than extract interpretable models from existing data.

To the best of our knowledge, no work has been explicitly devoted to symbolic regression for collective behaviors. Our main contribution is to propose the first method to perform this task. Our approach is composed of two phases:

1. In the first phase, the input data, both raw and post-processed, is used to train a graph neural network (GNN).
2. In the second phase, a symbolic expression is extracted using a nested genetic algorithm we refer to as *macro-micro evolution* (MME). The fitness of the symbolic expression is calculated using data generated by the GNN.

The power of our method comes from the combination of these two phases. GNNs offer embeddings that are ideal to capture the many facets of collective phenomena, such as pairwise interactions among agents, as well as diffusive and aggregative processes across agents. The MME decomposes the problem of system identification into two nested problems: *(i)* identification of the structure of a parametric expression; and *(ii)* estimation of the parameter values.

For validation, we show that our approach can capture three compelling variants of collective behaviors: *(i)* Hexagonal shape formation among homogeneous agents; *(ii)* Square shape formation among heterogeneous agents; *(iii)* Coordinated motion behaviors (i.e., boids [17]), which combine pairwise interactions and data aggregation.

We compare our approach with several state-of-the-art methods for symbolic regression. Our analysis reveals that, while hexagonal shape formation can be solved by most methods, our method solves it more efficiently. In addition, our method is capable to attack problems, such as square shape formation and coordinated motion, which are not solvable by existing methods.

Our paper is organized as follows: in Sect. 2 we review existing work on symbolic regression and highlight the novelty of our approach. In Sect. 3 we present our approach. In Sect. 4 we report the results of our analysis. We conclude the paper in Sect. 5.

2   Related Work

Symbolic regression is ubiquitous in science and engineering. Given a data set, the objective is to produce a symbolic expression (i.e., a mathematical formula) that closely fits the data. The constant growth, in both size and number, of available datasets makes it increasingly more desirable to automate this process. Depending on the nature and size of the dataset, the search for suitable symbolic

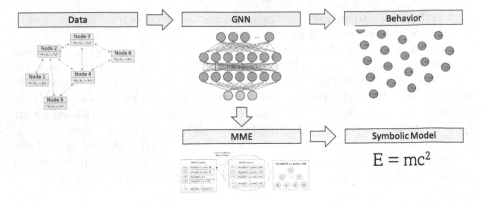

Fig. 1. Overview of our overall approach. An overview of MME can be seen in Fig. 2.

expressions can be hard. With complex, non-linear phenomena, the search space of possible expressions may suffer from combinatorial explosion.

A common approach to symbolic regression involves genetic algorithms (GAs) [16]. An expression is represented as a syntax tree formed by mathematical operators, fundamental functions, and operands. The GA modifies the expressions through mutation and crossover. At each iteration, the expressions are ranked according to metrics such as accuracy and expression complexity [4,9,14,23,24]. A prominent approach is Epsilon-Lexicase Selection [12].

AI Feynman [21] tames combinatorial explosion through a diverse suite of techniques. Extensive tests performed on well-known physics equations yielded near-perfect performance, surpassing Epsilon-Lexicase Selection. However, our analysis in Sect. 4 shows that the performance of AI Feynman on datasets of collective behaviors is far from satisfactory.

Neural networks [10,13,18,20,22] are another approach to model collective behaviors. In particular, Cranmer *et al.* proposed a method to perform symbolic regression in particle systems that uses a GNN as a surrogate model [6]. Similarly to our approach, the output of the GNN is fed to an GA designed for symbolic regression. Cranmer *et al.* employed *Eureqa* - a commercial suite of machine learning algorithms - and a self-developed Python-based library (*PySR*) [5]. Both Eureqa and PySR evolve the expression tree along with its parameters in a single step. We build upon this work to show that a *nested, hierarchical* GA greatly enhances the performance of symbolic regression.

3 Methodology

3.1 System Overview

As mentioned, our approach is comprised of two phases as shown in Fig. 1. In the first, we train a GNN to act as a surrogate model to replicate the target collective behavior. In the second, we employ a nested genetic algorithm, MME, to select appropriate symbolic expressions. The macro layer selects a parametric expression, while the micro layer tunes the expression's parameters. Data generated by the GNN is used in the MME to evaluate the fitness of each candidate expression. All code can be found at https://github.com/NESTLab/Extracting-Symbolic-Models-of-Collective-Behaviors.

3.2   Input: Data and Priors

Our approach accepts raw data as input. For example, in modeling collective motion, one could feed our approach with the poses of the individual agents. However, it is often possible to hypothesize that certain post-processed expressions of the raw data might be handy, e.g., distance between agents or its inverse. We call these expressions *priors*. Including priors eliminates the need to "rediscover" them, making symbolic regression faster and more accurate. We highlight that, in practice, there is no harm in providing priors that are unrelated to the final expression, because both phases are able to ignore the unnecessary inputs. This makes it possible to create "libraries" of common priors taken from the literature, taking advantage of our approach to identify the correct priors. This creates an interesting feedback loop for researchers engaged in model identification, as the type of inputs selected for the final expression offer insight on the nature of the mechanisms involved in the target collective behavior.

3.3   Phase 1: Graph Neural Networks

Graphs are natural models of swarm behaviors. Each node typically represents an agent and edges capture pairwise interactions and relationships. GNNs are neural networks superimposed on a graph structure. In a GNN, nodes, edges, and even the entire graph are associated with neural networks, respectively referred to as the *node model* (ϕ^n), the *edge model* or *message function* (ϕ^e), and the *graph model* (ϕ^g). The node model captures the individual behavior of an agent i as a result of internal state and pairwise interactions with neighbors, e.g., the sum of virtual forces in hexagonal formation. The output of the node model is the *node state* x_i. The edge model represents the interaction between two agents i and j, e.g., the Lennard-Jones potential [19]. Its output is called a *message* y_{ij}. The graph model aggregates the states x_i and messages y_{ij} to yield a swarm-level representation z, e.g., the regularity of the hexagonal pattern. These models are the ultimate targets of symbolic regression, depending on the application at hand. From a mathematical standpoint, a GNN can be formalized as follows:

$$x_i[t+1] = \phi^n(x_i[t], \sum_{j \in \mathcal{N}_i} y_{ij}[t])$$
$$y_{ij}[t+1] = \phi^e(x_i[t], x_j[t])$$
$$z[t+1] = \phi^g(x_i[t+1], \ldots, y_{ij}[t+1], \ldots)$$

where $\mathcal{N}_i$ indicates the neighborhood of agent i and t is the iteration index.

3.4   Phase 2: Symbolic Modeling with Macro-Micro Evolution

Fitness Function. MME is a nested evolutionary algorithm in which the outer (macro) evolution selects the structure of an expression λ, and the inner (micro) evolution tunes its parameters. Both evolutions use the same fitness function $f(\lambda)$, which linearly combines two functions $f^c(\cdot)$ and $f^a(\cdot)$ of the *complexity* and the *accuracy* of λ according to a weight $\rho \in [0, 1]$:

$$f(\lambda) = \rho \cdot f^c(\text{complexity}(\lambda)) + (1 - \rho) \cdot f^a(\text{accuracy}(\lambda)). \tag{1}$$

Complexity. To measure the complexity of an expression λ, we first associate a cost to each operator. For example, additions and subtractions, being simple operators, could be assigned a cost of 2; exponentiation of the form 2^λ could be assigned a cost of 20. The complexity of an expression is then calculated as the sum of the costs of each operator that appears in it. The user can define what operators should be considered, along with the costs to using them. As a parameter to MME, the user can also assign a target complexity τ for the final expression, which indicates the acceptable complexity of the final expression. Tuning τ is a way to prevent overfitting. The function $f^c(\cdot)$ that transforms the complexity is defined as

$$f^c(\lambda) = \frac{\max(0, \text{complexity}(\lambda) - \tau)}{\tau}.$$

Accuracy. We determine an individual's accuracy via the Mean Square Error (MSE) between the answers generated by an expression λ and the data generated by the GNN. Any expression λ that, once evaluated, results in an undefined or infinite value, or a complex number, is discarded. To prevent large values of MSE from rendering the contribution of complexity negligible, we define

$$h(\lambda) = \frac{\text{MSE}(\lambda)}{\text{MSE}(\lambda^{\text{worst}})}$$

where λ^{worst} represents the least accurate expression within the subset of surviving expressions of the generation.

Micro-Macro Evolution. At the start of each generation, MME performs *selection* and *duplicate removal*. Selection involves picking a subset of high-fitness expressions (the "parents") and the creation of "children" through crossover and mutation. Two individuals are considered duplicates if they share the same structure, regardless of the value of their parameters. Two passes of scoring then occur. The first pass ranks the new children and the surviving parents. Those that are bound to survive to the next generation are then run through the second pass, i.e., the micro-evolutionary algorithm, to determine the optimal parameter values as shown in Fig. 2. While this could theoretically result in long run times, in practice the micro evolution reaches convergence in a small number of generations. No automatic stopping criteria is used; MME is allowed to complete the number of generations specified.

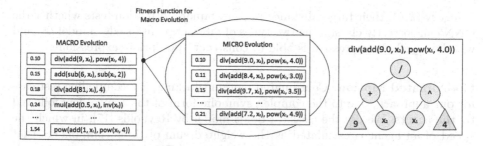

Fig. 2. Representation of the difference between macro and micro phases of MME. Circular nodes (structural) are modified in the macro phase while triangular nodes (parameters) are modified in the micro phase.

4 Experimental Evaluation

To validate the effectiveness of our approach, we considered three case studies with complementary features: hexagonal shape formation, square shape formation, and coordinated motion. A video that showcases the resulting collective behaviors found by our approach against the original models is available at https://youtu.be/r6r5GBH7Iuk.

Hexagonal Shape Formation. Shape formation is a well-studied problem in both natural and artificial swarms. The typical model that achieves hexagonal shapes imagines a swarm of identical agents immersed in an isotropic virtual potential field, in which the distance between pairs of agents induces an interaction force between them. The Lennard-Jones (LJ) potential [19] is one of the most common models of interaction due to its simplicity:

$$V_{\mathrm{LJ}}(r; \delta, \epsilon) = 4\epsilon \left(\left(\frac{\delta}{r} \right)^{12} - \left(\frac{\delta}{r} \right)^{6} \right)$$

where r is the current distance between the agents, δ is the distance at which the potential is zero, and ϵ is the depth of the minimum. Differently from the electric and gravity potentials, the LJ potential has both an attractive and a repulsive component. The LJ potential is a good testbed to verify that the edge model ϕ^e of a GNN can correctly capture the interaction force between identical individuals, and that MME can derive a satisfactory approximation of the virtual interaction force $F_{\mathrm{LJ}} = -\partial V_{\mathrm{LJ}}(r; \delta, \epsilon)/\partial r$.

Square Shape Formation. A straightforward extension of hexagonal formation is square formation. We divide the agents into two categories, e.g., by color, and use different LJ potentials depending on the color of the agents. If two interacting agents belong to different categories (i.e., have different colors, referred to as *non-kin*), their target distance is $\sigma = \sqrt[6]{\delta}$; if the agents belong to the same category (*kin*), their target distance is $\sqrt{2}\,\sigma$. Square formation tests whether the GNN can correctly classify the two types of interaction in its edge model ϕ^e, and whether symbolic regression is able to construct appropriate expressions.

Coordinated Motion. Coordinated motion (flocking) is a compelling test case for our approach, due to the complex symbolic form of the control law followed by the agents. We use the classical boids model by Reynolds [17], in which the speed of an agent is calculated as the weighted sum of three components that account for separation, alignment, and cohesion. For an agent, *separation* is defined as the average of the repulsion forces to neighbors that are closer than a certain threshold. *Alignment* is defined as the average of the velocities ($\vec{v}_j$) of the neighbors j of an agent. *Cohesion* is a unit vector that points to the centroid of the position of the neighbors. Combination of these three terms results in Eq. 2 where C, S, and A are user-defined weighted values of the cohesion, separation, and alignment terms respectively, $|\mathcal{N}|$ is the number of neighbors, $\vec{x}_j$ is the position of a neighbor in a boid's local coordinate frame, and $||\vec{x}_j||$ its length:

$$F_{\text{boids}}(\vec{x}_j, \ldots, \vec{v}_j, \ldots) = \frac{1}{|\mathcal{N}|} \sum_{j \in \mathcal{N}} \left(C\frac{\vec{x}_j}{||\vec{x}_j||} - S\frac{\vec{x}_j}{||\vec{x}_j||^2} + A\vec{v}_j \right). \qquad (2)$$

Coordinated motion allows us to verify the ability of a GNN to capture pair-wise inter-agent interaction in the edge model ϕ^e, as well as the aggregation of such interaction in the node model ϕ^n.

Data Generation. We followed a similar methodology across the three case studies. In all of them, we ran simulations to generate a sufficient amount of data. The agents were represented as holonomic point-masses operating in two dimensions with coordinates ranging between 0 and 1 m. Motion wrapped around the environment boundaries, making it a torus. For simplicity, the mass of each robot was set to 1 kg, and we used a double integrator to determine dynamics. The actuation was the acceleration vector of each robot. Sensing and communication were assumed noiseless, and their range was 0.5 m. The σ parameter for hexagonal shape formation was set to 0.13 m. For square shape formation, the parameters were $\sigma_{\text{kin}} = 0.13$ m and $\sigma_{\text{non-kin}} = \sqrt{2}\,\sigma_{\text{kin}}$. As for boids, we set $C = 2$, $S = 75$, and $A = 3$. We used 20 agents for the shape formation experiments and 50 for boids. Overall, for each setup, we ran 250 simulations, each 25 simulated seconds long. We recorded data at 10 Hz for shape formation experiments and 30 Hz for boids. After the simulations, we post-processed positional and angular data to be between 0 and 1 for all inputs. All data passed to the GNN was represented in Cartesian coordinates.

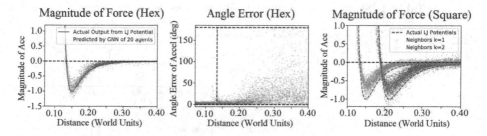

Fig. 3. The outputs of the GNN relative to the actual LJ potentials for the hexagonal (left) and square formations (right), as well as the errors of the angle of the output vector of the GNN in the hexagonal formation (middle)

4.1 Accuracy of GNN Models

GNN Configuration. We employed the same type of GNN in every experiment. The GNN used 4 fully connected layers: input and output layers whose sizes depend on the case study, and two hidden ones with 300 neurons each.

Hexagonal Lattice. We trained a GNN for 200 epochs with the Adam optimizer. To validate its performance, we ran the trained GNN with two inputs. The first input represents an agent at the origin of the world, and the second represents an agent at a random distance from the first. The output from the GNN represents the virtual force on the first agent expressed in Cartesian coordinates. Figure 3 (left) compares the magnitude of the force vector due to the original LJ potential used in simulation with 4,500 random outputs from the GNN, showing remarkable similarity between the two. Figure 3 (middle) reports the error in the angle of the force vector between the GNN and the reference vector. The error is next to zero in the range $[0, 0.2]$ m, which corresponds to the area where the interaction between agents is most significant. The error increases with distance beyond this range.

Square Lattice. We established the same setup for the square lattice case. We obtained the same amount of data as was obtained in the hexagonal lattice experiment, with the addition of edge attributes. Connections between kin neighbors were given an attribute of 1, while non-kin had an attribute of 2. We generated 10,000 pairs of nodes separated by random distances (between 0.07 m and 0.4 m) and provided them as input to the GNN. 5,000 data points contained edge attributes of 1, and 5,000 data points contained an edge attribute of 2. The magnitude of the forces generated by the GNN compared to the reference are reported in Fig. 3 (right). The GNN correctly categorized the kin and non-kin interactions, showing acceptable accuracy in capturing both potentials.

Table 1. Symbolic models found with the considered approaches.

Case study	Target equation	Algorithm	Resulting equation
Hex	$\left(\dfrac{1.2e-10}{x^{12}}\right) - \left(\dfrac{2.2e-5}{x^6}\right)$	MME	$\left(\dfrac{8e-9}{x^{10.07}}\right) - \left(\dfrac{9.8e-6}{x^{6.54}}\right)$
		PySR	$\dfrac{-\left(0.42 - \dfrac{0.06}{x}\right)}{(x-0.02)\left(8.14e8x^{11.66} - x + 0.272\right)} - 0.04$
		EpLex	$2.38x - 1.3 + \left(\dfrac{0.15}{x}\right)$
		AIF	$\left(5.6e-5\left(x + \dfrac{x^{0.5}}{-(x+2)}\right)\right)^{0.5}$
Square (Kin)	$\left(\dfrac{7.84e-9}{x^{12}}\right) - \left(\dfrac{1.7e-4}{x^6}\right)$	MME	$\left(\dfrac{6.8e-7}{x^{9.75}}\right) - \left(\dfrac{1.9e-5}{x^{7.75}}\right)$
Square (Non-Kin)	$\left(\dfrac{1.2e-10}{x^{12}}\right) - \left(\dfrac{2.2e-5}{x^6}\right)$	MME	$\left(\dfrac{1.58e-9}{x^{10.67}}\right) - \left(\dfrac{4e-6}{x^{6.79}}\right)$
Boids	$2\dfrac{\vec{x}}{||\vec{x}||} - \left(\dfrac{75}{||\vec{x}||}\right)\dfrac{\vec{x}}{||\vec{x}||} + 3\dot{\vec{x}}$	MME	$0.59\dfrac{\vec{x}}{||\vec{x}||} - \left(\dfrac{1}{||\vec{x}||}\right)\dfrac{\vec{x}}{||\vec{x}||} + \left(\dfrac{1}{||\dot{\vec{x}}||}\right)\dot{\vec{x}}$

Boids. For the boids experiment, we initially attempted to train the GNN using solely raw data, but observed degraded performance. We then decided to provide the network with priors. These were the distance and velocity vectors ($\vec{x}$ and $\dot{\vec{x}}$) of a neighbor relative to the individual of interest, as well as the magnitudes ($||\vec{x}||$ and $||\dot{\vec{x}}||$) and the inverse of the magnitudes($1/||\vec{x}||$ and $1/||\dot{\vec{x}}||$). We also included the normalized ($\vec{x}/||\vec{x}||$ and $\dot{\vec{x}}/||\dot{\vec{x}}||$) version of these vectors. An example of the resulting behavior compared to the reference is in the aforementioned video.

4.2 Symbolic Models

We compared MME to three other state-of-the-art symbolic regression algorithms: AIFeynman (AIF) [21], Epsilon-Lexicase (EpLex) [12], and PySR [5]. For all three evolutionary algorithms (MME, PySR, and EpLex), we used a population size of 4,000, and limited the operators to add, subtract, multiply, divide, and power. Each run was allowed a maximum of 200 generations. We capped to 3 and 15 the minimum and maximum number of operands in an expression for EpLex. AIFeynman was set up differently due to its capabilities. The algorithm—to the best of our knowledge—does not consider power operators; as such, the only operators given to it were add, subtract, multiply, divide, negate, and invert. We specified the maximum number of polynomial terms to 6, and allowed the interpolating neural network to train up to 200 epochs.

Hexagonal Lattice. To test the effectiveness of using symbolic regression to reverse engineer the data generated by a GNN, we reused the 4,500 points shown in Fig. 3 (left) as input to all four algorithms. Each algorithm was run 30 times on the same data. We set a target complexity τ of 12 for MME, where the average cost of operations used was equal to the arity of the operation, with the exception of the power operator in which the exponent was an operation instead of a constant being 20 instead of 2.

We calculated the error using the MSE in which all values were clipped between -1 and 1. These specific values allowed for easier analysis. PySR

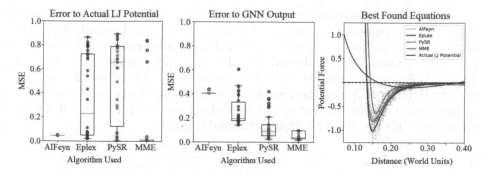

Fig. 4. The error from 30 runs of each evolutionary algorithm related to the actual Lennard-Jones expression (left) and the GNN-generated output (middle) as well as the best output equation from each algorithm (right).

and EpLex created several solutions containing asymptotic sections within the domain of interest. This yielded very high errors in these sections, which skewed the results significantly. The errors from the 30 experiments are shown in Fig. 4 in relation to the actual LJ potential used in simulation and also to the GNN-generated output data. The best expression plotted in Fig. 4 is that which has the lowest MSE relative to the GNN output data. The best expression found within the 30 runs for each of the four algorithms is also shown in Table 1. It should be noted that AIFeynman resulted in low MSE solely due to the fact that complex numbers were ignored in this analysis.

As seen in Table 1, the expressions generated by MME are remarkably similar to the target equation in structure. The only difference between the resulting expression and the target expression are the parameters, which, in a practical scenario, may be manually tuned as needed. No other state-of-the-art algorithm finds any expression remotely similar in structure to the target equation. Even if the found expressions are technically accurate in terms of MSE, they are unrecognizable when compared to the original reference.

Square Lattice. Considering the similarities between the square and hexagonal shape formations, only MME was tasked with finding the resulting equations shown in Table 1. Once again, MME finds symbolic expressions identical in structure to the target equations. This case, however, provides an interesting observation into the resulting expressions parameters. While the parameters between the resulting expressions and the target expressions are different, in each case, the ratio between kin and non-kin are very similar, which results in a behavior that is indistinguishable from the original.

Boids. We used MME to find a symbolic expression from the data from the GNN and the 12 priors described in Sect. 4.1. After running MME 10 times on this data, we sorted solutions by complexity first and then by MSE. The top equation was simplified manually and can be found in Table 1. While not identical to the target equation, the resulting expression shows a strong similarity—each of the three terms (cohesion, separation, and alignment) can be clearly seen in the final expression. The final expression does not fully reproduce the observed flocking behavior of boids, but we believe this to be due to the weights assigned to each term. Specifically, the weight of the separation term was found to be rather small compared to that of the original equation which results in a tight formation. This can easily be fixed by manual tuning.

5   Conclusion

We presented an automatic approach to extract symbolic models of collective behaviors. Our approach combines GNNs to approximate unknown network functions from data and grammatical evolution to manipulate symbolic expressions. By employing MME, a nested genetic algorithm, we reproduced expressions that closely match the references. We validated our approach using three non-trivial case studies: hexagonal and square pattern formation, and collective motion. Our approach works well where the state-of-the-art struggles.

Our approach does not remove the need for expert knowledge and ingenuity in deriving models of collective behaviors from real data. Hypothesis testing and experiment design remain in the hands of the researchers. However, automatically producing viable candidate expressions facilitates the job. The expressions we can produce are *compact*: our approach explicitly promotes short expressions, which are human-readable and easier to analyze. Furthermore, our approach offers the means to understand which parts of the input (i.e., raw data or priors with a generic set of functions) matter. This offers informative feedback to drive better hypothesis testing and experiment design.

Future work includes replacing the MSE with alternate methods of determining the accuracy of a signal, such as dynamic time warping and cross correlation coefficients. Other machine learning techniques such as Turing Learning and generative adversarial networks may also be used.

Acknowledgments. This work was funded by a DCRG grant from MathWorks, Inc. Results in this paper were obtained in part using a high-performance computing system acquired through NSF MRI grant DMS-1337943 to WPI.

References

1. Birattari, M., Ligot, A., Francesca, G.: AutoMoDe: a modular approach to the automatic off-line design and fine-tuning of control software for robot swarms. In: Pillay, N., Qu, R. (eds.) Automated Design of Machine Learning and Search Algorithms. NCS, pp. 73–90. Springer, Cham (2021). https://doi.org/10.1007/978-3-030-72069-8_5
2. Brown, D.S., Turner, R., Hennigh, O., Loscalzo, S.: Discovery and exploration of novel swarm behaviors given limited robot capabilities. In: Groß, R., et al. (eds.) Distributed Autonomous Robotic Systems. SPAR, vol. 6, pp. 447–460. Springer, Cham (2018). https://doi.org/10.1007/978-3-319-73008-0_31

3. Camazine, S., Deneubourg, J.L., Franks, N.R., Sneyd, J., Theraulaz, G., Bonabeau, E.: Self-Organization in Biological Systems. Princeton Studies in Complexity. Princeton (2003)
4. Chen, Q., Zhang, M., Xue, B.: Feature selection to improve generalization of genetic programming for high-dimensional symbolic regression. IEEE Trans. Evol. Comput. **21**(5), 792–806 (2017). https://doi.org/10.1109/tevc.2017.2683489
5. Cranmer, M.: PySR: fast & parallelized symbolic regression in Python/Julia (2020). https://doi.org/10.5281/zenodo.4041459
6. Cranmer, M.D., et al.: Discovering symbolic models from deep learning with inductive biases. CoRR abs/2006.11287 (2020). https://arxiv.org/abs/2006.11287
7. Ferrante, E., Duéñez-Guzmán, E., Turgut, A.E., Wenseleers, T.: GESwarm: grammatical evolution for the automatic synthesis of collective behaviors in swarm robotics. In: Proceedings of the 15th Annual Conference on Genetic and Evolutionary Computation, GECCO 2013, pp. 17–24. Association for Computing Machinery, New York (2013). https://doi.org/10.1145/2463372.2463385
8. Francesca, G., et al.: AutoMoDe-chocolate: automatic design of control software for robot swarms. Swarm Intell. **9**(2), 125–152 (2015). https://doi.org/10.1007/s11721-015-0107-9
9. Huang, Z., Zhong, J., Feng, L., Mei, Y., Cai, W.: A fast parallel genetic programming framework with adaptively weighted primitives for symbolic regression. Soft. Comput. **24**(10), 7523–7539 (2019). https://doi.org/10.1007/s00500-019-04379-4
10. Kaufmann, R., Gupta, P., Taylor, J.: An active inference model of collective intelligence. Entropy **23**(7) (2021). https://doi.org/10.3390/e23070830, https://www.mdpi.com/1099-4300/23/7/830
11. Kuckling, J., Ligot, A., Bozhinoski, D., Birattari, M.: Behavior trees as a control architecture in the automatic modular design of robot swarms. In: Dorigo, M., Birattari, M., Blum, C., Christensen, A.L., Reina, A., Trianni, V. (eds.) ANTS 2018. LNCS, vol. 11172, pp. 30–43. Springer, Cham (2018). https://doi.org/10.1007/978-3-030-00533-7_3
12. La Cava, W., Spector, L., Danai, K.: Epsilon-lexicase selection for regression. In: Proceedings of the Genetic and Evolutionary Computation Conference 2016 (2016). https://doi.org/10.1145/2908812.2908898
13. Li, Q., Gama, F., Ribeiro, A., Prorok, A.: Graph neural networks for decentralized multi-robot path planning. CoRR abs/1912.06095 (2019). http://arxiv.org/abs/1912.06095
14. Motta, F.A., Freitas, J.M.D., Souza, F.R.D., Bernardino, H.S., Oliveira, I.L.D., Barbosa, H.J.: A hybrid grammar-based genetic programming for symbolic regression problems. In: 2018 IEEE Congress on Evolutionary Computation (CEC) (2018). https://doi.org/10.1109/cec.2018.8477826
15. Neupane, A., Goodrich, M.: Learning swarm behaviors using grammatical evolution and behavior trees. In: Proceedings of the Twenty-Eighth International Joint Conference on Artificial Intelligence, pp. 513–520. International Joint Conferences on Artificial Intelligence Organization, Macao (2019). https://doi.org/10.24963/ijcai.2019/73
16. Orzechowski, P., La Cava, W., Moore, J.H.: Where are we now? In: Proceedings of the Genetic and Evolutionary Computation Conference (2018). https://doi.org/10.1145/3205455.3205539, http://dx.doi.org/10.1145/3205455.3205539
17. Reynolds, C.W.: Flocks, herds and schools: a distributed behavioral model. In: SIGGRAPH 1987: Proceedings of the 14th Annual Conference on Computer Graphics and Interactive Techniques, pp. 25–34 (1987). https://doi.org/10.1145/37401.37406

18. Ried, K., Müller, T., Briegel, H.J.: Modelling collective motion based on the principle of agency: General framework and the case of marching locusts. PLOS One **14**(2), 1–21 (2019). https://doi.org/10.1371/journal.pone.0212044
19. Smit, B.: Phase diagrams of Lennard-Jones fluids. J. Chem. Phys. **96**(11), 8639–8640 (1992). https://doi.org/10.1063/1.462271
20. Tolstaya, E., Gama, F., Paulos, J., Pappas, G., Kumar, V., Ribeiro, A.: Learning decentralized controllers for robot swarms with graph neural networks. In: Kaelbling, L.P., Kragic, D., Sugiura, K. (eds.) Proceedings of the Conference on Robot Learning. Proceedings of Machine Learning Research, 30 October–01 November 2020, vol. 100, pp. 671–682. PMLR (2020). https://proceedings.mlr.press/v100/tolstaya20a.html
21. Udrescu, S.M., Tegmark, M.: AI Feynman: a physics-inspired method for symbolic regression. Sci. Adv. **6**(16), eaay2631 (2020). https://doi.org/10.1126/sciadv.aay2631, https://www.science.org/doi/abs/10.1126/sciadv.aay2631
22. Ward, C.R., Gobet, F., Kendall, G.: Evolving collective behavior in an artificial ecology. Artif. Life **7**(2), 191–209 (2001). https://doi.org/10.1162/106454601753139005
23. White, T., Salehi-Abari, A.: A swarm-based crossover operator for genetic programming. Proceedings of the 10th Annual Conference on Genetic and Evolutionary Computation - GECCO 2008 (2008). https://doi.org/10.1145/1389095.1389356
24. Zhong, J., Feng, L., Cai, W., Ong, Y.: Multifactorial genetic programming for symbolic regression problems. IEEE Trans. Syst. Man Cybern. Syst. **50**, 4492–4505 (2020)

Learning Resilient Swarm Behaviors
via Ongoing Evolution

Aadesh Neupane[✉] and Michael A. Goodrich

Department of Computer Science, College of Physical and Mathematical Sciences,
Brigham Young University, Provo, UT, USA
adeshnpn@byu.edu, mike@cs.byu.edu

Abstract. Grammatical evolution can be used to learn bio-inspired solutions to many distributed mulitagent tasks, but the programs learned by the agents are often not resilient to perturbations in the world. Biological inspiration from bacteria suggests that ongoing evolution can enable resilience, but traditional grammatical evolution algorithms learn too slowly to mimic rapid evolution because they utilize only vertical, parent-to-child genetic variation. Prior work with the BeTr-GEESE grammatical evolution algorithm showed that individual agents who use both vertical and lateral gene transfer rapidly learn programs that perform one step in a multi-step problem even though the programs cannot perform all required subtasks. This paper shows that BeTr-GEESE can use ongoing evolution to produce resilient collective behaviors on two goal-oriented spatial tasks, foraging and nest maintenance, in the presence of different types of perturbation. The paper then explores when and why BeTr-GEESE succeeds, emphasizing two potentially generalizable properties: modularity and locality. Modular programs enable real-time lateral transfer, leading to resilience. Locality means that the appropriate phenotypic behaviors are local to specific regions of the world (spatial locality) and that recently useful behaviors are likely to be useful again in the near future (temporal locality).

1 Introduction

Bees, ants, termites, and other biological collectives efficiently solve complex problems without centralized control like finding a new site, foraging, nest-building, and protecting the colony, even when the environment fluctuates [21,60]. Such biological collectives *resiliently* accomplish tasks[1] in the presence of various perturbations that arise in the environment. Research has identified various resilience mechanisms including stress-induced adaptation [39,50], local interaction [21], task switching [59], lateral transfer [34], and modularity [71].

The purpose of this paper is to identify potentially generalizable properties that can enable grammatical evolution to use ongoing evolution to produce

---

[1] Resilient task performance differs from ecological resilience in which population sizes show resilience to variations [22] and from stability-based definitions of resilience in which some property of a collective remains in a locally stable region [24].

© Springer Nature Switzerland AG 2022
M. Dorigo et al. (Eds.): ANTS 2022, LNCS 13491, pp. 155–170, 2022.
https://doi.org/10.1007/978-3-031-20176-9_13

resilient swarm behaviors. Evolutionary approaches are powerful tools for learning bio-inspired swarm behaviors [12,15,79]. Grammatical evolution (GE) is a type of algorithmic evolution where evolutionary operators act on a given grammar to learn individual agent programs from the grammar. GE has been used to evolve swarm behaviors [18,43,44], and most demonstrations first evolve solutions and then deploy those learned solutions as fixed strategies. These fixed strategies can fail or degrade when perturbations are introduced into the environment.

Biology suggests solutions to overcome performance degradation of fixed strategies including stressed induced mutation, lateral gene transfer, and continuous evolution in bacteria [23]. A simple view of rapid adaptation is (a) that individual agents learn modular, circumstance-specific behaviors, and (b) that collective diversity allows suitable module exchange when circumstances change [30,76]. Ongoing evolution is unlikely to increase the resilience of many GE algorithms for two reasons. First, many GE algorithms learn too slowly to rapidly adapt, as demonstrated by the low rate of learning successful behaviors [19]. Second, the fitness of many collective behaviors requires significant coordination among agents, making it difficult to apportion fitness to the individual agents trying to learn how to contributed to the collective task. Carefully constructed fitness functions (e.g., intrinsic and extrinsic motivators [44,62,77]) help solve the second problem but are unlikely to be as useful in the presence of perturbations since new fitness functions might be needed for each perturbation type.

A curious phenomenon in prior work on the BeTr-GEESE grammatical evolution algorithm suggests that the algorithm can be adapted to successfully apply lateral gene transfer to produce collective resilience. Specifically, BeTr-GEESE agents successfully perform collective foraging and nest maintenance *while they are evolving*, but when learning stops the collective performs poorly [45]. Individual BeTr-GEESE agents do not learn programs that are sophisticated enough to perform all required subtasks but instead rapidly learn modular behaviors that perform only one subtask. The collective succeeds by using "time-multiplexing" in which agents switch behaviors by laterally exchanging modules, allowing all subtasks to be performed [45]. Time-multiplexing is a form of *lateral gene transfer* [48] in which genetic material transfers between organisms, in contrast to *vertical gene transfer* from parent to child.

This paper explores how BeTr-GEESE uses lateral gene transfer to produce resilient swarm behaviors in two distributed, *divisible and additive*[2] spatial tasks: foraging and nest maintenance. Resilience is first demonstrated by applying various types of perturbations during evolution and then measuring resulting performance. The concepts of *modularity* and *locality* are then used to explain how resilience emerges. *Modularity* in evolutionary algorithms means geneotype-to-phenotype mappings tend to associate specific phenotypic characteristics with specific genes, in contrast to "general purpose" genes that exhibit complex phenotypes [76]. The *divisible and additive* nature of foraging and nest maintenance mean that individual agents can evaluate the fitness of modular behaviors with-

---

[2] *Divisible* and *additive* multiagent tasks can be broken into subtasks achievable by individual programs that each contribute to the group problem to be solved [65].

out requiring the cooperation of many agents. *Locality* is a concept from the field of trace compression and cache design in computer architecture [57, 63] in which useful bytes of data cluster in time (temporal locality) and in adjacent memory cells (spatial locality). In a multiagent collective solving a spatial task, *temporal locality* means that a (modular) behavior that has been useful in the recent past is likely to be useful again soon, and *spatial locality* means that successful (modular) behaviors are likely to be localized to certain regions of the world.

2   Related Work

The ability of biological collectives to solve problems with partial, uncertain information has motivated AI researchers to mimic their behaviors [6, 40, 47, 55, 56]. One way to create collective algorithms is to collect data from natural colonies and then create mathematical models that can be used in algorithms [46, 67, 68]. Another way is to use evolutionary techniques to evolve agent behaviors [11].

Evolutionary robot systems require the creation of agent controllers: (i) state-machines [18, 29, 51, 52], (ii) neural networks [7, 14, 38, 72], (iii) behavior trees [32, 33], and (iv) controllers learned through genetic or grammatical evolution [4, 18, 31, 42]. Individuals in a swarm do not need to possess complex capabilities to evolve effective swarm behaviors [31]. Even with favorable controller choices, evolutionary algorithms, and fitness functions [41], evolved collective behaviors often degrade when tested with real robots or in presence of uncertainties [26].

Modularity contributes to evolving resilient behaviors because (i) modular organizations permit changes to one module without perturbing other modules and (ii) modules can be combined and reused to create new functions [1, 2, 76, 78]. In a modular system, a module has more frequent interaction within the subsystem than outside the subsystem [61], so *modularity* is the measure of interaction between different components in a system [53, 61]. For example, a highly modular grammar enabled a GE algorithm to evolve better multiagent solutions [69]. Evolving resilience might require additional evolutionary operations, such as lateral gene transfer [25, 35, 54]. Lateral transfer allows single agents to efficiently evolve complex behaviors when rewards are sparse and delayed [16, 37].

There are many evolutionary algorithms designed to learn resilient swarm and multiagent behaviors [3, 5, 27, 36, 74, 75]. Unfortunately, high fitness is not equivalent to resilient behaviors and fittest individuals are easily disrupted by genetic changes [64]. To the best of our knowledge, this paper is the first to evaluate the resilience of a grammatical evolution algorithm using ongoing evolution.

3   BeTr-GEESE Overview

BeTr-GEESE agents [45] use *sense-act-update* evolution steps to learn individual behaviors or "programs" from a bio-inspired task grammar. During the *sense* phase, agents exchange genes with (nearby) agents. The definition of "nearby" is controlled by the *grid size* (GS) parameter, and the willingness to transfer genes is controlled by the *interaction probability* (IP). During the *act* phase, an agent queries its storage pool to determine whether the pool size exceeds its *storage threshold* (ST) parameter. If the threshold is exceeded, agents apply the select-crossover-mutate genetic operations to the gene pool. During the *update* phase, an agent replaces its current gene if there is a new gene with higher fitness. BeTr-GEESE agents discard all other genes after updating and begin again.

Like other GE algorithms, BeTr-GEESE encodes genes as a sequence of integer *codons*. The codon sequence specifies the order in which grammar productions are used to produce the agent controller phenotype. The BeTr-GEESE grammar (see appendix) implements a behavior tree (BT) that has a postcondition, precondition, action (PPA) structure [8], with leaf nodes that either test basic properties of the environment (productions (7, 11)) or perform basic actions like moving or picking up objects (production (14)). The names in productions (7, 11, 15) are self-explanatory given the descriptions of foraging and nest maintenance in Sect. 4.1. Each BT returns a success, failure, or running status that encodes how successful the program has been in satisfying a post-condition.

Each agent acts in the environment using its phenotype program. BeTr - GEESE rewards behaviors that promote genetic diversity and world exploration, observe or accomplish subtasks, or avoid constraint violations. Phenotype fitness is subjectively defined as $A_t = 0.1(A_{t-1}) + (E_t + B_t)$, where $A_0 = D$. Phenotype fitness is evaluated over time, which is necessary because there is delay between acting and receiving a reward. When agents exchange genes, they also exchange the genes' fitness values, making it possible for an agent to avoid "testing" the phenotype because its fitness is known. *Diversity fitness*, D, promotes gene diversity and is used when a gene is first created ($t = 0$) from either the initial random population or through mutation and crossover of an existing gene pool [58,70,73]; D is defined as the total number of unique behavior nodes in the BT divided by the total possible behaviors. *Exploration fitness* [10], E, promotes visiting new locations, and is defined as the number of unique world locations visited by the agent. *BT feedback fitness*, B, is defined as the sum of post-condition, constraint, and BT root node rewards. For each post-condition or root node status returning *success*, a subjectively chosen reward of $+1$ occurs, and -2 reward occurs if a constraint node returns *failure*.

4   Resilience Experiments

This section demonstrates that, when the BeTr-GEESE algorithm uses ongoing evolution, agents are capable of solving problems that arise when the world or the agents are perturbed. The next section explores why.

4.1   Experiment Design

Experiments were conducted using two tasks: *foraging* and *nest maintenance*. Experiments use a population of 100 agents that move with speed of 2 units per time step in a 100×100 grid environment with agent neighborhood sensing defined by the *grid size* parameter GS = 10. A hub of radius ten is placed at the origin. A maximum of 12,000 evolution steps are allowed. Quoting from [45], *foraging* requires agents to retrieve food from a source to a hub. A single foraging site of radius ten with 100 "food" units is randomly placed at 30 units from the hub. Task performance is the percentage of food at the hub. *Nest maintenance* requires agents to move debris near the hub to anywhere farther than 30 units from the hub. 100 "debris" objects are placed within ten units of the hub.

Parameters	BeTr-GEESE
Parent-selection	Most fit 50%
Mutation probability	0.01
Crossover probability	0.9
Crossover	variable_onepoint [17, 49]
Maximum depth of derivation tree	10 levels

The parameters in the table above are used in the experiments. These parameters were subjectively selected from choices made in prior work on grammatical evolution. Maximum tree depth is a practical parameter that limits the effect of recursive dependencies in the grammar. *PonyGE2* [17] was used to implement GEESE-BT and BeTr-GEESE. BT controllers were created using *py_trees* [66], and the swarm simulation environment was created using *Mesa* [28]. Experiments ran on a machine with an i9 CPU, 64 GB RAM running 16 parallel threads.

The independent variable is perturbation type, described below [36]. The first dependent variable is the *power* resilience metric [36], defined as the peak success probability achieved before the maximum number of allowed evolution steps $T = 12000$. The second dependent variable is an affine transformation of the *time efficiency* (t_θ) resilience measure [36], which is defined as the time required for an algorithm to satisfy a given performance threshold $\theta = 80\%$. *Efficiency* is defined as $e = ((T_{\max} - t_\theta)/T_{\max}) * 100$ where $T_{\max} = 12000$. Efficiency is set to zero for trials in which the threshold is not met.

4.2   Results

The four upper (respectively, lower) sub-plots in Fig. 1 show power (respectively, efficiency) for each swarm task. Sixteen independent simulations were performed for each experiment condition described below.

Ablation. An *ablation* perturbation reduces information, control, or possibilities [36]. Adding obstacles is an ablation perturbation since obstacles reduce the navigable space for the agents. In experiments, $obs \in \{1, 2, \ldots, 5\}$ obstacles are added to the world at time $t \in \{1000, 2000, \ldots, 11000\}$. Obstacles remain in the world after their introduction. The experiment conditions are all combinations of t and obs. The first column of Fig. 1 shows mean power and efficiency.

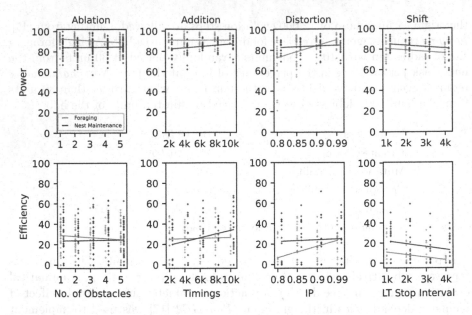

Fig. 1. Efficiency and power over a range of perturbations for foraging and next maintenance; IP = 0.85, ST = 7, and GS = 10.

Addition. An *addition* perturbation increases the set of observable states or actions [36]. An experiment was performed where new actions are added to the BeTr-GEESE BNF grammar in Appendix A as follows:

$\langle action \rangle ::= \langle motion \rangle | \langle nonmotion \rangle$ (1)

$\langle motion \rangle ::= \text{MoveTowards}\_\langle sobjects \rangle\_\langle motiontype \rangle | \text{Explore}\_0\_\langle motiontype \rangle |$ (2)
    $\text{MoveAway}\_\langle sobjects \rangle\_\langle motiontype \rangle$

$\langle motiontype \rangle ::= \text{Normal} | \text{Avoid}$ (3)

$\langle nonmotion \rangle ::= \text{CompositeSingleCarry}\_\langle dobjects \rangle | \text{CompositeDrop}\_\langle dobjects \rangle$ (4)

This modification increases an agent's action set by allowing an agent to choose between locomotion behaviors with/without obstacle avoidance. Two obstacles were randomly added to the environment at time $t \in \{1000, 2000, \ldots, 11000\}$. The second column of Fig. 1 shows mean power and efficiency.

Distortion. A *distortion* perturbation alters the probability with which states or actions occur [36]. Altering IP changes how frequently agents evolve, distorting probable states and actions. Experiment conditions used IP values in $\{0.8, 0.85, 0.9, 0.99\}$. The third column of Fig. 1 shows mean power and efficiency.

Shift. A *shift* perturbation combines the effects of multiple instances of ablation, addition, or distortion operations [36]. For the shift experiments, lateral transfer is initially turned *on* but turned *off* at time step 1000 for a duration of $\Delta \in \{1000, 2000, \ldots, 4000\}$ time steps, preventing an agent from collecting genes from neighbors. The fourth column of Fig. 1 shows mean power and efficiency.

4.3 Discussion

BeTr-GEESE agents show high resilience according to the power metric. Given sufficient time, agents evolve solutions when perturbations occur. High power persists across a range of perturbation types and parameters. The behaviors are inefficient because evolving revised solutions rarely occurs quickly. A power-efficiency tradeoff is observed, similar to optimality-robustness tradeoffs in control theory, where robust systems are often suboptimal [13,20]. Thus, ongoing evolution makes BeTr-GEESE agents inefficient but with high resilience power.

5 What Enables Resilience?

The section's goal is to identify properties of the BeTr-GEESE algorithm that could potentially generalize to other problems and GE swarm algorithms. Understanding these properties also sheds light on the limitations of using ongoing lateral transfer in GE to enable resilience.

5.1 Modularity

This subsection evaluates modularity properties of BeTr-GEESE. In prior work [45], two GE algorithms were compared: BeTr-GEESE and GEESE-BT. The two algorithms used the same genetic operators, the same parameter values (IP = 0.85, ST = 7, and GS = 10), the same form of lateral transfer between agents, the same basic actions, and the same preconditions and postconditions. The algorithms differed in three ways. First, BeTr-GEESE's grammar had a *CanMove* constraint necessary when obstacles are present in the world. Second, GEESE-BT's grammar produced traditional BTs and BeTr-GEESE's grammar produced PPA-style BTs [8]. Third, BeTr-GEESE used the fitness function described above, and GEESE-BT used both the fitness function above and task-specific motivators.

In the prior work, foraging (respectively, nest maintenance) was considered *successful* if more than 80% of the food is collected (respectively, debris is removed) during the time period when agents were evolving. *Success rate* was defined as the ratio of the number of successful evolution trials to the total number of trials. BeTr-GEESE's success rate was 75%, more than eight times higher than GEESE-BT even when GEESE-BT used the task-specific fitness functions. Note that success requires each basic action (production 15) in the grammar.

Having established that BeTr-GEESE performs successfully while learning, we now present new work that addresses whether the BeTr-GEESE grammar is more modular than GEESE-BT's grammar according to existing modularity metrics [9,53,61]. The BeTr-GEESE and GEESE-BT grammars have the same terminals with one exception: the *CanMove* constraint. The other terminals encode the basic actions, preconditions, postconditions, and constraints. The PPA structure encoded in BeTr-GEESE's grammar redundantly includes checks of constraints and postconditions, so 30 terminals appear on the right-hand-side (RHS) of productions in contrast to 24 for GEESE-BT. The PPA structure also produces "wider" trees, and this requires more non-terminals (20 to 11). BeTr-GEESE also has more productions and possible derivation trees, yielding a higher value of McCabe cyclomatic complexity (44 to 27). Finally, BeTr-GEESE averages fewer symbols on the RHS of productions (3.75 to 4.09) and produces programs that are more difficult to understand according to the Halstead effort metric (283.62 to 132.94). Thus, on one hand, these *size modularity metrics* suggest that BeTr-GEESE's grammar is less modular than GEESE-BT.

On the other hand, *structural modularity metrics* suggest that the BeTr-GEESE grammar is more modular. Specifically, derivation trees for BeTr-GEESE are more treelike (as opposed to more closely representing graphs) according to the tree impurity metric (7.6% to 15.56%). Additionally, related functionalities (non-terminals) in BeTr-GEESE are more logically grouped together according to the *nslev* clustering metric (8 to 6) and according to the *normalized count of levels* metric (40% to 36.36%). Derivation trees produced by the BeTr-GEESE grammar have higher correlations between non-terminals, and these correlations theoretically make it easier to learn syntactically correct programs.

Existing modularity metrics are ambiguous: BeTr-GEESE derivation trees are complex but have some structural correlations that might enable learning. An alternative notion of modularity is how well the task can be divided into "chunks". Both foraging and nest maintenance are *divisible* and *additive* [65]. They are divisible because the multistep mission of finding, moving, and dropping objects can be broken into subtasks. They are additive because individual agents can independently contribute to the cumulative success of the group. Agents need not all be coordinating to succeed, and no single agent has to perform all subtasks. Thus, for example, an agent can (incorrectly) move an object to an undesirable location, and another agent can move it to a desired location.

BeTr-GEESE uses the divisibility and additive properties to produce modular behaviors wherein genes only express simple actions. Each codon in a gene represents a production number in the grammar, so the sequence of codons in the gene encodes the derivation tree as a sequence of productions used to produce a valid PPA-style BT. The size modularity metrics indicate an important property of the derivation trees: many productions are needed for each simple action in the tree. The limited gene size, no more than 100 codons per gene, inhibits including all of the productions necessary for a valid, multi-action phenotype.

BeTr-GEESE limited gene expressiveness works well with its fitness function to learn single action phenotypes. Indeed, the prior work reported that 98% of the programs created by BeTr-GEESE had only one of the basic actions from production (15), while successful programs produced by GEESE-BT included all four. BeTr-GEESE fitness function includes feedback from the PPA-style BT phenotype, inhibiting constraint violations, promoting the use of basic actions, and rewarding successful subtask completion. Thus, even though BeTr-GEESE's derivation trees can be complex, the BT provides feedback that inhibit trees that do not perform any subtasks and promote trees that can perform single subtasks. Thus, BeTr-GEESE is modular in the sense that subtask-specific trees receive rapid feedback, which works well with divisible and additive collective tasks.

5.2 Locality

BeTr-GEESE allows modular behaviors to be quickly learned, but agents still need to be able to perform all subtasks to successfully forage or maintain the nest. This subsection shows that lateral transfer allows modular behaviors to be changed so that individual agents can find, carry, and drop objects, thus performing all necessary subtasks. The properties of lateral transfer is evaluated by describing the locality characteristics of the algorithm.

We begin with temporal locality. *Temporal locality* is the notion that a gene, and its associated phenotype, has a time window in which it is useful. A phenotype capable of performing a subtask must persist long enough for the subtask to be accomplished (e.g., explore until a site is found, travel from site to hub). But if an agent "holds onto" the gene too long then the agent cannot switch to the next needed subtask. Recall that after a BeTr-GEESE agent has received a sufficiently large number of genes through inter-agent interactions, it performs the standard genetic operators, selects the most fit, and then discards all but the most fit gene. Thus, how long a gene persists is determined by how frequently agents meet and exchange genes through lateral transfer. The lower bound on how long a gene persists is therefore controlled by: (i) how often agents are within close enough range to exchange genes (GS), (ii) how often agents with range exchange genetic information (IP), and (iii) the number of genes required before an agent applies the genetic operators (ST). How often the agent are in close range cannot be controlled directly, but IP and ST can be varied to control for how often agents meet each other.

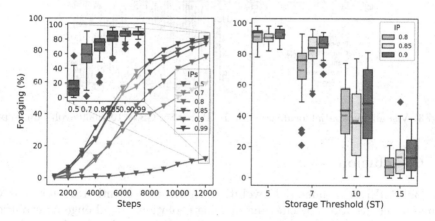

Fig. 2. a) Foraging (%) vs IP. ST = 7. b) Relationship between IP, ST, and foraging (%).

Sixteen independent foraging runs were conducted for each value of IP and ST, and the experiment results are summarised with box and whisker plots in Fig. 2. Figure 2a) shows that with a high willingness to transfer genes to other agents (IP > 0.8), the agents can change genes rapidly, promoting evolution through lateral and vertical transfer. When IP < 0.6, the agents persist with current behaviors too long, slowing down evolution. Figure 2b) shows that when ST is high, which means that agents must meet many other agents before evolving, agents are not able to change controllers quickly, and their performance goes down. Both figures show that too much persistence hinders evolution.

Figure 3 shows that BeTr-GEESE agents exhibit *spatial locality*. The colors in the figure indicate the most fit gene when agents perform the genetic operators. The figure is constructed from the first 3000 evolution steps in one successful simulation, but all successful simulations exhibit similar *locality* patterns. The most fit gene selected by BeTr-GEESE agents depends on the location of the environment. For example, the figure shows a uniform distribution of blue explore-the-world behaviors. The figure also shows yellow clusters of carry-an-object behaviors, green clusters of drop-an-object behaviors, and linear clouds of move-towards and move-away behaviors. Clusters and clouds form around and between the hub and food sites, enabling agents to meet and evolve relevant controllers to solve particular sub-tasks at particular locations. The meeting locations enable lateral transfer of useful genes, which tend to localize around those regions of the world where specific subtasks are needed.

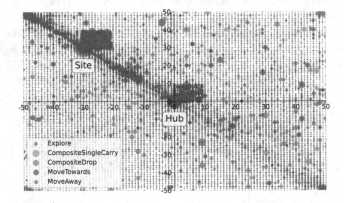

Fig. 3. Visualizing spatial locality: ST = 7, IP = 0.85, GS = 10, 3000 evolution steps.

6   Conclusion

The BeTr-GEESE grammatical evolution algorithm resiliently responds to environment perturbations by enabling ongoing evolution. Rapid ongoing evolution is possible because the algorithm uses a limited gene size, thereby producing agent programs that are modular in the sense that they can only perform single subtasks. These modular, subtask-specific programs can be exchanged through lateral transfer to sequentially perform all required subtasks, which produces resilient performance in divisible and additive group tasks like foraging and nest maintenance. Switching between subtasks is enabled by lateral gene transfer, but the behaviors of successful groups must exhibit temporal locality, meaning that an agent must persist in a behavior long enough to perform basic functions but also meaning that agents cannot persist too long or else evolution is too slow. Lateral transfer occurs at spatially local regions of the world where agents are likely to meet, allowing location-specific behaviors to be adopted by neighboring agents. Ongoing evolution through lateral transfer of simple modules exhibits resilience in the sense that agents can adapt to perturbations and still succeed in their tasks, but this adaptation might be inefficient. Future work should explore how modularity and locality in BeTr-GEESE can be applied not only to other GE algorithms and other types of multiagent problems, but also to designing efficient, fixed behaviors that produce resilient collective behaviors.

A   PPA Grammar

$\langle root \rangle ::= \langle sequence \rangle \mid \langle selector \rangle$ (1)

$\langle sequence \rangle ::=$ [Sequence]$\langle ppa \rangle$[/Sequence]| [Sequence]$\langle root \rangle \langle root \rangle$[/Sequence]   (2)
    [Sequence]$\langle sequence \rangle \langle root \rangle$[/Sequence]

$\langle selector \rangle ::=$ [Selector]$\langle ppa \rangle$[/Selector]|[Selector]$\langle root \rangle \langle root \rangle$[/Selector]   (3)
    [Selector]$\langle selector \rangle \langle root \rangle$[/Selector]

$\langle ppa \rangle ::=$ [Selector]$\langle postconditions \rangle \langle ppasequence \rangle$[/Selector]   (4)

$\langle postconditions \rangle ::= \langle SuccessNode \rangle \mid \langle ppa \rangle$ |[Sequence]$\langle postcondition \rangle$[/Sequence] (5)

$\langle postcondition \rangle ::= \langle postcondition \rangle$[PostCnd]$\langle postconditiont \rangle$ (6)
    [/PostCnd]|[PostCnd]$\langle postconditiont \rangle$[/PostCnd]

$\langle postconditiont \rangle ::=$ NeighbourObjects_$\langle objects \rangle$|NeighbourObjects_$\langle sobjects \rangle$| (7)
    IsCarrying_$\langle dobjects \rangle$|NeighbourObjects_$\langle dobjects \rangle$|
    DidAvoidedObj_$\langle sobjects \rangle$|IsVisitedBefore_$\langle sobjects \rangle$

$\langle ppasequence \rangle ::=$ [Sequence]$\langle preconditions \rangle$[Act]$\langle action \rangle$ [/Act][/Sequence]| (8)
    [Sequence]$\langle constraints \rangle$[Act]$\langle action \rangle$[/Act][/Sequence]|[Sequence]
    $\langle preconditions \rangle \langle constraints \rangle$[Act]$\langle action \rangle$[/Act][/Sequence]

$\langle preconditions \rangle ::=$ [Sequence]$\langle precondition \rangle$[/Sequence]   (9)

$\langle precondition \rangle ::= \langle precondition \rangle$[PreCnd]$\langle preconditiont \rangle$ [/PreCnd]| (10)
    [PreCnd]$\langle preconditiont \rangle$[/PreCnd]

$\langle preconditiont \rangle ::=$ IsDropable_$\langle sobjects \rangle$|NeighbourObjects_$\langle objects \rangle$_inv| (11)
    IsVisitedBefore_$\langle sobjects \rangle$_inv|IsCarrying_$\langle dobjects \rangle$_inv|
    IsVisitedBefore_$\langle sobjects \rangle$| IsCarrying_$\langle dobjects \rangle$|NeighbourObjects_$\langle objects \rangle$

$\langle constraints \rangle ::=$ [Sequence]$\langle constraint \rangle$[/Sequence]   (12)

$\langle constraint \rangle ::= \langle constraint \rangle$[Cnstr]$\langle constraintt \rangle$[/Cnstr]|[Cnstr]$\langle constraintt \rangle$ (13)
    [/Cnstr]

$\langle constraintt \rangle ::=$ CanMove|IsCarryable_$\langle dobjects \rangle$| IsDropable_$\langle sobjects \rangle$ (14)

$\langle action \rangle ::=$ MoveTowards_$\langle sobjects \rangle$|Explore|CompositeSingleCarry_$\langle dobjects \rangle$ (15)
    |CompositeDrop_$\langle dobjects \rangle$| MoveAway_$\langle sobjects \rangle$

$\langle objects \rangle ::= \langle sobjects \rangle \mid \langle dobjects \rangle$ (16)

$\langle sobjects \rangle ::=$ Hub|Sites   (17)

$\langle dobjects \rangle ::=$ Food|Debris   (18)

$\langle SuccessNode \rangle :: =$ [PostCnd]DummyNode[/PostCnd]   (19)

References

1. Bongard, J.: Morphological change in machines accelerates the evolution of robust behavior. Proc. Natl. Acad. Sci. **108**(4), 1234–1239 (2011)
2. Bongard, J.C.: Accelerating self-modeling in cooperative robot teams. IEEE Trans. Evol. Comput. **13**(2), 321–332 (2008)
3. Bredeche, N., Montanier, J.M., Liu, W., Winfield, A.F.: Environment-driven distributed evolutionary adaptation in a population of autonomous robotic agents. Math. Comput. Model. Dyn. Syst. **18**(1), 101–129 (2012)
4. Brooks, R.: A robust layered control system for a mobile robot. IEEE J. Robot. Autom. **2**(1), 14–23 (1986)
5. Canciani, F., Talamali, M.S., Marshall, J.A., Bose, T., Reina, A.: Keep calm and vote on: swarm resiliency in collective decision making. In: Proceedings of Workshop Resilient Robot Teams of the 2019 IEEE International Conference on Robotics and Automation (ICRA 2019), p. 4 (2019)
6. Cheng, J., Cheng, W., Nagpal, R.: Robust and self-repairing formation control for swarms of mobile agents. In: AAAI, vol. 5 (2005)
7. Cliff, D., Husbands, P., Harvey, I., et al.: Evolving visually guided robots. From Animals Animats **2**, 374–383 (1993)
8. Colledanchise, M., Ögren, P.: Behavior trees in robotics and al: an introduction (2018)
9. Črepinšek, M., Kosar, T., Mernik, M., Cervelle, J., Forax, R., Roussel, G.: On automata and language based grammar metrics. Comput. Sci. Inf. Syst. **14**, 309–329 (2010)
10. Črepinšek, M., Liu, S.H., Mernik, M.: Exploration and exploitation in evolutionary algorithms: a survey. ACM Comput. Surv. (CSUR) **45**(3), 1–33 (2013)
11. Doncieux, S., Bredeche, N., Mouret, J.B., Eiben, A.E.G.: Evolutionary robotics: what, why, and where to. Front. Robot. AI **2**, 4 (2015)
12. Doncieux, S., Mouret, J.B., Bredeche, N., Padois, V.: Evolutionary robotics: exploring new horizons. In: Doncieux, S., Bredèche, N., Mouret, J.B. (eds.) New Horizons in Evolutionary Robotics. Studies in Computational Intelligence, vol. 341, pp. 3–25. Springer, Heidelberg (2011). https://doi.org/10.1007/978-3-642-18272-3_1
13. Doyle, J.C., Francis, B.A., Tannenbaum, A.R.: Feedback Control Theory. Courier Corporation (2013)
14. Duarte, M., et al.: Evolution of collective behaviors for a real swarm of aquatic surface robots. PLoS One **11**(3), e0151834 (2016)
15. Eiben, A.E., Haasdijk, E., Bredeche, N.: Embodied, on-line, on-board evolution for autonomous robotics (2010)
16. Engebråten, S.A., Moen, J., Yakimenko, O., Glette, K.: Evolving a repertoire of controllers for a multi-function swarm. In: Sim, K., Kaufmann, P. (eds.) EvoApplications 2018. LNCS, vol. 10784, pp. 734–749. Springer, Cham (2018). https://doi.org/10.1007/978-3-319-77538-8_49
17. Fenton, M., McDermott, J., Fagan, D., Forstenlechner, S., Hemberg, E., O'Neill, M.: PonyGE2: grammatical evolution in Python. In: Proceedings of the Genetic and Evolutionary Computation Conference Companion, pp. 1194–1201 (2017)
18. Ferrante, E., Duéñez-Guzmán, E., Turgut, A.E., Wenseleers, T.: GESwarm: grammatical evolution for the automatic synthesis of collective behaviors in swarm robotics. In: Proceedings of the 15th Annual GECCO Conference, pp. 17–24. ACM (2013)

19. Ferrante, E., Turgut, A.E., Duéñez-Guzmán, E., Dorigo, M., Wenseleers, T.: Evolution of self-organized task specialization in robot swarms. PLoS Comput. Biol. **11**(8), e1004273 (2015)

20. Goh, C.K., Tan, K.C.: Evolving the tradeoffs between pareto-optimality and robustness in multi-objective evolutionary algorithms. In: Yang, S., Ong, Y.S., Jin, Y. (eds.) Evolutionary Computation in Dynamic and Uncertain Environments, vol. 51, pp. 457–478. Springer, Heidelberg (2007). https://doi.org/10.1007/978-3-540-49774-5_20

21. Gordon, D.M.: Ant Encounters. Princeton University Press, Princeton (2010)

22. Gunderson, L.H.: Ecological resilience-in theory and application. Annu. Rev. Ecol. Syst. **31**(1), 425–439 (2000)

23. Hall, J.P., Brockhurst, M.A., Harrison, E.: Sampling the mobile gene pool: innovation via horizontal gene transfer in bacteria. Philos. Trans. Roy. Soc. B: Biol. Sci. **372**(1735), 20160424 (2017)

24. Holling, C.S.: Engineering resilience versus ecological resilience. Eng. Ecol. Constraints **31**(1996), 32 (1996)

25. Jablonka, E., Lamb, M.J.: Evolution in Four Dimensions, Revised Edition: Genetic, Epigenetic, Behavioral, and Symbolic Variation in the History of Life. MIT Press, Cambridge (2014)

26. Jakobi, N., Husbands, P., Harvey, I.: Noise and the reality gap: the use of simulation in evolutionary robotics. In: Morán, F., Moreno, A., Merelo, J.J., Chacón, P. (eds.) ECAL 1995. LNCS, vol. 929, pp. 704–720. Springer, Heidelberg (1995). https://doi.org/10.1007/3-540-59496-5_337

27. Johnson, M., Brown, D.S.: Evolving and controlling perimeter, rendezvous, and foraging behaviors in a computation-free robot swarm. Technical report, Air Force Research Laboratory/RISC Rome United States (2016)

28. Kazil, J., Masad, D., Crooks, A.: Utilizing python for agent-based modeling: the mesa framework. In: Thomson, R., Bisgin, H., Dancy, C., Hyder, A., Hussain, M. (eds.) SBP-BRiMS 2020. LNCS, vol. 12268, pp. 308–317. Springer, Cham (2020). https://doi.org/10.1007/978-3-030-61255-9_30

29. König, L., Mostaghim, S., Schmeck, H.: Decentralized evolution of robotic behavior using finite state machines. Intl. J. Intell. Comput. Cybern. **2**(4), 695–723 (2009)

30. Koza, J.R.: Genetic programming as a means for programming computers by natural selection. Stat. Comput. **4**(2), 87–112 (1994)

31. Kriesel, D.M.M., Cheung, E., Sitti, M., Lipson, H.: Beanbag robotics: robotic swarms with 1-DoF units. In: Dorigo, M., Birattari, M., Blum, C., Clerc, M., Stützle, T., Winfield, A.F.T. (eds.) ANTS 2008. LNCS, vol. 5217, pp. 267–274. Springer, Heidelberg (2008). https://doi.org/10.1007/978-3-540-87527-7_26

32. Kucking, J., Ligot, A., Bozhinoski, D., Birattari, M.: Behavior trees as a control architecture in the automatic design of robot swarms. In: ANTS 2018. IEEE (2018)

33. Kuckling, J., Van P., V., Birattari, M.: Automatic modular design of behavior trees for robot swarms with communication capabilites. In: EvoApplications, pp. 130–145 (2021)

34. Lampe, D.J., Witherspoon, D.J., Soto-Adames, F.N., Robertson, H.M.: Recent horizontal transfer of mellifera subfamily mariner transposons into insect lineages representing four different orders shows that selection acts only during horizontal transfer. Mol. Biol. Evol. **20**(4), 554–562 (2003)

35. Lane, N.: The Vital Question: Energy, Evolution, and the Origins of Complex Life. WW Norton & Company (2015)

36. Leaf, J., Adams, J.A.: Measuring resilience in collective robotic algorithms. In: Proceedings of the 21st International Conference on Autonomous Agents and Multiagent Systems, pp. 1666–1668 (2022)
37. Lee, W.P.: Evolving complex robot behaviors. Inf. Sci. **121**(1–2), 1–25 (1999)
38. Lewis, M.A., Fagg, A.H., Solidum, A.: Genetic programming approach to the construction of a neural network for control of a walking robot. In: 1992 Proceedings of IEEE International Conference on Robotics and Automation, pp. 2618–2623. IEEE (1992)
39. Linksvayer, T.A., Janssen, M.A.: Traits underlying the capacity of ant colonies to adapt to disturbance and stress regimes. Syst. Res. Behav. Sci.: Off. J. Int. Fed. Syst. Res. **26**(3), 315–329 (2009)
40. Mlot, N.J., Tovey, C.A., Hu, D.L.: Fire ants self-assemble into waterproof rafts to survive floods. Proc. Natl. Acad. Sci. **108**(19), 7669–7673 (2011)
41. Nelson, A.L., Barlow, G.J., Doitsidis, L.: Fitness functions in evolutionary robotics: a survey and analysis. Robot. Auton. Syst. **57**(4), 345–370 (2009)
42. Neupane, A., Goodrich, M.A.: Designing emergent swarm behaviors using behavior trees and grammatical evolution. In: Proceedings of the 18th AAMAS Conference, pp. 2138–2140 (2019)
43. Neupane, A., Goodrich, M.A.: Learning swarm behaviors using grammatical evolution and behavior trees. In: IJCAI, pp. 513–520 (2019)
44. Neupane, A., Goodrich, M.A., Mercer, E.G.: GEESE: grammatical evolution algorithm for evolution of swarm behaviors. In: Proceedings of the 20th Annual GECCO Conference, pp. 999–1006 (2018)
45. Neupane, A., Goodrich, M.: Efficiently evolving swarm behaviors using grammatical evolution with PPA-style behavior trees. In: From Cells to Societies: Collective Learning Across Scales (2022)
46. Nevai, A.L., Passino, K.M., Srinivasan, P.: Stability of choice in the honey bee nest-site selection process. J. Theor. Biol. **263**(1), 93–107 (2010)
47. Noirot, C., Darlington, J.P.: Termite nests: architecture, regulation and defence. In: Abe, T., Bignell, D.E., Higashi, M. (eds.) Termites: Evolution, Sociality, Symbioses, Ecology, pp. 121–139. Springer, Dordrecht (2000). https://doi.org/10.1007/978-94-017-3223-9_6
48. Ochman, H., Lawrence, J.G., Groisman, E.A.: Lateral gene transfer and the nature of bacterial innovation. Nature **405**(6784), 299–304 (2000)
49. O'neill, M., Ryan, C., Keijzer, M., Cattolico, M.: Crossover in grammatical evolution. Genet. Program. Evolvable Mach. **4**(1), 67–93 (2003)
50. Perez, R., Aron, S.: Adaptations to thermal stress in social insects: recent advances and future directions. Biol. Rev. **95**(6), 1535–1553 (2020)
51. Petrovic, P.: Evolving behavior coordination for mobile robots using distributed finite-state automata. In: Frontiers in Evolutionary Robotics. InTech (2008)
52. Pintér-Bartha, A., Sobe, A., Elmenreich, W.: Towards the light-comparing evolved neural network controllers and finite state machine controllers. In: Proceedings of the Tenth Workshop on Intelligent Solutions in Embedded Systems, pp. 83–87. IEEE (2012)
53. Power, J.F., Malloy, B.A.: A metrics suite for grammar-based software. J. Softw. Maint. Evol. Res. Pract. **16**(6), 405–426 (2004)
54. Quammen, D.: The Tangled Tree: A Radical New History of Life. Simon and Schuster, New York (2018)
55. Reid, C.R., Lutz, M.J., Powell, S., Kao, A.B., Couzin, I.D., Garnier, S.: Army ants dynamically adjust living bridges in response to a cost-benefit trade-off. Proc. Natl. Acad. Sci. **112**(49), 15113–15118 (2015)

56. Rubenstein, M., Cornejo, A., Nagpal, R.: Programmable self-assembly in a thousand-robot swarm. Science **345**(6198), 795–799 (2014)
57. Samples, A.D.: Mache: No-loss trace compaction. In: Proceedings of the 1989 ACM SIGMETRICS International Conference on Measurement and Modeling of Computer Systems, pp. 89–97 (1989)
58. Schwander, T., Rosset, H., Chapuisat, M.: Division of labour and worker size polymorphism in ant colonies: the impact of social and genetic factors. Behav. Ecol. Sociobiol. **59**(2), 215–221 (2005)
59. Seeley, T.D.: The Wisdom of the Hive: The Social Physiology of Honey Bee Colonies. Harvard University Press (2009)
60. Seeley, T.D.: Honeybee Democracy. Princeton University Press, Princeton (2010)
61. Simon, H.A.: The Sciences of the Artificial, Reissue of the Third Edition with a New Introduction by John Laird. MIT Press, Cambridge (2019)
62. Singh, S., Lewis, R.L., Barto, A.G., Sorg, J.: Intrinsically motivated reinforcement learning: an evolutionary perspective. IEEE Trans. Auton. Ment. Dev. **2**(2), 70–82 (2010)
63. Sorenson, E.S., Flanagan, J.K.: Evaluating synthetic trace models using locality surfaces. In: Proceedings of the IEEE International Workshop on Workload Characterization, pp. 23–33 (2002)
64. Soule, T.: Resilient individuals improve evolutionary search. Artif. Life **12**(1), 17–34 (2006)
65. Steiner, D.I.: Group Process and Productivity. Academic Press, Cambridge (1972)
66. Stonier, D., Staniaszek, M.: Behavior Tree implementation in Python (2021). https://github.com/splintered-reality/py_trees/
67. Sumpter, D., Pratt, S.: A modelling framework for understanding social insect foraging. Behav. Ecol. Sociobiol. **53**(3), 131–144 (2003)
68. Sumpter, D.J.: Collective animal behavior. In: Collective Animal Behavior. Princeton University Press (2010)
69. Swafford, J.M., O'Neill, M.: An examination on the modularity of grammars in grammatical evolutionary design. In: IEEE Congress on Evolutionary Computation, pp. 1–8. IEEE (2010)
70. Toffolo, A., Benini, E.: Genetic diversity as an objective in multi-objective evolutionary algorithms. Evol. Comput. **11**(2), 151–167 (2003)
71. Toth, A., Robinson, G.: Evo-devo and the evolution of social behavior: brain gene expression analyses in social insects. In: Cold Spring Harbor Symposia on Quantitative Biology, vol. 74, pp. 419–426. Cold Spring Harbor Laboratory Press (2009)
72. Trianni, V., Groß, R., Labella, T.H., Şahin, E., Dorigo, M.: Evolving aggregation behaviors in a swarm of robots. In: Banzhaf, W., Ziegler, J., Christaller, T., Dittrich, P., Kim, J.T. (eds.) ECAL 2003. LNCS (LNAI), vol. 2801, pp. 865–874. Springer, Heidelberg (2003). https://doi.org/10.1007/978-3-540-39432-7_93
73. Ursem, R.K.: Diversity-guided evolutionary algorithms. In: Guervós, J.J.M., Adamidis, P., Beyer, H.-G., Schwefel, H.-P., Fernández-Villacañas, J.-L. (eds.) PPSN 2002. LNCS, vol. 2439, pp. 462–471. Springer, Heidelberg (2002). https://doi.org/10.1007/3-540-45712-7_45
74. Varughese, J.C., Thenius, R., Schmickl, T., Wotawa, F.: Quantification and analysis of the resilience of two swarm intelligent algorithms. In: GCAI, pp. 148–161 (2017)
75. Vistbakka, I., Troubitsyna, E.: Modelling autonomous resilient multi-robotic systems. In: Calinescu, R., Di Giandomenico, F. (eds.) SERENE 2019. LNCS, vol. 11732, pp. 29–45. Springer, Cham (2019). https://doi.org/10.1007/978-3-030-30856-8_3

76. Wagner, G.P., Altenberg, L.: Perspective: complex adaptations and the evolution of evolvability. Evolution **50**(3), 967–976 (1996)
77. Wang, J.X., et al.: Evolving intrinsic motivations for altruistic behavior. arXiv preprint arXiv:1811.05931 (2018)
78. Yamashita, Y., Tani, J.: Emergence of functional hierarchy in a multiple timescale neural network model: a humanoid robot experiment. PLoS Comput. Biol. **4**(11), e1000220 (2008)
79. Zahadat, P., Hamann, H., Schmickl, T.: Evolving diverse collective behaviors independent of swarm density. In: Proceedings of the Companion Publication of the 2015 Annual Conference on Genetic and Evolutionary Computation, pp. 1245–1246 (2015)

Mind the Gap! Predictive Flocking of Aerial Robot Swarm in Cluttered Environments

Giray Önür[1,3(✉)], Ali Emre Turgut[1,3], and Erol Şahin[2,3]

[1] Department of Mechanical Engineering, Middle East Technical University,
Ankara, Turkey
girayo@metu.edu.tr
[2] Department of Computer Engineering, Middle East Technical University,
Ankara, Turkey
[3] Center for Robotics and Artifical Intelligence (ROMER),
Middle East Technical University, Ankara, Turkey

Abstract. Flocking, coordinated movement of individuals, widely observed in animal societies, and it is commonly used to guide robot swarms in cluttered environments. In standard flocking models, robot swarms often use local interactions between the robots and obstacles to achieve safe collective motion using virtual forces. However, these models generally involve parameters that must be tuned specifically to the environmental layout to avoid collisions. In this paper, we propose a predictive flocking model that can perform safe collective motion in different environmental layouts without any need for parameter tuning. In the model, each robot constructs a search tree consisting of its predicted future states and utilizes a heuristic search to find the most promising future state to use as the next control input. Flocking performance of the model is compared against the standard flocking model in simulation in different environmental layouts, and it is validated indoors with a swarm of six quadcopters. The results show that more synchronized and robust flocking behavior can be achieved when robots use the predicted states rather than the current states of others.

1 Introduction

Flocking, the coherent motion of a group of individuals, is commonly encountered in animal societies [1] with schools of fish and flocks of birds demonstrating impressive examples of coordinated motion [10,11]. Flocking has also been an interest in artificial systems. One of the earliest attempts to implement flocking in artificial systems is due to Reynolds [13]. In his model, flocking is modeled using repulsion, velocity alignment, and attraction behaviors. Repulsion ensures collision avoidance, velocity alignment maintains the coherent motion, and attraction keeps the flock together. Numerous flocking models have been proposed based on these interactions to describe various systems such as animal groups [5] and migrating cells [9].

© Springer Nature Switzerland AG 2022
M. Dorigo et al. (Eds.): ANTS 2022, LNCS 13491, pp. 171–182, 2022.
https://doi.org/10.1007/978-3-031-20176-9_14

In the virtual force model [16], these behaviors are generated via virtual forces exerted on the agents where the magnitude and direction of the forces depend on the local interactions between neighboring agents. The virtual force model is often used for implementing robot swarms in cluttered or confined environments due to its reactivity, and low computational complexity [7,18]. However, these implementations frequently involve parameters that must be tuned specifically to the environmental layout. Consequently, sudden changes in the environmental layout may cause collisions or decrease flocking performance, which makes these models unreliable in real-world.

Recent studies [2,6] claim that natural swarms, such as schools of fish or swarms of bats, use predicted future states of their neighbors rather than the current states. In accordance with this claim, in [3] it was demonstrated that the neural activity in bat's brain encodes non-local navigational information up to a few meters away from the bat's present state during both random exploration and goal-directed motion.

Inspired by the natural swarms, predictive flocking models based on distributed model predictive control (DMPC) have emerged since DMPC can handle actuation constraints of robots and optimize flocking performance [8,14]. Previous work showed that aerial robot swarms using DMPC-based flocking model could perform safe collective motion with noisy sensor measurements in a cluttered environment [14] and in the presence of dynamic obstacles [8]. Although DMPC-based flocking models perform more robust collective motion compared to standard flocking models, their onboard implementation remains a challenge due to the computational complexity and the requirement of excessive communication between robots.

In this paper, we propose a novel flocking model based on a predictive search method that can perform safe collective motion in different environmental layouts without parameter tuning. In the proposed model, robots can sense obstacles and other robots within a limited range and only use the local information. Each robot constructs a search tree consisting of their possible future states and finds the trajectory that fulfills the flocking objectives by using a heuristic search algorithm to determine its next move.

2   Methodology

Consider a swarm consisting of N robots with a radius r_a moving in a 2D environment. Robots can sense obstacles and other robots within a limited range, r_s. At each time step, Δt, the next velocity of the robot is determined according to the updated information of the neighboring robots and obstacles. The number of neighbors and obstacles closest to robot i are indicated by M and O, respectively. Their values are limited to $M \leq M_{max}$ and $O \leq O_{max}$. The position and velocity of robot i are denoted by p_i and v_i. The position of the point closest to robot i on the boundary of obstacle k is indicated by o_k. The distance between robot i and its jth neighbor is denoted by $d_{ij} = \|p_i - p_j\| - 2r_a$ whereas the distance between robot i and obstacle k is indicated by $d_{ik} = \|p_i - o_k\| - r_a$.

(a)   (b)

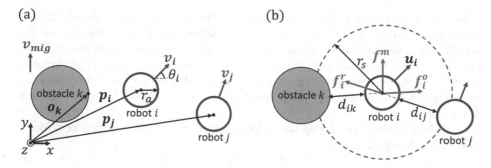

Fig. 1. Illustration of a robot swarm in a 2D environment with (a) robot's radius, heading angle, position and velocity vectors, (b) sensing range, heading, relative distances, and virtual forces.

v_{mig} is defined as the migration velocity to the robots. Each robot moves in the direction of its heading u_i, with the heading angle θ_i calculated with respect to the frame of reference (Fig. 1). Unit vectors along the x, y, and z-axis of the frame of reference are denoted by $\hat{x}$, $\hat{y}$ and $\hat{z}$. The common frame of reference is used for ease of description. In the following models, a robot can calculate its next velocity using a local frame of reference and relative positions and velocities of others.

2.1   Standard Flocking Model (SFM)

We extended the Active Elastic Sheet (AES) model [4], which uses spring-like virtual interaction forces between robots, by adding an obstacle avoidance force to prevent robot-obstacle collision and a migration force to provide migration velocity. The total force acting on robot i is obtained as the sum of three forces as:

$$f_i = f_i^r + f_i^o + f^m \tag{1}$$

where f_i^r is the inter-robot force, f_i^o is the obstacle avoidance force and f^m is the migration force (Fig. 1b).

The spring-like inter-robot force is calculated as:

$$f_i^r = \sum_{j=1}^{M} k^r (d_{ij} - d_{eq}) u_{ij} \tag{2}$$

where k^r is the inter-robot force gain, d_{eq} is the equilibrium distance and u_{ij} is the unit vector directed from robot i to its jth neighbor.

The obstacle avoidance force is calculated as:

$$f_i^o = \sum_{k=1}^{O} -k^o \frac{1}{d_{ik}^2} u_{ik} \tag{3}$$

where k^o is the obstacle avoidance force gain and $\boldsymbol{u}_{ik}$ is the unit vector directed from robot i to obstacle k. In [7], it has been shown that as the robot approaches an obstacle, the obstacle avoidance force must increase significantly compared to the inter-robot force to avoid the robot-obstacle collision. Thus, $\boldsymbol{f}_i^o$ designated as its magnitude increases exponentially as robot i gets closer to obstacle k, whereas the magnitude of $\boldsymbol{f}_i^r$ increases linearly as two robots get closer to each other.

The migration force keeps the velocity of robots at the migration velocity and it is calculated as:

$$\boldsymbol{f}^m = k^m \boldsymbol{v}_{mig} \tag{4}$$

where k^m is the migration force gain.

The linear speed of the robot is computed by projecting $\boldsymbol{f}_i$ onto $\boldsymbol{u}_i$ and multiplying it by the linear speed gain k^l as:

$$v_i = k^l(\boldsymbol{f}_i \cdot \boldsymbol{u}_i). \tag{5}$$

The angular speed of the robot is obtained by projecting $\boldsymbol{f}_i$ onto the vector perpendicular to its heading and multiplying it by the angular speed gain k^a as:

$$\omega_i = k^a(\boldsymbol{f}_i \cdot \boldsymbol{u}_i^\perp). \tag{6}$$

The linear speed is bounded between v_{min} and v_{max} whereas the angular speed is bounded between $-\omega_{max}$ and ω_{max}. Then, the linear and angular velocities of robot i are obtained as:

$$\boldsymbol{v}_i = v_i \boldsymbol{u}_i, \tag{7}$$

$$\boldsymbol{\omega}_i = \omega_i \hat{\boldsymbol{z}}. \tag{8}$$

2.2   Predictive Flocking Model (PFM)

The predictive flocking model searches for a trajectory that fulfills the flocking objectives only using local information. Each robot constructs a search tree consisting of nodes that contain its possible future position and velocity states where levels of the search tree represent future time steps.

Let the heading angle and speed of a parent node at the cth level of the search tree be denoted by θ^c and v^c, respectively. Then, the heading angle and speed values of its child nodes at the next level of the search tree are calculated as:

$$\theta_a^{c+1} = \theta^c + a\Delta\theta \qquad a \in \mathbb{Z} : -A \le a \le A, \tag{9}$$

$$v_b^{c+1} = v^c + b\Delta v \qquad b \in \mathbb{Z} : -B \le b \le B \tag{10}$$

where $\Delta\theta$ and Δv are the search step parameters, A and B are the parameters that determine the number of considered reachable heading angle and speed values at the next time step, respectively. Since the calculated heading angle

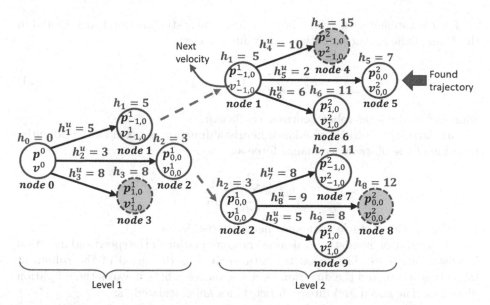

Fig. 2. Illustration of an example search tree for the parameters $\beta = 2$, $d = 2$, $A = 1$ and $B = 0$. p^0 and v^0 represent the current position and velocity of the robot. The gray nodes are pruned, and the remaining nodes are expanded. The next velocity of the robot is obtained as $v^1_{-1,0}$ which is the first velocity state of the found trajectory.

and speed values should satisfy the actuation constraints of the robot, the speed term v_b^{c+1} is bounded between v_{min} and v_{max}, and the parameters are selected as the constraints $A\Delta\theta \leq \omega_{max}\Delta t$ and $B\Delta v \leq a_{max}\Delta t$ are satisfied where ω_{max} and a_{max} are the maximum angular speed and the maximum acceleration of the robot. Then, the velocity and position states of the child nodes are calculated as:

$$v_{a,b}^{c+1} = v_b^{c+1}\big(cos(\theta_a^{c+1})\hat{x} + sin(\theta_a^{c+1})\hat{y}\big), \tag{11}$$

$$p_{a,b}^{c+1} = p^c + \Delta t v_{a,b}^{c+1} \tag{12}$$

where p^c is the position state of the parent node.

The positions of the neighboring robots at the cth level of the search tree are predicted assuming their velocities remain the same as:

$$p_j^c = p_j^0 + c\Delta t v_j^0 \tag{13}$$

where p_j^0 and v_j^0 are the current position and velocity of the jth neighboring robot.

The cost values of each node are calculated using the flocking heuristic functions. For the ith node at the cth level of the search tree, p_i and v_i are taken as the position and velocity states of the ith node whereas p_j taken as the predicted position of the jth neighboring robot at the cth level of the search tree.

For consistency with SFM, the inter-robot heuristic function is designated in the form of the spring potential energy function as:

$$h_i^r = \sum_{j=1}^{M} w^r \left(d_{ij} - d_{eq}\right)^2 \tag{14}$$

where w^r is the inter-robot heuristic coefficient.

Similarly, the obstacle avoidance heuristic function is taken as the potential function of the obstacle avoidance force as:

$$h_i^o = \sum_{k=1}^{O} w^o \frac{1}{d_{ik}} \tag{15}$$

where w^o is the obstacle avoidance heuristic coefficient.

The migration heuristic is taken as the combination of the speed and direction heuristic functions. The speed heuristic maintains the speed of the robots at migration speed, and the direction heuristic moves robots towards the migration direction. The speed and direction heuristics are calculated as:

$$h_i^s = w^s \left|\|\boldsymbol{v}_{mig}\| - \|\boldsymbol{v}_i\|\right|, \tag{16}$$

$$h_i^d = w^d \left(1 - \frac{\boldsymbol{v}_{mig} \cdot \boldsymbol{v}_i}{\|\boldsymbol{v}_{mig}\|\|\boldsymbol{v}_i\|}\right) \tag{17}$$

where w^s and w^d are the speed and direction heuristic coefficients, respectively.

The sum of the inter-robot, obstacle avoidance, speed, and direction heuristics is calculated as:

$$h_i^u = h_i^r + h_i^o + h_i^s + h_i^d. \tag{18}$$

The heuristic cost of the ith node is obtained as:

$$h_i = h_i^u + h_i^p \tag{19}$$

where h_i^p is the heuristic cost of the parent node of the ith node.

To find a trajectory that meets the flocking objectives, each robot utilizes a beam-search algorithm that expands only the β number of nodes with the lowest heuristic cost at each level of the search tree and prunes the remaining nodes to reduce the required time and memory for the search. The total number of levels in the search tree, which determines the total number of predicted future steps, is called the depth, d. The starting node of the search tree is represented as node 0, whose states are the current position and velocity of the robot, and its heuristic cost is taken as $h_0 = 0$ since its value does not affect the search result. The trajectory of the node with the smallest heuristic cost at the dth level of the search tree is taken as the found trajectory. Each robot repeats the search process within a short time interval, Δt, and takes its next velocity command as the first velocity state of the found trajectory, as illustrated in Fig. 2.

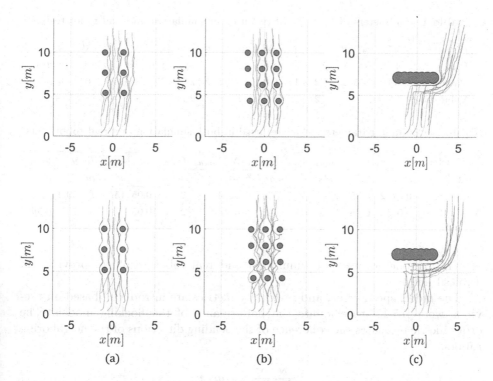

(a)   (b)   (c)

Fig. 3. Simulated trajectories of (top) PFM and (bottom) SFM in (a) the first, (b) second, and (c) third environment. Videos are available at https://tinyurl.com/Giray22.

3   Experimental Setup

We prepared three test environments consisting of a $L \times L$ rectangular arena with cylindrical obstacles to compare SFM and PFM in kinematic simulations. The first environment has low obstacle density, the second environment has high obstacle density, and the third environment contains a wall consisting of intertwined obstacles (Fig. 3).

2D Gaussian noise ($\mu = 0, \sigma_n = 0.02$) is added to the positions and velocities of the robots to test the robustness of the models. At the beginning of each test, robots are randomly placed in the environment. The tests are completed when all robots cross the finish line at y_f, and the maximum time allowed to complete a test is limited to t_{max}. Each test is repeated 10 times.

To test the applicability of PFM on real robots, we used a swarm of six Crazyflie 2.1 quadcopters[1] in an indoor flight arena populated with obstacles and communicated with them using the Crazyswarm platform [12]. Positions of the quadcopters are tracked using the Vicon motion capture system, and the velocity commands are computed on a single computer in different threads to mimic the decentralized behavior.

---

[1] https://www.bitcraze.io/products/crazyflie-2-1/.

Table 1. Parameters of PFM and SFM used in simulation and real robot tests.

Parameter	w^r	w^o	w^s	w^d	d_{eq}	$\Delta\theta$	Δv	β	d	A	B	k^r	k^o	k^m	k^l	k^a
Unit	$1/m^2$	m	s/m	–	m	rad	m/s	–	–	–	–	$1/m$	m^2	s/m	m/s	rad/s
Value (Sim.)	50	1.5	2	2	1	0.1	0.02	2	2	2	3	25	1.5	10	0.1	0.1
Value (Real)	25	3	4	2	1	0.15	0.1	2	2	2	1	–	–	–	–	–

Table 2. Common parameters that are used in both simulation and real robot tests.

Parameter	r_a	r_s	v_{min}	v_{max}	ω_{max}	a_{max}	N	M_{max}	O_{max}	Δt	t_{max}	L	y_f	v_{mig}
Unit	m	m	m/s	m/s	rad/s	m/s^2	–	–	–	s	s	m	m	m/s
Value (Sim.)	0.07	2	0.05	2	6	2	12	4	2	0.05	150	14	10.5	$1\hat{y}$
Value (Real)	0.07	2	0.05	2	6	2	6	4	2	0.05	150	8	7.5	$0.5\hat{y}$

The parameters used in simulation and real robot tests are provided in Tables 1 and 2.

The order, speed error, and proximity metrics are introduced based on previous work [15,17] to evaluate the performance of the flocking models. The order metric measures the coherence of the heading directions of the neighboring robots:

$$\Theta_{ord} = \sum_{i=1}^{N}\sum_{j=1}^{M} \frac{v_i \cdot v_j}{NM\|v_i\|\|v_j\|}. \tag{20}$$

Θ_{ord} becomes 1 when the neighboring robots are perfectly aligned, and it becomes -1 in case of complete disorder.

The speed error metric measures the normalized mean difference between the speed of the robots and the desired migration speed:

$$E_{spd} = \sum_{i=1}^{N} \frac{|\|v_{mig}\| - \|v_i\||}{N\|v_{mig}\|}. \tag{21}$$

E_{spd} becomes 0 when the robots' speed is equal to the migration speed, whereas its value gets larger when the difference between robots' speed and migration speed increases.

The proximity metric measures the normalized mean distance between the robots and their neighbors:

$$D_{prox} = \sum_{i=1}^{N}\sum_{j=1}^{M} \frac{d_{ij}}{NMd_{eq}}. \tag{22}$$

D_{prox} becomes 1 when the mean inter-robot distance is equal to the equilibrium distance. Its value decreases as the robots get closer to each other and increases as they move away from each other.

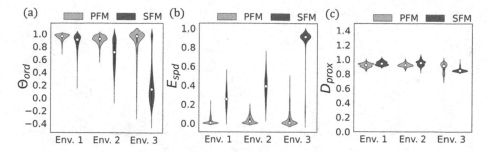

Fig. 4. (a) The order, (b) speed error, and (c) proximity metric values of PFM and SFM for the 10 times repeated tests in three different environments. Colored regions illustrate the data distribution, and white dots within the colored regions represent the median values.

4   Results and Discussion

The metric values of simulation tests for PFM and SFM in three different environments are depicted in Fig. 4 as violin plots. In violin plots, the first 0.5 seconds of each test are excluded in order to eliminate the initial transient period. PFM has order values close to 1 in all environments, whereas the order values of SFM decreased significantly in the second and third environments compared to the first one due to the change in environmental conditions (Fig. 4a). The effect of environmental change is further evident in the speed error metric; PFM has almost zero speed error values, whereas the SFM has significantly large speed error values in all environments (Fig. 4b). In the third environment, SFM only completed half of the tests within the maximum allowed time, t_{max}, and completed the remaining ones 3 to 6 times slower than PFM because of the highly reduced speed of the robots around the obstacle boundary. The performance of PFM and SFM is close in terms of cohesion; both models kept the proximity values close to 1 in all environments (Fig. 4c), and no collisions were observed throughout the tests.

For a more detailed comparison of PFM and SFM, trajectories of robots in three environments with the same initial positions are given in Fig. 3. While both models have smooth trajectories in the first environment (Fig. 3a), the trajectories of SFM are distorted near obstacle boundaries in the second and third environments (Fig. 3b, c). The order, normalized speed, and normalized inter-robot distance plots for both models in the second environment are given in Fig. 5. PFM completed the test faster than SFM by performing more ordered motion (Fig. 5a) and tracking the migration speed much better (Fig. 5b) while maintaining the mean inter-robot distance close to the equilibrium distance (Fig. 5c).

The results of the real robot test are given in Fig. 6. Similar to simulation tests, PFM completed the real robot test with nearly perfect order values (Fig. 6b) by tracking the migration speed with small errors (Fig. 6c) while keeping the mean inter-robot distance around the equilibrium distance (Fig. 6d).

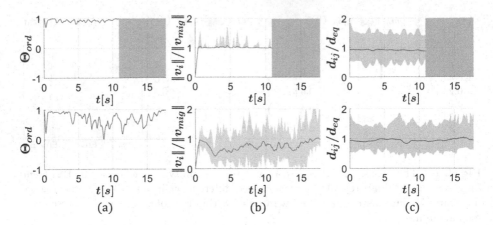

Fig. 5. (a) The order, (b) normalized speed, and (c) normalized inter-robot distance of (top) PFM and (bottom) SFM in the second environment. The plots are grey-scaled from the time PFM completes the task. In (b) and (c), solid lines are the mean values of the normalized speed and normalized inter-robot distance, whereas shades represent the maximum and minimum values. (Color figure online)

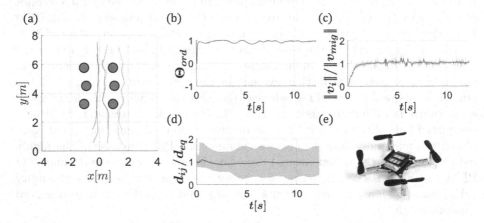

Fig. 6. (a) Trajectories of the quadcopters, (b) the order, (c) normalized speed, (d) normalized inter-robot distance of PFM in a real robot test, and (e) Crazyflie 2.1 quadcopter. In (c) and (d), solid lines are the mean values of the normalized speed and normalized inter-robot distance, whereas shades represent the maximum and minimum values. Video is available at https://tinyurl.com/Giray22.

Results of the tests showed that SFM might lead to oscillatory flocking behavior in cluttered environments due to its reactivity, and this behavior has a negative impact on the coherence of the robot swarm. Moreover, it is observed that the short-sightedness of SFM may cause robots to get stuck in obstacles and swarm speed to slow down drastically. On the other hand, it has been shown that PFM can achieve coherent flocking motion at desired migration speed in different environments by allowing the robot swarm to move according to predicted future states.

In this work, it is assumed that robots can only sense the closest point on the boundary of an obstacle. Since planning long-range trajectories without knowing the exact positions and shapes of the obstacles may be misleading, the depth of the search tree is kept small. Furthermore, it is observed that increasing the value of β does not improve the flocking behavior significantly for small depth values. Therefore, small β and d values are used in both simulation and real robot tests, reducing the required time for the trajectory search. Planning short-range trajectories also let robots use the constant velocity assumption for their neighbors, simplifying the prediction process and reducing the computational cost of PFM.

5 Conclusion

In this study, we proposed a novel search-based predictive flocking model (PFM) that only depends on local information of the neighboring robots and the environment. We compared PFM with the virtual force-based standard flocking model (SFM) in different environments based on order, speed error, and proximity metrics. Results showed that the proposed PFM could perform successful flocking behavior despite environmental differences, unlike SFM. We tested the applicability of PFM on real robots with a swarm of six quadcopters in a cluttered flight arena and validated that PFM works successfully with robot swarms as in simulation. Future work will include the dynamic obstacle avoidance and the application of the search-based prediction model for other collective behaviors such as aggregation and foraging.

Acknowledgements. This work was partially supported by the EU H2020-FET RoboRoyale (964492).

References

1. Camazine, S., Deneubourg, J.L., Franks, N.R., Sneyd, J., Theraula, G., Bonabeau, E.: Self-Organization in Biological Systems. Princeton University Press, Princeton (2020)
2. Couzin, I.D.: Synchronization: the key to effective communication in animal collectives. Trends Cogn. Sci. **22**(10), 844–846 (2018)
3. Dotson, N.M., Yartsev, M.M.: Nonlocal spatiotemporal representation in the hippocampus of freely flying bats. Science **373**(6551), 242–247 (2021)
4. Ferrante, E., Turgut, A.E., Dorigo, M., Huepe, C.: Elasticity-based mechanism for the collective motion of self-propelled particles with springlike interactions: a model system for natural and artificial swarms. Phys. Rev. Lett. **111**(26), 268302 (2013)
5. Fine, B.T., Shell, D.A.: Unifying microscopic flocking motion models for virtual, robotic, and biological flock members. Auton. Robot. **35**(2), 195–219 (2013)
6. Kong, Z., et al.: Perceptual modalities guiding bat flight in a native habitat. Sci. Rep. **6**(1), 1–10 (2016)

7. Liu, Z., Turgut, A.E., Lennox, B., Arvin, F.: Self-organised flocking of robotic swarm in cluttered environments. In: Fox, C., Gao, J., Ghalamzan Esfahani, A., Saaj, M., Hanheide, M., Parsons, S. (eds.) TAROS 2021. LNCS (LNAI), vol. 13054, pp. 126–135. Springer, Cham (2021). https://doi.org/10.1007/978-3-030-89177-0_13

8. Lyu, Y., Hu, J., Chen, B.M., Zhao, C., Pan, Q.: Multivehicle flocking with collision avoidance via distributed model predictive control. IEEE Trans. Cybern. **51**(5), 2651–2662 (2019)

9. Méhes, E., Vicsek, T.: Collective motion of cells: from experiments to models. Integr. Biol. **6**(9), 831–854 (2014)

10. Okubo, A.: Dynamical aspects of animal grouping: swarms, schools, flocks, and herds. Adv. Biophys. **22**, 1–94 (1986)

11. Parrish, J.K., Viscido, S.V., Grunbaum, D.: Self-organized fish schools: an examination of emergent properties. Biol. Bull. **202**(3), 296–305 (2002)

12. Preiss, J.A., Honig, W., Sukhatme, G.S., Ayanian, N.: Crazyswarm: a large nanoquadcopter swarm. In: 2017 IEEE International Conference on Robotics and Automation (ICRA), pp. 3299–3304. IEEE (2017)

13. Reynolds, C.W.: Flocks, herds and schools: a distributed behavioral model. In: Proceedings of the 14th Annual Conference on Computer Graphics and Interactive Techniques, pp. 25–34 (1987)

14. Soria, E., Schiano, F., Floreano, D.: Distributed predictive drone swarms in cluttered environments. IEEE Robot. Autom. Lett. **7**(1), 73–80 (2021)

15. Soria, E., Schiano, F., Floreano, D.: Predictive control of aerial swarms in cluttered environments. Nat. Mach. Intell. **3**(6), 545–554 (2021)

16. Spears, W.M., Spears, D.F., Hamann, J.C., Heil, R.: Distributed, physics-based control of swarms of vehicles. Auton. Robot. **17**(2), 137–162 (2004)

17. Vásárhelyi, G., Virágh, C., Somorjai, G., Nepusz, T., Eiben, A.E., Vicsek, T.: Optimized flocking of autonomous drones in confined environments. Sci. Robot. **3**(20), eaat3536 (2018)

18. Virágh, C., et al.: Flocking algorithm for autonomous flying robots. Bioinspir. Biomim. **9**(2), 025012 (2014)

Moving Mixtures of Active and Passive Elements with Robots that Do Not Compute

Gopesh Yadav Dosieah[1,4]([✉]), Anıl Özdemir[2,5], Melvin Gauci[3], and Roderich Groß[1]

[1] Department of Automatic Control and Systems Engineering,
The University of Sheffield, Sheffield, UK
r.gross@sheffield.ac.uk
[2] Department of Computer Science, The University of Sheffield, Sheffield, UK
[3] Amazon.com, Inc., Seattle, USA
[4] Dyson Technology Limited, Malmesbury, UK
[5] Zebra Technologies, London, UK

Abstract. This paper investigates the problem of moving a mixture of active and passive elements to a desired location using a swarm of wheeled robots that require only two bits of sensory input. It examines memory-less control strategies that map a robot's sensory input to the respective wheel velocities. Results from embodied simulations show that the problem can be solved without robots having (i) to discriminate between active and passive elements or (ii) sense other robots. Strategies optimized for moving passive elements, or mixtures of active and passive elements, performed robustly when changing the mixture of elements, or scaling up the number of robots (up to 25) or elements (up to 100). All strategies demonstrated to be fairly robust to noise and adaptable to active elements of different dynamics. Given the simplicity of the robot capabilities and strategies, our findings could be relevant in scenarios where microscopic swarm robots need to manipulate mixtures of elements of unknown dynamics, with potential applications in nanomedicine.

1 Introduction

Many studies examine the ability of swarms of robots to physically manipulate their environment. For example, this could concern the cooperative transport of an object that is too heavy to be effectively displaced by individual members of the swarm [1,4,5,11,25,28]. In the following, we specifically focus on the ability of swarms of robots to manipulate numerous elements at the same time.

In some application scenarios, the elements to be manipulated would be entirely *passive*, as exerting no control over their movement. This would be the case, for example, when collecting plastic waste in water bodies [20]. Beckers et al. [2] study a group of robots equipped with C-shaped pushers. The latter enable the robots to push and retain multiple, smaller objects even during turns. Each

© Springer Nature Switzerland AG 2022
M. Dorigo et al. (Eds.): ANTS 2022, LNCS 13491, pp. 183–195, 2022.
https://doi.org/10.1007/978-3-031-20176-9_15

robot moves in a straight line and rotates by a random angle when detecting an obstacle or when the resistance met by its pusher exceeds a threshold. The strategy is shown capable of clustering 81 objects in a bounded environment. Melhuish et al. [15] propose an extension of this strategy enabling a group of robots to spatially separate colored objects into distinct clusters. Kim and Shell [10, 21] studied a cluster task similar to [2]. As the robots are circular in shape, careful design is required to prevent the formation of (possibly separate) clusters along the boundary. The authors propose a strategy by which some robots are 'diggers', which follow walls and separate objects from the boundary, whereas others are 'twisters', which act on 'dug up' objects, and push them towards the center. This results in all objects ending up in a single cluster.

In other application scenarios, the elements to be manipulated may be *active*, as exerting control over their movements. This would be the case, for example, when shepherding groups of land mammals. The problem of *shepherding* a set of active elements to a goal region has been addressed using single-robot systems [3, 6, 22–24, 26, 27]. Vaughan et al. [26] propose a strategy to shepherd a flock of ducks towards a goal. An external system is used to determine the position of the flock, as well as the position and orientation of the robot. The robot is attracted towards the flock, the further the latter is away from the goal, the stronger the attraction. Moreover, it is repelled from the goal. This simple behavior succeeds in driving the flock towards the goal. A number of studies use distinct behaviors for (i) gathering the elements, and (ii) driving them towards the goal, which are executed either in alternation or simultaneously. Gathering maneuver include moving in arcs, zig-zags or orbiting. Driving maneuver include approaching the flock in a straight line from a position opposite to the goal, or performing gathering maneuver while gradually moving towards the goal [3, 6, 22, 24]. In [23], a robot shepherds a group of sheep agents. It relies only on local sensing. It moves repeatedly behind the sheep robot that is furthest away from the goal. Owing to a cohesion behavior however the sheep have no natural tendency to split into separate groups. Studies considering a group of shepherd robots include the work by Lien et al. [13] that demonstrated that a group of shepherds outperformed a single one. Other examples are Miki & Nakamura [16] and Lee & Kim [12] which study sets of simple rules to replicate common types of shepherding behaviors. They both demonstrated that the active elements could be herded by a swarm of robots without centralized coordination.

In our previous works [8], a computation-free paradigm for controlling swarms of simple robots was proposed. It was subsequently used to design computation-free controllers for swarms of robots to cluster passive elements [7], without specifying a desired goal region. Moreover, it was used to design computation-free controllers for swarms of robots to shepherd active elements towards a goal region [18].

This paper goes beyond prior work in swarm robotics by considering for the first time the problem of moving a loose mixture of active and passive elements towards a goal region. This problem is important for real-world applications, where the dynamics of the elements to be manipulated may not be known, or could

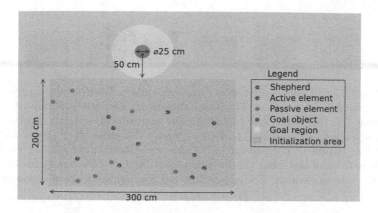

Fig. 1. A group of shepherd agents (red) is tasked to herd a mixture of elements of unknown dynamics towards a goal region (white) near a goal object (green). The elements can be actively moving (blue) or purely passive (orange). (Color figure online)

vary among the elements. We hypothesize that a single set of rules exists that requires no run-time memory and yet solves the problem irrespective of whether the elements to be manipulated are (i) passive, (ii) active, or (iii) a mixture of active and passive elements. We examine to what extent the controllers trained for any one of these sub-problems generalize to the respective other sub-problems, and hence, how the sub-problems compare in terms of complexity.

2   Methods

This section presents the problem formulation, the simulation setup used during design and validation, the control strategies of the shepherd agents, and the optimization process used for obtaining the parameters of the strategies.

2.1   Problem Formulation

The environment is an unbounded, planar, continuous space (see Fig. 1). It contains $m \geq 1$ shepherd agents, $n \geq 1$ elements, of which $n_a \geq 0$ are active and $n_p = n - n_a \geq 0$ are passive, as well as a goal object. The shepherd agents and all elements have cylindrical bodies of identical dimensions and mass. The goal object is stationary. It is also cylindrical, and assumed to be taller than the shepherd agents and elements.

Each shepherd agent has two wheels that are placed equidistant from its center. They can be controlled by setting a pair of normalized wheel speeds, $v_\ell, v_r \in [-1, 1]$, where -1 and 1 represent the maximum backward and forward speeds, respectively.

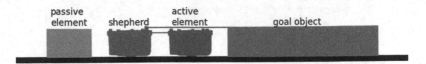

Fig. 2. Illustration of line-of-sight sensor implementation. Each shepherd agent obtains two bits of sensory information. The first indicates whether the goal object is in front of the robot (in the direct line of sight). The goal object is taller than any other object, which allows the shepherd to detect it even when some other agents or elements are placed in between. The second bit of sensory information indicates whether an element is in front of the robot (in the direct line of sight). This is only the case, if the nearest object is an element. The sensor does not distinguish between active or passive elements.

The shepherd agent has two line-of-sight sensors pointing forward, and assumed to have an infinite range.[1] The sensors are discrete; they only return the type of the first detected object in their direct line of sight (see Fig. 2). The first sensor is used to detect the goal which is taller than the shepherd agents and elements. This allows the shepherd agent to detect the goal if it is oriented towards the goal. The second sensor is used to detect the active and passive elements without distinguishing between them. For the sake of simplicity, we assume that the shepherd agent obtains a single, combined sensor reading,

$$I = \begin{cases} 0, & \text{if neither goal nor any element is detected;} \\ 1, & \text{if only an active or passive element is detected;} \\ 2, & \text{if only the goal is detected;} \\ 3, & \text{if both the goal and an active or passive element are detected.} \end{cases} \tag{1}$$

The objective for the shepherds is to herd all elements toward the goal. We define a goal region around the goal object (see Fig. 1) and assume that an element has been successfully moved towards the goal, as long as its center resides within the goal region at the end of the evaluation period. Note that the goal region is not detectable by any of the agents, it merely serves for evaluation purposes.

We consider three variants of the problem, also referred to as scenarios:

1. *Active only* scenario: all elements are active ($n_a = n$);
2. *Passive only* scenario: all elements are passive ($n_p = n$);
3. *Combined* scenario: elements of both types are present ($n_a \geq 1, n_p \geq 1$).

---

[1] Throughout this work, we assume an unlimited sensing range; in practice, however, nearly-identical results can be obtained if the sensing range is limited to a reasonably high value. The effects of a limited sensing range in a similar setting were studied in [8].

2.2 Setup for Computational Experiments

Open-source robot simulator Enki [14] was used for all computational experiments. All bodies are rigid. Their dynamics and kinematics are updated every 0.01 s. The sensors, control cycle, and actuation are updated every 0.1 s. The goal object is a cylinder of 12.5 cm radius and 5 cm height. The goal region is a disk of radius 50 cm. The shepherd agents are modelled as e-puck robots [17], which have cylindrical bodies of 3.7 cm radius and 4.7 cm height, and weigh 152 g. The active elements are modelled as e-puck robots too. The passive elements are cylindrical bodies of identical dimensions and mass. Their friction coefficient with the ground is 2.5.

The dynamics model of active elements are loosely inspired by the boids model [19]. It comprises three behavioral components:

1. To weakly repel from nearby active and passive elements;
2. To strongly repel from any nearby shepherd agent;
3. To move randomly.

All components rely only on local sensing: Active element i has two neighborhoods. The first, denoted by $\mathcal{N}_i^{\text{el}}$, comprises all other elements that are no more than $d^{\text{el}} = 10$ cm away. The second, denoted by $\mathcal{N}_i^{\text{sh}}$, comprises all shepherds that are no more than $d^{\text{sh}} = 50$ cm away. The repulsion components can then be expressed as

$$\mathbf{F}_i = k^{\text{el}} \sum_{j \in \mathcal{N}_i^{\text{el}}} \frac{\hat{\mathbf{r}}_{ji}}{||\mathbf{x}_j - \mathbf{x}_i||^2} + k^{\text{sh}} \sum_{j \in \mathcal{N}_i^{\text{sh}}} \frac{\hat{\mathbf{r}}_{ji}}{||\mathbf{x}_j - \mathbf{x}_i||^2}, \quad (2)$$

where coefficients $k^{\text{el}} = 100$ and $k^{\text{sh}} = 500$ model the strength of repulsion from other elements and shepherds, respectively, $\mathbf{x}_i$ is the position of focal element i, $\mathbf{x}_j$ is the position of any other element/agent within the corresponding neighborhood, and $\hat{\mathbf{r}}_{ji}$ is the unit vector from element/agent j to element i. We assume that the elements are indexed $1, 2, \ldots, n$ and shepherd agents are indexed $n+1, n+2, \ldots, n+m$. The wheel speeds for the active element are then calculated as:

$$\begin{pmatrix} v_l \\ v_r \end{pmatrix} = \begin{pmatrix} C_1 & C_2 \\ C_1 & -C_2 \end{pmatrix} \begin{pmatrix} f_x \\ f_y \end{pmatrix}, \quad (3)$$

where $C_1 = 2.0$ is a linear coefficient, $C_2 = 1.3$ is an angular coefficient, and f_x and f_y are the force components of $\mathbf{F}_i$ along the x- and y-axis in the focal element's coordinate frame (with the x-axis pointing towards the front of the robot).

The final behavioral component (random walk) is realized by adding random variables, which follow normal distributions $X \sim \mathcal{N}(0, 1)$, to the speed values of each wheel of the active element. Before applying the value to the actuator, it is truncated to half the maximum speed of the e-puck robot (12.8 cm/s). Therefore, in the default setup, the speed of the active elements are at most 50% of the maximally possible speed of the shepherd agents.

2.3   Control Strategies of the Shepherd Agents

Each shepherd uses the same controller. The controller is fully reactive, that is, it has no memory to store any values during run-time. It maps sensor reading I directly onto a pair of normalized wheel speeds $v_\ell, v_r \in [-1, 1]$.

The complete parameterized controller can be written as $\mathbf{v} = (v_{\ell_0}, v_{r_0}, v_{\ell_1}, v_{r_1}, v_{\ell_2}, v_{r_2}, v_{\ell_3}, v_{r_3})$, $\mathbf{v} \in [-1, 1]^8$, where (v_{ℓ_0}, v_{r_0}) is the left and right normalized wheel velocities when the combined sensor reading $I = 0$ and so on (for a definition of I, see Eq. 1).

We design three control strategies—one for each variant of the problem. We refer to them as `Controller A` (active only scenario), `Controller P` (passive only scenario), and `Controller A+P` (combined scenario). The controller variants only differ in the choice of parameter values.

2.4   Optimization Process

To optimize the parameter values of the controller, the Covariance Matrix Adaptation Evolution Strategy (CMA-ES) [9] is employed. CMA-ES is a stochastic method for optimization of non-linear, non-convex functions with continuous domains. It self-adapts the variance of decision variables and the co-variances between decision variables. In our case, the decision variables are the wheel speed pairs for every possible value of sensory input, that is, $\mathbf{v}$.

CMA-ES is conventionally unbounded, operating in the continuous space $\mathbb{R}^d$, where $d = 8$ is the problem dimension. However, as normalized wheel velocities are considered in the controller design, a way to map $\mathbb{R}^d \mapsto [-1, 1]^d$ is needed. This is achieved by using a sigmoid-based function on each wheel velocity, $sig(v) = \frac{1-e^{-v}}{1+e^{-v}}, \forall v \in \mathbb{R}$.

We set the initial solution to the zero vector $\mathbf{v}^{(0)} = \mathbf{0}$, population size to $\lambda = 20$, and the initial step size to $\sigma^{(0)} = 0.72$. These settings approximate a uniform distribution over $[-1, 1]^d$, as empirically demonstrated by Gauci et al. [7] using Monte Carlo simulations. Each evolution runs for 500 generations.

Fitness Function. To evaluate the utility of candidate solutions, a fitness function is used. For the problem considered here, the fitness function has a dual purpose. First, it shall reward candidate solutions that gather the elements, thereby providing cohesion. Second, it shall reward candidate solutions for moving elements near to the goal. A corresponding metric is established, which at time t is given by

$$f(t) = \frac{1}{4nr^2} \sum_{j=1}^{n} ||\overline{\mathbf{x}}(t) - \mathbf{x}_j(t)||^2 \cdot ||\overline{\mathbf{x}}(t) - \mathbf{g}||^2, \tag{4}$$

where r is the radius of the element body, $\overline{\mathbf{x}}(t)$ is the centroid of all elements at time t, $\mathbf{x}_j(t)$ is the position of element j at time t, and $\mathbf{g}$ is the position of the goal object.

Table 1. Best controller for each scenario.

Controller		$I = 0$	$I = 1$	$I = 2$	$I = 3$
Controller A (active elements only)	v_ℓ	0.459	0.995	0.738	−0.163
	v_r	0.983	0.161	−0.958	0.948
Controller P (passive elements only)	v_ℓ	0.997	0.925	−0.996	0.995
	v_r	0.632	1.000	−1.000	0.703
Controller A+P (combined scenario)	v_ℓ	0.592	1.000	0.729	0.794
	v_r	0.939	0.917	−0.998	0.983

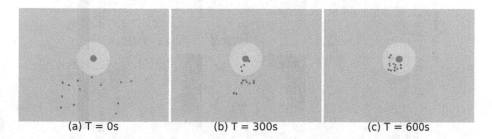

(a) T = 0s   (b) T = 300s   (c) T = 600s

Fig. 3. Sequence of snapshots showing three shepherd agents (red) moving five active (blue) and five passive (orange) elements to the goal object (green). The shepherds use controller A+P, which was specifically optimized for this scenario. (Color figure online)

Each simulation trial is associated with a weighted sum of the fitness values at times t,

$$F(T) = \sum_{t=1}^{T} t \cdot f(t),\qquad(5)$$

where $T = 600$ s is the total evaluation period (in simulated time). The weighted sum rewards the speed at which the elements are gathered and driven towards the goal while also rewarding 'convergence' towards a stable configuration.

The final fitness value is obtained as the mean $F(T)$ score across $N = 20$ independent simulation trials. In each trial, the starting locations of all agents and elements are sampled using a uniform distribution from within the initialization region denoted in Fig. 1.

3   Results

We performed 30 evolutionary runs for each of the three problem variants. In all simulation trials, $m = 3$ shepherd agents and $n = 10$ elements were used. The number of active (n_a) and passive (n_a) elements were as follows:

1. $n_a = 10, n_p = 0$ in the active only scenario (to synthesize Controller A);
2. $n_a = 0, n_p = 10$ in the passive only scenario (to synthesize Controller P);
3. $n_a = n_p = 5$ in the combined scenario (to synthesize Controller A+P).

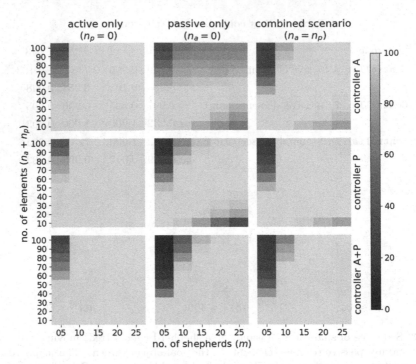

Fig. 4. Generalization and Scalability Analysis. Heat map showing the success rate grouped by controller type and scenario. Average rates over 100 trials in which m shepherd agents herd n_a active elements and n_p passive elements to the goal region.

For each scenario and for each of the 30 evolutionary runs, we post-evaluated the highest rated control strategy 100 times with random starting configurations. The best-rated controller from these post-evaluations is considered as the final controller for that scenario.

The evolved control parameters are shown in Table 1. Figure 3 shows a sequence of snapshots taken from a typical trial with `Controller A+P`. The shepherds tend to orbit around the elements and the goal. This helps to gather the elements and move them towards the goal region. A video showing representative trials for all controllers and scenarios is available on https://www.sheffield.ac.uk/naturalrobotics/supp/2022-001.

3.1 Generalization and Scalability Analysis

Each controller is examined in all three scenarios, thereby testing to what extent it generalizes beyond the specific scenario it was optimized for. For example, `Controller A`, which was trained in the active only scenario, is tested here in all three scenarios, including the passive only scenario and the combined scenario. Moreover, to test scalability of the controllers, a range of configurations is considered. Specifically, the number of shepherds is chosen as $m \in \{5, 10, 15, 20, 25\}$

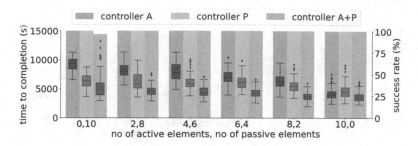

Fig. 5. Varying Ratio Analysis. Times to completion (box plots) and success rates (bar charts) for the three controllers as the ratio of active (n_a) to passive (n_p) elements is varied (100 trials per setup).

and the number of elements is chosen as $n \in \{10, 20, 30, \ldots, 100\}$ (for the combined scenario, we use $n_a = n_p = \frac{n}{2}$). Each of these configurations is tested against each of the three controllers. For each setup, 100 independent trials are conducted. Each trial lasts 1500 s.

Figure 4 shows the performance. Reported is the average *success* rate which is defined as the percentage of elements inside the goal region at the end of the trial. When only $m = 5$ shepherd agents are available, the performance of all three controllers decreases as the number of elements $n_a + n_p$ goes beyond 50. This can be attributed to the limited time available for five shepherds to move a relatively large herd, but possibly as well, though to a lesser extent, to the challenge of containing the herd, while elements move at random. The performance for Controller A and Controller P also drops when the number of shepherds m is similar to, or even exceeds, the number of elements $(n_a + n_p)$. Moreover, Controller A struggles in the passive only scenario when $n_p \geq 60$. This can be attributed to the behaviors being insufficiently optimized for handling passive elements: As the elements are no longer repelled by the shepherd, the latter has to push the elements for them to move. However, we found that this is not an issue in the combined scenario as the active elements help by pushing the passive elements and the passive elements prevent the active elements from dispersing. Controller A+P exhibited the best overall performance.

3.2   Varying Ratio Analysis

To analyse the controllers' performance with different ratio of active and passive elements, the latter is varied while keeping the total number of elements constant $(n_a + n_p = 10)$. The number of shepherds is set to $m = 3$. For each setup and controller, 100 independent trials are conducted.

Figure 5 shows the time to completion, that is, the time by which the last element enters the goal region, as well as the average success rates. As the fraction of active elements increases, the times to completion tend to become shorter, especially for Controller A and Controller A+P. For any pair of active and passive elements (n_a, n_p), Controller A+P outperforms the other two controllers

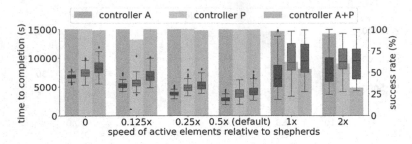

Fig. 6. Varying Speed Analysis. Times to completion (box plots) and success rates (bar charts) for the three controllers as the maximum speed of active elements is varied, expressed relative to the maximum speed of shepherd agents (100 trials per setup).

in terms of completion times. However, for the $(n_a = 0, n_p = 10)$ pair, its success rate (96%) was slightly lower than that of the other two controllers (100%).

3.3 Varying Speed Analysis

To further examine to what extent the evolved controllers cope with elements of different dynamic properties, we consider the impact of the maximum speed of the active elements. We use $m = 3$ shepherds, $n_a = 10$ active elements and no passive elements ($n_p = 0$). We choose the maximum speed of the active elements as $0 \times s, 0.125 \times s, 0.25 \times s, 0.5 \times s, 1 \times s, 2 \times s$, where $s = 12.8\,\mathrm{cm/s}$ is the maximum speed of the e-puck robot, and hence the maximum possible speed that any shepherd agent could move. For each setup and controller, 100 independent trials are conducted.

Figure 6 shows the times to completion and the average success rates. The performance is reasonably robust with respect to variations in speed. The best performance both in terms of completion times and success rates is obtained when the active elements use the default maximum speed ($0.5 \times s$). This could be because the controllers were specifically optimized for this setup. However, it is also plausible that when the active elements are too slow, they require to be *pushed* which may prove slightly less effective, whereas when the active elements are too fast, they may disperse faster (using Eq. 2), and hence make it more challenging to be contained by the shepherd agents.

3.4 Noise Analysis

To examine the robustness with respect to sensor noise, we conducted nine sets of experiments, testing each controller on each scenario. Each of the two binary sensor readings is subjected to (i) false-positive noise with probability $p \in [0, 1]$ (i.e. the sensors detect an object even though the object is not there) and (ii) false-negative noise with probability $p \in [0, 1]$ (i.e. the sensors do not detect an object even though it is present).

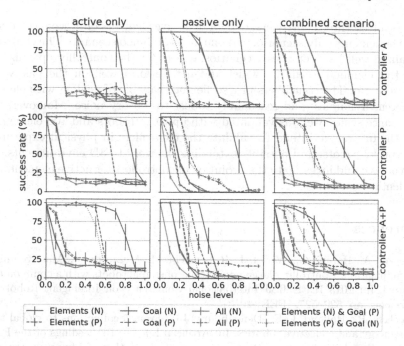

active only   passive only   combined scenario

noise level

— Elements (N)   — Goal (N)   — All (N)   — Elements (N) & Goal (P)
-+- Elements (P)   -+- Goal (P)   -+- All (P)   ⋯+⋯ Elements (P) & Goal (N)

Fig. 7. Noise analysis. Success rates for the three controllers when subject to false-positive (P) and false-negative noise (N); 100 trials per setup. (Color figure online)

Figure 7 shows the average success rates. All three controllers were particularly robust to false-negative noise on the goal sensor (solid blue line). To identify which conditions have the most adverse affect on performance, we ranked the conditions (per controller) by the lowest noise level that caused the success rate to drop to 50% (or below). `Controller A` and `Controller P` were most affected by false-positive noise on the goal sensor (irrespective of the type of noise affecting the element sensor). On the contrary, `Controller A+P` was most affected by false-negative noise on the element sensor (irrespective of the type of noise affecting the goal sensor).

4   Conclusions

This paper considered for the first time the problem of using a swarm of robots to move a mixture of active and passive elements to a goal region. It showed that this problem can be successfully addressed by robots that have only two binary sensors that detect the presence of the goal and of the elements in front of the robot, without having to distinguish between active and passive elements, and without needing to perceive the other robots in the swarm. Each robot has no run-time memory, and hence, on its own, is unable to learn the unknown dynamics of the elements during run-time.

We evolved three controllers, one for an active elements only scenario, one for a passive elements only scenario, and one for a combined scenario. The controllers generalized well between these scenarios, expect for the controller optimized for the active elements scenario, which did not perform well on the passive elements scenario. The controllers proved flexible, capable of dealing with elements of different dynamics, and reasonably robust to sensory noise. Moreover, their performance scaled well, as validated with up to 25 robots and 100 elements.

In the future, we intend to validate the controllers in physical experiments with e-puck2 robots, and possibly extending the work to 3D environments. Further studies could investigate the evolution of controllers for active elements with non-identical dynamics.

References

1. Becker, A., Habibi, G., Werfel, J., Rubenstein, M., McLurkin, J.: Massive uniform manipulation: Controlling large populations of simple robots with a common input signal. In: 2013 IEEE/RSJ International Conference on Intelligent Robots and Systems, pp. 520–527. IEEE (2013)
2. Beckers, R., Holland, O.E., Deneubourg, J.L.: From local actions to global tasks: stigmergy and collective robotics. In: Artificial Life IV: Proceedings of the Fourth International Workshop on the Synthesis and Simulation of Living Systems, pp. 181–189. MIT Press (1994)
3. Bennett, B., Trafankowski, M.: A comparative investigation of herding algorithms. In: Proceedings of the Symposium on Understanding and Modelling Collective Phenomena (UMoCoP), pp. 33–38 (2012)
4. Chen, J., Gauci, M., Li, W., Kolling, A., Groß, R.: Occlusion-based cooperative transport with a swarm of miniature mobile robots. IEEE Trans. Rob. **31**(2), 307–321 (2015)
5. Farivarnejad, H., Berman, S.: Multirobot control strategies for collective transport. Annu. Rev. Control Robot. Auton. Syst. **5**, 205–219 (2021)
6. Fujioka, K., Hayashi, S.: Effective shepherding behaviours using multi-agent systems. In: 2016 IEEE Region 10 Conference (TENCON), pp. 3179–3182 (2016)
7. Gauci, M., Chen, J., Li, W., Dodd, T.J., Groß, R.: Clustering objects with robots that do not compute. In: Proceedings of the 2014 International Conference on Autonomous Agents and Multi-Agent Systems, pp. 421–428. International Foundation for Autonomous Agents and Multiagent Systems (2014)
8. Gauci, M., Chen, J., Li, W., Dodd, T.J., Groß, R.: Self-organized aggregation without computation. Int. J. Robot. Res. **33**(8), 1145–1161 (2014)
9. Hansen, N., Ostermeier, A.: Completely derandomized self-adaptation in evolution strategies. Evol. Comput. **9**, 159–195 (2001)
10. Kim, J.H., Shell, D.A.: A new model for self-organized robotic clustering: understanding boundary induced densities and cluster compactness. In: Proceedings - IEEE International Conference on Robotics and Automation, pp. 5858–5863. IEEE (2015)
11. Kube, C.R., Bonabeau, E.: Cooperative transport by ants and robots. Robot. Auton. Syst. **30**(1–2), 85–101 (2000)
12. Lee, W., Kim, D.: Autonomous shepherding behaviors of multiple target steering robots. Sensors **17**, 2729 (2017)

13. Lien, J.M., Rodríguez, S., Malric, J.P., Amato, N.M.: Shepherding behaviors with multiple shepherds. In: Proceedings - IEEE International Conference on Robotics and Automation, pp. 3402–3407 (2005)
14. Magnenat, S., Waibel, M., Beyeler, A.: Enki: an open source fast 2D robot simulator (2009). https://github.com/enki-community/enki
15. Melhuish, C., Holland, O., Hoddell, S.: Collective sorting and segregation in robots with minimal sensing. In: From Animals to Animats 5: Proceedings of the Fifth International Conference on Simulation of Adaptive Behavior, pp. 465–470. MIT Press (1998)
16. Miki, T., Nakamura, T.: An effective simple shepherding algorithm suitable for implementation to a multi-mobile robot system. In: First International Conference on Innovative Computing, Information and Control, vol. 3, pp. 161–165 (2006)
17. Mondada, F., et al.: The e-puck, a robot designed for education in engineering. In: Proceedings of the 9th Conference on Autonomous Robot Systems and Competitions, vol. 1, pp. 59–65 (2009)
18. Özdemir, A., Gauci, M., Groß, R.: Shepherding with robots that do not compute. In: ECAL 2017: The Fourteenth European Conference on Artificial Life, pp. 332–339 (2017)
19. Reynolds, C.W.: Flocks, herds and schools: a distributed behavioral model. In: Proceedings of the 14th Annual Conference on Computer Graphics and Interactive Techniques, pp. 25–34. ACM (1987)
20. Rojas, J.: Plastic waste is exponentially filling our oceans, but where are the robots? In: 2018 IEEE Region 10 Humanitarian Technology Conference, R10-HTC, pp. 1–6 (2018)
21. Song, Y., Kim, J.-H., Shell, D.A.: Self-organized clustering of square objects by multiple robots. In: Dorigo, M., Birattari, M., Blum, C., Christensen, A.L., Engelbrecht, A.P., Groß, R., Stützle, T. (eds.) ANTS 2012. LNCS, vol. 7461, pp. 308–315. Springer, Heidelberg (2012). https://doi.org/10.1007/978-3-642-32650-9_32
22. Strömbom, D., et al.: Solving the shepherding problem: heuristics for herding autonomous, interacting agents. J. R. Soc. Interface 11, 20140719 (2014)
23. Sueoka, Y., Ishitani, M., Osuka, K.: Analysis of sheepdog-type robot navigation for goal-lost-situation. Robotics 7(2), 21 (2018)
24. Tsunoda, Y., Sueoka, Y., Sato, Y., Osuka, K.: Analysis of local-camera-based shepherding navigation. Adv. Robot. 32(23), 1217–1228 (2018)
25. Tuci, E., Alkilabi, M.H., Akanyeti, O.: Cooperative object transport in multi-robot systems: a review of the state-of-the-art. Front. Robot. AI 5, 59 (2018)
26. Vaughan, R., Sumpter, N., Frost, A., Cameron, S.: Robot sheepdog project achieves automatic flock control. In: Proceedings of the Fifth International Conference on Simulation of Adaptive Behavior on From Animals to Animats, vol. 5, pp. 489–493 (1998)
27. Vaughan, R., Sumpter, N., Henderson, J., Frost, A., Cameron, S.: Robot control of animal flocks. In: Proceedings of the 1998 IEEE International Symposium on Intelligent Control (ISIC) held jointly with IEEE International Symposium on Computational Intelligence in Robotics and Automation (CIRA) Intell, pp. 277–282 (1998)
28. Wilson, S., Pavlic, T.P., Kumar, G.P., Buffin, A., Pratt, S.C., Berman, S.: Design of ant-inspired stochastic control policies for collective transport by robotic swarms. Swarm Intell. 8(4), 303–327 (2014)

Real-Time Coordination of a Foraging Robot Swarm Using Blockchain Smart Contracts

Alexandre Pacheco$^{(\boxtimes)}$, Volker Strobel , Andreagiovanni Reina ,
and Marco Dorigo

IRIDIA, Université Libre de Bruxelles, Brussels, Belgium
{alexandre.melo.pacheco,volker.strobel,andreagiovanni.reina,
marco.dorigo}@ulb.be

Abstract. We present a novel control scheme for robot swarms that
exploits the computation layer of a blockchain to coordinate the actions of
individual robots in real-time. To accomplish this, we deploy a blockchain
smart contract that acts as a "decentralized supervisor" during a swarm
foraging task. Our results show that using blockchain-based global coordination rules can improve the foraging behavior of robot swarms, while
maintaining a decentralized, scalable, and democratic system in which
every robot contributes homogeneously to the decision-making process.

1 Introduction

The application of blockchain technology to robotic systems is a fast growing
research topic. Particularly, in swarm robotics, the most noteworthy advance-
ment was the recent introduction of a blockchain in order to achieve secure
consensus in the presence of Byzantine agents: in [19,27], it was shown that
blockchain-secured robot swarms can be deployed in situations where security
against unauthorized agents is paramount.

The introduction of a *decentralized* and *secure* database such as the blockchain might have a strong impact on the field of swarm robotics. However, further research is required to understand the extent of this impact, as well as its
potential drawbacks.

Ethereum [3] extended the application of blockchains from financial ledgers
to decentralized computing platforms. This means that the participants in the
Ethereum network can agree not only on the execution of financial transactions,
but also on the execution of computer programs known as *smart contracts*.

In this paper, we argue and validate the claim that smart contracts can be
very valuable when applied to the real-time coordination of robot swarms. In
this context, a smart contract is control code that is executed in a decentralized
manner by the swarm; that is, each robot executes the code independently and
the swarm comes to an agreement on its output. On a micro perspective, the
individual robots collect local information and deliver it to the smart contract by
broadcasting local messages. On a macro perspective, the smart contract extends

M. Dorigo et al. (Eds.): ANTS 2022, LNCS 13491, pp. 196–208, 2022.
https://doi.org/10.1007/978-3-031-20176-9_16

the swarms' ability to self-organize by aggregating the input of the robots and returning action policies on which the robots can act in real-time.

To demonstrate this, we deploy a blockchain smart contract to act as a "decentralized supervisor" during a collective foraging task in which the swarm needs to collect resources spread in an unknown environment. The robots broadcast messages—known as *transactions*—that contain information the robots obtained from scouting the environment for resources and that should be included in new blocks of the blockchain. The information about the environment contained in these transactions is aggregated by the smart contract into a shared database of resource locations. The blockchain consensus protocol guarantees that these transactions are executed orderly and conflict-free, and that all robots reach an agreement on the most recent state of this database. Furthermore, the smart contract distributes the available robots (recruits) to the various resources, while (i) prioritizing resources with better quality; and (ii) limiting the number of foragers per resource. These simple rules are shown to increase the resource collection rate and energy efficiency during the task. As consensus protocol we use proof-of-authority [29], which we have shown in previous research [19] to be suitable for robot swarms since it requires low power and is robust to network partitioning and temporary unavailability of robots.

The rest of the paper is organized as follows. In Sect. 2, we review related works. In Sect. 3, we introduce the foraging task, the environment, and other methods relevant for the implementation of the experiments: the simulations software, the robot's model, the blockchain, and the robot controllers. In Sect. 4, we present and discuss the experimental results. In Sect. 5, we deliver the conclusions of this study.

2   Related Work

Cooperation in Foraging Robot Swarms. Foraging is one of the most studied behaviors in swarm robotics because it models a wide range of application scenarios, such as search and rescue, agriculture, mining, waste cleaning, and planetary exploration. It can be described as the combination of two sub-tasks: searching the environment for objects, and performing actions on those objects (e.g., transportation, consumption, destruction, ...). In this work we focus on central place foraging [13], where agents are tasked with finding and transporting objects back to a target location (called "nest").

Inspired by the foraging behavior of ants, which deposit pheromones along paths leading to objects [5], robot swarm algorithms are most frequently based on indirect communications (stigmergy). Researchers have attempted to mimic ant behavior by using chemicals [24]; augmented reality pheromones [10]; and virtual pheromones, which are advertised locally by robots with the role of pheromone beacons [4,12,17]. The main advantages of these methods are scalability and robustness; however, their implementation either requires specific equipment and infrastructure (e.g., a smart environment or sensors/actuators for chemicals) or reduces efficiency by allocating part of the swarm to play the role of beacons.

Additionally, it has recently been shown that stigmergy is particularly fragile when malicious agents are present [1].

For these reasons, some researchers have employed forms of explicit communication to coordinate the collective foraging behavior, inspired by the recruitment dances that honeybees perform to signal foraging locations to peers [2,25].

Pitonakova et al. [21,22] compare swarms where robots recruit other robots at the nest with swarms of individualist foragers. They show that when resources are scarce or difficult to find, nest-site recruitment can be helpful to maximize the total resources collected. Conversely, if resources are abundant, it may be more advantageous to forage individually as this might prevent both *physical interference* (when robots foraging for the same resources collide) and *informational interference* (when robots are misguided by incorrect social information). Despite this insight, no coordination strategy nor methodology to enable the validation of the information are proposed in order to limit or reduce interference.

Applications of Blockchain to Swarm Robotics. The application of blockchain technology to robot swarms was demonstrated for the first time in [26–28], where the authors presented a proof-of-concept (in simulation) showing how blockchain-based smart contracts can be used to neutralize the negative effects of Byzantine robots in a consensus problem. In [19] the authors presented the first implementation of a blockchain in a swarm of real robots using proof-of-authority consensus [3,29], which is shown to be suitable to robot swarms given that it is energy efficient and robust to network partitioning.

Although these studies showcase the promise of smart contracts to achieve generic swarm-wide agreements, it is not yet clear whether the network consensus delay is too large to allow a wider range of applications—particularly, real-time control. Some researchers have presented control architectures in which the blockchain is maintained outside of the robot's network [9]. This design is akin to using an external control element (albeit, a distributed one in this case), and does not grant the autonomy and fault-tolerance properties warranted in a robot swarm. In this paper, we present a decentralized and autonomous robot swarm that uses blockchain smart contracts for real-time coordination.

3   Methods

Task. The goal of the swarm is to retrieve resources from the environment and deposit them at the nest. Resources have various qualities that yield a different reward when deposited. The performance of the swarm is measured in terms of the total *reward* collected, and of the *scouting efficiency*, which is the ratio between the reward collected and the distance traveled by the robots while exploring the environment. Each experiment lasts 15 min.

Environment. The environment consists of a square arena with the nest located at the center. The size of the arena is a function of the number of robots (i.e., we maintain a constant robot density of 3 robots per m^2), and the nest occupies

SSP (scattered, small)   SBP (scattered, big)   CSP (clustered, small)

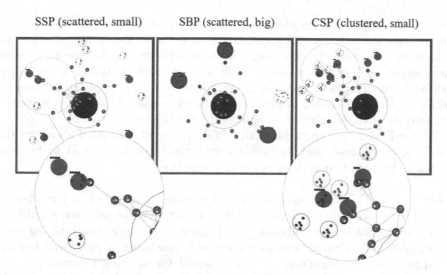

Fig. 1. A frame from a simulation run for each resource patch distribution: *SSP* (left), *SBP* (middle) and *CSP* (right). The patches are circles with items inside (the resources). A gray background means that the patch is included in the blockchain database, and the black dots above represent the remaining quantity of resources according to the blockchain database. The brown circle and annulus in the center are the nest and its deposit area, respectively. (Color figure online)

10% of the arena's total area. The nest is divided into two areas (Fig. 1): an external annulus, where robots can deposit resources; and an internal circle, where robots can idle. The nest broadcasts a homing signal which allows the robots to navigate to the nest from any location.

Resource *patches* are circular areas distributed randomly in an annulus centered on the nest and with radiuses 0.83 m and 1.44 m. *Resources* are individual items contained in a patch that the robots can collect and deposit at the nest. The patches can be of 4 different types (red, green, blue and yellow), and the resources collected from each type yield a different reward (2, 4, 6 and 8, respectively). Once a patch runs out of resources, an identical patch spawns elsewhere.

We consider three *distributions* of patches and resources in the environment. In all distributions, approximately 3% of the environment area is covered with patches, and there is an identical number of red, green, blue and yellow patches.

- **Scattered small patches (SSP)** The patches are distributed uniformly in the annulus, have a diameter of 16cm and contain 10 resources (Fig. 1, left).
- **Scattered big patches (SBP)** The patches are distributed uniformly in the annulus, have a diameter of 36cm and contain 15 resources (Fig. 1, middle).
- **Clustered small patches (CSP)** The patches are distributed according to a normal distribution that is biased towards the upper left quadrant of the arena, have a diameter of 16cm and contain 10 resources (Fig. 1, right).

Simulation Setup. The simulation setup consists of the swarm robotics simulation software ARGoS [20]; the blockchain software Ethereum [3]; and the virtualization software Docker [14]. The nodes of a custom Ethereum network are executed in Docker containers. Each ARGoS robot controller is associated with an Ethereum node, and can interact with the client application software (geth). In this way, ARGoS interacts with the client-side of Ethereum, while the maintenance of the blockchain is handled by the Docker containers.

We use Python wrappers for both ARGoS [11], and geth [8]. This allows the robot control routines and interactions with the blockchain client to be fully written in Python. Our code is available online [18].

Robot Model. The agent used in the simulations is a model of the *Pi-puck robot* [15]. In previous research, we showed that the Pi-pucks are capable of executing the blockchain software [19]. In order to perform the foraging task, the Pi-pucks use infrared sensors for obstacle avoidance; a range-and-bearing board for local peer discovery; a ground sensor for scouting resource patches; and two motors for locomotion. The manipulation of resources is not modeled.

Blockchain Protocol. For a thorough understanding of blockchain technology, we refer the readers to the papers on Ethereum [3] and Bitcoin [16]. Here we focus on the two components of blockchain technology which are most relevant for this work: *consensus protocols* and *smart contracts*.

The *consensus protocol* consists of the rules used by a blockchain network to agree on the addition of new blocks of information to the blockchain. In situations of conflict (known as blockchain *forks*), it also establishes the rule that defines what becomes the current accepted state of the blockchain. To accomplish this, proof-of-work, the original blockchain consensus protocol introduced with Bitcoin [16], requires the expenditure of computational resources. As such, it is often considered contraindicated for swarm robotics applications [23], which typically consider robots with limited capabilities and resources [6].

In our research, we have decided to use proof-of-authority [29] as an alternative to proof-of-work. Proof-of-authority keeps a core of authorized and accountable nodes which share the role of producing new blocks. In this protocol, anyone can create a block and propose it to be added to the chain, but in order to be considered a valid block three conditions must be met: (i) the difference between the timestamp of two consecutive blocks must be at least $t = T_b$ seconds (T_b is called the *block period*); (ii) the block must be correctly signed by an authorized node (known as a "sealer") using its private key; and (iii) a sealer can only sign one block every $\lfloor \frac{N}{2} \rfloor + 1$ blocks (N is the number of sealers).

Every node in the network checks if a proposed block meets these conditions. If this is the case, the node appends that block to its local copy of the blockchain. The consensus protocol establishes that the current version of the blockchain is the one which has the highest *cumulative difficulty*. Blocks which are signed *in-turn* (i.e., that are signed by an appointed preferred sealer for that block), contribute with a difficulty of 2; while other blocks contribute with 1.

When deploying a robot swarm it is important to consider that: (i) some robots may be unavailable when the network is partitioned; and (ii) some robots may join or leave the swarm during its operation. In the first situation, it is possible that the robots disconnected from the partition hosting the main blockchain (which has the highest cumulative difficulty) operate on a different version of the blockchain (i.e., a blockchain fork). Eventually, when the partitions reconnect, the main blockchain is established by consensus and the transactions included in the fork are rebroadcast. In the second situation, we note that the proof-of-authority consensus protocol allows current sealers to democratically elect or remove sealers, thus allowing for dynamic swarm sizes. In this paper, however, we maintain constant swarm sizes and every robot is a sealer throughout the duration of the experiment.

A *blockchain smart contract* is a computer program that is stored on the blockchain, and that encapsulates code (its functions) and data (its state). Network participants can execute its functions by broadcasting transactions to the smart contract address, which in turn will change its state. It is the role of the blockchain system to agree on the irrefutable execution of these state-altering transactions in a decentralized manner.

Our smart contract allows robots: (i) to store information regarding discovered resource patches; (ii) to enlist themselves as recruits in order to forage at a certain patch; and (iii) to query information about the known resource patches. Its programming code ensures that the information the robots provide is synchronized without conflicts; that the highest-reward resources are prioritized for foraging; and that there is a limit on the number of foragers per patch.

The robots can interact with functions by broadcasting *transactions* (to execute the function on the blockchain network), or by invoking *calls* (to execute the function locally and read its output). Our smart contract has 3 functions:

- `update_patches(patches[])` The input is a list of formatted strings which contain the relevant information about a patch: position, radius, quality, and quantity of resources. If the position is unique (within an error margin) a new resource is added to the database, otherwise an existing resource is updated.
- `assign_patch()` If there are available patches (i.e., patches with fewer foragers than the maximum number allowed), then the transacting robot is assigned as a forager to the highest quality patch.
- `query_patches()` Returns a database of resources, including the current foragers for each resource.

Robot Controller. The robots are controlled by a *finite-state machine*. At each simulation step, the robots perform a routine corresponding to their current state, as well as a *local peer discovery* routine.

The *finite-state machine* starts at the state Scout and is composed of 5 states:

- Idle Wait for 30 s; then, transition to Scout.
- Scout Perform a random-walk, with a duration sampled from $\mathcal{N}(\mu = 40$ s, $\sigma = 2$ s) and store the discovered patches in a list stored locally; then, broad-

cast a transaction to execute `update_patches(scouted_patches)`. Once the transaction is included in a block, delete the list and transition to `Plan`.

- `Plan` Return to the nest using the homing signal and invoke a call to `query_patches()`. If assigned to forage a resource, transition to `Search`; otherwise, broadcast a transaction to execute `assign_patch()`, and wait until it is included in a block. If the transaction fails (no resources available to forage), transition to `Idle`.
- `Search` Navigate from the nest towards the direction of the assigned patch and search its neighborhood for 10 s. If resources are found, transition to `Forage`; otherwise broadcast a transaction to execute `update_patches(depleted_patch)` and transition to `Scout`.
- `Forage` Collect a resource from the patch and navigate to the nest using the homing signal. Then, broadcast a transaction to execute `update_patches(current_patch)` to inform that one resource was removed. Once the transaction is included in a block, deposit the resource and, if there were more resources, transition to `Search`; otherwise, transition to `Scout`.

The *local peer discovery* routine enforces that all communications, including blockchain synchronization, occur locally (up to 30 cm). Within this range, the robots broadcast and receive IP addresses using infrared signals on the range-and-bearing board. After receiving an IP address, robots use TCP to share their *enode*—a unique URL used to identify and connect to nodes in the Ethereum network. If the infrared signal is lost, the robot disconnects from that peer on the blockchain network and deletes its IP address and enode from its local memory. This peering scheme serves two purposes: (i) to ensure that communications are only local and thus mimic a real-world swarm deployment where network partitioning can occur; and (ii) to provide an additional layer of security which prevents external agents from participating in the network (since the robots reject connections which are not accompanied by the short-range infrared greeting).

4   Results and Discussion

In general, our goal is to show that a blockchain can extend the swarm's ability to self-organize, and thus improve its collective performance, while maintaining the properties of a robot swarm: *decentralization, scalability* and *adaptability*.

The blockchain allows robots to agree on the state of the environment and on a coordination strategy, without the need for delegated supervisors (in contrast with centralized or hybrid control). Since the proof-of-authority consensus algorithm is robust to the unavailability of up to 50% of the network nodes, our blockchain-coordinated robot swarm does not have a singular point-of-failure and could be deployed in situations where a system that relies on information traveling to and from supervisors would fail (for example, in environments with limited or no communication infrastructure). In this sense, a blockchain enables a decentralized and democratic swarm, in which all robots contribute homogeneously to the decision-making process.

On the downside, it is important to analyze the impact of *consensus latency*, i.e., the time it takes for messages to be disseminated through the network and for robots to reach agreements in this democratic process—as well as the costs of *data storage*, since each robot keeps a local copy of the blockchain database. These aspects could raise scalability concerns in terms of communication and hardware requirements for robot swarms. In Sect. 4.1 we discuss these concerns, and show that they are manageable for swarms of different sizes.

In foraging, cooperation is not always an advantage [22]. Sharing information can lead to an increased rate of physical interference, for example, when the robots forage the same resources rather than finding a balance between exploitation and exploration. It may also lead to informational interference, which occurs when robots propagate incorrect or outdated information (e.g., if a resource patch becomes depleted during the time the information is being processed, or if the robots' sensors provide inaccurate positions).

The role of our smart contract supervisor is to improve the performance of the swarm (in terms of the *reward* collected and the *scouting efficiency*) by aggregating information about resource patches from the robot scouts, and assigning resource patches to robot recruits—thus minimizing the impact from both forms of interference. In Sect. 4.2 we report the performance results of a blockchain-coordinated robot swarm and we compare them to those obtained with a swarm of uncoordinated robots, which explore the environment and forage resources as they discover them individually, in environments with different resource distributions. In these experiments, we keep the swarm size constant (25 robots) and analyze how performance changes as the maximum number of foragers that the smart contract allows per patch increases.

4.1 Scalability

Consensus Latency. Figure 2 (left) shows the *Block Reception Delay*, which is the difference between the timestamp at the moment a robot receives a block and the timestamp at the moment the block was produced (in other words, the time it took for a block to be disseminated through the network from its producer to any other robot). Figure 2 (right) shows the *Block Production Delay*, which is the difference of the timestamps between two consecutive blocks on the final version of the blockchain. The first metric is calculated online by the robots, while the second is calculated offline after the experiment is finished.

The *block period* (T_b) parameter sets the minimum required difference between the timestamps of two consecutive blocks (see Sect. 3), and thus has a big effect on the information delay introduced by the blockchain: if it is too high, it reduces the possibility to employ the shared knowledge to perform time-critical tasks. Conversely, if it is too low, it increases the frequency of block production which leads to (i) higher costs of communication, computation, and data storage; and (ii) an increased rate of blockchain forks which contain redundant, or more dangerously, conflicting information. In Fig. 2 (left) we observe that a majority of blocks are received within 2 s. This observation justifies our choice of $T_b = 2$ s,

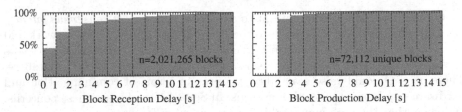

Fig. 2. The histograms represent cumulative probability distributions, and are generated from the combined data of all experiments performed in this study. Left: In 70% of the instances a robot received a block, that block was produced less than 2 s earlier; and in 100% of the instances, less than 15 s earlier. Right: The minimum and ideal production delay is equal to $T_b = 2$ s. An additional delay occurs due to network delays (e.g., temporary unavailability of the preferred block producer). In our experiments, 90% of the blocks were produced within 2 s to 3 s, which means that the blockchain is operating as designed.

as there is a high chance that the previous block has been disseminated through the network before it is time to produce the next block.

Data Storage. In previous research [19], we set the block period to 15 s. With a block period of 2 s, we expect that the cost of storing the blockchain will be higher since the amount of data stored depends on the number of blocks created (as well as on the number of transactions performed by the robots).

Figure 3 (left) shows the data storage required by each robot, which is seen to increase linearly with the number of robots in the swarm. On average, each robot requires 8 MB for 15 min of operation, which we consider reasonable given current data storage technology. Furthermore, the robots in our experiments are *full blockchain nodes*, i.e., each robot stores the complete blockchain history. In a real deployment this might not be necessary, since only the most recent information is relevant for the robots' operations, and the task of storing the blockchain history can be delegated to external agents when connection is available, or it can be segmented and stored by the robots in a distributed manner. In this case, the hardware-limited robots would host *light blockchain nodes* [7], while remaining able to verify the status of the blockchain and of the transactions by leveraging cryptographic primitives. For these reasons, we do not expect data storage to pose a scalability problem in a real deployment.

Performance. Figure 3 (right) shows that the swarm is capable of maintaining performance (the total reward collected increases with the number of robots) as the environment size, number of robots and quantity of resources scale accordingly. However, we also observe decreasing performance returns (the total reward collected increases sublinearly with the number of robots). Rather than a limitation of our blockchain-coordinated approach, this seems to occur due to the layout of the environment, which is prone to interference at the centrally located nest when the swarm size increases.

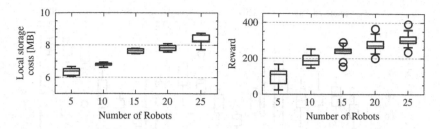

Fig. 3. Left: The storage space required for each robot grows linearly with the number of robots, at a rate of approximately 1 MB per 10 robots. Right: The collected reward grows sublineary with the number of robots, due to the increasing rate of physical interference at the centrally located nest. These experiments were repeated 25 times using the SSP distribution.

4.2   Performance in Different Distributions

SSP Distribution. In this environment there is a large number of patches randomly spread on the map. Previous research [22,30] indicates that individualist foragers tend to perform well, or even better than cooperating robots (when the benefits of cooperation do not overcome the negative effects of interference). In Fig. 4 (left) the total reward collected saturates at 2 foragers per patch, but is consistently higher than the non-collaborating swarm ('NC' in the x-axis). The scouting efficiency can be significantly higher but also has a high spread. This happens because cooperating robots, when lucky, will discover higher quality patches and better allocate foragers to those resources.

SBP Distribution. The blockchain-coordinated swarm is capable to retrieve 50% to 100% more reward, and to be twice more efficient in scouting for resources, as seen in Fig. 4 (middle). In this environment, the advantage of coordination is more pronounced since (i) the patches last longer as they contain more resources, and (ii) they are larger in size and there is therefore less interference.

CSP Distribution. The blockchain-coordinated swarm is capable to retrieve more than double of the reward and be 2 to 5 times more efficient during scouting, as seen in Fig. 4 (right) than non-collaborating swarms. This occurs because the scouting robots which move in the direction of the resource cluster are very successful, while others robots do not find any resources. The ability to aggregate and share information prevents unsuccessful robots from idling or wasting energy performing redundant exploration. Conversely, given the tight aggregation of resources, the foraging efficiency quickly drops as the number of recruits increases above 3 due to physical interference between robots.

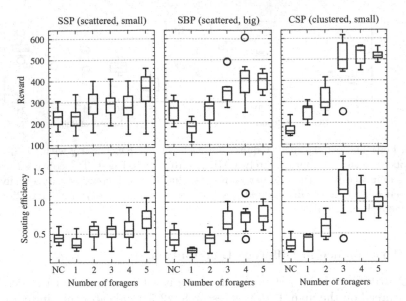

Fig. 4. Performance results for three distributions: SSP (left), SBP (middle) and CSP (right). The top row shows the reward collected by the swarm at the end of the experiment, and the bottom row the scouting efficiency. The x-axis (number of foragers) is a parameter in the smart contract which limits how many robots can be tasked as foragers for each resource patch. The uncoordinated robot swarm shows "NC". A swarm of 25 robots was used, and the experiments were repeated 10 times.

5   Conclusions

We showed that the coordination rules provided by a smart contract supervisor can improve the performance of the robot swarm during the foraging task, while keeping reasonable data storage costs and manageable delay in the control loop. These are positive results that showcase the potential of deploying blockchains for the real-time coordination of robot swarms in a wider range of scenarios.

The usage of a blockchain in a swarm robotics system enables a new class of distributed control algorithms that use explicit communication and coordination, while preserving decentralization and local exchanges of information. It is important to note the contrast between the macro perspective that is used when creating smart contract supervisors and the micro perspective that is more frequent in the design of robot swarm controllers. In our research, we present the two approaches as complementary since the behavior of individual robots emerges from local sensing and interactions, while the blockchain is regarded as an additional layer that is reserved for high-level decision making.

Acknowledgements. This work was partially supported by the program of Concerted Research Actions (ARC) of the Université libre de Bruxelles and by the Brussels-Capital Region via the Brussels International contract n. BI-MB-531-004021. A. Reina and M. Dorigo acknowledge support from the Belgian F.R.S.-FNRS, of which they are Chargé de Recherches and Research Director, respectively.

References

1. Aswale, A., López, A., Ammartayakun, A., Pinciroli, C.: Hacking the colony: on the disruptive effect of misleading pheromone and how to defend against it. In: Proceedings of the 21st International Conference on Autonomous Agents and MultiAgent Systems (AAMAS 2022), pp. 27–34. International Foundation for Autonomous Agents and Multiagent Systems, Richland (2022)
2. Biesmeijer, J.C., de Vries, H.: Exploration and exploitation of food sources by social insect colonies: a revision of the scout-recruit concept. Behav. Ecol. Sociobiol. **49**(2), 89–99 (2001). https://doi.org/10.1007/s002650000289
3. Buterin, V.: A next-generation smart contract and decentralized application platform. Technical report, Ethereum Foundation (2014). https://github.com/ethereum/wiki/wiki/White-Paper. Accessed 18 July 2019
4. Campo, A., et al.: Artificial pheromone for path selection by a foraging swarm of robots. Biol. Cybern. **103**(5), 339–352 (2010). https://doi.org/10.1007/s00422-010-0402-x
5. Deneubourg, J.L., Aron, S., Goss, S., Pasteels, J.M.: The self-organizing exploratory pattern of the argentine ant. J. Insect Behav. **3**(2), 159–168 (1990). https://doi.org/10.1007/BF01417909
6. Dorigo, M., Birattari, M., Brambilla, M.: Swarm robotics. Scholarpedia **9**(1), 1463 (2014)
7. Ethereum Foundation: Ethereum project (2017). https://ethereum.org
8. Ethereum Foundation: ethereum/web3.py: A Python interface for interacting with the Ethereum blockchain and ecosystem (2022). https://github.com/ethereum/web3.py
9. Fernandes, M., Alexandre, L.A.: Robotchain: using tezos technology for robot event management. Ledger **4** (2019). https://doi.org/10.5195/ledger.2019.175. https://www.ledgerjournal.org/ojs/ledger/article/view/175
10. Font Llenas, A., Talamali, M.S., Xu, X., Marshall, J.A.R., Reina, A.: Quality-sensitive foraging by a robot swarm through virtual pheromone trails. In: Dorigo, M., Birattari, M., Blum, C., Christensen, A.L., Reina, A., Trianni, V. (eds.) ANTS 2018. LNCS, vol. 11172, pp. 135–149. Springer, Cham (2018). https://doi.org/10.1007/978-3-030-00533-7_11
11. Hasselmann, K., Parravicini, A., Pacheco, A., Strobel, V.: KenN7/argos-python: python wrapper for ARGoS3 simulator (2022). https://github.com/KenN7/argos-python
12. Hoff, N., Wood, R., Nagpal, R.: Distributed colony-level algorithm switching for robot swarm foraging. In: Martinoli, A., et al. (eds.) Distributed Autonomous Robotic Systems, vol. 83, pp. 417–430. Springer, Heidelberg (2013). https://doi.org/10.1007/978-3-642-32723-0_30
13. Houston, A.I., McNamara, J.M.: A general theory of central place foraging for single-prey loaders. Theor. Popul. Biol. **28**(3), 233–262 (1985). https://doi.org/10.1016/0040-5809(85)90029-2
14. Merkel, D.: Docker: lightweight Linux containers for consistent development and deployment. Linux J. **2014**(239) (2014)

15. Mondada, F., et al.: The e-puck, a robot designed for education in engineering. In: Gonçalves, P.J.S., Torres, P.J.D., Alves, C.M.O. (eds.) Proceedings of the 9th Conference on Autonomous Robot Systems and Competitions, vol. 1, pp. 59–65. IPCB: Instituto Politécnico de Castelo Branco (2009)
16. Nakamoto, S.: Bitcoin: a peer-to-peer electronic cash system (2008). https:// bitcoin.org/bitcoin.pdf
17. Nouyan, S., Groß, R., Bonani, M., Mondada, F., Dorigo, M.: Teamwork in self-organized robot colonies. IEEE Trans. Evol. Comput. **13**(4), 695–711 (2009). https://doi.org/10.1109/TEVC.2008.2011746
18. Pacheco, A., Strobel, V.: teksander/geth-argos at ANTS2022. https://github.com/ teksander/geth-argos
19. Pacheco, A., Strobel, V., Dorigo, M.: A blockchain-controlled physical robot swarm communicating via an ad-hoc network. In: Dorigo, M., et al. (eds.) ANTS 2020. LNCS, vol. 12421, pp. 3–15. Springer, Cham (2020). https://doi.org/10.1007/978-3-030-60376-2_1
20. Pinciroli, C., et al.: ARGoS: a modular, parallel, multi-engine simulator for multi-robot systems. Swarm Intell. **6**(4), 271–295 (2012). https://doi.org/10.1007/ s11721-012-0072-5
21. Pitonakova, L., Crowder, R., Bullock, S.: Understanding the role of recruitment in collective robot foraging. In: Proceedings of the 14th International Conference on the Synthesis and Simulation of Living Systems (ALIFE 2014), pp. 264–271 (2014). https://doi.org/10.7551/978-0-262-32621-6-ch043
22. Pitonakova, L., Crowder, R., Bullock, S.: The information-cost-reward framework for understanding robot swarm foraging. Swarm Intell. **12**(1), 71–96 (2017). https://doi.org/10.1007/s11721-017-0148-3
23. Reina, A.: Robot teams stay safe with blockchains. Nat. Mach. Intell. **2**, 240–241 (2020). https://doi.org/10.1038/s42256-020-0178-1
24. Salman, M., Garzón Ramos, D., Hasselmann, K., Birattari, M.: Phormica: photochromic pheromone release and detection system for stigmergic coordination in robot swarms. Front. Robot. AI **7** (2020). https://www.frontiersin.org/article/10. 3389/frobt.2020.591402
25. Seeley, T.D.: Division of labor between scouts and recruits in honeybee foraging. Behav. Ecol. Sociobiol. **12**(3), 253–259 (1983). https://www.jstor.org/stable/ 4599586
26. Strobel, V., Castelló Ferrer, E., Dorigo, M.: Managing Byzantine robots via blockchain technology in a swarm robotics collective decision making scenario. In: Proceedings of the 17th International Conference on Autonomous Agents and MultiAgent Systems (AAMAS 2018), pp. 541–549. International Foundation for Autonomous Agents and Multiagent Systems, Richland (2018)
27. Strobel, V., Castelló Ferrer, E., Dorigo, M.: Blockchain technology secures robot swarms: a comparison of consensus protocols and their resilience to Byzantine robots. Front. Robot. AI **7**, 54 (2020). https://doi.org/10.3389/frobt.2020.00054
28. Dorigo, M., Birattari, M., Blum, C., Christensen, A.L., Reina, A., Trianni, V. (eds.): ANTS 2018. LNCS, vol. 11172. Springer, Cham (2018). https://doi.org/10. 1007/978-3-030-00533-7
29. Szilágyi, P.: EIP 225: clique proof-of-authority consensus protocol (2017). https:// github.com/ethereum/EIPs/issues/225. Accessed 10 May 2020
30. Wilson, E.O.: Sociobiology: The New Synthesis, Twenty-Fifth Anniversary Edition. Harvard University Press, Cambridge (2000)

Robot Swarms Break Decision Deadlocks in Collective Perception Through Cross-Inhibition

Raina Zakir[✉][iD], Marco Dorigo[iD], and Andreagiovanni Reina[iD]

IRIDIA, Université Libre de Bruxelles, Brussels, Belgium
{raina.zakir,marco.dorigo,andreagiovanni.reina}@ulb.be

Abstract. We study how robot swarms can achieve a consensus on the best among a set of n possible options available in the environment. While the robots rely on local communication with one another, follow simple rules, and make estimates of the option's qualities subject to measurement errors, the swarm as a whole is able to make accurate collective decisions. We compare the performance of two prominent decision-making algorithms that are based, respectively, on the direct-switching and the cross-inhibition models, both of which are well-suited for simplistic robots. Most studies used these models to let robots achieve consensus by solely relying on social interactions and ignored the aspect of enabling robots to self-source information from the environment. However, in order to select the best option, we deem sampling environmental information crucial for the successful performance of the task. Through robot-swarm simulations, we show that swarms programmed with the direct-switching model are only able to make consensus decisions in asymmetric environments where options have different quality values. Instead, using cross-inhibition, the robot swarm can also break decision deadlocks and reach a consensus in symmetric environments with equal quality options. We investigate the mechanistic causes of such differences and we find that the time the robots spend in a state of indecision is a key parameter to break the symmetry. This research highlights the importance of considering both social and environmental information when studying collective decision-making.

1 Introduction

Swarm robotics is the research field that studies how to apply principles of swarm intelligence [5] to the design of decentralised systems consisting of large numbers of relatively simple robots that collectively perform tasks or solve problems [8]. As the robots within a swarm do not have global knowledge, the swarm's collective behaviour emerges from the local interactions among the robots and from the interactions the robots have with their surrounding environment. Collective decision-making is a particular type of collective behaviour that is paramount to achieve group coordination—as such it is very often found in group-living animals [6]. For example, honeybees make consensus decisions on the site where to

© Springer Nature Switzerland AG 2022
M. Dorigo et al. (Eds.): ANTS 2022, LNCS 13491, pp. 209–221, 2022.
https://doi.org/10.1007/978-3-031-20176-9_17

build their nest among several alternative locations [26], ants are able to collectively select the shortest path from their nest to a profitable food source [10], and flocks of birds on the move select the same direction of motion in a decentralised way [3]. These natural systems have inspired the development of many different types of algorithms to enable robot swarms to make consensus decisions, such as selecting the aggregation site [27], selecting the direction of motion [7,9,17], selecting the predominant environmental feature [33], or selecting the shortest path for transporting items efficiently [29]. These algorithms need to be simple—to run on simple robots—and, at the same time, robust to robot malfunctions and flexible to changing environments—to work in real-life applications. A particularly important collective decision-making problem for swarm robotics is the so-called "best-of-n problem" [34], that is, how the swarm can select the best option among a set of n alternatives.

In this study, we consider the best-of-2 problem in which a minimalistic robot swarm is tasked with making a consensus decision on an environmental feature [33]. The environment floor is covered with yellow and blue tiles, and the environmental feature to decide on is which is the predominant colour. Therefore, the two colours represent the two alternative options to decide between, and the abundance of each colour (i.e. the proportion of yellow, or blue, tiles) represents the quality of the option. To achieve consensus on one of the two environmental features, the robots utilise a minimalistic decision-making algorithm. Each robot is committed to the option it considers the best and broadcasts voting messages about this option to its neighbours. Robots apply the decision-making algorithm to update their commitment to an option; the update can be based on either social information (received from neighbours as voting messages) or self-sourced information (obtained through independent exploration). Robots receiving voting messages from their peers update their opinion (i.e. the option to which they are committed) using minimalistic *opinion update models*. These models are minimalistic in nature and are therefore a viable solution for reaching consensus in simplistic robots. Periodically, robots choose to ignore social information and self-source information from the environment by independently switching their commitment to the option locally sensed in the environment. The individual self-sourcing of information through independent exploration of the environment can allow the swarm to achieve better adaptability in dynamic environments [2,30,36] where qualities of options may change over time. However, self-sourcing information is a form of asocial behaviour that also increases fluctuations (or noise) in the consensus formation [21,31] that may result in decision deadlocks in certain decision-making algorithms [12,16,21]. Hence, the opinion update models that are used in collective decision-making need to be resilient to decision deadlocks when the amount of noise increases, either due to the exploration of the environment to achieve adaptability or to other sources, such as malfunctioning sensors on the robots that make them asocial (stubborn or zealot) and threaten the resiliency of symmetry-breaking in collective decision-making [14,15].

Based on the literature, one of the most widespread models for updating a robot's opinion upon receiving new social information is direct-switching [35], in which a robot switches to a random neighbour's opinion during the voting phase. Direct-switching has been extensively used to engineer decentralised systems because of its simplicity and favourable tractability in minimalistic systems. However, theoretical studies on opinion dynamics [16] predict that direct-switching leads to decision deadlocks in presence of noise (e.g. self-sourcing environmental information). Despite being a highly relevant process in making decisions on the best option, there has been limited research focusing on the impact of self-sourcing environmental information on the collective dynamics of swarms using the direct-switching model. An alternative to the direct-switching model is the cross-inhibition model [18, 22, 23], which is inspired by the house-hunting process in honeybees [26]. The cross-inhibition model has comparable simplicity to direct-switching, and theory predicts a higher resilience to the presence of noise. Unlike what happens with the direct-switching model, when a robot using the cross-inhibition model receives a contrasting opinion from one of its neighbours, it gets uncommitted and remains without an opinion—i.e. it becomes undecided. Using robot swarm simulations, we estimate to what extent the decision-making algorithm based on the cross-inhibition model is resilient to increasing noise and show that the time spent by the robots in the uncommitted state is fundamental to the ability of being resilient to noise induced from the self-sourcing information.

The outline of the rest of the paper is as follows. Section 2 defines the best-of-n problem, the collective decision-making algorithms, and the mechanism to self-source information from the environment. In Sect. 3, we describe the experimental setup and explain the parameters that have been analysed in this study. In Sect. 4, we present the results, and finally, in Sect. 5, we conclude and discuss possible directions in which this work could be extended.

2 The Models

We consider the $n = 2$ instance of the best-of-n decision problem, in which the swarm has to converge to the best between two options, A or B. Each option has a quality, q_A and q_B, and the parameter $q = q_A/q_B$ represents the ratio between the two qualities. Without loss of generality, in our study, we assume that $q_A \geq q_B$. Each robot is committed to an option, which corresponds to the robot's opinion, or uncommitted, that is, without an opinion. The robot behaviour is based on the same finite state machine of [35] characterised by two continuously alternating states: exploration and dissemination shown in Fig. 1A. In the exploration state, the robots assess the quality q_i of their current opinion by sampling the environment (with $i = \{A,B\}$). The amount of time a robot stays in exploration is drawn randomly from an exponential distribution with a rate equal to λ^{-1}. In the dissemination state, the robots disseminate their opinion i locally to their neighbours. The amount of time a robot spends disseminating its opinion is drawn from an exponential distribution with a rate $q_i\, g$, which is directly proportional to the option's quality q_i and is scaled by the average duration of dissemination g. The parameter g is set based on the requirements of the considered scenario. By scaling the time spent in the dissemination state proportionally to the quality of the options assessed in the exploration state, the probability of receiving messages from peers committed to the best opinion increases because they disseminate for a longer time. As a result, it will be more likely to observe neighbours that are in favour of the best option than observing neighbours that are supporting the lower quality option. The dissemination state is followed by either a polling state or a self-sourcing state (see Fig. 1A). The decision to go to either states is random, based on the noise probability η. With probability η, the robot self-sources a new opinion from the environment, and with probability $(1 - \eta)$ polls other robots' information. In the self-sourcing state, the robot replaces its opinion with the option (i.e. the colour) found in its current location of the environment. Including the self-sourcing mechanism allows the robots to periodically monitor the environment and reconsider the best option with new environmental evidence. On the other hand, the polling state involves collecting the opinions of the neighbours, choosing one at random and then applying an opinion update mechanism—either direct-switching or cross-inhibition. In this study, to simplify the behaviour for minimalistic robots and minimise memory use, the robots in the polling state only consider the first message they receive from their neighbours. Finally, after either using social information or self-sourcing environmental information, a robot returns to the exploration state to continue the cycle.

Direct-Switching. When it uses direct-switching as its opinion update model, the robot reads the message of one randomly chosen neighbour (which is disseminating within its communication range) and adopts that neighbour's opinion regardless of whether it is the same or different from the robot's own opinion. This mechanism allows accurate consensus formation among neighbours [35]. However, it can also result in unstable group dynamics due to the formation of echo chambers among robots with the same opinion that can prevent consensus formation in the swarm [28].

Cross-Inhibition. According to the cross-inhibition model, the robot can either be committed to an option or uncommitted. During polling, when a committed robot reads a (randomly chosen) message from a robot committed to a different option (e.g. a robot committed to A reads a message from a robot committed to B), it gets inhibited and becomes uncommitted. When an uncommitted robot receives any opinion (A or B) from one of its neighbours, it gets recruited to the received option.

3   Experimental Setup

To analyse the models introduced in Sect. 2, we implement the collective decision-making behaviour on a swarm of $N = 100$ simulated robots. For this analysis,

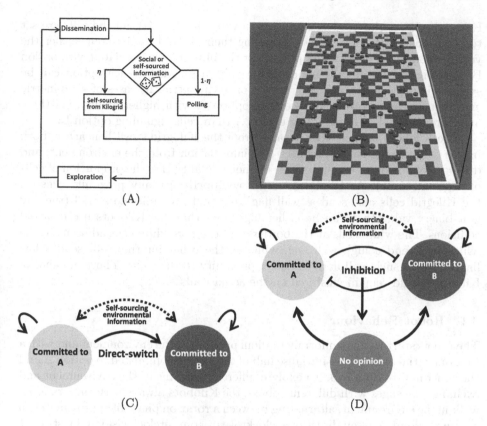

Fig. 1. (A) The finite state machine (FSM) describing the robots' behaviour, based on the FSM of [35] and extended to include the possibility of self-sourcing information. The rectangles represent the four FSM's states and the arrows represent the transitions among them. (B) Snapshot of an experiment showing 50 simulated Kilobots in the ARGoS Kilogrid arena comprising yellow and blue tiles. (C–D) Robot's opinion update model of direct-switching and cross-inhibition, respectively. The robot updates its opinion based on either social information (solid lines) or self-sourced environmental information (dashed lines). In direct-switching (C), the robot that gets recruited changes its commitment immediately. In cross-inhibition (D), when a committed robot receives a message from a robot committed to a different option, it resets its commitment (it gets inhibited). (Color figure online)

we use Kilobots [24]—small-sized and low-cost robots that communicate using infrared (IR) transceivers with other robots in a range of 10 cm, move at a speed of 1 cm/s and have a control loop of approximately 32 ms. We simulate the robot swarm in ARGoS, a state-of-the-art swarm robotics simulator [19, 20]. To provide robots with a virtual environment from which they can self-source information, we simulate the Kilogrid [1, 32]. The Kilogrid is an electronic table sized $[1 \times 2]\,\mathrm{m}^2$, composed of 800 cells that interact with the Kilobots through IR and that can be easily simulated in ARGoS [2]. With the exception of the

Kilogrid cells at the borders (depicted in white in Fig. 1B), all the cells are set to send constantly IR messages signalling their ID and their colour, either the yellow colour associated with option A or the blue colour associated with option B. The proportion of cells allocated to emit messages for each option can be symmetric (50% for A and 50% for B) or asymmetric. In cases of asymmetric environment, as a convention, we keep option A with higher quality, i.e. there are more Kilogrid cells signalling option A than cells signalling option B.

The Kilobots use the IR messages from the Kilogrid's cell beneath it both in the self-sourcing state to collect new information from the environment, and during exploration to estimate their opinion's quality (i.e. the proportion of cells of a given colour). As Kilobots are not equipped with any proximity sensors, the Kilogrid cells also send a 'wall flag' to signal proximity to a wall (the flag is a binary value that can be either high/low) that the Kilobots use to avoid collisions. The white cells at the borders and the non-white cells adjacent to the white cells send a high wall flag, while all the other internal cells send a low flag. Without such wall flags to detect proximity to the walls, a large number of Kilobots would remain clustered on the arena walls.

3.1 Robot Behaviour

The robots start from a uniformly random position in the environment and with a random initial opinion; we initialise half of the swarm committed to option A and the other half to option B. To explore different portions of the environment and exchange messages with different robots, the Kilobots always perform a random walk in the environment, alternating between a rotation phase of approximately 5 s (in a randomly chosen direction—clockwise or counterclockwise) and a straight motion phase of approximately 10 s. The random walk allows the robots to encounter different robots in their neighbourhood during the dissemination phase and allows more accurate estimation of the option qualities from the Kilogrid during the exploration phase.

A robot that receives a high wall flag from the Kilogrid executes—regardless of its state—a simple obstacle avoidance routine. The robot starts a random rotation phase of approximately 4 s followed by a straight motion phase of approximately 7 s. If the wall flag is detected again, the obstacle avoidance routine is reinitialised till the robot receives a low flag.

All robots start the experiment in an exploration state. During the exploration, a robot committed to i reads the Kilogrid messages to keep the count T_i of the number of cells it encountered (it uses the cell's ID to count each cell only once) and the count C_i of how many of the visited cells have the same colour as its own opinion i. At the end of the exploration cycle, the robot estimates the quality $q_i = \min(1, 2C_i/T_i)$, hence $0 \leq q_i \leq 1$. When $C_i/T_i \geq 0.5$, the quality is set to its maximum $q_i = 1$ as the goal is to select the predominant colour, and because the robot has found more than half of the readings have colour i, it assigns to i the maximum quality. For $C_i/T_i < 0.5$, the quality scales linearly in $[0, 1]$. The values T_i and C_i correspond to the counts of one exploration cycle only and are reset before entering the dissemination state.

Based on q_i, the robot computes the dissemination time using an exponential distribution with $\lambda_d^{-1} = q_i\, g_c$ where $g_c = 1\,300$ is the average number of control cycles in dissemination when $q_i = 1$, which corresponds to λ_d^{-1} of about 40 s. In case the robot is uncommitted, the parameter λ_d^{-1} is set to $0.5\,g_u$; using the default value for $g_u = 400$, the uncommitted robot spends an average of approximately 6 s in the dissemination state. At the end of the dissemination, the robot decides with probability η whether to perform either an individual environmental observation (enter the self-sourcing state) or a social interaction (enter the polling state). Once the environmental observation or the polling are terminated, the robot computes the exploration time and enters the exploration state again. A committed robot computes the exploration time using $\lambda_e = 0.0003$, resulting in an average exploration time of approximately 100 s. Instead an uncommitted robot uses the same rate used to compute the dissemination time, i.e. $\lambda_e^{-1} = \lambda_d^{-1} = 0.5\,g_u$, with $g_u = 400$. The total duration of each simulation run is 110 min.

4 Experiments and Results

We run simulations to test the effect of different values of the noise probability $\eta = 0$ (no noise), $\eta = 0.01$ (low), $\eta = 0.05$ (medium) and $\eta = 0.25$ (high), on both opinion update models for different quality ratios q. In the first set of experiments, we test direct-switching and cross-inhibition models in a symmetric environment (50% of the Kilogrid cells signal option A and 50% option B), i.e. $q = q_A/q_B = 1$. The second set of experiments includes the direct-switching and cross-inhibition model in asymmetric environments with three values of quality ratio q: 1.08 (Kilogrid cells: 52%A, 48%B), 1.22 (Kilogrid cells: 55%A, 45%B), and 1.5 (Kilogrid cells: 60%A, 40%B). For each condition, we run 50 simulations that we use to generate the histograms of Fig. 2. The histograms show how frequently the swarm distributes between robots supporting option A and B in the last 1 000 timesteps (approximately 30 s) of a run. For each timestep, we subtract the proportion of robots supporting option B from the proportion of robots supporting option A, i.e. (number robots for A - number robots for B)$/N$, and report the results as histograms in Fig. 2.

Figure 2 shows that when the environment is symmetric ($q = 1$), both models are able to break the symmetry in the absence of noise ($\eta = 0$). However, the performance of direct-switching deteriorates as soon as noise is introduced ($\eta \geq 0.01$), and the swarm cannot reach any agreement but remains in a state of decision deadlock. Direct-switching with noise $\eta > 0$ can only reach convergence to a stable majority towards the best option for a high quality ratio ($q = 1.22$ for low noise and $q = 1.5$ for medium noise); in all other conditions the swarm using direct-switching remains in an undecided state. Instead, the cross-inhibition is consistently able to break the symmetry for both low and medium levels of noise ($\eta \leq 0.05$) for any tested value of q. With higher levels of noise, both models fail to break the symmetry, even when the quality ratio increases. In summary, cross-inhibition is always better than direct-switching to break decision deadlocks and make consensus decisions, except for cases in which noise is very high.

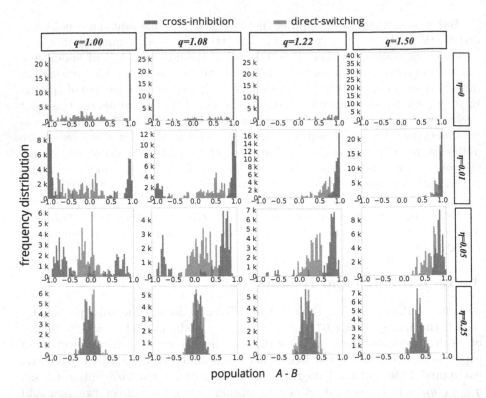

Fig. 2. Histograms for cross-inhibition and direct-switching models when $N = 100$, $g_c = 1300$ and $g_u = 400$ (statistics over 50 runs) showing the effect of increasing the probability of self-sourcing environmental information (η) and the quality ratio ($q = q_A/q_B$) on the collective decision-making process. The histograms are computed as the difference between the proportion of robots supporting A and B for each of the last 1 000 timesteps of every run ((A-B)/N on the x-axis).

To further analyse the mechanism through which the cross-inhibition model is resilient to decision deadlocks, we test the influence of the amount of time a robot spends in the uncommitted state and its ability to break the symmetry. To do so, we vary the average duration of dissemination and exploration of uncommitted agents by varying the parameter g_u from 0 to 2 000 (corresponding to an average temporal duration from 0 s to approximately 62 s). When $g_u = 0$, the voting mechanism becomes equivalent to direct-switching. Increasing g_u corresponds to increasing the time the robot spends in an uncommitted state, as g_u determines the average dissemination and exploration time of uncommitted robots. The change in dynamics with noise $\eta = 0.05$ and $q = 1$ is shown in Fig. 3A. When $g_u = 0$, the result obtained corresponds to dynamics similar to those observed in direct-switching with $\eta = 0.05$ in a symmetric environment (Fig. 2, $q = 1$ and $\eta = 0.05$); the swarm remains in a decision deadlock. As g_u increases, the bistability becomes more prominent, as observed in $\eta = 0.05$ in the symmetric

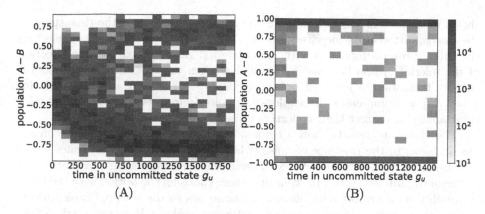

Fig. 3. (A) 2D-histogram for increasing g_u for $\eta = 0.05$ and $q = 1$ showcasing the shift from indecision to symmetry-breaking. (B) 2D-histogram for $\eta = 0$ and $q = 1.22$ showcasing the switch from consensus on the best option when $g_u = 0$ to bistability as g_u increases. The plots show how the distribution of robots supporting A and B (y-axis) change as g_u (x-axis) increases. We consider the last 1 000 timesteps (*e.g.* 6 s) of each of the 50 runs per g_u and subtract the proportion of robots supporting option B from the proportion of supporters for A (i.e. (number robots for A - number robots for B)/N) to plot the 2D-histograms.

environment (Fig. 2). The results of Fig. 3A show that the amount of time spent in an uncommitted state is the key to converging on a large majority for one of the two equivalent options.

The cross-inhibition model has dynamics that are much more stable than direct-switching [26]; therefore, the swarm reaches and maintains an agreement for either option. However, the high stability of the cross-inhibition model can also occasionally lock the system in a consensus for the inferior option (with lower quality), which may have been reached due to initial random fluctuations. Figure 2 shows that the system is in a bistability state (i.e. selection of both options is possible) when the options have similar qualities ($q \leq 1.08$ in the presence of noise) and is instead able to reliably select the superior alternative for larger quality differences. Differently, the direct-switching model, when it is able to break the symmetry, always selects the option with the highest quality. Interestingly, for $q = 1.22$, cross-inhibition's bistability exists for $\eta = 0$ and vanishes for higher levels of noise, $\eta = 0.01$ and $\eta = 0.05$. In this case, occasionally self-sourcing information helps in correcting initial mistakes.

To understand the accuracy of the two opinion update models in selecting the best option in the presence of similar quality options, we vary the time g_u when $q = 1.22$ and $\eta = 0$ (Fig. 3B). For $g_u = 0$, the swarm breaks the symmetry in favour of the option of highest quality (A) as the model is equivalent to direct-switching. When g_u increases, the system gradually moves towards a state of bistability. As observed in Fig. 2 ($q = 1.22$ and $\eta = 0$), cross-inhibition can occasionally select the inferior option due to its highly stable dynamics that lock the system into consensus for either option when qualities are similar. Figure 3B shows that bistability becomes more and more pronounced as the time spent in the uncommitted state increases, or, in other words, the probability of selecting the inferior option increases with increasing g_u. As noted earlier, the selection of the inferior option becomes less probable when the cross-inhibition model is subject to moderate levels of noise (compare Fig. 2 $\eta = 0$ and $\eta = 0.01$, for $q = 1.22$) as it increases the exploratory behaviour of the robots and enables their ability to correct their collective decision.

Therefore, our results show a trade-off between the ability to make consensus decisions in the presence of noise (when the robots spend long times in the uncommitted state) and the ability to avoid inaccurate decisions (for short times in the uncommitted state). In scenarios where choosing the option with the highest quality is an utmost requirement and noise is a factor not applicable, direct-switching is a better choice for collective decision-making. However, random fluctuations can be inevitable in systems operating in the real world, and we have shown how they can dramatically hamper the performance of direct-switching. Therefore, our study highlights the importance of using cross-inhibition to make collective decisions in realistic application scenarios.

5   Discussion and Conclusions

In this study, we investigated two prominent collective decision-making algorithms for the best-of-n problem in the presence of both social interactions and environmental information. The results of our simulations show that robot swarms running algorithms based on the direct-switching model fail to reach a consensus on the best option when robots use both social information and self-sourced information acquired through individual exploration of the environment. Self-sourcing information from the environment can also be modelled as noise, which is very likely to be present in most real-world scenarios, for example in the form of asocial robots or sensor failures [11]. Therefore, even if direct-switching has the desirable property of being very simple, to deploy systems in the real world the robot algorithms must be resilient to noise. We show that the cross-inhibition model serves as an ideal alternative to direct-switching. By letting robots inhibit each other and become uncommitted for some time, the cross-inhibition model enables stability and symmetry-breaking dynamics that prevent decision deadlocks. This work is limited to simulation; we plan as future work to conduct mathematical analyses based on ODEs and chemical reaction network models in order to understand better the role of the time spent in the uncommitted state for obtaining high stability and breaking symmetry. We also plan to validate our results through real-robot experiments on the real Kilogrid. Moreover, most of the collective decision-making research in swarm robotics is concentrated on binary best-of-n problems, with only a few studies exploring $n > 2$ [4,13,25,30]. Therefore, as future work, we also aim to expand our analyses and experiments to $n > 2$ scenarios and investigate if the robustness of the cross-inhibition model extends to non-binary environments, as theory predicts [22].

Acknowledgements. The authors thank Till Aust and Jonas Kuckling for the technical support on simulating the Kilogrid and running simulations on the HPC. This work was supported by Service Public de Wallonie Recherche under grant n° 2010235 - ARIAC by DigitalWallonia4.AI. M. Dorigo and A. Reina acknowledge support from the Belgian F.R.S.-FNRS, of which they are Research Director and Chargé de Recherches, respectively.

References

1. Antoun, A., Valentini, G., Hocquard, E., Wiandt, B., Trianni, V., Dorigo, M.: Kilogrid: a modular virtualization environment for the Kilobot robot. In: 2016 IEEE/RSJ International Conference on Intelligent Robots and Systems (IROS), pp. 3809–3814 (2016). https://doi.org/10.1109/IROS.2016.7759560
2. Aust, T., Talamali, M., Dorigo, M., Hamann, H., Reina, A.: The hidden benefits of limited communication and slow sensing in collective monitoring of dynamic environments. In: Dorigo, M., et al. (eds.) Swarm Intelligence (ANTS 2022). LNCS, vol. 13491. Springer, Cham (2022)
3. Ballerini, M., et al.: Empirical investigation of starling flocks: a benchmark study in collective animal behaviour. Anim. Behav. **76**(1), 201–215 (2008). https://doi.org/10.1016/j.anbehav.2008.02.004
4. Bartashevich, P., Mostaghim, S.: Multi-featured collective perception with evidence theory: tackling spatial correlations. Swarm Intell. **15**, 83–110 (2021). https://doi.org/10.1007/s11721-021-00192-8
5. Bonabeau, E., Dorigo, M., Theraulaz, G.: Swarm Intelligence: From Natural to Artificial Systems. Oxford University Press, New York (1999)
6. Bose, T., Reina, A., Marshall, J.A.R.: Collective decision-making. Curr. Opin. Behav. Sci. **6**, 30–34 (2017). https://doi.org/10.1016/j.cobeha.2017.03.004
7. Campo, A., Nouyan, S., Birattari, M., Groß, R., Dorigo, M.: Negotiation of goal direction for cooperative transport. In: Dorigo, M., Gambardella, L.M., Birattari, M., Martinoli, A., Poli, R., Stützle, T. (eds.) ANTS 2006. LNCS, vol. 4150, pp. 191–202. Springer, Heidelberg (2006). https://doi.org/10.1007/11839088_17
8. Dorigo, M., Birattari, M., Brambilla, M.: Swarm robotics. Scholarpedia **9**(1), 1463 (2014)
9. Ferrante, E., Turgut, A.E., Huepe, C., Stranieri, A., Pinciroli, C., Dorigo, M.: Self-organized flocking with a mobile robot swarm: a novel motion control method. Adapt. Behav. **20**(6), 460–477 (2012). https://doi.org/10.1177/1059712312462248
10. Goss, S., Aron, S., Deneubourg, J.L., Pasteels, J.: Self-organized shortcuts in the argentine ant. Naturwissenschaften **76**, 579 (1989). https://doi.org/10.1007/BF00462870
11. Khalil, N., Miguel, M.S., Toral, R.: Zealots in the mean-field noisy voter model. Phys. Rev. E **97**(1), 012310 (2018). https://doi.org/10.1103/physreve.97.012310
12. Khaluf, Y., Pinciroli, C., Valentini, G., Hamann, H.: The impact of agent density on scalability in collective systems: noise-induced versus majority-based bistability. Swarm Intell. **11**(2), 155–179 (2017). https://doi.org/10.1007/s11721-017-0137-6
13. Lee, C., Lawry, J., Winfield, A.F.T.: Negative updating applied to the best-of-n problem with noisy qualities. Swarm Intell. (2), 111–143 (2021). https://doi.org/10.1007/s11721-021-00188-4
14. Mobilia, M., Petersen, A., Redner, S.: On the role of zealotry in the voter model. J. Stat. Mech. Theory Exp. **2007**(08), P08029 (2007). https://doi.org/10.1088/1742-5468/2007/08/p08029

15. Mobilia, M.: Does a single zealot affect an infinite group of voters? Phys. Rev. Lett. **91**(2), 028701 (2003). https://doi.org/10.1103/physrevlett.91.028701

16. Mobilia, M.: Nonlinear q-voter model with inflexible zealots. Phys. Rev. E **92**(1), 012803 (2015). https://doi.org/10.1103/physreve.92.012803

17. Nouyan, S., Campo, A., Dorigo, M.: Path formation in a robot swarm: self-organized strategies to find your way home. Swarm Intell. **2**(1), 1–23 (2008). https://doi.org/10.1007/s11721-007-0009-6

18. Pais, D., Hogan, P.M., Schlegel, T., Franks, N.R., Leonard, N.E., Marshall, J.A.R.: A mechanism for value-sensitive decision-making. PLoS ONE **8**(9), 1–9 (2013). https://doi.org/10.1371/journal.pone.0073216

19. Pinciroli, C., Talamali, M.S., Reina, A., Marshall, J.A.R., Trianni, V.: Simulating Kilobots within ARGoS: models and experimental validation. In: Dorigo, M., Birattari, M., Blum, C., Christensen, A.L., Reina, A., Trianni, V. (eds.) ANTS 2018. LNCS, vol. 11172, pp. 176–187. Springer, Cham (2018). https://doi.org/10.1007/978-3-030-00533-7_14

20. Pinciroli, C., et al.: ARGoS: a modular, parallel, multi-engine simulator for multi-robot systems. Swarm Intell. **6**(4), 271–295 (2012). https://doi.org/10.1007/s11721-012-0072-5

21. Rausch, I., Reina, A., Simoens, P., Khaluf, Y.: Coherent collective behaviour emerging from decentralised balancing of social feedback and noise. Swarm Intell. (2), 321–345 (2019). https://doi.org/10.1007/s11721-019-00173-y

22. Reina, A., Marshall, J.A.R., Trianni, V., Bose, T.: Model of the best-of-N nest-site selection process in honeybees. Phys. Rev. E **95**(5), 052411 (2017). https://doi.org/10.1103/PhysRevE.95.052411

23. Reina, A., Valentini, G., Fernández-Oto, C., Dorigo, M., Trianni, V.: A design pattern for decentralised decision making. PLoS ONE **10**(10), e0140950 (2015). https://doi.org/10.1371/journal.pone.0140950

24. Rubenstein, M., Ahler, C., Nagpal, R.: Kilobot: A low cost scalable robot system for collective behaviors. In: 2012 IEEE International Conference on Robotics and Automation. IEEE Press, Piscataway (2012). https://doi.org/10.1109/ICRA.2012.6224638

25. Scheidler, A., Brutschy, A., Ferrante, E., Dorigo, M.: The k-unanimity rule for self-organized decision making in swarms of robots. IEEE Trans. Cybern. **46**, 1175 (2016). https://doi.org/10.1109/TCYB.2015.2429118

26. Seeley, T.D., Visscher, P.K., Schlegel, T., Hogan, P.M., Franks, N.R., Marshall, J.A.R.: Stop signals provide cross inhibition in collective decision-making by honeybee swarms. Science **335**(6064), 108–111 (2012). https://doi.org/10.1126/science.1210361

27. Sion, A., Reina, A., Birattari, M., Tuci, E.: Controlling robot swarm aggregation through a minority of informed robots. In: Dorigo, M., et al. (eds.) Swarm Intelligence (ANTS 2022). LNCS, vol. 13491. Springer, Cham (2022). https://doi.org/10.48550/arXiv.2205.03192

28. Starnini, M., Frasca, M., Baronchelli, A.: Emergence of metapopulations and echo chambers in mobile agents. Sci. Rep. **6**, 1–8 (2016). https://doi.org/10.1038/srep31834

29. Talamali, M.S., Bose, T., Haire, M., Xu, X., Marshall, J.A.R., Reina, A.: Sophisticated collective foraging with minimalist agents: a swarm robotics test. Swarm Intell. **14**(1), 25–56 (2019). https://doi.org/10.1007/s11721-019-00176-9

30. Talamali, M.S., Saha, A., Marshall, J.A.R., Reina, A.: When less is more: robot swarms adapt better to changes with constrained communication. Sci. Robot. **6**(56), eabf1416 (2021). https://doi.org/10.1126/scirobotics.abf1416

31. Tsimring, L.S.: Noise in biology. Reports on progress in physics. Phys. Soc. **77**(2), 026601 (2014). https://doi.org/10.1088/0034-4885/77/2/026601
32. Valentini, G., et al.: Kilogrid: a novel experimental environment for the kilobot robot. Swarm Intell. **12**(3), 245–266 (2018)
33. Valentini, G., Brambilla, D., Hamann, H., Dorigo, M.: Collective perception of environmental features in a robot swarm. In: Dorigo, M., et al. (eds.) ANTS 2016. LNCS, vol. 9882, pp. 65–76. Springer, Cham (2016). https://doi.org/10.1007/978-3-319-44427-7_6
34. Valentini, G., Ferrante, E., Dorigo, M.: The best-of-n problem in robot swarms: Formalization, state of the art, and novel perspectives. Front. Robot. AI **4**, 9 (2017). https://doi.org/10.3389/frobt.2017.00009
35. Valentini, G., Hamann, H., Dorigo, M.: Self-organized collective decision making: the weighted voter model. In: Proceedings of the 13th International Conference on Autonomous Agents and Multiagent Systems, AAMAS 2014, pp. 45–52. IFAA-MAS, Richland (2014)
36. Wahby, M., Petzold, J., Eschke, C., Schmickl, T., Hamann, H.: Collective change detection: adaptivity to dynamic swarm densities and light conditions in robot swarms. In: Artificial Life Conference Proceedings, pp. 642–649. MIT Press, Cambridge (2019). https://doi.org/10.1162/isal_00233

Self-organized Chain Formation
of Nano-Drones in an Open Space

Agata Barciś[1]([✉])[iD], Michał Barciś[1][iD], Enrico Natalizio[1,2][iD],
and Eliseo Ferrante[1,3][iD]

[1] Technology Innovation Institute, Autonomous Robotics Research Center,
Abu Dhabi, United Arab Emirates
{agata.barcis,michal.barcis,enrico.natalizio,eliseo.ferrante}@tii.ae
[2] Université de Lorraine, CNRS, Loria, Villers-lès-Nancy, France
[3] Vrije Universiteit Amsterdam, Amsterdam, Noord-Holland, The Netherlands

Abstract. We propose a method for the chain formation of multiple
agents in an open space. Chaining can be considered as a building block
for several application scenarios, including exploration, maintaining connectivity, or path formation. The proposed method was designed for
a very sensing and computationally constrained robot platform, more
specifically for nano-drones as they offer advantages in applications in
tight spaces or in the proximity of people. To enable portability to a
real platform, the method relies on a range and bearing sensing model
with a limited field of view that is susceptible to occlusions, which was
implemented both in simulation as well as on the real robot through a
camera coupled with LEDs. We analyze the method in the simulation-
based study. We show that the method works even in presence of noise in
sensing and actuation, which rather than being harmful to the chaining
performance has a positive effect. We analyze the performance in terms
of quality of final chain formation, and speed of convergence, and how
these two are affected by increasing swarm size. Finally, we present its
practical feasibility in a robotic proof-of-concept featuring nano-drones.

1 Introduction

The problem of chain formation is widely studied in swarm robotics, and fos-
ters many practical application scenarios. In fact, it enables path formation
in which the agents act as landmarks for other agents in foraging [14,18] or
task sequencing [6]. Chaining was also applied to navigation [5] and exploration
of tunnel-like environments (e.g., caves) with the requirement to keep connectivity [8,10]. Despite the advancements in the development of both chaining
methods and robot capabilities, most state-of-the-art solutions are designed for
ground robots, and there are still no reliable solutions available for drones.

In this work, we focus on chaining methods that would be suitable for nano-
drones. The main motivation for this choice is the capability of nano-drones to
explore tight spaces, e.g., underground tunnels, ventilation ducts, or pipes. Additionally, thanks to their low cost, they facilitate the development and deployment

© Springer Nature Switzerland AG 2022
M. Dorigo et al. (Eds.): ANTS 2022, LNCS 13491, pp. 222–233, 2022.
https://doi.org/10.1007/978-3-031-20176-9_18

of large groups of robots. Finally, they are safer than standard-size drones and can work even in proximity of people, for example, in warehouse inventory or factory surveillance, without disturbing their normal operations.

However, these advantages of nano-drones come at the price of numerous limitations and challenges. The noise in sensing and actuation, present in any robotic or especially drone system, might be increased due to the minimization of sensors. In general, nano-drones used for swarm robotics have much more limited sensing abilities compared to the ground counter-part, and standard swarm models developed for ground robots are not directly portable to nano-drones [2,3]. The small payload that the nano-drones can carry leads to two consequences: (i) the size of the battery carried by the drone is highly limited and so is its flight time, and (ii) the choice of sensors is quite narrow compared to the possibilities of larger platforms. In particular, equipping a nano-drone with an omni-directional sensor (for neighbor sensing) as the one normally considered in ground robots is very difficult. Most of the state-of-the-art approaches to chaining are infeasible for nano-drones because they have too complex sensing demands, e.g., they require omni-directional sensing [5,6,12–14], global positioning [17], they take too much time to converge [18], or rely on the assumption that the actuation noise is negligible [7].

In this paper, we present a method for open-space chaining that allows formation of the chain that does not require global positioning and that works even with limited sensing field of view (Sect. 2). We focus on realistic sensing conditions, so the method is robust against sensing and actuating noise. Additionally, the sensor used in this work is susceptible to occlusions that are often neglected by other swarming algorithms [16].

To analyze the proposed method we perform simulation-based experiments (Sect. 3). We study the convergence time of the proposed method, the quality of the chaining obtained, under the effect of different swarm sizes and of realistic sensing and actuation noise. Finally, we present the practical feasibility of chaining in a robotic proof of concept with nano-drones, in which sensing is done fully on-board (Sect. 4).

2 Method

The system consists of N agents. The position of agent i is denoted as $\mathbf{x}_i$ and its orientation, i.e. yaw angle, is θ_i. We denote the displacement vector from agent i to j as $\mathbf{x}_{i,j} = \mathbf{x}_j - \mathbf{x}_i$ and distance between them as $\|\mathbf{x}_{i,j}\|$. Agent i is controlled by setting its velocity ($\mathbf{v}_i$) and yaw rate ($\dot{\theta}_i$) in its own reference frame.

All of the agents are equipped with a field-of-view (FOV) sensor. We assume such a sensor is able to measure the range (r) and bearing (ϕ) to all agents in front of it, within limited viewing angle and range. In practice, such a sensor could be realized in multiple ways: using a camera, radar, LiDAR, sonar, etc. Many of these technologies are susceptible to *occlusions*: if multiple objects share exactly the same bearing, but are at different distances, they will be perceived as a single object. Our real-life realization of the FOV sensor is based on a camera (see Sect. 4.1 for details). It perceives multiple occluded objects as being closer than the closest of these objects. Our simulated setup models this behavior.

Note that the agents do not have access to the global positions of their peers or themselves. Therefore, whenever we mention the positions of other agents while calculating the update of agent i, we mean the relative positions with respect to the reference frame of agent i. Such positions are calculated based on the output of the FOV sensor $\mathbf{x}_j = \left[\cos \phi_j \cdot r_j, \sin \phi_j \cdot r_j\right]$.

The chain is parameterized with a desired distance d_0 that specifies the distance the agents should keep from their neighbors. The agents are deployed sequentially—as soon as agent i is positioned in the chain, agent $i + 1$ takes off. Sequential deployment is implemented manually in this paper, by having the current agent notifying the simulator or the operator when it has completed joining the chain. This assumption can be relaxed in future work by either implementing a self-organized communication scheme that monitors the status of chain formation, or by removing the sequential deployment assumption altogether.

We distinguish two agents with special roles:

- One agent is used to emulate the *target* t. Its only task is to hover in the same spot throughout the whole chain forming process. It can be considered external to the swarm.
- Another special agent is the *seed* s. It follows a different logic than all the other agents. Its goal is to find the target and keep a constant distance to it (1), at the same time keeping it in the middle of its field of view (2):

$$\mathbf{v}_s = P_{\mathbf{x}} \left(\mathbf{x}_t - \frac{\mathbf{x}_{t,s}}{\|\mathbf{x}_{t,s}\|} \cdot d_0 \right), \tag{1}$$

$$\dot{\theta}_s = P_\theta \phi_t, \tag{2}$$

where $P_{\mathbf{x}}$ and P_θ are the proportional controller settings for position and yaw, respectively. Since the agents have no sensor allowing them to distinguish the target, the seed agent assumes that the target is the closest agent out of the detected ones. This has no implications in the early phase of chain formation (when the seed is the deployed robot and only the target is hovering in the environment), while later in an experiment it can happen that the seed will seldom mistake another agent as the target.

In practical scenarios, the *target* agent could be replaced by some point of interest that the *seed* agent is able to detect (provided the target identification modules, out of scope for this paper, are implemented); or it could be used as a leader initiating the construction of a chain in a specific location determined by another criteria. The rest of agents are homogeneous and are guided by the procedure consisting of four main steps that are followed sequentially. The diagram explaining the behavior with possible transitions is depicted in Fig. 1. All controls described in the method are in the agent's relative frame, e.g., when the agent moves left, we mean that it moves to *its* left.

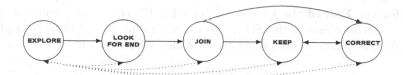

Fig. 1. Possible state transitions in the chaining algorithm.

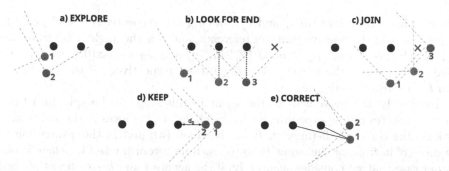

Fig. 2. An example of the chaining procedure. Black circles represent the part of the chain that is already formed. Dashed lines visualize the field of view of an agent, without showing the range limit. Blue circle represents an example of starting position of an agent in a given step and the red circle is the final position. In subfigures b) and c) an intermediate step is drawn with a purple color. (Color figure online)

Exploration (EXPLORE). At the beginning, just after being deployed, the agent i needs to find the chain. We assume, the chain is found if the agent detects at least two other agents in its field of view. In principle, any exploration strategy could be used for this step [11]. For the sake of simplicity, we assume the range of the FOV sensor is big enough to always detect a part of the chain from the place of the take-off, which is achieved by allowing the take off only within a specific area that has the target at its center. A possible take-off position and moment when the chain is detected are depicted in Fig. 2a as 1 and 2, respectively.

In the EXPLORE state, the agent just rotates around its center with yaw rate $\dot{\theta}_i = 0.2$ rad/s. When the agent detects another agent j in its field of view, it tries to keep it in the middle of its field of view, setting its yaw rate to $\dot{\theta}_i = P_\theta \cdot \phi_j$. Additionally, the agent moves left to go around the detected agent. It sets its velocity to $\mathbf{v}_i = [0, -0.2]$ m/s. If the detected agent is closer than d_c, the agent additionally moves back, so its velocity is $\mathbf{v}_i = [-0.1, -0.2]$ m/s. When the agent detects at least two agents in its field of view, it switches to the next step.

The agent can switch to the EXPLORE state from any of the other states if the required number of neighbors is not visible, and switches back to the state it comes from once enough neighbors are perceived. Effectively, this is used as a recovery strategy: The agent explores until it can see enough agents and continues with the execution of the previous state (transitions marked with dotted lines in Fig. 1).

Look for the End of the Chain (LOOK for END). We assume that agent k is the rightmost one in the FOV, and agent j is the second from the right in the FOV. The following equations describe movement of agent i:

$$\mathbf{v}_i = P_{\mathbf{x}} \mu_\beta \left[\min(r_j, r_k) - d_c, y_k \right] \tag{3}$$

$$\dot{\theta}_i = P_\theta \psi_\beta \cdot \arctan \left(\frac{y_{j,k}}{x_{j,k}} - \frac{\pi}{2} \right), \tag{4}$$

where y_k is a y coordinate of $\mathbf{x}_k$ and $x_{j,k}$ and $y_{j,k}$ are, respectively, x and y coordinates of $\mathbf{x}_{j,k}$ in the relative frame of reference, and β is the angle between agents i, j, k. The coefficients $\mu_\beta = \max(0.2, |\sin(\beta)|)$ and $\psi_\beta = \max(0.1, |\sin(\beta)|)$ are used to slow down the movement and rotation, respectively, if the agents i, j and k are close to being aligned.

Intuitively, the movement of the agent in this step can be split into three parts: it rotates to be perpendicular to the chain (4); it moves in the x direction to keep the constant distance d_c from the chain (3); and in the y direction to be directly in front of the agent k, so to reach its y coordinate (3). There is one corner case that we consider separately: if the agents j and k are almost aligned (difference of their bearings is smaller than 0.1 and hence it is likely there are occlusions), agent i moves with a constant speed to the left.

The distance d_c is chosen based on the FOV sensor viewing angle in such a way that the agent can see at least 3 agents that are in the chain (assuming they keep the desired distance d_0 from each other) with some safety margin for noise and disturbances caused by occlusions. The agent is moving to be directly in front of the rightmost visible agent (e.g., agent 2 in Fig. 2b). When there are no more agents on the right, it switches to the next step to join the chain. This final position is marked as 3 in Fig. 2b and the spot for the next agent in the chain is marked with a red cross.

Join the Chain (JOIN). To join the chain, the agent i is choosing the first two agents starting from the right of the FOV (the LOOK FOR END state guarantees that these are two agents at the end of the chain). We call these agents j and k, with k being the rightmost one (last in the chain). The agent rotates towards the point S in the middle between agents j and k

$$S = \frac{\mathbf{x}_j + \mathbf{x}_k}{2}, \tag{5}$$

$$\dot{\theta}_i = P_\theta \phi_S. \tag{6}$$

It calculates its desired position (marked with red cross in Fig. 2c) at the end of the chain:

$$\mathbf{x}_d = \mathbf{x}_k + d_0 \frac{\mathbf{x}_{j,k}}{\|\mathbf{x}_{j,k}\|} \tag{7}$$

and moves to the right with $\mathbf{v}_i = P_{\mathbf{x}} [0.25 \|\mathbf{x}_d\|, 0.5 \|\mathbf{x}_d\|]$. The movement in the x direction allows the agent to correct the distance from the chain on the way. The rotation combined with the motion result in the movement on an arc that brings the agent i to the position aligned with agents j and k. In this state, we say i is *aligned* with agents j and k if:

- bearing to j and k is equal when occlusions are not taken into account,
- the agents occlude each other and only one agent is detected.

Once the two closest agents are aligned, the agent is already considered to be a part of the chain and needs to remain in it, the procedure for this is described in the next step.

Keep the Chain (KEEP). When all the visible agents are aligned, the agent keeps the desired distance d_0 with the closest neighbor (see Fig. 2d). The behavior is the same as the one of seed (see equations (1) and (2)). However, if there are some disturbances (caused by noise or new agents trying to join the chain) and the agent detects some unaligned agents it switches to the next step.

Correct the Chain (CORRECT). Let us assume that agents j and k are the closest neighbors (the agents connected with black lines with agent 1 in Fig. 2e). The agent rotates towards the middle between two closest agents:

$$\dot{\theta}_i = P_\theta \cdot \frac{\phi_j + \phi_k}{2}. \tag{8}$$

At the same time, it moves towards the corrected position in a straight line:

$$\mathbf{v}_i = P_\mathbf{x}\mathbf{x}_d, \tag{9}$$

where $\mathbf{x}_d$ is defined as in Eq. (7). Once all the visible agents are aligned again, the agent switches back to the previous step (**KEEP**), this situation corresponds to the position marked with 2 in Fig. 2e.

3   Simulation Results

For the simulation study we use a custom kinematic-based simulator implemented in Python, designed to bridge the simulation to reality gap. In fact, exactly the same logic, programmed in Python, is executed both in simulation and during robotic experiments. In our simulations, agents take off at random positions drawn uniformly from a deployment area 10 m × 10 m. The *target* agent is placed exactly in the middle of the deployment area. To avoid disturbing the chain in the early stage of forming, a square 2 m × 2 m in the middle of the arena is excluded. If an initial position is chosen in this part of the area, the initial position is redrawn. Each agent is equipped in a FOV sensor with a viewing angle 90° and range 6 m. Such configuration of the sensor is motivated by our hardware setup. Furthermore, we assume the agents are not detected by the FOV sensor before takeoff. For each experiment we use five different configurations:

Idealized configuration is without any noise and with a sensor without occlusions that can "see through" the agents. It measures exact range and bearing to all the agents in range.

Occlusions configuration has no noise, but occlusions are taken into account.

Sensing noise adds sensing noise to the *Occlusions* configuration. The noise has two components: range noise $\eta_r \sim N(0, 0.1)$ and bearing noise $\eta_\phi \sim N(0, 0.05)$, which are added to the FOV sensor measurements.

Actuating noise adds actuating noise to the *Occlusions* configuration. Actuating noise is added to the agent's velocity $\eta_v \sim [N(0, 0.05), N(0, 0.05)]$ and its yaw rate $\eta_\dot{\theta} \sim N(0, 0.1)$.

Both noises adds sensing and actuating noise to the *occlusions* configuration.

3.1   Quality of the Chain Formation—Collinearity of Agents

We say that the chain formation is perfect if, at the end of an experiment, the agents are placed on a straight line. To measure how successful the agents are in forming the chain, we use the following order parameter.

For each triple of agents (including the ones that are still on the ground) we calculate the collinearity parameter.

$$C_{i,j,k} = \frac{\pi - \max(\alpha_{i,j,k}, \alpha_{k,i,j}, \alpha_{j,k,i})}{\pi}, \qquad (10)$$

where $\alpha_{i,j,k}$ is the angle between the agents, assuming that j is the vertex of the angle. It is calculated as:

$$\alpha_{i,j,k} = \arccos \frac{\mathbf{x}_{j,i} \cdot \mathbf{x}_{j,k}}{\|\mathbf{x}_{j,i}\| \|\mathbf{x}_{j,k}\|}. \qquad (11)$$

In the case when the agents are collinear, one of these angles is equal to π. Therefore, choosing the maximum of these angles allows us to determine how far are the agents from creating a straight line.

The collinearity of all the agents can be calculated as:

$$C = \frac{1}{\binom{N}{3}} \sum_{(i,j,k) \in \mathscr{C}(\{1,...,N\})} C_{i,j,k}, \qquad (12)$$

where $\mathscr{C}(\{1, \ldots, N\})$ is the set of all 3-combinations of agents.

In this experiment, we demonstrate how the metric C converges when the agents are creating the chain. We execute 50 runs for each configuration. The number of agents is constant and $N = 10$. The results are presented in Fig. 3. The line marks the median of the metric C for each simulation step from all 50 runs, whereas the colored area shows the range between first and third quartiles.

In all of the configurations the convergence curve of C has a similar shape and reaches a stable low value. This means that the agents manage to form the chain in a repeatable way. What is worth noting is that only in the setup with the idealized FOV sensor without occlusions the metric converges to 0, in the other plots it converges to a slightly greater value (around 0.03). The reason for that is that with occlusions the agents are not able to distinguish between an exactly straight and a slightly bent chain.

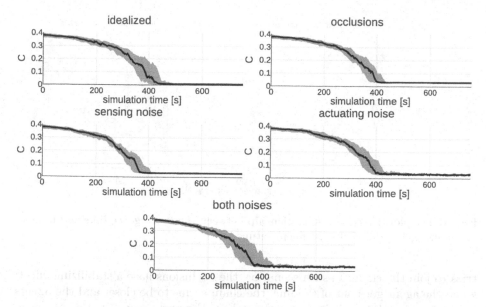

Fig. 3. The plot depicting convergence of order parameter C for five different experiment setups.

3.2   Convergence Time

In this experiment, we measured the time it takes for all the agents to detect they are in a chain (they are either in a KEEP or CORRECT state), and we use this also as a criteria to terminate the experiment. To avoid deadlocks, we assume that the maximum duration of an experiment is $2000 \cdot N$ simulation steps, after this time the experiment is stopped. By combining these two stopping criteria, we can easily distinguish the cases in which the chain converged to a low value of collinearity from the cases in which this did not happen (the experiment was stopped after $2000 \cdot N$, which corresponds to the dashed line in Fig. 4).

The experiment is run for different number of agents from $N = 10$ to $N = 100$, with the increment of 10 agents. For each number of agents we execute 25 runs for each of the five configurations of sensing capabilities and noise.

Figure 4 presents the results obtained in the course of the experiments. Each color represents a different configuration. The semi-transparent bars display the first and third quartile, with a median marked with a line. The line bars mark maximum and minimum or upper and lower fence. Additional points, not covered by the bars, indicate the outliers.

The worst performance is achieved in the setup without noise. With the sensor without occlusions, above 70 agents the chain is never achieved. Additional analysis of the failed runs of simulations showed that the agents fail to form a chain if one of them takes off between the agents that are already in the chain or very close to them. In this case, the agents try to keep the chain also with the new joiner, which results in the part of the chain following the agent that

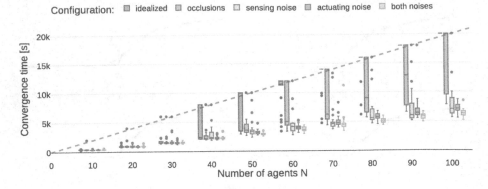

Fig. 4. The plot depicting the relationship between the convergence time and number of agents for five different experiment setups.

tries to join the chain. In such scenarios, the occlusions have a stabilizing effect: when the agent goes out of the line, the chain seems to be closer and the agents tend to stay with the chain rather than chase the new agent.

The setup with occlusions and no noise performs a bit better but, still, it is not perfect and in some runs the agents do not achieve the chain in the given time. The lack of convergence in this case is caused by deadlocks. A deadlock occurs when an agent takes off almost aligned with the chain. Depending on the direction it starts movement, the occlusions cause the other subset of agents to seem closer, which in turn causes the agent to move in the opposite direction. This procedure is continued until the end of the given simulation time.

Despite these shortcomings, in the setup with any kind of noise the agents almost always achieve chain, with only a few outliers. When the sensing and actuating noises are combined, the chain converges always and in the most efficient way. These results confirm that our solution can work in the realistic conditions and demonstrates its potential to be applied on nano-drones.

4   Proof of Concept

To show the practical applicability of the proposed method and that the simulated scenarios are realistic, we implemented a proof of concept on robots. We realized it using Crazyflie drones, a palm-sized, open-source flying robots.

To realize the proposed method in practice, we require a hardware implementation of the FOV sensor. We developed this sensor using a connected-component labeling algorithm implemented on AI-deck. AI-deck is an extension-board for Crazyflies that adds to it a HIMAX camera, GAP8 processor, and a WiFi module. For this work, we used the camera to capture pictures and the GAP8 processor to analyze them and estimate the range and bearing to all other agents in range. Then, this information is communicated to the main Crazyflie microcontroller as a sensor data. This sensor data is used in the control algorithm to coordinate the drone.

To facilitate the development and testing, the sensor data is communicated from the Crazyflie via radio to a laptop computer, where the control algorithm is running and sending the movement commands back to the Crazyflie. Such setup adds considerable latency to the control process, but allows for easier development. Furthermore, it shows the robustness of the proposed method. Even though we use a laptop computer, the logic is using only the information that would have been available on the drone. This, together with the fact that the method is not computationally intensive, allows to implement the whole solution fully on-board.

4.1   Camera-Based FOV Sensor

We develop a custom-made range and bearing sensor based on camera and LEDs. The drones are flying in the darkness with a 1W LED attached at the bottom to provide light for the optical flow sensor. The automatic exposure and gain (AEG) feature of the camera is turned off and the exposure and gain is tuned manually to achieve reproducible results for a fixed lighting conditions. In such setup, the only bright objects in a camera picture captured by a drone are the other drones.

To obtain range and bearing measurements to all visible drones from a camera picture, we use the following algorithm:

1. thresholding by discarding all pixels below a hand-tuned threshold,
2. expand the non-discarded areas by 4 pixels in all directions,
3. identify different drones by finding and labeling connected image components [15] using union-find data structure [4],
4. compute the centers and sizes of the connected components.

After that, we use the resulting centers of connected components to approximate the bearing ϕ to the other drone and the width of the component to approximate the distance d with the following equations:

$$d_i = \frac{1}{w_i} k, \tag{13}$$

$$\phi_i = \frac{x_i - \frac{1}{2}W}{W} A, \tag{14}$$

where w_i is the width of the i-th component and x_i is the center of this component in the horizontal direction. In our setup, $k = 15$ is a manually-tuned scaling factor dependent on the lighting conditions, $W = 255$ is the width of the camera image, and $A = 90°$ is the horizontal angle of view of the camera.

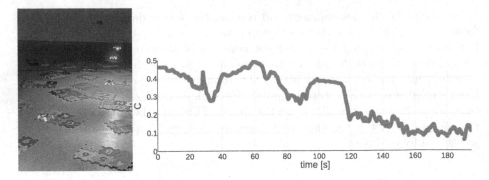

Fig. 5. (left) A photo of robots during an experiment. Three robots already formed a chain and the fourth one is joining it. (right) Convergence of the order parameter for a robotic experiment.

4.2 Results

We conducted experiments with four drones using the described setup and confirmed similar behavior as the one observed in the simulation. The main challenges were related to the fact that the FOV sensor requires that the only sources of light seen by the drones are the other agents. Additional sources of light and reflections from shiny surfaces negatively influence the sensor's measurements and might lead to a failed attempt. However, with some care to minimize these effects, we were able to successfully present the proof of concept.

We recorded the trajectories of robots using Qualisys motion capture system. Figure 5 shows the value of the order parameter C calculated based on the captured trajectories. It shows that the drones are able to construct and maintain the chain. The FOV sensor is able to provide around 1 measurement per second. The results show that even with such a low update rate the chaining algorithm performs well. We have published a video [1] presenting the proof of concept.

5   Conclusions and Outlook

We presented a method capable of building a chain of agents in an open space. It has a minimal sensing requirements with a limited field of view range and bearing sensor. The main advantage is its robustness against noise that enables real-life applications in robotic systems.

The future work on this topic will include exploration of the environment to connect target to a base, and the removal of the incremental deployment assumption. The real-life applications will benefit from improving the FOV sensor, it may include utilizing artificial intelligence methods [9].

References

1. Barciś, A., Barciś, M., Natalizio, E., Ferrante, E.: Video: Self-Organized Chain Formation of Nano-Drones in an Open Space (2022). https://youtu.be/Fqp-9Et3lmw

2. Brambilla, M., Ferrante, E., Birattari, M., Dorigo, M.: Swarm robotics: a review from the swarm engineering perspective. Swarm Intell. **7**(1), 1–41 (2013). https://doi.org/10.1007/s11721-012-0075-2

3. Coppola, M., McGuire, K.N., De Wagter, C., de Croon, G.C.H.E.: A survey on swarming with micro air vehicles: fundamental challenges and constraints. Front. Robot. AI **7**, 18 (2020). https://doi.org/10.3389/frobt.2020.00018

4. Cormen, T.H.: Data structures for disjoint sets. In: Introduction to Algorithms, 3rd edn, pp. 561–568. MIT Press, Cambridge (2009)

5. Ducatelle, F., Di Caro, G.A., Pinciroli, C., Mondada, F., Gambardella, L.: Communication assisted navigation in robotic swarms: self-organization and cooperation. In: 2011 IEEE/RSJ International Conference on Intelligent Robots and Systems, pp. 4981–4988 (2011). https://doi.org/10.1109/IROS.2011.6094454

6. Garattoni, L., Birattari, M.: Autonomous task sequencing in a robot swarm. Sci. Robot. **3**(20), eaat0430 (2018). https://doi.org/10.1126/scirobotics.aat0430

7. Jiang, Z., Wang, X., Yang, J.: Distributed line formation control in swarm robots. In: 2018 IEEE International Conference on Information and Automation (ICIA), pp. 636–641 (2018). https://doi.org/10.1109/ICInfA.2018.8812317

8. Laclau, P., Tempez, V., Ruffier, F., Natalizio, E., Mouret, J.B.: Signal-based self-organization of a chain of UAVs for subterranean exploration. Front. Robot. AI **8**, 614206 (2021)

9. Li, S., De Wagter, C., de Croon, G.C.H.E.: Self-supervised Monocular Multi-robot Relative Localization with Efficient Deep Neural Networks. arXiv:2105.12797 (2021)

10. Maxim, P.M., Spears, W.M., Spears, D.F.: Robotic chain formations. IFAC Proc. Vol. **42**(22), 19–24 (2009). https://doi.org/10.3182/20091006-3-US-4006.00004

11. Méndez, V., Campos, D., Bartumeus, F.: Random search strategies. In: Méndez, V., Campos, D., Bartumeus, F. (eds.) Stochastic Foundations in Movement Ecology. SSS, pp. 177–205. Springer, Heidelberg (2014). https://doi.org/10.1007/978-3-642-39010-4_6

12. Nouyan, S., Campo, A., Dorigo, M.: Path formation in a robot swarm. Swarm Intell. **2**(1), 1–23 (2008). https://doi.org/10.1007/s11721-007-0009-6

13. Nouyan, S., Dorigo, M.: Chain based path formation in swarms of robots. In: Dorigo, M., Gambardella, L.M., Birattari, M., Martinoli, A., Poli, R., Stützle, T. (eds.) ANTS 2006. LNCS, vol. 4150, pp. 120–131. Springer, Heidelberg (2006). https://doi.org/10.1007/11839088_11

14. Nouyan, S., Gross, R., Bonani, M., Mondada, F., Dorigo, M.: Teamwork in self-organized robot colonies. IEEE Trans. Evol. Comput. **13**(4), 695–711 (2009). https://doi.org/10.1109/TEVC.2008.2011746

15. Samet, H., Tamminen, M.: Efficient component labeling of images of arbitrary dimension represented by linear bintrees. IEEE Trans. Pattern Anal. Mach. Intell. **10**(4), 579–586 (1988). https://doi.org/10.1109/34.3918

16. Schilling, F., Soria, E., Floreano, D.: On the scalability of vision-based drone swarms in the presence of occlusions. IEEE Access **10**, 28133–28146 (2022). https://doi.org/10.1109/ACCESS.2022.3158758

17. Sousselier, T., Dreo, J., Sevaux, M.: Line formation algorithm in a swarm of reactive robots constrained by underwater environment. Expert Syst. Appl. **42**(12), 5117–5127 (2015). https://doi.org/10.1016/j.eswa.2015.02.040

18. Sperati, V., Trianni, V., Nolfi, S.: Self-organised path formation in a swarm of robots. Swarm Intell. **5**(2), 97–119 (2011). https://doi.org/10.1007/s11721-011-0055-y

The Hidden Benefits of Limited Communication and Slow Sensing in Collective Monitoring of Dynamic Environments

Till Aust[1,2]([⊠])(iD), Mohamed S. Talamali[3](iD), Marco Dorigo[1](iD),
Heiko Hamann[2](iD), and Andreagiovanni Reina[1]([⊠])(iD)

[1] IRIDIA, Université Libre de Bruxelles, Brussels, Belgium
mdorigo@ulb.ac.be, andreagiovanni.reina@ulb.be
[2] Institute of Computer Engineering, University of Lübeck, Lübeck, Germany
till.aust@student.uni-luebeck.de, hamann@iti.uni-luebeck.de
[3] Sheffield Hallam University, Sheffield, UK
s.talamali@shu.ac.uk

Abstract. Most of our experiences, as well as our intuition, are usually built on a linear understanding of systems and processes. Complex systems in general, and more specifically swarm robotics in this context, leverage non-linear effects to self-organize and to ensure that 'more is different'. In previous work, the non-linear and therefore counter-intuitive effect of 'less is more' was shown for a site-selection swarm scenario. Although it seems intuitive that being able to communicate over longer distances should be beneficial, swarms were found to sometimes profit from communication limitations. Here, we build on this work and show the same effect for the collective perception scenario in a dynamic environment. We also find an additional effect that we call 'slower is faster': in certain situations, swarms benefit from sampling their environment less frequently. Our findings are supported by an intensive empirical approach and a mean-field model. All our experimental work is based on simulations using the ARGoS simulator extended with a simulator of the smart environment for the Kilobot robot called Kilogrid.

1 Introduction

In our recent research about information spreading in groups of individuals [30], we discovered a counter-intuitive mechanism by which reducing interactions between the individuals makes the group more capable to adopt new better opinions. This effect, that we call *less is more*, manifests when groups need to make consensus decisions and individuals follow a relatively simple voting behavior. Such conditions can be particularly relevant for the design of algorithms for swarms of minimalistic robots that make best-of-n decisions [30]. Such algorithms are based on opinion dynamics models, in which every robot has an opinion about the option it currently considers the best (among n alternatives) and sends messages to neighboring robots to recruit them on that option [34].

© Springer Nature Switzerland AG 2022
M. Dorigo et al. (Eds.): ANTS 2022, LNCS 13491, pp. 234–247, 2022.
https://doi.org/10.1007/978-3-031-20176-9_19

In this study, we confirm the generality of our previous finding [30] by reproducing the *less is more* effect (LIME) in a different scenario: collective perception of an environmental feature, the so-called environmental element, in a dynamic environment. By studying this new scenario, we can control the speed of robot recruitment, that is the key parameter to trigger the LIME. Controlling this parameter was not possible in the previous study of Talamali et al. [30] as the recruitment speed was constrained by robot travel times to specific locations. These times also had high variance and depended, for example, on traffic congestion and robot density. The new scenario allows for a simplified analysis. Our results confirm and clarify the mechanisms. More importantly, we found a new surprising effect that was not reported earlier in this type of systems: the *slower is faster* effect [9,18,25–27] (SIFE). To adapt faster, recruited robots must be slower in disseminating their opinions and recruiting other robots. This is a second surprising and counter-intuitive mechanism of this simple voting system. The SIFE occurs when individuals are sparsely connected and make noisy estimates—two conditions commonly found in swarm robotics [10].

With this paper, we also release open-source code [2] supporting realistic simulations of the Kilogrid platform [1] (technology for Kilobots [21] to operate in smart environments) in ARGoS [15]. This simulation code, combined with the ARGoS Kilobot plugin [14], allows the use of identical code in simulation and reality (both for Kilobots and Kilogrid). Despite the limited adoption of the Kilogrid in other research labs than IRIDIA (ULB), we believe that supporting realistic physics-based simulations can help spreading the technology and encourage collaborations between laboratories with and without such equipment.

2   Collective Perception in a Dynamic Environment

In this paper, the task of the robot swarm is to make a consensus decision in favor of the predominant element of the environment [33]. We assume that the robots can individually estimate each element concentration (i.e., an element's relative frequency in the environment) to form their opinion which they share with each other. While individual estimates are noisy, the swarm collectively filters noise and converges to an accurate collective decision [33]. Individual estimation errors can be caused, for example, by simple error-prone sensing devices (readings distant from the ground truth, e.g., [11,13]), spatial correlations (clustered information in localised areas rather than uniformly in the environment, e.g., [3,4,29]), and limited sensing range. Our simulations allow us to control sources and levels of sampling errors as well as to disentangle the impact of sampling errors from other system dynamics of interest (e.g., recruitment time).

We conveniently model the collective perception problem in a similar way as done previously [33]. The to-be-estimated environmental element is the predominant color of the ground which is comprised of squared tiles ($5\,\mathrm{cm}^2$). We consider tiles with $n = 2$ colors: blue ■ and yellow ▨ (see Fig. 1a)[1]. The difficulty of the

---

[1] The current geopolitical situation motivated our choice of tile color ■▨.

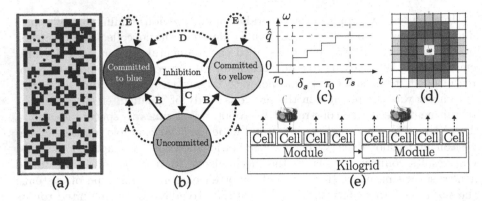

Fig. 1. (a) Collective perception scenario for the simulated Kilogrid in ARGoS (simulation code, see [2]), swarm of $N = 50$ Kilobots (small black circles); (b) robots controlled by a finite state machine with $n+1$ states (here $n = 2$); transitions: self-sourced (dashed arrows) or social (solid arrows) evidence; uncommitted→commit through (A) discovery or (B) recruitment; committed robots update their state by: (C) cross-inhibition, (D) direct switching, or (E) stay; (c) once recruited, robots gradually increase communication probability w for sampling time $\tau_s = s\,\delta_s$, s samples every δ_s seconds; (d) focal Kilogrid module receives Kilobot message and sends to all cells within communication range (proportional to parameter c; communication range r_c, $c = \{2, 3, 4, 5\}$); (e) robot-to-robot communication is virtualised using Kilogrid. (Color figure online)

perception problem $\kappa \in [0, 1]$ is determined by the ratio between the concentration of tiles in the two colors: $\kappa = q_b/q_y$ where q_b and q_y are the concentrations of blue and yellow tiles, respectively. Without loss of generality we assume that yellow ▨ is the predominant color in all our experiments, $q_y > q_b$. The concentration of blue/yellow tiles corresponds to the number of blue/yellow tiles divided by the total number of tiles in the environment. The tiles are uniformly randomly distributed, hence reducing spatial correlations. However, spatial correlations exist within the area of a single tile. Indeed, taking several samples from the same tile results in biased measurements (see Sect. 5.2).

We consider a virtual dynamic scenario. In all our experiments, the most frequent color is yellow ▨. However, the robot swarm is initialized to a state of full (100%) commitment in favor of blue ■ with every robot holding an estimate $q_b = 0.8$. This increases the task difficulty and can be considered a sudden change of colors from blue to yellow (■→▨) that happens right at the moment when we start our simulations. In the next section, we describe how robots reassess the environment's state and reconsider their opinion.

3   A Minimalist Behavior for a Rich Collective Response

The robots have minimal requirements in terms of memory, computation, sensing, and communication capabilities. Compared with previous work that investigated decentralized consensus decision making in the collective perception scenario, our algorithm has the fewest requirements, in line with our quest for minimalism. Different from previous work that required the storage of all available alternatives and all received messages [4, 23, 24], here the robots only store the information about a single opinion (i.e., the color considered predominant and its estimated concentration), the last received message from a neighbor, and a temporary variable to estimate possible environmental changes. Different from previous work requiring more advanced computation based on Bayesian inference [7, 8, 23, 24] or fusion operators from epistemic logic [4], our robot behavior is defined by a small finite state machine with reactive transitions. Different from previous work that required sensors capable of measuring a numerical value of the predominant element, such as an option quality, at every measurement step [7, 23, 24], here the robot can only sense the presence (■) or absence (not ■) of an element at a time. Different from previous work requiring maintenance of shared collective knowledge through rich inter-robot communication [28, 29], here the robots send simple messages with a few bits of information, only indicating their preferred element (i.e., their chosen color, for $n = 2$ that is one bit of information). Other works in collective perception that are comparable to ours in their simplicity of individual robot requirements are Valentini et al. [33] and Zakir et al. [35]. We extend previous analyzes by considering a dynamic environment which has only been considered in a few consensus decision making studies for the site selection scenario [6, 16, 17, 30], while here we consider the collective perception scenario.

Despite the minimalist robot control algorithm and the robots' noisy measurements, the swarm is able to collectively gather and process the data to make accurate consensus decisions (picking the dominant color). The robot's control algorithm is based on simple reactive rules, relies on limited memory, and can be described as four routines that are executed in parallel: motion, opinion update, sampling, and broadcasting.

The **motion routine** is independent of the other parts of the robot's behavior. The robot's motion is neither influenced by its opinion nor by social or environmental inputs. The motion routine is a random walk implemented as a random waypoint mobility model [5, 30]. However, it could be substituted by any other algorithm implementing random diffusion. Using the random waypoint model, robots select random positions as their destinations. Once the destination is reached, robots select the next random destination. Robots avoid collisions with surrounding walls by selecting random destinations that are at least three robot-body lengths (approximately 10 cm) away from walls. As robot's motion is subject to noise, the robot can still approach walls. Once it gets at a distance smaller than three robot-body lengths from any wall, the robot starts a wall avoidance manoeuvre by rotating away from the wall and moving straight. The robots have no proximity sensing, therefore they do not implement any obstacle avoidance to prevent collisions with each other. To avoid robots remaining stuck in traffic jams caused by groups of robots moving in opposite directions (or robots not moving due to malfunctioning motors), robots select new random destinations if the previous destination was not reached within two minutes.

The **opinion update routine** is essential to solve the collective perception task because it determines how robots change their opinions and, hence, defines the collective behavior. Robots change their opinion so that a large majority of the swarm reaches an agreement on the predominant color. While we present this routine for $n = 2$ colors, it does not require any changes to scale to numbers $n > 2$. Robots update their states every $\tau_u = 2$ s following the cross-inhibition update shown in Fig. 1b. Robots can be in $n + 1$ possible opinion states; in the investigated case of $n = 2$ colors they can be committed to blue, committed to yellow, or uncommitted. Transitions between states are triggered by new self-sourced or social evidence. Self-sourced evidence (dashed arrows in Fig. 1b) is available when, after a period of length τ_u, the robot completed sampling a color that is both different from and better than its current opinion (in case of uncommitted robots, any concentration estimate is considered as better). Hence, self-sourced evidence corresponds to discovering in the last τ_u a color that seems more frequent than the color of its current opinion. Social evidence (solid arrows in Fig. 1b) is available when after a period of length τ_u the robot received a message from a neighbor committed to a different color (if multiple messages have been received, only the most recent stays in memory). If both self-sourced and social evidence are available, the robot randomly selects one of the two, discarding the other. The new evidence triggers a state change: (a) committed robots with new social evidence become uncommitted—a *cross-inhibition* transition; (b) any robot with new self-sourced evidence becomes committed to the color corresponding to the new evidence—a *discovery* transition; (c) uncommitted robots with new social evidence, become committed as per the new evidence—a *recruitment* transition.

The **sampling routine** controls how information about the concentration of one element is collected from the environment. The robot continuously repeats sampling in cycles of collecting s samples. Each sample is a binary value indicating presence (1) or absence (0) of the environmental element of interest. Here, robots sample whether the color at their position is of a given color. The concentration estimate $\hat{q}_i$ is the proportion between the number of samples s_i^+ in which the element was present and the total number of samples s: $\hat{q}_i = s_i^+/s$. A new sampling cycle starts when the previous cycle has collected s samples, or when the robot changes opinion through social evidence. When the robot completes a sampling cycle or becomes uncommitted, it determines the new to-be-sampled color randomly. Here, the robot selects the color of the ground beneath itself. The random selection of the color to sample allows the robot either to update the color concentration estimate when it samples its commitment color, or to gather potential self-sourced evidence when it samples a different color. Instead, when a robot is recruited and commits to a new opinion i, it immediately starts to sample i to obtain the information needed to regulate its messaging frequency (weighted voting, as described in the broadcasting routine). This means that once a robot is recruited to i, it cannot instantaneously recruit other robots to i but a minimum amount of time is required to gather information about i first. The mathematical analysis of [30] showed that having this temporal delay between change of opinion through recruitment and recruitment of other robots—the sampling time τ_s—is the key mechanism that leads to the LIME. Therefore, the sampling time τ_s is the control parameter of this study and it corresponds to $\tau_s = s\,\delta_s$, where δ_s is the time between two samples. As analyzed in Sect. 5.2, the sampling parameters s and δ_s are also linked to the estimation noise and have a determining impact on the collective dynamics.

The **broadcasting routine** implements a continuous 'narrowcast' of recruitment messages, that is, a broadcast to all robots within communication range r_c (i.e., neighbors). The robot scales its frequency of communication proportionally to the estimated concentration of the environmental element. The higher the estimated concentration of i is, the more recruitment messages for color i the robot sends. The robot sends a message with a frequency of w/τ_m Hz where $1/\tau_m = 2\,\mathrm{Hz}$ is the maximum communication frequency of our robots and $w = \min(2\hat{q}_i, 1)$ is the concentration weight for color i. We multiply by two ($2\hat{q}_i$) because we need to find the predominant element and any concentration $>50\%$ represents the absolute majority. For lower concentrations, w scales linearly between 0 and 1. While in case of $n = 2$ a concentration $<50\%$ indicates predominance of the other color, this does not generalize to $n > 2$ and therefore we do not consider this deductive mechanism. A newly recruited robot does not have a concentration estimate yet. It gradually increments its communication frequency as it collects samples (see Fig. 1c). It computes $w = \min(2\hat{q}_i, 1)$ using $\hat{q}_i = s_i^+/s$ even if the collected samples are less than s. This mechanism helps avoiding situations of vocal minorities, that is, the situations in which a large proportion of the population changes their commitment and only a small proportion of robots communicates while the majority remain silent. In our implementation, just-recruited robots are not silent, yet less vocal. Uncommitted robots do not communicate until they get recruited or make a discovery transition.

4   Simulated Kilobots and Kilogrid

For our experiments, we use Kilobots which are cheap, simple, and small robots widely employed in swarm robotics [20–22,31]. By regulating the frequency of two vibration motors, the Kilobots move on a flat surface at speeds of about 1 cm/s in roughly straight motion and rotate at the spot at about 45 °/s. The Kilobot has a diameter of 3.3 cm, can display its internal state through a colored-LED, and can communicate with other robots and other devices through an infrared (IR) transceiver. The range of communication varies depending on lighting conditions and ground material [12]; in ideal conditions $r_c \approx 10\,\mathrm{cm}$. The Kilobot's control loop is executed at approximately 32 Hz.

Given these limited robot capabilities, researchers working with Kilobots have developed systems of augmented reality to allow Kilobots to interact with virtual environments [1,19,32]. We employ the Kilogrid system [32], which is a lattice of square electronic modules covered with a transparent glass. The Kilobots can move on the Kilogrid's glass surface while communicating with static modules beneath which are equipped with the same IR transceivers as the

Kilobots. Each $10 \times 10\,\mathrm{cm}^2$ module is composed of four smaller $5 \times 5\,\mathrm{cm}^2$ square cells. In our setup, we use a $1 \times 2\,\mathrm{m}^2$ rectangular Kilogrid composed of 10×20 modules for a total of 800 cells.

The collective perception scenario is implemented by assigning a color to each internal Kilogrid cell. In our environment there are 684 colored internal tiles and 116 non-colored tiles at the boundaries. Cells adjacent to walls are colorless because robots do wall avoidance when under two tiles away from any wall and should rarely visit these areas. All cells continuously signal their color to human observers using colored-LED and to the Kilobots via IR messages. The Kilogrid provides more information to the Kilobots to improve their movement which is subject to noise and unreliable [14]. The cell's IR messages contain the color, the cell's coordinates (x, y in the 20×40 Kilogrid's plane) and a wall flag. The coordinates are used to implement the above mentioned random waypoint mobility model [5,30] to let robots effectively diffuse in space. The 0/1 wall flag indicates a wall at distance $<10\,\mathrm{cm}$ and triggers wall avoidance.

The Kilogrid also allows extending the robot-to-robot communication range which is otherwise physically limited to $r_c \approx 10\,\mathrm{cm}$. Our robots communicate with each other via the Kilogrid. They send their IR messages to the cell beneath them. The cell sends the message to all the cells at an Euclidean distance $< c$ resulting in an effective range of $r_c \approx 2.5 + 5(c - 1)\,\mathrm{cm}$ (see Figs. 1d, e). Hence, we can test communication ranges beyond the Kilobot's limitations.

In this paper, we run experiments in simulation using an available ARGoS plugin that allows to run accurate simulations with the Kilobots [14], and a second ARGoS plugin for the simulation of the Kilogrid that we specifically developed for this study (open-source code available at [2]). The Kilogrid is programmed via code executed on each module. To simulate the Kilogrid, we developed an ARGoS loop function that runs the control cycle of all Kilogrid modules in each simulation step. Module-to-module communication is done by CAN bus, module-to-robot through IR messages, and modules can send data to the PC control station (e.g., log files). Following the ARGoS paradigm of using identical code for simulations and real-world experiments, we developed a simulated module interface that provides all functions available on the real Kilogrid module controller. The code for simulated and real modules has only minimal differences (documented in the code repository) that have been included to optimise simulation speed.

5   Results: Less is More and Slower is Faster

We test the ability of the robot swarm to adapt to sudden environmental changes. All robots start committed to blue ■ (predominant color before the change) with a high estimate $q_b = 0.8$, and hence $w = 1$. We assume the change ■→▨ happens right at the beginning of our experiment, which is initialized with an environment with more yellow than blue tiles. The swarm is expected to perceive the change, reconsider its previous decision, and converge to a large majority (consensus decision) in favor of yellow. We consider the swarm capable to adapt to the change when over a 5 min interval the mean of the number of robots committed to yellow is greater than 70% of the swarm size. In this way, we avoid to count short-lived random fluctuations as successful adaptations. Instead we want the swarm to reach a stable majority. The adaptation time is measured as the time it takes for at least 70% of the robots in the swarm to become committed to yellow at the beginning of the 5 min interval. We define "adaptation probability" as the proportion of simulation runs in which the swarm has successfully adapted. We run 30 simulations per condition.

5.1   When Recruitment is Slow do not be too Social, Less is More

We fix sample number $s = 15$ and time between two samples $\delta_s = 4\,\mathrm{s}$, and test different communication ranges $2.5\,\mathrm{cm} \leq r_c \leq 225\,\mathrm{cm}$ for problem difficulties $\kappa \in \{0.7, 0.8, 0.9\}$. Hence, once recruited, robots broadcast with low probability the new color until they complete the sampling cycle which lasts $\tau_s = s\,\delta_s = 60\,\mathrm{s}$ (see broadcast frequency diagram in Fig. 1c). Because the positive feedback (i.e., recruited robots recruit other robots) is slow, we expect to observe similar dynamics as reported in [30]. Figure 2a shows that also here we have the LIME, where more social interactions (large r_c) diminish the swarm's ability to adapt. Therefore, we confirm the predictions of [30] and show this is a general effect that can take place in scenarios different from collective site selection, where it was first observed. This counter-intuitive effect can be explained via the social impact of committed subpopulations of unbalanced sizes. A large majority is able to repeatedly mute minorities that make temporary discoveries of alternative options. The minority's opinion is slow to gain traction in the population as new recruits are slow in becoming vocal and are quickly reverted to the majority's opinion. When the communication range is large, or equivalently when the robot density is high, any minority is in contact with the large majority at all time. Instead, sparse connectivity, due to a small communication range or a low robot density, reduces the importance of subpopulation sizes. Interactions are sporadic (often limited to pairs) and the collective dynamics are governed by opinion quality (encoded via messaging frequency).

Unlike the site selection scenario [30], where the positive feedback delay was hard to manipulate, here the delay consists in the sampling time $\tau_s = s\,\delta_s$ and can easily be studied. We investigate how the collective performance varies for different sampling times and for different levels of robot connectivity. We study sampling time by varying values s as well as δ_s, and robot connectivity by varying both communication range and robot density (proportional to swarm size as environment size is constant). Figs. 2b–d show that the LIME on robot connectivity is present in parameter regions of slow recruitment (top part of the plots) and gradually vanishes when recruitment is quick. This result is in agreement with theory, as quick recruitment enables positive feedback cascades and allows well connected swarms to react fast to environmental changes. While Figs. 2b–d only show results for problem difficulty $\kappa = 0.9$, we observed qualitatively equivalent dynamics for any κ tested.

We model the collective adaptation dynamics using a mean-field model built as a system of ODEs that describes the proportion of robots in each opinion state [30]. Let x_i be the proportion of robots committed to the environmental element i and let x_u be the proportion of uncommitted robots, with $x_u + \sum_i x_i = 1$. The opinion dynamics model reads as

$$\dot{x}_i = \underbrace{\frac{q_i}{\tau_s} x_u}_{A} + \underbrace{\frac{1}{\tau_s} \frac{k\, r_c^2\, N\, x_u}{1 + k\, r_c^2\, N\, x_u} q_i\, x_i}_{B} - \underbrace{\frac{k\, r_c^2\, N\, x_i}{1 + k\, r_c^2\, N\, x_i} \sum_{j \neq i} q_j\, x_j}_{C}$$

$$+ \underbrace{\frac{q_i}{\tau_s} \sum_{j \neq i} [x_j\, \mathcal{H}(\hat{q}_i - \hat{q}_j)] - \frac{x_i}{\tau_s} \sum_{j \neq i} [q_j\, \mathcal{H}(\hat{q}_j - \hat{q}_i)]}_{D} , \tag{1}$$

where $\mathcal{H}$ is the unit step function, and k is a proportionality factor to fit the ODE system to the observed dynamics of the simulated swarm robotics system (e.g., speed of robots, communication frequency, robots' opinion update time). The four terms on the rhs of Eq. (1) model discovery, recruitment, cross-inhibition, and direct switching transitions (capital letters below each term correspond to the transitions depicted in Fig. 1b, for more details see [30]).

The model of Eq. (1), as previously published [30], describes 'slow' (i.e., not instantaneous) recruitment through the Holling function type 2. As the sampling time τ_s is decreased, the recruitment becomes quicker and the effect of the Holling function reduces. As a result the recruitment rate becomes approximately linear on neighborhood size. Through bifurcation analysis in the case of $n = 2$, we identify two states of the system as a function of the communication range (in Fig. 2e), or equivalently of the swarm density (not shown). Prior to the subcritical bifurcation (low r_c or N), the system has a single stable equilibrium that represents a consensus decision for the color with the highest concentration, therefore, in this parameter range adaptation is guaranteed. After the bifurcation (high r_c or N), a second stable equilibrium appears representing a consensus decision for the inferior alternative. In this parameter range, the swarm when initialized at equilibrium for the inferior color can only switch between the coexisting attractors through high random fluctuations and the swarm may take longer to adapt. The bifurcation analysis of Fig. 2e shows results that are qualitatively equivalent to the dynamics observed in simulations (see Fig. 2g).

5.2   With Noisy Estimates and Few Neighbors, Slower is Faster

The results of Figs. 2b–d also show new interesting dynamics that were not found in the previous study [30]. When robot connectivity is low (i.e., sporadic social interactions) the swarm is only able to adapt when the sampling time is high (either the number of samples s or the time between readings δ_s are large). This mechanism corresponds to the SIFE [9,18,25–27] by which the swarm is able to adapt at a quicker speed (i.e., within 40 min) when the robots perform their task of estimating the environmental element concentration at a slower pace.

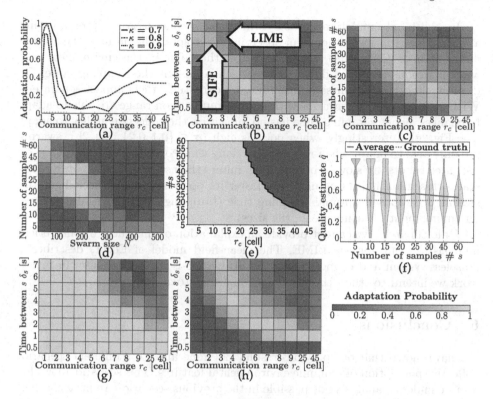

Fig. 2. (a, b, c) Smaller communication ranges lead to higher adaptation probability. This effect happens only when recruitment is slow, i.e., in the top part of panels (b, c), for high sampling times $\tau_s = s\,\delta_s$, which can be caused by (b) large times between samples δ_s (with fixed $s = 15$) or (c) high numbers of samples s (with fixed $\delta_s = 1$). (b–c) When communication is limited, slower sampling time leads to higher probability of adapting. (d) The same two effects can be observed for fixed communication range ($r_c \approx 12.5$ cm for $c = 3$) and increasing robot density, which we control by modifying the swarm size N in an environment with a fixed size; (e) the ODE model (Eq. (1)) predicts results qualitatively similar to simulations without noise (g) ($N = 50$, $\kappa = 0.9$, $k = 4 \times 10^{-6}$); (f) sampling times τ_s influence the noise, because accuracy increases when robots collect more samples s; (g) when estimation noise is independent of sampling and low ($\sigma = 0$) the SIFE disappears; (h) when estimation noise is independent of sampling and high ($\sigma = 0.1$) both effects are present; if not specified, swarm size $N = 50$, difficulty $\kappa = 0.9$, 30 simulations each; color-maps show probability to adapt.

To study this phenomenon, we ran additional simulations. Slowing down the sampling process has the double effect of slowing down the recruitment and of reducing errors on the color concentration. Increasing either the sample number s or the time between samples δ_s reduces the estimation noise because the robot respectively collects more samples (see Fig. 2f) or reduces sample correlation. Therefore, we investigate whether adaptation of sparse swarms is limited by high noise or quick recruitment.

In additional simulations, robots estimate color concentration ($\hat{q}_b$ or $\hat{q}_y$) using a normal distribution rather than observing tile colors. The mean of the normal distribution is the correct concentration of the color in the environment and we test various standard deviations σ which represent the sampling noise. By disentangling noise from sampling time, we can study their impact separately. Without noise ($\sigma = 0$), swarms with low communication range are able to adapt to changes, hence sampling time has no impact on the collective ability to adapt (see Fig. 2g). Interestingly, when noise is high ($\sigma \in \{0.1, 0.2\}$, Fig. 2h), swarms are only able to adapt when robots take a long time to make their estimate (i.e., recruited robots are slow in becoming recruiters themselves). The slower a robot starts disseminating its opinion, the faster its opinion spreads throughout the swarm. A supposed optimal sampling time (sampling rate) might also depend on environmental features (e.g., tile sizes).

Unfortunately, we cannot provide an explanation of this effect by theoretical analysis as done for the LIME. The mean-field model of Eq. (1) describes a noiseless system and cannot model the SIFE that is driven by noise. In future work we intend to study this phenomenon using stochastic models.

6   Conclusions

We have shown that our previous results [30] generalize to a different scenario: collective perception of dynamic environmental features. This scenario allows for a more in-depth analysis not possible in the previous scenario. We have clarified the relationship between recruitment speed and ability to collectively adapt to environmental changes. The collective task that we study here is equivalent to enabling the swarm to revise an incorrect collective decision that led the swarm to reach a consensus for the inferior alternative and avoids lock-in states.

Our results explain the importance of considering the interplay between sampling time and the communication range when designing the robot behavior as it can have a paramount effect on the collective dynamics. Through rigorous mathematical and computational analysis, we explain the mechanisms that cause the LIME, which is triggered by slow recruitment. During our investigations, we also stumbled upon a new effect: slower individual dissemination enables faster global agreement. We are unable, for the moment, to explain mathematically the SIFE. However, our computational analysis confirms that the results on speed are not confounded with estimation noise. Our future research will investigate the mechanisms causing such unexpected dynamics which are highly relevant for swarm robotics studies as they manifest when swarm connectivity is sparse and robots follow a simple behavior subject to high levels of noise.

Acknowledgements. The authors thank Anthony Antoun, Marco Trabattoni, and Jonas Kuckling for technical support concerning Kilogrid and simulations on HPC. MD and AR acknowledge support from the Belgian F.R.S.-FNRS, of which they are Research Director and Chargé de Recherches, respectively.

References

1. Antoun, A., Valentini, G., Hocquard, E., Wiandt, B., Trianni, V., Dorigo, M.: Kilogrid: a modular virtualization environment for the Kilobot robot. In: 2016 IEEE/RSJ International Conference on Intelligent Robots and Systems (IROS), vol. 1, pp. 3809–3814. IEEE (2016). https://doi.org/10.1109/IROS.2016.7759560
2. Aust, T., Reina, A.: Open-source code for simulating the Kilogrid in ARGoS. https://github.com/tilly111/adaptive_symmetry_breaking
3. Bartashevich, P., Mostaghim, S.: Benchmarking collective perception: new task difficulty metrics for collective decision-making. In: Moura Oliveira, P., Novais, P., Reis, L.P. (eds.) EPIA 2019. LNCS (LNAI), vol. 11804, pp. 699–711. Springer, Cham (2019). https://doi.org/10.1007/978-3-030-30241-2_58
4. Bartashevich, P., Mostaghim, S.: Multi-featured collective perception with evidence theory: tackling spatial correlations. Swarm Intell. **15**(1), 83–110 (2021). https://doi.org/10.1007/s11721-021-00192-8
5. Bettstetter, C., Hartenstein, H., Pérez-Costa, X.: Stochastic properties of the random waypoint mobility model. Wirel. Netw. **10**(5), 555–567 (2004). https://doi.org/10.1023/B:WINE.0000036458.88990.e5
6. Soorati, M.D., Krome, M., Mora-Mendoza, M., Ghofrani, J., Hamann, H.: Plasticity in collective decision-making for robots: creating global reference frames, detecting dynamic environments, and preventing lock-ins. In: 2019 IEEE/RSJ International Conference on Intelligent Robots and Systems (IROS), vol. 1, pp. 4100–4105. IEEE (2019). https://doi.org/10.1109/IROS40897.2019.8967777
7. Ebert, J.T., Gauci, M., Mallmann-Trenn, F., Nagpal, R.: Bayes bots: collective Bayesian decision-making in decentralized robot swarms. In: 2020 IEEE International Conference on Robotics and Automation (ICRA), pp. 7186–7192. IEEE (2020). https://doi.org/10.1109/ICRA40945.2020.9196584
8. Ebert, J.T., Gauci, M., Nagpal, R.: Multi-feature collective decision making in robot swarms. In: Proceedings of the 17th International Conference on Autonomous Agents and Multiagent Systems (AAMAS), Richland, SC, vol. 3, pp. 1711–1719 (2018)
9. Gershenson, C., Helbing, D.: When slower is faster. Complexity **21**(2), 9–15 (2015). https://doi.org/10.1002/cplx.21736
10. Hamann, H.: Swarm Robotics: A Formal Approach. Springer, Cham (2018). https://doi.org/10.1007/978-3-319-74528-2
11. Lee, C., Lawry, J., Winfield, A.F.: Negative updating applied to the best-of-n problem with noisy qualities. Swarm Intell. **15**(1), 111–143 (2021). https://doi.org/10.1007/s11721-021-00188-4
12. Nikolaidis, E., Sabo, C., Marshal, J.A.R., Reina, A.: Characterisation and upgrade of the communication between overhead controllers and Kilobots. Technical report, White Rose Research Online (2017)
13. Parker, C.A.C., Zhang, H.: Biologically inspired decision making for collective robotic systems. In: 2004 IEEE/RSJ International Conference on Intelligent Robots and Systems (IROS) (IEEE Cat. No. 04CH37566), vol. 1, pp. 375–380. IEEE (2004). https://doi.org/10.1109/IROS.2004.1389381
14. Pinciroli, C., Talamali, M.S., Reina, A., Marshall, J.A.R., Trianni, V.: Simulating Kilobots within ARGoS: models and experimental validation. In: Dorigo, M., Birattari, M., Blum, C., Christensen, A.L., Reina, A., Trianni, V. (eds.) ANTS 2018. LNCS, vol. 11172, pp. 176–187. Springer, Cham (2018). https://doi.org/10.1007/978-3-030-00533-7_14

15. Pinciroli, C., et al.: ARGoS: a modular, parallel, multi-engine simulator for multi-robot systems. Swarm Intell. **6**(4), 271–295 (2012). https://doi.org/10.1007/s11721-012-0072-5

16. Prasetyo, J., De Masi, G., Ferrante, E.: Collective decision making in dynamic environments. Swarm Intell. **13**(3), 217–243 (2019). https://doi.org/10.1007/s11721-019-00169-8

17. Prasetyo, J., De Masi, G., Ranjan, P., Ferrante, E.: The best-of-n problem with dynamic site qualities: achieving adaptability with stubborn individuals. In: Dorigo, M., Birattari, M., Blum, C., Christensen, A.L., Reina, A., Trianni, V. (eds.) ANTS 2018. LNCS, vol. 11172, pp. 239–251. Springer, Cham (2018). https://doi.org/10.1007/978-3-030-00533-7_19

18. Rahmani, P., Peruani, F., Romanczuk, P.: Flocking in complex environments-attention trade-offs in collective information processing. PLoS Comput. Biol. **16**(4), 1–18 (2020). https://doi.org/10.1371/journal.pcbi.1007697

19. Reina, A., Cope, A.J., Nikolaidis, E., Marshall, J.A.R., Sabo, C.: ARK: augmented reality for Kilobots. IEEE Robot. Autom. Lett. **2**(3), 1755–1761 (2017). https://doi.org/10.1109/LRA.2017.2700059

20. Reina, A., Ioannou, V., Chen, J., Lu, L., Kent, C., Marshall, J.A.: Robots as actors in a film: no war, a robot story. arXiv preprint arXiv:1910.12294 (2019)

21. Rubenstein, M., Ahler, C., Hoff, N., Cabrera, A., Nagpal, R.: Kilobot: a low cost robot with scalable operations designed for collective behaviors. Robot. Auton. Syst. **62**(7), 966–975 (2014). https://doi.org/10.1016/j.robot.2013.08.006

22. Rubenstein, M., Cornejo, A., Nagpal, R.: Programmable self-assembly in a thousand-robot swarm. Science **345**(6198), 795–799 (2014). https://doi.org/10.1126/science.1254295

23. Shan, Q., Mostaghim, S.: Collective decision making in swarm robotics with distributed Bayesian hypothesis testing. In: Dorigo, M., et al. (eds.) ANTS 2020. LNCS, vol. 12421, pp. 55–67. Springer, Cham (2020). https://doi.org/10.1007/978-3-030-60376-2_5

24. Shan, Q., Mostaghim, S.: Discrete collective estimation in swarm robotics with distributed Bayesian belief sharing. Swarm Intell. **15**(4), 377–402 (2021). https://doi.org/10.1007/s11721-021-00201-w

25. Slobodkin, L.B.: Growth and Regulation of Animal Populations. Holt, Rinehart and Winston, New York (1961)

26. Stark, H.U., Tessone, C.J., Schweitzer, F.: Decelerating microdynamics can accelerate macrodynamics in the voter model. Phys. Rev. Lett. **101**(1), 018701 (2008). https://doi.org/10.1103/PhysRevLett.101.018701

27. Stark, H.U., Tessone, C.J., Schweitzer, F.: Slower is faster: fostering consensus formation by heterogeneous inertia. Adv. Complex Syst. **11**(4), 551–563 (2008). https://doi.org/10.1142/S0219525908001805

28. Strobel, V., Castelló Ferrer, E., Dorigo, M.: Managing byzantine robots via blockchain technology in a swarm robotics collective decision making scenario. In: Proceedings of the 17th International Conference on Autonomous Agents and Multiagent Systems (AAMAS), Richland, SC, vol. 3, pp. 541–549 (2018)

29. Strobel, V., Castelló Ferrer, E., Dorigo, M.: Blockchain technology secures robot swarms: a comparison of consensus protocols and their resilience to Byzantine robots. Front. Robot. AI **7**, 54 (2020). https://doi.org/10.3389/frobt.2020.00054

30. Talamali, M.S., Saha, A., Marshall, J.A.R., Reina, A.: When less is more: robot swarms adapt better to changes with constrained communication. Sci. Robot. **5**(56), eabf1416 (2021). https://doi.org/10.1126/scirobotics.abf1416

31. Valentini, G., Hamann, H., Dorigo, M.: Self-organized collective decision-making in a 100-robot swarm. In: Proceedings of the Twenty-Ninth AAAI Conference on Artificial Intelligence (AAAI 2015), pp. 4216–4217. AAAI Press (2015)
32. Valentini, G., et al.: Kilogrid: a novel experimental environment for the Kilobot robot. Swarm Intell. **12**(3), 245–266 (2018). https://doi.org/10.1007/s11721-018-0155-z
33. Valentini, G., Brambilla, D., Hamann, H., Dorigo, M.: Collective perception of environmental features in a robot swarm. In: ANTS 2016. LNCS, vol. 9882, pp. 65–76. Springer, Cham (2016). https://doi.org/10.1007/978-3-319-44427-7_6
34. Valentini, G., Ferrante, E., Dorigo, M.: The best-of-n problem in robot swarms: formalization, state of the art, and novel perspectives. Front. Robot. AI **4**, 9 (2017). https://doi.org/10.3389/frobt.2017.00009
35. Zakir, R., Dorigo, M., Reina, A.: Robot swarms break decision deadlocks in collective perception through cross-inhibition. In: Dorigo, M., et al. (eds.) ANTS 2022. LNCS, vol. 13491, pp. 209–221. Springer, Cham (2022)

A Novel Time-of-Flight Range and Bearing Sensor System for Micro Air Vehicle Swarms

Cem Bilaloğlu[1,4]([✉]), Mehmet Şahin[1,4], Farshad Arvin[2], Erol Şahin[3], and Ali Emre Turgut[1,4]

[1] Department of Mechanical Engineering, Middle East Technical University, Ankara, Turkey
{cembi,aturgut,mesahin}@metu.edu.tr
[2] Department of Computer Science, Durham University, Durham, UK
farshad.arvin@durham.ac.uk
[3] Department of Computer Engineering, Middle East Technical University, Ankara, Turkey
erol@metu.edu.tr
[4] Center for Robotics and Artificial Intelligence (ROMER), Middle East Technical University, Ankara, Turkey

Abstract. In this paper, we propose a novel range and bearing sensing (RnB) system for micro-air vehicle (MAV) swarms. The RnB system uses 12 infrared (IR) time-of-flight (ToF) sensors and measures the range and bearing of obstacles and other MAVs. The system incorporated hardware and software filtering to remove ambient noise and interference between different sensors to distinguish between obstacles and kin MAVs. The overall system is 50 mm wide and weighs 12.5 gram. We have installed the system on 5 indoor quadrotors and demonstrated the performance of the RnB system using flocking behavior. To the best of our knowledge, our system is the first IR ToF sensor-based RnB system designed specifically for swarms that enabled the first decentralized flocking on indoor MAVs using only on-board resources.

1 Introduction

MAVs are small flying robots that create minimal aerodynamic effects [15] and enable indoor swarm operation mostly in the form of agile quadrotors [7]. These robot collectives are suitable for robotic missions that leverage scalability, ranging from bio-inspired flocking behavior [22] to high-level mapping [1], surveillance [20] and search [16] tasks. However, the advantages of MAVs introduce many challenges in terms of payload and on-board resources. Accordingly, in most real-robot scenarios, external motion capture systems (Vicon [8], Optitrack [13], Loco Position [2], Lighthouse [6]) provide robot positions to coordinate swarms. External sensing limits MAVs to structured environments and static obstacles far simpler than realistic scenarios. Thus, it is essential to develop on-board relative positioning sensors for decentralized swarm scenarios and existing efforts mainly concentrate on ranging-based ultra-wideband (UWB), vision, and IR RnB systems.

© Springer Nature Switzerland AG 2022
M. Dorigo et al. (Eds.): ANTS 2022, LNCS 13491, pp. 248–256, 2022.
https://doi.org/10.1007/978-3-031-20176-9_20

UWB, a short-range communication technology frequently used for global positioning with anchors in the environment [2], was recently adapted to omni-directional relative positioning [2,4,9,17,24]. Although these systems can sense the relative position of robots with respect to each other, they cannot sense the position of the obstacles in the environment.

Vision-based methods using camera and image processing in contrast, is practical for sensing obstacles [11,25] but challenging for relative positioning of MAVs [14,19]. Such methods are computationally expensive and without markers on MAVs [21] the processing requirements are very high.

Multiple classical IR receiver-emitter pairs which measure range using the intensity of the reflected light, provide a simple solution for ground swarm robots [5,10,23]. These planar systems are called "range and bearing" (RnB) sensors which measure the relative position vector of an object where the range is the magnitude and bearing is the angle of the vector relative to the robot's heading. The only extension of IR RnB to a flying swarm is the Eye-bot [18], using tens of receivers for spatial coverage and weighing hundreds of grams.

A modern and lightweight version of IR pairs uses time of flight (ToF) to estimate range by measuring the travel time of reflected IR light from an object. These sensors are robust against object reflectivity and ambient light compared to classical IR pairs. Although there have been studies to use these sensors on MAVs [3,12] to sense the obstacles, there are no studies to sense other robots.

In this paper, we propose a novel RnB system for MAV-swarms using ToF sensors (see Fig. 1). We exploit these sensors to distinguish robots from obstacles and measure relative position in a challenging environment of a swarm with excessive interference. The result is a stand-alone on-board system with a decentralized and scalable robot detection strategy that does not require additional sensing or communication. We present our open-source[1] hardware and software, and we demonstrate the performance of the system in an actual swarm behavior[2] with 5 Tello quadrotors (Ryze Technology, Shenzhen, CN).

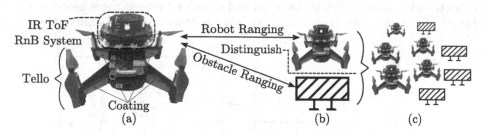

Fig. 1. a) RnB system with IR ToF sensors on a Tello quadrotor b) Ranging measurements from robots and obstacles and distinguishing robots from obstacles c) RnB in decentralized swarm scenarios, defining distinct robot-robot and robot-obstacle interactions such as self-organized flocking

---

[1] Link to open source hardware/software repository.

[2] Link to experiment videos with 5 MAVs.

2   Range and Bearing System

The RnB system consists of a mainboard with a dedicated controller (STM32F1) and 12 IR ToF sensors (VL53L1) equally spaced on the circumference. The system can work with any host capable of I2C communication and supplying a current of 170 mA at 3.3 V (Fig. 2).

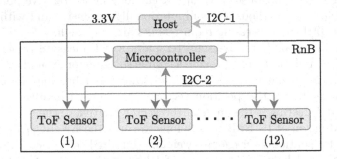

Fig. 2. Flow diagram of the RnB system and connections with a host robot

2.1   Ranging Sequence of Time of Flight Sensor

A single ranging sequence of the ToF sensor is composed of three phases as shown in Fig. 3b. During the *ambient* phase, the receiver senses IR light with an inactive emitter. In the *signal* phase, the emitter sends a pulse, and the receiver senses again IR light. These two phases are followed by a random delay phase during which the ToF sensor neither emits nor collects any signal. After each ranging sequence, ToF sensors report an *ambient* indicating the background noise, a *signal* corresponding to the intensity of the reflected light from the object, and a *range* which is the estimated distance between the sensor and the target object. Notably, these phases are always consecutive and immutable.

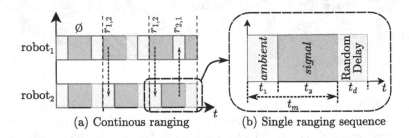

Fig. 3. Ranging sequences of RnB systems on $robot_1$ and $robot_2$ where blue arrows denote the robot detection. Symbol ∅ denotes a false negative robot detection and $r_{i,j}$ denotes that $robot_i$ detected $robot_j$ (Color figure online)

2.2 Robot Detection and Ranging in a Swarm

The RnB system distinguishes kin robots using the same system from passive obstacles, which we refer to as 'robot detection'. To perform robot detection, we assume that there are no external emitters other than the RnB system of the robots in the environment. Accordingly, if a sensor collects a non-zero *ambient* reading, then there should be at least one nearby robot in the FoV of the sensor.

An interference scenario in the ranging of two RnB systems occurs when they have a synchronous operation, as seen in the first ranging sequence of $robot_1$ and $robot_2$ in Fig. 3a. Consequently, both systems' *ambient* and *signal* phases fully overlap, and neither detects the other, resulting in 'false negative' robot detection. During the *signal* phase, RnB systems emit pulses simultaneously, and in addition to reflections, they collect the pulses emitted by the other RnB systems. We refer to this event as 'signal collision' that affects the ranging measurement adversely. Notably, we want to avoid this 'in-sync interference' (ambient-ambient and signal-signal) and seek 'out-of-sync interference' (ambient-signal) both for robot detection and for ranging.

2.3 Random Delay and Filtering

We minimize false-negative robot detection and signal collision with: (i) adding a random delay block of fixed duration with a probability of 0.5 to the ranging sequence of the sensors, (ii) filtering the data collected in circular buffers to eliminate noisy readings. The random delay phase shifts any two sensors out-of-sync and ensures that the *ambient* measurement of one sensor coincides with the *signal* measurement of the other sensor (see Fig. 3a).

The *range*, *ambient* and *isRobot* readings are stored in circular buffers for filtering. The median and interquartile range (IQR) of these buffers are used to estimate *range* and *isRobot* information as outlined in Algorithm 1.

Algorithm 1: Robot detection, random delay and filtering (see footnote 1)

```
range=maxRange; // Initially no object detected
isRobot=false; // Initially no robot detected
if iqrAmbient > ambientThresh then
    circularBuffIsRobot.update(true);// Update with robot detection
else
    circularBuffIsRobot.update(false);// Update with no robot detection
if circularBuffIsRobot.any() then
    isRobot = true; // At least one robot detection in buffer
if (iqrRange < rangeThresh) and (signal > signalThresh) then
    range = medianRange; // Valid object range
if randomBool() and !isWait then
    isWait = true; // Will delay in next cycle
```

2.4　Design

The RnB system have 12 sensors separated by $\beta = 30°$ (see Fig. 4) and it calculates the bearing of an object seen by the ith sensor as $i \cdot \beta$. The FoV of the sensor $\phi = 27°$, is smaller than the offset between the sensors β, thus the width of the blind zones w increases with inter-robot distance d by the relation $w = 2d \left[\tan\left(\beta/2\right) - \tan\left(\phi/2\right) \right] + 11.2$ mm. At $d = 0$ the width of the blind zone is equal to the gap between two sensors 11.2 mm and at $d_{max} = 1300$ mm the width of the blind zones becomes ≈ 90 mm. We regarded this value acceptable for the target robot Tello with 195 mm horizontal span.

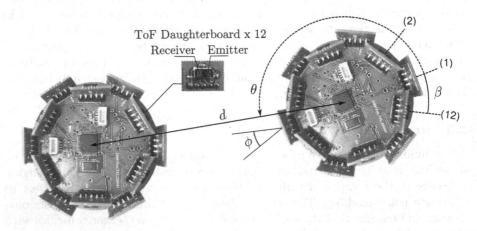

Fig. 4. Two RnB systems with the planar relative pose variables $\{d, \theta\}$, the cone angle ϕ determining the FoV of the sensor and the angle between sensors β

The FoV of the sensor also sets the allowable altitude deviation between MAVs. This deviation increases with inter-robot distance according to the relation $\Delta h = \pm d \cdot \tan\left(\phi/2\right)$ which corresponds to $\Delta h < \pm 174$ mm at $d = 650$ mm and $\Delta h < \pm 348$ mm at $d_{max} = 1300$ mm. We considered these values acceptable for target quadrotor Tello, capable of controlling its altitude in the interval $\Delta h < \pm 50$ mm with its on-board sensor.

We should also note that without any modification, the ranging performance of ToF sensors is not adequate for indoor quadrotors with tiny cross-sections. We overcame that problem by increasing the reflectance of the robots with retro-reflective folio coating, as shown in Fig. 1a. A similar approach can be used to detect smaller quadrotors such as Crazyflie (Bitcraze AB, Malmö, SE).

3　Results and Discussion

In all the experiments, we set the length of the circular buffers to 5 and set the duration of the random delay to $t_d = 5$ ms with measurement duration $t_m = 20$ ms (see Fig. 3b).

3.1 Controlled Experiments

In order to characterize the performance, we controlled the relative pose (d, θ) of two MAVs with the RnB system, and we measured their actual values using a Vicon motion capture system (Vicon Motion Systems Limited, Oxford, UK). We synchronized the ground truth information from Vicon with the readings collected from both of the RnB systems.

In the first experiment, we measured the ranging and robot detection performance of the RnB with and without introducing the random delay phase and plotted *ambient range* and *isRobot* values in Fig. 5. As depicted in the plots, our method eliminated periodic ranging errors and false negatives in robot detection.

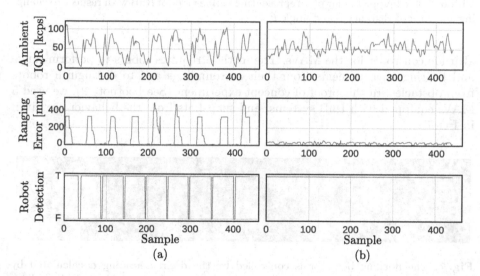

Fig. 5. Line plots showing *ambient* reading *range* error and robot detection performance a) without random delay phase b) with random delay phase

For the second experiment, we set θ to angles in the interval $[0, \beta/2]$ and we changed d continuously up to d_{max}. The collected data spans the whole operational range of the RnB system because the sensors are axis-symmetric and consecutive sensors are separated by β. We plot the results for d and θ on a polar plot with over 17000 data points in Fig. 6. The sensor measured up to its maximum range $d_{max} = 1300$ mm and half FoV angle $\phi/2 = 13.5°$. On the blind zones, from $\phi/2 = 13.5°$ to $\beta/2 = 15°$ maximum distance that the sensor can measure decreased, and the ranging error increased.

3.2 Self-organized Flocking with Micro Air Vehicles

In order to verify the RnB system in a swarm setting, we implemented a flocking method [23] without any modifications apart from an additional closed-loop

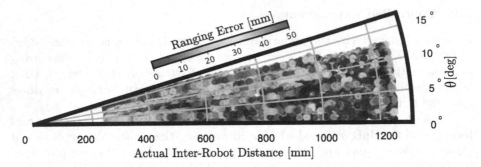

Fig. 6. Color-mapped polar plot representing *range* error of RnB with respect to changing inter robot distance d and angle θ

altitude controller for the MAVs. The method requires robots to perform range and bearing measurements from their surroundings and to distinguish robots from obstacles. In this proof of concept experiment (See Footnote 2), we used 5 MAVs equipped with RnB systems, and snapshots from the behavior are given in Fig. 7.

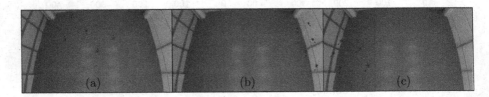

Fig. 7. The flocking behavior is controlled by the desired heading a calculated by weighted sum $a = h + \beta p$. h is the resultant direction of neighbors and used for aligning robots. p is the resultant proximal control vector computed using virtual forces f_i, minimizing $|range - \sigma_{des}|$ for each RnB sensor. The desired equilibrium point σ_{des} is set for both cohesion and collision avoidance

4   Conclusion

This paper introduces a novel RnB system for MAVs, using IR ToF sensors. We proposed a method based on random delay and filtering to have a fully scalable and decentralized robot detection and ranging. Then, we verified our method and measured the effect of relative pose on sensing performance with a set of controlled experiments. Lastly, we demonstrated the RnB system in a flocking scenario with 5 MAVs using only on-board resources.

Acknowledgements. This work was partially supported by the EU H2020-FET RoboRoyale (964492).

References

1. Achtelik, M., et al.: SFly: swarm of micro flying robots. In: 2012 IEEE/RSJ International Conference on Intelligent Robots and Systems, pp. 2649–2650, October 2012
2. Cai, X., Ye, L., Zhang, Q.: Ensemble learning particle swarm optimization for real-time UWB indoor localization. EURASIP J. Wirel. Commun. Netw. **2018**(1), 125 (2018)
3. Duisterhof, B.P., et al.: Tiny robot learning (tinyRL) for source seeking on a nano quadcopter. In: 2021 IEEE International Conference on Robotics and Automation (ICRA), pp. 7242–7248, May 2021
4. Guo, K., Qiu, Z., Meng, W., Xie, L., Teo, R.: Ultra-wideband based cooperative relative localization algorithm and experiments for multiple unmanned aerial vehicles in GPS denied environments. Int. J. Micro Air Veh. **9**(3), 169–186 (2017)
5. Gutierrez, A., Campo, A., Dorigo, M., Donate, J., Monasterio-Huelin, F., Magdalena, L.: Open E-puck range bearing miniaturized board for local communication in swarm robotics. In: 2009 IEEE International Conference on Robotics and Automation, pp. 3111–3116, May 2009
6. Kilberg, B.G., Campos, F.M.R., Schindler, C.B., Pister, K.S.J.: Quadrotor-based lighthouse localization with time-synchronized wireless sensor nodes and bearing-only measurements. Sensors **20**(14), 3888 (2020)
7. Kumar, V., Michael, N.: Opportunities and challenges with autonomous micro aerial vehicles. Int. J. Robot. Res. **31**(11), 1279–1291 (2012)
8. Kushleyev, A., Mellinger, D., Powers, C., Kumar, V.: Towards a swarm of agile micro quadrotors. Auton. Robot. **35**(4), 287–300 (2013). https://doi.org/10.1007/s10514-013-9349-9
9. Li, J., Bi, Y., Li, K., Wang, K., Lin, F., Chen, B.M.: Accurate 3D localization for MAV swarms by UWB and IMU fusion. In: 2018 IEEE 14th International Conference on Control and Automation (ICCA), pp. 100–105, June 2018
10. Liu, Z., West, C., Lennox, B., Arvin, F.: Local bearing estimation for a swarm of low-cost miniature robots. Sensors **20**(11), 3308 (2020)
11. McGuire, K., de Croon, G., De Wagter, C., Tuyls, K., Kappen, H.: Efficient optical flow and stereo vision for velocity estimation and obstacle avoidance on an autonomous pocket drone. IEEE Robot. Autom. Lett. **2**(2), 1070–1076 (2017)
12. Mcguire, K., De Wagter, C., Tuyls, K., Kappen, H., Croon, G.: Minimal navigation solution for a swarm of tiny flying robots to explore an unknown environment. Sci. Robot. **4**, eaaw9710 (2019)
13. Michael, N., Mellinger, D., Lindsey, Q., Kumar, V.: The GRASP multiple micro-UAV testbed. IEEE Robot. Autom. Mag. **17**(3), 56–65 (2010)
14. Nägeli, T., Conte, C., Domahidi, A., Morari, M., Hilliges, O.: Environment-independent formation flight for micro aerial vehicles. In: 2014 IEEE/RSJ International Conference on Intelligent Robots and Systems, pp. 1141–1146, September 2014
15. Powers, C., Mellinger, D., Kushleyev, A., Kothmann, B., Kumar, V.: Influence of aerodynamics and proximity effects in quadrotor flight. In: Desai, J., Dudek, G., Khatib, O., Kumar, V. (eds.) Experimental Robotics. STAR, vol. 88, pp. 209–302. Springer, Heidelberg (2013). https://doi.org/10.1007/978-3-319-00065-7_21
16. Pugh, J., Martinoli, A.: Inspiring and modeling multi-robot search with particle swarm optimization. In: 2007 IEEE Swarm Intelligence Symposium, pp. 332–339, April 2007

17. Queralta, J.P., Almansa, C.M., Schiano, F., Floreano, D., Westerlund, T.: UWB-based system for UAV localization in GNSS-denied environments: characterization and dataset. In: 2020 IEEE/RSJ International Conference on Intelligent Robots and Systems (IROS), pp. 4521–4528, October 2020
18. Roberts, J.F., Stirling, T., Zufferey, J.C., Floreano, D.: 3-D relative positioning sensor for indoor flying robots. Auton. Robot. **33**(1), 5–20 (2012). https://doi.org/10.1007/s10514-012-9277-0
19. Roelofsen, S., Gillet, D., Martinoli, A.: Reciprocal collision avoidance for quadrotors using on-board visual detection. In: 2015 IEEE/RSJ International Conference on Intelligent Robots and Systems (IROS), pp. 4810–4817, September 2015
20. Saska, M., Vonásek, V., Chudoba, J., Thomas, J., Loianno, G., Kumar, V.: Swarm distribution and deployment for cooperative surveillance by micro-aerial vehicles. J. Intell. Robot. Syst. **84**(1), 469–492 (2016). https://doi.org/10.1007/s10846-016-0338-z
21. Schilling, F., Schiano, F., Floreano, D.: Vision-based drone flocking in outdoor environments. IEEE Robot. Autom. Lett. **6**(2), 2954–2961 (2021)
22. Soria, E., Schiano, F., Floreano, D.: Predictive control of aerial swarms in cluttered environments. Nat. Mach. Intell. **3**(6), 545–554 (2021)
23. Turgut, A.E., Çelikkanat, H., Gökçe, F., Şahin, E.: Self-organized flocking in mobile robot swarms. Swarm Intell. **2**(2), 97–120 (2008). https://doi.org/10.1007/s11721-008-0016-2
24. van der Helm, S., Coppola, M., McGuire, K.N., de Croon, G.C.H.E.: On-board range-based relative localization for micro air vehicles in indoor leader–follower flight. Auton. Robot. **44**(3), 415–441 (2019). https://doi.org/10.1007/s10514-019-09843-6
25. Xiao, F., Zheng, P., di Tria, J., Kocer, B.B., Kovac, M.: Optic flow-based reactive collision prevention for MAVs using the fictitious obstacle hypothesis. IEEE Robot. Autom. Lett. **6**(2), 3144–3151 (2021)

An Adaptive Metric Model for Collective Motion Structures in Dynamic Environments

Stef Van Havermaet[1]($\boxtimes$)(iD), Pieter Simoens[1](iD), and Yara Khaluf[2](iD)

[1] Department of Information Technology–IDLab, Faculty of Engineering
and Architecture, Ghent University–imec, Ghent, Belgium
`{stef.vanhavermaet,pieter.simoens}@ugent.be`
[2] Department of Social Sciences – INF, Applied Information Science,
Wageningen University and Research, Wageningen, The Netherlands
`yara.khaluf@wur.nl`

Abstract. Robot swarms often use collective motion. Most models generate collective motion using the repulsion zone, alignment zone, and attraction zone. Despite being widely used, these models have a limited capacity for generating group structures in response to environmental stimuli. Enabling robot swarms to display proper spatial structures is crucial for several swarm robotics tasks. In this paper, we focus on three spatial structures that allow the swarm to adapt its aggregation (coverage) and alignment (order) in response to environmental changes. We show that the metric and long-range models are unable to generate every structure. We propose an extension to the metric model that allows the swarm to display the three structures, which is demonstrated in a simulated dynamic environment where different stimuli appear over time.

1 Introduction

Collective motion is nature's most fundamental demonstration of coordinated activity, performed by bird flocks, fish shoals, and human crowds [25]. Emergent behavior results from individuals' interactions to perform tasks like foraging or migrating. Collective motion is important in artificial systems like robot swarms, which simulate social animal behavior. Individual robots have basic abilities, but when they work together in groups, they can perform more complex behaviors like foraging [7,16,17,19], exploration [10,20], and collective perception [12,23].

Many activities in robot swarms need collective motion. Navigation from a source to a destination, forming topologies, tracking targets, and moving objects are among the examples. Depending on the particular task, specific structures need to be displayed in the swarm. For example, the swarm needs to aggregate while navigating through narrow paths, and to expand while exploring new environments. A large number of theoretical [4,6] and empirical [3,11] studies have proposed models to generate collective motion. Most of these models consider short-range repulsion and long-range attraction among the individuals, in addition to the alignment of velocities along with the their (nearest) neighbors [25]. These models show high efficiency in generating aligned motion based on simple individual rules. However, there is little to no evidence on whether such models can modify spatial features of the group (e.g., structure) as a response to environmental stimuli.

In this study, we use two system measures to define our target structures: swarm order (an expression of alignment degree) and swarm relative coverage (an expression of compactness). The swarm displays three target structures based on environmental stimuli: (a) high coverage, low order (HCLO), (ii) high coverage, high order (HCHO), and (iii) low coverage, high order (LCHO). Individuals have different orientations in HCLO to maximize coverage (low order). This structure is desired for exploration tasks, where robots must observe the environment in all directions and maximize inter-individual distance. HCHO is a high-order, high-coverage swarm. This structure navigates tasks while maximizing coverage (e.g., navigation with exploration). In LCHO, the swarm aggregates, maintaining a high order and high density. This structure can transport items or navigate narrow spaces. All three structures require swarm connectivity (i.e., remain in a single cluster). The aforementioned tasks can also be combined (e.g. search and rescue), which requires the swarm to adapt its structure based on observed stimuli in the dynamic environment.

We consider two models of collective motion: the metric model, where each individual interacts within a defined radius, and the long-range model, where short-interactions occur topologically and long-range interactions randomly. Our results highlight the metric model and long-range model's limitations to generate the above-mentioned structures. We propose an extension to the metric model that allows the swarm to switch between the three structures. We test our extended metric model (EMM) in a simulated dynamic environment, where different stimuli appear over time and are perceived by few individuals.

We show how HCLO, HCHO, and LCHO emerged and how EMM scales with system size. This paper continues as follows. In Sect. 2, we review collective motion models. In Sect. 3, we describe the other models we use. In Sect. 4, we discuss the key results. Section 5 concludes this paper.

2   Related Work

To generate collective motion and group cohesion, many models have been proposed. Models from biology and physics [8,9,13,21,24] suggest simple rules of interaction among individuals can induce collective motion. Such rules capture attraction, repulsion, and alignment [21]. Most of these models use metric distance. These models assume individuals align and attract each other, and that interaction declines with distance. Vicsek model [25] uses neighbor's velocity to exploit individuals' alignment. The Couzin model [5] is used in theoretical biology and group robotics. This paper uses the Couzin model.

Special cases of the metric model were suggested and became widely used, such as the topological model [1,2], in which each individual interacts with a

fixed number of neighbors. The topological model was suggested based on experimental findings of birds flocking [1]. The model proposed in [18] accounts for
sensory-imposed interaction limitations, and is a special-case of the metric model.
Individuals only interact with visually observable neighbors. In [26], the authors
show how long-range models, which introduce long-range alignment interactions
between individuals, prevents group dispersion in open spaces.

Several studies have examined spatial structures in natural organisms. [14]
studied Zebrafish shoals and schools. This work investigated model parameters
other than group density that may impact these two structures. Both [5, 22]
studied how individual heterogeneity affects spatial position in the group, leading
to specific structures. In [15], the authors highlight the importance of system size
and the number of influential neighbors on the emergence of different structures.
Despite interesting results, the work doesn't explain how the model can generate
spatial structures. The obtained structures were dispersed rather than clustered.

3 Model

3.1 Metric and Long-Range Model

Each individual i updates its direction of motion based on the neighbors' poses
in the three non-overlapping behavioral zones around i. Each behavioral zone
corresponds to a distinct interaction; (i) repulsion from others inside the circular
zone with radius ZoR, (ii) alignment of orientation with others inside the zone
with width ZoO, and (iii) attraction to others inside the zone with width ZoA.

The metric and long-range models differ from each other by neighbor selec-
tion. For the metric model, the neighbors $\mathcal{N}_i$ of individual i consists of all individuals within the interaction-radius $RoI = ZoR + ZoO + ZoA$ [5]. For the
long-range model, the neighbor set $\mathcal{N}_i$ is the union of the set of m nearest neigh-
bors $\mathcal{M}_i$ and κ_i randomly selected neighbors of $\mathcal{N}_i \backslash \mathcal{M}_i$ [26], where κ_i is sampled
from a Poisson distribution with average κ.

Let $\mathcal{N}_i^r$, $\mathcal{N}_i^o$, and $\mathcal{N}_i^a$ denote the distinct subsets of neighbors by separating
$\mathcal{N}_i$ based on the repulsion, orientation, and attraction zones respectively. Let us
define r_{ij} as the relative position of individual j from i, and q_i as the direction
vector. The new direction computed with weights $\alpha_r \geq 0$, $\alpha_o \geq 0$ and $\alpha_a \geq 0$ as:

$$\hat{q}_i(t) = -\alpha_r \sum_{j \in \mathcal{N}_i^r} \frac{r_{ij}(t)}{\|r_{ij}(t)\|} + \alpha_o \sum_{j \in \mathcal{N}_i^o} \frac{q_j(t)}{\|q_j(t)\|} + \alpha_a \sum_{j \in \mathcal{N}_i^a} \frac{r_{ij}(t)}{\|r_{ij}(t)\|} \quad (1)$$

3.2 System Measures

To quantify whether all individuals move in approximately the same direction, we
measure the amount of order Ψ defined as $\Psi(t) = \frac{1}{N} \| \sum_{i=1}^{N} q_i(t) \|$. Furthermore,
we define the relative coverage as $\Omega(t) = \frac{A(t)}{A(t_0)}$, with A as the area of the convex
hull of the set of robots and t_0 as the starting time step. Finally, the number
of clusters is measured where individuals i and j are part of the same cluster if
their relative distance is lower than the interaction-radius RoI.

3.3 Extended Metric Model (EMM)

Our proposed model, the extended metric model (EMM), relies on adapting the impact of the behavioral orientation zone while following the same neighbor selection approach as the metric model. In order to obtain a relative coverage $\Omega > 1$ with low order $\Psi \approx 0$, we maintain the width of the orientation zone ZoO, but set $\alpha_o = 0$ in Eq. (1)—i.e., deactivating the orientation zone. Consequently, individuals are able to spread out until attraction interactions ensure that they remain cohesive. Transitioning to high relative coverage $\Omega > 1$ and high order $\Psi \approx 1$ is then accomplished by resetting $\alpha_o > 0$ (i.e., activating the orientation zone). To obtain a low relative coverage $\Omega < 1$ with high order $\Psi \approx 1$, the width ZoO is decreased while keeping the zone activated ($\alpha_o > 0$).

4 Results and Discussion

We simulate a robot swarm of size N in 2D open space environment. At the beginning of a simulation, robots are placed within a confined box of the size $(\frac{N}{\rho})^{\frac{1}{2}}$ with initial density $\rho = 0.01$. Within this box, both the robots' positions and moving directions are initially uniformly distributed. All simulations are run with $w = \frac{\pi}{2}$, $v = 2$, $\sigma = 0.05$, $\alpha_r = 100$, $\alpha_o = 50$, and $\alpha_a = 1$ based on preliminary simulations to obtain a system of a single cluster. Unless varied, the system size is $N = 100$.

We start with the metric model, looking at the swarm order Ψ, group relative coverage Ω, and the number of clusters (NoC). The emergence of the target structures (i.e., HCLO, HCHO, and LCHO) is investigated using a combination of these system measures. We enable the width of the orientation zone (ZoO) and the attraction zone (ZoA) to vary over the range of [0–100] in Figs. 1A, B, C, while keeping the width of the repulsion zone constant ($ZoR = 1$). Structures that arise while the swarm is preserved in a single connected cluster (light-gray color in Fig. 1), have a low relative coverage and a high group order, which corresponds to the target structure (LCHO). We note that the swarm splitting in numerous clusters fits with the structure of high coverage and low order (HCLO) (left-bottom corner). Finally, the high-coverage, high-order (HCHO) structure is completely absent. The width of the repulsion zone (ZoR) and the orientation zone (ZoO) are then varied throughout a range of [5–30] and [0–200], respectively, while the width of the attraction zone remains constant ($ZoA = 50$). The LCHO structure is formed when high order corresponds with low relative coverage, as seen in Figs. 1D, E, F. However, given a medium level of order with a possibility of more than one cluster, the right-bottom corner shows a likelihood of a high coverage, low order (HCLO) to emerge. Finally, the high-coverage, high-order (HCHO) structure is again absent.

Next, we perform an analysis of the long-range model. The results are shown in Fig. 2 for $\kappa = 0.05$ and $\kappa = 0.9$. Our results for $\kappa = 0.05$, in Figs. 2A, B, C, show that the swarm can move in a single cluster, while maintaining a low relative coverage, and a high swarm order. This aligns with the structure of low coverage, high order (LCHO). The other two structures of HCLO and HCHO are

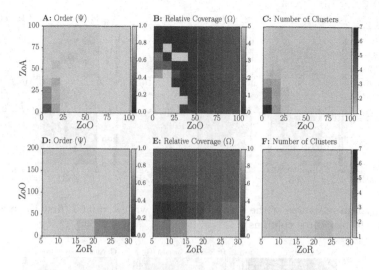

Fig. 1. System measures of the metric model.

fully absent. In Figs. 2D, E, F, we can notice an evidence of high relative coverage with high order in the right-bottom corner (while maintaining a single cluster). This corresponds to the structure of HCHO. The long-range model shows similarly to the metric model the ability to generate low coverage, high order structures (LCHO). The structure of high coverage, low order (HCLO) is missing. As the average long-range connectivity κ increases, the long-range model's ability to create a high coverage, high order (HCHO) decreases, as demonstrated in Fig. 2G–L. The low coverage, high order (LCHO) structure becomes the only one that the long-range model can generate. Hence, the emergence of the high coverage, high order (HCHO) is κ-dependent for the long-range model. So far, we have demonstrated that while, both, the metric and the long-range models are suitable to generate the low coverage, high order (LCHO) structures, they are not suitable for generating the other two structures (i.e., HCHO, HCLO). In the following we show the system measures resulting from applying the extended metric model (EMM). Figure 3 demonstrates how the EMM can display the three target structures, while maintaining the group moving in a single cluster for all structures (Fig. 3 right column). Figures 3A, B show the system measures when deactivating the orientation zone. Hence the values at the y-axis define the distance at which the attraction zone starts. These two figures show the possibility to generate the HCLO structure through expanding the swarm coverage while pushing the attraction zone away by increasing the width of the deactivated orientation zone. Figures 3D, E are obtained after activating the orientation zone. They show the ability of the EMM model to display, both, the HCHO and the LCHO structures. The HCHO (LCHO) structure is achieved by increasing (decreasing) the width of the activated orientation zone. Both results

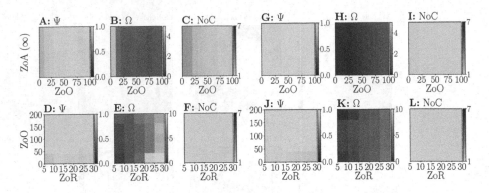

Fig. 2. System measures of the long-range model with $\kappa = 0.05$ (first three columns) and $\kappa = 0.9$ (last three columns).

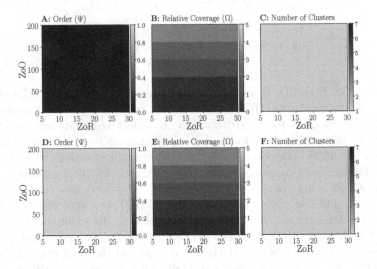

Fig. 3. System measures of the proposed model (EMM).

in Figs. 3A, B and in Figs. 3D, E show that the emerging structure is independent of the width of the repulsion zone (ZoR).

Next, we simulate a swarm of robots using the EMM model to perform the following sequential set of tasks: (i) explore the environment looking for a particular stimulus (**stimulus A**) that define the direction they need to move into. (ii) Navigate in the direction of stimulus A until a **stimulus B** appears. (iii) As a response to stimulus B (e.g., a narrow path) the swarm needs to shrink in coverage while still navigating to its target. Figure 4(left) shows the system measures recorded over 7×10^3 simulated time steps. The swarm order Ψ starts low as the robots are initialized with random directions. Following the EMM model, every robot deactivates its orientation zone, whose width is set to 200, aiming for the HCLO structure. In a few time steps, the relative coverage increases to

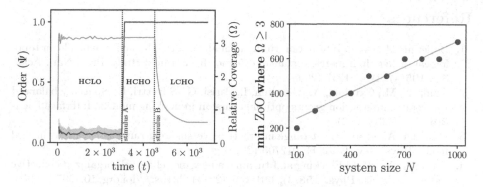

Fig. 4. Further analysis of the proposed model (EMM)

$\Omega = 3$, while the system maintains a low order. At time step 3×10^3, stimulus A (which triggers the swarm to navigate into one direction) is introduced and perceived by a single robot, who spreads the message to its neighbors. As the message spreads, robots start activating their orientation zone (see Fig. 3D, E). This enables the swarm to converge to the HCHO structure after introducing stimulus A, as shown in Fig. 4(left). Thanks to activating the orientation zone, fluctuations in both system measures disappear. Finally, at time step 4.5×10^3 stimulus B is introduced and perceived by a single robot, who spread it further. The system converges to the LCHO structure when informed robots reduce the width of their orientation zone. (In this paper, we reduce ZoO to 50 based on findings where we varied ZoO in [5–200]). Finally, Fig. 4(right) shows that the minimum width of the orientation zone, that is needed to create the HCLO and the HCHO structures, scales linearly with the system size.

5   Conclusions

We studied in this paper the emergence of three target structures based on the swarm order and relative coverage; HCLO, HCHO, and LCHO. These structures are fundamental for a large set of robot tasks such as exploration, navigation, and moving through narrow paths. First, we demonstrated that even across a wide range of parameter values, the widely-used metric model and the recently proposed long-range model are unable to generate all three structures. We proposed an extension of the metric model (EMM) that adapts the activation state and width of the orientation zone to dynamically generate the three target structures. We showed that EMM displays each of the three structures in different parameter ranges, and is capable of producing the required structure based on different stimuli introduced in a dynamic environment scenario. We finally show how our model parameter scales linearly with the system size.

References

1. Ballerini, M., et al.: Interaction ruling animal collective behavior depends on topological rather than metric distance: evidence from a field study. Proc. Natl. Acad. Sci. **105**(4), 1232–1237 (2008)
2. Camperi, M., Cavagna, A., Giardina, I., Parisi, G., Silvestri, E.: Spatially balanced topological interaction grants optimal cohesion in flocking models. Interface Focus **2**(6), 715–725 (2012)
3. Cavagna, A., et al.: Short-range interactions versus long-range correlations in bird flocks. Phys. Rev. E **92**(1), 012705 (2015)
4. Cavanga, A., et al.: Flocking and turning: a new model for self-organized collective motion. J. Stat. Phys. **158**(3), 601–627 (2014). https://doi.org/10.1007/s10955-014-1119-3
5. Couzin, I.D., Krause, J., James, R., Ruxton, G.D., Franks, N.R.: Collective memory and spatial sorting in animal groups. J. Theor. Biol. **218**(1), 1–11 (2002)
6. Dossetti, V., Sevilla, F.J.: Emergence of collective motion in a model of interacting brownian particles. Phys. Rev. Lett. **115**(5), 058301 (2015)
7. Font Llenas, A., Talamali, M.S., Xu, X., Marshall, J.A.R., Reina, A.: Quality-sensitive foraging by a robot swarm through virtual pheromone trails. In: Dorigo, M., Birattari, M., Blum, C., Christensen, A.L., Reina, A., Trianni, V. (eds.) ANTS 2018. LNCS, vol. 11172, pp. 135–149. Springer, Cham (2018). https://doi.org/10.1007/978-3-030-00533-7_11
8. Grégoire, G., Chaté, H.: Onset of collective and cohesive motion. Phys. Rev. Lett. **92**(2), 025702 (2004)
9. Huth, A., Wissel, C.: The simulation of the movement of fish schools. J. Theor. Biol. **156**(3), 365–385 (1992)
10. Kegeleirs, M., Garzón Ramos, D., Birattari, M.: Random walk exploration for swarm mapping. In: Althoefer, K., Konstantinova, J., Zhang, K. (eds.) TAROS 2019. LNCS (LNAI), vol. 11650, pp. 211–222. Springer, Cham (2019). https://doi.org/10.1007/978-3-030-25332-5_19
11. Kelley, D.H., Ouellette, N.T.: Emergent dynamics of laboratory insect swarms. Sci. Rep. **3**(1), 1–7 (2013)
12. Khaluf, Y., Allwright, M., Rausch, I., Simoens, P., Dorigo, M.: Construction task allocation through the collective perception of a dynamic environment. In: Dorigo, M., et al. (eds.) ANTS 2020. LNCS, vol. 12421, pp. 82–95. Springer, Cham (2020). https://doi.org/10.1007/978-3-030-60376-2_7
13. Kunz, H., Hemelrijk, C.K.: Artificial fish schools: collective effects of school size, body size, and body form. Artif. Life **9**(3), 237–253 (2003)
14. Miller, N., Gerlai, R.: From schooling to shoaling: patterns of collective motion in zebrafish (Danio rerio). PLoS One **7**(11), e48865 (2012)
15. Mirabet, V., Auger, P., Lett, C.: Spatial structures in simulations of animal grouping. Ecol. Model. **201**(3–4), 468–476 (2007)
16. Nauta, J., Simoens, P., Khaluf, Y.: Group size and resource fractality drive multimodal search strategies: a quantitative analysis on group foraging. Phys. A Stat. Mech. Appl. **590**, 126702 (2022)
17. Nauta, J., Van Havermaet, S., Simoens, P., Khaluf, Y.: Enhanced foraging in robot swarms using collective lévy walks. In: 24th European Conference on Artificial Intelligence (ECAI), vol. 325, pp. 171–178. IOS (2020)
18. Poel, W., Winklmayr, C., Romanczuk, P.: Spatial structure and information transfer in visual networks. Front. Phys. **9**, 623 (2021)

19. Rausch, I., Khaluf, Y., Simoens, P.: Scale-free features in collective robot foraging. Appl. Sci. **9**(13), 2667 (2019)
20. Rausch, I., Simoens, P., Khaluf, Y.: Adaptive foraging in dynamic environments using scale-free interaction networks. Front. Robot. AI **7**, 86 (2020)
21. Reynolds, C.W.: Flocks, herds and schools: a distributed behavioral model. In: Proceedings of the 14th Annual Conference on Computer Graphics and Interactive Techniques, pp. 25–34 (1987)
22. Romey, W.L.: Individual differences make a difference in the trajectories of simulated schools of fish. Ecol. Model. **92**(1), 65–77 (1996)
23. Valentini, Gabriele, Brambilla, Davide, Hamann, Heiko, Dorigo, Marco: Collective perception of environmental features in a robot swarm. In: Dorigo, M., et al. (eds.) ANTS 2016. LNCS, vol. 9882, pp. 65–76. Springer, Cham (2016). https://doi.org/10.1007/978-3-319-44427-7_6
24. Vicsek, T., Czirók, A., Ben-Jacob, E., Cohen, I., Shochet, O.: Novel type of phase transition in a system of self-driven particles. Phys. Rev. Lett. **75**(6), 1226 (1995)
25. Vicsek, T., Zafeiris, A.: Collective motion. Phys. Rep. **517**(3–4), 71–140 (2012)
26. Zumaya, M., Larralde, H., Aldana, M.: Delay in the dispersal of flocks moving in unbounded space using long-range interactions. Sci. Rep. **8**(1), 1–9 (2018)

An Extension of the iMOACO$_\mathbb{R}$ Algorithm Based on Layer-Set Selection

Ashraf M. Abdelbar[1]($\boxtimes$)(iD), Thomas Humphries[2](iD),
Jesús Guillermo Falcón-Cardona[3](iD), and Carlos A. Coello Coello[4](iD)

[1] Department of Mathematics and Computer Science, Brandon University,
Brandon, MB, Canada
abdelbara@brandonu.ca
[2] David R. Cheriton School of Computer Science, University of Waterloo,
Waterloo, ON, Canada
thomas.humphries@uwaterloo.ca
[3] Tecnologico de Monterrey, School of Engineering and Sciences,
Ave. Eugenio Garza Sada 2501, 64849 Monterrey, NL, Mexico
jfalcon@tec.mx
[4] Computer Science Department, CINVESTAV-IPN, Mexico City, Mexico
ccoello@cs.cinvestav.mx

Abstract. iMOACO$_\mathbb{R}$ is an ant colony optimization algorithm designed to tackle multi-objective optimization problems in continuous search spaces. It is built on top of ACO$_\mathbb{R}$ and uses the $R2$ indicator (to improve its performance on high-dimensional objective function spaces) to rank the pheromone archive of the best previously-explored solutions. Due to the utilization of an $R2$-based selection mechanism, there are typically a large number of tied-ranks in iMOACO$_\mathbb{R}$'s pheromone archive. It is worth noting that the solutions of a specific layer share the same importance based on the $R2$ indicator. A critical issue due to the large number of tied-ranks is a reduction of the algorithm's exploitation ability. In consequence, in this paper, we propose replacing iMOACO$_\mathbb{R}$'s probabilistic solution selection mechanism with a mechanism tailored to these layer-sets. Our proposed layer-set selection uses rank-proportionate (roulette wheel) selection to select a layer, with all the solutions in the layer sharing equally in the layer's probability. Our experimental evaluation indicates that our proposal, which we call iMOACO$'_\mathbb{R}$, performs better than iMOACO$_\mathbb{R}$ to a statistically significant extent on a large number of benchmark problems having from 3 to 10 objective functions.

1 Overview

Multi-objective optimization problems (MOP) [3,16] are a class of problems that require the simultaneous optimization of multiple objective functions which are mutually conflicting. Due to this conflict, the solution of a MOP is composed of a set of solutions that represent the best possible trade-offs among the objective functions. The bio-inspired metaheuristics are promising techniques to

© Springer Nature Switzerland AG 2022
M. Dorigo et al. (Eds.): ANTS 2022, LNCS 13491, pp. 266–274, 2022.
https://doi.org/10.1007/978-3-031-20176-9_22

solve MOPs. Among these techniques, those based on the behavior of colonies of ants have recently attracted the attention of the community to solve continuous MOPs. iMOACO$_\mathbb{R}$ [7] is an ant colony algorithm [6] for multi-objective optimization in continuous spaces, and is designed specifically for problems with four or more objective functions. iMOACO$_\mathbb{R}$ uses the $R2$ indicator [2] to rank solutions, and is built on top of ACO$_\mathbb{R}$ [13], a well-established ant colony algorithm for continuous-domain optimization.

As a consequence of using an $R2$-based selection mechanism, there are typically a large number of tied-ranks in iMOACO$_\mathbb{R}$'s archived population. A tie would require the fitness function values for two archived solution to be exactly the same, which is unlikely to happen very often in a typical real optimization problem with a real-valued objective function. For this reason, the handling of tied ranks is not a very important issue for most single-objective optimization applications of ACO$_\mathbb{R}$, and does not seem to have received much attention in the literature. However, in iMOACO$_\mathbb{R}$, the archive is typically made up of a number of layers, with the set of solutions at each layer having the same $R2$ indicator value. The number of distinct layers can be much smaller than the population size. For example, we have found that in a population of 220 solutions, it is not uncommon for the number of layer-sets (distinct ranks) to be no more than 50 for most of the computation. The problem is that tied ranks smooth out the probability distribution used for selection. This results in an algorithm with lower exploitation than the same algorithm with a uniquely ranked population.

In this paper, we propose replacing iMOACO$_\mathbb{R}$'s probabilistic solution selection mechanism with a mechanism tailored to layer-sets. Our proposed layer-set selection mechanism uses roulette wheel selection to select a layer, with all the solutions in the layer sharing equally in the layer's probability. We evaluate our proposal with respect to standard iMOACO$_\mathbb{R}$ using the same suite of problems and experimental settings adopted in [7]. Our results indicate that our proposal, which we call iMOACO$'_\mathbb{R}$, performs better than standard iMOACO$_\mathbb{R}$ to a statistically significant extent in several state-of-the-art benchmark problems, with the number of objective functions varying from 3 to 10.

2 Background

The unconstrained multi-objective optimization problem is mathematically defined as follows: $\min_{x \in \Omega} f(x) := [f_1(x), f_2(x), \ldots, f_m(x)]^T$, where $x \in \Omega$ is an n-dimensional vector of decision variables and $\Omega \subseteq \mathbb{R}^n$ is the decision space. $f_i : \Omega \to \mathbb{R}$, $i = 1, \ldots, m$ are the objective functions. When solving a MOP, the aim is to find in Ω a subset of solutions x^* that yield the optimum values for all the objective functions (i.e., the particular set that represents the best possible trade-offs among the objective functions). In furtherance of determining which solutions are optimal, the most common binary order relation used in multi-objective optimization is the Pareto dominance relation. Given two vectors of decision variables $x, y \in \Omega$, we say that x **dominates** y (denoted by $x \prec y$) if $f_i(x) \leq f_i(y)$ for $i = 1, \ldots, m$ and there exists at least an index $j \in \{1, \ldots, m\}$

such that $f_j(x) < f_j(y)$. Based on the Pareto dominance relation, we say that a vector of decision variables $x^* \in \Omega$ is **Pareto optimal** if there does not exist another $x \in \Omega$ such that $x \prec x^*$. The set that contains all the Pareto optimal solutions is known as the **Pareto Optimal Set** and its image in the objective functions space is known as the **Pareto Front**.

In order to assess the performance of MOEAs, a wide variety of quality indicators (QIs) have been proposed in the specialized literature [17]. Among the plethora of available QIs, the most relevant are those that assess the convergence of a Pareto front approximation to the true Pareto front $\mathcal{PF}^*$. One of these QIs is the discrete unary $R2$ indicator [2] that assesses the convergence of an approximation set $\mathcal{A}$ (containing a finite set of objective vectors that approximate $\mathcal{PF}^*$), using scalarizing functions. The discrete unary $R2$ indicator is defined as follows:

$$R2(\mathcal{A}, W) = -\frac{1}{|W|} \sum_{w \in W} \max_{a \in \mathcal{A}} \{u_w(a)\}, \tag{1}$$

where W is a set of m-dimensional convex weight vectors and $u_w : \mathbb{R}^m \to \mathbb{R}$ is a scalarizing function, parameterized by $w \in W$, that assigns a real value to each objective vector in $\mathcal{A}$.

3   The iMOACO$_\mathbb{R}$ Algorithm

In 2017, Falcón-Cardona and Coello Coello proposed the indicator-based many-objective ant colony optimizer for continuous search spaces (iMOACO$_\mathbb{R}$) [7] which is based on the ACO$_\mathbb{R}$ [13–15] search engine. The most important element of every ACO-based algorithm is the design of the pheromone matrix since it stores knowledge throughout the search process to solve the optimization problem [6]. The pheromone matrix of ACO$_\mathbb{R}$ is an archive that stores the best N solutions found so far and it sorts them according to the quality of the objective function. However, this scheme cannot be directly implemented in iMOACO$_\mathbb{R}$ since the Pareto dominance relation does not establish a total order. Hence, Falcón-Cardona and Coello Coello proposed to use the $R2$ indicator [2] to transform the multi-objective problem into a single-objective one and, thus, imposing a total order. For this purpose, the $R2$-ranking algorithm [10] was employed to rank the population in a similar fashion to the nondominated sorting algorithm [5] and, then, the best N solutions are stored according to the rank assigned. For each solution $x^j, j = 1, \ldots, N$, the auxiliary fields store its vector of objective values, the rank assigned and a weight value ω_j.

For each solution x^j in the archive, let r_j denote the rank of x^j. At each iteration, the weights $\omega_j, j = 1, \ldots, N$ are computed using the following formula:

$$\omega_j = \gamma(r_j - 1; 0, qN) \tag{2}$$

where $q > 0$ is a parameter that controls the diversification process of the search, r_j denotes the rank of archived solution x^j where a rank of 1 denotes the best solution, and $\gamma(a; b, c) = \frac{1}{c\sqrt{2\pi}} e^{-\frac{(a-b)^2}{2c^2}}$ denotes the Gaussian function.

To create new solutions, all k^{th} components of the N solutions are employed to define a Gaussian-kernel probability density function $G^k(y) = \sum_{j=1}^{N} \omega_j g_j^k(y) = \sum_{j=1}^{N} \omega_j \gamma(y; \mu_k^j, \sigma_k^j)$, where $k = 1, \ldots, n$, and $G^k(y)$ depends on three parameter vectors: ω is the vector of weights associated with the individual Gaussian functions, μ_k is the vector of means, and σ_k is the vector of standard deviations. $\mu_k = \{\mu_k^1, \mu_k^2 \ldots, \mu_k^N\} = \{x_k^1, x_k^2, \ldots, x_k^N\}$, and each $\sigma_k^j \in \sigma_k$ is computed as follows: $\sigma_k^j = \xi \sum_{l=1}^{N} \frac{|x_k^l - x_k^j|}{N-1}$, where $\xi > 0$ is a parameter that controls the convergence rate, simulating the evaporation of pheromones.

After computing the weights, each of the M ants performs n construction steps to create a new solution x^{new}, where each component x_k^{new} is drawn by sampling the bth Gaussian function that is part of G^k. The index $b \in \{1, \ldots, N\}$ is selected with probability $\Pr(\text{select } b) = \frac{\omega_b}{\sum_{l=1}^{N} \omega_l}$. Finally, the M newly created solutions compete with the ones in the pheromone matrix to be part of the pheromone matrix in the next iteration.

4   Our Proposed Approach

In typical continuous-domain single-objective optimization applications of ACO$_\mathbb{R}$, tied ranks in the archive are usually quite rare. For this reason, the handling of tied ranks is not a very important issue for most single-objective optimization applications of ACO$_\mathbb{R}$, and does not seem to have received much attention in the literature. But, in iMOACO$_\mathbb{R}$, there will typically be many tied ranks since any set of solutions with the same $R2$ value will have the same rank. The solution archive can be thought of as being made up of a number of layers, where each layer consists of a set of solutions that are tied for the same rank—and thus, have the same value of ω_r and the same probability of selection.

We recorded the number of distinct ranks in the population at each iteration for a single run of iMOACO$_\mathbb{R}$ on the DTLZ5 problem instance with 10 objectives, using the experimental settings described in Sect. 5, and used this data to construct the plot shown in Fig. 1. In this figure, the x-axis represents the iteration number and the y-axis represents the number of distinct ranks in the population for that iteration. The figure indicates that for most of the computation, the

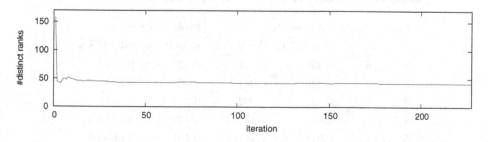

Fig. 1. Plot of the number of distinct ranks (y-axis) versus iteration number (x-axis), in a single run of iMOACO$_\mathbb{R}$ on the DTLZ5 problem instance with (10 objectives).

number of distinct ranks is around 50 (in a population of size 220). Hence, this is a clear drawback of iMOACO$_\mathbb{R}$ that results in a decrease of its exploitation ability.

We propose iMOACO$'_\mathbb{R}$, a variation in which the ACO$_\mathbb{R}$'s rank-proportionate selection mechanism is applied at the level of the layers rather than at the level of individual solutions, with all the solutions in a given layer sharing the probability of selection of their layer. Specifically, we propose replacing Eq. (2) with the following:

$$\omega_j = \frac{\gamma(r_j - 1, 0, cqR)}{N_{r_j}} \qquad (3)$$

where R is the number of distinct ranks in the population, N_r is the number of solutions tied for rank r, and c is an additional parameter that is needed to compensate for the fact that a value of q that is appropriate for standard iMOACO$_\mathbb{R}$ may not be the most appropriate for the modified iMOACO$'_\mathbb{R}$. (We use a value of $c = 2$).

Equation (3) computes the weight ω_j of a solution of rank b (i.e., $r_j = b$). Let us assume that there is a set of solutions of size N_b tied for rank b. All solutions in that set will have equal weight. That weight is determined first by calculating the weight of selection of the set (which is the numerator of the formula in Eq. (3)), then dividing that weight by the size of the set (the denominator N_b).

Consider the following numerical example. Suppose we have a population of 30 solutions, consisting of: 6 solutions tied for rank 1, 4 tied for rank 2, 7 for rank 3, 6 for rank 4, and 7 for rank 5. Table 1 compares selection probabilities under iMOACO$_\mathbb{R}$ and iMOACO$'_\mathbb{R}$ for this population. Each row corresponds to a rank layer-set. The first two columns show the rank and the number of solutions in that rank-set. The next two columns show the individual probability of selection of each of the solutions at that rank. The last two columns show the overall probability that one of the solutions in that layer-set will be selected. The table indicates that the probability of selection of layer 1 is much higher under iMOACO$'_\mathbb{R}$, the probability of selection of layer 2 is similar, and the probability of subsequent layers is much smaller under iMOACO$'_\mathbb{R}$ and drops rapidly as k increases.

Table 1. Numerical example showing a population of 30 solutions.

Layer	#sols	Prob. of sol.		Prob. of layer	
		iMOACO$_\mathbb{R}$	iMOACO$'_\mathbb{R}$	iMOACO$_\mathbb{R}$	iMOACO$'_\mathbb{R}$
1	6	0.055	0.134	0.327	0.805
2	4	0.046	0.044	0.185	0.180
3	7	0.034	0.002	0.245	0.015
4	6	0.024	7.4E−05	0.142	4.5E−04
5	7	0.014	7.1E−07	0.101	4.9E−06

The rapid decline, under iMOACO$'_\mathbb{R}$, of the probability of selection of a layer k, as k increases, is not specific to the given numerical example. In general, if we define z_k as the ratio of the probability of selection of layer k to the probability of selection of layer 1, then it is possible to obtain

$$z_k = \frac{\gamma(k-1, 0, cqR)}{\gamma(0, 0, cqR)} = e^{-\frac{k-1}{cqR}} \tag{4}$$

indicating that z_k decays exponentially with k. This is consistent with the spirit of ACO$_\mathbb{R}$. If we assume that ties in a typical single-objective application of ACO$_\mathbb{R}$ are negligibly rare, and define z_k for ACO$_\mathbb{R}$ as the ratio of the probability of selection of the kth best solution in the archive to the probability of selection of the best solution in the archive, then it is possible to obtain $z_k = e^{-\frac{k-1}{qN}}$ indicating that z_k also decays exponentially with k in ACO$_\mathbb{R}$.

In terms of Holland's classical exploitation-exploration trade-off [11], iMOACO$'_\mathbb{R}$ is more exploitative (in the same spirit as ACO$_\mathbb{R}$) than iMOACO$_\mathbb{R}$.

5   Experimental Methodology and Discussion of Results

Our experimental methodology is based on that of Falcón-Cardona and Coello Coello [7]. We used the test suites Deb-Thiele-Laumanns-Zitzler (DTLZ) [4] and Walking-Fish-Group (WFG) [12]. For each problem, we set the number of objective functions (m) to 3, 5, 7, and 10. With $m = 3$, we set the population size N to 120, the maximum number of generations G_{max} to 416, and h to 14; with $m = 5$, we set: $N = 126, G_{max} = 396$, and $h = 5$; with $m = 7$: we set $N = 85, G_{max} = 595$, and $h = 7$; with 10 objectives, we set: $N = 220, G_{max} = 227$, and $h = 19$. Moreover, we set $q = 0.1$, $\xi = \alpha = 0.5$, and $\epsilon = 0.5$. For each instance, we performed 30 independent runs of each of iMOACO$_\mathbb{R}$ and iMOACO$'_\mathbb{R}$.

In our comparison, performance is assessed with the hypervolume (HV) indicator [1]. We used the HV implementation of [8], available in [9]. Computing the HV requires that a reference vector be supplied by the user. This was set to $(1, 1, \dots)$ for DTLZ1, $(2, 2, \dots)$ for DTLZ2 and DTLZ4, $(7, 7, \dots)$ for DTLZ3, $(4, 4, \dots)$ for DTLZ5, $(11, 11, \dots)$ for DTLZ6, $(1, 1, \dots, 21)$ for DTLZ7, and $(3, 5, 7, \dots, 2m + 1)$ for all WFG problems. Occasionally, particularly for DTLZ1 and DTLZ3, the reference vector dominates all the solutions returned by the algorithm under evaluation; in such cases, HV is taken as zero.

We ran iMOACO$_\mathbb{R}$ and iMOACO$'_\mathbb{R}$ for 30 independent trials on each of the 64 problem instances in our test suite, and computed the value of the hypervolume (HV) indicator in each case. Table 2 reports the mean and standard deviation of HV for each algorithm for each problem instance. In each row, the better mean HV value is underlined.

The table indicates that iMOACO$'_\mathbb{R}$ had better performance on 36 instances, and worse on 20 instances, with 8 ties. Considering the 28 DTLZ instances alone: iMOACO$'_\mathbb{R}$ had 13 wins, 7 losses, and 8 ties; for the 36 WFG instances: iMOACO$'_\mathbb{R}$ had 23 wins, 13 losses, and 0 ties. For the 3-objective instances alone:

Table 2. The mean and standard deviation of HV for the original iMOACO$_\mathbb{R}$ and our proposed modified iMOACO$'_\mathbb{R}$.

Prob.	m	Mean		Std. dev.		Prob.	m	Mean		Std. dev.	
		Mod.	Orig.	Mod.	Orig.			Mod.	Orig.	Mod.	Orig.
DTLZ1	3	0	0	0	0	WFG2	3	<u>9.786e1</u>	9.744e1	7.9e−1	5.5e−1
	5	0	0	0	0		5	<u>9.947e3</u>	9.707e3	1.0e2	9.1e1
	7	0	0	0	0		7	<u>1.742e6</u>	1.694e6	3.3e4	2.8e4
	10	0	0	0	0		10	<u>9.882e9</u>	9.467e9	2.3e8	1.3e8
DTLZ2	3	7.420	<u>7.420</u>	2.5e−4	3.1e−4	WFG3	3	<u>7.256e1</u>	7.245e1	2.6e−1	2.5e−1
	5	<u>3.165e1</u>	3.165e1	2.6e−3	2.0e−3		5	5.202e3	<u>5.391e3</u>	2.8e2	2.5e2
	7	<u>1.277e2</u>	1.272e2	9.8e−3	1.4		7	7.793e5	<u>7.839e5</u>	2.8e4	2.0e4
	10	<u>1.023e3</u>	1.014e3	4.7e−1	3.0e1		10	4.688e9	<u>4.800e9</u>	1.1e8	2.4e8
DTLZ3	3	0	0	0	0	WFG4	3	7.060e1	<u>7.067e1</u>	3.5e−1	3.5e−1
	5	0	0	0	0		5	7.611e3	<u>7.615e3</u>	1.7e2	1.6e2
	7	0	0	0	0		7	<u>1.271e6</u>	1.242e6	4.6e4	5.1e4
	10	0	0	0	0		10	<u>7.437e9</u>	7.219e9	3.2e8	3.1e8
DTLZ4	3	7.419	<u>7.419</u>	1.1e−3	9.2e−4	WFG5	3	<u>6.847e1</u>	6.831e1	7.0e−1	7.1e−1
	5	<u>3.164e1</u>	3.163e1	4.4e−3	5.2e−3		5	<u>4.838e3</u>	4.786e3	2.0e2	1.7e2
	7	<u>1.277e2</u>	1.265e2	7.1e−3	4.2		7	6.784e5	<u>6.938e5</u>	3.6e4	3.4e4
	10	<u>1.024e3</u>	1.003e3	4.0e−3	4.2e1		10	4.271e9	<u>4.326e9</u>	1.9e8	2.1e8
DTLZ5	3	5.984e1	<u>5.984e1</u>	1.0e−2	7.9e−3	WFG6	3	<u>7.425e1</u>	7.414e1	4.7e−1	3.6e−1
	5	<u>9.379e2</u>	9.374e2	1.5	9.1e−1		5	<u>7.201e3</u>	6.674e3	5.9e2	3.4e2
	7	1.434e4	<u>1.438e4</u>	9.3e1	1.1e2		7	<u>8.779e5</u>	8.466e5	7.3e4	7.4e4
	10	9.291e5	<u>9.362e5</u>	4.7e3	6.3e3		10	<u>4.847e9</u>	4.796e9	3.4e8	2.4e8
DTLZ6	3	<u>1.318e3</u>	1.316e3	3.8e−1	1.3	WFG7	3	<u>7.545e1</u>	7.522e1	2.6e−1	2.6e−1
	5	1.562e5	<u>1.568e5</u>	1.6e3	1.0e3		5	<u>7.419e3</u>	7.214e3	2.4e2	2.7e2
	7	<u>1.783e7</u>	1.734e7	3.2e5	1.9e6		7	1.074e6	<u>1.086e6</u>	6.3e4	6.0e4
	10	<u>2.425e10</u>	2.386e10	3.7e8	1.4e9		10	6.903e9	<u>6.961e9</u>	3.4e8	2.7e8
DTLZ7	3	1.624e1	<u>1.625e1</u>	1.0e−1	6.0e−2	WFG8	3	<u>6.547e1</u>	6.541e1	5.1e−1	3.0e−1
	5	<u>1.259e1</u>	1.256e1	1.2e−1	1.1e−1		5	<u>5.272e3</u>	5.158e3	3.2e2	2.7e2
	7	<u>8.278</u>	8.239	1.5e−1	1.9e−1		7	7.571e5	<u>7.797e5</u>	8.2e4	6.8e4
	10	<u>2.414</u>	1.464	1.8e−1	7.5e−1		10	5.037e9	<u>5.181e9</u>	5.7e8	4.1e8
WFG1	3	<u>4.420e1</u>	4.417e1	8.8e−1	7.0e−1	WFG9	3	6.594e1	<u>6.594e1</u>	2.5e−1	1.8e−1
	5	<u>3.973e3</u>	3.923e3	1.3e2	9.2e1		5	5.828e3	<u>5.851e3</u>	4.4e2	4.0e2
	7	<u>6.776e5</u>	6.693e5	4.0e4	3.3e4		7	<u>7.405e5</u>	7.114e5	1.3e5	1.0e5
	10	<u>3.992e9</u>	3.969e9	3.8e7	2.1e7		10	<u>4.400e9</u>	4.162e9	5.0e8	3.5e8

iMOACO$'_\mathbb{R}$ had 8 wins, 6 losses, and 2 ties; for the 5-objective instances: 10 wins, 4 losses, and 2 ties; for the 7-objective instances: 9 wins, 5 losses, and 2 ties; for the 10-objective: 9 wins, 5 losses, and 2 ties. Thus, iMOACO$'_\mathbb{R}$ performs better on each of these subgroups of the test suite.

A one-tailed Wilcoxon signed-rank test applied to the results of Table 2 produced a p-value of 0.031, indicating a statistically significant difference.

Finally, we note that our proposed layer-set selection mechanism can generally be applied to other situations where ACO$_\mathbb{R}$ is used in an application with a non-negligible frequency of tied-ranks.

Acknowledgements. The last author acknowledges support from CONACyT project no. 1920.

References

1. Brockhoff, D., Friedrich, T., Neumann, F.: Analyzing hypervolume indicator based algorithms. In: Rudolph, G., Jansen, T., Beume, N., Lucas, S., Poloni, C. (eds.) PPSN 2008. LNCS, vol. 5199, pp. 651–660. Springer, Heidelberg (2008). https://doi.org/10.1007/978-3-540-87700-4_65
2. Brockhoff, D., Wagner, T., Trautmann, H.: On the properties of the R2 indicator. In: Proceedings 2012 Genetic and Evolutionary Computation Conference (GECCO-2012), Philadelphia, PA, USA, pp. 465–472. ACM Press, July 2012
3. Coello Coello, C.A., Lamont, G.B., Van Veldhuizen, D.A.: Evolutionary Algorithms for Solving Multi-Objective Problems. Springer, New York (2007). https://doi.org/10.1007/978-1-4757-5184-0
4. Deb, K., Thiele, L., Laumanns, M., Zitzler, E.: Scalable multi-objective optimization test problems. In: Proceedings 2002 IEEE Congress on Evolutionary Computation (CEC 2002), Piscataway, NJ, USA, vol. 1, pp. 825–830. IEEE Press (2002)
5. Deb, K., Pratap, A., Agarwal, S., Meyarivan, T.: A fast and elitist multiobjective genetic algorithm: NSGA-II. IEEE Trans. Evol. Comput. **6**(2), 182–197 (2002)
6. Dorigo, M., Stützle, T.: Ant Colony Optimization. MIT Press, Cambridge (2004)
7. Falcón-Cardona, J.G., Coello Coello, C.A.: A new indicator-based many-objective ant colony optimizer for continuous search spaces. Swarm Intell. **11**(1), 71–100 (2017). https://doi.org/10.1007/s11721-017-0133-x
8. Foncesca, C.M., Paquete, L., López-Ibáñez, M.: An improved dimension-sweep algorithm for the hypervolume indicator. In: Proceedings 2006 IEEE Congress on Evolutionary Computation (CEC-2006), Piscataway, NJ, USA, pp. 1157–1163. IEEE Press (2016)
9. Fonsesca, C.M., López-Ibáñez, M., Paquete, L., Guerreiro, A.P.: Computation of the hypervolume indicator. http://iridia.ulb.ac.be/manuel/hypervolume. Accessed May 2017
10. Hernández Gómez, R., Coello Coello, C.A.: Improved metaheuristic based on the R2 indicator for many-objective optimization. In: Proceedings 2015 Genetic and Evolutionary Computation Conference (GECCO-2015), Madrid, Spain, pp. 679–686. ACM Press, July 2015
11. Holland, J.H.: Adaptation in Natural and Artificial Systems: An Introductory Analysis with Applications to Biology, Control, and Artificial Intelligence. University of Michigan Press, Ann Arbor (1975)
12. Huband, S., Hingston, P., Barone, L., While, L.: A review of multiobjective test problems and a scalable test problem toolkit. IEEE Trans. Evol. Comput. **10**, 477–506 (2006)
13. Liao, T., Socha, K., de Oca, M.M., Stützle, T., Dorigo, M.: Ant colony optimization for mixed-variable optimization problems. IEEE Trans. Evol. Comput. **18**, 503–518 (2014)

14. Socha, K., Blum, C.: An ant colony optimization algorithm for continuous optimization: application to feed-forward neural network training. Neural Comput. Appl. **16**, 235–247 (2007). https://doi.org/10.1007/s00521-007-0084-z
15. Socha, K., Dorigo, M.: Ant colony optimization for continuous domains. Eur. J. Oper. Res. **185**, 1155–1173 (2008)
16. Tian, Y., et al.: Evolutionary large-scale multi-objective optimization: a survey. ACM Comput. Surv. **54**(8), 1–34 (2021)
17. Zitzler, E., Thiele, L., Laumanns, M., Fonseca, C.M., da Fonseca, V.G.: Performance assessment of multiobjective optimizers: an analysis and review. IEEE Trans. Evol. Comput. **7**(2), 117–132 (2003)

Binary Particle Swarm Optimization for Selective Cell Switch-Off in Ultra-Dense 5G Networks

Juan Jesús Espinosa-Martínez[1], Jesús Galeano-Brajones[1]([✉]) [iD],
Javier Carmona-Murillo[1] [iD], and Francisco Luna[2] [iD]

[1] Department of Computing and Telematics System Engineering, Centro
Universitario de Mérida, Universidad de Extremadura, Mérida, Spain
jespinosv@alumnos.unex.es, {jgaleanobra,jcarmur}@unex.es
[2] School of Computer Science and Engineering, Universidad de Málaga,
Málaga, Spain
flv@lcc.uma.es

Abstract. The massive deployment of small base stations is one of the main pillars for the new generations of mobile networks to meet the expected growing in data traffic demands. This densification entails high energy consumption that needs to be minimized to ensure system sustainability in a context of reduced environmental impact. To address this issue, optimization algorithms that will rely on metaheuristics can be used due to the complexity and the large instance size of the problem. Therefore, it is a multi-objective optimization problem in which not only the energy efficiency criteria is taken into account, but also the service provided to the users in terms of capacity is considered. In this context, the aim of this work is to evaluate the performance of Binary Particle Swarm Optimization (BPSO) in solving this multi-objective problem, using a V-shaped function to deal with binary codification. The performance of our proposed solution is compared with the results obtained by MOCell and NSGA-II in our previous works. In addition, the performance of the hybridization with specific operators proposed in one of our previous works is tested. The research showed that the hybridization brought very significant benefits to the algorithm's searches.

1 Introduction

The deployment of the fifth generation (5G) of cellular networks is expected to address the increasing demand for services with strict requirements for low latency and high reliability (e.g., autonomous driving), high bandwidth (e.g., Virtual Reality/Augmented Reality) and resilience to support scenarios with an extremely high density of devices connected. In this scenario, the massive

Supplementary Information The online version contains supplementary material available at https://doi.org/10.1007/978-3-031-20176-9_23.

deployment of many Small Base Stations (SBSs) per km^2, known as Ultra Dense Networks (UDNs) [4], is becoming one of the mainstays of 5G networks due to the reuse of the electromagnetic spectrum and the increase in the network capacity that it provides. However, this densification implies a rise in the network power consumption, which is accentuated in periods of low demand in which some SBSs are switched on without serving any user.

Thus, in order to address this issue, the standardized strategy known as Cell Switch-Off (CSO) was proposed [1]. This strategy consists of selective switching off/on of SBSs to minimize the energy consumption of the network, but simultaneously trying to maximize the Quality of Service for the existing demand. This is a multi-objective combinatorial optimization problem that has been demonstrated as NP-complete [5] and whose resolution has been proposed in the literature with the use of multi-objective metaheuristics [7,14]. Moreover, the UDNs are heterogeneous because they contain SBSs with different transmission power, cell size and working frequency due to different radio technologies.

In our previous work [8], we have proposed the hybridization of two well-known multi-objective metaheuristics, MOCell [11] and NSGA-II [3], with two specific operators that aim to improve the performance of these algorithms in the CSO problem. The research showed that the hybridization brought very significant benefits to the algorithm's search. The work presented in this paper builds on our previous work by evaluating the performance of Binary Particle Swarm Optimization (BPSO), using a V-shaped function to deal with binary codification. Furthermore, this work compares the BPSO performance with MOCell and NSGA-II, and hybridizes it with both of the proposed specific operators. The results show that BPSO intensifies the search in the objective of minimizing consumption better than the rest of the metaheuristics, and that the hybridization improves the BPSO search, but not significantly. In the literature, we can find proposals where PSO is used to optimize the CSO problem [2,12,13], but none of them compare its performance with other metaheuristics or hybridize it with specific operators.

The remainder of the paper is structured as follows. In Sect. 2, the optimization problem addressed has been formulated. The mechanism to adapt the PSO algorithm to the binary codification is described in Sect. 3. Section 4 details the experimental methodology and the detailed analysis of the results obtained. Finally, the last section includes the main conclusions reached, as well as the lines of future work that remain open.

2 The CSO Problem

Due to the limited length of this document, the modelling of the UDNs is available as supplementary material. For this reason, references to equations in this section refer to that material[1].

---

[1] https://doi.org/10.6084/m9.figshare.19682955.v2

Let $\mathcal{B}$ be the set of the SBSs randomly deployed. A solution to the CSO problem is a binary string $s \in \{0,1\}^{|\mathcal{B}|}$, where s_i indicates whether SBS i is activated or not. The first objective to be minimized is therefore computed as:

$$\min f_{Power}(s) = \sum_{i=1}^{|\mathcal{B}|} s_i \cdot P_i \qquad (1)$$

where P_i is the power consumption of SBS i (Eq. sup. 7). Note that P_i includes both the transmission power on every cell contained in i and the maintenance power of the SBS.

Let $\mathcal{U}$ be the set of the UEs also deployed as described in the supplementary material and $\mathcal{U}$ the whole set of Cells contained in $\mathcal{B}$. Subsequently, in order to compute total capacity of the system, UEs are first assigned to the active Cell that provides it with the highest SINR. Let $\mathcal{A}(s) \in \{0,1\}^{|\mathcal{U}| \times |\mathcal{C}|}$ be the matrix where $a_{ij} = 1$ if $s_j = 1$ and the Cell j serves UE i with the highest SINR, and $a_{ij} = 0$ otherwise. Then, the second objective to be maximized, which is the total capacity provided to all the UEs, is calculated as:

$$\max f_{Cap}(s) = \sum_{i=1}^{|\mathcal{U}|} \sum_{j=1}^{|\mathcal{C}|} s_j \cdot a_{ij} \cdot BW_i^j \qquad (2)$$

where BW_i^j is the shared bandwidth of Cell j provided to UE i (Eq. sup. 6). We would like to remark that these two problem objectives are clearly conflicting one each other, since switching off base stations leads to a reduction of the power consumption of the network, but it also damages the capacity received by the user, as the UE-Cell distance increases (rising the propagation losses) at the same time as the available bandwidth to serve users is reduced.

3   Binary PSO

3.1   BPSO Modelling

The swarm consist of n particles, each one defined by a d-dimensional vector that represents all the SBSs present in the scenario, some being active and the rest switched off. Therefore, each position in the particle's position vector, x_{id}^k, represents one single SBS, that can be turned on (1) or turned off (0). Thus, for each particle i in a specific iteration k, the position vector is defined as $X_i^k = (x_{i1}^k, x_{i2}^k, ..., x_{id}^k)$, and the velocity vector is $V_i^k = (v_{i1}^k, v_{i2}^k, ..., v_{id}^k)$, where $i \in [1, 2, ..., n]$, $d \in [1, 2, ..., L]$, being L the number of SBSs, $x_{ij} \in \{0,1\}$ and $V_{min} \leq v_{ij}^k \leq V_{max}$. The fitness value of each particle is F_i and the algorithm stores the best value for each particle, known as local best (P_{best}), and the best value of the whole swarm, known as global best (G_{best}).

3.2 Initialization and Update

The first step is to set up the parameters of the BPSO. This must be done carefully since these parameters will heavily influence the behaviour of BPSO. For this project, the parameters were selected according to the literature recommendations [9]: the swarm size is 100 particles; the inertia weighs are $\omega_{max} = 0.9$ and $\omega_{min} = 0.4$; the acceleration coefficients are $c_1 = c_2 = 2.0$; and the velocity thresholds are $V_{min} = 0.0$ and $V_{max} = 4.0$. Regarding the updating process, the velocity update is defined as follows:

$$v_{id}^{k+1} = \omega^k \cdot v_{id}^k + c_1 \cdot rand_1(P_{best,id}^k - x_{id}^k) + c_2 \cdot rand_2(G_{best} - x_{id}^k) \quad (3)$$

where c_1 and c_2 are acceleration coefficients, $rand_1$ and $rand_2$ are two random numbers in $[0, 1]$ and ω is the inertia weight which is updated with the following equation:

$$\omega^k = \omega_{max} - k \cdot \left(\frac{\omega_{max} - \omega_{min}}{k_{max}} \right) \quad (4)$$

where ω_{max} and ω_{max} the inertia weighs, k is the current iteration and k_{max} is the maximum number of iterations. The velocity threshold control is applied as follows:

$$v_{id}^k = \begin{cases} V_{max}, & \text{if } v_{id}^k > V_{max} \\ V_{min}, & \text{if } v_{id}^k < V_{min} \\ v_{id}^k, & \text{otherwise} \end{cases} \quad (5)$$

Nevertheless, the velocity defined in Eq. 3 as a continuous value can not be directly applied to update the discrete space that represents the particle's position. Therefore, a V-shaped function [10] is used to re-define velocity in terms of probability, and it is defined as

$$f(v_{id}^k) = |tanh(v_{id}^k)|. \quad (6)$$

Finally, the position update is defined as follows:

$$x_{id}^k = \begin{cases} 0, & \text{if } f(v_{id}^k) < rand \\ 1, & \text{if } f(v_{id}^k) \geq rand \end{cases} \quad (7)$$

where $rand$ is a random number in $[0, 1]$. Here, this work differs from the use that [10] gives to the V-shaped function so that the probability output from $f(v_{id}^k)$ is directly associated with the x_{id}^k value (the higher the probability, the higher the chance of x_{id}^k to be 1). Thus, the velocity is also directly associated with the value of x_{id}^k.

4   Experimentation

4.1   Methodology

Based on the nine scenarios described in Sect. 2 and the stochastic nature of the metaheuristics, 50 seeds for each type of scenario have been addressed in the experimentation[2]. This ensures that all algorithms face the same set of problem instances. In order to obtain fair comparative results between algorithms, these use the same population/swarm size of 100 solutions and the same genetic operators: binary tournament selection, two points crossover with crossover rate of 0.9, and bit flip mutation with a mutation rate of $1/L$, being L the number of cells in the scenario. The BPSO is the exception, as it does not use a crossover operator. Regarding the specific operators [8], we use the application rates 0.1 and 0.01 to be consistent with previous work. The stopping condition is defined by the number of evaluations of the objective function but, in order to ensure that the algorithms reach convergence, this limit is linked to the density of the instances. Since the size of the search space lies in the density of BSs, the following stopping conditions have been defined: for L{X} (being X the three values for the UEs densities), 100000 evaluations; for M{X}, 150000 evaluations; and for H{X}, 250000 evaluations. These numbers are the result of a preliminary analysis of the convergence of the algorithms. The quality of the Pareto front approximations has been measured with the Hypervolume [15] and the attainment surfaces [6]. Since the Hypervolume value is highly dependent on the arbitrary scaling of the objectives, a normalization process with respect to a reference front composed by all the non-dominated solutions found by all the algorithms for the same scenario has been carried out before calculating it.

4.2   Results

4.3   PSO Performance

In this new work, we start from a slightly different network modelling. Previously, we worked with omnidirectional SBSs, i.e., antennas radiating in all directions. Now, we use antennas that can generate very narrow beams, allowing them to be grouped into matrixes or arrays. This allows us to have much more precise control because these beams consume much less power. Due to this change, the density of SBSs has increased by three times, thus generating a larger search space. For this reason, the results of MOCell and NSGA-II are different.

Table 2 in the supplementary material shows the HV performance for the nine scenarios and the three algorithms, where the cells with a grey background indicate the best result for each scenario. According to HV, the algorithm that best approximates the fronts is BPSO, followed by NSGA-II in seven scenarios, and MOCell in the remaining two. The reason for this result can be better understood by looking at the Fig. 1. BPSO explores much more the solutions with lower power consumption, and the rest of the algorithms achieve a more

---

[2] The source code is available at https://github.com/galeanobra/CSO_BPSO.git

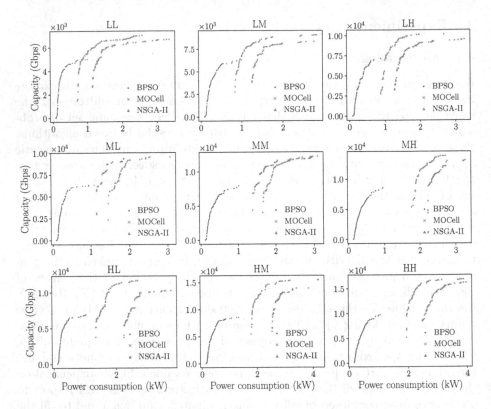

Fig. 1. Attainment surfaces of the three algorithms for each scenario.

equal compromise between both objectives. The reason for the difference in HV is due to the fact that the generated RPF is very vertical, i.e., it covers very little of the consumption objective, so BPSO is always covered by the RPF and the other two algorithms only partially. This can be seen in the MOCell result from the MH scenario.

4.4   Specific Operators in PSO

As discussed above, in [8] we present the hybridization of MOCell and NSGA-II with two specific operators that seek to bring expert knowledge of the problem to the search of the algorithms. We compare the performance of the operators directly with the algorithms without hybridization, using the same indicators as in this work. In the conference paper, we showed that the application of the operators contributed to the search by obtaining better solutions in both objectives. The HV results for each of the above-mentioned algorithms are shown in the Tables 3, 4 and 5 of the supplementary material. As we demonstrated in the previous work, MOCell and NSGA-II obtain a very significant improvement in HV when hybridized with both specific operators. In the case of BPSO, hybridization with these operators generates a less significant improvement. Of the nine density combinations with which we have experimented, in six, BPSO improves due to hybridization. Even so, the improvement obtained is slight and not very significant.

Finally, Fig. 2 shows the attainment surfaces for scenario HH. The results are similar for the nine scenarios, but for space reasons we only show the most relevant one. Thanks to this indicator, we can observe the results of HV directly extrapolated to fronts. Thus, it can be observed that the performance of MOCell and NSGA-II with hybridization is significantly better, while the improvement in BPSO is not significant. After analysing the solutions, we can conclude that the BPSO performance is caused because it reaches sparse solutions, i.e., solutions containing too few active SBSs. This makes it difficult for specific operators to switch off more cells, and therefore does not improve the performance of the algorithm. Regarding the statistical significance tests, we found that for BPSO there are no significant differences between the application or not of the hybridization. In contrast, both MOCell and NSGA-II obtain significantly better performance when hybridization is applied. For more information, please see the supplementary material[3].

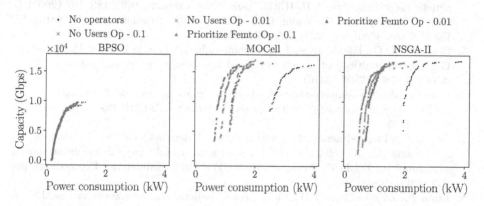

Fig. 2. Attainment surfaces of the three algorithms for scenario HH.

5   Conclusions

The Ultra-Dense Networks are a key building block for 5G and Beyond 5G networks, but they also have a power consumption problem that needs to be addressed. This problem has been formulated in the literature as a multi-objective optimization problem that selectively switches off a subset of Small Base Stations in these networks, aiming to reduce the power consumption while maximizing the QoS of the demands. This work continues a previous one, analysing the performance of the Binary PSO in this multi-objective problem,

---

[3] https://doi.org/10.6084/m9.figshare.19682955.v2

as well as the hybridization with the previously proposed operators. The results show that this algorithm obtains solutions with larger energy savings, although worse QoS, and the hybridization with these specific operators improves the search, but not significantly. As future work, it is proposed to study different mechanisms for PSO to deal with binary codification, as well as its hybridization with new specific operators that would improve the algorithm search.

Acknowledgements. This research was funded in part by the Spanish Ministry of Science and Innovation, grant number PID2020-112545RB-C54, and the Regional Government of Extremadura, Spain, grant numbers IB18003 and GR21097.

References

1. 3GPP: small cell enhancements for E-UTRA and E-UTRAN-physical layer aspects. Technical report, 3rd Generation Partnership Project (3GPP) (2014)
2. Alsharif, M.H., Kelechi, A.H., Kim, J., Kim, J.H.: Energy efficiency and coverage trade-off in 5G for eco-friendly and sustainable cellular networks. Symmetry **11**(3), 408 (2019)
3. Deb, K., Pratap, A., Agarwal, S., Meyarivan, T.: A fast and elitist multiobjective genetic algorithm: NSGA-II. IEEE Trans. Evol. Comput. **6**(2), 182–197 (2002)
4. Ge, X., Tu, S., Mao, G., Wang, C.X., Han, T.: 5G ultra-dense cellular networks. IEEE Wirel. Commun. **23**(1), 72–79 (2016)
5. González, D.G., Hämäläinen, J., Yanikomeroglu, H., García-Lozano, M., Senarath, G.: A novel multiobjective cell switch-off framework for cellular networks. IEEE Access **4**, 7883–7898 (2016)
6. Knowles, J.: A summary-attainment-surface plotting method for visualizing the performance of stochastic multiobjective optimizers. In: 5th ISDA, pp. 552–557. IEEE (2005)
7. Luna, F., Luque-Baena, R., Martínez, J., Valenzuela-Valdés, J., Padilla, P.: Addressing the 5G cell switch-off problem with a multi-objective cellular genetic algorithm. In: IEEE 5G World Forum, 5GWF 2018 - Conference Proceedings, pp. 422–426 (2018)
8. Luna, F., Zapata-Cano, P.H., Palomares-Caballero, Á., Valenzuela-Valdés, J.F.: A capacity-enhanced local search for the 5G cell switch-off problem. In: Dorronsoro, B., Ruiz, P., de la Torre, J.C., Urda, D., Talbi, E.-G. (eds.) OLA 2020. CCIS, vol. 1173, pp. 165–178. Springer, Cham (2020). https://doi.org/10.1007/978-3-030-41913-4_14
9. Mejia, V.D.L.: A modified binary particle swarm optimization algorithm to solve the thermal unit commitment problem. Master's thesis (2018)
10. Mirjalili, S., Lewis, A.: S-shaped versus V-shaped transfer functions for binary particle swarm optimization. Swarm Evol. Comput. **9**, 1–14 (2013)
11. Nebro, A.J., Durillo, J.J., Luna, F., Dorronsoro, B., Alba, E.: MOCell: a cellular genetic algorithm for multiobjective optimization. Int. J. Intell. Syst. **24**(7), 726–746 (2009)
12. Venkateswararao, K., Swain, P.: Binary-PSO-based energy-efficient small cell deployment in 5G ultra-dense network. J. Supercomput. **78**(1), 1071–1092 (2021). https://doi.org/10.1007/s11227-021-03910-5

13. Kang, M.W., Chung, Y.W.: An efficient energy saving scheme for base stations in 5G networks with separated data and control planes using particle swarm optimization. Energies **10**(9), 1417 (2017)
14. Zapata-Cano, P., Luna, F., Valenzuela-Valdés, J., Mora, A.M., Padilla, P.: Metaheurísticas híbridas para el problema del apagado de celdas en redes 5G. In: XIII MAEB, pp. 665–670 (2018) (in Spanish)
15. Zitzler, E., Thiele, L.: Multiobjective evolutionary algorithms: a comparative case study and the strength pareto approach. IEEE Trans. Evol. Comput. **3**(4), 257–271 (1999)

Choeur Synthétique: An Art Installation Based on Swarm Robotics

Muhanad Alkilabi[1,2], Arnaud Eeckhout[3], Mauro Vitturini[3], Marie du Chastel[4], Marine Warzée[4], Jean-Yves Rousseaux[4], Antoine Hubermont[1], Timoteo Carletti[1], and Elio Tuci[1(✉)]

[1] Faculty of Computer Science, University of Namur, Namur, Belgium
muhanad.hayder@uokerbala.edu.iq,
{antoine.hubermont,timoteo.carletti,elio.tuci}@unamur.be
[2] Faculty of Computer Science and Information Technology,
Department of Computer Science, University of Kerbala, Karbala, Iraq
[3] The Collective VOID, Brussels, Belgium
collectivevoid@hotmail.com
[4] TRAKK, Namur, Belgium
{marie,marine,jean-yves}@kikk.be

Abstract. A robot swarm is a self-organising system in which a global cooperative response emerges from the local interactions between the robots and their social and physical environment. This paper describes an art-science collaboration project called "Choeur Synthétique", a swarm robotics based artwork in which acoustic patters emerge from the behaviour of mobile robots that form random aggregates within a close arena. The contribution of this paper is in describing the motivations of this artistic work and in the illustration of its artistic elements and of the technical specifications.

1 Introduction

The aim of this paper is to illustrate the "Choeur Synthétique" (Synthetic Choir), that is an art-science collaboration project based on a particular type of multi-robot system generally referred to as swarm robotics system [5], which is characterised by the fact that each robot autonomously produces its actions with an on-board control structure that reads the activity of the sensors mounted on the robot's body and sets the state of the robot actuators.

The swarm robotics technology has been recently used by the artist Sofian Audry to build an installation called "Vessels" [2]. This installation is made of a swarm of small robot vessels, located in a water tank, that generate their movements and their individual behaviour based on data they collect related to the quality of their environment (e.g., quality of the water/air). Each robot behaves as a single entity, but each action from one robot causes a reaction that influences the entire group and contributes to the emergence of the group movement. Another example comes from "Lasermice" by the artist So Kanno [7]. The artist puts together 60 robots and made their communication method (infrared)

© Springer Nature Switzerland AG 2022
M. Dorigo et al. (Eds.): ANTS 2022, LNCS 13491, pp. 284–291, 2022.
https://doi.org/10.1007/978-3-031-20176-9_24

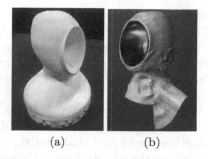

(a)   (b)

Fig. 1. (a) Image of the robot with the base holding the sensors and the anthropomorphic bust. The silicon skin and the decoration of the inner part of the bust cavity are missing. (b) Drawing of the an anthropomorphic bust with the silicon realistic skin, and the inner cavity coated with gold.

visible by adding a visible laser, thus creating continuous laser-line drawings in the space, all enhanced by a solenoid who makes a noise every time a robot sees another and changes direction. Another art installation based on swarm robotics technology is "Empathy Swarms" from the artist duo Hochschuh and Donovan who built and programmed a swarm of small hexagonal vehicles that operates in a place shared with people. The objective of this installation is to create an emotional experience in the observes through the perception of the spatial and visual patters made by the robots [6]. The collective WERC created "PIXI" an installation of digital organisms called pixi, built to operate in a natural environment. Each Pixi can emit a pulsating light. The global visual pattern created by the observation of multiple Pixi generates the impression of a coherent flock of elements, a phenomena that is greater than the sum of its constitutive parts.

A special mention must be done for an artist that is certainly an inspiration: Céleste Boursier-Mougenot. Even though he did not use robot technology, he managed somehow to generate an emergent phenomenon that could have been made in a much more complex way by using robots. The works "Liquide Liquide" and "From Here to Ear" are two beautiful examples of how to create random acoustic events using nature [3,4]. In "Liquide liquide", the water current of a warm pool moves and let collide porcelain bowls. The sound generated by the collisions reverberates in the space creating a very hypnotic atmosphere; in "From Hear to Ear" instead, guitars and cymbals are played randomly by birds who have their nest and food all around the exhibition space, thus creating a musical aleatory improvisation together with the birds' tweets.

Choeur Synthétique is part of a research on voice and language that the artists of the Collective VOID has been doing since few years. Each of the 15 mobile robots of the Choeur Synthétique can move independently and avoid collisions using ultrasound sensors, and they can communicate using infrared signals (see Fig. 1a, and Sect. 2 and 3 for the robot's technical specifications). As soon as two or more robots get closer than a certain distance to each another they can stop moving and start emitting sound. The response of a robot upon the perception of a swarm mate is a stochastic response that can happen with a certain probability. The group formation process is an emergent phenomenon generated by random encounters between the robots during their erratic navigation within a close arena. The continuous random interactions between the 15 robots generates a self-organised audio and visual experience that resembles to an ever-aleatory voice composition.

Each robot carries a file with a voice singing a single note or a single noise. The notes are the voices of the Namur choir. Each note and each voice is different. The installation puts together the typical characteristics of the swarm robotics approach like autonomy of movement, stochastic dimension of the movement, casual encounters, the always changing dynamics of the swarm to create an ever changing combination of sounds based on voices recorded by professional singers. Each robot carries an anthropomorphic bust, a mix between a human head, made out of silicon realistic skin, with a cavity resembling a gramophone, coated with gold (see Fig. 1b). The notes resonate through busts as they meet, create clusters and harmonising or "cacophonising" the space. These visually disturbing objects move around in a mechanical yet humanised way, chasing pavements, looking for meaning, while keeping a sort of authoritarian look. The sound they generate can be filling, can be pleasant or can be disturbing. But hearing a voice singing can release endorphins in our brains. Hearing voices coming together and forming chords, can have the same effect on us than singing in groups, that is the release of serotonin and oxytocin. That is why we can find ourselves attracted and enchanted sometimes by hearing the sound of one or more voices singing. One of art concerns is to stimulate, is to create accidents, to lay and display things in order to trigger something in the onlooker. VOID believes that good art is about that, and rather than sending a precise message it contains a whole lot of messages, a whole lot of thoughts, non-thought, emotions, irrationality, ideas, suggestions, visions, and it puts it out there. It is to each one of us to make good use of it. At the time of writing this paper, few elements of the artistic part have to be completed. In particular, some of the anthropomorphic busts have not being decorated yet, and the registration of the notes by the Namur's Choir is not completed yet. However, the reader can access a first and partial demonstration of this art installation at https://youtu.be/k-rUGShq-Hs.

2   The Robots' Hardware

This section describes the hardware configuration of the robots used for to create the art installation Choeur Synthétique. Figure 2a shows a simplified diagram of the main robot's hardware components which are the following:

Mechanics. The robot's structure is made of two parts (see Fig. 2b):
  – A laser cut circular wooden base (diameter of 300 mm) made of Medium-Density Fiberboard (MDF) material. The robot base is the core of the mechanical structure that holds the battery, the DC motors, all other electronic circuits and a 3D printed ring. The two DC motors are fixed

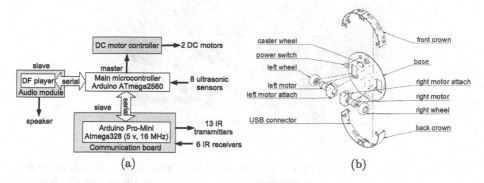

Fig. 2. (a) Diagram of the robots' hardware components. (b) The mechanical structure of the robot in an exploded view.

into the robot's base using a 3D printed motor attach made of two pieces (see Fig. 2b). The wheels are attached to the DC motors' shafts.

- A 3D printed ring, divided in two parts (i.e., the front and the back crown), that holds the IR-LEDs, IR-sensors, ultrasonic sensors, charging port and a USB port (see Fig. 2b). The USB is the main user interface to program the robot. The material of the ring is Polylactic Acid (PLA). The two parts of the rings are fixed to the base. The height of the ring is 50 mm height.

The materials of the base and of the ring have been chosen to reduce the manufacturing costs while maintain the mechanical specifications of the design objectives.

Microcontroller. The main microcontroller of the robot is an Arduino Mega 2560 Rev3 based on ATmega2560. It has 8 kB SRAM and 256 kB flash memory. The CPU is 16 bits processor runs at 16 MHz speed (for more details see [1]). The microcontroller is supported by the open-source Arduino Software (IDE) which facilitates the development of the firmware and the uploading of the software into the robot.

Sensors. Each robot is equipped with two types of sensor:

- Eight HC-SR04 ultrasonic distance measuring sensors connected directly to the main microcontroller. The ultrasonic sensors can detect an obstacle up to a distance of 1 m. The position of these sensors on the robots' ring is indicated in Fig. 3a. The sensors are placed close to the robot base in order to detect short obstacles (10 mm height from the ground) that are used to delimit the perimeter of the robots' arena.
- Six TSOP1838 InfraRed (IR) sensors that receive a frequency modulated IR signal at 38 KHz transmitted by neighbouring robots. These sensors are connected directly to the communication board (see Fig. 2a) and are positioned at the top of the front-facing ultrasonic sensors. The position of these sensors on the robot base is shown in Fig. 3a.

Actuator. Each robot is equipped with the following actuators:

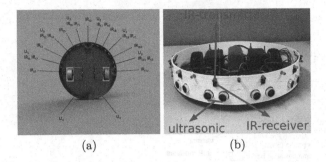

(a)   (b)

Fig. 3. (a) Image showing the positions, on the robots' ring, of the ultrasonic sensors U_i with $i \in [0, 7]$ and of the IR transmitter IR_{ti} with $i \in [0, 12]$ and of the receivers IR_{ri} with $i \in [0, 5]$. (b) Image of the robot base with the ring holding the sensors.

- Two *Greartisan* DC 12 V high torque DC motors that provide the robot with differential drive kinematics. The motor maximum speed is 100 RPM and the maximum torque is 2.2 Kg.cm. The gear reduction ratio is 1:22.
- 13 InfraRed LEDs emitting IR signals at 880 nm wavelength. The IR-LEDs are positioned on the robot base as shown in the Fig. 3b. The range of IR-LEDs transmition cover the front half circle of the robot at 50 cm distance. The transmition is directly control by the communication board.
- A speaker with 8 Ω and 5 W connected to the Mini MP3 DFPlayer audio module via digital audio amplifier providing high quality sound. The audio module offers the capability to manage audio tracks (i.e., play, stop, pause, etc.) from the software. The main microcontroller controls the audio module through software serial communication (see Fig. 2a).

Communication board. This is an important hardware component which has been developed to offer a simple method for communication with the neighbouring robots using IR signals. The board uses Arduino Pro Mini microcontroller as the main processing unit. A full software communication protocol is implemented for this hardware module. The communication protocol encodes the data to be transmitted (i.e., the robot's id, the robot's state, and its intention to sing) with a frequency modulated IR signal and broadcasts it (via IR-LEDs) to any neighbouring robots located at less than 50 cm distance from the emitter. This board also decodes the received messages (via IR-receivers) from other robots and sends it to the main microcontroller via serial communication (see Fig. 2a). This simple method of communication is designed to be more reliable and more economic from an energy perspective than alternative methods (e.g., a communication system based on vision and colour LEDs). Since the art installation is supposed to be shown in multiple exhibition spaces under different lighting conditions, the robustness to varying lighting conditions is particularly important as well as the level of energy consumption given that robots are required to operate for 6 to 8 h a day.

Battery. Each robot is equipped with 7800 mAh, 7.4 V Lithium Ion battery made of six cells. The battery offers 10 h of full operation.

3   The Robot Firmware

Choeur Synthétique refers to a group of autonomous mobile robots that navigate a close environment and interact with each others. As soon as two or more robots get closer to each other, they stop and exchange IR signals which communicate the robots' intention to form an aggregate and to sing together. Those robots that agree to sing together start emitting their own sound. The combination of sounds emitted by the potentially many robots' aggregates that emerge in a self-organised way generates the Choeur Synthétique.

Each robot is controlled by a Finite State Machine made of the following five states:

Random walk. All robots start their life in this state. When in this state, a robot moves according to an isotropic random walk, with a fixed step length (4 s, at 20 cm/s), and turning angles chosen from a wrapped Cauchy probability distribution characterised by the following PDF [8]:

$$f_\omega(\theta, \mu, \rho) = \frac{1}{2\pi} \frac{1 - \rho^2}{1 + \rho^2 - 2\rho\cos(\theta - \mu)}; \tag{1}$$

where $\mu = 0$ is the average value of the distribution, and $\rho \in [0, 1]$ determines the distribution skewness. For $\rho = 0$ the distribution becomes uniform and provides no correlation between consecutive movements, while for $\rho = 1$ a Dirac distribution is obtained, corresponding to straight-line motion. While in this state, a robot broadcasts through its infrared emitters signals communicating its intention to form an aggregate and to sing together with other robots. Note that the infrared signals can only be perceived when robots are sufficiently closer to detect each other through their ultrasounds as potential obstacles.

Refrain. A robot transitions into this state from state Play after having sung as a member of an aggregate. A robot in this state behaves as if it was in state Random walk but without emitting infrared signal. Thus, the robot moves but is not available to form aggregate. Any time it gets closer to another robot, it treats it as an obstacle to be avoided. This states facilitates the spatial distribution of the robots within the arena. A robot remains in this state for 30 s. When this interval expires, the robot transitions to the state Random Walk.

Obstacle avoidance. A robot transition to this state, if while in Random Walk or Refrain, it detects an obstacle (i.e., another robot or the arena walls) closer than certain distance using its ultrasonic sensors. If the robot previously was in state Refrain or the obstacle is an arena wall or another robot that does not signal with its infrared the intention to aggregate, then an obstacle avoidance manoeuvre is activated. This manoeuvre takes the robot away from the obstacle. If the robot previously was in state Random walk and the obstacle is another robot that signals with the infrared its intention to form an aggregation, then the robot transitions to state Stop.

Stop. A robot transition into this state when it receives infrared signals from one or more group mates communicating their intention to form an aggregate. Note that, infrared signals are perceived only when robots are closer than 50 cm. The robot stays still while in this state without emitting any sound. A robot can remain in this state for a maximum of 3 s. During this time, the robot keeps on exchanging messages with the neighbouring robot/s to verify their intentions to sing. If after 3 s no agreement is found, the robot moves back to the state Random walk. If instead agreement is found, the robot moves to state Play.

Play. While in this state, the robot emits sound while staying still. It remains in this state until the play timeout expires. At this point the robot transitions to state Refrain.

4   Conclusions

We have illustrated the Choeur Synthétique, an art-science collaboration project based on the use of the swarm robotics technology. We have shown that the possibility to work with self-organising robot-based systems in which the global response emerges from the local interactions of relatively simple units is particularly appealing to artists. This is because the contribution of the artist in determining what is perceived by an observer of the artist's work is subordinate to the actions of the laws of nature that ultimately determine the unpredictable and ever-changing global organisation of the swarm robotics based art installation. We have briefly reviewed those art-science projects that have exploited the swarm robotics technology to generate self-organising visual and/or acoustic patters. We have discussed the motivations of the collective VOID in contributing to this art installation in which the self-organisation of the swarm robotics system concerns the acoustic patters generated by singing robots that form random aggregates within a close arena. We have illustrated the artistic contributions and the technical specifications of the robots' hardware and firmware.

Acknowledgements. Dr Alkilabi thanks the Research Institute naXys, University of Namur (BE), and the Iraqi MOHER for the financial support. TRAKK, the Research Institute naXys and the Faculty of Computer Science from the University of Namur (BE) have managed the fundraising and has coordinated the collaborative activities between the scientists and the artists.

References

1. arduino.cc: Arduino mega specs (2021). https://store.arduino.cc/products/arduino-mega-2560-rev3
2. Audry, S.: Vessels (2010). https://sofianaudry.com/fr/works/vessels

3. Boursier-Mougeno, C.: From here to ear (2016). https://www.e-flux.com/announcements/72780/cleste-boursier-mougenotfrom-here-to-ear/
4. Boursier-Mougeno, C.: Liquide Liquide (2019). https://www.fondationfrancoisschneider.org/en/celeste-boursier-mougenot-liquid/
5. Dorigo, M., Şahin, E.: Guest editorial. special issue: swarm robotics. Auton. Robots **17**(2–3), 111–113 (2004)
6. Hochschuh, K., Donovan, A.: Empathy swarm (2021). https://hochschuh-donovan.com/portfolio/empathy-swarm/
7. Kanno, S.: Lasermice (2018). https://www.kanno.so/project/lasermice
8. Kato, S., Jones, M.: An extended family of circular distributions related to wrapped Cauchy distributions via Brownian motion. Bernoulli **19**(1), 154–171 (2013)

Component Swarm Optimization Using Virtual Forces for Solving Layout Problems

Juliette Gamot[1,2]($\boxtimes$), Romain Wuilbercq[1], Mathieu Balesdent[1], Arnault Tremolet[1], Nouredine Melab[2], and El-ghazali Talbi[2]

[1] ONERA, Université Paris-Saclay, Palaiseau, France
[2] INRIA, Université de Lille, Villeneuve-d'Ascq, France
juliette.gamot@onera.fr

Abstract. The optimal layout of a system involves placing a given number of components in a container in order to optimize one or several objectives while respecting some geometrical and functional constraints. This paper proposes a new method to solve the problem of optimal layout of a satellite module that relies on a virtual-forces system. The proposed method is compared to a genetic algorithm illustrating its performance.

1 Introduction

The layout design of a system consists in placing a number of components within a container as a means to optimize one or several objectives while respecting some functional and geometrical constraints [3,9,17]. In the present work, the layout optimization of a simplified satellite module is used as an illustrative example of an optimal layout problem [9]. This problem consists in finding the layout of N components (which can usually be cylinders or cuboids) on bearing plates that minimizes the inertia of the whole module. A number of geometrical constraints must be enforced such as no overlapping between components, no overlapping between the components and the container, and the center of gravity must be accurately located at the geometrical centroid of the container [9,14]. Several improvements are introduced in terms of modeling of the optimal layout problem to enhance the representativity of the problem with respect to classical satellite layout optimal problem [9]. The problem which is considered in this paper is:

$$
\begin{cases}
\text{Minimize } I_{tot}(\mathbf{x}) \\
\text{where: } \mathbf{x} \in \mathbb{R}^{N_{design}} \\
\text{subject to :} \\
\mathbf{h_{container}}(\mathbf{x}) = 0 \\
\mathbf{h_{overlap}}(\mathbf{x}) = 0 \\
\mathbf{g_{CG}}(\mathbf{x}) \leq 0 \\
\mathbf{g_{functional}}(\mathbf{x}) \leq 0
\end{cases}
$$

where I_{tot} is the global inertia corresponding to the objective function. It takes as arguments the continuous positions of the centers of inertia $\mathbf{p}$ and orientations α of the components, $\mathbf{x} = (\mathbf{p}, \alpha)$ (the cardinal of the design variables vector $\mathbf{x}$ is written N_{design}). Four constraints are considered:

© Springer Nature Switzerland AG 2022
M. Dorigo et al. (Eds.): ANTS 2022, LNCS 13491, pp. 292–299, 2022.
https://doi.org/10.1007/978-3-031-20176-9_25

- Three geometrical constraints: $h_{container}$ which correspond to no overlap between the components and the container and exclusion zones, $h_{overlap}$ which corresponds to no overlap between the components, g_{CG} which translates the fact that the center of mass of the module must be in a tolerance zone centered on the geometrical center of the container.
- One functional constraint: $g_{functional}$ which ensures a certain distance between some components for functional reasons.

Most of the methods employed to solve this problem are meta-heuristics [14] and can lead to difficulties to satisfy the constraints according to the problem definition. In this paper, a component swarm optimization algorithm using virtual forces (CSO-VF) is proposed in order to solve the constraints easily. To the best of our knowledge, this kind of methods has never been explored for solving optimal layout problems. The rest of the paper is organized as follows: Sect. 2 reviews the main methods employed in the literature. In Sect. 3, the proposed algorithm is described. The proposed method is applied to the satellite module and the experimental results are reported and discussed in Sect. 4.

2   State of the Art

Because the optimal layout problem belongs to the NP-hard class of problems, it is not solvable by exact methods [17]. Consequently, various approximate methods have been developed in order to solve layout optimization problems first defined by Cagan et al. [2].

Mostly, metaheuristic methods have been explored [14]. For example, Jacquenot used a genetic algorithm (GA) enhanced by a separation algorithm to facilitate the resolution of overlapping constraints [6]. Meller et al. used a simulated annealing algorithm to solve facility layout problems [10]. Particle Swarm Optimization (PSO) has also been investigated. Mohammed et al. proposed a study about PSO methods in order to solve facility layout problems [11].

With the increase in the number of constraints, design variables or the number of objectives, other methods have been introduced to improve the computational performance of metaheuristic techniques. Among them, Potter and De Jong [12] introduced cooperative co-evolutionary algorithms based on the divide and conquer paradigm along with the biological model of co-evolution of cooperating species [3,15]. Metaheuristic methods have also been often hybridized between themselves. In [8], a GA is hybridized with differential evolution, artificial bee colony and PSO. In [7], evolutionary algorithms are hybridized with heuristic rules and applied to the layout optimization of a satellite module. Other methods than metaheuristics have been applied to layout optimization problems even if they are less investigated [1,16].

Finally, Rashedy et al. introduced a gravitational search algorithm based to evolve a swarm of masses providing better results than former heuristic algorithms [13]. Guo et al. proposed methods based on a virtual-forces system in order to solve architectural layout problems [5]. Dirafzoon et al. proposed a virtual force-based individual particle optimization for coverage in wireless sensor networks [4]. The proposed methodology which will be detailed in the next section is in line with those last techniques as it has not been explored for optimal layout problems.

3   The CSO-VF Algorithm

In the CSO-VF algorithm, each component corresponds to a particle and different forces and operators are applied to each of them in order to evolve the swarm. This model is used in order to make it easier to deal with the constraints. One can note that this kind of algorithm is different from PSO, indeed in PSO each particle corresponds to an entire solution of the problem to be evolved. Moreover, this swarm intelligence algorithm is deterministic.

3.1   The Particle

At each step of the resolution a particle i is described by its translation acceleration $\mathbf{a_i}$, its rotational acceleration L_i, its translation speed $\mathbf{v_i}$ and its rotational speed ω_i, the position of its center of inertia $\mathbf{p_i}$ and its orientation (for cuboid components) α_i. Attractive and repulsive forces of resultant $\mathbf{F_i}$ as well as a torque T_i are applied to each particle in order to update those previous parameters knowing that the velocity, the rotational speed, the angle as well as the forces and torques are bounded by their respective global maximum values $v_{max}, \omega_{max}, \alpha_{max}, f_{max}, t_{max}$. Figure 1 illustrates a particle. The pink zone represents a forbidden zone.

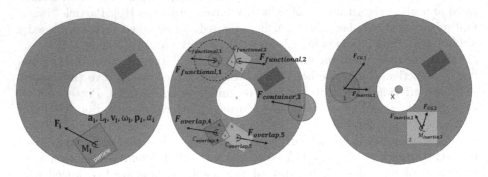

Fig. 1. Particle   **Fig. 2.** Attractive and repulsive forces   **Fig. 3.** Gradient-based forces

3.2   Virtual Forces System

The forces applied to each particle at each step aims at optimizing the objectives and satisfying the constraints defined in the introduction. They are split into 3 categories and will be detailed in the case of the optimal layout problem of the satellite module, without loss of generality.

Attractive Forces. If a particle i does not belong entirely to the container then an attractive force directed towards the geometric center of the module $\mathbf{p_c}$ is applied. It corresponds to the constraints $h_{container}$ and is defined as follows:

$$\mathbf{F}_{container,i}(\mathbf{p_i}) = \frac{\mathbf{p_c} - \mathbf{p_i}}{|\mathbf{p_c} - \mathbf{p_i}| + \epsilon}v_{max} - v_i \tag{1}$$

where ϵ ensures numerical stability. This force is illustrated on Fig. 2 with the 3rd particle. Red zones represent the violation of the constraints.

Repulsive Forces. If a particle i overlaps another one j then a repulsive force is applied and corresponds to the constraint $h_{overlap}$. The point of application of this force is initially the barycenter of the overlap polygon of the two particles. A change of point of this torsor is carried out in order to transfer the forces to the centers of inertia of both particles. Consequently, a moment appears on each of the particles noted $C_{overlap,i}$. The expression of the force related to the overlap between two particles i and j is as follows:

$$\mathbf{F}_{overlap,i,j}(\mathbf{p_i}, \mathbf{p_j}) = -\frac{\mathbf{p_j} - \mathbf{p_i}}{|\mathbf{p_j} - \mathbf{p_i}| + \epsilon}v_{max} - v_i \tag{2}$$

If $N_{overlap}^i$ particles overlap the ith particle then the total overlap force applied to this particle is calculated as $\mathbf{F}_{overlap,i} = \sum_{j=1}^{N_{overlap}^i} \mathbf{F}_{overlap,i,j}$.

   This force is illustrated on Fig. 2 with particles 4 and 5. If an energy component is too close to a fuel component then a repulsive force directed along the line formed by the center of inertia of both components involved is applied with an expression similar to $\mathbf{F}_{overlap,i}$. This force is intended to satisfy the constraint $g_{functional}$. This force is illustrated on Fig. 2 with particles 1 and 2.

Gradient-based Forces. In order to take into account the objective function minimization into CSO-VF, a force along the opposite of the gradient of the inertia according to the position of the center of inertia of each component and a torque proportional to the gradient of the inertia according to the orientation of each component are applied:

$$\mathbf{F}_{inertia,i}(\mathbf{p_i}) = -\beta_1 \nabla I_{tot}(\mathbf{p_i}) \quad (3) \qquad \mathbf{M}_{inertia,i}(\alpha_i) = -\beta_2 \nabla I_{tot}(\alpha_i) \quad (4)$$

   In the same way, a force along the opposite of the gradient of the position of the global center of mass according to the position of the center of inertia of each component is applied in case the global center of mass is located outside of the tolerance zone, and expressed as:

$$\mathbf{F}_{CG,i}(\mathbf{p_i}) = -\beta_3 \nabla g_{CG}(\mathbf{p_i}) \tag{5}$$

β_i $(i \in \{1,2,3\})$ are hyperparameters of the algorithm. The gradient-based forces are illustrated on Fig. 3. The dotted line corresponds to the functional zone of influence of a component.

Between the steps s and $s + 1$, the Fundamental Principle of Dynamics is applied in order to update the parameters of each particle i (with a mass m_i and geometric inertia I_i) between two steps (separated by Δt) according to the following equations:

$$a_{i,s+1} = \frac{F_i}{m_i} \quad (6) \qquad\qquad L_{i,s+1} = \frac{C_i}{I_i} \quad (9)$$

$$v_{i,s+1} = v_{i,s} + a_{i,s+1}\Delta t \quad (7) \qquad \omega_{i,s+1} = \omega_{i,s} + L_{i,s+1}\Delta t \quad (10)$$

$$p_{i,s+1} = p_{i,s} + v_{i,s+1}\Delta t \quad (8) \qquad \alpha_{i,s+1} = \alpha_{i,s} + \omega_{i,s+1}\Delta t \quad (11)$$

The Swap Operator: Every N_{swap} steps, the swap operator allows two components to exchange their positions in pairs if it enables an improvement of the objective function while not deteriorating the resolution of the constraints.

The Stagnation Rule: If the position of one or more particles does not evolve during a certain amount of steps, the forces linked to the geometrical constraints of overlapping as well as the functional constraint are set to 0. Only the gradient-based forces (center of mass and inertia) are responsible of the swarm evolution. It allows the swarm to escape from zones where the forces may be antagonistic and promote exploration and diversity.

4   Implementation and Results

The proposed method is applied to the satellite layout model adapted from [3,9,17]. Table 1 sums up the geometrical configurations of the problems to solve. Two occupation rates of the container are studied: 30% and 50%. The occupation rate is defined as the area of the components over the area available in the container. Table 2 sums up the configuration of the hyper-parameters of the algorithm.

Configuration 1: Occupation Rate of the Plate = 30%: CSO-VF is run on 10 random initializations. Figure 4 shows the converging curves of the the best feasible layout. All the runs manage to find a feasible solution. In order to evaluate the proposed method, a comparison with a GA is conducted. To do so, the CSO-VF algorithm is ran over 500 layout initialized independently. The same geometric configuration is implemented in a GA. Moreover, the GA is initialized with the same 500 individuals generated by the swarm initialization. The convergence curves obtained by both CSO-VF and the GA for the same configuration are shown on Fig. 5. For the CSO-VF algorithm the convergence curve corresponds to the mean of the convergence curves over the 500 runs. The best run is also shown. For the GA, the convergence curve corresponds to the best feasible individual at each generation. Figure 6 shows the best layout obtained amongst the 500 runs and this occupation rate. Green, yellow and blue components correspond respectively to fuel, energy and other components. The dotted lines represent the zone of influence of some components useful for the functional constraint.

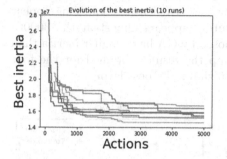

Fig. 4. Convergence curves for 10 random initializations.

Fig. 5. Proposed method + GA

Table 1. Geometrical configuration of the module.

Container	One one-sided bearing plate
Exclusion zones	One central bus and one rectangular electronic bus
Components	12 (30% compactness) or 24 (50% compactness)

Table 2. Hyperparameters of the algorithm

Parameters	Symbol	30%	50%
Maximum force	f_{max}	400	254
Maximum speed	v_{max}	11	10
Maximum angle	α_{max}	1	6.5
Maximum rotational speed	ω_{max}	54	63
Maximum tork	T_{max}	55	30
Gradient-based forces parameters	$\beta_1, \beta_2, \beta_3$	$693, 0.16, 97$	$554.5, 0.24, 99$
Swap operator's call frequency	N_{swap}	60	60

Table 3. Results for both occupation rates and both methodologies.

Configuration/Method	30		50	
	CSO-VF	GA	CSO-VF	GA
Mean fitness	1.57e7	1.54e7	2.43e7	2.7e7
Standard deviation	7.59e5	1.4e4	7.05e5	2.95e5
Best individual	1.4e7	1.53e7	2.29e7	2.51e7

Configuration 2: Occupation Rate of the Plate = 50%: In this case, the constraints are more difficult to satisfy. The same experiments as for the 30% occupation rate are conducted. Again, the runs manage to find a feasible solution. In the same way, the GA is used to solve the 50% occupation rate problem with an initial population of 500 individuals to be compared with CSO-VF over the same 500 initializations. The method exposed in this paper enables to solve the constraints easily compared to the GA: feasible solutions appear earlier than for GA (the first feasible solution appears almost at the 3000th generation). Moreover the best layout proposed by GA has a higher inertia than the one found by CSO-VF. Table 3 sums up the results obtained for the four methods and two occupation rates. Figure 6 shows the best layout.

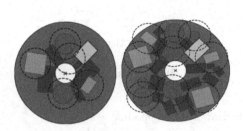

Fig. 6. Best layouts, at left: compactness of 30%, at right:compactness of 50%

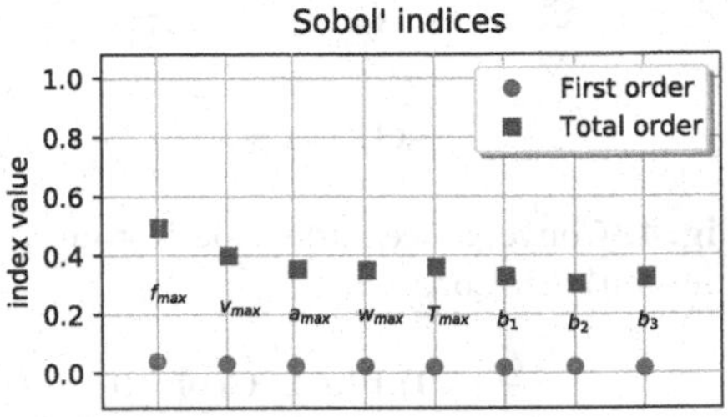

Fig. 7. Sensitivity analysis

In order to analyze the sensitivity of the different tuning parameters on the algorithm efficiency, a global sensitivity analysis has been carried out. The Sobol' indices have been computed as a by-product of a chaos polynomial surrogate model built from a Design of Experiments of 1000 i.i.d. random samples on the tuning parameters. As it can be seen on Fig. 7, the total Sobol' indices for the different parameters are quite equal, that traduce the fact that the parameters have the same overall effect on the algorithm performance. Furthermore, the first order Sobol indices are close to zero, that traduces the fact that the tuning parameters have strong interaction.

5   Conclusion

In this paper, a swarm intelligence algorithm based on a virtual-forces system named CSO-VF is proposed in order to solve optimal layout problems and to contribute to make it easier to satisfy the many constraints involved in the problem definition. It has been successfully applied to the optimal layout problem of a satellite module. To assess the efficiency of the method a comparison with a GA was conducted. The increase in the occupation rate of the container proves that the more the constraints are difficult to solve, the better the CSO-VF algorithm manages to find feasible solutions and converges compared to the GA. Comparisons with other methods reviewed are currently being conducted as well as additional experiments on higher occupation rates.

References

1. Burggräf, P., Wagner, J., Heinbach, B.: Bibliometric study on the use of machine learning as resolution technique for facility layout problems. IEEE Access 9, 22569–22586 (2021)
2. Cagan., J., Szykman, S.: Constrained three-dimensional component layout using simulated annealing. ASME. J. Mech. Des. 119(1), 28–35 (1997)
3. Cui, F.Z., Zhong, C.Q., et al., X.K.W.: A collaborative design method for satellite module component assignment and layout optimization. Proc. Inst. Mech. Eng. Part G: J. Aerosp. Eng. 233(15), 5471–5491 (2019)
4. Dirafzoon, A., Salehizadeh, S., Emrani, S., Menhaj, M.: Virtual force based individual particle optimization for coverage in wireless sensor networks. In: 23rd Canadian Conference on Electrical and Computer Engineering (CCECE) Calgary, Canada, pp.1–4 (2010)
5. Guo, Z., Li, B.: Evolutionary approach for spatial architecture layout design enhanced by an agent-based topology finding system. Front. Architectural Res. 6, 53–62 (2016)
6. Jacquenot, T.G.: Méthode générique pour l'optimisation d'agencement géométrique et fonctionnel. PhD thesis (in French), Ecole Centrale de Nantes (ECN) (2010)
7. Li, Z., Zeng, Y., Wang, Y., Wang, L., Song, B.: A hybrid multi-mechanism optimization approach for the payload packing design of a satellite module. Appl. Soft Comput. 45, 11–26 (2016)
8. Lim, Z.Y., Ponnambalam, S.: et Kazuhiro Izui: multi-objective hybrid algorithms for layout optimization in multi-robot cellular manufacturing systems. Know.-Based Syst. 120, 87–98 (2017)
9. Liu, J.F., Hao, L., Li, G., Xue, Y., Liu, Z.X., Huang, J.: Multi-objective layout optimization of a satellite module using the Wang-landau sampling method with local search. Front. Inf. Technol. Electron. Eng. 17(6), 527–542 (2016)
10. Meller, R.D., Bozer, Y.A.: A new simulated annealing algorithm for the facility layout problem. Int. J. Prod. Res. 34(6), 1675–1692 (1996)
11. Mohammed, M.A., Hasan, R.A.: Particle swarm optimization for facility layout problems FLP - a comprehensive study. In 2017 13th IEEE International Conference on Intelligent Computer Communication and Processing (ICCP) Cluj-Napoca, Romania, pp. 93–99 (2017)
12. Potter, M.A., De Jong, K.A.: A cooperative coevolutionary approach to function optimization. In: Davidor, Y., Schwefel, H.-P., Männer, R. (eds.) PPSN 1994. LNCS, vol. 866, pp. 249–257. Springer, Heidelberg (1994). https://doi.org/10.1007/3-540-58484-6_269
13. Rashedi, E., Nezamabadi-Pour, H., Saryazdi, S.: Gsa: a gravitational search algorithm. Inf. Sci. 179(13), 2232–2248 (2009)
14. Singh, S.P., Sharma, R.R.K.: A review of different approaches to the facility layout problems. Int. J. Adv. Manuf. Technol. 30(5), 425–433 (2006)
15. Teng, H.F., Chen, Y., et al., W.Z.: A dual-system variable-grain cooperative coevolutionary algorithm: satellite-module layout design. IEEE Trans. Evol. Comput. 14(3), 438–455 (2009)
16. Vashisht, D., et al.: Placement inintegrated circuits using cyclic reinforcement learning and simulated annealing. arXiv preprintarXiv:2011.07577 (2020)
17. Wang, Y.S., Teng, H.F., Shi, Y.J.: Cooperative co-evolutionary scatter search for satellite module layout design. Eng. Comput. 26(7), 761–785 (2009)

Constant Bearing Flocking

Cristino de Souza Junior[1]([⊠])(iD), Tiziano Manoni[1,2], and Eliseo Ferrante[1,2](iD)

[1] Technology Innovation Institute, Abu Dhabi, UAE
{cristino.dsouza,tiziano.manoni,eliseo.ferrante}@tii.ae
[2] Vrije Universiteit Amsterdam, Amsterdam, The Netherlands
{t.manoni,e.ferrante}@vu.nl

Abstract. In this paper, we present "bearing-and-range-only" approach for a self-organized flocking, which allows the flocking alignment without the assumption of measuring agent's velocity or orientation. This last assumption challenges the implementation with real robot, since common off-the-shelf sensors do not provide such information unless inter-agent communication is used. To overcome the above issue, we propose a flocking behavior based on the "constant bearing rule", which is known geometrical concept commonly used for missile guidance. The proposed behavior is described by a steering law and a velocity law. In the first one, the agent tries to keep constant bearing towards the target (if informed), or towards the center of mass of the perceived neighbors (if not informed). The second law allows the agent to regulate its linear velocity to keep a minimal safety distance towards the closest agent. Together, the two laws combined realize alignment. We perform simulation experiments to evaluate the new method and we compare the results with a "range-and-bearing" state of the art method.

1 Introduction

Flocking can be defined as the cohesive and aligned motion of a group of individuals in a common direction, achieved only through local interactions and possibly also local communication. This rich collective behavior has been subject of interest in many disciplines in the last few decades. These efforts have also lead to real robot implementations even on unmanned aerial vehicles (UAVs), such as the work in [1,8,9,11], where several dozen quadcopters were able to display amazing formations in an open sky.

Nevertheless, the above implementations rely on communication between neighbors, sharing position or velocities in the inertial frame. In contrast, biological examples shows flocking being achieved even in very simplistic living organism [10], and where very few interaction is needed, such as described in [12]. Similar conversely, natural swarms seem to use many vision-based perception to implement the interactions required for flocking, such as pointed in [2,7].

However, the limitation of the current approaches, for a communication-less flocking, is the requirement of the alignment (or friction) term, which is, either too heavy too process if relying on vision, or requires more information than what a common RaB sensor can offer.

© Springer Nature Switzerland AG 2022
M. Dorigo et al. (Eds.): ANTS 2022, LNCS 13491, pp. 300–307, 2022.
https://doi.org/10.1007/978-3-031-20176-9_26

It is therefore challenging to design a self-organized flocking motion without heading alignment and without the necessity to have all agents informed about the desired target direction. In the literature, so far we find only one method able to achieve this objective: the active elastic model proposed in [4]. In this method, agents implement simple virtual potential functions to achieve a cohesive formation. Assuming a non-holonomic differential-drive kinematic model of motion, they then convert the virtual forces into forward and angular velocity in a way to achieve spontaneous alignment in a random direction (when no informed agents are present) or in the desired target direction (with small proportions of informed agents). This model assumes omni-directional sensing with limited sensing range and is designed for a achieving cohesive formation, therefore alignment is an emergent phenomenon for which it is hard to control the convergence speed and also the final motion speed of the swarm.

In this paper, we propose a flocking algorithm where, similar to the active elastic model, neighbors' velocity or orientation do not require to be measured. Therefore, the method relies only on range and bearing information of the neighbors that are inside the limited field-of-view (FoV). Differently from most of the literature, in our approach the range and bearing information is not used only to achieve cohesion, but also to achieve alignment. The proposed method, which we call constant bearing (CB) flocking, is composed by two feedback laws. The first one is inspired by methodologies utilized for missiles navigation [5] and is also observed in real-life animals [3]: the agent tries to keep a constant bearing with respect to either the target (if it is informed about it) or to the estimated centroid of the perceived neighbors. The second law regulates the velocity of the agent in order to keep a minimal safety distance towards the closest agent. The application of these laws leads to the alignment of the agents' headings. Finally, differently from our previous work [6], which also uses guidance-laws for modeling the multi-agent behavior, this new approach considers limited neighbors' perception and does not require global knowledge of the target's.

The new algorithm has been extensively tested in a simulated environment. Specifically, we study the effect of the swarm size, of the proportion of informed robots, and of two different kinds of FoVs: omnidirectional versus constrained to 180° pointing towards the direction of motion (e.g. akin to a front-facing fish-eye camera). In all the experiments, we compare the new constant bearing method against the active elastic model. The remaining of the paper is organized as follows. In Sect. 2, the flocking problem is formulated and the investigated methodologies are presented. First the Constant Bearing (CB), the novelty of this paper; and second, the Active Elastic, the baseline for the further analysis. Following, the experimental setup and the used metrics are described in Sect. 3. Finally, the results are discussed in Sect. 4, and the final remarks are summarized in Sect. 5.

2   Constant Bearing (CB) Flocking

The proposed behavioral approach is composed of a steering law (ω) and a velocity regulation law ($\mathbf{v}$), which are the inputs for the focal agent. The general form of the algorithm is given below:

$$\omega = \sigma_a\left(f_\lambda\right) + \sigma_b\left(f_\beta\right) \tag{1a}$$

$$\mathbf{v} = \sigma_c\left(f_{v_i}\right) \tag{1b}$$

The steering law (ω) is composed by two terms: the constant bearing term (f_λ) and the field-of-view restriction term (f_β). Since both terms are unbounded functions, they are saturated in a and b, respectively, by the saturation function $\sigma_\epsilon(.)$. This is basically to avoid unfeasible outputs and to assure the predominance of second term over the first one. Additionally, the velocity term (1b) is also bounded in c by the saturation function described bellow:

$$\sigma_\epsilon(x) = \begin{cases} x, & \text{if } |x| \leq \epsilon \\ sgn(x), & \text{if } |x| > \epsilon \end{cases} \tag{2}$$

where, the ϵ stands for the saturation boundary.

2.1   Constant Bearing Term (f_λ)

It is responsible for keeping constant the bearing angle (λ_{iO}) towards the object of interest. This term, which is the core of the algorithm, is the equivalent of the known guidance law Proportional Navigation (ProNav), which is commonly used in guided missiles. More details about the ProNav can be obtained in [5]. The simplest version of this guidance can be stated as below:

$$f_\lambda = \eta * \dot{\lambda}_{iO}, \tag{3a}$$

$$\lambda_{iO} = \begin{cases} \lambda_{iT}, & \text{if agent informed.} \\ \lambda_{iC}, & \text{if agent NOT informed.} \end{cases} \tag{3b}$$

where, λ_{iT} is the bearing angle between pursuer and target, and λ_{iC} denotes the bearing angle towards the centroid of the perceived agents. Also, η is a constant and positive gain, commonly called navigation gain in the guidance literature.

Assuming that the distances (r_{ij}) and the bearing angle towards the neighbors (λ_{ij}) are known, we easily can obtain the λ_{iC}:

$$\lambda_{iC} = \arctan\left(\frac{\sum_{i \in FoV} r_{ij} \sin \lambda_{ij}}{\sum_{i \in FoV} r_{ij} \cos \lambda_{ij}}\right). \tag{4}$$

2.2 Velocity Regulation (v):

The goal of this term is to keep a minimal safety distance towards the closest interacting agent. Therefore, a possible implementation for this law can be seem bellow:

$$f_{v_i} = \gamma * \Theta \left(r_{min} \right), \tag{5}$$

where γ is the positive gain, and r_{min} is the distance to the closest perceived agent. Also, $\Theta(.)$ is a saturated linear function, which regulates velocity. It is defined as:

$$\Theta(x) = \begin{cases} 0, & \text{if } x \leq R_{saf} \\ y(x), & \text{if } R_{saf} < x < R_{int} \\ 1, & \text{if } x \geq R_{int} \end{cases} \tag{6a}$$

$$y(x) = \frac{x}{R_{int} - R_{saf}} + \frac{R_{saf}}{R_{int} - R_{saf}} \tag{6b}$$

where, R_{saf} denotes the closest safety distance between two agents, and R_{int} is the radius of interaction. This function makes the pursuer start to brake from R_{int} linearly until it achieves R_{saf}.

2.3 Alignment Emergence:

As stated in the introduction, the combination of the laws (3)-a and (5), is responsible for the emergence of the behaviors of aggregation and alignment:

- **Aggregation**, occurs when the bearing angle is constant ($\dot{\lambda}_{iO} = 0$) and the range to object of interest is decreasing ($\dot{r}_{iO} < 0$).
- **Alignment**, occurs when the bearing angle is constant ($\dot{\lambda}_{iO} = 0$) and the range to object of interest is constant ($\dot{r}_{iO} = 0$).

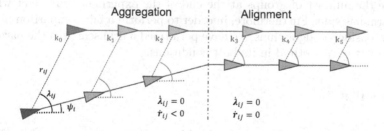

Fig. 1. Illustration of the "constant bearing" rule being applied for the two distinct behavior: aggregation and alignment. The figure describe the spatial displacement of two agents, a "leader" and a "follower" over six sequential timestamps (K). The follower is described by the blue triangle, and the target by the red triangle. (Color figure online)

An illustration of the above statement can be seen in Fig. 1, where the focal agent i is following another agent j, which for this specific example is doing the role of "leader".

Finally, the **Heading restriction term**, (f_β), is an additional term to the law (3), which is responsible for keeping the object of interest, i.e., target or centroid of the flocking, inside the FoV. This term is need to compensate (3)-a, where abrupt changes in λ_{iO} may lead to angular rate output that takes the object of interest out of the FOV. Therefore, the chosen function for this term implementation is:

$$f_\beta = \mu * \tan\left(\frac{\alpha_{iO}}{\beta * \pi^{-1}}\right), \tag{7a}$$

$$\alpha_{iO} = \psi_i - \lambda_{iO}, \tag{7b}$$

where the lead angle (α_{iO}) is composed by the subtraction of the heading angle (ψ_i) and the bearing (λ_{iO}). Besides, μ represents a constant positive gain, and β is the opening angle of the FOV.

3   Experimental Setup

We study the proposed method in a multi-agent simulator that has been developed internally. The agent is modelled as a differentially-driven two-wheels robot, with both omnidirectional sensing, with a FoV of 360°, and a restricted FoV of 180 (like a frontal camera). This sensor measures the range and bearing of the robot detected, without any information related to the identity. Besides, we then add a Gaussian noise to the distance equals to $\mathcal{N}(0, 0.01)$ and Gaussian noise equals to $\mathcal{N}(0, 0.02)$ for the bearing.

To provide a comparison with previous works, we select as a baseline is the minimalistic version studied in Ferrante et al. [4], which is based on potential-field forces. Furthermore, to evaluate the performance of our algorithm, we use the same metrics used in [4]: order, accuracy, and travelled distance. We also measure the number of groups at the end of the experiment to detect whether the swarm has split. Furthermore, in order to perform a fair comparison between the two considered algorithms, we have performed a grid search in the parameter space to put each method in its best conditions.

4   Results

Effects of the Swarm Size: In the Fig. 2, we selected two swarm sizes, $N = 20$ and $N = 100$, to compare the performance of CB with the baseline method AE. In the first plot, for 20 agents, we see no statistical difference on the accuracy for both the methods. However, for 100 agents, CB outperforms clearly the baseline algorithm. The under-performance of AE is mainly explained by its initially design for a omnidirectional sensor (FoV = 360). In the baseline, the alignment is achieved as by-product of the aggregation and interactions; consecutively, it

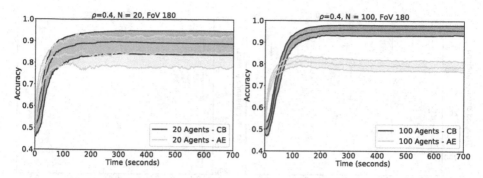

Fig. 2. ACCURACY for 20 and a 100 agents with % 40 % informed with FoV of 180°C and different swarm sizes

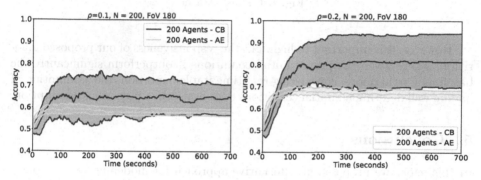

Fig. 3. Effects of the informed rate for 200 swarm sizes.

suffers much more with the reduction on the field-of-view, where less information are available for the interaction.

Effects of the Informed Rate: In Fig. 3, we have the comparison of CB with the baseline algorithm for two informed rate ($\rho = 0.1$ and $\rho = 0.2$). From both plots, we can confirm the direct relation between informed rate and accuracy; and also we observe the same tendency happening for the baseline algorithm. Besides, we can also remark CB's high dependency on the initial condition of the experiment, which is evidenced for lower rate of informed, where there is large variability between runs.

Traveled Distance and Clusters: In Fig. 4, we can see the comparison of the travelling distance for both approaches. We can see that, although CB outperforms AE in average values for all cases, it has again a much higher variability between runs. It reinforces once more the dependency of algorithm in the initial conditions (position and orientation) of the agents. It is highly evidenced in for the case of 20% of informed ($\rho = 0.2$) in both plots, where while the upper-bound evidenced the existence of runs with high performance travelled distance, the lower-bound indicate runs where all the agents kept essentially stuck along the whole experiment.

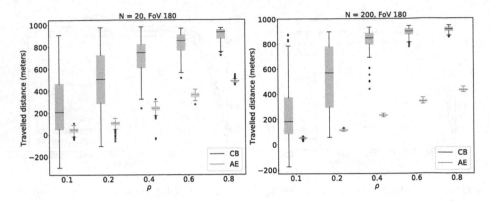

Fig. 4. Distance travel

However, it is important to highlight the responsiveness of our proposed algorithm, where given the proper initial conditions it outperform significantly the baseline. Furthermore, considering real-time implementation, the assumption of having well determined initial conditions does not seem a precarious assumption.

5   Conclusions

In this paper we proposed an alternative approach for modelling self-organized agents relying only range-and-bearing measurement. We showed that our method allow the flock to achieve aligned motion without requiring on neighbors' velocity or orientation measurement, which is a common assumption in most of the state-of-the-art algorithms. This released assumption can ease the implementation with real-time robots, since this information can be obtained by off-the-shelf sensors. Furthermore, our approach is consider limited fiel-of-view, which is also a common feature in most robotic platforms.

We evaluated numerically our method under variable swarm-size, proportion of informed agents, and type of field-of-view. Besides, we also provided quantitative comparison with a state-of-art approach. As result, our new method tends to outperform the baseline under limited field-of-view configuration; which is even more evidenced for higher swarm-size and proportion of informed. Besides, our approach significantly outperforms the baseline regarding the total distance travelled. Nevertheless, our approach tends to be very sensitive to the initial conditions, which causes a high variation between runs. This short-come, together with the real-time implementation, are the main improvements envisaged for future works.

References

1. Balázs, B., Vásárhelyi, G., Vicsek, T.: Adaptive leadership overcomes persistence-responsivity trade-off in flocking. J. R. Soc. Interface **17**(167), 20190853 (2020)
2. Bastien, R., Romanczuk, P.: A model of collective behavior based purely on vision. Sci. Adv. **6**(6), eaay0792 (2020)
3. Brighton, C.H., Thomas, A.L., Taylor, G.K.: Terminal attack trajectories of peregrine falcons are described by the proportional navigation guidance law of missiles. Proc. Natl. Acad. Sci. **114**(51), 1–6 (2017)
4. Ferrante, E., Turgut, A.E., Huepe, C., Stranieri, A., Pinciroli, C., Dorigo, M.: Self-organized flocking with a mobile robot swarm: a novel motion control method. Adapt. Behav. **20**(6), 460–477 (2012)
5. Shneydor, N.A.: Missile Guidance and Pursuit: Kinematics. Dynamics and Control. Horwood Publishing, Chichester (1998)
6. de Souza, C., Castillo, P., Vidolov, B.: Local interaction and navigation guidance for hunters drones: a chase behavior approach with real-time tests. Robotica **40**, 1–19 (2022)
7. Strandburg-Peshkin, A.: Visual sensory networks and effective information transfer in animal groups. Curr. Biol. **23**(17), R709–R711 (2013)
8. Vásárhelyi, G., et al.: Outdoor flocking and formation flight with autonomous aerial robots. In: 2014 IEEE/RSJ International Conference on Intelligent Robots and Systems, pp. 3866–3873. IEEE, Chicago, Illinois (2014)
9. Vásárhelyi, G., Virágh, C., Somorjai, G., Nepusz, T., Eiben, A.E., Vicsek, T.: Optimized flocking of autonomous drones in confined environments. Sci. Robot. **3**(20), eaat3536 (2018)
10. Vicsek, T., Zafeiris, A.: Collective motion. Phys. Rep. **517**(3–4), 71–140 (2012)
11. Virágh, C., et al.: Flocking algorithm for autonomous flying robots. Bioinspiration Biomimetics **9**(2), 1–15 (2014)
12. Wang, W., Escobedo, R., Sanchez, S., Sire, C., Han, Z., Theraulaz, G.: The impact of individual perceptual and cognitive factors on collective states in a data-driven fish school model. PLoS Comput. Biol. **18**(3), e1009437 (2022)

Distributed Sorting in Complex Environments

Mohammed Abdullhak[1] and Andrew Vardy[2]([✉])

[1] Department of Computer Science, Memorial University of Newfoundland,
St. John's, Canada
mabdullhak@mun.ca
[2] Department of Computer Science, Department of Electrical and Computer
Engineering, Memorial University of Newfoundland, St. John's, Canada
av@mun.ca

Abstract. We introduce an algorithm allowing a robot swarm to sort objects in complex environments. In this task, objects of different types are scattered around the environment and there is a specific goal area for each object type. The robots orbit the environment looking for objects and gather each class of objects into their designated area by physically pushing them around obstacles and towards their goals. The robots utilize a distributed collision avoidance algorithm for avoiding collisions with obstacles and among themselves based on the concept of buffered Voronoi cells. The robots decide which objects to target based on buffered Voronoi cell occupancy, thus preventing contention between robots. Global planning to determine the direction to move an object towards its goal along the shortest path is performed using goal maps generated from the distance transforms of these goal areas. The proposed algorithm is fully distributed and requires no central control or communication between robots. We evaluate the performance of our algorithm using an open-source web-based simulator and validate the real-world performance of the proposed algorithm in live experiments.

1 Introduction

Our focus is on object sorting as a distributed task, where a swarm of simple robots incrementally push objects towards their goals, even within complex environments where the straight-line path from object to goal is occluded. This task is solved while avoiding collisions between robots and handling contention over objects. We propose a distributed sorting algorithm with no communication requirements. The robots are assumed to have plans of their environments, including the desired location for each class of objects. We also assume the robots can localize and determine the relative positions of nearby robots and objects. This assumption could be met via an external localization system [7] or by self-localization by reference to sensor cues [10]. We make use of our previously developed local planning and collision avoidance algorithm [1] based on the concept of buffered Voronoi cells proposed by Zhou et al. [17]. This algorithm guides robots to arbitrary goal positions in a collision-free manner.

Object sorting has been studied by many researchers, starting with the seminal work of Deneubourg et al. who proposed a distributed sorting algorithm

© Springer Nature Switzerland AG 2022
M. Dorigo et al. (Eds.): ANTS 2022, LNCS 13491, pp. 308–315, 2022.
https://doi.org/10.1007/978-3-031-20176-9_27

inspired by how ant colonies sort their brood [2]. Sorting objects of multiple classes has been studied by many researchers [4,5,11,13,14] but always in simple obstacle-free environments and under the condition that like objects should be gathered together into homogeneous clusters whose locations emerge from the system's dynamics. However, real-world applications may require user control over the process. For example, in recycling the user will want to specify the goal location for each material. When these goal locations are specified, the task becomes synonymous with foraging with multiple collection points [3,15,16].

2   Collision Avoidance with Buffered Voronoi Cells

For a set of n disk-shaped robot with a radius of R, the Voronoi diagram partitions the environment into a set of non-overlapping regions. The region for each robot consists of all the points in the environment closer to it than any other robot [8]. Each region is called a *Voronoi cell* [6]. Assuming the robots are in a collision-free configuration (the distance between any two robots is larger than $2R$), the buffered Voronoi cell (BVC) as proposed by Zhou et al. [17] of a robot is its Voronoi cell retracted by its radius R, so that if the center of the robot is within its BVC, the entirety of its body lies within its Voronoi cell. If each robot's incremental movements are restricted to lie within its own BVC, then the possibility of collision is excluded [17]. Our algorithm utilizes the local planning algorithm we previously proposed [1] which operates as follows: at each time step t, each robot calculates its BVC, then it selects a waypoint within its BVC which is chosen to avoid deadlock configurations.

3   Sorting Algorithm

In this section we will discuss the sorting algorithm whose purpose is to target objects (pucks) and push them towards their goals. We first discuss the orbiting behavior which guides a robot in the absence of viable targets. Then we consider how to select pucks and the strategy for pushing them towards their goals. Finally, we consider obstacles lying in between the pucks and their goals.

We are assuming that the robots have a map of the environment, and know the desired final position for each class of targets. We also assume that the robots can localize themselves within their environment and can sense the position of nearby robots, targets, and static obstacles. The algorithm is fully distributed; each robot works independently without any need for communication.

3.1   Orbiting Behavior

The default behavior for robots with no suitable targets is to follow the periphery of the environment looking for new targets—we refer to this behavior as *orbiting* as it was inspired by our previously proposed orbital construction algorithm [12]. The purpose of orbiting is to traverse the environment looking for opportunities where the robot is well-positioned to push a puck towards its goal.

We generate a policy that maps between robot position and orbit direction. We define the *orbit border* as the set of points which are at least R distance away from the border of the environment and any static obstacle. See Fig. 1(a) for an example. We then compute the distance from all points to the orbit border using the fast marching method [9]. We define the orbit direction vector $\vec{d_r}$ for each position as the negative of the gradient. To establish clockwise orbiting we further define $\vec{b}$ for each vector by rotating $\vec{d_r}$ by 90° for all points within the orbit border and by −90° for all points outside of the orbit border. By adding the two vectors $\vec{d_r}$ and $\vec{b}$ for all points in the environment and smoothing the resulting array using a Gaussian filter we reach a smooth orbiting behavior. An example of the vector field corresponding to this policy is shown in Fig. 1(d).

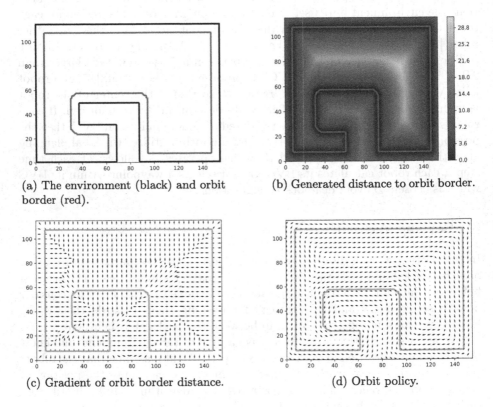

(a) The environment (black) and orbit border (red).

(b) Generated distance to orbit border.

(c) Gradient of orbit border distance.

(d) Orbit policy.

Fig. 1. Computing the orbit policy from the orbit border.

3.2   Target Selection

Let Q_t be the set of all nearby targets detected at time t. In order to avoid target conflicts, where multiple robots compete to push the same target, only targets located within the robot's current Voronoi cell V_t are considered. We define T_t as the set of detected targets that lie within the current Voronoi cell,

$T_t = \{n_i \mid n_i \in Q_t , \ p_i \in V_t\}$, where p_i is the position of target n_i. If no targets lie within the current Voronoi cell V_t, the robot falls back to orbiting the environment as described in Sect. 3.1.

For each target n_i in T_t, the robot retrieves $\overrightarrow{d_i}$, the direction towards which the target should be pushed and calculates the goal position for this target $g_i = p_i + \overrightarrow{d_i}$. We then calculate two metrics. First, the distance d_i between the robot's current position P and the target's current position p_i. Second, the angle a_i which is calculated from the angle $\angle Pp_i g_i$ between the robot's current position P, the target's current position p_i, and the target's goal g_i. The angle a_i for each target is then converted to the $[0°, 180°]$ range: $a_i = |\angle Pp_i g_i - 180|$. The target with the smallest angle a_i is then selected as the best target W_t with the distance used to resolve ties. See Fig. 2(a) for an illustrative example.

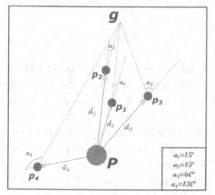

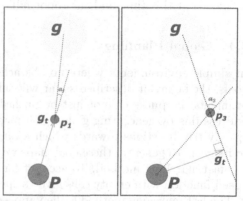

(a) Example of how distance d_i and angle a_i are used to select the best target: p_1.

(b) **left:** Angle $a_1 = 15° \leq c_1°$ so the robot's local goal g_t is set to the current position of the puck. **right:** Angle $c_1 \leq a_3 = 60° \leq c_2$ so the goal is set to the projection of the robot's position onto the line.

Fig. 2. Examples of target selection (a) and computing the goal for a target (b).

3.3 Target Pushing Strategy

After the robot selects its target, it chooses one of two goal positions based on the angle a_i of the target. If the angle a_i is smaller than a specific threshold c_1 ($c_1 = 15°$ in our experiments), then the robot is already well positioned to directly push the target towards it goal. Thus, the robot moves directly towards the target by setting the target's current position p_i as its goal. If the angle a_i is larger than c_1 but is still smaller than another threshold c_2 ($c_2 = 75°$ in our experiments), then the robot needs to perform a maneuver to better position itself. In this case, the chosen goal position is the point g_i' that is closest to the robot's current position P from the line connecting the target's current position and the target's current local goal $\overline{p_i g_i}$. Figure 2(b) shows both of these scenarios.

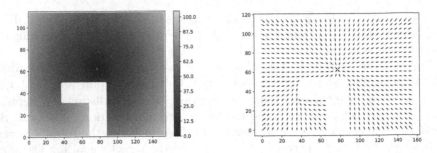

Fig. 3. left: Distance to goal array. **right:** Direction to goal vectors.

If the angle a_i is larger than c_2 then the current target is not well positioned to be moved at this time and the robot falls back to orbiting the environment.

3.4 Global Planning

In simple environments where no obstacles exist between the pucks and their goals, the behavior described so far will suffice. However, in more complex environments the pucks cannot just be pushed blindly towards their goals. We will address this by generating global goal maps for each target group. These maps specify the directions towards which a target located should move to get closer to its goal. To generate these goal maps we use the goal position as the source for the fast marching method. To account for the presence of obstacles we define a speed function with empty cells given a speed of 1 while occupied cells a speed of 0. The fast marching method is then applied to generate a distance function. The negative gradient of the distance function corresponds to the direction that a puck at this position should be moved to reach its goal while avoiding obstacles. Figure 3 provides an example.

4   Results

4.1   Simulation

The simulations were performed using an open source web-based simulation platform[1]. We simulate a set of disk-shaped robots with static obstacles and multiple groups of pucks. Each group has a unique goal area. We performed two sets of experiments; for each one, the proposed algorithm is compared against a baseline algorithm where a core feature of the proposed algorithm is disabled. Two metrics are tracked: the total distance between all pucks and their goal areas, and the number of pucks outside of their goal areas at each time step. First, we measure the impact of the proposed target conflict avoidance mechanism. We disable this feature in the baseline algorithm by allowing any pucks within the

---

[1] https://github.com/m-abdulhak/SwarmJS.

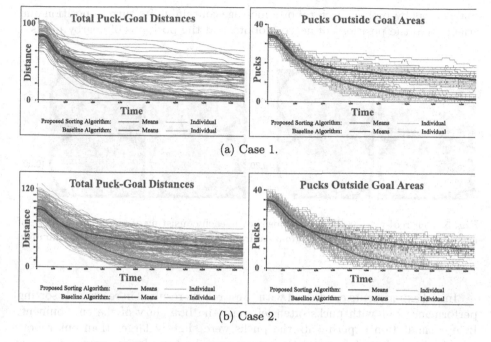

Fig. 4. Simulation results for case 1 (a) and case 2 (b).

sensing distance to be valid targets for a robot, instead of only the ones within the BVC of the robot. We repeated each experiment 100 times in a 800×500 cm empty environment with a set of 25 robots having a radius of 8 cm, and two groups of pucks each having 20 pucks with a radius of 10 cm. Figure 4(a) shows the results of this experiment (case 1). In the second experiment, we assess the impact of the orbiting behavior. We compare the full proposed algorithm against a baseline algorithm where the robots pursue random points in the environment when no suitable targets are found. The results are shown in Fig. 4(b), clearly demonstrating the advantage of orbiting in complex environments.

4.2 Real-World Validation

Our experimental platform is a set of Pololu 3pi robots fitted with Raspberry Pi 3 A+ single-board computers. A unique AprilTag [7] is fitted to each robot to identify it by an overhead tracking system that provides localization and sensing to the robots. The robots are autonomous, but have no on-board localization or sensing capability. They connect to a central server remotely over WiFi to continuously request location and sensing data. The server continuously processes the images received from the attached overhead camera, an Intel Real-sense D435. The server detects the positions and orientations of the robots and the positions of the pucks. It uses this data to simulate the values detected by each robot's virtual sensors by passing each robot a message containing its current position and orientation, the positions of nearby robots, and the positions of nearby pucks.

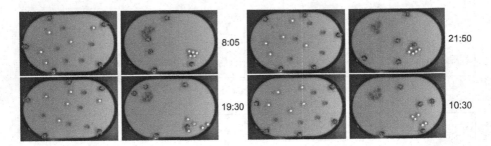

Fig. 5. Four real-world validation trials shown, each consisting of an overhead image of the initial environment state, the final environment state, and time elapsed in minutes.

Initial experiments conducted with these robots resulted in reasonable sorting performance but with pucks often left near the boundary of the environment. In our simulation experiments the pucks were slightly larger than our robots allowing the robots to extract the pucks from the boundaries. However, in our physical setup the robots were slightly larger than the pucks making them very difficult to extract. Rather than modifying the pucks' size, we added 'tails' to the robots and modified the algorithm to trigger an in-place turn whenever a robot is sufficiently close to both the boundary and a puck. The tails are not actuated and are composed of paper wrapped in tape, designed to flick pucks while spinning but to bend out of the way of other robots.

The proposed algorithm was tested on a set of 5 robots, tasked with sorting 5 red and 5 green pucks into their respective goal areas. Figure 5 shows the initial and final states of four trials, along with the execution time. The robots were able to gather all pucks into their goal areas in all four trials.

5   Conclusions

This paper presented a distributed sorting algorithm for sorting objects into specified goal areas. The simulations showed that the proposed algorithm works reliably even in complex environments, and the physical experiment validated its performance on real robots with simulated sensing. In the future, we are interested in testing this algorithm on robots using on-board sensing and localization. This should be feasible since the locally relevant subset of the Voronoi diagram can be generated using only the distances to nearby robots and obstacles.

References

1. Abdullhak, M., Vardy, A.: Deadlock prediction and recovery for distributed collision avoidance with buffered voronoi cells. In: 2021 IEEE/RSJ International Conference on Intelligent Robots and Systems (IROS), pp. 429–436 (2021). https://doi.org/10.1109/IROS51168.2021.9636609
2. Deneubourg, J.L., Goss, S., Franks, N., Sendova-Franks, A., Detrain, C., Chrétien, L.: The dynamics of collective sorting robot-like ants and ant-like robots. In: From Animals to Animats: Proceedings of the First International Conference on Simulation of Adaptive Behavior, pp. 356–365 (1991)
3. Lu, Q., Fricke, G.M., Ericksen, J.C., Moses, M.E.: Swarm foraging review: closing the gap between proof and practice. Current Robot. Rep. 1(4), 1–11 (2020). https://doi.org/10.1007/s43154-020-00018-1
4. Melhuish, C., Holland, O., Hoddell, S.: Collective sorting and segregation in robots with minimal sensing. In: Proceedings of 5th International Conference on Simulation of Adaptive Behaviour, pp. 465–470 (1998)
5. Melhuish, C., Sendova-Franks, A.B., Scholes, S., Horsfield, I., Welsby, F.: Ant-inspired sorting by robots: the importance of initial clustering. J. Roy. Soc. Interface 3(7), 235–242 (2006)
6. Okabe, A., Boots, B., Sugihara, K., Chiu, S.: Spatial Tessellations: concepts and applications of Voronoi diagrams. Wiley Series in Probability and Statistics, Wiley (2009). https://books.google.ca/books?id=dT7YH3mjeeIC
7. Olson, E.: AprilTag: a robust and flexible visual fiducial system. In: 2011 IEEE International Conference on Robotics and Automation, pp. 3400–3407 (2011). https://doi.org/10.1109/ICRA.2011.5979561
8. Sack, J.R., Urrutia, J.: Handbook of Computational Geometry. Elsevier, Amsterdam (1999)
9. Sethian, J.A.: A fast marching level set method for monotonically advancing fronts. Proc. National Acad. Sci. 93(4), 1591–1595 (1996)
10. Thrun, S., Burgard, W., Fox, D.: Probabilistic Robotics. MIT Press, Cambridge, MA (2005)
11. Vardy, A.: Accelerated patch sorting by a robotic swarm. In: 2012 Ninth Conference on Computer and Robot Vision, pp. 314–321. IEEE (2012)
12. Vardy, A.: Orbital construction: swarms of simple robots building enclosures. In: 2018 IEEE 3rd International Workshops on Foundations and Applications of Self* Systems (FAS* W), pp. 147–153. IEEE (2018)
13. Vardy, A., Vorobyev, G., Banzhaf, W.: Cache consensus: rapid object sorting by a robotic swarm. Swarm Intell. 8(1), 61–87 (2014). https://doi.org/10.1007/s11721-014-0091-5
14. Wang, T., Zhang, H.: Multi-robot collective sorting with local sensing. In: IEEE Intelligent Automation Conference (IAC). Citeseer (2003)
15. Winfield, A.F.: Foraging Robots, pp. 3682–3700. Springer, New York, New York, NY (2009). https://doi.org/10.1007/978-0-387-30440-3_217
16. Zedadra, O., Jouandeau, N., Seridi, H., Fortino, G.: Multi-agent foraging: state-of-the-art and research challenges. Complex Adapt. Syst. Model. 5(1), 1–24 (2017)
17. Zhou, D., Wang, Z., Bandyopadhyay, S., Schwager, M.: Fast, on-line collision avoidance for dynamic vehicles using buffered voronoi cells. IEEE Robot. Autom. Lett. 2(2), 1047–1054 (2017). https://doi.org/10.1109/LRA.2017.2656241

Effect of Different Communication Affordances on the Emergence of Collaboration Strategies in an Online Multiplayer Game

Hala Khodr[✉], Nicolas Wagner, Barbara Bruno, Aditi Kothiyal,
and Pierre Dillenbourg

School of Computer and Communication Sciences, Ecole Polytechnique Fédérale de
Lausanne, Écublens, Switzerland
hala.khodr@epfl.ch

Abstract. In a group, the collective dynamics is governed by the inter-actions between individuals, which can manifest differently depending on the available means of communication. In this paper, we compare 3 conditions of communication affordances (global chat, local chat and no chat) in an online multiplayer game and investigate their effect on team performance. An experiment involving a total of 108 participants (grouped in teams of 6 players) revealed that while the three conditions allow for the emergence of different communication systems, they yield no significant difference on the time taken to complete the task.

1 Introduction

Collective behaviours are ubiquitous in nature, ranging from animal swarms to human crowds. In such systems, multiple agents have to coordinate and collaborate in a flexible and robust manner to achieve a shared goal. The communication between the agents is an essential factor affecting the interaction between them and therefore influencing the collective performance of the group. As a consequence, communication and its role in collective behaviours have been studied in many different domains and under a variety of perspectives.

A first lens for analysis focuses on the *medium of communication*, with verbal [14] and haptic [6] mediums being among the most commonly considered. In a collaborative virtual 2D pointing task between 2 dyads, Jinling et al. compared verbal, haptic, and a combination of both modalities. Their outcomes indicate that participants using verbal only and haptic+verbal communication performed equally well while participants using haptic only communication took more time and had longer path lengths [14]. Conversely, and quite interestingly, in a study on decision taking, haptically coupled dyads were found to solve a perceptual discrimination task more accurately than their best individual members and five times faster than dyads using verbal communication [10].

A second perspective is the analysis of the *emergence of communication* systems in collaborative tasks. An example of this phenomenon is the emergence of

© Springer Nature Switzerland AG 2022
M. Dorigo et al. (Eds.): ANTS 2022, LNCS 13491, pp. 316–323, 2022.
https://doi.org/10.1007/978-3-031-20176-9_28

simple language (common code) when participants are involved in a coordination game with no common language made available in the beginning [12]. Such a behaviour requires humans to know that communicative behaviour is indeed communicative in nature. [11] investigates this assumption through an ad-hoc designed experimental game. The authors found that the emergence of a communication system usually involves a bootstrapping process, and that this process has an impact on the final form of the communication system. Moreover, a sufficient common ground is observed to be a necessity for the recognition of signalhood, and the emergence of dialogue is seen as the key step in the development of a system that can be employed to attain shared goals. In [8], through a maze game task, the authors present how particular environmental affordances (such as the structure of the mazes) drive the emergence of different communicative conventions in otherwise identical tasks, suggesting that linguistic adaptations are highly sensitive to factors of the shared task environment.

A third key aspect is the analysis of the *effects of communication on team performance*, in organizational contexts. A meta-analysis reveals that communication quality has a significantly stronger relationship with team performance than communication frequency [7]. Although communication can be positively correlated with team performance, the advantages of communication are dependent on the task characteristics as well as the type of communication used [9].

Finally, the *scope of communication* is a crucial topic in all domains involving swarms of artificial agents, such as swarm robotics, where the locality of interactions and communication has a beneficial effect on the scalability and robustness of the system, and is thus generally preferred over the use of global communication and sensing [4]. Local communication is then further divided in 1) direct robot-to-robot communication, either using explicit messages or implicitly detecting the existence and relative location of other robots in the immediate vicinity, and 2) stigmergic communication relying on the modification of the environment (e.g. pheromones) [13].

While, as the review above highlights, each of the key aspects concerning communication in collective behaviours has been extensively studied, less is known about their interplay. In an effort towards bridging this gap and further expanding our understanding of the role of communication, in this paper, we consider the above four perspectives together, specifically investigating the effect of different communication affordances (different mediums and scope) on the emergence of collaboration strategies and team performance in an online multiplayer game.

2   Methodology

For our study, we designed an online collaborative game where human participants interact via a robot avatar in a controlled experimental setup. Similar to HuGoS [5], our online environment can capture all the interaction details among participants throughout the game. Three versions of the game, respectively allowing no verbal communication, local verbal (chat-based) communication and global verbal (chat-based) communication among participants were designed, to allow for investigating the effects of communication medium and scope on the emerging communication system and team performance.

2.1 Game Design

Game Mechanics. Our online multiplayer game is based on the Unity game engine and the Photon Unity Networking [2] package for multiplayer games. The game involves 6 players, each represented by an avatar which is chosen to be a virtual robot [15] of a unique colour and a limited field of view set to 5% of the total map size. The game's goal is to move boxes to goal positions indicated by red dots as fast as possible. There are a total of 12 boxes in the environment whose positions are not all visible to all players, with some that a player can move alone and others that require the joint action of 3 (medium boxes) or even 6 players. Players can control their avatars via the arrow keyboard keys. A player can move a box by: 1) *Pushing the box*: the player's avatar applies a repulsion force on the box when it is inside the halo surrounding the box or by 2) *Pulling the box*: the player's avatar applies an attraction force on the box when it is inside the halo surrounding the box and the SHIFT key is pressed. The game is organized in three stages. In the first stage, each player is in a room alone and must move a small box to its goal position to unlock a door and access the second stage. In the second stage, three players are in the same part of the environment, and they must move together two medium boxes, while the three others have the same task in another part of the environment. In the third stage, all six players are in the same space and must move two large boxes to their goals.

Game Deployment. The game is deployed on WebGL and accessible at https://ants-cellulo-game.web.app. The advantage of using WebGL is that all files are hosted on the website, thus allowing players to play the game via their browsers, with no local download or installation needed. The game data we log include: the positions and the ping of all movable objects in the game, the chat messages, the timer. The data is logged every tenth of a second and uploaded to a Firebase storage [1] every 1 min. The game is standalone, self-explanatory and can be played without the intervention of an experimenter.

Communications Affordances. We implement three versions of the game, exclusively differing from one another in terms of the communication affordances provided to the players:

1. *Global Chat:* In this condition, a chat is included in the game. All players can communicate with everyone else by typing and receiving messages.
2. *Local Chat:* In this condition, only the players who are in the neighbourhood of the sending player can receive the message. On the top of the chat box, each player can see with whom they can communicate. The communication range is set to be 20% of the dimension of field of view.
3. *No Chat:* In this condition, players cannot communicate through chat.

2.2 Experiment Design

We designed the study as a between-groups experiment, with the communication affordance as manipulated variable (thus yielding the three conditions described in Sect. 2.1) and team performance (here intended as the time taken to complete the task) as main outcome variable. The study[1] involved 108 participants recruited via Prolific[2] [3], an online recruitment platform. They self-organized in teams of 6 as described in Sect. 2.1 and the teams were split equally and randomly across the three conditions, thus yielding 6 teams per condition. We collected age, gender, major and degrees as background info of the participants. The mean age of all participants was 24.8 years old (SD = 5.9) with 39 females, 67 males and 2 others. The participants included 44 who finished high school, 33 with a Bachelor degree, 26 with Masters, 4 with PhD and 1 other.

3 Results

We compare quantitatively the teams' performance in the three conditions in terms of their time of completion. To complement the statistical analyses correlating chat data with team performance, we implemented a replay tool allowing us to perform qualitative observation of players' behaviour during the game.

3.1 Effects of Communication Affordances on Team Performance

The mean time to complete the task, across all conditions, was 17.2 ($\pm$4.5) min. The fastest team took 9.6 min and the slowest one 25.5 min. Although the Local condition has the lowest average time among the three conditions, a Kruskal Wallis[3] test shows no significant difference in performance among the three conditions (df = 2, H = 3.94, p = .14). This result is interesting as it contradicts the common-sense hypothesis that having a (global) communication would lead to better performance. While representing more than 100 participants, this analysis (which is done at team level), actually only accounts for 6 data points per condition: collecting more data in future studies will thus be crucial to either confirm this result (i.e., the lack of an effect of the communication affordance on performance) or reveal significant differences (e.g., between the local condition and the others).

3.2 Emerging Communication System Analysis - Global Condition

Although no direct correlation was found between communication affordance and team performance, a deeper analysis on the communication type which emerged in each condition provides useful insights on the possible causes of that result.

First of all, in the Global condition, a significant positive correlation (Spearman's ρ = .94, p = .005, power = .9) is found between the total number of messages sent during the game and the time taken to complete the task. In

---

[1] This study was approved by our institutions Human Research Ethics Committee with reference number No 022-2021.

[2] The average reward was set to 6 £/hr. A bonus incentive was given to groups who finish the fastest.

[3] Chosen since the normality assumption of the data is not satisfied.

Fig. 1. Global condition   **Fig. 2.** Local condition

other words, better performing teams (low time) send less messages over chat. At the same time, no significant correlation is found between the chatting frequency (i.e. number of messages sent per minute, on average) and the time taken to complete the task. These results suggest that (1) chatting more doesn't seem to help complete the task faster and rather (2) teams seem to chat "while" playing, rather than "to" play, thus sending more messages when they take longer to finish the game. In synthesis, global communication doesn't seem to have an impact on the teams' ability to coordinate actions and perform the task better.

To complement the above analysis on the volume of the messages, we also analyzed their content. Figure 1 shows the word cloud of all chats in the Global condition. The two most recurrent words are "need" and "push". The next recurrent words are "one", "left", and "pull". This shows that the players mainly use the chat to ask for help ("need", "one"), or give orders for the actions to be done related to the game ("push","pull") and agree on directions ("left").

3.3   Emerging Communication System Analysis - Local Condition

The total number of messages shared by teams in the Local condition is significantly lower compared to the Global condition (ttest: $t[10] = -2.3$, p =.04, Cohen-d = 1.33), thus suggesting that this communication modality, by design, induces a smaller volume of messages to be shared.

Contrary to the Global condition, no significant correlation is found here between the total number of messages sent during the game and the time taken to complete the task. At the same time, no significant correlation is found between chatting frequency and completion time either. Quite interestingly, however, a median split reveals that the 3 top performing teams are also the ones with the smallest overall number of messages sent as well as the lowest chatting frequency.

These results, somewhat hinting at the importance of sharing "the right information at the right time" motivate us to look into the timing of the messages. By comparing the game events with the chat messages, we notice two trends concerning when a chat is initiated: 1) Prior to acting, e.g. before moving a box or going on search for the goal position/missing players. 2) In response to certain events, e.g. to help a player or solve a conflict. Some examples are shown is

Table 1. Examples of chats initiated in response to an event/conflict

	Sender	Message	Receiver(s)
Example 1	Green	its stuck	Red
	Red	pull with shift	Green
	Green	oh ..	
Example 2	Yellow	from the top	Orange, purple
	Purple	can't fit	Yellow, orange
	Yellow	and then left to right	Orange, purple
	Purple	isn't it better to push to left from the right	Yellow, orange

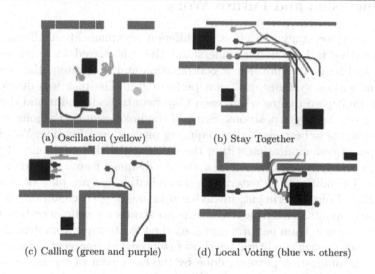

(a) Oscillation (yellow)   (b) Stay Together

(c) Calling (green and purple)   (d) Local Voting (blue vs. others)

Fig. 3. Emergent behaviours in the non-chat condition

Table 1. On average, teams had 2.3 chats per game initiated prior to acting and 2.8 initiated in response to an event/conflict, with the difference between the two not being significant. Concerning the content of the messages, Fig. 2 shows the word cloud of all chats in the Local condition.

3.4 Emerging Communication System Analysis - No Chat Condition

In this condition, communication is only possible implicitly, via the movement of the players' avatars. The qualitative inspection of the games' replays allowed us to identify a number of emerging behaviours and communication mechanisms.

1. "Oscillating behaviour": A player moves their avatar back and forth, in a way which we hypothesize to be an indication of the direction in which they want to go (Fig. 3a).

2. Once together, players stay and navigate together (Fig. 3b).
3. "Calling behaviour": A player moves close to another player, stops, then moves, to signal to the other player to follow them (Fig. 3c).
4. "Local voting system": this behaviour is particularly noticeable when the 6 players need to decide which of the two large boxes to move first. If divided between the two boxes, players in the minority group tend to go and join the majority around the other box (Fig. 3d). This behaviour also appears when choosing in which direction to move the box. Each player chooses one side of the box and they eventually all converge to a same side.

4   Conclusion and Future Work

In this paper we study the effect of different communication affordances on a collaborative task to better understand the role played by communication medium and scope on multi-agent coordination and, concretely, the emergence of communication systems and team performance. The task was developed as an online multiplayer game where each player controls an avatar and the goal is to move boxes to target positions. Some of the boxes require the joint action of multiple players to be moved, thus requiring players' coordination. We allow for three types of communication within the game: a global chat among all players, a local chat among players within a certain distance from each other and no chat. In all conditions, no external communication among players is allowed. The results of our experiment, involving 6 teams in each condition for a total of 108 participants, show that there was no significant difference between the three conditions in team performance (i.e., the time taken to complete the task). Going deeper in each condition, we show few observed emergent behaviours and implicit communication patterns done by the movement of the player when no chat was allowed. In the global condition, a significant positive correlation is found between the total number of messages and the time taken to complete the task, suggesting that chatting is not necessarily helpful towards coordination. Following a similar trend, the 3 best performing teams in the Local condition were also the ones with the lowest number of exchanged messages, and the lowest chatting frequency. Further observation of the game replays showed the emergence of two distinct triggers for initiating communication: either to agree on an action before taking it, or in response to a conflict/difficulty. A similar qualitative analysis of the players' behaviour in the No-Chat condition revealed the emergence of signalling and coordination mechanisms, based on the avatars' movements and for agreeing on an action.

Acknowledgements. This work was supported as a part of NCCR Robotics, a National Centre of Competence in Research, funded by the Swiss National Science Foundation (grant number 51NF40_185543). I thank my brothers, colleagues and friends who participated in playing and testing the game.

References

1. Get started with cloud storage on web | firebase documentation. https://firebase. google.com/docs/storage/web/start
2. Photon unity 3D networking framework SDKs and game backend | photon engine. https://www.photonengine.com/pun
3. Prolific. quickly find research participants you can trust. https://www.prolific.co/
4. Bayindir, L., Şahin, E.: A review of studies in swarm robotics. Turk. J. Electr. Eng. Comput. Sci. **15**(2), 115–147 (2007)
5. Coucke, N., Heinrich, M.K., Cleeremans, A., Dorigo, M.: HuGoS: a virtual environment for studying collective human behavior from a swarm intelligence perspective. Swarm Intell. **15**(4), 339–376 (2021)
6. Khodr, H., Kianzad, S., Johal, W., Kothiyal, A., Bruno, B., Dillenbourg, P.: Allo-Haptic: robot-mediated haptic collaboration for learning linear functions. In: 2020 29th IEEE International Conference on Robot and Human Interactive Communication (RO-MAN), pp. 27–34. IEEE (2020)
7. Marlow, S.L., Lacerenza, C.N., Paoletti, J., Burke, C.S., Salas, E.: Does team communication represent a one-size-fits-all approach?: a meta-analysis of team communication and performance. Organ. Behav. Hum. Decis. Process. **144**, 145–170 (2018). https://doi.org/10.1016/j.obhdp.2017.08.001
8. Nölle, J., Fusaroli, R., Mills, G.J., Tylén, K.: Language as shaped by the environment: linguistic construal in a collaborative spatial task. Palgrave Commun. **6**(1), 1–10 (2020)
9. O'Bryan, L., Beier, M., Salas, E.: How approaches to animal swarm intelligence can improve the study of collective intelligence in human teams. J. Intell. **8**(1), 9 (2020). https://doi.org/10.3390/jintelligence8010009
10. Pezzulo, G., Roche, L., Saint-Bauzel, L.: Haptic communication optimises joint decisions and affords implicit confidence sharing. Sci. Rep. **11**(1), 1–9 (2021)
11. Scott-Phillips, T.C., Kirby, S., Ritchie, G.R.S.: Signalling signalhood and the emergence of communication. Cognition **113**(2), 226–233 (2009). https://doi.org/10.1016/j.cognition.2009.08.009
12. Selten, R., Warglien, M.: The emergence of simple languages in an experimental coordination game. Proc. Nat. Acad. Sci. **104**(18), 7361–7366 (2007). https://doi.org/10.1073/pnas.0702077104
13. Svennebring, J., Koenig, S.: Building terrain-covering ant robots: a feasibility study. Auton. Robot. **16**(3), 313–332 (2004)
14. Wang, J., Chellali, A., Cao, C.G.: A study of communication modalities in a virtual collaborative task. In: 2013 IEEE International Conference on Systems, Man, and Cybernetics, pp. 542–546 (2013). https://doi.org/10.1109/SMC.2013.98
15. Özgür, A., et al.: Cellulo: versatile handheld robots for education. In: 2017 12th ACM/IEEE International Conference on Human-Robot Interaction HRI, pp. 119–127 (2017)

Generating and Analyzing Collective Step-Climbing Behavior in a Multi-legged Robotic Swarm

Daichi Morimoto[1(✉)], Motoaki Hiraga[1], Kazuhiro Ohkura[1],
and Masaharu Munetomo[2]

[1] Graduate School of Advanced Science and Engineering, Hiroshima University,
Hiroshima, Japan
{morimoto,hiraga}@ohk.hiroshima-u.ac.jp, kohkura@hiroshima-u.ac.jp
[2] Information Initiative Center, Hokkaido University, Hokkaido, Japan

Abstract. This paper focuses on generating and analyzing collective step-climbing behavior in a multi-legged robotic swarm. The multi-legged robotic swarm is expected to climb obstacles that are hard for a single robot by using other robots as stepping stones. However, designing a robot controller for a multi-legged robotic swarm becomes a challenging problem because it designs not only a gait for the basic movement of robots but also the behavior of robots to exhibit collective behavior. This paper employs the evolutionary robotics (ER) approach for designing a robot controller that consists of a recurrent neural network. The controllers are evaluated in the collective step-climbing task conducted by computer simulations. The results show that the ER approach successfully designed the robot gait to achieve the task. Additionally, the results of the analysis confirm that the robot obtained the actions to support other robots along with climbing other robots.

1 Introduction

Swarm robotics (SR) [2] is the study of how to design collective behaviors with a large number of autonomous robots. The basic collective behaviors such as aggregation [4,7], path formation [16], collective transport [8], and collective decision-making [15,17] are discussed in SR. Many studies in SR are conducted with flat fields, using mobile robots driven by wheels. In these studies, designers can focus on designing collective behavior by reducing efforts on designing the basic movement of the robot. However, the field where the robots can operate is limited to relatively flat terrain. Therefore, the collective behavior is also limited to the two-dimensional space.

This paper focuses on designing a three-dimensional collective behavior of a multi-legged robotic swarm. The multi-legged robot is expected to operate in rough terrain fields [13]. Additionally, the multi-legged robotic swarm is expected to climb obstacles that are hard for a single robot by using other robots as stepping stones. The robot system for climbing other robots is discussed in modular

© Springer Nature Switzerland AG 2022
M. Dorigo et al. (Eds.): ANTS 2022, LNCS 13491, pp. 324–331, 2022.
https://doi.org/10.1007/978-3-031-20176-9_29

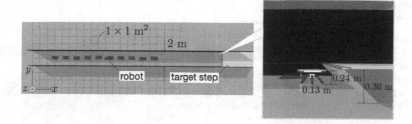

Fig. 1. The experimental environment. In this paper, the evolution process starts from the situation where the robots can walk along the x-axis and form a line. The preliminary evolution for obtaining walking and forming a line is conducted like [11].

robots or cellular robotics [6,10,14]. Compared with related fields, the multi-legged robotic swarm is expected to operate in a wide range of task scenarios by improving the mobility of a unit robot.

On the other hand, designing a controller of a multi-legged robotic swarm becomes a challenging problem because it requires not only a basic gait but also the behavior of robots to exhibit collective behavior. This paper focuses on the evolutionary robotics(ER) approach [12]. The ER approach is utilized for designing a gait of a multi-legged robot [9,18]. The ER approach is also used for designing collective behavior of a robotic swarm [4,16]. This paper is the hybridization between designing a gait of a multi-legged robot and designing a collective behavior of a robotic swarm using the ER approach. In this paper, the recurrent neural network is utilized as the robot controller. The robot controller is evaluated in a simple step-climbing task similar to [11]. The result shows that the ER approach succeeded to generate a collective step-climbing behavior. Additionally, not only the action of climbing objects but also the actions seem to be useful for achieving the task(e.g., positioning next to other robots for making the wide stepping stone, keeping a posture, and so on)are obtained. This paper introduces measurement factors for the position and the orientation of robots and analyzes the obtained behavior. The result shows that, in addition to climbing objects, the actions to support other robots for achieving the task are obtained.

The rest of this paper is organized as follows. Section 2 describes the settings of experiments, and Sect. 3 describes measurement factors. Section 4 shows the results of the experiments. Finally, Sect. 5 concludes this paper.

2   Settings of the Experiment

This experiment aims to generate collective step-climbing behavior of a multi-legged robotic swarm by using the evolutionary robotics approach. The experiment also focuses on analyzing the obtained behavior. The experiments are carried out in computer simulations with Bullet 3D physics engine [3].

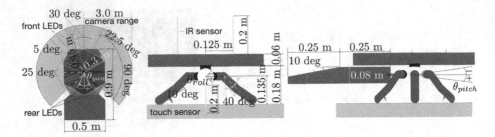

Fig. 2. Settings of the robot. Cyan dotted lines indicate the movable range of the joint. The gray circular sector shows the visible range of the camera. (Color figure online)

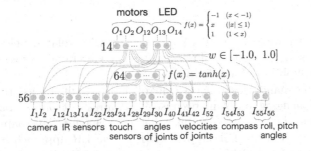

Fig. 3. Structure of the robot controller.

2.1 Task Settings

Figure 1 shows the environmental settings of the experiment. In this paper, the evolution process starts from the situation where the controller can make robots walk and form a line. The target step is higher than a single robot. Therefore, robots have to utilize other robots as stepping-stones for achieving the task. The target step has an acute angle on the surface. The robots should keep their posture for becoming a stepping stone. If the robot climbs the step, it will be replaced at 5 m in front of the step and join the task again.

2.2 Robot Settings

The robot configuration is illustrated in Fig. 2. Each leg has two joints, and therefore the robot has a total of twelve joints. The movable ranges of each joint are shown by cyan dotted lines. The robots have a shell and a tail part to support other robots climbing themselves. The robot is also equipped with LEDs, a camera, infrared (IR) sensors, touch sensors, and an electric compass. The camera has a visible range divided into six regions. Each region detects the colored LEDs on the front and back of the robot independently; in total, twelve binary signals are obtained. The value from the IR sensor is normalized into [0,1]. IR sensors can distinguish between robots and other objects. Touch sensors are equipped at the end of each leg. Each touch sensor returns 1 when it detects collisions with other objects and 0 otherwise. The electric compass shows sine and cosine values of the direction the robot is facing.

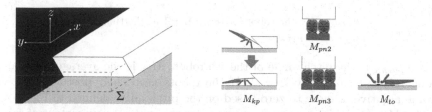

Fig. 4. Illustrations about the measurement factors. *Left*: The cuboid space specified by Σ. *Right*: The robot's situations corresponding to measurement factors.

2.3 Controller

The robot controller is illustrated in Fig. 3. The controller is the recurrent neural network that contains direct connections from the input layer to the output layer. In the output layer, twelve neurons decide the target angular velocity of joints, and the remaining two decide the activation of LEDs. A total of 9360 synaptic weights are optimized by a (μ, λ)-evolution strategy(ES) [1,5]. The numbers of parents(μ) and offspring(λ) are 64 and 192, respectively. The fitness function consists of three parts; $fitness_1$ for walking, $fitness_2$ for following the other robots, and $fitness_3$ for climbing the step. These settings are designed based on [11]. This experiment mainly uses $fitness_3$ for evolving step-climbing behavior.

3 Measurement Factors

This paper also focuses on analyzing obtained behavior of robots. The action of robots in front of the step is important to understand the physical interactions between robots. Therefore, Σ is introduced to describe the position and orientation of robots in front of the step, which is defined as follows:

$$
\Sigma = \begin{cases} 1 & \text{if} \quad x_\Sigma < x \quad \text{and} \quad z < z_\Sigma \quad \text{and} \\ & \quad |\theta_{roll}| < \theta_{r\_\Sigma} \quad \text{and} \quad |\theta_{pitch}| < \theta_{p\_\Sigma} \quad \text{and} \quad |\theta_{yaw}| < \theta_{y\_\Sigma} \\ 0 & \text{otherwise} \end{cases} \tag{1}
$$

where x and z are the coordinate values of the robot. The θ_{roll}, θ_{pitch}, and θ_{yaw} are the orientation angles of the robot. The x_Σ, z_Σ, θ_{r_Σ}, θ_{p_Σ}, and θ_{y_Σ} are threshold values. The Σ judges whether or not the robot is standing in front of the step and facing toward the step. Figure 3 shows the cuboid space specified by Σ. The thresholds are set as follows; $x_\Sigma = 15.2$ [m], $z_\Sigma = 0.19$ [m], $\theta_{r\_\Sigma} = 40$[deg], $\theta_{p\_\Sigma} = 30$[deg], $\theta_{y\_\Sigma} = 60$[deg].

Four measurement factors are introduced for detecting the situations of robots. Figure 3 illustrated the robot's situations corresponding to measurement factors. These situations are determined by the observation of robots in preliminary experiments. The M_{kp} is the measurement of keeping the posture of the robot, which is calculated by the following equations:

$$
M_{kp} = \frac{1}{N_r} \sum_t^T \sum_i^{N_r} f_{kp,t,i} \tag{2}
$$

$$f_{kp,t,i} = \begin{cases} \theta_{pitch,i} & \text{if} \quad \text{the robot } i \text{ satisfies } \Sigma = 1 \text{ at the timestep } t \\ 0 & \text{otherwise} \end{cases}$$

where $\theta_{pitch,i}$ is the pitch angle of the ith robot. M_{kp} is the average pitch angle among robots that satisfy $\Sigma = 1$. If the robots keep their posture, M_{kp} will become negative or close to zero based on the pitch angle defined in Fig. 2.

The M_{pn2} and M_{pn3} are measurements for the spatial arrangement of robots in front of the step. M_{pn2} is calculated by the following equations:

$$M_{pn2} = \sum_t^T f_{pn2,t} \tag{3}$$

$$f_{pn2,t} = \begin{cases} 1 & \text{if} \quad \text{robot } i, j(i \neq j) \text{ satisfy } \Sigma = 1 \quad \text{and} \\ & \theta_{pitch,i},\ \theta_{pitch,j} \in (\underline{\theta}_{p\_pn},\ \overline{\theta}_{p\_pn}) \quad \text{and} \\ & \|x_i - x_j\|_2 < r_{pn2} \\ 0 & \text{otherwise} \end{cases}$$

where $\underline{\theta}_{p\_pn}$ and $\overline{\theta}_{p\_pn}$ are thresholds about the pitch angle. The r_{pn2} is the threshold for the distance between robot i and j. The absolute values of $\underline{\theta}_{p\_pn}$ and $\overline{\theta}_{p\_pn}$ are set to smaller values than the θ_{p_Σ}. Therefore, M_{pn2} sets a more narrow range about the pitch angle than Σ. The M_{pn2} detects the situation where two robots are positioned next to each other, as illustrated at M_{pn2} of Fig. 3. The M_{pn2} is calculated when just two robots satisfy $\Sigma = 1$. Each thresholds are set as follows; $\underline{\theta}_{p\_pn} = -45[\text{deg}]$, $\overline{\theta}_{p\_pn} = 15[\text{deg}]$, $r_{pn2} = 0.8$ [m].

The M_{pn3} detects the situation where three robots are positioned next to each other, as illustrated in Fig. 3. M_{pn3} is calculated by the following equations:

$$M_{pn3} = \sum_t^T f_{pn3,t} \tag{4}$$

$$f_{pn3,t} = \begin{cases} 1 & \text{if} \quad \text{robot } i, j, k(i \neq j \neq k) \text{ satisfy } \Sigma = 1 \quad \text{and} \\ & \theta_{pitch,i},\ \theta_{pitch,j},\ \theta_{pitch,k} \in (\underline{\theta}_{p\_pn},\ \overline{\theta}_{p\_pn}) \\ 0 & \text{otherwise.} \end{cases}$$

The values of $\underline{\theta}_{p\_pn}$ and $\overline{\theta}_{p\_pn}$ are the same as M_{pn2}. The M_{pn3} is calculated when just three robots satisfy $\Sigma = 1$. The M_{pn2} and M_{pn3} show the total timesteps that robots are placed like M_{pn2} and M_{pn3} in Fig. 3.

The M_{to} detects the turnovered robots, which is calculated by the following:

$$M_{to} = \frac{1}{N_r} \sum_t^T \sum_i^{N_r} f_{to,t,i} \tag{5}$$

$$f_{to,t,i} = \begin{cases} 1 & \text{if} \quad \theta_{r\_to} < |\theta_{roll,i}| \\ 0 & \text{otherwise} \end{cases}$$

where $\theta_{roll,i}$ is the roll angle of the ith robot. The θ_{r_to} is the threshold of the turnover. θ_{r_to} is set to 135[deg]. The M_{to} is calculated regardless of the Σ.

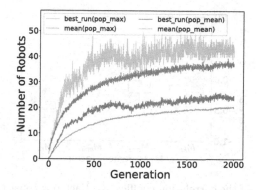

Fig. 5. The number of robots that have climbed the step. The dashed lines are mean values over ten evolution trials. The solid lines show the best run.

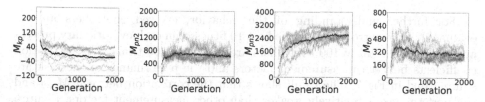

Fig. 6. The transitions of measurement factors. All measurement factors are calculated as the mean value of the population. Dashed lines are the results of each trial. The black solid line is the mean value over ten evolutionary trials.

4   Results and Discussion

In this paper, a total of ten evolutionary processes are conducted. Figure 5 shows the number of robots that have climbed the step in each generation. Figure 5 shows the evolutionary robotics approach succeeded to evolved a robot controller for achieving the task. Fig. 6 shows the transitions of measurement factors. Figure 4 shows the mean value of M_{kp} decreased. This means the robots stopped tilting forward at the front of the step and kept their posture flat or behaved like a slope. This behavior seems to be better for achieving the task because the robot tilting forward becomes an additional obstacle. The values of M_{pn2} and M_{pn3} are shown in Fig. 4 and Fig. 4. The value of M_{pn3} becomes higher than M_{pn2}. This shows that the situation of M_{pn3} occurred more frequently in evolutionary processes. Figure 4 shows that M_{to} increased steeply in the initial generations and slightly decreased after around 500 generations. In the initial generation, the robots cannot climb the step. Therefore, robots do not turn over frequently. Through the evolution process, robots tried to climb other robots or the step, and the risk of turnover also has increased. Subsequently, the turnovers are decreased by the selection pressure. The result of measurement factors shows that the robot obtained behavior to support other robots along with behavior to climb objects.

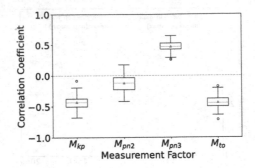

Fig. 7. The box plot of the correlation coefficients. Each box consists of 100 correlation coefficients. Each coefficient is calculated by 100 scores of each controller.

For further understanding of the behavior, evolved controllers are re-evaluated. The controllers with the best 10 fitnesses in each evolutionary process are selected. A total of 100 controllers are tested for 100 trials. The correlation coefficients between measurement factors and the performance of the task are summarized in Fig. 7. The result shows that the correlation between M_{pn2} and the performance is relatively weaker than other measurement factors. Figure 6 shows that the situation of M_{pn3} occurs more frequently than M_{pn2}. Therefore, M_{pn2} seems to have little effect on the performance. The remaining factors(M_{kp}, M_{pn3}, and M_{to}) indicate a correlation coefficient of approximately 0.4 with a positive or negative sign. Figure 7 shows that the robot behaviors corresponding to M_{kp}, M_{pn3}, and M_{to} contribute to achieving the task. However, correlations are not so strong.

5   Conclusions

This paper focuses on generating and analyzing a collective step-climbing behavior in a multi-legged robotic swarm. The evolutionary robotics approach is applied to designing a robot controller. The results show that the (μ, λ)-ES successfully evolved the robot controller. In addition, measurement factors are introduced to analyze the robot's behavior. The results show that the actions to support other robots for achieving the task are obtained. The results also show that the measurement factors are correlated to the achievement of the task.

This paper only focused on limited situations for supporting other robots. The next question is how many kinds of behavior are switched during the task, and what is the trigger for switching them. Additionally, contributions from the embodiment of robots will be discussed in future work.

Acknowledgments. This work was partially supported by the Hokkaido University Information Initiative Center and by JSPS KAKENHI Grant Number JP21J23095.

References

1. Beyer, H.G., Schwefel, H.P.: Evolution strategies-a comprehensive introduction. Nat. Comput. **1**(1), 3–52 (2002)
2. Brambilla, M., Ferrante, E., Birattari, M., Dorigo, M.: Swarm robotics: a review from the swarm engineering perspective. Swarm Intell. **7**(1), 1–41 (2013)
3. Coumans, E., Bai, Y.: Pybullet, a python module for physics simulation for games, robotics and machine learning. (2016–2021). https://pybullet.org
4. Dorigo, M., et al.: Evolving self-organizing behaviors for a swarm-bot. Autono. Rob. **17**(2–3), 223–245 (2004)
5. Eiben, A.E., Smith, J.E.: Introduction to Evolutionary Computing. Springer, Cham (2003)
6. Fukuda, T., Kawauchi, Y.: Cellular robotic system (CEBOT) as one of the realization of self-organizing intelligent universal manipulator. In: Proceedings., IEEE International Conference on Robotics and Automation, pp. 662–667. IEEE (1990)
7. Gauci, M., Chen, J., Dodd, T.J., Groß, R.: Evolving aggregation behaviors in multi-robot systems with binary sensors. In: Ani Hsieh, M., Chirikjian, G. (eds.) Distributed Autonomous Robotic Systems. STAR, vol. 104, pp. 355–367. Springer, Heidelberg (2014). https://doi.org/10.1007/978-3-642-55146-8_25
8. Groß, R., Dorigo, M.: Towards group transport by swarms of robots. Int. J. Bio-Inspired Comput. **1**(1–2), 1–13 (2009)
9. Hornby, G.S., Takamura, S., Yamamoto, T., Fujita, M.: Autonomous evolution of dynamic gaits with two quadruped robots. IEEE Trans. Robot. **21**(3), 402–410 (2005)
10. Malley, M., Haghighat, B., Houe, L., Nagpal, R.: Eciton robotica: Design and algorithms for an adaptive self-assembling soft robot collective. In: 2020 IEEE International Conference on Robotics and Automation (ICRA), pp. 4565–4571. IEEE (2020)
11. Morimoto, D., Hiraga, M., Shiozaki, N., Ohkura, K., Munetomo, M.: Evolving collective step-climbing behavior in multi-legged robotic swarm. Artif. Life Robot. **27**, 1–8 (2022). https://doi.org/10.1007/s10015-021-00725-8
12. Nolfi, S., Floreano, D.: Evolutionary Robotics: The Biology, Intelligence, and Technology of Self-organizing Machines. MIT press, Cambridge (2000)
13. Ozkan-Aydin, Y., Goldman, D.I.: Self-reconfigurable multilegged robot swarms collectively accomplish challenging terradynamic tasks. Sci. Rob. **6**(56), eabf1628 (2021)
14. Romanishin, J.W., Gilpin, K., Rus, D.: M-blocks: momentum-driven, magnetic modular robots. In: 2013 IEEE/RSJ International Conference on Intelligent Robots and Systems, pp. 4288–4295. IEEE (2013)
15. Scheidler, A., Brutschy, A., Ferrante, E., Dorigo, M.: The k-unanimity rule for self-organized decision-making in swarms of robots. IEEE Trans. Cybern. **46**(5), 1175–1188 (2015)
16. Sperati, V., Trianni, V., Nolfi, S.: Self-organised path formation in a swarm of robots. Swarm Intell. **5**(2), 97–119 (2011)
17. Valentini, G., Ferrante, E., Hamann, H., Dorigo, M.: Collective decision with 100 Kilobots: speed versus accuracy in binary discrimination problems. Auton. Agents Multi-Agent Syst. **30**(3), 553–580 (2016)
18. Valsalam, V.K., Hiller, J., MacCurdy, R., Lipson, H., Miikkulainen, R.: Constructing controllers for physical multilegged robots using the ENSO neuroevolution approach. Evol. Intell. **5**(1), 45–56 (2012)

Modeling Immune Search Through the Lymphatic Network

Jannatul Ferdous[1]([⊠]), G. Matthew Fricke[1,2], and Melanie E. Moses[1,3,4]

[1] Department of Computer Science, University of New Mexico, Albuquerque, USA
jannat@unm.edu
[2] Center for Advanced Research Computing, University of New Mexico, Albuquerque, USA
[3] Biology Department, University of New Mexico, Albuquerque, USA
[4] Santa Fe Institute, Santa Fe, USA

Abstract. The lymphatic system is a networked structure used by billions of immune cells, including T cells and Dendritic cells, to locate and identify invading pathogens. Dendritic cells carry pieces of pathogens to the nearest lymph node, and T cells travel through the lymphatic vessels and search within lymph nodes to find them. Here we investigate how the topology of the lymphatic network affects the time for this search to be completed. Building on prior work that maps out the human lymphatic network, we develop and extend a method to infer the lymphatic network topology of mice. We compare search times for the modeled and observed topologies and show that they are similar to each other and consistent with observed immune response times. This is relevant for translating immune response times in mice, where most experimental work occurs, into expected immune response times in humans. Our analysis predicts that for large systemic infections, the topology of the lymphatic network allows immune response times to remain fast even as animal mass increases by orders of magnitude. This work advances our understanding of how the structure of the lymphatic network supports the swarm intelligence of the immune system. It also elucidates general principles relating swarm size and organization to search speed.

1 Introduction

Adaptive immunity evolved in vertebrates to recognize and remember novel pathogens, enabling a faster response time to subsequent infections. In contrast to most biological rates, which are systematically slower in larger animals (scaling as $M^{1/4}$, where M is body mass [2,11,26]), the adaptive immune response time is relatively invariant across several orders of magnitude of mammalian body mass [4,6]. Immune response is a swarm intelligence problem with billions of interacting agents searching for pathogens without central control, and it is a model for scale-invariant search in swarms.

T cells are adaptive immune cells that can recognize novel pathogens in lymph nodes, and then replicate and disperse into tissues to find and kill cells

© Springer Nature Switzerland AG 2022
M. Dorigo et al. (Eds.): ANTS 2022, LNCS 13491, pp. 332–340, 2022.
https://doi.org/10.1007/978-3-031-20176-9_30

infected by those pathogens. The movement of T cells through the lymphatic system increases contact with antigens and amplifies the immune response [23]. Similar to eusocial insects, information transmission in this liquid brain [21] is mediated through direct agent contact and chemical signals among agents that navigate complex and varied environments [16].

Each T cell can bind to a particular subset of cognate antigens. Dendritic cells (DCs) gather antigen from tissues, travel to and enter nearby lymph nodes (LNs) through the lymphatic network, and display the antigen on their surfaces. T cells search LNs for DCs displaying cognate antigen, and if a match is made, the T cells activate, proliferate, and circulate to the site of infection where they kill infected cells. The time it takes to initiate an adaptive immune response depends on two factors: 1) the speed with which T cells travel through the lymphatic system to LNs containing DCs displaying antigen, and 2) how quickly T cells find those DCs once inside the LN.

In this work, we analyze T cell travel time through the lymphatic network to find DC's in mice and humans by extending the algorithm of Savinkov et al. [20], that models only the human lymphatic networks. While most lab studies that show how the immune system works are conducted on mice, most of the literature on modeling the lymphatic network is based on humans. The lack of data makes it challenging to build a general model of lymphatic networks for mice and other mammals.The model parameters are updated based on best-fit values by comparing empirically observed anatomical data with the graph resulting from the algorithm. We expand the network metrics used by the algorithm to better fit the model to empirical data. Using the inferred network model we compute the expected time for T cells to find LNs containing DCs presenting cognate antigen. We run a random walk search on the simulated and observed lymphatic networks to find the average time T cells need to reach the LNs containing cognate DCs. We find that the generated and actual anatomical graphs have similar statistics. The resulting search time over the network is similar in mice and humans for systematic or mass-dependent infections, but it is longer in humans than in mice for small infections that only reach a single LN.

2   Related Work

Several studies have modeled the human lymphatic system [19,20,24]. In [24], the authors use computational geometry to build graph models of the human lymphatic network in order to explain the general features underlying the 3D structural organization of the lymphatic system. The model is based on available anatomical data (from the PlasticBoy project [1]), which estimates the lymphatic system's structure and analyzes the topological properties of the resulting models. In [20], the authors developed and implemented a computational algorithm to generate the algorithm-based random graph of the human lymphatic system. Some fundamental characteristics of the observed data-based graph [24] and the algorithm-based graph of human lymphatic system graph models are analyzed.

In [27] Wiegel and Perelson hypothesize that LN number and size evolved to minimize two competing goals: the time to transport antigen from an infected

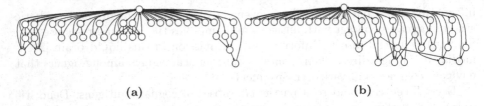

Fig. 1. Comparison of simulated and observed lympahtic networks. **(a)** Mouse lymphatic network graph based on anatomical data with 36 nodes and 49 edges. edges. **(b)** Example simulated graph of the mouse lymphatic system. Algorithm parameters: $N_v = 36$, $N_{inp} = 13$, $N_l = 5$, $P_e = 0.851$, $P_o = 0.66$.

area to the nearest LN and the time for immune cells to find the antigen inside the LN. Banerjee and Moses [3] use an ODE model to estimate that, empirically, immune response times are independent of host body size.

3   Methods

3.1   Lymphatic Network Simulation Algorithm

Savinkov et al. [20] developed an algorithm that generates a random directed human lymphatic network graph with no cycle from a reference human graph. We extend their work by adding another step to the algorithm to simulate T cells traveling through the circulatory system to enter LNs. The steps are given in Algorithm 1. We used data from [9] to create a reference graph of mice to compare with the simulated graph. Out of 5 input parameters in the algorithm, three parameters, number of nodes N_v, number of input nodes N_{inp}, and number of layers N_l are explicitly set to match the anatomy-based graph's properties. Based on the comparison metrics characterizing the topology of an anatomy-based graph (described in Sect. 3.2), the value of the other two parameters, probability of new edge creation P_e at each step and probability that the created edge connects nodes from different layers P_o, are set to produce graphs with similar topological structures.

3.2   Comparing Simulated Graphs to Observation

We have used the following topological properties defined in [20] to compare the observed graph with the current state of the simulated graph for humans and mice: *The number of input nodes N_{inp}, Maximum degree of graph ΔG, Girth of the graph, g, The diameter of the graph, D, Radius of the graph, r, Average path length, I_G, The energy of the graph, E_n, The spectral radius of the graph, ρ, Edge density of the graph, ρ_d, The clustering coefficient, C (transitivity)*. We also introduced the following graph properties to the list: *Number of separators, n_{sep}*: is the number of nodes removal of which disconnects the graph n_{deg_i}: is the number of nodes with degree i. G_l: is the average degree of of nodes in each layer l and, n_l: is the number of nodes in each layer l.

Since number of node connections and layers are larger in larger animals, n_{deg_i} and n_l are also larger. Thus, the objective function has more parameters in larger animals. To produce a similar graph that matches these topological properties, we tune the parameters P_e and P_o. We collect these parameter values for the minimum value of the objective function, ω. For a number of properties, the objective function is defined as:

$$\omega = \sum_{i=1}^{a} \left(\frac{s_i(G) - s_i(G*)}{s_i(G*)} \right)^2 \tag{1}$$

where $s(G) = (n, m, n_{inp}, \Delta G, g, D, r, I_G, E_n, \rho, \rho_d, C, n_{sep}, n_{deg_1}, .., n_{deg_{max}}, G_1, .., G_l, n_1, .., n_l)^T$

This objective function penalizes the topological discrepancies of graph G from the target graph $G*$ and weighs them with $(s_i(G*))^{-2}$ to bring discrepancies of different components of vector s to a single scale.

3.3   Search Algorithm

To run the search algorithm, we randomly choose a source node n_s from which the T cell initiate a random walk through the graph. We consider that the LNs that contain matching DC, designated $V' \in V$, are distributed within the lymphatic network in three ways for different kinds of infections.

- *Random Systemic:* Systemic infections can spread to multiple lymph nodes throughout the body, i.e., in HIV. For this case, we assume that the V' are distributed randomly over the lymphatic network.
- *Clustered:* A cluster of LN can contain antigen if an animal gets a vaccine injection with inoculation dose adjusted to size, or if an animal breathes in a respiratory virus where the amount of inhaled virus is proportional to lung size. For such cases, we distribute the V' nodes in clusters. We randomly pick one node and run Breadth-First Search (BFS) to make the clusters. We exclude the circulation node 0 from being in the cluster.
- *Single:* If an animal steps on a thorn and gets a local infection of a fixed size, or a mosquito bite transmits an illness into the blood, then the same small amount of infection is injected into the animal regardless of its size. For both of these cases, we randomly pick one node $|V'| = 1$ that contain cognate DC.

We compute the time it takes for each T cell using a random walk to reach the first LNs that contains DCs holding cognate antigen. We follow Perelson and Weigel's prediction that the number of LNs in mammals scale with $\propto M^{\frac{1}{2}}$ [18], for the random systemic and clustered scenarios, $|V'| \propto M^{\frac{1}{2}}$. For the uniform random and clustered V', we assume the number of LNs that are bearing the cognate antigen-bearing DCs ($|V'|$ are 5 and 275 in mice and humans, respectively representing 7% and 3.6% of LN.

Table 1. Summary statistics for observed and simulated graphs of mice and humans characterizing their topological properties. For the predicted graphs, we present the statistics obtained over 10,000 graphs for human and 500 for mice.

Parameter	Mice observed graph	Mice simulated graph	Human observed graph	Human simulated graph
$G(n, m)$	(36, 53)	(36, 49)	(996, 1117)	(996, 1029)
N_{inp}	13	13	357	357
Maximum degree, ΔG	24	26	8	16
Girth, g	3	3	3	4
Diameter, D	4	4	40	39.96
Radius, r	3	3	30	28
Average path length, l_G	1.34	1.42	12.79	15.3
Energy, E_n	37.17	36.40	1224.5	1190
Spectral radius, ρ	5.81	5.91	3.51	4.18
Edge density, ρ_d	0.04	0.04	0.001127	0.001038
Clustering coefficient, C	0.12	0.11	0.027	0.0004
Number of separators, n_{sep}	5	9	401	496

4 Results

4.1 Modeled Lymphatic Network

We run the extended algorithm to generate lymphatic networks for humans and mice. Figure 1a, and Fig. 1b show the resulting observed and simulated graphs for mice. The first three parameters of the algorithm for mice are collected from [9]. For P_0 and P_e, we take their values that give the objective function's minimum value in Eq. (1). They are compared numerically in Table 1 based on the topological properties, described in Sect. 3.2.

From Table 1 we can see that the properties are very similar for observed and simulated graphs for mice and humans. Some properties vary slightly, but the statistic from the objective function gives the overall best match of the simulated graph to the observed graph. We collect the time data the DC takes in humans and mice respectively to reach the LN containing cognate T cell from the infected area after running the random walk, shown in Fig. 2. The time for T cells to encounter a target LN is shorter in humans than in mice for random and clustered target LNs. That is because there are more target LN in humans, and we consider only the time to find the first target LN. The search to find a single V', takes much longer in humans because there are many more LN in humans (996) compared to mice (36).

4.2 Predicted Time

We compare the search time of a single T cell to find a target LN to actual immune response times to determine if our model predictions are reasonable. We calculate times from hop counts and estimates of the time between hops,

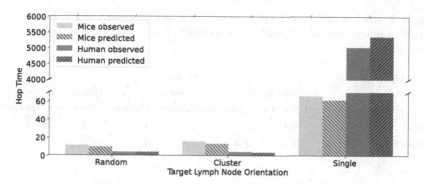

Fig. 2. Average Number of Hops to Find a LN with Cognate Antigen after running the random walk on 500 observed and algorithm-based graph of mice and human. The **random bars** represent that $|V'|$ are randomly distributed over the graphs. There are 275 LNs containing the cognate T cell out of 996 LNs in human and 5 LNs out of 36 LNs in mice. The **cluster bars** represent $|V'|$ are distributed in clusters over the graphs. There are 275 LNs containing the cognate T cell out of 996 LNs in human and 5 LNs out of 36 LNs in mice. The **single bars** represent that there is only one LN ($|V'| = 1$) chosen at random carrying the cognate T cell out of 996 LNs in human and 36 LNs in mice.

shown in Table 2. Since we only model a portion of the overall adaptive immune response, that is, the time taken for a single T cell to conduct a random walk through the lymphatic network to find an infection, we cannot predict the speed of the overall immune response. For mice LN mean residence time in LN per hop is approximately 13 h [23], and for sheep 19 h [14]. Since sheep and humans masses are similar (40 kg–160 kg for sheep [5] and 43 kg–140 kg for humans) [25], we approximate residence times in humans with those of sheep. Multiplying these residence times by the hop counts from Fig. 2 results in Table 2. We find that the predicted time for a single T cell to find a LN with cognate antigen is on the same order as observed immune response times for systemic infections in mice and humans. According to [7,10,15,17,22] the mean adaptive immune response time in mice for influenza and LCMV infection is 5.3 days and in humans for SARS-CoV2 its 5.1 days [8,12,13]. This means that for systemic or whole-organ infections (where the number of LN increases with body mass), typical T cells can find the a LN with antigen during the time available to proliferate and amplify the growing immune response. In contrast, the time to find a single LN with antigen is orders of magnitude longer. This suggests that not many T cells would reach the single LN during the time of adaptive immune amplification. However, in small infections, a global response is likely not to be needed. We expect the T cells that reside in the local LN to be sufficient to respond to small local infection [3]. The actual timing depends on many factors, including the fraction of LN containing target DCs, V' and the number of cognate T cells searching for those DCs. We do not consider lymph vessel or blood residency times in these estimates, because those times are small relative to the time within LN [23].

Table 2. Predicted times for T cell to enter LN containing cognate DC based on hop count. *H. sapiens* and *M. musculus* LN residence times are taken to be 19 h. Time given in days (d).

| | M. musculus | | | | H. sapiens | | | |
| | Observed | | Simulated | | Observed | | Simulated | |
	Random	Clustered	Random	Clustered	Random	Clustered	Random	Clustered
Hops	11	15	9.3	13	3.8	4.1	3.9	3.4
Time	5.9 d	8.3 d	5 d	7 d	3 d	3.3 d	3 d	2.7 d

5   Discussion

We simulated the lymphatic network for mice, ran a random walk process on the resulting graph, and predicted the time for a typical T cell, searching that graph for a LN with cognate antigen. We examined three scenarios corresponding to different infection patterns: random systemic infection, clustered infection, and infection in a single LN. Our results show that the time for each T cell to search for clustered and randomly distributed systemic infections in lymph nodes are on the same order as observed immune response times to systemic infections such as influenza and COVID-19 in humans and mice. In contrast, the time for a T cell to find a single LN is far longer, requiring thousands of network hops that would take years of search time in humans or a month in a mouse. However, we suggest that such long search times for small localized infections may be adaptive. For systemic infections that require a large response, T cells quickly discover LN with DCs presenting antigen, but T cells are not recruited to small local infections when they are not needed – local infections are responded to only by the small number of T cells that already reside in the lymph node where the infection is presented on DC.

This analysis shows that the physical structure of the lymphatic network facilitates scale invariant immune response. For large and systemic infections that require a large and fast response, T cells navigate the lymphatic network to find infected LN equally fast in large and small animals. In one sense, the adaptive immune system exemplifies the kind of decentralized control typical in swarm intelligence: immune response is fast and adaptable based on the independent action of billions of immune cells that communicate locally and navigate complex tissue environments. However, the decentralized search is constrained by the network structure of the lymphatic system that provides a form of global guidance in physical space. That structure contributes to the extraordinary scalability of response.

Acknowledgements. We thank the UNM Center for Advanced Research Computing, supported in part by the NSF, for high performance computing resources, and NSF awards 2030037 & 2020247 for funding.

References

1. Human lymphatic system 3D model. https://www.plasticboy.co.uk/store/Human_Lymphatic_System_no_textures.html. Accessed 30 Apr 2022
2. Banavar, J.R., et al.: A general basis for quarter-power scaling in animals. Proc. Natl. Acad. Sci. **107**(36), 15816–15820 (2010)
3. Banerjee, S., Moses, M.: Scale invariance of immune system response rates and times: perspectives on immune system architecture and implications for artificial immune systems. Swarm Intell. **4**(4), 301–318 (2010). https://doi.org/10.1007/s11721-010-0048-2
4. Banerjee, S., Perelson, A.S., Moses, M.: Modelling the effects of phylogeny and body size on within-host pathogen replication and immune response. J. R. Soc. Interface **14**(136), 20170479 (2017)
5. Burrill, M.J.: Sheep. In: World Book. World Book Inc (2004)
6. Cable, J.M., Enquist, B.J., Moses, M.E.: The allometry of host-pathogen interactions. PLoS ONE **2**(11), e1130 (2007)
7. De Boer, R.J., Homann, D., Perelson, A.S.: Different dynamics of cd4+ and cd8+ t cell responses during and after acute lymphocytic choriomeningitis virus infection. J. Immunol. **171**(8), 3928–3935 (2003)
8. Iyer, A.S., et al.: Dynamics and significance of the antibody response to sars-cov-2 infection. MedRxiv (2020)
9. Kawashima, Y., Sugimura, M., Hwang, Y.C., Kudo, N.: The lymph system in mice. Jpn. J. Vet. Res. **12**(4), 69–78 (1964)
10. Keating, R.: Potential killers exposed: tracking endogenous influenza-specific cd8+ t cells. Immunol. Cell Biol. **96**(10), 1104–1119 (2018)
11. Kleiber, M.: Body size and metabolic rate. Physiol. Rev. **27**(4), 511–541 (1947)
12. Koblischke, M., et al.: Dynamics of cd4 t cell and antibody responses in covid-19 patients with different disease severity. Front. Med. **7** (2020)
13. Lei, Q., et al.: Antibody dynamics to SARS-COV-2 in asymptomatic COVID-19 infections. Allergy **76**(2), 551–561 (2020)
14. McDaniel, M.M., Ganusov, V.V.: Estimating residence times of lymphocytes in ovine lymph nodes. Front. Immunol. **10**, 1492 (2019)
15. Miao, H.: Quantifying the early immune response and adaptive immune response kinetics in mice infected with influenza a virus. J. Virol. **84**(13), 6687–6698 (2010)
16. Moses, M.E., Cannon, J.L., Gordon, D.M., Forrest, S.: Distributed adaptive search in t cells: lessons from ants. Front. Immunol. **10**, 1357 (2019)
17. Owens, S.L., Osebold, J., Zee, Y.: Dynamics of b-lymphocytes in the lungs of mice exposed to aerosolized influenza virus. Infect. Immun. **33**(1), 231–238 (1981)
18. Perelson, A.S., Wiegel, F.W.: Scaling aspects of lymphocyte trafficking. J. Theor. Biol. **257**(1), 9–16 (2009)
19. Reddy, N.P., Krouskop, T.A., Newell, P.H., Jr.: A computer model of the lymphatic system. Comput. Biol. Med. **7**(3), 181–197 (1977)
20. Savinkov, R., Grebennikov, D., Puchkova, D., Chereshnev, V., Sazonov, I., Bocharov, G.: Graph theory for modeling and analysis of the human lymphatic system. Mathematics **8**(12), 2236 (2020)
21. Solé, R., Moses, M., Forrest, S.: Liquid brains, solid brains (2019)
22. Tamura, S.i., Kurata, T.: Defense mechanisms against influenza virus infection in the respiratory tract mucosa. Jpn. J. Infect. Dis. **57**(6), 236–47 (2004)
23. Textor, J., et al.: Random migration and signal integration promote rapid and robust t cell recruitment. PLoS Comput. Biol. **10**(8), e1003752 (2014)

24. Tretyakova, R., Savinkov, R., Lobov, G., Bocharov, G.: Developing computational geometry and network graph models of human lymphatic system. Computation **6**(1), 1 (2017)
25. Walpole, S.C., Prieto-Merino, D., Edwards, P., Cleland, J., Stevens, G., Roberts, I.: The weight of nations: an estimation of adult human biomass. BMC Pub. Health **12**(1), 1–6 (2012)
26. West, G.B., Brown, J.H., Enquist, B.J.: A general model for the origin of allometric scaling laws in biology. Science **276**(5309), 122–126 (1997)
27. Wiegel, F.W., Perelson, A.S.: Some scaling principles for the immune system. Immunol. Cell Biol. **82**(2), 127–131 (2004)

Optimization of a Self-organized Collective Motion in a Robotic Swarm

Mazen Bahaidarah[1,2]([✉]), Fatemeh Rekabi Bana[3], Ali Emre Turgut[4],
Ognjen Marjanovic[1], and Farshad Arvin[3]

[1] Department of Electrical and Electronic Engineering,
The University of Manchester, Manchester, UK
mazen.bahaidarah@manchester.ac.uk

[2] Department of Electrical and Electronics Engineering, King Abdulaziz University,
Jeddah, Saudi Arabia

[3] Department of Computer Science, Durham University, Durham, UK

[4] Center for Robotics and AI (ROMER), Middle East Technical University,
Ankara, Turkey

Abstract. A novel collective organization method is proposed in this paper to improve the performance of the former Active Elastic Sheet (AES) algorithm by applying the Particle Swarm Optimization technique. Replacing the manual parameters tuning of the AES model with an evolutionary-based method leads the swarm to remain stable meanwhile the agents make a perfect alignment exploiting less energy. The proposed algorithm utilizes a hybrid cost function including the alignment error, interaction force, and time to consider all the important criteria for perfect swarm behavior. The Monte-Carlo simulation evaluated the algorithm's performance to establish its effectiveness in different situations.

1 Introduction

Flocking is a prevalent collective behavior that can be observed in many phenomena [4]. The main idea is a group of organisms moving together cohesively to form a particular shape using local interactions. Reynolds [18] has precisely described the three key factors to attain the flocking mechanism, which are: alignment, separation, and cohesion.

Vicsek model [19], presented in 1995, developed based on the self-propelled particles approach to use orientations for velocity alignment and steering the agents towards their neighbours' headings. Several collective motion models [5,6,11] have considered the Vicsek model and mostly depend on sharing orientations between the robots. Other studies, in contrast, did not rely on exchanging robots' orientation explicitly. For example in [15], collective motion is attained due to pairwise repulsive forces and implicitly leads to the velocity-alignment rule. In [10], isotropic agents interact using the inelastic collision method without sharing orientation among agents. Although the approach is applicable for simple systems, many practical challenges, such as energy consumption, communication issues, and obstacle avoidance capability, persuade

© Springer Nature Switzerland AG 2022
M. Dorigo et al. (Eds.): ANTS 2022, LNCS 13491, pp. 341–349, 2022.
https://doi.org/10.1007/978-3-031-20176-9_31

researchers to develop more sophisticated methods to improve collective behavior in a realistic environment.

Ferrante et al. [8,9] introduced the Active Elastic Sheet (AES) flocking model developed based on an elasticity approach. This approach is a position-based model. Exchanging the relative positions solely between the neighbours is beneficial in practical scenarios. Therefore, several studies have investigated the feasibility of the AES method in swarm robotic systems. In [20], the AES model is applied using a swarm of seven e-pucks robots to achieve self-organized collective motion in a real-world scenario. This paper presents remarkable results in the presence of measurement noise. However, it does not consider a specific level of accuracy or energy consumption, and the suggested algorithm is not capable of avoiding the obstacles merely. Accordingly, other studies endeavour to add the obstacle avoidance feature utilising external forces related to the distance between the robots and obstacles [2,14]. Furthermore, in [17], two external forces are added to the AES model to overcome the same problem. Although these studies demonstrated substantial improvements regarding the original algorithm, they did not investigate the effect of critical parameters on precision and required power for long-term applications. In contrast, in [3], the AES model was applied to a group of e-pucks using Webots simulator [16] to study the effect of other factors, such as time and population size and investigated the scalability of this approach. Nevertheless, this study did not consider energy consumption a constraining factor for long-term scenarios.

Evolutionary techniques could play a significant role in optimizing the swarm behavior by selecting the best value of the controller parameters to reduce the robots' energy consumption. The Particle Swarm Optimization (PSO) algorithm [12] is widely used because of its simplicity, rapid convergence rate, and the low computational burden. Several researchers have utilised PSO to tune the flocking controllers' parameters and optimize the swarm's self-organization behavior [13]. In [1], PSO is used in the multi-agent system to nominate an agent in a cluster as the best solution to facilitate obtaining the system's leader afterwards to achieve collective motion. These results imply the PSO's capability for optimization purposes considered in this paper.

Accordingly, this paper attempts to establish the collective performance improvement utilising PSO on the original AES model [8] and the optimized version using Tabu Continuous Ant Colony System (TCACS) [17]. The suggested approach generates a tuning strategy for specific parameters affecting the energy consumption and accuracy level by applying the PSO. As a result, the main contributions of this paper are summarised as follows: i) State and solve a hybrid optimization problem to minimize the required power and maximize precision using the PSO, ii) Establish the effectiveness of the suggested optimization method with the Monte-Carlo simulation approach.

2   Collective Motion

This section presents the theoretical background utilised to develop the optimized AES model for collective control of a swarm system.

2.1   Active Elastic Sheet

This paper considers a swarm system of N robots that move in a two-dimensional arena, where the motion of ith robot is determined by attraction-repulsion forces originated from its closest neighbours. The robots' positions $\vec{x}_i$ and orientations θ_i can be calculated mathematically [8,9]. The robots are deployed in a perfect environment and accordingly the noise level is negligible regarding to original signals. Therefore, it is possible to eliminate the disturbance terms and make a modified model as presented in Eq. (1) as follows:

$$\dot{\vec{x}}_i = (v_0 + \alpha \, \vec{F}_i.\hat{n}_i)\hat{n}_i \, , \; \dot{\theta}_i = \beta \, \vec{F}_i.\hat{n}_i^{\perp} \, , \; \hat{n}_i = \left[\cos(\theta_i) \, \sin(\theta_i) \right]^T , \qquad (1)$$

According to Eq. (1), α and β are inverse transitional and rotational parameters, and v_0 is a biasing speed. $\hat{n}_i$ is a unit vector pointing parallel to the heading direction of the robot i, and $\hat{n}_i^{\perp}$ is a unit vector pointing perpendicular to it. The interactions between robot i and its neighbours s_i will generate a linear force $\vec{F}_i$ to maintain the distance among the swarm. This force can be obtained using Eq. (2):

$$\vec{F}_i = \sum_{j \in S_i} -\frac{k}{l_{ij}}(|\vec{r}_{ij}| - l_{ij})\frac{\vec{r}_{ij}}{|\vec{r}_{ij}|} \, , \; \psi = \frac{1}{N} \left\| \sum_{i=1}^{N} \hat{n}_i \right\| , \qquad (2)$$

where, $\frac{k}{l_{ij}}$ is the spring constant, and l_{ij} is the natural length that connects robots i and j. The distance between i^{th} and j^{th} robots is represented as $\vec{r}_{ij} = \vec{x}_j - \vec{x}_i$. The ith robot is connected with its neighbouring robots S_i initially, through virtual springs by predetermining the formation of the robots at $t = 0$ s. Therefore, this spring connection will remain constant, regardless of the change in distance between robots during the experiments.

The alignment of the entire group determines the collective flock's performance. The degree of alignment ψ is the metric used to show the alignment status of the robots. The minimum value, ($\psi = 0$), indicates the robots are non-aligned, and the maximum, ($\psi = 1$), means they are aligned perfectly.

According to [17], two main objectives should to be applied to maintain the stability of the collective motion. Minimising the total force of each robot that leads, and maximising the degree of alignment of the entire swarm. The PSO algorithm is applied to tune the decision parameters α and β of the AES model and achieve these two objectives.

2.2   Parameters Optimization

This section expresses the optimization procedure based on PSO approach and the mechanism of the objective function.

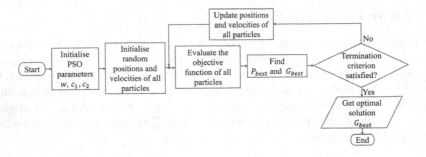

Fig. 1. The flowchart of PSO algorithm used in this study.

Particle Swarm Optimization (PSO). Each particle in a swarm is placed at a random location in a search space to seek the optimal solution. The positions and velocities of the particles will be updated to obtain better objective function values. Therefore, the position x and the velocity v of each particle can be calculated as follows:

$$v_{k+1}^i = w \, v_k^i + c_1 \, r_1 \, (P_{best} - x_k^i) + c_2 \, r_2 \, (G_{best} - x_k^i), \tag{3}$$

The new particle position is calculated as $(x_{k+1}^i = x_k^i + v_{k+1}^i)$ for $i = \{1, 2, 3, \ldots, N\}$ where N is the swarm size, and $k = \{1, 2, 3, \ldots, T\}$ where T is the number of iterations. r_1 and r_2 are random parameters between 0 and 1 to make the PSO algorithm acts naturally. P_{best} is best local position of a particle i, and G_{best} is the best global position of the entire swarm. The most significant control parameters are: i) the inertia weight w, ii) acceleration constant c_1 that is related to the local best, and iii) acceleration constant c_2 that is related to the global best. The three control parameters have remarkable influence to the PSO algorithm performance therefore, adjusting the proper values of the parameters is crucial. Clerc and Kennedy [7] have introduced a mathematical model to calculate the appropriate values of w, c_1 and c_2 by defining new parameters called Constriction Coefficients as presented in Eq. (4):

$$\chi = \frac{2 \, k}{|2 - \phi - \sqrt{\phi^2 - 4 \, \phi}|}, \tag{4}$$

where k value is any value from 0 to 1, and $\phi = \phi_1 + \phi_2$ in which $(\phi > 4)$. So, the controller parameters will be obtained according to Eq. (4) as follows: the inertia weight $w = \chi$, first acceleration constant $c_1 = \chi \, \phi_1$, and the second acceleration constant $c_2 = \chi \, \phi_2$. The flowchart of PSO mechanism is shown in Fig. 1.

Objective Function. Designing an objective function to optimize a particular system is the key factor that influence the improvement of the system performance. In this paper, three objectives are considered to enhance the AES flocking behavior: i) Minimising the attractive/repulsive forces of each robot, ii) Maximising the degree of alignment, and iii) minimising the alignment time. As a result,

the mathematical expression of the uniform minimisation objective function is
as follows:

$$J = \sum_{t=0}^{T_{max}} \left[w_1 \sum_{i=1}^{N} F_i + w_2 \, \psi_{error} + w_3 \, t^2 \right] \tag{5}$$

As depicted in Eq. (5), T_{max} is the simulation time in seconds and N is the
swarm size. F_i is calculated using Eq. (2), and $\psi_{error} = (1 - \psi)^2$ is the difference
between the degree of alignment at time t that is calculated in Eq. (2) and 1
which represents the maximum value of alignment. w_1, w_2, and w_3 are weighting
parameters of the objective function.

2.3 Experimental Setup

The "Mobile Robotics Simulation Toolbox" was used in Matlab to investigate
the performance of the collective motion. The robots locations are initialised with
random orientations to form a rectangular shape in an $L \times L$ arena. Accordingly,
robot's status in the arena is represented as $[x, y, \theta]^T$. The essential parameters
have been initialised, such as the swarm size $N = \{60, 100\}$, arena length $L =$
70 m, the number of steps $T_{max} = 300$ s, sensing radius $R = 7.1$ m.

Some assumptions are considered in this work: i) the simulations are conducted without taking into account the effect of noises, ii) l_{ij} is set as the initial
distance between robot i and robot j. In this paper, a swarm of $N = \{60, 100\}$
robots are located in a square arena $L \times L$ in a random orientations and predefined positions to form a rectangle shape. The experiments are conducted for
50 simulations, where each simulation runs from $t = 0$ to T_{max}. In addition, the
configuration of PSO parameters is set to tune the decision parameters of the
AES model α and β. The maximum iteration number to explore in the search
space is 100, and the particle size is 200. For each point in the search space,
the objective function takes the force F_i and degree of alignment ψ as inputs,
and the cost values are output. Then, the PSO algorithm evaluates these values
to obtain the optimal solution. Three weighting parameters are defined in the
objective function w_1, w_2, and w_3.

To verify the development of the AES method after applying the PSO algorithm, we compare the performance of the original configuration of AES [8] and
the optimized version of AES using TCACS [17].

3 Results and Discussion

This study aims to reduce the required power consumption by maximising the
degree of alignment and minimising the force between the robots. Applying
the PSO algorithm resulted in the values for parameters as: $\alpha = 0.18082$ and
$\beta = 0.81649$. In the experiments, the robots mainly deployed within a rectangle
shape for $N = \{60, 100\}$ robots.

This configuration gives a noticeable optimized outcomes compared to the results obtained from the previous methods presented in [8,17]. The values of w_1, w_2, and w_3 are set according to the variation bound and the importance of the corresponding criteria in the objective function.

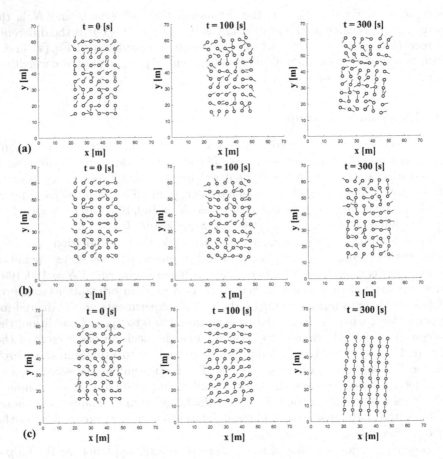

Fig. 2. The collective motion of 60 robots for three different AES configurations: (a) Original parameters, (b) TCACS parameters, and (c) PSO parameters.

Figure 2 demonstrates three different simulations to compare the configurations mentioned previously. In Fig. 2(a), AES model runs using $\alpha = 0.01$ and $\beta = 0.12$ as suggested in [8]. It can be seen that the flock struggle to move cohesively. In Fig. 2(b), AES model runs using $\alpha = 0.066$ and $\beta = 0.97$ as suggested in [17]. It shows remarkable improvement in comparison to Fig. 2(a), where shape of the swarm stays steady, but at $t = 300$ s, the robots are not fully aligned. In Fig. 2(c), it shows significant enhancement by using the optimized parameters, $\alpha = 0.18082$ and $\beta = 0.81649$. It is clear that the swarm alignment reaches the best point in $t = 300$ s. The optimized AES model outperforms the other two simulations, where the collective motion is fulfilled accurately.

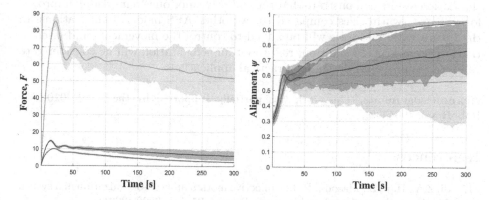

Fig. 3. The results of 50 simulations of F and ψ for original AES (green), optimized AES with TCACS (blue), and optimized AES with PSO (red) for $N = 100$ robots. (Color figure online)

In Fig. 3, the green line represents the original AES model configurations, the blue line depicts the AES model optimized by TCACS, and the red line demonstrates the AES model using PSO for $N = 100$. The results of all implementations that are conducted in this study will be available in GitHub[1]. The experiment is conducted for 50 simulations, each of which runs for $t = 300$ s. Hence, in these shaded plots, the middle line is the mean value, the upper and lower bounds introduce the third quartile and the first quartile respectively. Figure 3, shows that the results of optimized parameters by PSO outperforms the other two configurations, where the minimum value of the force is $F = 2.51$ and the maximum value of alignment is $\psi = 0.95$. The presented results also suggest exceptional robustness against the variation in environmental conditions causes different initial alignments for the robots. According to the results, it is evident that applying the optimized decision parameters, reduced the required power for the AES model to manipulate the swarm collective behaviour as precise as possible. Furthermore, reducing the internal energy level causes a much smoother dynamic response and prevents the system from unnecessary transient oscillations and makes the system work more coherently.

4   Conclusion

This paper addressed the development of the AES model that achieves the collective motion using an optimized elasticity approach for a swarm robotic system. This study aims to utilize the PSO algorithm to optimize the value of AES

---

[1] https://github.com/mbahaidarah/AES_PSO.

decision parameters α and β, which will improve the robots' motion, alignment, and power consumption. Reducing the interaction forces between the robots decreases the required energy and increases the swarm stability. The numerical simulation results demonstrate that the collective motion is remarkably improved for different swarm sizes compared to two other AES model configurations. In the future, external forces will be added to control the movements and orientations of the swarm. In addition, real-robot implementation will be considered to validate the proposed design for practical applications.

Acknowledgements. This work was partially supported by the EU H2020-FET RoboRoyale (964492).

References

1. Ali, Z.A., Han, Z., Masood, R.J.: Collective motion and self-organization of a swarm of UAVs: a cluster-based architecture. Sensors **21**(11), 3820 (2021)
2. Ban, Z., Hu, J., Lennox, B., Arvin, F.: Self-organised collision-free flocking mechanism in heterogeneous robot swarms. Mob. Netw. Appl. **26**, 1–11 (2021)
3. Ban, Z., West, C., Lennox, B., Arvin, F.: Self-organised flocking with simulated homogeneous robotic swarm. In: Gao, H., Wang, X., Iqbal, M., Yin, Y., Yin, J., Gu, N. (eds.) CollaborateCom 2020. LNICST, vol. 350, pp. 3–17. Springer, Cham (2021). https://doi.org/10.1007/978-3-030-67540-0_1
4. Camazine, S., Deneubourg, J.L., Franks, N.R., Sneyd, J., Theraula, G., Bonabeau, E.: Self-organization in biological systems. In: Self-organization in Biological Systems. Princeton University Press (2020)
5. Cavagna, A., et al.: Flocking and turning: a new model for self-organized collective motion. J. Stat. Phys. **158**(3), 601–627 (2015)
6. Chaté, H., Ginelli, F., Grégoire, G., Raynaud, F.: Collective motion of self-propelled particles interacting without cohesion. Phys. Rev. E **77**(4), 046113 (2008)
7. Clerc, M., Kennedy, J.: The particle swarm-explosion, stability, and convergence in a multidimensional complex space. IEEE Trans. Evol. Comput. **6**(1), 58–73 (2002)
8. Ferrante, E., Turgut, A.E., Dorigo, M., Huepe, C.: Collective motion dynamics of active solids and active crystals. New J. Phys. **15**(9), 095011 (2013)
9. Ferrante, E., Turgut, A.E., Dorigo, M., Huepe, C.: Elasticity-based mechanism for the collective motion of self-propelled particles with springlike interactions: a model system for natural and artificial swarms. Phys. Rev. Lett. **111**(26), 268302 (2013)
10. Grossman, D., Aranson, I., Jacob, E.B.: Emergence of agent swarm migration and vortex formation through inelastic collisions. New J. Phys. **10**(2), 023036 (2008)
11. Ihle, T.: Chapman–Enskog expansion for the Vicsek model of self-propelled particles. J. Stat. Mech: Theory Exp. **2016**(8), 083205 (2016)
12. Kennedy, J., Eberhart, R.: Particle swarm optimization. In: Proceedings of ICNN 1995-International Conference on Neural Networks, vol. 4, pp. 1942–1948. IEEE (1995)
13. Lim, S., Song, Y., Choi, J., Myung, H., Lim, H., Oh, H.: Decentralized hybrid flocking guidance for a swarm of small UAVs. In: 2019 Workshop on Research, Education and Development of Unmanned Aerial Systems (RED UAS), pp. 287–296. IEEE (2019)

14. Liu, Z., Turgut, A.E., Lennox, B., Arvin, F.: Self-organised flocking of robotic swarm in cluttered environments. In: Fox, C., Gao, J., Ghalamzan Esfahani, A., Saaj, M., Hanheide, M., Parsons, S. (eds.) TAROS 2021. LNCS (LNAI), vol. 13054, pp. 126–135. Springer, Cham (2021). https://doi.org/10.1007/978-3-030-89177-0_13

15. Menzel, A.M., Ohta, T.: Soft deformable self-propelled particles. EPL (Europhys. Lett.) **99**(5), 58001 (2012)

16. Michel, O.: Cyberbotics Ltd. Webots^{TM}: professional mobile robot simulation. Int. J. Adv. Robot. Syst. **1**(1), 5 (2004)

17. Raoufi, M., Turgut, A.E., Arvin, F.: Self-organized collective motion with a simulated real robot swarm. In: Althoefer, K., Konstantinova, J., Zhang, K. (eds.) TAROS 2019. LNCS (LNAI), vol. 11649, pp. 263–274. Springer, Cham (2019). https://doi.org/10.1007/978-3-030-23807-0_22

18. Reynolds, C.W.: Flocks, herds and schools: a distributed behavioral model. In: Proceedings of the 14th Annual Conference on Computer Graphics and Interactive Techniques, pp. 25–34 (1987)

19. Vicsek, T., Czirók, A., Ben-Jacob, E., Cohen, I., Shochet, O.: Novel type of phase transition in a system of self-driven particles. Phys. Rev. Lett. **75**(6), 1226 (1995)

20. Zheng, Y., Huepe, C., Han, Z.: Experimental capabilities and limitations of a position-based control algorithm for swarm robotics. Adapt. Behav. **30**, 19–35 (2020)

Response Threshold Distributions to Improve Best-of-N Decisions in Minimalistic Robot Swarms

Swadhin Agrawal[1]([✉]) [ID], Sujit P. Baliyarasimhuni[1] [ID],
and Andreagiovanni Reina[2] [ID]

[1] MOON Lab, IISER Bhopal, Bhopal, India
{swadhin20,sujit}@iiserb.ac.in
[2] IRIDIA, Université Libre de Bruxelles, Brussels, Belgium
andreagiovanni.reina@ulb.be

Abstract. We aim to design algorithms that allow robot swarms to solve the best-of-n problem using as little resources as possible. Our minimalistic approach aims to create solutions suitable for simple robots with fewer memory and computational requirements than the state of the art algorithms require. While the long term goal is to implement decentralised algorithms for best-of-n decision making based on heterogeneous response thresholds, here we focus on what threshold distribution allows the swarm to best distinguish between options' qualities, in order to select the option with the highest quality. Each robot estimates the quality of a random option and gives a binary response—accept or reject—depending on the quality being above or below its threshold. This study investigates the normal distribution of thresholds that maximises the probability that the majority of the swarm favours the best alternative. We conduct our analysis for various types of environments, by considering different options' quality distributions and number of options. Our results form the basis to develop future decentralised algorithms for swarms of reactive binary robots able to make best-of-n decisions.

1 Introduction

The design of systems composed of minimalistic units can be advantageous to operate in application scenarios where there are limitations on energy and equipment [11,14,36]. For example, future nanorobots that operate in blood vessels must follow behaviours based on minimalistic computation due to limitation on their hardware. Similarly, environmental monitoring through biodegradable robots with limited operational time-span benefits from minimalistic design for affordable large-scale production. We aim to design minimalistic solutions for a basic form of coordination in robot swarms, i.e. best-of-n decision making, where the swarm must reach a consensus on the best option among n alternatives.

Several works investigated swarm robotics solutions for best-of-n problems [22,30]. Existing solutions that we believe have the fewest requirements on the individual robots, in terms of communication, computation, and memory, are based on simple voting algorithms combined with quality-based frequency of communication [3,19,29,31,32,37]. Through these methods, robots search for available options, and once they find one, they make an individual estimate of the option's quality and use this quality to regulate their communication frequency. Robots keep memory of a single option (and its quality), and broadcast to nearby robots the chosen option only (without quality). Robots update their opinion based on other robots' messages, and reach an agreement in favour of the best option by sending messages with frequency proportional to the self-estimated option's quality. Despite the robots' estimate are subject to measurement errors, this strategy allows the swarm to filter out noise and achieve high accuracy levels [20,28].

Our hypothesis is that methods based on heterogeneous response thresholds can suffice to solve best-of-n problems and remove the need to modulate communication based on quality, hence, removing the need to process and memorise quality measurements. Behaviours based on response thresholds have a reactive binary (yes/no) response determined by the stimulus intensity (or option quality) being above or below a threshold, and can be observed in several eusocial insect species [8,18,24,25,27,34]. Despite individuals' simplicity, systems composed of response threshold units can display accurate and rational collective behaviour [9,17,24,35], which is enabled by a crucial element of such systems, the heterogeneity of their individuals, each having a different threshold [8,18].

The division of labour in ants, regulated by heterogeneous response thresholds, has inspired the design of several multirobot systems to tackle task allocation problems [1,4,6,12,13,15,16,26]. However, despite its potential, only limited attention has been devoted to apply response thresholds to the design of consensus decision making systems [9,23]. While the long term objective is the deployment of minimalistic binary robots for best-of-n decisions, this paper only focuses on the relationship between threshold distribution and environmental stimuli in order to improve the collective ability to distinguish between options and select the best. Understanding this relationship is the basis of future research aimed to develop decentralised algorithms for autonomous binary robots that adapt their thresholds to what is best for the given decision conditions.

2   Characterisation of the Problem

Robots operate in a world with n options, each characterised by its quality $\{q_1, q_2, \ldots, q_n\}$. The qualities are random variables with probability distribution function $\mathcal{D}_q$; i.e. we assume that in a given environment the n options' qualities are randomly distributed according to $\mathcal{D}_q$. We assume that the swarm is composed of $S = n \times m$ robots that operate in a symmetric environment, hence, during the exploration of the environment, the robots are equally likely to discover any of the n options and distribute in n subgroups of similar size $\approx m$, with each subgroup estimating the quality of one option. To reduce variability among experiments, we fix the size of all robot subgroups to exactly m. Robots are characterised by a response threshold h which is a stochastic variable with Gaussian probability distribution $\mathcal{D}_h = \mathcal{N}(\mu_h, \sigma_h)$. Each robot either accepts or rejects the option that it has estimated by comparing the estimated quality $\tilde{q}_i$ with its response threshold (accepts if $\tilde{q}_i \geq h$, otherwise, rejects the option). For simplicity, but without loss of generality, we do not assume estimation errors ($\tilde{q}_i = q_i$). Our vision is that robots which accepted an option will engage in voting in support of that option, while robots which rejected the option will not vote. Previous studies showed that simple local voting mechanisms (e.g. the voter model [5,10]) can consistently lead to a consensus in favour of the option that is voted by the initial relative majority [21]. While this study does not include the voting phase, we aim to obtain a proportion of acceptance across the n available options that will allow the voting process to select the best option. In this study, a process is considered successful if the most accepted option (i.e. the largest number of robots accepted it) matches the highest quality option. Whenever more than one option has the maximum number of accepting robots, one of the options in the tie is chosen at random. When no robots accept any option—i.e. all robots have their threshold above the estimated quality—the process is considered unsuccessful as no robot will be able to vote for any options.

Our goal is to identify what values of μ_h and σ_h (i.e. which response threshold distribution $\mathcal{D}_h$) maximise the probability of success given a known number of options n and distribution of options' quality $\mathcal{D}_q$. Past experiments only considered Gaussian distributions of the options' qualities [9,24,35], however, environments with other distributions may exist. In our analysis, we consider three types of quality distributions $\mathcal{D}_q \in \{\mathcal{U}, \mathcal{N}, \mathcal{K}\}$: the uniform distribution $\mathcal{U}(\mu_q, \sigma_q)$, the Gaussian distribution $\mathcal{N}(\mu_q, \sigma_q)$, and the bimodal distribution $\mathcal{K}(\mu_q', \mu_q'', \sigma_q', \sigma_q'')$. The bimodal distribution $\mathcal{K}(\mu_q', \mu_q'', \sigma_q', \sigma_q'')$ models environments with subgroups of good or bad options, that we implement as the sum of two Gaussians with equal standard deviation $\sigma_q = \sigma_q' = \sigma_q''$ and mean $\mu_q' = \mu_q + \delta$ and $\mu_q'' = \mu_q - \delta$ for a fixed $\delta = 2.5$. Therefore, hereafter we indicate $\mathcal{K}(\mu_q, \sigma_q)$ in terms μ_q and σ_q only. It is out of the scope of this study to implement the voting algorithm or let the robots autonomously set their thresholds; here we only focus on understanding which threshold distribution improves the ability to distinguish options.

Highest Average Rate of Success (HARS). In order to study the relationship between the probability distribution functions (PDFs) of the options' qualities $\mathcal{D}_q$ and of the robots' thresholds $\mathcal{D}_h$, we run simulations for a large set of combinations of the two PDFs (i.e. by varying their mean $\{\mu_q, \mu_h\}$ and standard deviation $\{\sigma_q, \sigma_h\}$) and computing the average rate of success (i.e. the proportion of successful runs) for each combination. All our simulation code is available at [2]. The average rate of success is displayed as colourmaps in Fig. 1. To identify which value of μ_h (or σ_h) maximises the average rate of success for a given μ_q (or σ_q), we compute the *highest average rate of success* (HARS), which is the simplest curve (in all considered cases, a straight line) that traverses the region with the highest success rate. We computed the HARS line using a standard

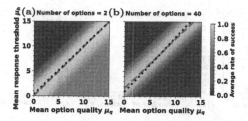

Fig. 1. We test all combinations of the mean options' quality $\mu_q \in [0, 15]$ and the mean response threshold $\mu_h \in [0, 15]$, and we report the average rate of success (500 runs per combination) as a colourmap, for $\mathcal{D}_h = \mathcal{N}(\mu_h, \sigma_h)$ and $\mathcal{D}_q = \mathcal{N}(\mu_q, \sigma_q)$. We fix swarm size to $S = 100n$ and standard deviations to equal values $\sigma_h = \sigma_q = 1$. We test (a) $n = 2$ options and (b) $n = 40$ options. The diagonal light band represents the region of high success. The black dotted line indicates the highest average rate of success (HARS line, see Sect. 2), and the red dashed line is the predicted best mean μ_h^*, computed with Eq. (1). The two lines show a linear relationship between μ_q and μ_h with slope ≈ 1. The dark area in the bottom right of each plot indicates an average success rate of $\approx 1/n$, because approximately all robots accept any of the n options, which are therefore indistinguishable and the expected outcome of the voting phase is random. Instead, the dark area in the top left of each plot indicates an average success rate of zero because all n options are rejected by all robots and no decision is made. (Color figure online)

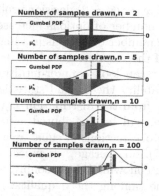

Fig. 2. Increasing the number of samples n drawn from a PDF increases the expected value of q' (the sample with the highest value) [7]. The bottom half of each panel shows a Gaussian distribution $\mathcal{N}(\mu = 10, \sigma = 1)$ sliced in n slices with equal area in terms of CDF. Each panel's top half shows, through a histogram, the proportion of times (out of 10^3 runs) q' lays in each of the n bottom slices. We also include the Gumbel distribution (solid line on top halves) parameterised following generalised extreme value distribution (GEVD) theory [7]. Our reasoning, which led to Eq. (1) (red dashed line), is in good agreement with results from simulations and GEVD theory. (Color figure online)

differential evolution method (from the SciPy library [33]) that ranks each line with the sum of success rate in all points crossed by the line (normalised by the line length) and returns the highest score line (black dotted lines in Fig. 1).

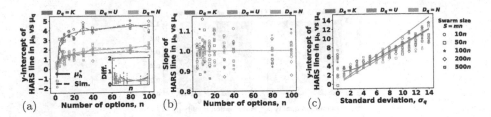

Fig. 3. (a) y-intercept and (b) slope of HARS lines for μ_h^* computed as a function of μ_q, for varying n (on x-axis) and S (markers), for $\sigma_h = \sigma_q = 1$. (c) y-intercept for varying std. dev. σ_q (on x-axis) for $n = 5$, $\sigma_h = 1$. In (a), the dashed lines show the average for all S and in all plots, the solid lines show the predicted μ_h^* with Eq. (1). The inset of (a) shows the absolute difference between predicted and fitted HARS lines.

3   Finding the Best Mean Response Threshold μ_h^*

We investigate how μ_h^*—the best mean of the probability distribution of the robots' response thresholds $\mathcal{D}_h = \mathcal{N}(\mu_h, \sigma_h)$—varies for different options' qualities distributions $\mathcal{D}_q \in \{\mathcal{U}(\mu_q, \sigma_q), \mathcal{N}(\mu_q, \sigma_q), \mathcal{K}(\mu_q, \sigma_q)\}$ and different number of options n. While our first intuition suggested that the best results would be obtained when the thresholds' mean is equal to the qualities' mean, i.e. $\mu_h^* = \mu_q$, we find that this is true for binary ($n = 2$) decision problems (e.g. see Fig. 1a) but it is not the case when the number of options increases, $n > 2$, e.g. see Fig. 1b. Therefore, we find that the number of options is a highly relevant parameter in setting the best mean μ_h^* of the response threshold distribution.

This result, that at first can look counter-intuitive, can be explained with a reasoning based on probability theory and statistics. When drawing a large number of quality values n from the distribution $\mathcal{D}_q$, we can expect that each of these values, on average, will be distributed according to the PDF of $\mathcal{D}_q$. Therefore, if we slice $\mathcal{D}_q$ into n sections of equal area $\frac{1}{n}$ in terms of cumulative distribution function (CDF), on average, we expect that each of the n drawn values lies in a distinct slice. Following this reasoning, we expect that, on average, the maximum quality value (among the n qualities) lies in the last slice and that the second-to-best value lies in the second-to-last slice. Figure 2 shows this mechanism numerically for the representative example of a Gaussian $\mathcal{D}_q$, however the same mechanism also holds for other PDFs, in agreement with results from the generalised extreme value distribution theory [7]. Most times the highest value among n random draws falls in the slice with the highest value range. As we are interested in distinguishing the best option from the others, ideally a large proportion of thresholds should lay between the highest quality value, which we identify with the letter q', and the second highest quality value, which we identify with q''. Therefore, the best mean μ_h^* of $\mathcal{D}_h$ lays between the expected value of q' and q'', which we can compute through the inverse of the CDF of $\mathcal{D}_q$, as the μ_h^* that satisfies the following equation:

$$\int_{-\infty}^{\mu_h^*} \mathcal{D}_q(x|\mu_q, \sigma_q)dx = 1 - \frac{1}{n}, \tag{1}$$

where $\mathcal{D}_q(x|\mu_q, \sigma_q)$ is the PDF of $\mathcal{D}_q$ at x given μ_q and σ_q. Equation (1) is dependent on the number of options n. As n increases, the area of the slices decreases and, in turn, both the expected highest value $E(q')$ and the best threshold mean μ_h^* increase. This result gets more accurate as the number of options gets larger [7].

Accuracy of Our Prediction of μ_h^*. Through simulations, we show that the prediction of Eq. (1) matches the highest average rate of success (HARS lines in Fig. 1 and Fig. S4 in [2]). Figure 3 shows that the obtained results generalise to a large set of conditions, for different PDFs and for different swarm sizes. The intercept of the HARS lines (Fig. 3a) quickly increases for low n, and it then asymptotically saturates to a constant value for large n.

Figure 3b shows that the slope of the HARS lines remains constant to ≈ 1 for all tested types of quality PDFs and values of n and S. Thus, we can consider the predicted and fitted lines parallel to each other, and use the distance between them (inset of Fig. 3a) as the measure for accuracy of Eq. (1), showing low absolute difference and good accuracy in all tested combinations. Equation (1) generalises to systems with different variability of the quality values, σ_q, as shown in Fig. 3c for $n = 5$, where the mean μ_h^* increases with σ_q as predicted by theory.

4   Finding the Best Std Dev. σ_h^* for Response Thresholds

A method to determine the optimal standard deviation of the response threshold distribution is as important as determining its mean, because the right amount of variability can optimise the number of robots required to deal with the stochastic nature of the best-of-n decision making process. When the thresholds' mean is far from optimal (e.g. $\mu_h = \mu_q$ for $n \gg 2$), σ_h can play an important role in discerning between high quality options. When σ_h is much smaller than σ_q, the probability that robots will have their response thresholds between q' and q'' is almost null, and all high quality options will be indistinguishable during the voting phase (Fig. S5 in [2]). Having $\sigma_h > \sigma_q$ can reduce this problem because the thresholds are more spread, however is also a waste of resources, as several thresholds are set to values much lower than necessary and only a small percentage of robots have a determining role in the collective decision making. Differently, when μ_h is set to close to the optimal value μ_h^*, the influence of σ_h is much reduced. Some variability among response thresholds is always necessary, however the standard deviation can have relatively low values ($\sigma_h < \sigma_q$), and still cover the relevant quality range, as confirmed by the fitted HARS lines of Fig. S6a which always have a slope smaller than 1, for $\mu_h = \mu_h^*$.

While for μ_h^* we derived Eq. (1) from first principles, we did not succeed for σ_h^*. Differently, we numerically fitted curves on simulation results and we report

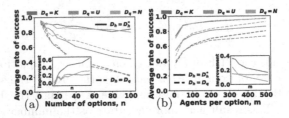

Fig. 4. Accuracy for $\mu_q = 5$ and $\sigma_q = 2$, averaged (a) over different $S = mn$ with $m \in \{10, 50, 100, 200, 500\}$, and (b) over different $n \in \{2, 5, 8, 10, 15, 20, 30, 40, 80, 100\}$, when the parameters are optimally tuned using our equations (solid lines) compared with the case when the distributions are set equal to each other (dashed lines). The two insets show the benefits of employing μ_h^* and σ_h^* as (a) the number of options n increases and (b) the swarm size S decreases.

results in Figs. S6-c and mathematical equations in Eq. S(1) in the supplementary material [2]. Differently from μ_h^*, where the slope was approximately constant and intercept largely varied (see Fig. S2), for σ_h vs σ_q the intercept has negligible values close to zero (except for small $n \leq 3$), while the slope varies and is sufficient to determine the relationship between σ_h and σ_q as a function of n (see Figs. S6b–c). Similar to the analysis of μ_h vs μ_q, the HARS lines of σ_h vs σ_q do not show noteworthy changes with varying number of robots in both cases of $\mu_h = \mu_q$ and $\mu_h = \mu_h^*$ in σ_h vs σ_q, also when $\sigma_h = \sigma_q$ in μ_h vs μ_q (see respectively Fig. S3 and Fig. S1 in [2]).

5   Discussion and Conclusion

Minimalistic robots, e.g. organic nanorobots with basic functionalities, have the potential to disrupt several fields such as medicine, agriculture, and environmental preservation [11,14,36]. However, designing solutions for robotic systems limited in memory, communication, and computation is challenging. In our research, we explore the possibility of using heterogeneous response thresholds to make best-of-n decisions. We envision the possibility of simplifying the existing algorithms used in collective decision making in the context of best-of-n [3,19,23,28,29,31,32,37], by removing the (currently necessary) robots' ability of (i) scaling the estimated option's quality in a normalised quality range, and (ii) memorise the option's quality in order to modulate the communication frequency (i.e. weighted voting). Our vision consists in building binary reactive robots that engage in a unweighted voting without keeping track of options' qualities [5,10]. Each robot uses a simple binary response threshold to accept/reject the sensed option [9,24], and only accepting robots begin the voting process. In order to allow the swarm to converge towards the best of the n alternatives, the (unweighted) voting must begin from a state of relative majority in favour of the best option [21]. This paper investigates which response threshold distribution to choose to increase the probability of having such a condition.

We investigated the relationship between $\mathcal{D}_h$ (PDF) and various types of environments, characterised by different $\mathcal{D}_q$ (PDF) and the number of options. The collective accuracy improved almost by 20% for all the tested PDFs when we tuned the $\mathcal{D}_h$ to the optimal value predicted by our theory, compared against the naive setting of $\mathcal{D}_h = \mathcal{D}_q$, especially for large number of options (Fig. 4a), and small swarm sizes (Fig. 4b). The relative improvement reduces with increasing swarm size because in very large systems, accuracy approximates 100% for both optimal and suboptimal response threshold distributions. Nevertheless, we do not rule out the possibility that the result of reduced benefits for larger swarms may change once we will include, as planned future work, the subsequent voting phase. These results will be the starting point for future research aimed to design decentralised algorithms that allows robots to autonomously vary their thresholds using simple reactive rules and collectively approximate the values derived in our study. We believe that this study is a necessary preliminary step towards the development of minimalistic robot swarms based on adaptive response thresholds, capable of solving the best-of-n decision problem.

Acknowledgements. S. A. acknowledges full support from IISER Bhopal. A. R. acknowledges support from F.R.S.-FNRS, of which he is a Chargé de Recherches.

References

1. Agassounon, W., Martinoli, A.: Efficiency and robustness of threshold-based distributed allocation algorithms in multi-agent systems. In: Proceedings of the First International Joint Conference on Autonomous Agents and Multiagent Systems (AAMAS 2002), pp. 1090–1097. ACM Press, New York, USA (2002). https://doi.org/10.1145/545056.545077
2. Agrawal, S., Baliyarasimhuni, S.P., Reina, A.: Supplementary materials of the article "Response threshold distributions to improve best-of-n decisions in minimalistic robot swarms". https://github.com/zorawar12/ycsnounits.git
3. Aust, T., Talamali, M.S., Dorigo, M., Hamann, H., Reina, A.: The hidden benefits of limited communication and slow sensing in collective monitoring of dynamic environments. In: Sasireka, B. (ed.) Swarm Intelligence (ANTS 2022). LNCS, vol. 13491, pp. 234–247. Springer, Cham (2022)
4. Castello, E., et al.: Adaptive foraging for simulated and real robotic swarms: the dynamical response threshold approach. Swarm Intell. **10**(1), 1–31 (2016). https://doi.org/10.1007/s11721-015-0117-7
5. Clifford, P., Sudbury, A.: A model for spatial conflict. Biometrika **60**, 581–588 (1973). https://doi.org/10.1093/biomet/60.3.581
6. Ferreira, P.R., Boffo, F.S., Bazzan, A.L.C.: Using Swarm-GAP for distributed task allocation in complex scenarios. In: Jamali, N., Scerri, P., Sugawara, T. (eds.) AAMAS 2007. LNCS (LNAI), vol. 5043, pp. 107–121. Springer, Heidelberg (2008). https://doi.org/10.1007/978-3-540-85449-4_8
7. Hansen, A.: The three extreme value distributions: an introductory review. Front. Phys. **8**, 604053 (2020). https://doi.org/10.3389/fphy.2020.604053
8. Hasegawa, E., Ishii, Y., Tada, K., Kobayashi, K., Yoshimura, J.: Lazy workers are necessary for long-term sustainability in insect societies. Sci. Rep. **6**(1), 20846 (2016). https://doi.org/10.1038/srep20846

9. Hasegawa, E., et al.: Nature of collective decision-making by simple yes/no decision units. Sci. Rep. **7**, 14436 (2017). https://doi.org/10.1038/s41598-017-14626-z
10. Holley, R.A., Liggett, T.M.: Ergodic theorems for weakly interacting infinite systems and the voter model. Ann. Probab. **3**, 643–663 (1975). https://doi.org/10.1214/aop/1176996306
11. Jafferis, N.T., Helbling, E.F., Karpelson, M., Wood, R.J.: Untethered flight of an insect-sized flapping-wing microscale aerial vehicle. Nature **570**(7762), 491–495 (2019). https://doi.org/10.1038/s41586-019-1322-0
12. Kanakia, A., Klingner, J., Correll, N.: A response threshold sigmoid function model for swarm robot collaboration. In: Chong, N.-Y., Cho, Y.-J. (eds.) Distributed Autonomous Robotic Systems. STAR, vol. 112, pp. 193–206. Springer, Tokyo (2016). https://doi.org/10.1007/978-4-431-55879-8_14
13. Krieger, M.J., Billeter, J.B.: The call of duty: self-organised task allocation in a population of up to twelve mobile robots. Robot. Auton. Syst. **30**(1–2), 65–84 (2000). https://doi.org/10.1016/S0921-8890(99)00065-2
14. Kriegman, S., Blackiston, D., Levin, M., Bongard, J.: Kinematic self-replication in reconfigurable organisms. Proc. Natl. Acad. Sci. **118**(49), e2112672118 (2021). https://doi.org/10.1073/pnas.2112672118
15. Labella, T.H., Dorigo, M., Deneubourg, J.L.: Division of labor in a group of robots inspired by ants' foraging behavior. ACM Trans. Auton. Adapt. Syst. **1**(1), 4–25 (2006). https://doi.org/10.1145/1152934.1152936
16. Liu, W., Winfield, A.F.T., Sa, J., Chen, J., Dou, L.: Towards energy optimization: emergent task allocation in a swarm of foraging robots. Adapt. Behav. **15**(3), 289–305 (2007). https://doi.org/10.1177/1059712307082088
17. Marshall, J.A.R., Brown, G., Radford, A.N.: Individual confidence-weighting and group decision-making. Trends Ecol. Evol. **32**(9), 636–645 (2017). https://doi.org/10.1016/j.tree.2017.06.004
18. Masuda, N., O'Shea-Wheller, T.A., Doran, C., Franks, N.R.: Computational model of collective nest selection by ants with heterogeneous acceptance thresholds. R. Soc. Open Sci. **2**(6), 140533 (2015). https://doi.org/10.1098/rsos.140533
19. Parker, C.A.C., Zhang, H.: Cooperative decision-making in decentralized multiple-robot systems: the best-of-n problem. IEEE/ASME Trans. Mechatron. **14**(2), 240–251 (2009). https://doi.org/10.1109/TMECH.2009.2014370
20. Parker, C.A.C., Zhang, H.: Biologically inspired collective comparisons by robotic swarms. Int. J. Robot. Res. **30**(5), 524–535 (2011). https://doi.org/10.1177/0278364910397621
21. Redner, S.: Reality-inspired voter models: a mini-review. Comptes Rendus Phys. **20**(4), 275–292 (2019). https://doi.org/10.1016/j.crhy.2019.05.004
22. Reina, A., Ferrante, E., Valentini, G.: Collective decision-making in living and artificial systems: editorial. Swarm Intell. **15**(1), 1–6 (2021). https://doi.org/10.1007/s11721-021-00195-5
23. Reina, A., Valentini, G., Fernández-Oto, C., Dorigo, M., Trianni, V.: A design pattern for decentralised decision making. PLoS ONE **10**(10), e0140950 (2015). https://doi.org/10.1371/journal.pone.0140950
24. Robinson, E.J.H., Franks, N.R., Ellis, S., Okuda, S., Marshall, J.A.R.: A simple threshold rule is sufficient to explain sophisticated collective decision-making. PLoS ONE **6**(5), e19981 (2011). https://doi.org/10.1371/journal.pone.0019981
25. Sasaki, T., Pratt, S.C.: Emergence of group rationality from irrational individuals. Behav. Ecol. **22**(2), 276–281 (2011). https://doi.org/10.1093/beheco/arq198

26. Scheidler, A., Merkle, D., Middendorf, M.: Stability and performance of ant queue inspired task partitioning methods. Theory Biosci. **127**(2), 149–161 (2008). https://doi.org/10.1007/s12064-008-0033-0

27. Seeley, T.D.: Social foraging in honey bees: how nectar foragers assess their colony's nutritional status. Behav. Ecol. Sociobiol. **24**(3), 181–199 (1989). https://doi.org/10.1007/BF00292101

28. Talamali, M.S., Marshall, J.A.R., Bose, T., Reina, A.: Improving collective decision accuracy via time-varying cross-inhibition. In: 2019 International Conference on Robotics and Automation (ICRA), pp. 9652–9659 (2019). https://doi.org/10.1109/ICRA.2019.8794284

29. Talamali, M.S., Saha, A., Marshall, J.A.R., Reina, A.: When less is more: robot swarms adapt better to changes with constrained communication. Sci. Robot. **6**(56), eabf1416 (2021). https://doi.org/10.1126/scirobotics.abf1416

30. Valentini, G., Ferrante, E., Dorigo, M.: The best-of-n problem in robot swarms: formalization, state of the art, and novel perspectives. Front. Robot. AI **4**, 9 (2017). https://doi.org/10.3389/frobt.2017.00009

31. Valentini, G., Ferrante, E., Hamann, H., Dorigo, M.: Collective decision with 100 Kilobots: speed versus accuracy in binary discrimination problems. Auton. Agent. Multi-Agent Syst. **30**(3), 553–580 (2016). https://doi.org/10.1007/s10458-015-9323-3

32. Valentini, G., Hamann, H., Dorigo, M.: Self-organized collective decision making: the weighted voter model. In: Proceedings of the 2014 International Conference on Autonomous Agents and Multi-Agent Systems, AAMAS 2014, pp. 45–52. International Foundation for Autonomous Agents and Multiagent Systems, Richland (2014)

33. Virtanen, P., et al.: SciPy 1.0: fundamental algorithms for scientific computing in Python. Nat. Methods **17**, 261–272 (2020). https://doi.org/10.1038/s41592-019-0686-2

34. Weidenmüller, A.: The control of nest climate in bumblebee (Bombus terrestris) colonies: interindividual variability and self reinforcement in fanning response. Behav. Ecol. **15**(1), 120–128 (2004). https://doi.org/10.1093/beheco/arg101

35. Yamamoto, T., Hasegawa, E.: Response threshold variance as a basis of collective rationality. R. Soc. Open Sci. **4**(4), 170097 (2017). https://doi.org/10.1098/rsos.170097

36. Yasa, I.C., Ceylan, H., Bozuyuk, U., Wild, A.M., Sitti, M.: Elucidating the interaction dynamics between microswimmer body and immune system for medical microrobots. Sci. Robot. **5**(43), eaaz3867 (2020). https://doi.org/10.1126/scirobotics.aaz3867

37. Zakir, R., Dorigo, M., Reina, A.: Robot swarms break decision deadlocks in collective perception through cross-inhibition. In: Sasireka, B. (ed.) Swarm Intelligence (ANTS 2022). LNCS, vol. 13491, pp. 209–221. Springer, Cham (2022)

Stability-Guided Particle Swarm Optimization

Andries Engelbrecht[✉][iD]

Department of Industrial Engineering, and Computer Science Division,
Stellenbosch University, Stellenbosch, South Africa
engel@sun.ac.za

Abstract. Particle swarm optimization (PSO) performance has been shown to be sensitive to control parameter values. To obtain best possible results, control parameter tuning or self-adaptive PSO implementations are necessary. Theoretical stability analyses have produced stability conditions on the PSO control parameters to guarantee that an equilibrium state is reached. Should control parameter values be chosen to satisfy a stability condition, divergent and cyclic search behaviour is prevented, and particles are guaranteed to stop moving. This paper proposes that control parameter values be randomly sampled to satisfy a given stability condition, removing the need for control parameter tuning. Empirical results show that the resulting stability-guided PSO performs competitively to a PSO with tuned control parameter values.

1 Introduction

The performance of particle swarm optimization (PSO) [28] algorithms is sensitive to control parameter values [4,6,7,38]. Literature has suggested various control parameter configurations that result in good PSO performance [32]. However, for best performance, the PSO control parameters require tuning for each problem [27,38]. Various tuning approaches are available [3–5,13,29,37]. These approaches can be computationally expensive. Tuning of PSO control parameters prior to solving an optimization problem has recently been shown to not necessarily result in best performance due to the time-dependence of control parameter optimality [20]. An alternative to control parameter tuning is to deterministically adjust or self-adapted control parameter values during the search process. Though, recent studies have shown these dynamic and self-adaptive approaches are mostly inefficient [16,19,21].

Theoretical analyses of PSO algorithms provided a good understanding of PSO behavior [6,8,11,33,34,38], specifically the impact of control parameters [10,20,22–25]. These theoretical studies provided stability conditions derived on the values of the PSO control parameters, giving guarantees under which conditions particle swarms will reach an equilibrium state. An important outcome of these stability conditions is formal guidance on the setting of PSO control parameter values. This paper proposes that control parameter values be

© Springer Nature Switzerland AG 2022
M. Dorigo et al. (Eds.): ANTS 2022, LNCS 13491, pp. 360–369, 2022.
https://doi.org/10.1007/978-3-031-20176-9_33

randomly selected to satisfy a provided stability condition. The resulting PSO algorithms are referred to in this paper as stability-guided PSO algorithms. Results show that these algorithms are very competitive to that of a PSO algorithm with tuned control parameters.

Section 2 discusses the PSO algorithm on which this work is based. Stability conditions are reviewed in Sect. 3. The stability-guided PSO algorithms are summarized in Sect. 4. The empirical process is provided in Sect. 5, and the results are presented and discussed in Sect. 6.

2   Particle Swarm Optimization

The first PSO algorithm was proposed by Kennedy and Eberhart [28]. While various variations of the PSO algorithm have been developed, the focus of this paper is on the inertia weight PSO developed by Shi and Eberhart [36]. For the inertia weight PSO, particle positions are updated using

$$\mathbf{x}_i(t+1) = \mathbf{x}_i(t) + \mathbf{v}_i(t+1) \tag{1}$$

The velocity is calculated using

$$\mathbf{v}_i(t+1) = w\mathbf{v}_i(t) + c_1\mathbf{r}_{1,i}(t) \odot (\mathbf{y}_i(t) - \mathbf{x}_i(t)) + c_2\mathbf{r}_{2,i}(t) \odot (\hat{\mathbf{y}}_i(t) - \mathbf{x}_i(t)) \tag{2}$$

where $\odot$ is the Hadamard product, $w \in [0,1]$ is the inertia weight, c_1 and c_2 are acceleration coefficients, $\mathbf{r}_{1,i}(t)$ and $\mathbf{r}_{2,i}(t)$ are vectors of random values sampled from an n_x-dimensional uniform distribution over $[0,1]$, n_x is the number of decision variables, $\mathbf{y}_i(t)$ and $\hat{\mathbf{y}}_i(t)$ are the personal and global best positions.

3   Stability Conditions

This paper focuses only on the following two stability conditions: Referred to as SC1, Van den Bergh and Engelbrecht [38] derived under both the deterministic and stagnation assumption [8,9] that

$$c_1 + c_2 < 2(1+w), \quad c_1 > 0, \quad c_2 > 0, \quad 0 < w < 1 \tag{3}$$

The same stability condition was derived by Cleghorn and Engelbrecht [8] under the deterministic and weak chaotic assumption [8,9]. Referred to as SC2, Poli and Broomhead [33,34] derived under the stagnation assumption that

$$c_1 + c2 = \frac{24(1-w^2)}{7-5w}, \quad -1 < w < 1 \tag{4}$$

4   Stability-Guided Particle Swarm Optimization

The stability-guided PSO algorithms presented in this paper are not the first approaches towards random selection of control parameters to satisfy stability conditions. Erwin and Engelbrecht [17] presented a similar approach for a multi-objective PSO algorithm, i.e. the multi-guide PSO (MGPSO) [35]. It was shown that the stability-guided MGPSO performed on par with a tuned MGPSO.

The stability-guided PSO algorithms are variations of the global best inertia weight PSO algorithm, with control parameter values randomly sampled to satisfy a given stability condition. The first variation samples the control parameters to satisfy the stability condition of Eq. (3). The second variation samples the control parameter values to satisfy the stability condition of Eq. (4). Note that though the stability condition by Poli and Broomhead allows for $w \in [-1, 1]$, the sampling algorithm considers only values of $w \in [0, 1]$.

The control parameter sampling is done before the particle velocity update. Each particle samples its own values for the control parameters.

5 Empirical Process

This section outlines the empirical process. Section 5.1 summarizes the benchmark functions used, Sect. 5.2 lists the algorithms used and discusses the tuning process, and Sect. 5.3 provides the performance measures and the statistical tests used.

Table 1. List of benchmark functions (* indicates that the function was generalized for $n_x \geq 1$)

Function	Domain	Reference	Function	Domain	Reference
Ackley 1	[−32, 32]	[26]	Paviani	[2.001, 9.999]	[26]
Alpine 1	[−10, 10]	[26]	Penalty 1	[−50, 50]	[18]
Bohachevsky 1*	[−15, 15]	[26]	Penalty 2	[−50, 50]	[18]
BMF	[−5, 5]		Pinter 2	[−10, 10]	[26]
Brown	[−1, 4]	[26]	Price 2*	[−10, 10]	[26]
CosineMixture	[−1, 1]	[26]	Qings	[−500, 500]	[26]
CrossInTray	[−10, 10]	[26]	Quadric	[−100, 100]	[15]
Discus	[−100, 100]	[30]	Rana	[−500, 500]	[26]
DropWave*	[−5.12, 5.12]	[2]	Rastrigin	[−5.12, 5.12]	[1]
Easom*	[−100, 100]	[26]	Riple 25*	[0, 1]	[26]
Elliptic	[−100, 100]	[15]	Rosenbrock	[−30, 30]	[26]
EggCrate*	[−5, 5]	[26]	Salomon	[−100, 100]	[26]
EggHolder	[−512, 512]	[26]	Schwefel 1	[−100, 100]	[26]
Exponential	[−1, 1]	[26]	Schwefel 2.26	[−500, 500]	[26]
Giunta*	[−1, 1]	[26]	Shubert 4	[−10, 10]	[26]
Levy 3	[−10, 10]	[1]	Step 3	[−100, 100]	[26]
LevyMontalvo	[−5, 5]	[18]	Trigonometric	[−10, 10]	[26]
Mishra 1	[0, 1]	[26]	Vincent	[0.25, 10]	[15]
Mishra 4	[−10, 10]	[26]	Weierstrass	[−0.5, 0.5]	[26]
Mishra 7	[−10, 10]	[26]	XinSheYang 1	[−5, 5]	[26]
NeedleEye	[−10, 10]	[2]	XinSheYang 3	[−20, 20]	[26]
Norwegian	[−5, 5]	[15]	XinSheYang 4	[−10, 10]	[26]

5.1 Benchmark Functions

Each of the algorithms have been evaluated on 30-dimensional instances of the 44 benchmark functions listed in Table 1. Note that the LevyMontalvo function is a generalization of the Levy 13 function [18]. The BonyadiMichalewicz function (BMF) is defined as $f(\mathbf{x}) = \frac{\prod_{j=1}^{n_x}(x_j+1)}{\prod_{j=1}^{n_x}((x_j+1)^2+1)}$.

5.2 Algorithms

The stability-guided PSO algorithms are compared with two versions of the standard inertia weight PSO algorithm: (1) PSO_s, where the control parameters are static and set to $w = 0.7, c_1 = 1.4$ and $c_2 = 1.4$ [12,14]; (2) PSO_t, with tuned control parameters using the grid search process outlined in Algorithm 1.1. The found best control parameter configurations are listed in Table 2. These values serve as additional confirmation of the strong dependence of the control parameter values on achieving best results.

Algorithm 1.1. Control Parameter Tuning Process

1: **for** $w = 0$ to $w = 1$ in increments of 0.05 **do**
2:   **for** $c_1 = 0$ to $c_1 = 2 * w - 2$ in increments of 0.2 **do**
3:     **for** $c_2 = 2 - c_1$ to $c_2 = 2 * w - 2 - c_1$ in increments of 0.2 **do**
4:       Execute $PSO(w, c_1, c_2)$ for 10 independent runs
5:     **end for**
6:   **end for**
7: **end for**
8: **return** Control parameter configuration that resulted in best average solution

---

The two stability-guided PSO algorithms are respectively referred to as PSO_{sc1} and PSO_{sc2}.

The swarm size for each algorithm was set to 30 particles, and each algorithm was executed on each problem for 1000 iterations.

In order to show proof of concept, it is sufficient to compare the stability-guided PSO algorithms with a tuned PSO. It should be noted that recent analyses of dynamic and self-adaptive approaches to PSO control parameter setting have shown that existing approaches do not perform well [19,21]. An approach to random sampling of the inertia weight was shown to provide the best performance, though not statistically significantly better than the PSO_s approach [19]. All other approaches were shown not to perform significantly better than statically assigned control parameter values as for PSO_s.

5.3 Performance Measure and Statistical Tests

The quality of the global best position after 1000 iterations, averaged over 30 independent runs, was used to rank the algorithms per benchmark problem based

Table 2. Tuned control parameter values

Function	w, c_1, c_2	Function	w, c_1, c_2	Function	w, c_1, c_2
Ackley 1	0.6, 2.0, 1.8	Levy 3	0.8, 1.8, 1.0	Rastrigin	0.85, 1.4, 0.4
Alpine 1	0.65, 1.6, 1.8	LevyMontalvo	0.8, 2.0, 0.8	Ripple 25	0.8, 0.8, 1.8
Bohachevsky 1	0.75, 1.2, 2.0	Mishra 1	0.75, 2.0, 1.0	Rosenbrock	0.85, 1.2, 1.0
BMF	0.55, 1.8, 1.8	Mishra 4	0.85, 1.2, 0.8	Salomon	0.75, 1.6, 1.4
Brown	0.6, 1.8, 1.6	Mishra 7	0.8, 0.2, 1.6	Schwefel 1	0.5, 2.0, 1.8
CosineMixture	0.8, 0.2, 1.8	NeedleEye	1.0, 0.2, 0.2	Schwefel 2.26	0.8, 0.2, 2.0
CrossInTray	0.75, 2.0, 0.4	Norwegian	0.65, 0.6, 2.0	Shubert 4	0.8, 0.2, 2.0
Discus	0.75, 2.0, 1.0	Paviani	0.6, 1.4, 1.8	Step 3	0.15, 2.0, 2.0
DropWave	0.8, 2.0, 0.6	Penalty 1	0.4, 2.0, 2.0	Trigonometric	0.8, 1.8, 0.6
Easom	0.8, 1.0, 0.4	Penalty 2	0.7, 1.8, 1.5	Vincent	0.55, 1.8, 1.8
Elliptic	0.5, 1.6, 2.0	Pinter 2	0.8, 2.0, 0.8	Weierstrass	0.9, 2.0, 1.0
EggCrate	0.85, 1.8, 0.2	Price 2	0.65, 1.2, 1.8	XinSheYang 1	0.85, 1.6, 0.6
EggHolder	0.8, 0.2, 2.0	Qings	0.5, 1.6, 2.0	XinSheYang 3	0.75, 0.2, 2.0
Exponential	0.45, 1.8, 2.0	Quadric	0.6, 1.4, 1.8	XinSheYang 4	0.6, 1.0, 2.0
Giunta	0.8, 2.0, 0.8	Rana	0.8, 0.2, 2.0		

on a wins-losses approach. For each pair of algorithms, a Mann-Whitney U test (at confidence level of 0.05) was applied to determine if there is a statistical significant difference in performance. If so, the winning algorithm is scored a win and the loosing algorithm a loss. The ranking is done on the differences between the wins and losses, with a lower rank indicating better performance. To determine the extend to which one algorithm is better than another, the ratio A_1/A_2 is reported for each function, where A_1 and A_2 refer to two different algorithms. A ratio close to one indicates similar performance. A ratio greater than one indicates the extend to which algorithm A_1 is worse than algorithm A_2. A ratio less than one indicates the extent to which algorithm A_1 is better than algorithm A_2.

6   Results

Table 3 summarizes the ranks per function as well as the average rank over all of the functions. The first observation from Table 3 is that the static approach, PSO_s, ranked the worst, with only one function for which it ranked best (i.e. NeedleEye), though together with the other algorithms. PSO_t ranked on average the best over all of the problems. The ranks for PSO_{sc1} and PSO_{sc2} are very close, and close to that of the tuned PSO_t. For nine of the problems (i.e. BonyadiMichalewicz, Exponential, NeedleEye, Price 2, Qings, Rosenbrock, Salomon, Step 3, and Vincent) there is no significant difference between the stability-guided PSOs and the tuned PSO. For the rest of the problems, both stability-guided PSOs ranked best for two problems (i.e. CosineMixture and XinSheYang 4); PSO_t and PSO_{sc1} ranked both best for one problem (i.e. Mishra 7); PSO_t and PSO_{sc2} ranked both the best for one problem (i.e. Schwefel 2.26).

Table 3. Ranks based on solution quality and performance ratios

Function	PSO_s	PSO_t	PSO_{sc1}	PSO_{sc2}	$\frac{PSO_{sc1}}{PSO_t}$	$\frac{PSO_{sc2}}{PSO_t}$	$\frac{PSO_{sc2}}{PSO_{sc1}}$
Ackley 1	3	1	2	2	4.87E+00	4.78E+00	9.80E−01
Alpine 1	4	1	2	3	5.98E−01	4.89E+01	8.18E+01
Bohachevsky 1	3	1	2	2	2.32E+00	2.59E+00	1.12E+00
BonyadiMichalewicz	2	1	1	1	1.00E+00	1.00E+00	1.00E+00
Brown	4	3	2	1	1.10E−48	3.83E−48	3.47E+00
CosineMixture	3	2	1	1	1.04E+00	1.04E+00	1.00E+00
CrossInTray	4	1	3	2	7.60E−01	8.81E−01	1.16E+00
Discus	4	1	3	2	9.27E−48	7.41E−49	8.00E−02
DropWave	4	1	3	2	6.71E−01	7.61E−01	1.13E+00
Easom	3	1	3	2	1.02E+00	1.01E+00	9.97E−01
Elliptic	4	1	3	2	3.97E−27	1.02E−23	2.57E+03
EggCrate	4	1	3	2	4.97E+00	4.11E+00	8.26E−01
EggHolder	3	1	2	2	9.05E−01	9.51E−01	1.05E+00
Exponential	2	1	1	1	1.00E+00	1.00E+00	1.00E+00
Giunta	3	1	2	2	9.88E−01	9.92E−01	1.00E+00
Levy 3	3	1	2	2	1.50E+00	2.50E+00	1.67E+00
LevyMontalvo	3	1	2	2	1.29E+00	8.23E−01	6.36E−01
Mishra 1	4	3	1	2	9.80E−01	9.80E−01	1.00E+00
Mishra 4	3	1	2	2	9.18E−01	8.97E−01	9.77E−01
Mishra 7	3	1	1	2	1.00E+00	1.00E+00	1.00E+00
NeedleEye	1	1	1	1	1.00E+00	1.00E+00	1.00E+00
Norwegian	2	3	1	4	1.04E+00	8.56E−01	8.22E−01
Paviani	4	3	1	2	1.22E+00	1.22E+00	1.00E+00
Penalty 1	4	1	3	2	1.08E+00	1.35E+00	1.25E+00
Penalty 2	3	1	2	2	4.06E+00	7.67E+01	1.89E+01
Pinter 2	3	1	2	2	2.03E+00	1.97E+00	9.68E−01
Price 2	1	1	1	1	1.00E+00	1.00E+00	1.00E+00
Qings	2	1	1	1	2.02E−01	1.04E+03	5.11E+03
Quadric	2	1	3	4	7.36E+05	9.37E+06	1.27E+01
Rana	4	1	3	2	9.04E−01	9.48E−01	1.05E+00
Rastrigin	4	1	3	2	1.54E+00	1.15E+00	7.46E−01
Ripple 25	4	2	3	1	9.82E−01	1.00E+00	1.02E+00
Rosenbrock	2	1	1	1	9.16E−01	6.40E−01	6.99E−01
Salomon	2	1	1	1	1.08E+00	1.05E+00	9.66E−01
Schwefel 1	4	1	3	2	3.03E+54	1.42E+59	4.68E+04
Schwefel 2.26	3	1	2	1	1.20E+00	1.09E+00	9.11E−01
Shubert 4	4	2	3	1	1.05E+00	1.00E+00	9.58E−01
Step 3	2	1	1	1	2.53E+00	1.88E+00	7.45E−01
Trigonometric	4	1	3	2	1.00E+00	1.00E+00	1.00E+00
Vincent	2	1	1	1	1.00E+00	1.00E+00	1.00E+00
Weierstrass	3	4	1	2	7.21E−01	7.31E−01	1.01E+00
XinSheYang 1	3	1	2	2	8.19E+00	6.38E+00	7.78E−01
XinSheYang 3	3	2	1	2	4.16E−16	7.94E+22	1.91E+38
XinSheYang 4	3	2	1	1	2.65E−14	1.55E−13	5.87E+00
Average	3.02	1.37	1.96	1.83			
Deviation	0.91	0.74	0.84	0.77			

For the 22 problems where the tuned PSO ranked better than the stability-guided PSO algorithms, the question is whether the stability-guided PSO algorithms showed totally unacceptable performance or not. To answer this question, refer to the performance ratios provided in Table 3. It is only for two problems (i.e. Quadric and Schwefel 1) that the performance of the stability-guided PSO algorithms were order of magnitude worse than that of the tuned PSO. For the rest of these problems, the performance of the algorithms are in the same order of magnitude.

Where PSO_{sc1} is better than PSO_t, it is to a great extend for five problems (i.e. Brown, Discus, Elliptic, XinSheYang 3, and XinSheYang 4). The same applies for PSO_{sc2}, except for XinSheYang 3 for which PSO_{sc2} performed significantly worse than PSO_t. Where PSO_{sc2} is worse than PSO_{sc1}, it is notably so for seven problems (i.e. Alpine 1, Elliptic, Penalty 2, Qings, Quadric, Schwefel 1, and XinSheYang 3). PSO_{sc1} is significantly worse than PSO_{sc2} for only one problem (i.e. Discus).

7   Conclusions

This paper proposed that values for the three particle swarm optimization (PSO) control parameters be sampled randomly such that a given theoretically derived stability condition is satisfied. Because the stability conditions guarantee that an equilibrium state will be reached, such random sampling is then also ensures that an equilibrium state will be reached. The resulting stability-guide PSO algorithms are then offered as alternatives to having to tune control parameters prior to application of the PSO, and to currently available inefficient self-adaptive PSO algorithms. The empirical analysis of the performance of the stability-guided PSO algorithms has shown that these algorithms perform very competitively in comparison to a well-tuned PSO algorithm. It is only for two problems out of the studied 44 problems that the tuned PSO outperformed the stability-guided PSO algorithms with orders of magnitude.

This paper analyzed the performance of the stability-guided PSO algorithms only on 30-dimensional instances of the benchmark problems. Future studies will evaluate performance on larger-scale problems. Recent research has shown a preference for control parameter values that facilitate exploitative search behavior when PSO is applied to solve large-scale optimization problems [31]. Future work will determine the regions of the stability region that facilitates exploitative behavior, and will develop stability-guide PSO algorithms that bias sampling of control parameter values towards values that facilitate exploitation. The current approaches sample control parameter values per particle. Future work will explore the potential benefit of sampling control parameter values per dimension. Lastly, for the Poli and Broomhead stability conditions, values for the inertia weight were restricted to be in $[0, 1]$, despite the condition allowing values in $[-1, 1]$. Future work will evaluate the impact if random sampling allows negative inertia weight values.

References

1. Adorio, E.: MVF – Multivariate Test Functions Library in C for Unconstrained Global Optimization. Technical report. University of the Philippines Diliman (2005)
2. Al-Roomi, A.: Unconstrained Single-Objective Benchmark Functions Repository (2015). https://www.al-roomi.org/benchmarks/unconstrained
3. Balaprakash, P., Birattari, M., Stützle, T.: Improvement strategies for the F-Race algorithm: sampling design and iterative refinement. In: Bartz-Beielstein, T., et al. (eds.) HM 2007. LNCS, vol. 4771, pp. 108–122. Springer, Heidelberg (2007). https://doi.org/10.1007/978-3-540-75514-2_9
4. Beielstein, T., Parsopoulos, K.E., Vrahatis, M.N.: Tuning PSO parameters through sensitivity analysis. Universitätsbibliothek Dortmund (2002)
5. Birattari, M., Stëtzle, T., Paquete, L., Varrentrapp, K.: Racing algorithm for configuring metaheuristics. In: Proceedings of the Genetic and Evolutionary Computation Conference, pp. 11–18 (2002)
6. Bonyadi, M.R., Michalewicz, Z.: Impacts of coefficients on movement patterns in the particle swarm optimization algorithm. IEEE Trans. Evol. Comput. $21(3)$, 378–390 (2016)
7. Bratton, D., Kennedy, J.: Defining a standard for particle swarm optimization. In: 2007 IEEE Swarm Intelligence Symposium, pp. 120–127. IEEE (2007)
8. Cleghorn, C., Engelbrecht, A.: A generalized theoretical deterministic particle swarm model. Swarm Intell. $8(1)$, 35–59 (2014)
9. Cleghorn, C., Engelbrecht, A.: Particle swarm convergence: an empirical investigation. In: Proceedings of the IEEE Congress on Evolutionary Computation (2014)
10. Cleghorn, C., Engelbrecht, A.: Particle swarm optimizer: the impact of unstable particles on performance. In: Proceedings of the IEEE Swarm Intelligence Symposium (2016)
11. Cleghorn, C., Engelbrecht, A.: Particle swarm stability a theoretical extension using the non-stagnate distribution assumption. Swarm Intell. $12(1)$, 1–22 (2018)
12. Clerc, M., Kennedy, J.: The particle swarm-explosion, stability, and convergence in a multidimensional complex space. IEEE Trans. Evol. Comput. $6(1)$, 58–73 (2002)
13. Dobslaw, F.: A parameter tuning framework for metaheuristics based on design of experiments and artificial neural networks. Int. J. Aerosp. Mech. Eng. 64, 213–216 (2010)
14. Eberhart, R., Shi, Y.: Comparing inertia weights and constriction factors in particle swarm optimization. In: Proceedings of the IEEE Congress on Evolutionary Computation (2000)
15. Engelbrecht, A.: Particle swarm optimization with crossover: a review and empirical analysis. Artif. Intell. Rev. $45(2)$, 131–165 (2016)
16. Engelbrecht, A.: Inertia weight control strategies: particle roaming behavior. In: International Conference on Soft Computing and Machine Intelligence (2017)
17. Erwin, K., Engelbrecht, A.: A tuning free approach to multi-guide particle swarm optimization. In: Proceedings of the IEEE Swarm Intelligence Symposium (2021)
18. Gavana, A.: Global Optimisation Benchmarks. http://infinity77.net/global_optimization/index.html. Accessed 31 Mar 2022

19. Harrison, K., Engelbrecht, A., Ombuki-Berman, B.: Inertia control strategies for particle swarm optimization: too much momentum, not enough analysis. Swarm Intell. **10**(4), 267–305 (2016)
20. Harrison, K., Engelbrecht, A., Ombuki-Berman, B.: Optimal parameter regions and the time-dependence of control parameter values for the particle swarm optimization algorithm. Swarm Evol. Comput. **41**, 20–35 (2018)
21. Harrison, K., Engelbrecht, A., Ombuki-Berman, B.: Self-adaptive particle swarm optimization: a review and analysis of convergence. Swarm Intell. **12**, 187–226 (2018)
22. Harrison, K., Ombuki-Berman, B., Engelbrecht, A.: Optimal parameter regions for particle swarm optimization algorithms. In: Proceedings of the IEEE Congress on Evolutionary Computation (2017)
23. Harrison, K.R., Ombuki-Berman, B.M., Engelbrecht, A.P.: An analysis of control parameter importance in the particle swarm optimization algorithm. In: Tan, Y., Shi, Y., Niu, B. (eds.) ICSI 2019. LNCS, vol. 11655, pp. 93–105. Springer, Cham (2019). https://doi.org/10.1007/978-3-030-26369-0_9
24. Harrison, K., Ombuki-Berman, B., Engelbrecht, A.: The parameter configuration landscape: a case study on particle swarm optimization. In: Proceedings of the IEEE Congress on Evolutionary Computation (2019)
25. Jain, N., Nangia, U., Jain, J.: Impact of particle swarm optimization parameters on its convergence. In: Proceedings of the 2nd IEEE International Conference on Power Electronics, Intelligent Control and Energy Systems, pp. 921–926 (2018)
26. Jamil, M., Yang, X.S.: A literature survey of benchmark functions for global optimization problems. Int. J. Math. Model. Numer. Optim. **4**(2), 150–194 (2013)
27. Jiang, M., Luo, Y., Yang, S.: Stochastic convergence analysis and parameter selection of the standard particle swarm optimization algorithm. Inf. Process. Lett. **102**(1), 8–16 (2007)
28. Kennedy, J., Eberhart, R.: Particle swarm optimization. In: Proceedings of ICNN 1995-International Conference on Neural Networks, vol. 4, pp. 1942–1948. IEEE (1995)
29. Klazar, R., Engelbrecht, A.: Parameter optimization by means of statistical quality guides in F-Race. In: Proceedings of the IEEE Congress on Evolutionary Computation (2014)
30. Liang, J., Qu, B., Suganthan, P.: Problem definitions and evaluation criteria for the CEC 2014 special session and competition on single objective real-parameter numerical optimization. Technical report. Tech. Rep. 201311. Zhengzhou University and Nanyang Technological University (2013)
31. Oldewage, E., Engelbrecht, A., Cleghorn, C.: Movement patterns of a particle swarm in high dimensions. Inf. Sci. **512**, 1043–1062 (2020)
32. Pedersen, M.: Good parameters for particle swarm optimization. Technical report. HL1001. Hvass Laboratories (2010)
33. Poli, R.: Mean and variance of the sampling distribution of particle swarm optimizers during stagnation. IEEE Trans. Evol. Comput. **14**(4), 712–721 (2009)
34. Poli, R., Broomhead, D.: Exact analysis of the sampling distribution for the canonical particle swarm optimiser and its convergence during stagnation. In: Proceedings of the Genetic and Evolutionary Computation Conference, pp. 134–141 (2007)
35. Scheepers, C., Engelbrecht, A.P., Cleghorn, C.W.: Multi-guide particle swarm optimization for multi-objective optimization: empirical and stability analysis. Swarm Intell. **13**(3–4), 245–276 (2019)

36. Shi, Y., Eberhart, R.: A modified particle swarm optimizer. In: Proceedings of the IEEE International Conference on Evolutionary Computation Proceedings, pp. 69–73 (1998)
37. Smith, S., Eiben, A.: Comparing parameter tuning methods for evolutionary algorithms. In: Proceedings of the IEEE Congress on Evolutionary Computation (2009)
38. Van den Bergh, F., Engelbrecht, A.: A study of particle swarm optimization particle trajectories. Inf. Sci. **176**(8), 937–971 (2006)

Correction to: Decentralized Multi-Agent Path Finding in Warehouse Environments for Fleets of Mobile Robots with Limited Communication Range

Abderraouf Maoudj[✉] and Anders Lyhne Christensen

Correctin to:
Chapter "Decentralized Multi-Agent Path Finding in Warehouse Environments for Fleets of Mobile Robots with Limited Communication Range" in: M. Dorigo et al. (Eds.): *Swarm Intelligence*, **LNCS 13491, https://doi.org/10.1007/978-3-031-20176-9_9**

The originally published version of chapter 9 contained inaccurate calculations caused by an inadvertent error in the software code. The quantitative results have been revised to accurately reflect the research findings.

The obtained results are presented in Fig. 3. The first clear trend is that the *DCMAPF* performs well in terms of success rate in all maps no matter the map size or the number of robots. Secondly, a prominent trend observed in all plots of the metric *sum-of-costs* is that *DCMAPF* outperforms the prioritized planners *PIBT* and *PIBT+* for small fleet sizes. Additionally, it is evident that the *sum-of-costs* of *DCMAPF* tends to increase relative to the other planners as the maps become more challenging with higher numbers of robots.

In maps with low obstacle densities, such as *empty-48-48*, all planners have very high success rates, except CBS that has lower success rate in most experiments involving more than 100 robots due to its computational complexity. In terms of solution cost, *DCMAPF* outperforms *PIBT* and *PIBT+* when the number of robots is less than 450 since in conflict resolution, robots with low priority have enough space to quickly give way to higher priority robots. However, when the robot count hits 450, we notice that the performance of *DCMAPF* is slightly worse than *PIBT* and *PIBT+*. On the random-32-32-20 map and on the random-64-64-20 map, a similar, but more pronounced trend is observed. This is due to the decentralized nature of *DCMAPF* where each robot relies only on a partial observation of the environment. This can make it difficult to resolve conflicts that involve large numbers of robots and can result in robots getting stuck in undesirable looping behavior. The looping behavior could potentially be corrected by introducing a mechanism to detect and avoid this undesirable behavior. Importantly, the success rate on the random-32-32-20 map reached 100% and is high for both the empty-48-48 map and the random-64-64-20 map. Interesting results can be observed for the warehouse map, where *DCMAPF* shows high performance and outperforms *PIBT* and *PIBT+*, and yields similar results

The updated original version of this chapter can be found at
https://doi.org/10.1007/978-3-031-20176-9_9

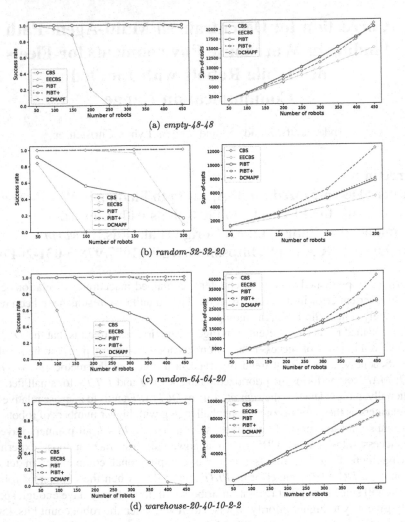

(a) *empty-48-48*

(b) *random-32-32-20*

(c) *random-64-64-20*

(d) *warehouse-20-40-10-2-2*

Fig. 3. Comparative results in terms of *success rate* and *sum-of-costs* of successful runs on four benchmark maps.

to those of the sub-optimal planner *EECBS* and the optimal planner *CBS*, further substantiating the efficacy of *DCMAPF*.

In summary, the performance of *DCMAPF* compares well to that of centralized planners, except for scenarios with very high robot densities. Its solution quality is better than that of the prioritized planners *PIBT* and *PIBT+* with a high success rate in multiple scenarios. The one exception is the particularly constrained scenario of the small map *random-32-32-20*, where *DCMAPF*'s performance is worse than the other planners, specifically when the robot count exceeds 150. Notwithstanding the increase in sum-of-costs in this map, the 100% success rates demonstrate the robustness of *DCMAPF* in demanding circumstances. In a nutshell, the obtained results highlight the effectiveness of *DCMAPF* and that decentralized coordination is a promising approach to solve *MAPF* problems. Example runs can be found in the supplementary video: https://youtu.be/5_5TdVuM8kI.

Animals Are Not Particles: Towards a Second Generation of 'Hetero-Swarm' Robotics

Marina Papadopoulou(✉)(iD), Ines Fürtbauer(iD), and Andrew J. King(iD)

Biosciences, Faculty of Science and Engineering, Swansea University, Swansea, UK
{marina.papadopoulou,i.fuertbauer,a.j.king}@swansea.ac.uk

Swarm robotic systems tend to be decentralized, distributed, and homogeneous, inspired by mathematical and computational models of animal collective behavior [4]. These models usually comprise coordinated groups of simple, autonomous agents that are identical in their underlying rules of motion and interaction. With recent advances in laboratory and field observation techniques, however, behavioral scientists are identifying individual heterogeneity in almost every collective behavior system they study [3, 6]. Theoretical models of collective behavior are therefore being revised, altering our view of how animal collectives form and function. In a new project, we will explore if and how swarm robotic systems can be improved by considering this individual heterogeneity.

First, using high-resolution data describing the movement of individuals within groups (collected through video tracking and GPS collars) we will quantify the role of heterogeneity on group organization (Fig. 1A) during collective motion. We will focus on fish shoals [2], goat herds [8] and baboon troops [1] which are expected to represent animal systems that range from low to high heterogeneity, respectively (Fig. 1A). An example of our ongoing analysis of the underlying interaction rules of baboons (based on pairwise interactions) is given in Fig. 1B and C.

Second, to gain the theoretical understanding of how the identified heterogeneity influences the collective properties of a group, we will use the empirical data to develop a new computational (agent-based) model for each of our study species. Such species-specific approach, previously used to model bird flocks [5], allows for individual variation in model parameters (e.g. [7]) or in the rules that control each agent's motion.

Third, we will use the new agent-based models in existing swarm robotics set-ups [4]. For example, e-puck2 robots with omni-direction camera extension can be programmed according to traditional homogeneous models, or our new "hetero-swarm" models. This approach will allow us to measure simple aspects of performance related to control (e.g. leader-follower, heading consensus), or flexibility (e.g. collision avoidance) for swarms following fish- or baboon-like models, compared to traditional swarm robot models. In this way, we aim to create a repository of "second-generation" bio-inspired swarm behaviors for the community to test and use.

© Springer Nature Switzerland AG 2022
M. Dorigo et al. (Eds.): ANTS 2022, LNCS 13491, pp. 371–372, 2022.
https://doi.org/10.1007/978-3-031-20176-9

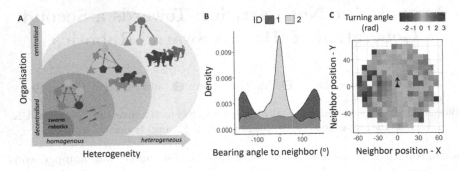

Fig. 1. A. Expected level of heterogeneity and organisation in each of our three study systems: shoals of three-spined sticklebacks (*Gasterosteus aculeatus*, a highly gregarious fish with differentiated leader-follower dynamics), flocks of sheep (*Ovis aries*, that have preferential associations during flocking), and troops of chacma baboons (*Papio ursinus*, that form complex social groups with relationships that affect their collective decision-making processes). **B.** Distribution of the relative position of a neighbor (angle between an individual's heading and its neighbor's position) for a pair of female baboons over 12 h. Angles close to 0° indicate that the neighbor is in front. **C.** Interaction plot for the pair of baboons: turning angle in relation to their relative position (m). A focal individual (triangle heading up) turns more when its neighbor is on its side.

Acknowledgements. This work is supported by an Office of Naval Research (ONR) Global Grant (2G-SWARM project) awarded to A.J.K.

References

1. Bracken, A.M., Christensen, C., O'Riain, M.J., Fürtbauer, I., King, A.J.: Flexible group cohesion and coordination, but robust leader-follower roles, in a wild social primate using urban space. Proc. R. Soc. B Biol. Sci. **289**(1967), 20212141 (2022)
2. Georgopoulou, D.G., King, A.J., Brown, R.M., Fürtbauer, I.: Emergence and repeatability of leadership and coordinated motion in fish shoals. Behav. Ecol. **33**(1), 47–54 (2022)
3. Jolles, J.W., King, A.J., Killen, S.S.: The role of individual heterogeneity in collective animal behaviour. Trends Ecol. Evol. **35**(3), 278–291 (2020)
4. Oh, H., Ramezan Shirazi, A., Sun, C., Jin, Y.: Bio-inspired self-organising multi-robot pattern formation: a review. Robot. Auton. Syst. **91**, 83–100 (2017)
5. Papadopoulou, M., Hildenbrandt, H., Sankey, D.W.E., Portugal, S.J., Hemelrijk, C.K.: Self-organization of collective escape in pigeon flocks. PLoS Comput. Biol. **18**(1), e1009772 (2022)
6. Quque, M., et al.: Hierarchical networks of food exchange in the black garden ant Lasius Niger. Insect Sci. **28**(3), 825–838 (2021)
7. Saffre, F., Hildmann, H., Deneubourg, J.L.: Can individual heterogeneity influence self-organised patterns in the termite nest construction model? Swarm Intell. **12**(2), 101–110 (2018). https://doi.org/10.1007/s11721-017-0143-8
8. Sankey, D.W.E., et al.: Consensus of travel direction is achieved by simple copying, not voting, in free-ranging goats. R. Soc. Open Sci. **8**(2), 201128 (2021)

Applying PSO to Find Optimal Strategy for 3D Chip Layout Design

Katarzyna Grzesiak-Kopeć and Maciej Ogorzałek(✉)

Institute of Applied Computers Science, Jagiellonian University, Kraków, Poland
{katarzyna.grzesiak-kopec,maciej.ogorzalek}@uj.edu.pl

One of the most challenging engineering design tasks is a chip layout design. It involves enormous number of components and their interconnections. It also carries with it a very large number of frequently conflicting requirements and design goals. In this paper we propose a computational intelligent method to automatically find and tune a universal designer strategy for a 3D chip layout design problem. We use the concept of playing a 3D layout design game as introduced in [1]. We proposed to animate the physical chip modules and made them autonomous agents that navigate around their world using steering behaviours to find a globally near-optimal solution. The constraints and goals given by the designer were mapped to adequate flock behaviors, namely *separation*, *cohesion* and *alignment*. The proposed *layout optimization game* approach has been implemented in Godot and illustrated by the application to the MCNC benchmark circuits. The main difficulty was indicating the right blending factors for all possible movements for each agent. In this paper a particle swarm optimization (PSO) algorithm is proposed to solve this problem.

The goal is to minimize the chip volume and the total wire-length. Each agent entering the game scene has to find its preferable position. Three parameters were adopted to constitute *the heuristic evaluation function*: (1) *layout bounding box*, (2) *layout proportion* and (3) *neighborhood range*. The effectiveness of the proposed approach has been verified independently of the game world. The prototype software was implemented in Python with a use of JupyterLab and the PySwarms research toolkit for the particle swarm optimization. The main question was whether there is such a blending of these three factors that its minimization: (1) will actually minimize the total wire-length in the chip, (2) may be applied to different chip examples with satisfactory performance. PSO is used to fine-tune blending weights for the proposed three heuristic functions. Each particle in the swarm represents a candidate solution to the optimization problem and the swarm navigate in a three dimensional parameters space. Like in other games, it is highly probable that there is no single winning strategy, but we are interested in any of them. Then, the final solution is rated according to its total wire-length. For a wire-length calculation the basic half-perimeter model (HPWL) was applied, where the wire-length of a net is a half of the perimeter of the bounding rectangle that encloses all the pins of the net. Without loss of generality, the pins positions were estimated by the centers of their modules. The approach is one of the most widely used approximation schemes. The most common set of benchmark circuits for floor-planning and placement problems,

© Springer Nature Switzerland AG 2022
M. Dorigo et al. (Eds.): ANTS 2022, LNCS 13491, pp. 373–374, 2022.
https://doi.org/10.1007/978-3-031-20176-9

namely the MCNC benchmark circuits, was selected. Since three of the examples out of five are more or less of the same size, the number of modules for a chip to design was set to 10. Because a single chip layout design is computationally expensive, the increasing of the number of iterations was selected at the expense of the flock size. The swarm was set to 5 particles and the number of epochs for the gbest PSO was set to 100. The experiment was repeated with different *cognitive component* and *social component* contributions. The chip definition (modules sizes and connections) was randomized for every single design. Because all numerical values were drawn from a given range (which holds true in a real-life problems), the algorithm always converged to some point of stagnation. The higher contribution of the social component to the particle velocity the faster convergence behavior of the swarm. On average, moving from 2D to semi-3D (using chip layers) can improve the total wire-length by 28% to 51% and we confirmed this premise in [2]. But moving from 2D to really 3D chip design gives more spectacular results. In our research, the resulting blending vector from each experiment (different results have been obtained with different experiments) was afterwards applied to *apte*, *xerox* and *hp* instances from the MCNC benchmark. The final chip solution for different optimized blending vectors was the same. And the estimated total wire-length in the case of *apte* fell from optimal result in 2D which is $513,061\,\mu$m down to $10,202\,\mu$m, for *xerox* fell from $370,993\,\mu$m to $77,346.5\,\mu$m and in the case of *hp* fell from $153,328\,\mu$m to $32,872\,\mu$m. That means that the proposed method succeeded in constructing a general winning strategy for the 3D chip layout design task with given heuristic evaluation functions.

The paper presents an original design paradigm to engineering design problem. Depicted by the simplified 3D chip layout design example it offers an innovative method to tackle various space arrangement tasks. Instead of optimizing particular design parameters, it proposes to redefine a design process itself with a use of the particle swarm optimization. The process is a game played by a designer who defines the game entities that constitute the final design components. These entities are autonomous agents that navigate the game world in order to meet design requirements. Its actions are the resultant of the design goals and constraints and the current state of the game environment. The outcome of the experiments confirms, that given the domain expert knowledge in a form of heuristic functions, it is possible to find a design strategy that will not only shorten the computations but improve the final design quality.

References

1. Grzesiak-Kopeć, K., Nowak, L., Ogorzałek, M.: 3D integrated circuits layout optimization game. In: Rutkowski, L., Korytkowski, M., Scherer, R., Tadeusiewicz, R., Zadeh, L.A., Zurada, J.M. (eds.) ICAISC 2017. LNCS (LNAI), vol. 10246, pp. 444–453. Springer, Cham (2017). https://doi.org/10.1007/978-3-319-59060-8_40
2. Grzesiak-Kopeć, K., Ogorzałek, M.: 3D IC optimal layout design. A parallel and distributed topological approach (2019). arXiv:1911.11768

Particle Swarm Optimization Applied to the Direct Aperture Optimization Problem on Radiotherapy

Gonzalo Tello-Valenzuela[1]⬤, Mauricio Moyano[1](✉)⬤, Keiny Meza-Vasquez[2]⬤, and Guillermo Cabrera-Guerrero[1]⬤

[1] Gcuela de Ingeniería Informática, Facultad de Ingeniería, Pontificia Universidad Católica de Valparaíso, Valparaíso, Chile
gonzalo.tello.v@mail.pucv.cl, mauricio.moyano@pucv.cl
[2] Departamento de Ciencias Biomédicas e Imágenes, Facultad de Ciencias Médicas, Universidad Nacional Autonoma de Honduras, Tegucigalpa, Honduras

The direct aperture optimization (DAO) problem is a Mixed-Integer optimization problem used in the Intensity-modulated radiotherapy (IMRT) to generate treatment plans. The aim of DAO is to determine a set of aperture shapes with corresponding intensities that consider the physical restrictions of the delivery machine. In this work, We propose combining the Particle Swarm Optimisation algorithm (PSO) with mathematical programming to solve the DAO. We compare the treatment plans obtained by our algorithm with those obtained with the traditional sequential approach used in IMRT. Results show that our algorithm is quite competitive w.r.t. state of the art for DAO.

In DAO, the generation of a treatment plan is composed of a set of apertures and their corresponding intensities. The shape of each aperture was encoded as a 0/1 two-dimensional matrix. The process of adjusting this matrix is called aperture shape optimization. Then, when the shapes are modified, it is necessary to adjust the associated intensities. This process is called aperture weight optimisation [4]. To solve this, we use a PSO algorithm [3] to solve the aperture shape optimization. In each iteration of PSO, we optimize the intensities of each particle using a mathematical programming model. This interaction is shown in Fig. 1. This process is repeated until PSO does not obtain any improvement.

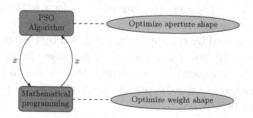

Fig. 1. Interaction between PSO algorithm and mathematical programming model.

The performed experiments over the test instance set to evaluate the algorithm's overall performance on prostate case instance *CERR package* [2]. Table

© Springer Nature Switzerland AG 2022
M. Dorigo et al. (Eds.): ANTS 2022, LNCS 13491, pp. 375–377, 2022.
https://doi.org/10.1007/978-3-031-20176-9

1 and 2 report the results obtained by the traditional approach used in IMRT, and the PSO approaches when applied over the CERR. The traditional approach obtains a fluence map optimizing solving the Fluence map optimization problem. Then, the sequencing problem is solved for the resulting fluence maps using a well-known efficient algorithm [1].

Table 1. Average results reported by the traditional two-step approach for CERR.

Instances	$z(x^*)$	$z(r(x^*))$	# ap	$z(r_2(x^*))$	#ap	$z(r_4(x^*))$	# ap
CERR	43.32	44.70	144.57	49.30	89.42	66.79	50.14

In the Table 1, $z(x*)$ corresponds to the cost of the optimal fluence map using. We report the mean value over the 14 beam angle configuration instances of CERR where columns $z(r(x*))$, $z(r_2(x*))$ and $z(r_4(x*))$ correspond to the cost of the fluence maps with intensities rounded to the nearest integer, the nearest multiple of 2, and the nearest multiple of 4, respectively. Also, we report the number of apertures generated by the MLC sequencing algorithm (#ap).

Table 2. Results reported using the PSO algorithm for CERR.

Instances	$z(x^*)$	# ap
CERR	56.34	12.48

Table 2 reports the results obtained by our PSO algorithm. Due to its stochastic nature, the strategy was run 30 times on each instance. We report the mean value over the 14 instances of CERR and the number of apertures generated.

When comparing our algorithm with the traditional approach to the problem, the results show that the proposed algorithm can obtain competitive results in relation to the values of the objective function when the fluence map is rounded to a multiple of 4. However, the difference with the optimal solution generated by the traditional approach is still significant. Further, even though our algorithm is not better than the $z(r_2(x*))$ treatment plan (w.r.t. the objective function value), the number of aperture shapes needed by our solutions is always smaller than the apertures needed by the solutions obtained by the traditional sequential approach. This needs to be in consideration because the number of apertures impacts the delivery time, and large delivery time leads to inaccuracies in the delivery of treatment plans due to patient movements and reduces the number of patients that can be treated per day.

References

1. Baatar, D., Hamacher, H., Ehrgott, M., Woeginger, G.: Decomposition of integer matrices and multileaf collimator sequencing. Discrete Appl. Math. **152**, 6–34 (2005). https://doi.org/10.1016/j.dam.2005.04.008

2. Deasy, J.O., Blanco, A.I., Clark, V.H.: CERR: a computational environment for radiotherapy research. Med. Phys. **30**(5), 979–985 (2003). https://doi.org/10.1118/1.1568978, https://aapm.onlinelibrary.wiley.com/doi/abs/10.1118/1.1568978
3. Kennedy, J., Eberhart, R.: Particle swarm optimization. In: Proceedings of ICNN 1995-International Conference on Neural Networks, vol. 4, pp. 1942–1948. IEEE (1995)
4. Romeijn, H.E., Ahuja, R.K., Dempsey, J.F., Kumar, A.: A column generation approach to radiation therapy treatment planning using aperture modulation **15**(3), 838–862 (2005)

Search Space Illumination of Robot Swarm Parameters for Trustworthiness

James Wilson[1,2]([✉]) [iD] and Sabine Hauert[1,2] [iD]

[1] Bristol Robotics Laboratory, Bristol, UK
[2] Department of Engineering Mathematics, University of Bristol, Bristol, UK
{j.wilson,sabine.hauert}@bristol.ac.uk

Human control presents an interesting challenge in swarm robotics. Swarms can benefit from the additional context provided by human input [3]. However, the volumes of agents within a swarm can present difficulty; with more agents acting within a system, the more complex manually controlling the entire swarm will be, potentially surpassing the cognitive limit of the operator [4].

When producing an effective swarm system, the level of control an operator has over a swarm is a key consideration [1]. Too much human influence (e.g. excessive/ineffective override of collective swarm behaviors) can negatively impact swarm performance. This is referred to as 'neglect benevolence' [6]. An effect in which swarms can be observed to operate more effectively with less interference from a human operator. Even so, there is a demand for human supervision of robot swarms [2]. In addition to providing swarms with context, operators play an important role in reassuring the public that the system is run with human oversight. Operators can make ethical considerations in scenarios that current levels of autonomy cannot adequately resolve.

In many cases the trustworthiness of a system is subjective, depending on the opinion of the users and the scenario it is being used for. Therefore, to create a system deemed trustworthy, user input is needed to navigate the space of possible swarm controllers and tension trade-offs. In this paper, we hope to add an element of trustworthiness to swarm systems by providing characteristic metrics in simple terms which have been measured and tested based on sets of generated, low level, swarm parameters. When it comes to deployment, this means that an operator can simply express their use-case's characteristic priorities, and select a set of parameters for their swarm which represent an intuitive set of trade-offs. An illustration of our target interface can be seen in Fig. 1.

We produced such a system by creating a multi-dimensional array of swarm characteristics which represent high performing sets of swarm parameters. This array provides users with the ability to explore specific combinations of trustworthiness characteristics (energy consumption, robot safety and robustness), with any given cell in the array providing the user with a tested swarm behavior known to achieve good results for the specified characteristic requirements.

We produce the multidimensional array of characteristics using the search space illumination algorithm 'Map-Elites' [5]. This algorithm mutates the parameters of our swarm simulation (max speed, avoidance distance, maximum time spent holding a box, and number of swarm agents), runs an experimental trail (a simulated box collection task) in which performance and characteristics are

© Springer Nature Switzerland AG 2022
M. Dorigo et al. (Eds.): ANTS 2022, LNCS 13491, pp. 378–379, 2022.
https://doi.org/10.1007/978-3-031-20176-9

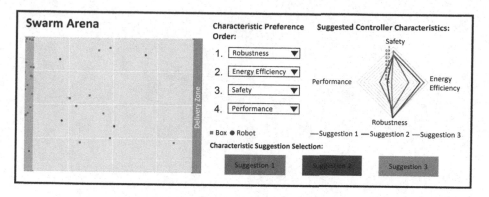

Fig. 1. Illustration of target interface displaying the behavior of the swarm and displaying available characteristic sets to the user based on their preference selection.

measured, and then records parameter sets that outperform prior characteristic sets or identify new characteristic combination niches. The algorithm then iterates, expanding and improving upon available characteristic combinations.

Through the deployment of Map-Elites we were able to find a wide set of characteristics that provided a spectrum of performances, showing a clear tradeoff between safety, robustness and energy efficiency. These characteristic combinations will undergo future testing to ensure they transfer to high fidelity simulations and hardware. We also plan to conduct a user study to identify the benefits this system may provide.

References

1. Ashcraft, C.C., Goodrich, M.A., Crandall, J.W.: Moderating operator influence in human-swarm systems. In: 2019 IEEE International Conference on Systems, Man and Cybernetics (SMC), pp. 4275–4282. IEEE (2019)
2. Carrillo-Zapata, D., et al.: Mutual shaping in swarm robotics: user studies in fire and rescue, storage organization, and bridge inspection. Front. Robot. AI **7**, 53 (2020)
3. Kapellmann-Zafra, G., Salomons, N., Kolling, A., Groß, R.: Human-robot swarm interaction with limited situational awareness. In: Dorigo, M., et al. (eds.) ANTS 2016. LNCS, vol. 9882, pp. 125–136. Springer, Cham (2016). https://doi.org/10.1007/978-3-319-44427-7_11
4. Lewis, M.: Human interaction with multiple remote robots. Rev. Hum. Fact. Ergon. **9**(1), 131–174 (2013)
5. Mouret, J.B., Clune, J.: Illuminating search spaces by mapping elites. arXiv preprint arXiv:1504.04909 (2015)
6. Walker, P., Nunnally, S., Lewis, M., Kolling, A., Chakraborty, N., Sycara, K.: Neglect benevolence in human control of swarms in the presence of latency. In: 2012 IEEE International Conference on Systems, Man, and Cybernetics (SMC), pp. 3009–3014. IEEE (2012)

Author Index

Printed in the United States
by Baker & Taylor Publisher Services

Printed in the United States
by Baker & Taylor Publisher Services